Lecture Notes in Artificial Intelligence   2702

Edited by J. G. Carbonell and J. Siekmann

Subseries of Lecture Notes in Computer Science

Springer

Berlin
Heidelberg
New York
Hong Kong
London
Milan
Paris
Tokyo

Peter Brusilovsky   Albert Corbett
Fiorella de Rosis (Eds.)

User Modeling 2003

9th International Conference, UM 2003
Johnstown, PA, USA, June 22-26, 2003
Proceedings

 Springer

Series Editors

Jaime G. Carbonell, Carnegie Mellon University, Pittsburgh, PA, USA
Jörg Siekmann, University of Saarland, Saarbrücken, Germany

Volume Editors

Peter Brusilovsky
University of Pittsburgh
School of Information Sciences
Department of Information Science and Telecommunications
135 North Bellefield Avenue, Pittsburgh, PA 15260, USA
E-mail: peterb@mail.sis.pitt.edu

Albert Corbett
Carnegie Mellon University
Human Computer Interaction Institute
Pittsburgh, PA 15213, USA
E-mail: corbett+@cmu.edu

Fiorella de Rosis
University of Bari
Intelligent Interfaces
Department of Informatics
Via Orabona 4, 70126 Bari, Italy
E-mail: derosis@di.uniba.it

Cataloging-in-Publication Data applied for

A catalog record for this book is available from the Library of Congress.

Bibliographic information published by Die Deutsche Bibliothek
Die Deutsche Bibliothek lists this publication in the Deutsche Nationalbibliografie;
detailed bibliographic data is available in the Internet at <http://dnb.ddb.de>.

CR Subject Classification (1998): H.5.2, I.2, H.5, H.4, I.6, J.4, J.5, K.4, K.6

ISSN 0302-9743
ISBN 3-540-40381-7 Springer-Verlag Berlin Heidelberg New York

Springer-Verlag Berlin Heidelberg New York
a member of BertelsmannSpringer Science+Business Media GmbH

http://www.springer.de

© Springer-Verlag Berlin Heidelberg 2003
Printed in Germany

Typesetting: Camera-ready by author, data conversion by PTP-Berlin GmbH
Printed on acid-free paper   SPIN: 10928677   06/3142   5 4 3 2 1 0

Preface

The International User Modeling Conferences are the events at which research foundations are being laid for the personalization of computer systems. In the last 15 years, the field of user modeling has produced significant new theories and methods to analyze and model computer users in short- and long-term interactions. A user model is an explicit representation of properties of individual users or user classes. It allows the system to adapt its performance to user needs and preferences. Methods for personalizing human-computer interaction based on user models have been successfully developed and applied in a number of domains, such as information filtering, adaptive natural language and hypermedia presentation, tutoring systems, e-commerce and medicine. There is also a growing recognition of the need to evaluate the results of new user modeling methods and prototypes in empirical studies and a growing focus on evaluation methods.

New trends in HCI create new and interesting challenges for user modeling. While consolidating results in traditional domains of interest, the user modeling field now also addresses problems of personalized interaction in mobile and ubiquitous computing and adaptation to user attitudes and affective states. Finally, with the spread of user modeling in everyday applications and on the Web, new concerns about privacy preservation are emerging.

All these topics are covered in the proceedings of UM 2003, the 9th International Conference on User Modeling. This is the latest in a conference series begun in 1986, and follows recent meetings in Sonthofen (2001), Banff (1999), Sardinia (1997), Hawaii (1996) and Cape Cod (1994). Previous successes in user modeling research reflect the cooperation of researchers in different fields, including artificial intelligence, human-computer interaction, education, cognitive psychology and linguistics. User Modeling 2003 followed the tradition of the earlier International User Modeling Conferences in providing a forum in which researchers and practitioners with different backgrounds can exchange their complementary insights.

The UM 2003 conference included 3 invited talks, 26 full paper presentations, 28 poster presentations, 9 doctoral consortium presentations, 7 workshops and 2 tutorials. The full text of all presented papers appear in these proceedings, along with summaries of the posters and doctoral consortium papers and abstracts of the invited talks. UM 2003 received 106 submissions to the main technical program from 24 countries. The selection criteria were stringent, and the 24.5% acceptance rate for full papers is quite typical for the User Modeling series and its traditional approach to assembling a high-quality technical program. The following list provides the distribution of all submissions accepted for the technical program (papers, posters and doctoral consortium papers) by region of origin: Australia and New Zealand (6), Canada and USA (28), Europe and Israel (28), and Japan (1).

The three invited talks provided insights across a broad range of user modeling issues:

- *Adaptive Interfaces for Ubiquitous Web Access*, by Michael Pazzani;
- *Computers That Recognize and Respond to User Emotion*, by Rosalind Picard;
- *The Advantages of Explicitly Representing Problem Spaces*, by Kurt VanLehn.

In addition to the contributions featured in this volume, UM 2003 offered two tutorials:

- *Evaluating the Effectiveness of User Models by Experiments*, presented by David Chin;
- *Systems That Adapt to Their Users: An Integrative Overview*, presented by Anthony Jameson.

Seven workshops form the final major component of UM 2003. Their proceedings can be accessed via http://www.um.org, the website of User Modeling, Inc. The workshop topics were:

- Workshop on *Adaptive Hypermedia and Adaptive Web-Based Systems*, organized by Paul De Bra and Judy Kay;
- 3rd Workshop on *Assessing and Adapting to User Attitudes and Affect: Why, When and How?*, organized by Cristina Conati, Eva Hudlicka and Christine Lisetti;
- 2nd Workshop on *Empirical Evaluation of Adaptive Systems*, organized by Stephan Weibelzahl and Alexandros Paramythis;
- MLIRUM 2003: 2nd Workshop on *Machine Learning, Information Retrieval and User Modeling*, organized by Sofus Macskassy, Ross Wilkinson, Ayse Goker and Mathias Bauer;
- TV 2003: 3rd Workshop on *Personalization in Future TV*, organized by Liliana Ardissono and Mark Maybury;
- Workshop on *User and Group Models for Web-Based Adaptive Collaborative Environments*, organized by Jesús Boticario, Elena Gaudioso, Mathias Bauer and Gal Kaminka; and
- Workshop on *User Modelling for Ubiquitous Computing*, organized by Keith Cheverst, Berardina Nadja De Carolis and Antonio Krüger.

UM 2003 was hosted by the University of Pittsburgh under the auspices of User Modeling, Inc.

We hope that these proceedings will be a useful support both in discussing presentations at the conference and in communicating advances in the domain to those who were unable to attend. Organizing a conference is many months of work, which may make differences among the chairs emerge. In our case, harmonic and friendly sharing of duties was the principle and practice of our work.

Acknowledgements

A great many people contributed to the high quality of this conference. We owe special thanks to the members of the Program Committee for their unstinting efforts in reviewing the paper and poster submissions, selecting the winners of the best paper awards, and selecting the invited speakers.

David Albrecht, Australia
Liliana Ardissono, Italy
Mathias Bauer, Germany
Sandra Carberry, USA
Noelle Carbonell, France
Keith Cheverst, UK
David Chin, USA
Cristina Conati, Canada
Piotr Gmytrasiewicz, USA
Brad Goodman, USA
Haym Hirsh, USA
Kristina Höök, Sweden
Eric Horvitz, USA
Anthony Jameson, Germany
Judy Kay, Australia

Alfred Kobsa, USA

Antonio Krüger, Germany
Diane Litman, USA
Gordon McCalla, Canada
Kathleen McCoy, USA
Antonija Mitrovic, New Zealand
Riichiro Mizoguchi, Japan
Helen Pain, UK
Cécile Paris, Australia
Barry Smyth, Ireland
Constantine Stephanidis, Greece
Carlo Tasso, Italy
Julita Vassileva, Canada
Gerhard Weber, Germany
Ingrid Zukerman, Australia

We also thank the external reviewers:

Mitsuru Ikeda
Akiko Inaba
Carl Kadie

Akihiro Kashihara
Frank Wittig

The Doctoral Consortium program was co-chaired by Sandra Carberry, USA and Cristina Conati, Canada. They were assisted by the following committee:

Joseph Beck, USA
Susan Bull, UK
Giuseppe Carenini, Canada
Abigail Gertner, USA
James Greer, Canada
Eva Hudlicka, USA
Neal Lesh, USA

Frank Linton, USA
Christine Lisetti, USA
Lisa Michaud, USA
Eva Millán, Spain
Tanja Mitrovic, New Zealand
Jack Mostow, USA
Kurt VanLehn, USA

Frank Wittig and Anthony Jameson, Germany co-chaired the efforts of the workshop organizers:

Liliana Ardissono, Italy
Mathias Bauer, Germany

Jesus Boticario, Spain
Keith Cheverst, UK

Cristina Conati, Canada
Paul DeBra, The Netherlands
Berardina Nadja De Carolis,
Italy
Elena Gaudioso, Spain
Ayse Goker, UK
Eva Hudlicka, USA
Gal Kaminka, USA
Judy Kay, Australia
Antonio Krüger, Germany

Christine Lisetti, USA
Sofus Macskassy, USA
Mark Maybury, USA
Alexandros Paramythis,
Austria
Stephan Weibelzahl,
Germany
Ross Wilkinson, Australia

We also extend our thanks to

- The Local Advisory Committee, Jack Mostow, Christian Lebiere and Ken Koedinger;
- The Publicity Chair, Ayse Goker;
- Sergey Sosnosvsky for maintaining the conference website;
- Valeria Carofiglio, Angela Wagner and Mary Scott for helping us in managing the submissions and producing the proceedings;
- Susan Strauss Williams and Heather Frye for their assistance with financial planning and arrangements.

Special thanks to Julita Vassileva, Mathias Bauer and Anthony Jameson for helping to insure a continuity in the UM organization and for assisting with suggestions in critical situations.

Generous financial support provided by Microsoft Research made it possible for several doctoral students to attend the conference. And we are grateful to both Kluwer Academic Publishers for sponsoring the best paper award and to the James Chen family for sponsoring best student paper awards.

April 2003

Peter Brusilovsky
Albert Corbett
Fiorella de Rosis

Table of Contents

Natural Language and Dialog

Plan Recognition

Evaluation

Emerging Issues of User Modeling

Group Modeling and Cooperation

Applications

Student Modeling Methods

Learning Environments: Natural Language and Pedagogy

Mobile and Ubiquitous Computing

Doctoral Consortium Papers

Adaptive Interfaces for Ubiquitous Web Access

Michael Pazzani

Information and Computer Science Department, University of California, USA
http://www.ics.uci.edu/~pazzani/

The World Web Wide gives unprecedented access to Newspapers, magazines, shopping catalogs, restaurant guides, and classified ads and other types of information. All this information, however, used to be accessible only while users are tethered to a computer at home or in an office. Wireless data and voice access to this vast store allows unprecedented access to information from any location at any time.

The presentation of this information must be tailored to the constraints of mobile devices. Although browsing and searching are the acceptable methods of locating information on the wired web, those operations soon become cumbersome and inefficient in the wireless setting and impossible in voice interfaces. Small screens, slower connections, high latency, limited input capabilities, and the serial nature of voice interfaces present new challenges. Agents that select information for the user are a convenience when displaying information on a 19-inch desktop monitor accessed over a broadband connection; they are essential on a handheld wireless device. This talk discusses adaptive personalization technology that makes all of this information available to the mobile user. The goal of adaptive personalization is to increase the usage and acceptance of mobile access through content that is easily accessible and personally relevant.

P. Brusilovsky et al. (Eds.): UM 2003, LNAI 2702, p. 1, 2003.
© Springer-Verlag Berlin Heidelberg 2003

Computers That Recognize and Respond to User Emotion

Rosalind Picard

MIT Media Laboratory, USA
http://web.media.mit.edu/~picard/

Did you like that or not? Did the system's choice of adaptation aggravate you more, or did it bring about an expression of gratefulness? Does this interest you or bore you? Recognition of the effects an action has on a user is a key part of adapting successfully to users; how can machines be enabled to recognize affective expressions such as frustration, interest, anger, or joy? And, what are guidelines for designing their response, especially given that recognition is likely to not be perfect? This talk will present new technologies under development for sensing and responding appropriately to human affective expressions. Current applications include usability feedback, health behavior change, learning companions, and human-robot interaction.

P. Brusilovsky et al. (Eds.): UM 2003, LNAI 2702, p. 2, 2003.
© Springer-Verlag Berlin Heidelberg 2003

The Advantages of Explicitly Representing Problem Spaces

Kurt VanLehn

Computer Science Department, University of Pittsburgh, USA
http://www.pitt.edu/~vanlehn/

Newell and Simon (1972) coined the term "problem space" for a virtual structure: all possible lines of reasoning that can be employed by an agent to solve a problem. For certain toy problems (e.g., Tower of Hanoi), the problem space can be represented explicitly as labeled, directed graph. For non-toy problems, cognitive scientists have sometimes employed the concept of a problem space to analyze tasks, but seem to feel that explicit representation of the whole problem space for a problem is probably not worthwhile, and perhaps not even feasible. I will present techniques developed over a decade of research that make explicit representation of large problem spaces feasible. I will demonstrate how explicit representations of problem spaces have been used in systems that do non-trivial user modeling, task analysis, intelligent tutoring, and natural language dialogues.

P. Brusilovsky et al. (Eds.): UM 2003, LNAI 2702, p. 3, 2003.
© Springer-Verlag Berlin Heidelberg 2003

The Three Layers of Adaptation Granularity

Alexandra Cristea[1] and Licia Calvi[2*]

[1] Faculty of Computer Science and Mathematics, Eindhoven University of Technology
Postbus 513, 5600 MB Eindhoven, The Netherlands
+31-40-247 4350
a.i.cristea@tue.nl
http://wwwis.win.tue.nl/~alex/

[2] Dept. of Eng. and Systems Science, University of Pavia
Via Ferrata 1, 27100 Pavia, Italy
+39-0382-505370
licia.calvi@unipv.it

Abstract. In spite of the interest in AHS, there are not as many applications as could be expected. We have previously pinpointed the problem to rely on the difficulty of AHS authoring. Adaptive features that have been successfully introduced and implemented until now are often too fine grained, and an author easily loses the overview. This paper introduces a three-layer model and classification method for adaptive techniques: *direct adaptation rules*, *adaptation language* and *adaptation strategies*. The benefits of this model are twofold: on one hand, the granulation level of authoring of adaptive hypermedia can be precisely established, and authors therefore can work at the most suitable level for them. On the other hand, this is a step towards standardization of adaptive techniques, especially by grouping them into a higher-level adaptation language or strategies. In this way, not only *adaptive hypermedia authoring*, but also *adaptive techniques exchange between adaptive applications* can be enabled.

1 Introduction

The ever-growing interest in AHS research [1,2,3,4,6,7,9,11,12,23,24,25] is not always counterbalanced by a deep investigation into its foundations and principles to go beyond both existing applications and accepted methodologies. What is felt as being missing is, on the one hand, more writing possibilities and facilities for authors and, on the other hand, the recognition of established standards to perform adaptivity. This paper aims at contributing to this basic discussion by introducing the idea of the granularity in adaptivity treatment and by modeling such granularity in a three-layer model.

The paper is structured as follows: in Section 2, we will better motivate the reason behind adaptivity granularity. In Section 3, we will present these three levels and discuss them in some details. In Section 4, we will discuss them in a current application, the system MOT, developed at the Eindhoven University of Technology.2   Motivation

---

[*] Licia Calvi is also affiliated to the University of Parma, Dept. of Italian.

P. Brusilovsky et al. (Eds.): UM 2003, LNAI 2702, pp. 4–14, 2003.

2 Motivation

Previously [6] we have already noticed, in concordance with other authors [1], that the transition from linear, book-like hypermedia authoring is not easy. Authors are confronted with the heavy task of designing contents alternatives, adaptation techniques and ultimately, the whole user-interaction mechanism. It becomes unrealistic therefore to assume that they would not need support in this process. We already deduced that for adaptive courseware the authoring tool would have to offer tunable complexity and automatically perform many of the authoring tasks. The solution we offered [6] was to divide the authoring process into a layered model, grouped (for educational purposes) into *conceptual, lesson* and *adaptation and presentation* layer and to design the respective help and feedback for each layer, concentrating on automatizing tasks which are repetitive from one author to another. Here we concentrate on one specific layer, the *adaptation* layer. In this paper, we propose a three-layer model and classification method for adaptive techniques and populate the different levels: *direct adaptation rules, adaptation language* and *adaptation strategies*. This model is aimed at standardizing adaptation techniques at the different levels and therefore works towards exchanging adaptive techniques between different applications, as well as helps the authors of adaptive hypermedia by giving them higher-level handlers of low-level adaptation techniques. Authors therefore could only specify adaptation at the level of adaptation strategies and let the system "handle the details", i.e., fill-in the adaptation language and respective adaptation rules. Note that for adaptive hypermedia this idea of separation of the adaptation authoring into different design steps is not new. In AHAM, already a distinction is made between the initialization of the user model (IU), updating the user model (UU), and the generation of the adaptation (GA) [25] at the execution phase of the adaptation model. However, this division, although necessary, comes at a too late stage and is not expressive enough for the authoring process.

3   The Three Levels of Adaptation Model

These levels represent the dynamic behavior of the adaptive hypermedia. The static relations are represented as concept maps, and treated elsewhere [6,7].

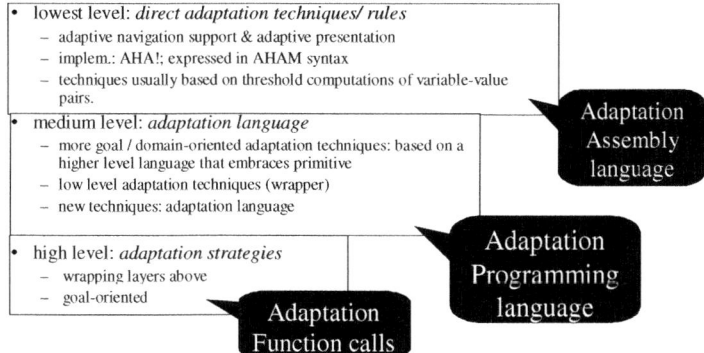

Fig. 1. The three layers of adaptation

3.1 Low Level Adaptation: *Direct Adaptation Techniques*

Low-level adaptation techniques are all types of techniques previously used in adaptive hypermedia applications (*content adaptation* – adaptive presentation: inserting/removing of fragments, altering fragments, stretchtext, sorting fragments, dimming fragments - and *link adaptation* techniques: adaptive guidance – adaptive navigation support: direct guidance, link sorting, link hiding/ removal/ disabling, link annotation, link generation, map adaptation), summarized in [1,25].

They are usually determined by a mixture of fine-grained elements of the domain model (DM), user model (UM), adaptation model (AM), optionally (instantiated) goal model (GM) [7] and optional presentation model (PM). The adaptation engine (AE) works on these models, represented by all sort of types of links and concepts, variables or attributes[1] and their values, etc.

Adaptation at this level means defining a function a:

$$a : \{\textbf{DM, UM, AM, PM}\} \rightarrow \{[\textbf{DM}], \textbf{UM}, [\textbf{AM}], \textbf{PM}\} \quad (1)$$

Function a can furthermore be divided into a set of sub-functions:

$$a = \{update, generate\} \quad (2)$$

where:

$$update : \{\textbf{DM, UM, AM, PM}\} \rightarrow \{[\textbf{DM}], \textbf{UM}, [\textbf{AM}]\}$$
$$generate : \{\textbf{DM, UM, AM, PM}\} \rightarrow \{\textbf{PM}\} \quad (3)$$

Note that by defining a as a function, we already include the assumption that for each instance of the input values set $\{DM_i, UM_i, AM_i, PM_i\}$ the output $\{[DM_o]^2, UM_o, [AM_o], PM_o\}$ is uniquely determined, and thus *confluence* exists [23].

All these adaptivity functions a can be written as (are equivalent to) IF-THEN rules or Condition-Action rules as defined in [23].

3.2 Medium Level Adaptation: *Adaptation Language*

This level is determined by grouping the above into typical adaptation mechanisms and constructs (rules into higher-level adaptation rules; operators or language constructs and variables into adaptation language interface variables). The result is a 'programming language' for adaptation strategies [3], as listed in the following.

Most adaptive systems are rule-based and adaptation is mainly triggered by conditional rules. The mother of all rules is indeed a:

```
IF <PREREQUISITE> THEN <ACTION>                    (4)
```

rule. We can however elaborate on this rule and introduce a number of modifications that give rise to a set of additional adaptive rules. In [3] we presented a preliminary set

---

[1] In the case of attributes, volatile and non-volatile [25] attributes are treated together.
[2] Normally, the AM and DM instances do not change as a result of applying a.

of such conditional rules[3] and we showed their implementation in the AHA! system. One important derived rule is, for instance, a *level rule* [8], expressed as:

$$\text{IF ENOUGH (<PREREQUISITES>) THEN <ACTION>} \qquad (5)$$

where ENOUGH = function of number and quality of prerequisites; true when, e.g., a given number of prerequisites from a PREREQUISITES set is fulfilled.

This type of relaxation of the prerequisites is intuitive[4], in the sense that it allows the author to write simplified rules, instead of writing a great number of complex ones.

Other rules that we have defined in [3] and that belong to the medium level of adaptivity, i.e., the adaptation language, are:

- A *temporal* rule: to capture unbound minimization, we need to add the WHILE construct in the original rule.

$$\text{WHILE <CONDITION> DO <ACTION>} \qquad (6)$$

- A *repetition* rule: to indicate for how long a certain operation has to last before the reader can move on to another one.

$$\text{FOR <i=1...n> DO <ACTION>} \qquad (7)$$

- An *interruption* command: to stop the user's current action.

$$\text{BREAK <ACTION>} \qquad (8)$$

- A *generalization* command: to show the user a more general concept compared to the one s/he is currently reading.

$$\text{GENERALIZE (COND, COND}_1\text{, ..., COND}_n\text{)} \qquad (9)$$

- A *specialization* command: to show the user a more specific concept compared to the one s/he is currently reading.

$$\text{SPECIALIZE (COND, COND}_1\text{, ..., COND}_n\text{)} \qquad (10)$$

All these other possible rules (e.g., generalization, temporal, repetition, etc.) that can be developed from the original IF-THEN rule can be considered as deriving from Goldstein's Genetic Graph [14], because they, as well as Goldstein' graph, model the evolution of the user's knowledge during knowledge acquisition (e.g., abstraction, exemplification, generalization, etc.) and prescribe accordingly several ways in which the information nodes can be connected. In [3], we essentially concentrated on literary examples of this kind of practice simply to show, in a domain that follows rather peculiar strategies and design guidelines, how adaptivity may be considered in more generic terms and therefore applied to many more domains than the "simple" educational domain, which represents the most common exemplification of the adaptation philosophy. Such conditional rules allow more freedom, both in authoring as well as in navigating in this type of environment. They provide authors with more tools to express the kind on knowledge relationships they want to represent depending both on the inherent meaning they intend to deliver as well as on its context. At the same time,

---

[3] Based, among others, on [14,19,20].

[4] The idea is derived from game levels.

these rules are modeled according to the user's cognitive style and strategy in a way that we will make more explicit in the next section, where we will present some examples of the possible match between some adaptive strategies with possible cognitive styles.

3.3 Highest Level of Adaptation: *Adaptation Strategies*

There are several ways of modeling user's information processing strategies and cognitive styles. In [7], an overview of some of these models was discussed. Most of them rely however on the different ways in which people perceive and process information. In this sense, the four-parameter matrix we can derive looks like depicted in Fig. 2.

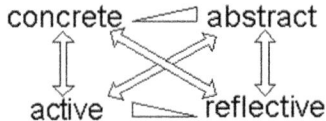

Fig. 2. The four-paradigm matrix for cognitive style modeling.

Here, the *concrete* users are those who need to comprehend information by doing, the *abstract* users are those who instead need more analytic insight, *active* users are those who need to see in practical use the new information they just acquired and the *reflective* ones are those who need to process and "metabolize" information before they can use it in practice.

To define how this model applies to all possible content domains, we would first need to identify for each such domain the specific function it satisfies. We can refer to this end to Jakobson's model [15], and extrapolate, from the functions he identifies, the three functions most information domains can be ascribed to: to *persuade*, to *inform*, to *instruct*. In an *instructional domain*, for example, we can assume that the adaptive strategies should be modeled so that:

1. Concrete students would get many practical drills and examples to work out.
2. Abstract students would be applied to an adaptation strategy that relies on generalization and specification rules.
3. Active students would get an adaptation strategy relying on exemplification.
4. Reflective students would be applied to an adaptation strategy that relies on generalization and specification rules and some examples.

These learning strategies can be complemented by some cognitive styles and some learning strategies considerations. So, in the first case, the adaptation strategies could be adjusted depending on the verbal or visual style (something that in the adaptive hypermedia literature is referred to as *preferences*) and on the either heuristic or systematic procedure the student chooses to process information. Verbal and visual learning modalities and heuristic and systematic learning strategies can also be orthogonally combined to fit all the four learning styles mentioned above.

So, for instance, a heuristic learning approach certainly fits the *converger* student profile [7]. For this profile, the adaptation strategy should therefore foresee a logically structured content, a series of learning tasks oriented towards learning to do, and self-assessment questionnaires. The *diverger* profile [7] would most probably feel more at ease with a systematic learning approach. Also in this case, learning tasks would mainly support learning-to-do. This will result in a mainly non-propositional [16] level of representation, where emphasis lies in the activation of the right sequence of operations to perform the task at hand. The *assimilator* profile [7] would be associated with learning-to-recall tasks due to its mainly theoretical orientation. Because of the emphasis on the construction of meaning, this kind of profile is linked to a mainly semantic, propositional level of representation [17,18]. In this case, the adaptation strategy would rely more on the use of generalization/exemplification rules to foster the student's deductive abilities and his/her attitude towards the creation of semantic associations between concepts. Finally, the *accommodator* profile [7] would be associated with a learning-to-do task and a trial and error learning strategy.

How to determine which user is what is beyond the scope of this paper. Here we will treat only the case in which this has been established by a previous mechanism.

3.4 Examples

In the following part, we will show some schematic practical examples[5] of our model.

Table 1. Adaptive strategy for cognitive style: converger (abstract, active)

medium_increase() : *generate adaptive presentation with (obviously) increasing difficulty*

1. Explanation: Convergers are *abstract* and *active*; they like to feel in control; start with course for intermediates at medium adaptivity level, repeat for a number of times:
  -    evaluate state of learner and start increasing difficulty & decreasing adaptivity level if result=good
  -    evaluate state of learner and start decreasing level if result=bad

2. Translation at medium level: (ENOUGH shows here that the result is above an average result) AdaptLevel= 5; N=AskUser(); # this is to let user feel and be in control; levels: (1=min to 10=max) FOR <I=1..N> DO {   SPECIALIZE (ENOUGH(Result)); IF (AdaptLevel>1) AdaptLevel--;   GENERALIZE (NOT(ENOUGH(Result))); IF (AdaptLevel<5) AdaptLevel++; } # Note that adaptation level is not allowed to increase too much

3. Translation at low level: (the average can be implemented but takes more space)
DiffLevel = 3; AdaptLevel= 5; # note that here there is no predefined number of repetitions
IF <ACTION> THEN # Note that above we don't need the action of the user for triggering;
{   IF (Result1 +Result2)/2>5 AND DiffLevel<10 THEN # Note that 'enough' and specialize
    { DiffLevel++; IF (AdaptLevel>1) AdaptLevel--;}   # must be redefined each time
    IF (Result1 +Result2)/2<5 AND DiffLevel>1 THEN {DiffLevel--; IF (AdaptLevel<5) AdaptLevel++;}
}

4   MOT and the Three Layers of Adaptation

In the following, we present the integration of the three layers of adaptation in an implementation example. We point at how these layers are reflected in the MOT sys-

---

[5] We keep the examples on purpose simple, enough just to compare at a glance the three levels.

tem, an adaptive hypermedia authoring system developed at the Technical University of Eindhoven, and give some details of functionality for each layer.

Table 2. Adaptive strategy for cognitive style: diverger (concrete, reflective)

low() : *generate adaptive presentation with adaptively increasing difficulty*
Explanation: start with course for beginners at high level of adaptation, from general issues + examples, down + rest as in Table 1
2. Translation at medium level: (ENOUGH same as in Table 1)   AdaptLevel= 10; GENERALIZE();   WHILE (not_finished) DO   { SPECIALIZE (ENOUGH(Result)); IF (AdaptLevel>5) AdaptLevel--; # Note that we keep adaptation   GENERALIZE (NOT(ENOUGH(Result))); IF (AdaptLevel<10) AdaptLevel++; } # level high here

3. Translation at low level:
 DiffLevel = 1; AdaptLevel= 10;
 IF <ACTION> THEN
 { IF (Result1 +Result2)/2>5 AND DiffLevel<10 THEN { DiffLevel++; IF (AdaptLevel>5) AdaptLevel--;}
   IF (Result1 +Result2)/2<5 AND DiffLevel>1 THEN {DiffLevel--; IF (AdaptLevel<10) AdaptLevel++;}}

Table 3. Adaptive strategy for cognitive style: assimilator (abstract, reflective)

high() : *generate adaptive presentation with high difficulty and little adaptivity*
1.   Explanation: start with course for intermediates at high level adaptation + similar Table 1
2. Translation at medium level: (ENOUGH same as in Table 1)   SPECIALIZE(); AdaptLevel= 1;   WHILE (not_finished) DO { GENERALIZE(ENOUGH(Result));   SPECIALIZE (NOT(ENOUGH(Result))); }

3. Translation at low level:
 DiffLevel = 10; AdaptLevel= 1;
 IF <ACTION> THEN
 { IF (Result1 +Result2)/2>5 AND DiffLevel<10 THEN DiffLevel++;
   IF (Result1 +Result2)/2<5 AND DiffLevel>1 THEN DiffLevel--; }

Table 4. Adaptive strategy for cognitive style: accommodator (concrete, active)

medium_decrease() : *generate adaptive presentation with (obviously) decreasing difficulty*
-      1. Explanation: Accomodators like to feel in control; they want first examples and then theory.
2. Translation at medium level: (ENOUGH same as in Table 1)   AdaptLevel= 5; N=AskUser(); # this is to let user feel and be in control;   FOR <I=1..N> DO   { SPECIALIZE (ENOUGH(Result)); IF (AdaptLevel>1) AdaptLevel--;   GENERALIZE (NOT(ENOUGH(Result))); IF (AdaptLevel<5) AdaptLevel++; }

3. Translation at low level: (the average can be implemented but takes more space)
 DiffLevel = 8; AdaptLevel= 5;
 IF <ACTION> THEN
 { IF (Result1 +Result2)/2>5 AND DiffLevel<10 THEN {DiffLevel++; IF (AdaptLevel>1) AdaptLevel--;}
   IF (Result1 +Result2)/2<5 AND DiffLevel>1 THEN {DiffLevel--; IF (AdaptLevel<5) AdaptLevel++;}}

4.1 Low Level Adaptation

As it can be seen from the description in section 3 and in [1, 25], generation of low level adaptation techniques means defining the constituting elements of DM, UM, AM (or *a*), PM. MOT is implementing each of these models separately, as described in [9].

The DM is actually divided into two layers, a *domain* (or concept) layer and a *goal* (in particular, for educational applications, *lesson*) layer, as defined in our previous research [6]. These two layers are implemented with the help of concept maps. Concept maps are tuples <C, L>, where C represents the set of concepts and L the set of links (CM⊆**CM**, the set of all concept maps of the AHS).

Concepts in the domain layer are tuples $< A_c, C_c >$ where A_c ($A_c \neq \varnothing$) is a set of attributes and C_c a set of sub-concepts; concepts in the goal layer (*GM*) are defined by the tuple $< A_g, C_g >$ where A_g (card(A_{min})=2) [6] is a set of attributes and C_g a set of sub-concepts. The detailed definitions are contained in another paper [9]. An example of domain and goal layer concepts can be seen in Figure 3. As can bee seen in Figure 3 (right side), the goal layer already implements AND-OR connections and allows weights for the different concepts. It is the role of the AM to give the interpretation of these weights and AND-OR connections, based on the existing goal layer and the UM. In this way, for the same domain and goal model, different presentations can be generated by the AE. For MOT, we plan to connect the system to different adaptive presentation engines, including AHA! [11]. In this way, we can let the PM be generated by the AHA! AE, AM and UM, all working at the low level of adaptivity.

4.2 Medium Level Adaptation

MOT doesn't allow direct programming of adaptive rules at the medium level of adaptation, mostly due to the fact that the adaptive layer in MOT is not yet developed. We are planning to explicitly introduce such constructs, to test the possible enhancement of authoring ease. This level is for authors who want to design new strategies.

4.3 Highest Level of Adaptation: Adaptation Strategies

As said, MOT allows a goal (or lesson) level, where the adaptation strategies can be implemented. Each "lesson" at this level is goal-oriented and can represent a specific adaptation strategy. At the level of the adaptation strategy, the AND-OR connections in Fig. 3 have a meaning (*semantics*).

For instance, the selection in Fig. 3 right side is the basis of adaptation for *diverger* or *assimilator* users. It is a no-frills text-based content-oriented selection. For *converger* or *accommodator* users, a selection based on examples would be more beneficial. The level selections (generalization, specialization) such as described in tables 1-4 can be translated in MOT into attribute selections for the lesson level, which can already be done easily (and automatically) in MOT (Figure 3, right side). We are planning to introduce more refined versions of automatic high level adaptation strategy implementations (tables 1-4), to make the task of the adaptive hypermedia designers easy.

---

[6] Each *GM* concept has only 2 attributes: '*name*' and '*contents*'.

At the moment, the connection with the adaptation model and user model is not yet made.

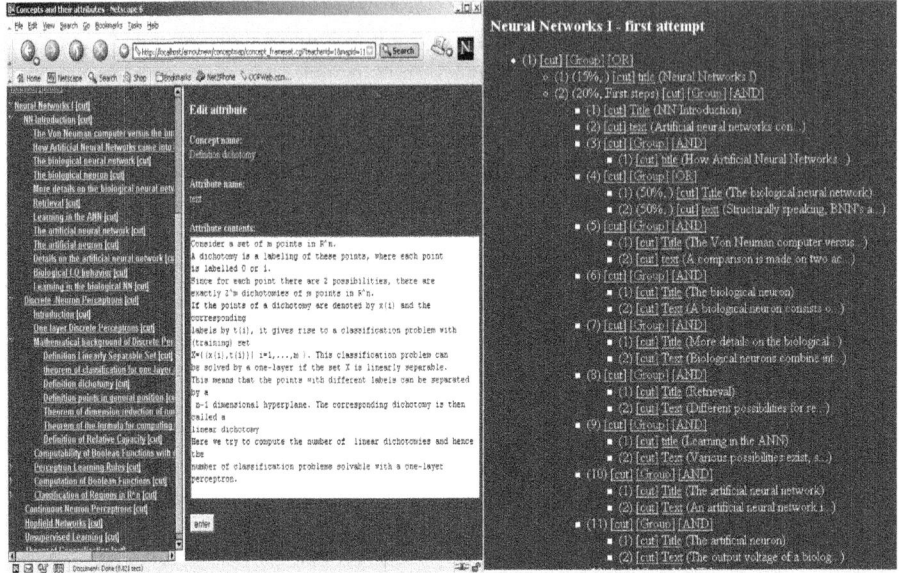

Fig. 3. Domain layer and goal layer concept editing in MOT

5 Conclusion

It is beneficial, especially for authoring purposes, to approach adaptation techniques from a higher level of semantics [3,25]. Next to the inherent difficulties of authoring adaptive hypermedia already highlighted in [3,6,25], the semantics of adaptation is difficult to follow at a low level of granularity of the implementation. In such cases, typical problems of CA can appear, such as no guarantee of termination and confluence [23,25]. These kinds of problems can be bypassed by allowing authors a gradual access to the adaptivity engine. For this purpose, we have defined three levels of adaptation: *direct adaptation techniques, adaptation language* and *adaptation strategies.* Moreover, these levels were instantiated with some examples based on MOT, a system implemented at the Eindhoven University of Technology. MOT is gradually implementing each of these layers.

The levels of adaptation that we have proposed therefore group adaptive techniques according to their *implementation form* (adaptation language) or *purpose* (adaptive strategies). In this way, we actually label the (groups of) adaptive techniques for further usage (re-implementation for authoring purposes or re-usage for exchange of adaptive techniques between adaptive applications). We are therefore working towards creating an ontology of adaptive techniques and integrating them in the new generation of meaningful Web [22], the semantic web [21].

References

1. Brusilovsky, P.: Adaptive hypermedia, User Modeling and User Adapted Interaction, Ten Year Anniversary Issue (Alfred Kobsa, ed.) 11 (1/2) (2002) 87–110
2. Brusilovsky, P., Eklund, J., and Schwarz, E.: Web-based education for all: A tool for developing adaptive courseware, in Computer Networks and ISDN Systems, Proceedings of Seventh International WWW Conference (14-18 April 1998) 30 (1–7), 291–300
3. Calvi, L., and Cristea, A.I.: Towards Generic Adaptive Systems Analysis of a Case Study, in Proceedings of AH'02, LNCS 2347, Springer, (Malaga, Spain, May 2002) 79–89
4. Carro, R. M., Pulido, E. Rodríguez, P.: Designing Adaptive Web-based Courses with TANGOW, in proceedings of ICCE'99, V. 2 (Chiba, Japan, November 1999) 697–704
5. Cristea A.I., Okamoto, T.: Considering automatic educational validation of computerized educational systems, IEEE ICALT2001, Madison, USA, Okamoto T., Hartley R., Kinshuk & Klus J. (Eds.) (2001), CA (ISBN 0-7695-1013-2)
6. Cristea, A.I., and Aroyo, L.: Adaptive Authoring of Adaptive Educational Hypermedia, in Proceedings of AH 2002, LNCS 2347, Springer, 122–132
7. Cristea, A.I., and De Bra, P.: Towards Adaptable and Adaptive ODL Environments, in Proceedings of AACE E-Learn'02 (Montreal, Canada, October 2002), 232–239
8. Cristea, A., Okamoto, T.: MyEnglishTeacher – A WWW System for Academic English Teaching, in Proceedings of the ICCE 2000 Conference (Taipei, Taiwan, 2000)
9. Cristea, A., De Mooij, A.: Adaptive Course Authoring: MOT, My Online Teacher, in Proceedings of ICT-2003, IEEE LTTF, "Telecommunications + Education" Workshop (Feb 23 - March 1, 2003 Tahiti Island in Papetee - French Polynesia) (in press)
10. Cristea, A.I., Okamoto, T., and Kayama, M.: Considerations for Building a Common Platform for Cooperative & Collaborative Authoring Environments, in Proceedings of AACE E-Learn'02 (Montreal, Canada, October 2002), 224–231
11. De Bra, P. and Calvi, L.: AHA! An open Adaptive Hypermedia Architecture, The New Review of Hypermedia and Multimedia, V. 4, Taylor Graham Publishers (1998) 115–139
12. European Community Socrates-Minerva project (project reference number 101144-CP-1-2002-NL-MINERVA-MPP). http://wwwis.win.tue.nl/~alex/HTML/Minerva/index.html
13. Frasincar, F., Houben, G.J., Vdovjak, R., and Barna P.: RAL: An Algebra for Querying RDF, in Proceedings of WISE 2002 (Singapore, December 2002)
14. Goldstein, I.: The genetic graph: a representation for the evolution of procedural knowledge, In D. Sleeman and J.S. Brown (eds.), ITS, Academic Press, (1982)
15. Jakobson, R.: Closing Statements: Linguistics and Poetics, in T. A. Sebeok (ed.), *Style in Language,* MIT Press, Cambridge, (1960)
16. Johnson-Laird, P.N.: Mental Models: Towards a Cognitive Science of Language, Inference, and Consciousness, Cambridge University Press, Cambridge, MA (1983)
17. Kintsch, W.: The role of knowledge in discourse comprehension: A construction-integration model, Psychological Review, 95 (1988) 163–182
18. Kintsch, W and van Dijk T. A. Toward a Model of Text Comprehension and Production. Psychological Review, 85 (1978) 363–394
19. Lughi, G. Parole on line. Dall'ipertesto all'editoria multimediale. Guerini e Assoc., 2001.
20. Trigg, R.H. A network-based approach to text handling for the online scientific community. PhD thesis, Dept. of Computer Science, University of Maryland, (1983)
21. WC3, Semantic Web. http://www.w3.org/2001/sw/
22. W3C, Requirements for a Web Ontology Language, http://www.w3.org/TR/webont-req/

23. Wu, H., De Bra, P.: Sufficient Conditions for Well-Behaved Adaptive Hypermedia Systems, in Proceedings of WI'01, LNAI V.2198, Springer (Maebashi, October 2001) 148–152
24. Wu, H., De Kort, E., De Bra, P.: Design Issues for General-Purpose Adaptive Hypermedia Systems, in Proceedings of the ACM Conference on Hypertext and Hypermedia (Aarhus, Denmark, August 2001) 141–150
25. Wu, H.: A Reference Architecture for Adaptive Hypermedia Applications, doctoral thesis, Eindhoven University of Technology, The Netherlands, ISBN 90-386-0572-2, (2002)

Adaptive Presentation of Multimedia Interface Case Study: "Brain Story" Course

Halima Habieb-Mammar, Franck Tarpin-Bernard, and Patrick Prévôt

ICTT, INSA de Lyon
20 Avenue Jean Capelle, 69211 Villeurbanne Cedex - FRANCE
{habieb, tarpin, prevot}@gprhp.insa-lyon.fr

Abstract. The paper presents the development of a multimedia adaptive interface based on the cognitive profile of a user. It describes the cognitive profile and the document architecture that have been adopted. Indeed, the user profile is generated in a stage former to the adaptation, it is structured into a separate database. As for the document, it is presented in XML files. The paper describes in detail the way these components are combined ; it presents the adaptive process. During this process, the combination of medias that best fits the cognitive profile of each user is selected. This technique is applied on a hypermedia course called "Saga du Cerveau" (*The Brain Story*).

1   Introduction

Research on adaptive interfaces and user modeling has attracted attention for more than a decade and seems to have recently aroused a renewal of interest, mainly thanks to hypermedia. As the amount of on-line information grows at an astonishing speed, people feel overwhelmed by the information currently available, and the corresponding media landscape [7]. This clearly leads to a need of automated methods, commonly referred to as adaptive interfaces, which present information with respect to the user profile[2][3]. As adaptive interfaces aim at automatically adapting to individual users, the development of appropriate user modeling techniques is of great importance[4]. Techniques dealing with user profile construction are drawn from work in cognitive psychology and human computer interface.

We first describe the supervised cognitive training program called HAPPYneuron™. This program enables the construction of the cognitive profile of users. We then investigate adaptive techniques using this profile. We focus our first work on output media in the context of hypermedia. We have chosen XML and ASP technologies to implement the system.

P. Brusilovsky et al. (Eds.): UM 2003, LNAI 2702, pp. 15–24, 2003.

2 Description of HAPPYneuron TM

We have been working since 2000, in collaboration with the SBT company, on an interactive web site proposing a supervised cognitive training: www.happyneuron.com [11]. Mainly dedicated to seniors, this website provides exercises that train and evaluate cognitive abilities. During each training session (i.e. each connection), the user performs a set of exercises suggested by the system. Exercises have a playful dimension and vary in difficulty level, speed... in order to entertain the user [9]. Normalized data is stored into a database (means and standard deviations) for each variant of exercise and family of population distinguishing gender, educational level and age [11]. Current statistics show that since the web site was open to the general audience (summer 2001), the number of performed exercises has exceeded 1,800,000 and the population of players is well distributed between 15 and 80 years of age. Comparing the trainee's results and normalized data, we are able to progressively build the user cognitive profile. It then enables the system to advise the user in his choice of exercises.

In this context, we have built an evaluation module composed of ten precise exercises that enables to quickly build a cognitive profile. Then, this profile, which is quite stable, can be used in very different contexts. Our first purpose is to elaborate an adaptive multimedia course on the brain. Depending on one's profile, the lesson will be presented using the most adapted media.

Before describing the adaptation process module, we give hereafter the definition of the cognitive styles we adopted in our model.

3 Some Cognitive Styles

Cognitive styles induce people to adopt similar attitudes and behaviors in a variety of domains [1]. Cognitive styles are important in determining the most effective interface for a particular category of user, especially in the formative stages of an interaction [8][10]. For instance, we can quote *Field Independent* (FI) and *Field Dependent* (FD). FI people tend to have good analytical and cognitive restructuring skills. They will actively reorganize information according to contextual demands and impose structure when necessary according to their experience. They are likely to form a mental model of the situation before proceeding with their task. FI people seem to follow a restructuring approach more easily and use internal referents in other situations [1]. FD people tend to adopt a passive approach in learning and problem solving. They prefer to be guided and to rely on external referents. Lesser use of restructuring may handicap field dependent people in unstructured situations. Field dependent people may need more explicit instructions in problem-solving strategies or more accurate definitions of performance outcome than field independent people, who may even perform better when allowed to develop their own strategies [9].

Three main kinds of data can be used to measure cognitive styles: behavioral, self-report, and physiological [1]. In our approach, we use the first technique. Indeed, the *Behavioral data* can be obtained by recording the final result of a given task or the procedure followed in performing the task. The task may consist in filling out a paper-

and-pencil test or a sorting test, in carrying out trials by means of an experimental apparatus, or in interacting with a computer like during exercise running [10]. For an example, to assess whether a person is a visualizer or a verbalizer, it is possible to present him/her with tasks which can be performed through both visual and verbal strategies and to record the extent to which each of the two kinds of procedures has been followed.

4   Our Approach

The two important steps adopted in our approach are structured as shown in Fig. 1.

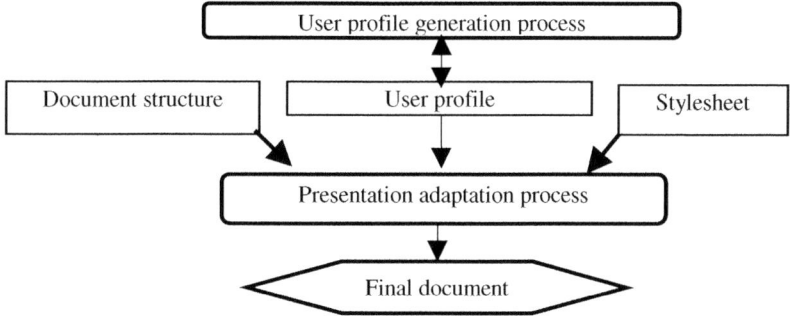

Fig. 1. User profile generation and presentation adaptation process

4.1   The User Profile Generation Process

The process consists in executing a sequence of interactive exercises then computing the cognitive profile. The main components of the output profile are the cognitive indicators dispatched into 5 sectors: *memory, attention, executive functions, language and visual & spatial capacities* [11]. In detail, 25 indicators have been determined. In our process, we are not using all the indicators. However, the most used were: working memory (verbal, visual or auditory), memory (long term and short term), categorization, comprehension, inhibition, visual and spatial exploration, form recognition and glossary.

Using the cognitive indicators, we have modeled the cognitive sectors that are most called upon while performing an exercise. However, in practice, an exercise cannot imply a unique sector. Every cognitive activity results from a parallel or hierarchical processing of a lot of cognitive abilities. For each exercise, we have determined the different solicited indicators and chosen weight factors ($0 \leq p_i \leq 10$). After each exercise running, the performance (P) of the user is computed using the average performance (M) and the standard deviation (σ) of this performance that are stored in our database and result from other users which have the same characteristics (age, gender and level of education). A user with an average performance will obtain a score of 50 (the default value) and someone with a very good performance of $M+2\sigma$ will obtain 90 (2.5 % of the population) [9][11].

4.2 Presentation of the Adaptation Process

As described in figure 1, the user profile generation process yields a user profile which constitutes the input data for the adaptation process. Indeed, this profile enables the selection of the most adapted output media. The multimedia document is structured in an XML document [9].

Prior to any process, each stylesheet contains the layout of a complete page to be presented. For a specific subject, the final layout of this page is brought through the adaptive process. This page is the most suitable one to the user profile.

In the XML document, the page may fall under many blocks. Each one may be presented according to different elements. Every element is structured in turn according to different media. Each media has an attribute called **signature** which is a representation of the "level of complexity" ranged [0,5]. The first value of the attribute is defined by the course author. It stands for the quantity of either verbal, visual or musical information that the element contains i.e. the difficulty of the text (the term "difficulty" is related to the difficulty encountered to understand the text), the quantity of information the image contains, the quantity of noise and the language in which the message is expressed. This level enables the selection of the best combination according to the user profile. Later the system modifies each attribute by computing an other level. For textual modality, this level refers to the length of the text. For the image, the level of complexity concerns its dimension. As for the sound modality, it concerns its duration. $T[x]$ stands for Textual elements with the level x, $G[x]$ for Graphical element and $S[x]$ for Sound element (music, jingle, recorded voice etc.).

To illustrate the adaptation process, we hereafter give an example of a page dealing with the *Memory* item.

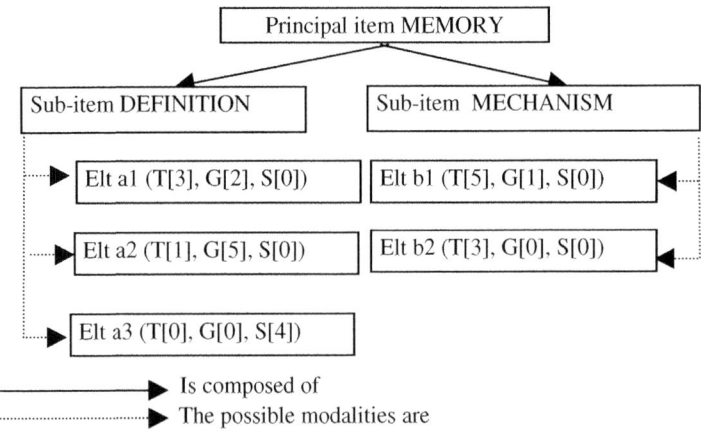

Fig. 2. XML document structure

This page presents two sub-items : "definition of memory" and "mechanism of memory". In the XML document, the page may fall under two blocks (see Fig. 2).

The issue is to find the "best" combination of media according to the will of the designer and the abilities of the reader. According to the XML structure, the possible combinations are: (Elt a1, Elt b2), (Elt a2, Elt b2), (Elt a3, Elt b1), etc.

On the other hand, we build a compatibility matrix whose lines correspond to criteria extracted from the user profile components (cognitive styles and interaction styles) and whose rows are the possible combinations of media.

For each combination and each criteria (e.g. capacity to manage more than one media, respect of preferred media, field-dependency...) a compatibility factor is calculated using an arithmetic formula that combines the user profile and the characteristics of the combination. The combination of media that results in the biggest sum is considered as the most compatible one.

Indeed, an ASP program on the server side builds an enriched XML document that contains the whole page to be presented. Each part, which is presented as a tag, has an attribute called *state*. This attribute may hold the 0 or 1 values, where 0 indicates the disabled state and 1 the enabled one of the corresponding tag. Thanks to the user profile and the items priority (i.e. the important items which have to be shown), the ASP program includes the state values into each tag.

From the other side, the user profile which contains the indicators to be explored is structured into a database and constitutes the second input for the presentation adaptation process. The last input of the process is the stylesheet which transforms the final XML document and presents it as the final adapted page.

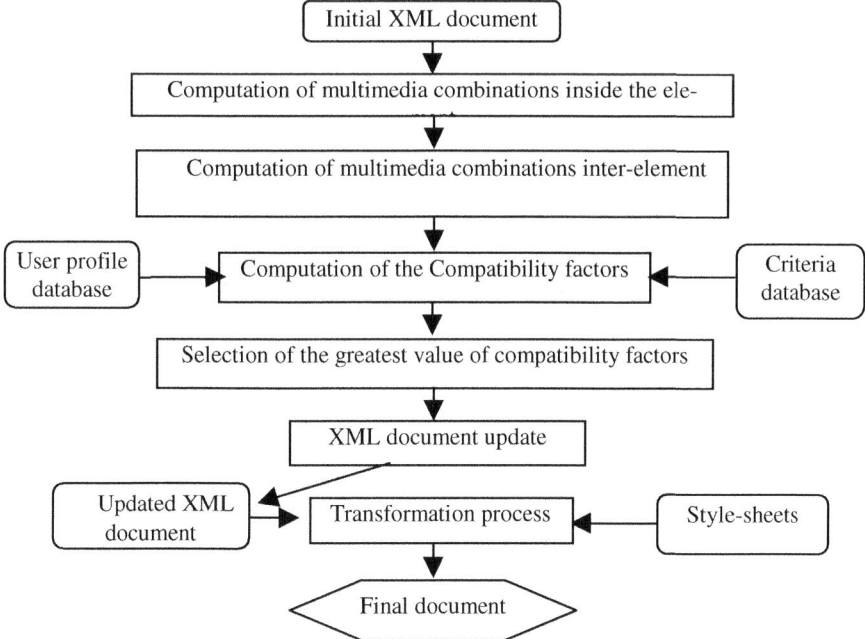

Fig. 3. The algorithm steps in selecting the "best" multimedia combination

Step 1 :

The first step consists in computing the combinations inside the element itself. Indeed, the designer brings each block of the document in terms of set of elements. All the elements have the same content but are presented into different media (Fig. 2).

Step 2 :

In the second step, there are the multimedia combinations inter-elements which are computed through the first combinations.

Step 3 :

For each combination, the compatibility factor is calculated by evaluating criteria related to user profile (visual or verbal, how much he/she can manage two media, etc.) and the document itself (number of media, level of complexity for every media, etc). As an example, these are the first criteria we used :

$$(Nb\_Vi*Sc\_Vi+Nb\_Ve*Sc\_Ve)/(Nb\_Vi+Nb\_Ve) \tag{1}$$

$$100*(Nb\_Vi+Nb\_Ve+Nb\_S)/Nb\_Max \tag{2}$$

The first criterion is used for computing the best combination that fits the profile. The second one is used to favor the selection of a multimedia combination. These criteria use the following variables which are the visual and the verbal scores :

$$Sc\_Vi=(WM\_Vi+STM\_Vi+LTM\_Vi+Rec+Exp)/5 \tag{3}$$

$$Sc\_Ve=(STM\ \_Ve+STM\_Ve+LTM\_Ve+Glos+Cat+Comp)/6 \tag{4}$$

$$Nb\_Max = Max(Nb\_Vi+Nb\_Ve+Nb\_S) \tag{5}$$

Where:

WM_Ve : Verbal Working Memory
STM_Ve/ Vi : Verbal/ Visual Short Term Memory
LTM_Ve/Vi : Verbal/Visual Long Term Memory
Rec : Form Recognition
Exp: Visual and spatial Exploration
Glos : Glossary
Cat : Category
Comp : Comprehension
Nb_Ve/ Vi : Weight of Verbal/ Visual media
Sc_Vi/ Sc_Ve: Visual / Verbal score calculated using the formula (3) / (4)
Nb_Vi/Ve/S: respectively the number of Visual, Verbal and Sound media

Each criterion is attributed a factor to weigh it.

Step 4 :

This step consists in selecting the combination for which the sum is the greatest one.

Step 5 :

Changes the state value (inside the XML document) for every element where the signature belongs to the selected combination.

Step 6 :

Transforms the selected elements using an XSLT document.

4.3 Results

We present hereafter some results obtained by the algorithm given above applied to 3 users. The document contains 2 blocks (B1,B2) with 3 elements, whose signatures are :

B1 (E1:T[3]G[2]S[0] + E2:T[1]G[5]S[0] + E3:T[0]G[0]S[4]),
B2 (E1:T[5]G[0]S[0] + E2:T[3]G[0]S[0] + E3:T[0]G[4]S[0]).

Each table displays the combinations, the criteria and their evaluation, and the "best" combination for each profile. The following table shows the profile of 3 virtual users:

Table 1. Cognitive profile for three users

Indicator	Wm_ve	Stm_ve	Stm_vi	Ltm_ve	Ltm_vi	Rec
Profile 1	70	70	30	70	30	50
Profile 2	50	50	70	30	70	50
Profile 3	30	30	50	30	50	50

Indicator	Glos	Cat	Exp	Comp	Sc_ve	Sc_vi
Profile 1	70	70	50	50	66	38
Profile 2	30	50	70	50	43	66
Profile 3	50	30	30	50	36	46

The "best" combination for every user is shown in the following table. The score values are the average of the criteria given above.

Table 2. Scores related to every profile and the "best" combination for each profile

N°	Combinations	Score Pr1	Score Pr2	Score Pr3
0	B1(E2+E3), B2(E1+E3)	49,47	56,93	42,27
1	B1(E2+E3),B2(E2+E3)	46,82	**59,03**	43,12
2	B1(E2+E3),B2(E1+E2)	56,43	51,43	40,00
3	B1(E1+E3), B2(E1+E3)	54,38	53,05	40,67
4	B1(E1+E3), B2(E2+E3)	52,33	54,67	41,33
5	B1(E1+E3), B2(E1+E2)	62,26	46,82	38,10
6	B1(E1), B2(E1+E3)	53,93	53,41	40,81
7	B1(E1), B2(E2+E3)	50,29	56,29	42,00
8	B1(E1), B2(E1+E2)	**66,67**	43,33	36,67
9	B1(E2), B2(E1+E3)	49,47	56,93	42,27
10	B1(E2), B2(E2+E3)	46,82	59,03	**43,13**
11	B1(E2), B2(E1+E2)	56,43	51,43	40,00
12	B1(E3), B2(E1+E3)	54,38	53,05	40,67
13	B1(E3), B(E2+E3)	52,33	54,67	41,33
14	B1(E3), B(E1+E2)	62,26	46,82	38,10

Scores are computed using the two criteria given above, the maximum value enables the choice of the "best" combination. Hereafter, we show an example of the output documents for the block 1 only. In the first image (Fig. 4), the two media (text and image) are chosen with the levels 1 and 5 respectively which corresponds to the profile of the **score Pr3**. In the second image the two selected media appear but this time with the levels 3 and 2 respectively which corresponds to the profile of the **score Pr1** (Fig. 5).

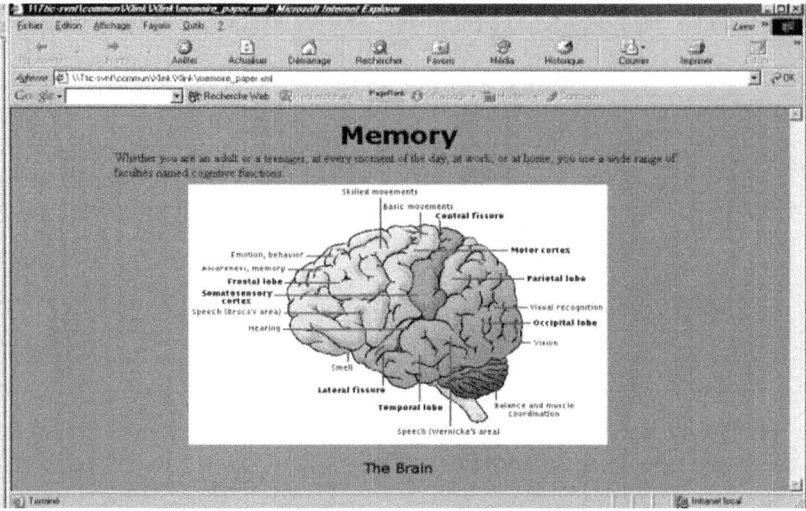

Fig. 4. Output document with the T3 and G2 media

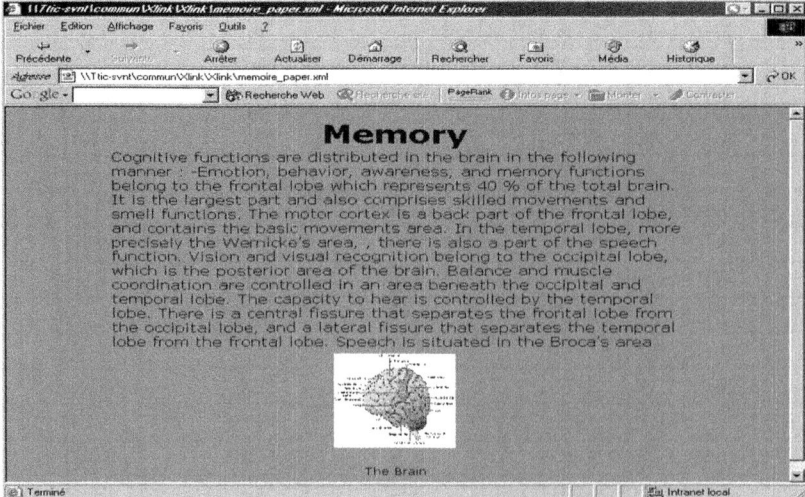

Fig. 5. Output document with media T5 and G1

5   Experimental Plan Description

Our experimental plan starts by selecting a population of 24 students to evaluate the system. First, they execute a module that enables us to build their cognitive profile. Then we create two groups according to the scores they got for verbal and visual media. The basic idea is to divide each group into two sub-groups, where the student of the first group explore the "Brain Story" document adapted to their cognitive profile whereas the second one explore the document that is not adapted to their cognitive profile.

Before the exploration, a pre-test related to the "Brain Story" document is applied to all the students in order to evaluate their knowledge of the subject. During twenty minutes, every student explores the document entirely. At the end of the test, every student fills a questionnaire for an evaluation of :

- knowledge that students acquired (quantitative evaluation i.e. the quantity of information they learned);
- easiness during the document exploration (qualitative evaluation).

The evaluation enables the validation of the adaptive process we adopted, especially selection criteria and their weights.

6 Conclusion and Future Work

In this paper, we have described how to generate and then incorporate the cognitive profile into adaptive multimedia interfaces. The first step consists in building the user cognitive model through a set of interactive exercises. Based on demographic data, this model contains 25 cognitive indicators dispatched into 5 sectors: *memory, attention, executive functions, language and visual & spatial capacities*. This profile is the input of the last step of the adaptation process, where the couples (criteria, multimedia combinations) are evaluated with weighting factors. These factors enable the selection of most compatible output documents.

The first working track has been defined, experimentation and validation work are currently in progress especially to improve the criteria and especially their weights to make the adaptation more reliable. On the other side, we are working on transformation process with XSLT to adapt the transformation to the document.

To evaluate the adaptation process, as described above, we are going to compare the amount of learned information and how much the use of adapted multimedia interfaces was easy for several populations confronted to different presentations of our document. This experimentation is planned in March 2003. Adapted presentations and non adapted presentations will be proposed and results will be compared.

According to theories, guidelines and to our preliminary work, we can say that this research field is promising and fertile with new developments. This work has been possible by adopting a multidisciplinary approach i.e. computer science, cognitive psychology and neuro-psychology.

References

1. Antonietti, A. Colombo, B. Net surfing and thinking style research and innovation. In Research Workshop of European Distance Education Network (EDEN), Prague 2000. (URL: http://www.eden.bme.hu/CodeSig/reports.htm)
2. Brusilovsky, P., Su, H.-D. Adaptive Visualization Component of a Distributed Web-based Adaptive Educational System. In: Intelligent Tutoring Systems. Vol. 2363, (Proceedings of 6th International Conference on Intelligent Tutoring Systems, ITS'2002, Biarritz, France, June 2–7, 2002) Berlin: Springer-Verlag, pp. 229–238.
3. Brusilovsky, P. Methods and Techniques of Adaptive Hypermedia. User Modeling and User-Adapted Interaction, 6, pp. 87–129. 1996 (Reprinted in Adaptive Hypertext and Hypermedia, Kluwer Academic Publishers, 1998, pp. 1–43).
4. De-Bra, P., Brusilovsky, P., Houben, G.J. Adaptive Hypermedia: From Systems to Framework. ACM Computing Surveys 31:4. (URL: http://www.cs.brown.edu/memex/ACM_HypertextTestbed/papers/25.html).
5. De-Bra, P., & Calvi, L. a Generic Adaptive Hypermedia System. 2nd Workshop on Adaptive Hypertext and Hypermedia, pp. 1–10. (URL: http://wwwis.win.tue.nl/ah98/DeBra.html)
6. Dufresne, A., Turcotte, S. Cognitive style and its implications for navigation strategies. In B. d. Boulay, & R. Mizoguchi (Ed.), Artificial Intelligence in Education: Knowledge and Media in Learning Systems (pp. 287–293). Amsterdam: IOS Press. AI-ED'97 Conference, Kobe, Japan, 1997.
7. Elting, C. Zwickel, J. Malaka, R. Device-Dependant Modality Selection for User-Interface An Empirical Study. In IUI'02, San Francisco, USA, 2002.
8. Furtado, E. Incorporating human factors into a method for designing of adaptive user interface. In Tools for Working with Guidelines, pp. 147–156, 2000.
9. Habieb-Mammar, F. Tarpin-Berbard, P. Prévôt Modelisation XML des interfaces adaptatives integrant le profil cognitif de l'utilisateur . *DVP'2002 Documents Virtuels Personnalisables.* Brest. p. 8. Juillet 2002.
10. Laroussi M, Conception et Réalisation de Système Didactique Hypermédia Adaptatif : CAMELEON, Ph.D. thesis, Manouba University, Manouba, Tunisia, 2001.
11. Tarpin-Bernard, F. Habieb Mammar, H. Croisile, B. Noir, M. (2001). A supervised Program for Cognitive e-Training. WebNet'2001, World Conference on Web technologies. Orlando. October 2001.
12. Witkin, H. A., Goodenough, D. R. Cognitive Styles: Essence and Origins. New York: Int. Universities Press 1981.
13. Witkin, H. A., Moore, C. A., Goodenough, D. R., Cox, P. W. Field-Dependent and Field-Independent Cognitive Styles and Their Educational Implications. Review of Educational Research, 47 (1) (1977) 1–64.
14. Language XML- W3C Recommandation http://www.w3.org/xml/
15. XSL Transformations (XSLT) http://www.w3.org/Style/xsl/

Discovering Prediction Rules in AHA! Courses

Cristóbal Romero[1], Sebastián Ventura[1], Paul de Bra[2], and Carlos de Castro[1]

[1]University of Córdoba, Campus Universitario de Rabanales, 14071, Córdoba, España
{cromero,sventura,cdecastro}@uco.es
[2]Eindhoven University of Technology (TU/e), PO Box 513, Eindhoven, The Netherlands
debra@win.tue.nl

Abstract. In this paper we are going to show how to discover interesting prediction rules from student usage information to improve adaptive web courses. We have used AHA! to make courses that adapt both the presentation and the navigation depending on the level of knowledge that each particular student has. We have performed several modifications in AHA! to specialize it and power it in the educational area. Our objective is to discover relations between all the picked-up usage data (reading times, difficulty levels and test results) from student executions and show the most interesting to the teacher so that he can carry out the appropriate modifications in the course to improve it.

1 Introduction

Web-based education is a current research area, due to its benefits such as independence in physical localization and platform. Especially Web-based Adaptive Educational Hypermedia Systems [2] have many advantages because they can adapt the course to each specific student. They build an individual user model and they use it to adapt the application to the user, for example, they adapt the content of a hypermedia page to the knowledge or objective of the user, or they suggest the most relevant links to follow. But the methodology used to elaborate them is accustomed to being static, that is, when the course elaboration is finished and published on the Internet it is never modified again. The teacher only accesses the student's evaluation information obtained from the course to analyze the student's progress. We propose, a dynamic elaboration methodology, where the usage information is used by the teacher to modify the course and to improve its performance for a better student's learning. Our approach is to use data mining [12] in order to discover useful information to help in decision making processes. Nowadays some researches are beginning to use different data mining techniques in web-learning activities [11]. Concretely we propose an evolutionary algorithm for discovering prediction rules. To do it we use the student's usage information obtained from a Web-based Adaptive Hypermedia Course. The discovered rules could then be shown to the teacher in order to help him decide how the course could be modified to obtain best performance.

P. Brusilovsky et al. (Eds.): UM 2003, LNAI 2702, pp. 25–34, 2003.

Below we are going to describe our dynamic construction methodology, and then we describe the architecture of the AHA! courses and the modifications we have done. Next we'll describe the student's usage information obtained with it. Then we'll introduce the evolutionary algorithms for predictioning rule mining. And finally we'll describe the implementation, main conclusion and the current state of our work.

2 Methodology

The dynamic construction methodology of Web-based Adaptive Courses that we propose [9] is recurrent, evolutionary and while the number of students who use the system increases, more information is available to the teacher to improve it. In our methodology we can distinguish four main steps:

1. Construction of the course. The teacher builds the Hypermedia Adaptive Course providing information of the domain model, the pedagogic model and the interface module. An authoring tool is usually used to facilitate this task. The remaining information: tutor model is usually given by the system itself and the student model is acquired in execution time. Once the teacher and the authoring tool finish the elaboration of the course, then, all contents may be published on a web server.
2. Execution of the course. Students execute the course using a web navigator and in a transparent way the usage information is picked up and stored in the server in the log file of each student.
3. Prediction Rule Mining. After log files have been transferred to a database the teacher can apply the evolutionary algorithms to discover important relationships among the data picked up. We want to discover relations between knowledge levels, times and scores. To do this task, he can use a generic data mining tool or he can use our specific visual tool (EPRules).
4. Improving the course. The teacher using the discovered relationships carries out the modifications that he believes more appropriate to improve the performance of the course. For example he can modify the course's original structure (joining concepts, changing concepts from level or chapter, etc.) and content (eliminating or improving bad questions, bad pages, etc.). To do it, he uses again the authoring tool.

3 Architecture of Modified AHA!

In order to test our methodology and our algorithms for discovering prediction rules we have developed an adaptive web-course to obtain the necessary usage information. We have chosen AHA! [4] to build our course because it lets us convert into adaptive all type of web-based applications, its adaptation characteristics, it stores usage information in log files and the source code is available. We have to do some modifications in order to specialize it in education. We want to adapt the course to each particular user depending on his knowledge level. The architecture of the modified AHA! consists of domain model, user model and adaptation engine.

3.1 Domain Model

The domain model in the AHA system [4] consists of concepts and relations between them. One concept is a component that represents an information abstract element and it has identification, a set of pair attributes values and a set of links. One concept has one o several related web pages. Each web page is a XML file with conditionally included fragments and hypertext links.

The AHA modified domain model that we are going to use is based on the typical structure of the educational material in which one course consists of several chapters that have several concepts and subconcepts. Another important characteristic that we have added to the AHA domain model is the classification of concepts by difficulty levels (novice, medium and expert). In this way each chapter can have tree different difficulty levels, each one with different concepts.

3.2 User Model

The user model in AHA [4] consists of a set of pair attributes-values about knowledge, time and visit. In the case of knowledge, each attribute is associated to one concept of the domain model. For each user the system has a board in which the values of the attributes are stored. In AHA the knowledge attributes values vary from 0 to 100. They show the knowledge level that the student has on that concept and they change as the student visits the concepts. AHA also has another attribute that indicates if the student has read or not the concept (values 0 or 1). Finally for each page, AHA stores the time the user spend visiting it.

Our AHA modified student model is practically the same with the difference in the way of calculating the knowledge attribute and the values that it can have. In our systems we calculate the knowledge variable basing on the obtained score in the question associated to the concepts. In AHA the value is only increased as the user reads the pages about the concepts. Also in our system the variable can only have four values: 0 (no level of knowledge. No test done yet.), 10 (low level of knowledge), 50 (medium level of knowledge) and 100 (high level of knowledge).

3.3 Adaptation Engine

In AHA [4] the information content adaptation of a hypermedia document and the links structure is carried out using a set of rules. These rules will specify the relation structure between the domain model and user model, that is, the personalized presentation generated for each student. The adaptation rules are defined by the author of the course. Applying these rules we will obtain the adaptation that will be shown to the user.

Our AHA modified adaptation engine uses rules also for adapting the presentation and navigation to the specific knowledge level of each student. But in AHA all the rules are located in the same domain content files. In our system we have created a new type of files named chapter evaluation files. These files contain all the necessary rules to adapt a specific chapter. So, in the XML domain files have only content without rules, separating in this way the content from the adaptation. The adaptation we have implemented in our system is: if the level of knowledge of the student in a chapter is high then the content will be shown in a high level. If the student increases or decreases his level in the chapter, then the content will be increased or decreased too. In Figure 1 it is shown the specific adaptation of a chapter in our system.

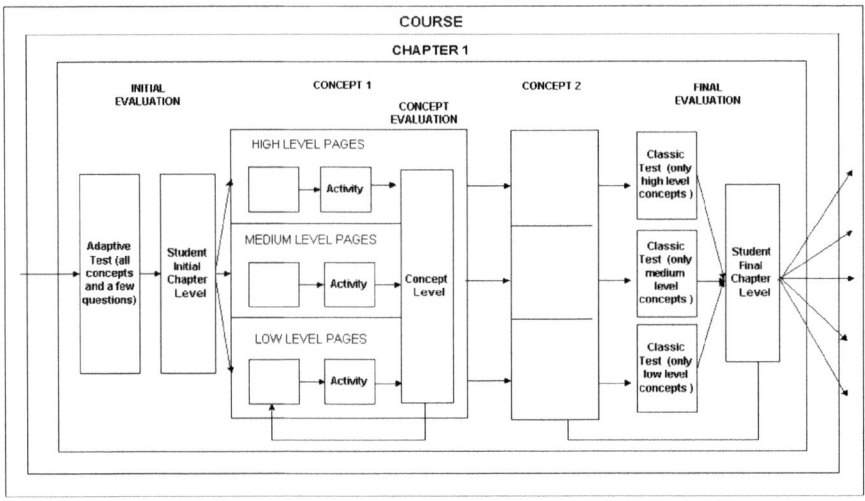

Fig. 1. Adaptation of one chapter in modified AHA!

In the previous figure we can see that in order to know the student knowledge level in each chapter, first the student has to do an adaptive initial test that determines the initial level to be show in the chapter. Next, the system obtains the progression through the activities and finally it obtains the final level through a classic final test. In order to finish a chapter the student has to get the expert level, that is, if initially the student obtained a low level, he would have to overcome the medium level and then the expert level. When the student finishes a chapter in expert level, he can go to the next chapters and all starts again (firstly doing an initial test, next the activities and then the final test).

4   Usage Information

The usage information we are going to use for discovering prediction rules is the information picked up from the courses developed with the modified AHA! system. The AHA system stores the usage information in two web log files (logs and model files) in which the information about the user navigation and the user knowledge is respectively stored. But we have added one more log file (test file) to store the scores of the questions (activities and tests). Before applying our prediction rules algorithm we have moved all that information stored in the logs files to tables and columns of a database. We have done it to facilitate and to increase the speed of the data mining algorithms.

During this translation process we have carried out a pre-processing of the data (attribute selection, noise elimination, etc.). So the three logs files (logs, model and test) are converted in three tables of a data base.

- Times. It's created from the logs file and it contains information about the XML pages (content, question, etc.) and the accurate time in which the student has accessed to them.
- Levels. It's created from the model file and it contains information about the knowledge level (high, medium, low) that the student has in each concept.
- Success. It's created from the test file and it contains information about the success or failure of the students in the questions (tests or activities).

5   Prediction Rule Mining

We have used an evolutionary algorithm to obtain prediction rules [7] from the usage data of a web-based adaptive course. The prediction rules show important dependence relations between data that can be used for decision making. The general form of a prediction rule is:

$$\text{IF Cond}_1 \text{ AND } \dots \text{ Cond}_n \dots \text{ AND Cond}_m \text{ THEN Pred} \tag{1}$$

This kind of rule consists of two parts. The rule antecedent (the IF part) contains a conjunctions of m conditions about values of predictor attributes, whereas the rule consequent (the THEN part) contains a prediction about the value of a goal attribute. We have chosen this type of knowledge representation because it is intuitively comprehensible for most users.

On the other hand evolutionary algorithms are a paradigm based on the Darwin evolution process, where each individual codifies a solution and evolves to a better individual by means of genetic operators (mutation and crossover). In general the main motivation for using evolutionary algorithms for rule discovery is that they perform a global search and cope better with attribute interaction than greedy rule algorithms often used in data mining [5]. Most data mining methods are based on the rule induction paradigm, where the algorithm usually performs a kind of local search (hill climbing). Also the fitness function in evolutionary algorithm evaluates the individual as a whole, i.e. all the interactions among attributes are take into account. In contrast, most rule induction methods selects one attribute at a time and evaluate partially constructed candidates rule, rather than full candidate rule. The Genetic Process we have used consists of the following steps [6]: The first step is Initialization, next Evaluation, Selection and Reproduction steps are repeated until the Finalization condition is fulfilled (see Figure 2).

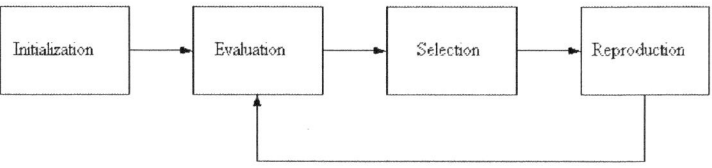

Fig. 2. Evolutionary Process.

- Initialization consists of generating a group of initial rules specified by the user. They are generated starting from the most frequent values in the database. We use a Michigan approach in which each individual (chromosomes) encodes a single rule. We use encoding value in which a rule is a linear string of conditions, where each condition is a variable-value pair. The size of the rules is dynamically depending of the number of elements in antecedent and the last element always represents the consequent. The generic format of the rules we are going to discover in Backus Naur Form (BNF) is:

<rule>::= IF <antecedent> THEN <consequent>
<antecedent>::= <condition> AND <antecedent> | <condition>   (2)
<consequent>::= <condition>
<condition>::= <attribute> <operator> <value>
<attribute>::= <type>.<name> | <type>.<name>(<number>)
<type>::= TIME | SUCCES | LEVEL
<name>::= STRING
<number>::= INTEGER
<operator>::= ≤ | ≥ | =
<value>::= INTEGER | YES | NO | LOW | MEDIUM | HIGH

- Evaluation consists of calculating the fitness of the current rules and keeping with the best ones (overcome a minimum value specify). Our evaluation function can use the measures directly chosen by the user instead of using only the typical confidence and support (the support is a measure of the number of data that fulfill the rule and the confidence is a measure of the correlation between antecedent and consequent). We have implemented a lot of rule evaluation measures [10] arise from statistic, machine learning and data mining areas (certainty factor, correlation, interest, Laplace, conviction, Gini, J-measure, etc.). The rules that overcome a minimum value specified by for the chose measure are directly stored in the final rule vector. This rule vector is show to the user at the end of the evolutionary process.
- Selection chooses rules from the population to be parents to crossover or mutate. We use rank-based selection that first ranks the population and then every rule receives fitness from its ranking. The worst will have fitness 1, second worst 2, etc. and the best will have fitness N (number of rules in population). Parents are selected according to their fitness. With this method all the rules have a chance to be selected.
- Reproduction consists of creating new rules, mutating and crossing current rules (rules obtained in the previous evolution step). Mutation consists of the creation of a new rule, starting from an older rule where we change a variable or value. We randomly mutate a variable or values in the consequent or antecedent. Crossover consists of making two new rules, starting from the crossing of two existent rules. In crossing the antecedent of a rule is joined to the consequent of another rule in order to form a new rule and vice versa (the consequent of the first rule is joined to an antecedent of the second).
- Finalization is the number of steps or generations that will be applied to the genetic process. We could also have chosen to stop when a certain number of rules are added to the final rule vector.

6 Implementation and Results

We have developed a specific visual tool (EPRules: Educational Prediction Rules) in Java to facility the process of discovering interesting prediction rules (see Figure 3). This Tool is oriented to the teacher so it is more easy to use, more comprehensible and more intuitive than other current generic data mining tools.

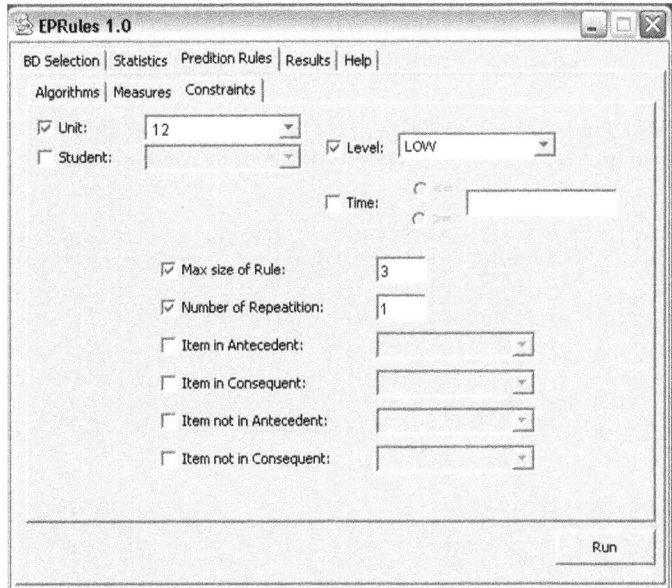

Fig. 3. Visual Tool for discovering prediction rules.

The main tasks of EPRules are:
- Selection and Preprocessing. You can select an existing database or the AHA logs files you want to preprocess and convert them in the database of usage information.
- Statistics. You can select the basic statistics (maximum, minimum, mean, mode, etc.) of the times, scores and levels obtained by students in the pages and questions of the course.
- Prediction rules. You can select the parameters of the evolutionary algorithm (population size, crossover and mutation probability, number or evolution, etc.) the measures to use (support, confidence, interest, etc.) and constraints (unit, student, level, time, etc.) to apply in the prediction rules.
- Results. You can visualize the statistics (in numerical and graphical way) and the prediction rules (antecedent, consequent and measures values).

We have used the data picked-up from a Linux course developed with modified AHA!. The course has been used by 50 student of Computer Science in the University of Cordoba. To test our evolutionary algorithm we have compared it with an Apriori algorithm [1] that is a classical algorithm for discovering rules. The specific parameter used for the two algorithms are shown in Table 1.

Table 1. Parameters of Evolutionary and Apriori algorithms.

Evolutionary Algorithm	Apriori Algorithm
Size of rule = 3	Size of rule = 3
Min Support = 0.8	Min Support = 0.8
Min Chose-Measure = 0.8	Min Confidence = 0.8
Size of population = 100	
Number of evolution = 50	
Crossover Probability = 0.8	
Mutation Probability = 0.2	

We have compared the Apriori algorithm that only uses confidence and support with our evolutionary algorithm using one different measure each time (Figure 4).

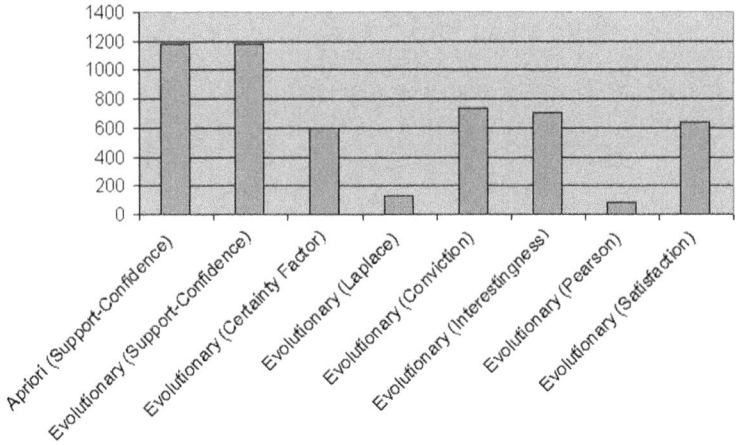

Fig. 4. Evolutionary versus Apriori algorithm.

We have compared the average execution time and the average number of discovered rules, and the Apriori algorithm was always faster and it found much more rules than our evolutionary algorithm. But wasn't a bad result, because on one side it was expected that evolutionary algorithm was slower but on the other side it is very good that the evolutionary algorithm can discover a small number of rules. Due to the completeness nature of the Apriori algorithm it discovers all the possible rules and there are a lot of redundant and not interesting rules. And if there are so many rules it is difficult to the teacher to understand and to identify what the really interesting rules are. This problem has been named like interestingness problem of association rules [8] and to resolve it the use of a lot of different measures have been proposed. Our solution to this problem is that the own teacher choose the measure in what he is interested. In this way all the discovered rules will be interesting for him. The objective is to show only a few interesting rules to the teacher. To do it we use the chose measure and constraints. So the teacher can specify some conditions or filters that the discovered rules have to fulfill. These conditions are about chapters (in what chapter he is interested), students (in whom student or students he is interested in), levels (in which level he is interested), etc. The discovered rules show relations about tree types of relation (time, success and level) depending on the type of the condiciont of the rule consequence:

- Time. It shows conditions (antecedent items) that have an effect in a time condition (consequent item).
- Level. It shows conditions (antecedent items) that have an effect in a level condition (consequent item).
- Success. It shows conditions (antecedent items) that have an effect in a success condition (consequent item).

In the Table 2 we show several interesting examples of discovered prediction rules with size 2 and with its support and interestingness measure.

Table 2. Example of Discovered Prediction Rules.

Antecedent	Consequent	Sup	Int
TIME.testi3-0(3)>60	SUCCESS.testi3-0(3)=NO	0.8	0.93
LEVEL.historia1-0=HIGH	LEVEL.intro1-2=HIGH	0.85	0.95
SUCCESS.ftp12-2(1)=YES	SUCESS.telnet11-1(2)=YES	0.85	0.91
LEVEL.testf14-1=LOW	LEVEL.testf6-1=LOW	0.8	0.93

Firstly, we have to know the exact meaning of the nomenclature we have used to name the concepts so we can understand the rules correctly. The name of a concept consist of the page name (the string after the dot), the chapter number (after the page name), slash delimiter, the level number (0 low, 1 medium and 2 high) and the question number in brackets if it is a question not a content page. The first rule shows that students have problems (time and failure) with the question 3 of the initial test in chapter 3, so the teacher should modify it. The second rule shows a relation between two concepts of the same chapter 1 but in a different level (0:low and 2:high), so the teacher should put them together in the same level. The third rule shows a relation between two questions of different chapters, so the teacher should verify that there are really different questions. And finally the fourth rule shows a relation between the final levels of two chapters, so the teacher can add a direct link between these two chapters if there isn't any yet.

7 Conclusions

In this paper we have described a methodology to develop web-based adaptive hypermedia courses using AHA system as base. We have modified the AHA! functionality to specialize it in educational environment. In short we have added level of knowledge (low, medium and high) so that we can adapt the presentation and navigation of the course depending on the level of each student in each chapter. But our objective is to be able to improve the performance of the developed courses applying evolutionary algorithms to discover prediction rules among all the usage data. These rules will be shown to the teacher so he can decide what change can do in the course.

We have tested our evolutionary algorithms with the data obtained from the Linux course and we have shown that they can produce potentially useful results. We have compared it with a classic algorithm for discovering rules like Apriori and we have shown that our evolutionary algorithm is a good alternative for extracting a small set of interesting rules, which is very important for decision-making. To achieve it, we have used the constraints and measures that the teacher selects more important to him.

We are now developing a more sophisticated evolutionary algorithm with multiobjective optimization techniques [3], to obtain more interesting rules. The idea is to use not only one measure for finding the rules but also to use several different metrics at the same time. We are also developing a new evolutionary algorithm using grammar-based genetic programming. We have shown that the rules can directly be represented like a grammar, so we can implement them easily. Using this type of representation the form of the rules is more flexible and modifiable.

References

1. Agrawal R., Srikant R. (1994) Fast Algorithms for Mining Association Rules. Conf. on Very Large Databases. Santiago de Chile.
2. Brusilovsky, P. (1998) Adaptative Educational Systems on the World-Wide-Web: A Review of Available Technologies. Conf. on ITS. San Antonio.
3. Coello, C.A. (1999) An Updated Survey of Evolutionary Multiobjetive Optimization Techniques: State of the Art and Future Trends. IEEE pp. 3–13.
4. De Bra P., Ruiter J. (2001). AHA! Adaptive Hypermedia for All. Conf. on WebNet. Orlando, Florida.
5. Freitas, A. A. (2002) A survey of evolutionary algorithms for data minig and knowledge discovery. Advances in Evolutionary Computation. Springer-Verlag.
6. Michalewicz, Z. (1996) Genetic Algorithms + Data Structures = Evolution Programs. 3rd edn. Springer-Verlag, Berlin Heidelberg New York
7. Noda E., Freitas A., Heitor S.L. (1999) Discovering Interesting Prediction Rules with a Genetic Algorithm. Conf. on Evolutionary Computation. Washington DC.
8. Piatesky-Shapiro G., Matheus J. (1994) The interestingness of deviations. Proceedings of the AAAI-94 Workshop on KDD. Seattle, Washington.
9. Romero, C., De Castro, C., Ventura, S. Hall W., Hong M. (2002). Using Genetic Algorithms for Data Mining in Web-based Educational Hypermedia System. Workshop on Adaptive Systems for Web-based Education. Malaga.
10. Tan, P., Kumar V. (2000) Interesting Measures for Association Patterns: A Perspective. TR00-036. Department of Computer Science. University of Minnesota.
11. Zaïne, O. R. (2001) Web Usage Mining for a Better Web-Based Learning Environment. Conf. on Advanced Technology for Education, Banff, Alberta.
12. Zytkow J., Klosgen W. (2001) Handbook of Data Mining and Knowledg Discovery. Oxford University Press.

Word Weighting Based on User's Browsing History

Yutaka Matsuo

National Institute of Advance Industrial Science and Technology,
y.matsuo@aist.go.jp,
http://www.carc.aist.go.jp/~y.matsuo

Abstract. We developed a word-weighting algorithm based on the information access history of a user. The information access history of a user is represented as a set of words, and is considered to be a user model. We weight words in a document according to their relevancy to the user model. The relevancy is measured by the biases of co-occurrence, called *IRM* (Interest Relevance Measure), between a word in a document and words in the user model. We evaluate *IRM* through a constructed browsing support system, which monitors word occurrences on the user's browsed Web pages and highlights keywords in the current page. Our system consists of three components: a proxy server that monitors access to the Web, a frequency server that stores the frequencies of words appearing on the accessed Web pages, and a keyword extraction module.

1 Introduction

Currently, many information support systems combined with natural language techniques use *tfidf* to measure the weight of words. *Tfidf*, based on statistics of word occurrence on a target document and a corpus, has been shown to be effective in many practical systems including summarization systems and retrieval systems [7]. Its effectiveness is also supported from an information theoretical view [1].

However, a word that is important to one user is sometimes not important to others. Let us take the newspaper article "Suzuki hitting streak ends at 23 games", for example. Ichiro Suzuki is a Japanese Major League Baseball player who was recognized as MVP in 2001. A user who is greatly interested in Major League Baseball would be interested in the phrase such as "hitting streak ends," because he/she would know that Suzuki was achieving the longest hitting streak in the majors in that year. On the other hand, a user who has no interest in MLB at all would note the words "game" or "Seattle Mariners" as the informative words, because those words would indicate that the subject of the article was baseball, and that knowledge would be sufficient.

Current systems utilize the weight of words to represent a user profile, and to compare a document profile with a user profile. However, word weighting and keyword selection that reflect a user's interest are important because appropriate selection of keywords improves the accurcy of the comparison between a document profile and a user profile.

P. Brusilovsky et al. (Eds.): UM 2003, LNAI 2702, pp. 35–44, 2003.
© Springer-Verlag Berlin Heidelberg 2003

Table 1. Frequency and probability distribution.

Frequent word	a	b	c	d	e	f	g	h	i	j	Total
Frequency	203	63	44	44	39	36	35	33	30	28	555
Probability	0.366	0.114	0.079	0.079	0.070	0.065	0.063	0.059	0.054	0.050	1.0

a: *machine*, b: *computer*, c: *question*, d: *digital*, e: *answer*, f: *game*, g: *argument*, h: *make*, i: *state*, j: *number*

In order to measure the weight of words more correctly, contextual information about a user is necessary. This paper shows one approach to address context-based word weighting, focusing on the statistical feature of word occurrence: If a user is not familiar with the topic, he/she may think general words related to the topic are important. On the other hand, if a user is familiar with the topic, he/she may think more detailed words are important.

The rest of the paper is organized as follows. In the next section, we explain *IRM*. We evaluate IRM by constructing the browsing support system shown in Sections 3 and 4. We discuss our approach in Section 5 and offer concluding remarks.

2   Weighting Words

2.1   Weighting by Co-occurrence Biases

IRM is based on a word-weighting algorithm applied to a single document. We first introduce the method [5].

A document consists of sentences. Here, two words[1] in the same sentence are considered to co-occur once. By counting the word frequencies, we can obtain frequent words. Let us take a very famous paper by Alan Turing [10] as an example. Table 1 shows the top ten frequent words (denoted as G) and the probability of occurrence, normalized so that the sum is to be 1.

Next, a co-occurrence matrix is obtained by counting frequencies of pairwise word co-occurrence, as shown in Table 2. For example, word a and word b co-occur in 30 sentences in the document. Let N denote the number of different words in the document. Because the word co-occurrence matrix is an $N \times N$ symmetric matrix, Table 2 shows only a part of the whole – an $N \times 10$ matrix. We do not define diagonal components here.

Assuming that word w_i appears independently from frequent words G, the distribution of co-occurrence of word w_i and any of the frequent words is similar to the unconditional distribution of occurrence of the frequent words, which is shown in Table 1. Conversely, if word w_i has a semantic relation with a particular set of words $g \in G$, co-occurrence of word w_i and g is greater than expected; the probability distribution is biased.

---

[1] In this paper, we refer to a word as a word or a word sequence.

Table 2. A co-occurrence matrix.

	a	b	c	d	e	f	g	h	i	j	Total
a	—	30	26	19	18	12	12	17	22	9	165
b	30	—	5	50	6	11	1	3	2	3	111
c	26	5	—	4	23	7	0	2	0	0	67
d	19	50	4	—	3	7	1	1	0	4	89
e	18	6	23	3	—	7	1	2	1	0	61
f	12	11	7	7	7	—	2	4	0	0	50
g	12	1	0	1	1	2	—	5	1	0	23
h	17	3	2	1	2	4	5	—	0	0	34
i	22	2	0	0	1	0	1	0	—	7	33
j	9	3	0	4	0	0	0	0	7	—	23
...											...
u	6	5	5	3	3	18	2	2	1	0	45
v	13	40	4	35	3	6	1	0	0	2	104
w	11	2	2	1	1	0	1	4	0	0	22
x	17	3	2	1	2	4	5	0	0	0	34

u: *imitation*, v: *digital computer*, w:*kind*, x:*make*

Looking at Table 2, a general word such as 'kind" or "make" is used relatively impartially with each frequent word, while a word such as "imitation" or "digital computer" shows co-occurrence especially with particular words. These biases are derived from either semantic, lexical, or other kinds of relation between two words.

Therefore, the degree of biases of co-occurrence can be used as a surrogate for word importance. In order to evaluate the statistical significance of biases, we use the χ^2 test. We denote the unconditional probability of a frequent word $g \in G$ as the expected probability p_g, and the total number of co-occurrences of word w_i and any of the frequent words G as $f_G(w_i)$. The frequency of co-occurrences of word w_i and word $g \in G$ is written as $freq(w_i, g)$. The statistical value of χ^2 is defined as follows.

$$\chi_i^2 = \sum_{g \in G} \frac{(freq(w_i, g) - f_G(w_i)p_g)^2}{f_G(w_i)p_g} \tag{1}$$

The word $f_G(w_i)p_g$ represents the expected frequency of co-occurrence, and $(freq(w, g) - f_G(w_i)p_g)$ represents the difference between expected and observed frequencies. Therefore, large χ_i^2 indicates that co-occurrence of word w_i shows a strong bias.

Table 3 shows words with high χ^2 values in Turing's paper. Generally, words with large χ^2 are relatively important in the document; words with small χ^2 are relatively trivial. This method performs better than *tf*, and comparably to *tfidf* [5].

Table 3. Words with high χ^2 value.

χ^2 value	frequency	label
196.9	16	imitation game
88.9	15	play
62.4	9	human computer
60.1	3	card
57.1	4	future
50.4	10	logic
45.1	7	identification
44.4	6	universality
42.7	30	state

2.2   Interest Relevance Measure

In the above method, the selection of frequent words G is essential to the resultant weight, because for each word, the co-occurrence with $g \in G$ is counted and contributes to the χ^2 value. If we set G differently, the obtained weighting will also become different.

For example, if we add the word "logic" to the frequent words G in Turing's paper, we get the result shown as in Table 4. "logic system" and "proposition" have high values because these words co-occur with "logic". If we add the word "God" to G, we get the result shown in Table 5. Now "animal," "woman," and "book" appear because these words co-occur selectively with "God". By adding the word w to G, words relevant to w appear important because they co-occur with w. This agrees with our intuition: for example, if a user is interested in motorbikes, he/she would likely pay attention to words related to motorbike; thus, these words would have a high weight.

Therefore, we focus on "familiar words" of the user, instead of "frequent words" in the document. Familiar words are the words which a user has frequently seen in the past. They can be obtained by, for example, monitoring the user's browsing behavior using a proxy server as discussed below. Frequency of co-occurrence with the familiar words is measured for each word, and the bias is calculated in order to measure the weight of words for a user. The bias shows the selective relevance of these words to the familiar words; if a word co-occurs selectively with several familiar words, it is of importance to the user. On the other hand, if a word does not co-occur, or co-occurs impartially, with each of the familiar words, it may not be important to the user.

Definition 1. Interest Relevancy Measure*(IRM) is defined as follows. For word w_i for user k,*

$$IRM_{ik} = \sum_{h \in H_k} \frac{(freq(w_i, h) - f_G(w_i)p_h)^2}{f_G(w_i)p_h}, \qquad (2)$$

Table 4. Words with high χ^2 value on the frequent words + "logic"

χ^2 value	frequency	label
196.6	16	imitation game
88.5	15	play
84.4	3	logic system
62.2	9	human computer
60.0	3	card
57.0	4	future
44.9	7	identification
44.2	6	proposition
43.9	5	limitation

Table 5. Words with high χ^2 value on the frequent words + "God"

χ^2 value	frequency	label
196.2	16	imitation game
113.8	6	animal
88.2	15	play
62.0	9	human computer
59.9	3	card
56.9	4	future
49.8	10	logic
44.7	7	identification
43.9	5	woman
40.8	5	book

where H_k is a set of familiar words for user k, $freq(w_i, h)$ is the frequency of co-occurrence of words w_i and h, $f_G(w_i)$ is the total number of occurrences of word w_i, and p_h is the expected probability of word h to appear.

If the value of *IRM* is large, word w_i is relevant to the user's familiar words. The word is relevant to the user's interests, so it is a keyword for the user. Conversely, if the value of *IRM* is small, word w_i is not specifically relevant to any of the user's familiar words.

3   Evaluation

It is difficult to evaluate *IRM* objectively because the weight of words depends on a user's familiar words, and therefore varies among users.

Therefore, we evaluate *IRM* by constructing a Web browsing support system. In our system, Web pages accessed by a user are monitored by a proxy server. Then the count of each word is stored in a database. The system, as shown in Fig. 1, consists of three components: a proxy server, a frequency server, and a keyword extraction module.

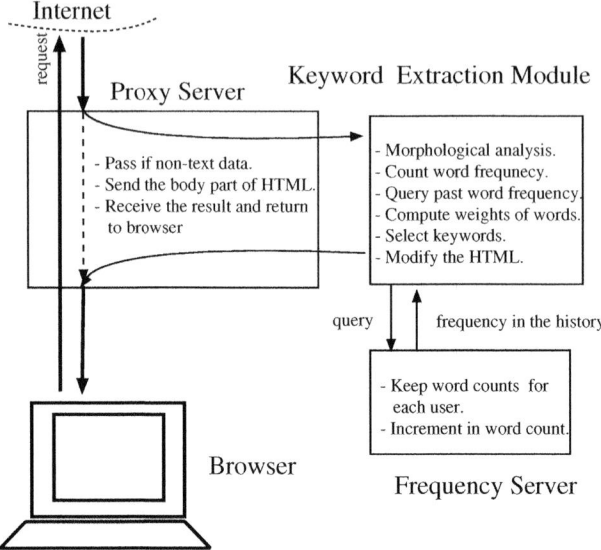

Fig. 1. System architecture.

3.1   Proxy Server

The Proxy Server inspects the browser's HTTP requests. When the response is returned, it judges whether the page is html/text. If it is a non-text file, or the length of the text is too short, it forwards the page to the browser without making any changes. Otherwise, it sends the body part of the page to the Keyword Extraction Module. Then it receives the modified contents in which the keywords are highlighted, and forwards it to the browser. Because the proxy server creates new threads to handle the browser's requests, it allows multiple pending requests from multithreaded browsers.

3.2   Keyword Extraction Module

The Keyword Extraction Module first performs morphological analysis, and counts the word frequencies on a page. Then it queries the Frequency Server in order to obtain the word frequency of the past for the user. Based on current and past word counts, the *IRMs* of various words are calculated. A given number of selected words are highlighted as keywords in a bold, red, larger font by inserting `<b><font size=+1 color=red>` and `</b></font>` tags.

3.3   Frequency Server

The Frequency Server keeps a record of the total number of browsed pages and a count of each word for each user. In other words, it manages user profiles. Particular words are defined as stop words; This includes the stop list by Salton [8], and words common to Web pages, such as "copyright," "page," "link," "news," "search," "mail," and so on.

Using this system, a user can browse the Web as usual. The difference is that some words are highlighted as described. Users can grab the overview quickly and locate possibly interesting words at once.

4   Evaluation

For purposes of evaluation, ten people each tried this system for more than one hour. We asked them to evaluate the system. Three methods were implemented for comparison, all using the same stop list: The weight of a word was calculated by (I) word frequency, (II) $tf \cdot idf$ measure, and (III) *IRM* measure. System (I) simply highlights the most frequent words in the document in red, and the most familiar words in blue. System (II) highlights the words with highest $tf \cdot idf$ value in red, and the most familiar words in blue. In our case, the $tf \cdot idf$ value is calculated using the past frequency of word w_i for user k, $f_{past}(w_{ik})$, and the number of browsed pages n_k, as follows:

$$tfidf_{ik} = f(w_i) \cdot \left(\log_2 \frac{n_k}{f_{past}(w_{ik})} + 1 \right).$$

System (III) highlights the words with highest *IRM* value in red, and the most familiar words in blue. The participants are kept blind to the weighting algorithm of the system. Note that in all three systems, the words in blue are extracted in the same manner.

After the user had tried each system, we asked him/her following questions. Answers to the questions were made on a 5-point Likert-scale from 1 (not at all) to 5 (very much).

Q1 Did this system help you browse the Web?
Q2 Are the words in red of interest to you?
Q3 Do the interesting words appear in red?
Q4 Are the words in blue of interest to you?
Q5 Do the interesting words appear in blue?

After the user had evaluated all three systems, we asked him/her the following two questions.

Q6 Which system assisted your browsing the most?
Q7 Which system best detected your interests?

The results are shown in Tables 6 and 7. With regard to the types of system support (Q1), the difference among them was small. *Tfidf* and *IRM* were comparable. The questions regarding the red-highlighted words (Q2 and Q3) demonstrated differences. Though *tfidf* performed as well as *IRM* with respect to precision, it performed worse with respect to recall. Q4 and Q5 about blue-highlighted words were similarly extracted in the three systems. Nevertheless,

Table 6. Average point of participants.

	Q1	Q2	Q3	Q4	Q5
(I) Word frequency	2.8	3.2	2.9	2.7	2.7
(II) *tfidf*		3.2	4.0	3.3	2.5	2.5
(III) **IRM**		3.2	4.1	3.8	2.0	2.4

Table 7. Cast ballots.

	Q6	Q7
(I) Word frequency	1	0
(II) *tfidf*	3	2
(III) **IRM**	6	8

IRM was evaluated as worse than the other systems. (Hopefully, this is because the words highlighted in red were better selected.) Overall, *tfidf* and *IRM* performed well. However, in terms of catching the user's interest, *IRM* performed best.

Q6 and Q7 are more straightforward questions. Obviously, word frequency is the least useful. Although a couple of participants chose *tfidf* as most effective, the majority of users agreed that *IRM* could best detect words of interest to the user.

None of the users negatively remarked the processing time, because the average processing time is less than a second. However, did remark some that changing fonts in HTML had a destructive effect on the design of the page. The performance of those three systems appeared useful for Web pages with relatively long text – for example, news articles.

5 Discussion and Related Work

Although *IRM* and *tfidf* are different algorithms, they have several qualitative properties in common.

- If a word appears relatively infrequently in a document, its weight is small: Because *IRM* measures the significance of biases, a small number of appearances of a word often implies small significance.
- If a word is familiar to the user (i.e., frequently appeared in the past), its weight is small.

The main difference of *IRM* to *tfidf* is the following.

- Even if a word appears frequently in a document, the weight of the word is small if it is not relevant to user's interests (i.e., if it does not co-occur with any familiar words).

This merit of *IRM* is reflected in Q2 in the previous section.

In recent years, various systems have been developed that utilize user models for personalization: Letizia [4] learns the interests of a user by observing his/her browsing behavior. Then it recommends links to follow. WebACE [3] proposes an agent for exploring and categorizing documents on the Web. It uses the *tfidf* measure for the feature vector of documents, and clusters these documents. Somlo presents an agent that maintains a history list with addresses of all the sites visited by a user [9]. If repetition occurs, the agent will learn this and add the address to the user profile. The profile categories are based on the *tfidf* measure. Web Personae, a personalized search and browsing system, models users with multiple profiles, each corresponding to a distinct topic or domain [6]. WebMate [2] is an agent that assists the user in browsing and searching. It represents different domains of user interest using multiple word vectors.

The above mentioned systems basically use word frequency or *tfidf* measure. Our *IRM* measure may contribute weight to words based both on their frequency in the documents and the user's interests.

Though each individual user may have a number of unrelated interests, our system can properly handle these; If a word co-occurs selectively with some familiar words, it is highlighted. Other familiar words have little effect on the bias.

6   Conclusions

In this paper, we proposed a new word-weighting algorithm called *IRM* for measuring the relevance of a word and a user's interests. We developed a browsing support system to evaluate *IRM*, which monitors a user's access to the Web and highlights keywords. Although the importance of a document or a sentence is not the summation of the weight of the words used in it, it is useful to calculate the weight of words in order to gauge a user's interests and consequently personalize retrieval or summarization systems.

References

1. A. Aizawa. The feature quantity: An information theoretic perspective of *thidf*-like measures. In *Proc. of SIGIR 2000*, pages 104–111, 2000.
2. L. Chen and K. Sycara. WebMate: A personal agent for browsing and searching. In *Proc. 2nd International Conference on Autonomous Agents (Agents '98)*, 1998.
3. E. Han, D. Boley, M. Gini, R. Gross, and K. Hastings. WebACE: A web agent for document categorization and exploration. In *Proc. 2nd International Conference on Autonomous Agents (Agents '98)*, 1998.
4. H. Lieberman. Letizia: An agent that assists Web browsing. In *Proc. 14th International Joint Conference on Artificial Intelligence (IJCAI-95)*, pages 924–929, 1995.
5. Y. Matsuo and M. Ishizuka. Keyword extraction from a document using word co-occurrence statistical information. *Transactions of the Japanese Society for Artificial Intelligence*, 17(3), 2002.

6. J. P. McGowan, N. Kushmetrick, and B. Smyth. Who do you want to be to-day? Web Personae for personalised information access. In *Proc. International Conference on Adaptive Hypermedia and Adaptive Web-Based Systems*, 2002.
7. A. Pretschner and S. Gauch. Personalization on the web. Technical Report ITTC-FY2000-TR-13591-01, The University of Kansas, 1999.
8. G. Salton. *Automatic Text Processing*. Addison-Wesley, MA., 1989.
9. G. L. Somlo and A. E. Howe. Agent-assisted internet browsing. In *Workshop on Intelligent Information Systems (AAAI-99)*, 1999.
10. A. M. Turing. Computing machinery and intelligence. *Mind*, 59:433–450, 1950.

SNIF-ACT: A Model of Information Foraging on the World Wide Web

Peter Pirolli and Wai-Tat Fu

[1] PARC, 3333 Coyote Hill Road, Palo Alto, California 94304
pirolli@parc.com, wfu@gmu.edu

Abstract. SNIF-ACT (Scent-based Navigation and Information Foraging in the ACT architecture) has been developed to simulate users as they perform unfamiliar information-seeking tasks on the World Wide Web (WWW). SNIF-ACT selects actions based on the measure of information scent, which is calculated by a spreading activation mechanism that captures the mutual relevance of the contents of a WWW page to the goal of the user. There are two main predictions of SNIF-ACT: (1) users working on unfamiliar tasks are expected to choose links that have high information scent, (2) users will leave a site when the information scent of the site diminishes below a certain threshold. SNIF-ACT produced good fits to data collected from four users working on two tasks each. The results suggest that the current content-based spreading activation SNIF-ACT model is able to generate useful predictions about complex user-WWW interactions.

1   Introduction

Over the course of the past decade and a half, vast amounts of content in the form of hypermedia have become available to the average computer user, primarily through the World Wide Web (WWW). Over this time, there has been limited progress towards a deep scientific understanding of the psychology of human interaction with the WWW. Detailed cognitive models are difficult to create, and unlike most models in human-computer interaction, the analysis of human-WWW interaction requires modeling user interaction with the semantics of Web content. Although difficult, there are many potential payoffs to developing a scientific foundation in this area. Such cognitive models could provide insights and engineering principles for improving usability. More directly they could provide automated cognitive engineering tools. They could serve as the basis for user models embedded in systems and devices to improve interaction, and they could serve as the basis for helping people to learn how to find, make sense of, and use information to improve solutions to significant everyday problems involving health, finance, career, and so on. The purpose of this paper is to present a computational cognitive model that simulates fine-grained human data collected from WWW users studied in a laboratory setting using realistic tasks. The model is based on a theoretical integration of *Information Foraging*

P. Brusilovsky et al. (Eds.): UM 2003, LNAI 2702, pp. 45–54, 2003.

Theory [1] and ACT-R [2]. Particularly important is the concept of *information scent*, which characterizes how users evaluate the utility of hypermedia actions. SNIF-ACT has been developed with a *user-trace methodology* [3] for studying and analyzing the psychology of users performing ecologically valid WWW tasks (i.e. tasks that are representative of what real users perform). A *user trace* is a record of all significant states and events in the user-WWW interaction based on eye tracking data, application-level logs, and think-aloud protocols. A *user-tracing architecture* has been implemented for developing simulation models of user-WWW interaction and for comparing SNIF-ACT simulations against user-trace data. The user tracing architecture compares each action of the SNIF-ACT simulation directly against observed user actions.

Previous cognitive models of HCI have mainly been developed to deal with the analysis of expert performance on well-defined tasks involving application programs [4]. These have had limited applicability to understanding foraging through content-rich hypermedia, and consequently new theories are needed. An attempt [5] at developing a GOMS model [6] of WWW users failed to have a significant correlation with user behavior [7]. That model's behavior was based purely on the structure of pages and links—none of the behavior was determined by the semantics of page content. A day-in-the-life protocol analysis of real users engaged in their own tasks with the WWW [8] showed that the majority of user time was devoted to processing WWW content. Recent work [9] involving comprehension-based models of exploration (that use Latent Semantic Analysis) has achieved some promising success in modeling limited WWW interaction. These results lead us to conclude that a realistic user model of WWW interaction will have to deal with how user behavior depends on content. Under this rationale, the results reported in this paper focus on behavior of novice users on novel tasks – situations under which the major controlling variable is the semantic content of the WWW. This minimizes the effect of specific user's traits and properties (e.g. domain-specific knowledge) to the WWW interactions.

2   SNIF-ACT

The goal of our modeling effort is to develop a computer program than simulates step-by-step user behavior in enough detail to reproduce the user data. SNIF-ACT (Figure 1) is the model that we are currently developing to simulate WWW users. SNIF-ACT is an extension of the ACT-R theory and simulation environment [2], a general *production system* architecture designed to model human psychology. By using this system to model WWW behavior, we link our analysis to the same principles used to model cognitive behavior in general. ACT-R contains principles concerning: (1) knowledge representation, (2) knowledge deployment (performance), and (3) knowledge acquisition (learning). There are two major components in the ACT-R architecture: a *declarative knowledge* component and a *procedural knowledge* component. Declarative knowledge corresponds to things that we are aware we know and that can be easily described to others, such as the content of WWW links, or the functionality of browser buttons. Procedural knowledge specifies how declarative knowledge is transformed into active behavior. Procedural knowledge is represented as condition-action pairs, or *production rules* (see Figure 1).

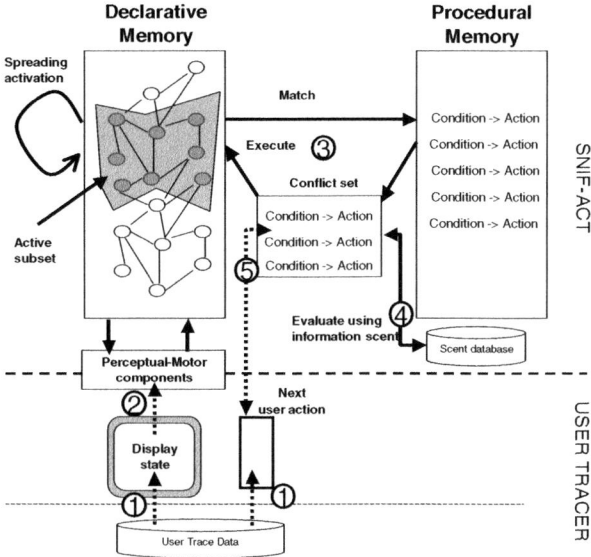

Fig. 1. The structure of the SNIF-ACT model and the User-Tracing Architecture. The numbers indicate the order of the steps in each cycle of the SNIF-ACT simulation. Due to space limitation, details of the user-tracing architecture can be found in [3].

For instance, our SNIF-ACT simulation contains the production rule *Use-Search-Engine* (see below). The production applies in situations where the user has a goal to go to a WWW site, has processed a task description, and has a browser in front of them. The production rule specifies that a subgoal will be set to use a search engine. The condition (*IF*) side of the production rule is matched to the current goal and the active chunks in declarative memory, and when a match is found, the action (*THEN*) side of the production rule will be executed.

> *Use-Search-Engine:*
> *IF   the goal is Goal*Start-Next-Patch*
> *& there is a task description*
> *& there is a browser*
> *& there is a search engine name in memory*
> *& the browser is not at the search engine*
> *THEN   Set and push a subgoal Goal*Use-Search-Engine*
> *to the goal stack*

Roughly, the idea is that each elemental step of cognition corresponds to a production. At any point in time, a single production fires. When there is more than one match, the matching rules form a *conflict set*, and a mechanism called *conflict resolution* is used to decide which production to execute (see Figure 1). The conflict resolution mechanism is based on a utility function. The expected utility of each matching production is calculated based on this utility function, and the one with the highest expected utility will be picked. In modeling WWW users, the utility function is provided by information foraging theory, and specifically the notion of *information scent* [1]. This constitutes a major extension of the ACT-R theory and is described in greater detail below.

2.1   Utility: Information Scent

As users browse the WWW, they make judgments about the utility of different courses of action available to them. Typically, they must use local cues, such as link images and text, to make navigation decisions. Information scent refers to the local cues that users process in making such judgments. The analogy is to organisms that use local smell cues to make judgments about where to go next (for instance in pursuing some prey). In earlier work [1, 10] we extended ACT-R to produce a theory called ACT-IF (where IF stands for "information foraging"). ACT-IF included a formal model of information scent that predicted how users would use text presented in browsers to make navigation decisions. The model of users' judgments of information scent is based on spreading activation. The basic idea is that a user's information goal activates a set of chunks in a user's memory, and text on the display screen activates another set of chunks. Activation spreads from these chunks to related chunks in a *spreading activation network*. Through this spreading activation network, the amount of activation accumulating on the goal chunks and display chunks is an indicator of their mutual relevance. The spreading activation network is therefore content-based, as mutual relevance of user goals and contents are calculated each time the display changes. The amount of activation is used to evaluate and select productions. The activation of content-dependent chunks matched by production rules can be used to determine the utility of selecting those production rules dynamically.

The spread of activation from one cognitive structure to another is determined by weighting values on the associations among chunks. These weights determine the rate of activation flow among chunks. In the context of WWW browsing, we assume that activation spreads from the user's goal, which is the focus of attention, through memory associations to words and images that the user sees on WWW pages. Associations have *strengths* or *weights* that determine the amount of activation that flows from one chunk to another. If the user reads some link text on a WWW page, and the link text is strongly associated to the user's goal, then we expect the user to judge the link as being highly relevant to the goal. The association strengths among words in human memory are assumed to be related to the probabilities of word occurrences and of word co-occurrences. Consequently, the spreading activation computation of information scent in SNIF-ACT requires these estimates. In past research [1, 10], we derived these estimates from the Tipster corpus [11]. This database contained statistics relevant to setting the base-level activations of 200 million word tokens and the inter-word association strengths of 55 million word pairs.

Unfortunately, the Tipster corpus does not contain many of the novel words that arise in popular media such as the WWW. For instance, the movie title "Antz" does not occur in the Tipster corpus. Consequently, we augment the statistical database derived from Tipster by estimating word frequency and word co-occurrence statistics from the WWW itself using a program that calls on the AltaVista search engine to provide data. As indicated in Figure 1, the spreading activation networks needed to perform the scent computations are stored in a *scent database* that is accessed when production evaluations are computed by SNIF-ACT. The model is initialized with a goal that consists of a set of chunks. Each goal chunk represents a content word in a task description provided to users in our study. When the model "sees" a web page, each link is represented as a set of chunks, with each link chunk representing a concept (e.g., a word) presented by the link. The activation received by a goal chunk, i, from link chunks j, will be:

$$A_i = B_i + \sum_j W_j S_{ji},$$
(1)

where B_i is the base-level activation of i, S_{ji} is the association strength between an associated chunk j and chunk i, and W_j reflects attention (*source activation*) on chunk j. One may interpret Equation 1 as reflection of a Bayesian prediction of the log posterior odds of one chunk in the context of other chunks. A_i in Equation 1 is interpreted as reflecting the log posterior odds that i is likely, B_i is the log prior odds of i being likely, and S_{ji} reflects the log likelihood odds ratios that i is likely given that it occurs in the context of chunk j. This version of spreading activation was used in the past [1, 10] to develop models of information scent. The summed activation of all chunks composing a goal (e.g., summed over all chunks i) is treated as a measure of the utility of the perceived link.

2.2   Predictions

There are two main predictions of the SNIF-ACT model that derive from the utility predictions of the information scent computations, and from the patch model of Information Foraging Theory [1]. In the patch model, information sources are assumed to be distributed in some hierarchical "patches" in the external environment. The first main prediction concerns link-following behavior. Novice users working on unfamiliar tasks are expected to choose links that have high information scent. Basically, users will be performing a kind of hill-climbing with information scent as the heuristic for choosing the next step to take. The second prediction concerns the points at which users will give up on WWW sites. A user's information environment has a patchy structure, with information collected together on bookshelves, piles on desks, in folders on personal computers, libraries, etc. Information is encountered at a denser rate when a user is "in" a patch (e.g., viewing a set of WWW search results) as opposed to "between" patches (e.g., formulating a search query and waiting on search results). WWW sites are considered information patches. The conventional model of foraging in information patches predicts that users will leave an information patch when the expected utility of the site diminishes below the utility of moving to another site.

3   Experiment

3.1   Tasks and Users

Tasks for our study were selected from a database collected by a survey of over 2000 WWW users [12]. The two analyzed in details are:

Antz Task: After installing a state of the art entertainment center in your den and replacing the furniture and carpeting, your redecorating is almost complete. All that remains to be done is to purchase a set of movie posters to hang on the walls. Find a site where you can purchase the set of four Antz movie posters depicting the princess, the hero, the best friend, and the general.

City Task: You are the Chair of Comedic events for Louisiana State University in Baton Rouge, LA. Your computer has just crashed and you have lost several advertisements for upcoming events. You know that The Second City tour is coming to your theater in the spring, but you do not know the precise date. Find the date the comedy troupe is playing on your campus. Also find a photograph of the group to put on the advertisement.

Four users were solicited from PARC and Stanford. Users were encouraged to perform both tasks as they would typically, but they were also instructed to think out loud [13] as they performed their tasks.

3.2   User Trace Comparator

Figure 1 shows how the User Trace Comparator controls the SNIF-ACT simulation model and matches the simulation behavior to the user trace data (each step is indicated by a circle in Figure 1):

1. Parse the User Trace Database to determine the next display state and the next user action that occurs at that display state.
2. If the display state has changed, then indicate this to the SNIF-ACT system. SNIF-ACT contains production rules that actively perceive the display state and update declarative memory to contain chunks that represent the perceived portions of the display.
3. Run SNIF-ACT so that it runs spreading activation to identify the active portion of declarative memory and matches productions against working memory to select a conflict set of production rules.
4. SNIF-ACT evaluates the productions in the conflict set using the information scent computations. At the end of this step, one of the rules in the conflict set will be identified as the production to execute.

5. Compare the production just selected by SNIF-ACT to the next user action and record any statistics (notably whether or not the production and action matched). If there is a match, then execute the production selected by SNIF-ACT. If there is a mismatch, then select and execute the production that matches the user action.
6. Repeat Steps 1 - 5 until there are no more user actions.

4   Results

The predictions made by the SNIF-ACT model were tested against the log files of all data sets. The major controlling variable in the model is the measure of information scent, which predicts two major kinds of actions: (1) which links on a web page people will click on, and (2) when people decide to leave a site. These kinds of actions were therefore extracted from the log files and compared to the predictions made by the model. We call the first kind of actions *link-following* actions, which were logged whenever a participant clicked on a link on a web page. The second kind of actions was called *site-leaving* actions, which were logged whenever a participant left a web site (and went to a different search engine or web site). The two kinds of actions made up 72 % (48% for link-following and 24% for site-leaving actions) of all the 189 actions extracted from the log files.

4.1   Link-Following Actions

The SNIF-ACT model was matched to the link-following actions extracted from the N = 8 (2 tasks x 4 participants) data sets. The user trace comparator was used to compare each action from each participant to the action chosen by the model. Whenever a link-following action was encountered, the SNIF-ACT model ranked all links on the web page according to the information scent of the links. We then compared the links chosen by the participants to the predicted link rankings of the SNIF-ACT model. If there were a purely deterministic relationship between predicted information scent and link choice, then all users would be predicted to choose the highest ranked link (i.e rank=0). However, we assume that the scent-based utilities are stochastic and subject to some amount of variability due to users and context (which is consistent with ACT-R [2]). Consequently we expect the probability of link choice to be highest for the links ranked with the greatest amount of scent-based utility, and that link choice probability is expected to decrease for links ranked lower on the basis of their scent-based utility values.

Fig. 2 shows that link choice is strongly related to scent-based utility values. Links ranked higher on scent-based utilities tend to get chosen over links ranked lower. There are a total of 91 link-following actions collected from all users in Figure 2. The distribution of the predicted link selection was significantly different from random selection $\chi 2$ (30) = 18589.45, p < 0.0001. This result replicates a similar analysis made by Pirolli and Card [1] concerning the ACT-IF model prediction of cluster selection in the Scatter/Gather browser.

4.2   Site-Leaving Actions

To test how well information scent is able to predict when people will leave a site, site-leaving actions were extracted from the log files and analyzed. Site-leaving actions are defined as actions that led to a different site (e.g. when the participants used a different search engine, typed in a different url to go to a different web site, etc.).

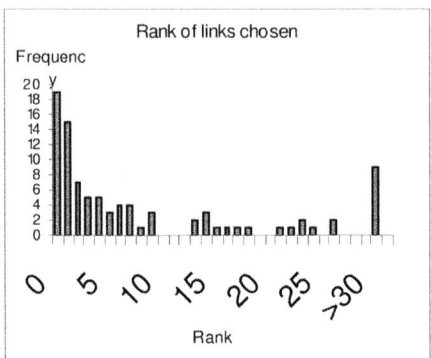

Fig. 2. Frequency that SNIF-ACT productions match link-following actions. The SNIF-ACT production rankings are computed at each simulation cycle over all links on the same web page and all productions that match.

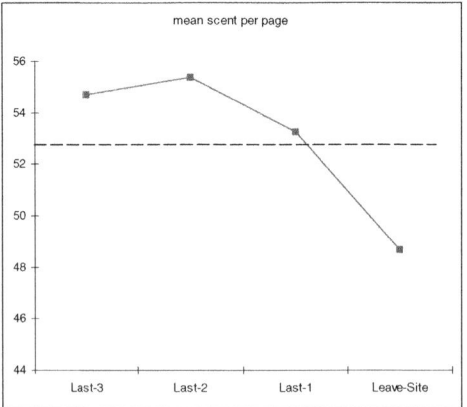

Fig. 3. Mean information scent on the web page as a function of distance from the last web page before the users left the site. The dotted line represents the mean scent of the next site the participants went to after they left the current site.

The results were plotted in Fig. 3. The x-axis shows the four web pages the participants visited before they left the site (i.e. Last-3, Last-2, Last-1, and Leave-

Site). There were 12 site-leaving actions in the whole data set. For each of the 12 site-leaving actions, the average of the information scent of all the links on the page was calculated to represent the information scent of the page. Each point in Fig. 3 is the mean information scent of the 12 pages. It shows that initially the mean information scent of the web page was high, and right before the participants left the site, the mean information scent dropped. Fig. 3 also shows the mean information scent of the web pages right after the participants left the site (the dotted line in Fig. 3). It shows that the mean information scent on the page right after they left the site tended to be higher than the mean information scent before they left the site. This is consistent with the information foraging theory which states that people may switch to another "information patch" when the expected gain of searching in the current patch is lower than the expected gain of searching for a new information patch. In fact, from the verbal protocols, we often found utterances like "it seems that I don't have much luck with this site", or "maybe I should try another search engine" right before participants switch to another site. It suggests that the drop in information scent on the web page could be the factor the triggered participants' decision to switch to another site.

5   General Discussion

We have described the user modeling and tracing techniques using SNIF-ACT. The system demonstrates how cognitive models can be used to understand real-world user-WWW interactions. We have shown that for general information-seeking tasks in unfamiliar domains, user-WWW interactions depend heavily on the content of the WWW pages. Using the measure of information scent, mutual relevance between the user goals and web contents were captured and stored in scent information databases. The use of information scent, together with the ACT cognitive architecture was shown to predict user actions well. We believe the SNIF-ACT system has provided a good user model of the participants. Elsewhere [14], stochastic simulation models have been developed based on the information scent concept presented here. The Bloodhound project [14] does not simulate the detailed cognition of individual users, but instead makes predictions about the probability of users choosing a given link from a set of links on a page. These probabilities are predicted on the basis of a given task and an information scent analysis. Bloodhound is a system designed to predict the flow of users through a WWW site (assuming a given task) and to identify usability problems based on the predicted flow patterns. The Bloodhound system currently does not deal with individual differences in background knowledge, detailed effects of WWW page design, or learning. Because SNIF-ACT was built on a detailed theory of cognition that is intended to address knowledge, learning, and perception, we expect that SNIF-ACT could be used to gain insights that could feed into systems such as Bloodhound.

Acknowledgements. This work is supported by an Office of Naval Research contract No. N00014-96-C-0097 to P. Pirolli and S. Card and Advanced Research and Development Activity, Novel Intelligence from Massive Data Program, Contract No, MDA904-03-C-0404 to S.Card and P. Pirolli. We thank Ed Chi for assistance in generating the Scent Databases for SNIF-ACT.

References

1. Pirolli, P. and S.K. Card, Information foraging. Psychological Review, 1999. 106: p. 643–675.
2. Anderson, J.R. and C. Lebiere, The atomic components of thought. 2000, Mahwah, NJ: Lawrence Erlbaum Associates.
3. Pirolli, P., et al. A user-tracing architecture for modeling interaction with the World Wide Web. in Advanced Visual Interfaces, AVI 2002. 2002. Trento, Italy: ACM Press.
4. Pirolli, P., Cognitive engineering models and cognitive architectures in human-computer interaction, in Handbook of applied cognition, F.T. Durso, et al., Editors. 1999, John Wiley & Sons: West Sussex, England. p. 441–477.
5. Lynch, G., S. Palmiter, and C. Tilt. The Max model: A standard web site user model. in Human Factors and the Web. 1999.
6. Card, S.K., T.P. Moran, and A. Newell, The psychology of human-computer interaction. 1983, Hillsdale, New Jersey: Lawrence Erlbaum Associates.
7. Pirolli, P., A web site user model should at least predict something about users. internetworking, 2000. 3.
8. Byrne, M.D., et al. The tangled web we wove: A taxonomy of WWW use. in Human Factors in Computing Systems, CHI '99. 1999. Pittsburgh, PA: ACM Press.
9. Blackmon, M.H., et al. Cognitive Walkthrough for the Web. in Human Factors in Computing Systems, CHI 2002. 2002. Minneapolis, MN: ACM Press.
10. Pirolli, P. Computational models of information scent-following in a very large browsable text collection. in Conference on Human Factors in Computing Systems, CHI '97. 1997. Atlanta, GA: Association for Computing Machinery.
11. Harman, D. Overview of the first text retrieval conference. in 16th Annual International ACM/SIGIR Conference. 1993. Pittsburgh, PA: ACM.
12. Morrison, J.B., P. Pirolli, and S.K. Card. A taxonomic analysis of what World Wide Web activities significantly impact people's decisions and actions. in Conference on Human Factors in Computing Systems, CHI '01. 2001. Seattle, WA: ACM Press.
13. Ericsson, K.A. and H.A. Simon, Protocol Analysis: Verbal reports as data. 1984, Cambridge, MA: MIT Press.
14. Chi, E.H., et al. The Bloodhound Project: Automating discovery of Web usability issues using the InfoScent simulator. in Conference on Human Factors in Computing Systems, CHI 2003. 2003. Fort Lauderdale, FL: ACM Press.

Adapting to the User's Internet Search Strategy

Jean-David Ruvini

e-lab Bouygues SA
1 avenue Eugène Freyssinet, 78061 St Quentin en Yvelines, France
jdruvini@bouygues.com
http://e-lab.bouygues.com

Abstract. World Wide Web search engines typically return thousands of results to the users. To avoid users browsing through the whole list of results, search engines use ranking algorithms to order the list according to predefined criteria. In this paper, we present Toogle, a front-end to the Google search engine for both desktop browsers and mobile phones. For a given search query, Toogle first ranks results using Google's algorithm and, as the user browses through the result list, uses machine learning techniques to infer a model of her search goal and to adapt accordingly the order in which the results are presented. We describe preliminary experimental results that show the effectiveness of Toogle.

1 Introduction

Today World Wide Web search engines like Google, Altavista or AllTheWeb among others search documents for user specified keywords and return a list of document snippets (called results) where the keywords were found. With the vast amount of on-line information sources available on the web, this list typically contains thousands of results.

To deal with this amount of information, users have two choices : to browse through the list of results which is often a tedious task or to repeatedly select new keywords and query the search engine until they estimate they have selected the right keywords and... it's worth browsing the list! This problem is particularly critical on small devices offering web browsing (like mobile phones) which generally have limited display and input capabilities, making browsing a very difficult task.

To limit the browsing process and to help users quickly locate relevant documents, search engines use ranking algorithms to order the list according to certain criteria, presenting relevant documents in the top of the list and less relevant documents below. Criteria can include the number of keywords matched, proximity and frequency of keywords, document length, number of links made to a document, number of times a document is accessed from a result list and other factors. Alternatively, [8] proposed to learn the ranking function from clickthrough data (the logfile of results the users clicked on) of a group of users.

These ranking algorithms have two major limitations. First, they are global to all users and do not adapt to a specific user and to a specific search session or query.

P. Brusilovsky et al. (Eds.): UM 2003, LNAI 2702, pp. 55–64, 2003.

Second, they are exclusive in that they cannot be combined with - or, more precisely - benefit from other ranking algorithms.

In this paper, we present ongoing research efforts to overcome these limitations that leaded to the implementation of Toogle, an intelligent front-end to the Google search engine. The Toogle hypothesis is that a typical browsing session over a list of results where the user clicks on some results and ignore some others, conveys information about his search goal. Toogle first ranks search results using Google's algorithm and, as the user steps through the result list, uses machine learning techniques to infer a model of the user's search goal from clickthrough data and to adapt accordingly the order in which results are presented. Toogle is available for both desktop computer and wireless device web browsers but has been mainly designed to improve usability of small devices.

This paper is structured as follows: First, we present Toogle's interface. Second we explain how it works. Third, we report preliminary experimental results for wireless device web browsers. Fourth, we discuss related research. The paper concludes with a summary of contributions and plans for future research.

2   Toogle: An Intelligent Front-End to Google

As we mentioned above, Toogle, as Google, is accessible from desktop internet browsers and mobile phone offering web browsing, namely i-mode mobile phone. First introduced in Japan in February 1999 by NTT DoCoMo, i-mode is one of the world's most successful services (currently more than 41 millions subscribers in Japan) offering wireless World Wide Web (WWW) access and e-mail from mobile phones. It was launched in France by Bouygues Telecom by November 2002.

For both their desktop and i-mode versions there is almost no difference, from the user perspective, between Toogle and Google. Toogle is accessed from a web browser and its homepage is a clone of Google's homepage. To query Toogle, the user just has to type in some keywords and to press the "Google Search" button exactly as he uses to do with Google. Similarly, Toogle's results are displayed in the same format as Google's results, grouped into pages that can be accessed individually from links located at the bottom of the current result page. Figure 1(a)[1] shows the homepage of Toogle i-mode. Figure 1(b) and 1(c) show the result page of Toogle i-mode for the query "korean restaurant new york". Figure 1(b) presents the first lines of that result page; on Figure 1(c) the user has scrolled down this page to review the first result.

There are few differences between desktop and i-mode versions of Toogle (respectively Google). The main noticeable one is the number of results displayed on each result page. Whereas desktop browser version displays 10 results per page, i-mode version displays only 5 results per page. In the following we use "page" to refer with no distinction to a list of 5 or 10 results.

---

[1] The i-mode emulator shown in Figure 1 is WAPAG (see http://www.wapag.com/).

The main reason why we have chosen to emulate Google rather than any other search engine is that Google can be accessed programmatically using a web service programming toolkit (released by the Google corporation). This toolkit makes possible a simple proxy architecture for Toogle. When the user initiates a search query, the query is first sent to Toogle and then forwarded to Google. The results returned by Google are first processed by Toogle which then display them in the user's browser. Similarly, when the user clicks a proposed result to examine the corresponding document, the document request is processed by Toogle. This architecture allows Toogle to record the list of results presented to the user and which results she actually examined. It uses this information in the adaptation process described in the next section.

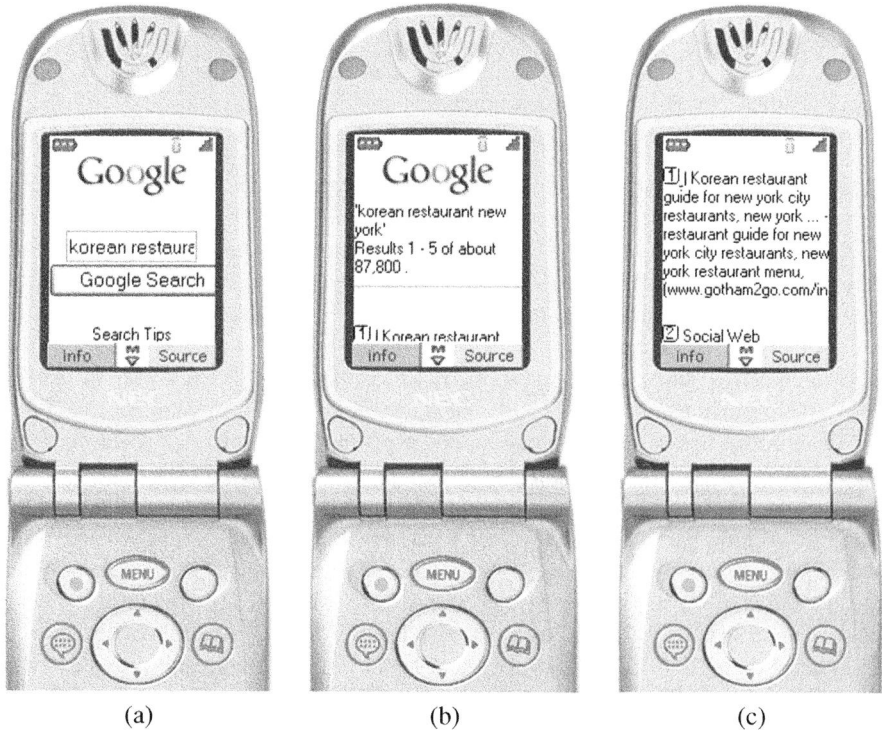

(a)   (b)   (c)

Fig. 1. The homepage (a) and a result page (b) and (c) of the i-mode versions of Google and Toogle.

3   Adapting to the User's Search Strategy

Toogle is based on the observation that there is not an exact mapping between search queries and search goals. Since result lists typically present a lot of different information, users may type the same query for accessing different documents and, as a consequence, exhibit different browsing behaviors for that query. In other words, the browsing behavior of the user for a given query depends on his search goal (or interest).Toogle elaborates on this observation to infer, for a each search query, a model of the user interest and to adapt the list of results accordingly. More precisely, it first presents to the user the list of results proposed by Google with no modification. As the user browses through the list, Toogle tries to infer a model of his search goal from his browsing actions. It then uses this model to reorder the list of results the user has not yet considered in order to present most relevant results first. In the following we explain how Toogle builds a model of the user's interest and how and when it uses this model to reorder the list.

3.1   Building a Model of the User's Interest

Toogle's goal is to build, for a given user U, a search query Q and its corresponding list of results L, the following target function:

$$ResultInterest_{U,Q,L} : Result \rightarrow \{0,1\}$$

Given a result, the value of $ResultInterest_{U,Q,L}$ is interpreted as a measure of the interest the user has in it. A value of 1 indicates that he has a strong interest in it and is likely to click it to examine the corresponding document, whereas a value of 0 indicates that he is not likely to examine the document.

Toogle uses a machine learning approach to build the $ResultInterest_{U,Q,L}$ function. More precisely, because results are textual data, it employs a text classifier to learn it. This approach requires to identify positive examples of results the user is likely to click and negative examples i.e. results he is not likely to click. Remember that Toogle (as Google) groups results into pages. For a given search query, Toogle considers, within all the result pages the user has visited, results he has clicked as positive examples and the results he has not clicked as negative examples. Suppose for example that, using an i-mode web browser (5 results per page), the user has clicked the results ranked in position 3, 5 (first page) and 8 (second page) in the list. Toogle considers results 3, 5 and 8 as positive examples and results 1, 2, 4, 6 and 7 as negative examples. The reason why Toogle uses the document snippets (results) rather than the documents themselves is straightforward: whereas a click on a result provides an explicit indication of the interest the user has in it, it is difficult to draw any conclusion about the content of a document from the fact that the user read it. Also, working with results is possible even if some documents are not available ("page not found" status).

Once it has identified the examples, Toogle represents them in a text classifier exploitable form, namely the bag-of-words representation. It this representation, a result is encoded as a feature vector, with each feature indicating the presence or absence of a word. Table 1 shows an example of a Google result for the search query "french food". A result is made of five main parts : the title of the document referenced by the result, a snippet of the document where the keywords composing the search query were found, a summary of the document, its category and its url. Some of these parts may be absent from the result and it is often the case for the summary and the category. Toogle makes no difference between the five parts of the results in the encoding.

Finally, if Toogle could identify at least one positive example and one negative example, it invokes the text classifier to build the model of the user's interest. Of course, result pages the user has not visited are not taken into account in the learning process (no example is extracted from them).

Since Toogle only uses document snippets, the problem has a small dimensionality (the examples contain few words) and Toogle can learn very quickly with most of the algorithms classically used for text classification. As a consequence, it can build a model or revised a learned model, whenever it identifies a new positive example that is to say whenever the user clicks a result. In its current implementation, Toogle's learning algorithm is the Support Vector Machine [16] which has been shown to achieve excellent performances on textual data [4].

The learned $ResultInterest_{U,Q,L}$ function can be seen as a model of the user's interest relatively to the search query Q and the corresponding result list L. It is a short term model since it is valid only in the lifetime of the query Q. In the next section we explain how this model is used.

Table 1. A Google result for the search query "french food"

French Food and Cook : **French** Dinner
French Food and Cook : the authentic **French** cuisine site. Best typical **French** recipes and advice on **French** cooking. ... **French Food** and Cook : Home Page. ... Description: Complete information on how to organize and cook a dinner, including recipes. Category: Home > Cooking > World Cuisines > European > French www.ffcook.com/Cadres/Dinner.htm - 21k - Cached - Similar pages

3.2 Reordering the Result List

To avoid disturbing the user by modifying the ranking of results on a page she has visited, Toogle reorders only pages she has not visited yet. The reordering occurs whenever she requests a new result page and involves three steps.

First, Toogle queries Google for more results and loads them in memory. However, it does not load a single result page but several pages. The number of pages loaded determines the number of results Toogle is able to take into account in the adaptation process. Since the results are obtained from Google, the loaded list is ordered according to the Google's ranking criteria, from the most relevant to the least relevant result.

Second, it uses the text classifier and the learned user's model to classify the loaded results. It then reorders the result list according to the predicted label : every result classified as a positive example is considered as a potentially interesting one and is moved to the top of the list (high ranks). Toogle locally preserves Google's ranking in that it does not perturb the relative ordering of positive examples and the relative ordering of negatives examples : if results r is ranked higher than r' in Google's ordering and r and r' have the same predicted label then r is ranked higher than r' in Toogle's ordering.

Finally, Toogle displays the 5 (i-mode) or the 10 (desktop browser) most relevant results to the user, presenting the most relevant at the top of the result page and the least relevant at the bottom. Suppose for example that, using an i-mode web browser (5 results per page), the user has requested the result page number 3 (results 11 to 15).

Suppose also that Toogle has predicted that results 12, 17 and 23 (according to Google's ordering) may be of interest to the user. Toogle will display a result page presenting (from top to bottom) results 12, 17, 23, 11 and 13. Results 11 and 13 are negative examples but since they are the negative examples with the highest rank in the Google's ordering they are presented before any other negative example.

Of course, when the user submits a new search query to Toogle, it forgets everything it has previously learned and start learning a new model specific to the new query and the new search goal.

The next section presents preliminary experimental results.

Table 2. Toogle's predictive accuracy and browsing gain for eight queries

		Q1	Q2	Q3	Q4	Q5	Q6	Q7	Q8	Mean
Pos. ex.		5	4	7	5	5	11	3	4	5.50
Neg. ex.		10	16	16	10	14	7	9	8	11.25
Predictive accuracy		i-mode								
	NBC	22	93	77	50	50	58	71	14	54.48
	SVM	100	80	100	80	72	54	72	100	82.25
		Desktop								
	NBC	100	89	61	60	44	71	100	50	71.92
	SVM	40	100	89	100	78	75	50	100	79.00
Browsing gain		i-mode								
	Page	1	0	3	1	2	1	0	1	1.125
	Ratio	0.0	1.0	0.0	0.0	0.0	0.0	1.0	0.0	0.25

4   Experiment

The goal of the experiment presented here is to show that Toogle facilitates browsing through a list of search engine results by reducing user's efforts and information overload. More precisely, it is to answer the two following questions :

1. Can text classification algorithms successfully learn the user's interest from click-through data?
2. Does Toogle reduce the number of result pages users have to browse?

We conducted a preliminary experiment by submitting to two users eight search tasks using Google on an i-mode emulator. To avoid query formulation bias, the eight search queries (and the corresponding search goals) were given to the users. One of the users was a researcher of our laboratory while the other was a female computer novice with no prior knowledge about i-mode. For the eight queries, the two users exhibited the same browsing behavior (they clicked the same results).

Using a proxy architecture similar to the Toogle's architecture, we recorded users' browsing actions. Using these records we then simulated the users to feed Toogle with their browsing actions and analyzed Toogle's behavior. The results of this experiment are presented in Table 2.

Column labels Q1 to Q8 refer to the eight queries used in the experiment. The table comprises three parts. The first part, composed of the first two rows, lists the number of positive (first row) and negative (second row) examples of each query. For a given query, the positive examples are all the results the user clicked during the browsing session and the negative examples all the results (up to the last positive example) she did not click.

The second part gives the predictive accuracy of Toogle for both i-mode and desktop browsers for two learning methods: the Support Vector Machine (SVM) and the Naïve Bayes Classifier (NBC) [6]. We used the SVM-Light [7] implementation for the SVM, and the Bow toolkit [14] for NBC.

To evaluate predictive accuracy, we split the example set in two sets : a training set and a test set. For i-mode, the training set was constituted of the five first examples (according to Google's ranking), and of the ten first examples for desktop browser. The training set was used to learn a user's model and the test set to evaluate the performance of this model. The predictive accuracy is the percent of examples of the test set which label ("positive" or "negative") was correctly predicted. This Table shows that Support Vector Machines achieve good performances (around 80%) for both i-mode and desktop browsers. This is an interesting finding (which requires further investigation) because it suggests that this method is able to learn a good user's model even when few training data are available which is often the case in the area of User Modeling and Adaptive Interfaces. This is particularly true for the i-mode version where the training set contained only five examples. Note that, although SVM are known to be theoretically longer to train, we observed no significant difference between NBC and SVM training time. As we mentioned earlier this is due to the fact that the problem has a small dimensionality (few examples, few features).

The third part proposes an evaluation of the browsing gain for the end user of Toogle, in term of "page gain" and of gain "ratio" on the basis of the SVM algorithm. The page gain is defined as the difference between Google's ordering and Toogle's ordering in the number of result pages the user has to visit to be able to click all the interesting results (i.e. the positive examples). For instance, suppose that, on i-mode, the last result the user has clicked is ranked in position 20 by Google and in position 7 by Toogle. Since an i-mode result page presents 5 results, result 20 appears on Google's page 4 whereas result 7 appears on Toogle's page 2. In that case, the page gain is 2.

The page gain must be considered with respect to the maximum possible gain. The gain ratio measures how far from this optimal Toogle reordering is. Let G_T be Toogle's page gain and G_{Opt} be the maximum possible page gain for a given query. The gain ratio is defined as: $$Ratio = 1 - \frac{G_T}{G_{Opt}}$$

Concerning i-mode, results presented in Table 2 are very encouraging. They show that there is a real gain in using Toogle (page gain is optimal) for more most of the queries (6 out of 8).

Since Toogle has been mainly designed to improve usability of i-mode WWW search engines, the queries used in the experiment were strongly biased in disfavor of desktop browsers. More precisely, since the search tasks submitted to the users required them to examine less than 21 results for most of the queries (the only exception is query Q3), they had to visit only 2 result pages. Because in that case the page gain can only be 0, results are not presented for desktop browsers in Table 2. However, because Toogle exhibits a high prediction accuracy, we believe that further experiments will show that its effectiveness on i-mode generalizes to desktop browsers.

Another interesting fact that does not appear in Table 2 is that Toogle is very conservative. There are two observations that support this claim. First, Toogle incorrectly ranked a result lower than it was in Google's ordering only once. It occurs for query Q6 on desktop browser: result ranked 16 by Google was ranked 17 by Toogle. Second, there is a particular case where Toogle's prediction errors do not penalize the user: when it predicts the same label for all the examples of the test set (all positive or all negative). In that case Toogle's reordering is identical to Google's ordering. This occurs for queries Q2 and Q7 where gain ratio is equal to 100%. In other words, when Toogle is unsure about the user's interest, it does not reorder the results.

The results of the preliminary experiment presented in this section show that Toogle is clearly effective on i-mode browsers where it decreases the users' information overload. The next section details related systems.

5   Related Work

Besides Toogle illustrates the application of adaptive hypermedia techniques [3] to search engines, works related to Toogle can be grouped in four categories: browsing assistants, small device usability, search engine optimization and relevance feedback.

Browsing assistants like Letizia [10], WebWatcher [9], SurfLen [5] or PageGather [15] are similar to Toogle in that they recommend yet-unseen documents. As opposed to WebWatcher, SurfLen and PageGather who incorporate knowledge about other users, Letizia (like Toogle) estimates the visitor interest based solely on its actions (links he followed, documents he bookmarked, etc.). Whereas these agents act as guides and explicitly recommend documents to the user, Toogle is invisible and unobtrusive and, as a consequence, has been integrated into a small device with limited display capabilities.

Concerning small device usability, [1] proposed an algorithm for automatically suggesting shortcut links in real time to users of wireless PDAs or cell phones. The algorithm finds shortcuts by using a model of web visitor behavior learned on server access logs. They have shown that using a mixture of Markov models, their algorithm can save wireless visitors more than 40% of the possible link savings. This value can be put in parallel with Toogle's gain ratio of 25% which means that Toogle saves users near 75% of the possible information overload saving.

Several techniques have been proposed to optimize search engines. [12] built (from search engine access logs) Bayesian networks to model the dynamics of users' search activities. They have shown that these models can be used successfully to infer the probability of the user's next action, the time delay before taking the action and the user's informational goal. [2] used clickthrough data for identifying clusters of similar queries and similar URLs. More recently, [13] proposed to use common sense reasoning to translate any search query into an effective query. Closer to Toogle, [8] proposed to use clickthrough data to optimize the order in which results are presented to the user. However, the proposed approach differs from our approach in that its goal is not to adapt the ordering to a single user within the context of a specific search query, but to learn a ranking algorithm from the browsing habits of a group of users, independently of their queries. Another advantage of our approach over Joachims's approach is that Toogle elaborates on an existing ordering and can benefit from any search engine ranking algorithm (including Joachims's algorithm) whereas Joachims's learned algorithm is used in replacement of any other ranking algorithm.

The closest work to Toogle [17] comes from relevance feedback research. Relevance feedback in document retrieval systems is an iterative process wherein the set of retrieved documents is updated based on the user's feedback. The update phase typically consists in augmenting the user's query with terms extracted from documents marked as relevant by the user. In [17], the authors investigate implicit relevance feedback where relevance is inferred from the user's behavior. As Toogle, their system first displays an ordered list of documents summaries and re-orders the list as the user interacts with it. As opposed to Toogle it bases its implicit feedback model around summary viewing time and uses term extraction techniques to infer user's search goal. Also, the authors do not address on search engine optimization and browsing gain, particularly in the context of small devices.

6 Conclusion

In this paper, we presented Toogle, a front-end to the Google search engine, that reduces search engine users information overload by adapting to the user's inferred search goal the order in which search results are presented. Toogle first ranks results using Google's algorithm and, as the user steps through the result list, uses machine learning techniques to build a model of his search goal and reorders the list of results accordingly. A preliminary experiment shows that Toogle performs well in practice on wireless phones offering WWW browsing, reducing substantially the number of result pages the user has to visit. Toogle is unobtrusive and, since it elaborates over an existing ordering and locally preserve this ordering, can benefit from any ranking algorithm.

Although the experimental results presented in this paper are encouraging, we need to evaluate Toogle in depth through extensive experiments and user tests. We are currently carrying these experiments. There are several possible directions of research to improve Toogle. One direction is to increase the informative value of the text composing the search results in order to facilitate the learning of the user's search goal model. For example, this can be done by adding a field "keywords" to the result description, containing the most informative words of the document referred by the result in respect with the other documents proposed in the result page. Since result pages typically presents less than a dozen of results, these keywords could be extracted very efficiently using classical term extraction. Another direction is to "take advantage of the user think time" [11] to refine the learned model and increase the predictive performance of Toogle. Several techniques have been proposed in the area of machine learning (ensemble methods, re-sampling) to achieve this goal.

64   J.-D. Ruvini

References

1. Anderson C. R, Domingos P. and Weld D. S. Adaptive web navigation for wireless devices. In Proceedings of the International Conference on Artificial Intelligence, Morgan Kaufmann, (2001).
2. Beeferman D. and Berger A. Agglomerative clustering of a search engine query log. In Proceedings of the International Conference on Knowledge Discovery and Data Mining, ACM, (2000).
3. Brusilovsky, P. Methods and Techniques of Adaptive Hypermedia. User Modeling and User-Adapted Interaction 6(2–3), (1996), 87–129.
4. Dumais S., Platt J., Heckerman D. and Sahami M. Inductive Learning Algorithms and Representations for Text Classification. In Proceedings of the International Conference on Information and Knowledge Management, ACM, (1998), 148–155.
5. Fu X., Budzik, J. and Hammond K.J. Mining navigation history for recommendation. In Proceedings of the International Conference on Intelligent User Interfaces, ACM, (2000).
6. Good I.J. The Estimation of Probabilities: An Essay on Modern Bayesian Methods. MIT Press, (1965).
7. Joachims T. SVM-Light Support Vector Machine, (1999). http://svmlight.joachims.org/.
8. Joachims T. Optimizing Search Engine using Clickthrough Data. In Proceedings of the ACM Conference on Knowledge Discovery and Data Mining, ACM, (2002).
9. Joachims T., Freitag D. and Mitchell T. WebWatcher: A Tour Guide for the World Wide Web. In Proceedings of the Fifteenth International Conference on Artificial Intelligence, Morgan Kaufmann, (1997).
10 Lieberman H. Letizia: An Agent That Assists Web Browsing. In Proceedings of the Fifteenth International Conference on Artificial Intelligence, Morgan Kaufmann, Montreal, Canada, (1995).
11. Lieberman, H. Autonomous Interface Agents. In Proceedings of the International Conference on Human Computer Interaction, ACM, (1997).
12. Lau T. and Horvitz E. Patterns of Search: Analyzing and Modeling Web Query Refinement. In Proceedings of the International Conference on User Modeling, ACM, (1998).
13. Liu H., Lieberman H. and Selker T. GOOSE: A Goal-Oriented Search Engine With Commonsense. In Proceedings of the International Conference on Adaptive Hypermedia and Adaptive Web Based System, LNCS 2347, p. 253, (2002).
14. McCallum A. K. Bow: A toolkit for statistical language modeling, text retrieval, classification and clustering, 1996. http://www.cs.cmu.edu/~mccallum/bow.
15. Perkowitz M. and Etzioni O. Towards adaptive web sites: conceptual framework and case study. Artificial Intelligence Journal, 118(1–2), (2000).
16. Vapnik V. The Nature of Statistical Learning Theory. Springer-Verlag, New-York, (1995).
17. White R. W., I. Ruthven and J. M. Jose. Finding Relevant Documents Using Top Ranking Sentences: An Evaluation of Two Alternative Schemes. In Proceedings of the 25th International Conference on Research and Development in Information Retrieval, ACM, 2002.

Learning a Model of a Web User's Interests

Tingshao Zhu[1], Russ Greiner[1], and Gerald Häubl[2]

[1] Dept. of Computing Science, University of Alberta, Canada T6G 2E1
{tszhu, greiner}@cs.ualberta.ca
[2] School of Business, University of Alberta, Canada T6G 2R6
Gerald.Haeubl@ualberta.ca

Abstract. There are many recommender systems that are designed to help users find relevant information on the web. To produce recommendations that are relevant to an individual user, many of these systems first attempt to learn a model of the user's browsing behavior. This paper presents a novel method for learning such a model from a set of annotated web logs — *i.e.*, web logs that are augmented with the user's assessment of whether each webpage is an *information content (IC)* page (*i.e.*, contains the information required to complete her task). Our systems use this to learn what properties of a webpage, within a sequence, identify such IC-pages, and similarly what "browsing properties" characterize the words on such pages ("IC-words"). As these methods deal with *properties* of webpages (or of words), rather than specific URLs (words), they can be used anywhere throughout the web; *i.e.*, they are not specific to a particular website, or a particular task. This paper also describes the enhanced browser, AIE, that we designed and implemented for collecting these annotated web logs, and an empirical study we conducted to investigate the effectiveness of our approach. This empirical evidence shows that our approach, and our algorithms, work effectively.

1 Introduction

The World Wide Web has become the largest information source for most people in the world. Unfortunately, it can be difficult for a web user to locate the information she[1] finds relevant. As different users will want different data, this paper provides a way to learn this user-specific relevance information, based on the user's current click stream, and a general user model. A browser that incorporates this learning facilty could adapt to the user, and enable her to find information that is relevant to her, more efficiently.

Our goal is a recommender system that can suggest *Information-Content (IC)* pages to the user — *i.e.*, the webpages that the user must examine to complete her task. Our *IcFinder* system (including the *IcURLPredictor* and *IcWordFinder* subroutines) uses a sample of "annotated web logs" (which label each page as IC or not; see Section 3) to learn a general model that characterizes how users seek relevant information. Given a new sequence of webpages visited by a user, this model will help identify which further pages this particular user will find useful. We also explore ways to use the annotated web logs from one user, or from a small cluster of users, to learn a recommender model specific to an individual user.

---

[1] We will use the female pronoun ("she", "her") when referring to users of either gender.

P. Brusilovsky et al. (Eds.): UM 2003, LNAI 2702, pp. 65–75, 2003.

IcURLPredictor takes as input annotated sequence of pages $U^\pm = \{\langle U_1, \pm_1 \rangle, \ldots, \langle U_t, \pm_t \rangle\}$ and a target URL V, as well as a learned page-recommender model M_P, and predicts whether V is an IC-page — *i.e.*, if V contains information relevant to the user who has just visited U. This M_P model examines properties of the webpages, both in the target V and sequence $U^\pm$, such as the domain type, whether it followed a search engine, etc., to learn rules of the form

> any URL whose domain has been accessed more than 10 times,
> and whose depth is more than 3   (1)
> is likely to be an IC-page

Notice this rule is not about any specific page — *e.g.*, it is not about `http://www.cs.ualberta.ca` — but instead identifies a page based on the user's browsing patterns. Although this system is fairly accurate, it does require the user to annotate the pages (in $U^\pm$) while she is browsing.

IcWordFinder takes as input an *unannotated* sequence of visited webpages $U = \langle U_1, \ldots, U_n \rangle$ as well as a learned word-recommender model M_W, and returns a list of IC-words — *i.e.*, words that are likely to appear within the IC-page associated with U (and that, presumably, reflect the user's information need). In particular, it considers every word w that appears in any U_i, then assigns "browsing properties" to this w based on how w appears within this session — *e.g.*, did w appear in the title of any webpage, did it ever appear as a query to a search engine, etc. *IcWordFinder* then uses M_W to classify each w, determining the chance that a word with these browsing properties will be an IC-word. Notice that this classifier bases its decisions on the browsing properties of a word, rather than on the word itself; *i.e.*, it might claim that

> any word that appears in at least two titles in the session,
> but was never part of a seach engine query,   (2)
> is likely to be an IC-word

but it will not make claims about, say, the IC-word-ness of "moose", nor will it build association rule [1] like "given moose, Alberta will be an IC-word".

The models used by *IcWordFinder* (resp., *IcURLPredictor*) were learned from annotated webpages. Hence different users, who visit different webpages and give different annotations, can produce different models, and so obtain very different classifiers.

The general *IcFinder* system can use these subroutines to help find the IC-pages associated with a sequence of (un)annotated webpages: For example, it could obtain the likely IC-words from *IcWordFinder*, send these word to a search engine (such as Google), and then recommend the top-ranked returned pages. Alternatively, *IcFinder* could start from the user's current page and "scout" out ahead: following every link in that page, then every link on each of those "1-step away" pages, and so forth to some depth, stopping when *IcURLPredictor* thinks that the visited page qualifies as an IC-page, or when the words in that scouted page match the *IcWordFinder* results.

Section 2 surveys other approaches to building recommender systems, and notes how they differ from our method. In particular, it explains why many of the standard recommender systems, such as collaborative filtering and association rules, are not applicable to our situation. Section 3 describes the tool that we developed (AIE) and the study we conducted to collect the labeled data required in our research. Section 4 describes our actual *IcURLPredictor* and *IcWordFinder* techniques. This section also discusses some of the challenges we faced (such as dealing with an imbalanced dataset), and presents the empirical results of our algorithms, emphasizing their ability to produce effective user models. (For more information about the study we performed, the data we collected, and our analyses, please see [12].)

2   Related Work

There is a great deal of research on generating recommendations for web users. This section will summarize several related approaches, and discuss how they differ from our approach.

Zukerman [15] distinguishes two main approaches to learning which pages will appeal to a user: A *content-based* system tries to learn a model based on the contents of the webpage, while a *collaborative* system bases its model on finding "similar" users, and assuming the current user will like the pages that those similar users have visited.

Recall that our goal is to find pages that contain information the user needs to complete her task. This differs from the implicit goal of standard collaborative systems, which is to identify pages that other similar users have visited, as those visited pages may correspond simply to irrelevant pages on the paths that others have taken towards their various goals, or worse, simply to standard dead-ends that everyone seems to hit. (This is why we need to use explicitly annotated web logs; see below.)

Our systems are basically content-based, as their decisions are based on the information within each webpage. However, our approach differs from the *standard* content-based systems: As many such systems are restricted to a single website, their classifiers can be based on a limited range of words or URLs; this means they can make predictions about the importance of specific URLs (see association rules [1]), or of specific hard-selected words [3,6,2]. We did not want to restrict ourselves to a single website, but wanted a system that could recommend pages anywhere on the web, which could therefore involve an unrestricted range of words. For this reason, we built our content-based classifiers based on characteristics ("browsing properties") of the words, or of the URLs. (E.g., *IcURLPredictor* may learn patterns like Equation 1 and *IcWordFinder* may find rules like Equation 2.) Notice this means our system is not restricted to predefined words, nor to webpages that already have been visited by this user, nor even to webpages that have been visited by similar users. As these browsing properties will appear across different websites, we expect them to be useful even in novel web environments.

3   AIE and Empirical Study

3.1   Specific Task

Recall that our overall goal is to determine which pages are IC — *i.e.*, which contain the information required to complete a task. To do this, we collected a set of *annotated web-logs*; each being a sequence of webpages that a user has visited, where each page is labeled (by the user) with a bit that indicates whether she views this page as an IC-page. We collected data from 129 participants (undergraduate business students), asking each participant to perform the following task:

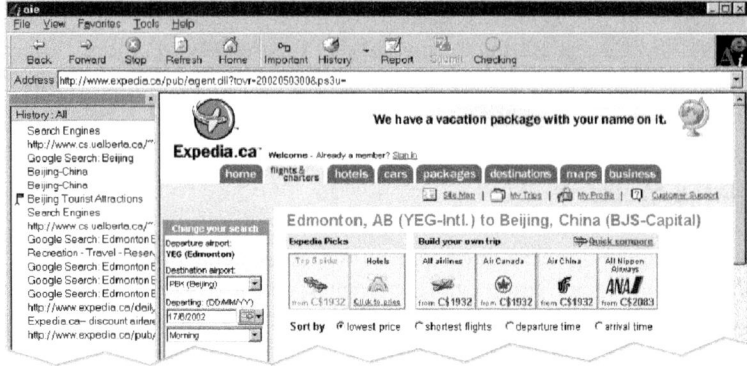

Fig. 1. AIE Browser

1. Identify 3 novel vacation destinations — *i.e.*, places not visited in the past
2. Plan a *detailed* vacation to each destination, choosing specific travel dates, flight numbers, accomodations (hotels, campsites, . . .), activities, etc.

Subjects were given access to our augmented browsing tool (AIE; see Section 3.2), which recorded their specific web-logs, and required them to provide the "IC-page" annotation. The participants also had to produce a short report summarizing the vacation plans, and citing the specific important webpages that were involved in these decisions — these, of course, are IC-pages. To help motivate the participants to take this exercise seriously, they knew that two of them, selected at random, would win up to $500 towards one of the three specific vacations they were about to plan.

3.2   AIE: Annotation Internet Explorer

To help us collect the relevant information, we built an enhanced version of INTERNET EXPLORER, called AIE (shown in Figure 1) which we installed on all of the computers in the lab used in our study. As with all browsers, the user can see the current webpage. In addition, this tool incorporates several relevant extensions — see the toolbar across the top of Figure 1. First, the user can declare the current page to be an "IC-page", by clicking the *Important* button on the top bar. Second, the *History* button on the toolbar brings up the left side-panel (as shown in Figure 1), which shows the user the set of all pages seen so far, with a flag indicating which pages the user tagged as IC. The *Report* button will switch the browse view to the report editor, which subjects used to enter their reports.

After completing their reports, users submitted entire session using the *Submit* button. This recorded the entire sequence of web-sites visited, together with the user's IC-page annotations, as well as other information, such as time-stamps for all pages.

3.3   Some Aspects of the Web Log Data

The 129 study participants collectively requested 15,105 pages, involving 5,995 distinct URLs; hence each URL was requested 2.52 times on average. (If we disregard the

3,039 pages corresponding to 11 search engine pages, each of the remaining URLs was requested only 2.02 times on average.) We found that 82.39% of the URLs were visited only once or twice — hence very few URLs had strong support in this dataset. The subjects labeled 1,887 pages as IC, which corresponds to 14.63 IC-pages per participant.

4 Learning Task

As noted above, we use these annotated web logs to train our classifiers: *IcURLPredictor* for predicting which URLs will be IC-pages, and *IcWordFinder* to identify which words will be IC-words.[2] We first extracted certain "browsing features" of the URLs and the words from the raw data, and labeled each page (resp., word) to indicate whether it is an IC-page (resp., IC-word). We summarize these features in Sections 4.2 and 4.3.

To better describe the performance of our predictors, we computed precision and recall values for both prediction tasks, where "IC-Precision" is TrueIC/PredictedAsIC and "Recall" is TrueIC/AllRealIC; see [10]. We similarly define nonIC-Precision and nonIC-Recall for non-IC-pages.

4.1 Data Cleaning

Our system parses the log files to produce the sequence of pages that have been downloaded. Unfortunately some of these pages are just advertisements. As these ads do not contribute to the participant's information needs, leaving them in the training data might confuse the learner. We therefore assembled a list of advertisement domain names (such as: ads.orbitz.com, ads.realcities.com, etc.), and had our algorithms ignore a URL if its domain name is in this list.

While we did record time information, we were unable to use it in the learning process. This is because many subjects switched modes (to "Report mode") on finding each IC-page, which means that much of the time between requesting an IC-page and the next page was not purely viewing time, but also includes the time spent writing this part of the report. Unfortunately, as we did not anticipate this behavior, we did not record the time spent in Report mode.

4.2 IC-Page Prediction

An IC-page classifier tries to determine whether the current URL is an IC-page, based on the available information. That is, assume the user has visited the "annotated page sequence" $\langle (U_1, \pm_1), (U_2, \pm_2), (U_3, \pm_3), \ldots, (U_{t-1}, \pm_{t-1}), U_t \rangle$, where each $\pm_i$ is "$+$" if this page was deemed an IC-page and "$-$" otherwise. The challenge is to use this information (augmented with other data, see below) to determine whether U_t is an IC-page — *i.e.*, the value of $\pm_t$.

Our *IcURLPredictor* tries to learn this IC-page classifier: Given a number of such annotated web logs, learn a classifier M_P that can take an annotated page sequence as input, and determine whether the final page is IC or not.

---

[2] This is just for the training phase; *IcWordFinder* will later use *unannotated* web logs to make its predictions.

Attributes Used: There are many attributes we could extract from the pages in the web sequence. We considered many of them, but after some preliminary analyses, we selected the 14 attributes shown below, which we compute during a preprocessing step during both training and testing.

Note that a "site-session" is the click stream within a single web domain — *i.e.*, a new site-session begins whenever the user enters a new website. The site-session is only a click stream segmentation method; we do not assume that each site-session concentrates on exactly one task.

1. *URL Properties of target webpage, U_t*
   This set consists of some general features of the current URL, including: **URL-type** (search engine, dynamic, static, etc.), **DomainType** (edu, com, net, org, gov, etc.), and **URL-depth** (Number of "/"'s in the URL).

2. *User Click Stream $\langle U_1, U_2, \dots, U_{t-1} \rangle$ vs U_t*
   FollowSearchEngine: Does U_t immediately follow some search engine?
   isLastEntry: Is U_t the last one in the site-session?
   inTotalNumberofPage: the number of pages that have been visited within this site-session.
   inTotalNumberofICPage: the number of pages, within this site-session, that have been labeled as IC
   inLastIC: the number of pages that have been visited since the last IC-page within this site-session.
   TotalNumberOfPages: the number of pages that have been visited.
   TotalNumberOfICPages: the number of IC-pages that have been visited.
   LastIC: the number of pages that have been visited since the last IC-page.
   PercentageDomain: the percentage of the pages that have the same domain as U_t
   PercentageIC: percentage of IC-pages
   PercentageSameDomainIC: percentage of IC-pages that have the same domain as U_t

Empirical Results for *IcURLPredictor*: As only 10% of the pages are IC, there is a trivial way to obtain 90% accuracy: simply returning "Not IC" on each instance. Of course, this will not serve our needs. To address this problem of "imbalanced data" [9], we used oversampling to generate testing and training data [5]: Form a 200-element testing set by randomly selecting (with replacement) 100 IC-pages and 100 non-IC-pages. (Notice some IC-pages may appear several times in a single training sample.)

After data preparation, we ran several classification algorithms on the data set, producing decision tree (C4.5) [8], NaïveBayes (NB) [4], and Boosted NaïveBayes (BNB) [11]. In all cases, we performed 10-fold cross validation. The results, averaged over all 10 CV folds, appear in Table 1 in the form of "mean±standard-deviation". Notice that BNB has the best "worst-case" over these 4 values, averaging around 65%.

4.3   IC-Word Prediction: *IcWordFinder*

This section describes the *IcWordFinder* subroutine, which learns a classifier (M_W) that can predict whether a word will be an IC-word. Here too we first pre-processed the

Table 1. Empirical Results for Predicting IC (nonIC) Pages

	IC-page		non IC-page	
	Precision	*Recall*	*Precision*	*Recall*
C4.5	0.712 ± 0.063	0.27 ± 0.05	0.5486 ± 0.02	0.89 ± 0.02
NaïveBayes	0.594 ± 0.035	0.82 ± 0.03	0.7075 ± 0.06	0.46 ± 0.12
BNB	0.669 ± 0.048	0.70 ± 0.04	0.6861 ± 0.04	0.65 ± 0.07

annotated web logs: We first segmented the user's entire click stream into *IC-sessions* — sequences of webpages that end with an IC-page; see below. For each IC-session, we then extract all the words in the pages except the last one (which is an IC-page), compute various browsing features of each word, and label each word as an IC-word or not. *IcWordFinder* uses this information to train a classifier to predict when a word will be an IC-word.

IC-session Identification: An "IC-session" is a consecutive sequence of pages that ends with an IC-page, or the end of the user's entire session. While we expect that each IC-session pertains to a single information seeking task or one aspect of such a task, we never explicitly use this assumption.

To identify meaningful IC-sessions, we used the heuristic that if the page after an IC-page is a new search query, this indicates the start of a new session, since it is very common that when one task has been done, users will go to a search engine to begin the next task.

We defined each IC-session as composed of *pageviews*, where a *pageview* is what the user actually sees. In the case of frames, a pageview can be composed of a number of individual URLs. When a frame page is being loaded, all of its child pages will be requested by the browser automatically; and thus instead of recording only the frame page in the log file, all of its child pages were recorded also.

Attribute Extraction: We consider all words that appear in all pages, removing stop words and stemming [7]. We next compute the 25 attributes, for each remaining word, from each IC-session. (This section only sketches the attributes; see [12,14].)

Search Query Category: As our data set includes many requests to search engines, we include several attributes that relate to the words in search-result pages. We consider only information produced by every search engine: the title (*i.e.*, the first line of the result) and the snippet (*i.e.*, the text below the title). We can tag each entry in each search-result page as one of the following: *Chosen*, *Skipped*, and *Untouched*. If the user follows a link, the words in its title and snippet will be considered "*Chosen*". The words that appear in the links that the user did not follow, before the last chosen one, will be deemed "*Skipped*", and all entries after the last chosen link will be considered "*Untouched*".

Most of these search query attributes are the number of times the word appears in each state — *e.g.*, how many times the word is in {*Skipped*, *Chosen*, *Untouched*} title/snippet, the number of times that it appears within the query's keyword list, etc.

Sequential Attributes: Each of the sequential features is extracted from each page in an IC-session, except search-result pages and the last destination page. If the URL refers to a frame page, we determine the features based on that pageview.

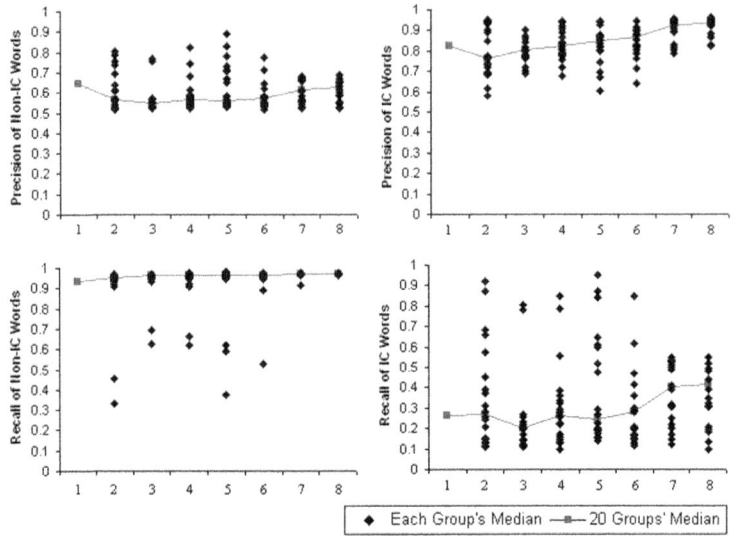

Fig. 2. IC-word Prediction: Testing Result

Many features are based on the "weight" of a word, which is basically the word's frequency in the page, but with addition weight based on the word's location and layout in the webpage — *e.g.*, if the word is in the title, is in bold, etc.

We say a hyperlink (in page U) is "*backed*" if the user followed that link to a page, but went back to page U later. A page is "*backward*" if that page has been visited before; otherwise we say a page is "*forward*"; and one URL may be a forward page at first, but later a backward page elsewhere in the sequence. (Note we record every URL requested, even if it has been accessed before.) Sequential attributes are mainly the features for the weights of the words in the IC-session, such as the average/variance of a word's weight in all the pages, backward pages, and forward pages, how many times the word is in the anchor text of the followed hyperlink, how many times the word is in the page's title, etc.

We compute these attributes for each word in an IC-session, and we also know whether it appears in the IC-page or not. When we train the classifier, we do not need the words themselves, just these attributes and whether the word appears in the IC-page.

Empirical Results for *IcWordFinder*: After preparing the data, our *IcWordFinder* used Weka [13] to produce a NaïveBayes (NB) classifier [4]. For each IC-session, let w_{seq} denotes all the words in the sequence except the last page (which is an IC-page), and w_{dest} denotes the words in that final IC-page. We focus on only those sessions with $w_{dest} \subseteq w_{seq}$. We ran our test on $(8 \times 20) + 1$ subject groups, where each group involved $N \in \{1, 2, \ldots, 8\}$ subjects. For $N = 1$, we took each individual as a 1-user group; and for the other $N \in \{2, 3, \ldots, 8\}$, we randomly selected 20 different groups from the set of participants. Note that we allowed overlap among these 20 groups. For each group, we built 10-fold training/testing datasets, and computed the median value of these 10 results as the final score for this group. (We report medians because they are

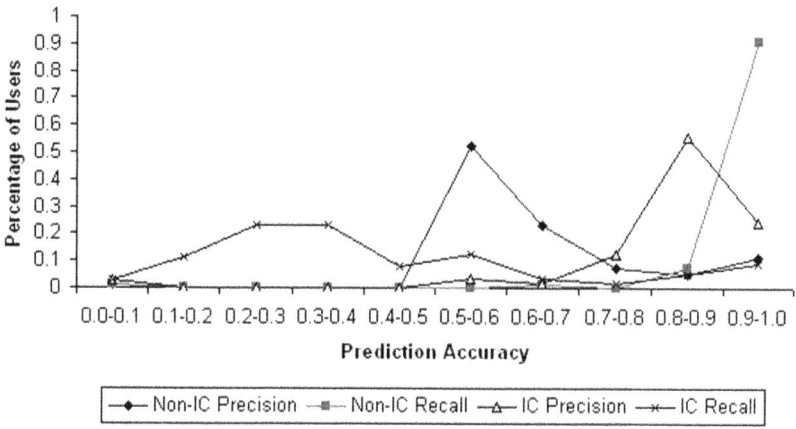

Fig. 3. Prediction result for individual users

less sensitive to outliers than means.) To generate the training and testing data, we used the oversampling technique described earlier.

Here, we found an average accuracy of around 65–70%; the precision and recall results appear in Figure 2. Even though the average recall of IC-words is only about 45%, we anticipate this will be sufficient to to find IC-pages, which of course is our ultimate goal. Recall the two methods (from Section 1) for locating IC-pages given IC-words. *IcFinder* can scout ahead to find the IC-pages that match the predicted IC-words; knowing 45% of the words on that page makes it easy for the scout to correctly identify the page based on its content, or at least some pages very similar to it. Alternatively, *IcFinder* might try to build search queries using the predicted IC-words. Given the high precision of our IC-word prediction, even with recall around 45%, we can anticipate finding tens of words that will surely be in the IC-page. Since the predicted IC-words are exclusive of stop words, they will be quite relevant to the IC-page's content. We therefore suspect that a query with these relevant words will help retrieve the relevant IC-page.

The single-user case ($N = 1$) is perhaps the most relevant, as it shows how well our system, trained on a single user, will perform for that user. Here, for each user, we compute 10-fold training/testing; a histogram showing the median values for all 4 cases (Precision vs Recall; and IC vs non-IC) appears in Figure 3. The results indicate that some individual users are very predictable; note the very high precision and recall in many cases. This suggests that there is a general model of web user's information search — one not based on a particular website or a specific set of words, but a general model that describes how individuals find useful information.

5   Conclusion and Future Work

Future Work: We collected annotated web data only for a single task — travel planning. As we suspect that other tasks may have different characteristics, we plan to conduct further empirical studies based on other tasks; *e.g.*, producing a research report by probing academic websites. We will also investigate ways to learn models for individual users, or small clusters of users, extending Figure 3. Here, we will explore ways to combine a general model, over all users, with the details relevant to an individual user. We will also experiment with yet other learning algorithms, as well as other techniques for dealing with imbalanced datasets.

Contributions: This paper provides two tools that can help web users find the information they need to complete their task: *IcURLPredictor*, which learns a classifier for identifying IC-pages, and *IcWordFinder*, which learns a classifier for identifying IC-words. Like many other webpage recommendation systems, our tools first learn a general user model from a large quantity of user data. As many of these alternative recommendation systems use specific pre-defined URLs or words, they are most effective when applied in the same environment as the training scenario, but much less helpful in a new environment. By contrast, our tools first extract "browsing features" of the words or pages, then learn user-specific *characteristics* of words (or pages) that make them IC for the current user, based on these features. While the models we learn are general to a class of users, the performance systems then uses the actual webpages in the user's current session to produce recommendation specific to that person, in the current context, with the goal of retrieving the information that is most relevant to her. As our systems are also independent of any specific URL or word, these classifiers will be able to help users even in arbitrary novel websites.

To learn such browsing behavior, we first collected annotated web log data by conducting an empirical study, using a browsing tool, AIE, developed for this task. We then built our models M_P and M_W (used by *IcURLPredictor* and *IcWordFinder*) based on the observed browsing features: attributes of the visited URLs and of the words that appear in the annotated web log. The testing results show that our systems produce reasonably accurate predictions, in situations for which no other technique even applies.

Acknowledgments. The authors gratefully acknowledge the generous support from Canada's Natural Science and Engineering Research Council, the Alberta Ingenuity Centre for Machine Learning (http://www.aicml.ca), and the Social Sciences and Humanities Research Council of Canada *Initiative on the New Economy* Research Alliances Program (SSHRC 538-2002-1013).

References

1. R. Agrawal and R. Srikant. Fast algorithms for mining association rules. In *Proc. of the 20th Int'l Conference on Very Large Databases (VLDB'94)*, Santiago, Chile, Sep 1994.
2. C. Anderson and E. Horvitz. Web montage: A dynamic personalized start page. In *Proceedings of the 11th World Wide Web Conference (WWW 2002)*, 2002.
3. D. Billsus and M. Pazzani. A hybrid user model for news story classification. In *Proceedings of the Seventh International Conference on User Modeling (UM '99)*, Banff, Canada, 1999.
4. R. Duda and P. Hart. *Pattern Classification and Scene Analysis*. Wiley, 1973.
5. N. Japkowicz. The class imbalance problem: Significance and strategies. In *Proceedings of the 2000 International Conference on Artificial Intelligence (ICAI 2000)*, 2000.
6. A. Jennings and H. Higuchi. A user model neural network for a personal news service. *User Modeling and User-Adapted Interaction*, 3(1):1–25, 1993.

7. M. Porter. An algorithm for suffix stripping. *Program*, 14(3):130–137, Jul 1980.
8. J. Ross Quinlan. *C4.5: Programs for Machine Learning*. Morgan Kaufmann Publishers, San Mateo, 1992.
9. C. Ling R. Holte, N. Japkowicz and S. Matwin. *AAAI'2000 Workshop on Learning from Imbalanced Data Sets*. AAAI Press, 2000.
10. C. Rijsbergen. *Information Retrieval*. 2nd edition, London, Butterworths, 1979.
11. R. E. Schapire. Theoretical views of boosting and applications. In *Tenth International Conference on Algorithmic Learning Theory*, 1999.
12. http://www.cs.ualberta.ca/~greiner/web-user-model.html.
13. I. Witten and E. Frank. *Data Mining: Practical Machine Learning Tools and Techniques with Java Implementations*. Morgan Kaufmann, OCT 1999.
14. T. Zhu, R. Greiner, and G. Häubl. An effective complete-web recommender system. In *The Twelfth International World Wide Web Conference (WWW2003)*, Budapest, May 2003.
15. I. Zukerman and D. Albrecht. Predictive statistical models for user modeling. *User Modeling and User-Adapted Interaction*, 11(1-2):5–18, 2001.

Modelling Users' Interests and Needs for an Adaptive Online Information System*

Enrique Alfonseca and Pilar Rodríguez

Computer Science Department, Universidad Autonoma de Madrid,
Carretera de Colmenar Viejo, km. 14,5,
28043 Madrid, Spain
{Enrique.Alfonseca, Pilar.Rodriguez}@ii.uam.es
http://www.ii.uam.es/~ealfon

Abstract. A system has been built that adapts the contents of existing web sites to the needs of the users. With this system, it is possible to define the user interests about any kind of topic, and they are used to filter the information from the site. To do it, we have used topic identification and document classification techniques. As an additional functionality, a summarisation system has been integrated with the system, and the user can specify which is the level of compression to be performed on the original hypertext pages from the static web site. In a preliminary evaluation the system was well received among potential users.

1 Introduction

The World Wide Web has made hypermedia a widely used mean for conveying information. However, the quantity of data available on the Internet continues growing steadily, and the large amounts of information can pose potential problems to the web surfer [10]: firstly, static web sites offer the same information to all kinds of users, independently of their interests (the so-called *"one size fits all"* paradigm). Secondly, web pages can also produce *comprehension problems* if some users find that some piece of information is too basic for them, or when they cannot understand the contents of a web page because they don't have the required background.

An architecture has been built for adapting the contents of a web site to different users according to their interests and needs. Using the system, static web sites are analysed, and different contents are shown to different users according to their profile, while maintaining the hypertext structure as much as possible. This paper discusses the design of the user model, and how the user features affect the presentation of contents in the adapted web site. This work has been applied to a system for automatically generating hypermedia sites [2], so as to make those sites adaptive. Some experiments have been performed with a pool of graduates. In general, they considered the application useful and provided feedback for improving it.

---

* This work has been sponsored by CICYT, project number TIC2001-0685-C02-01.

P. Brusilovsky et al. (Eds.): UM 2003, LNAI 2702, pp. 76–80, 2003.

2   User Modelling Based on Interests and Available Time

The aim of the system is the transformation of a static web site into an adaptive site that shows different kinds of information to different users. To do that, the contents of the web site will be modified, but the link structure will be kept the same as much as possible. There are two kinds of transformations that are performed to the textual contents: a filtering of the information that is deemed irrelevant, and a summarisation of the remaining information, according to the instructions provided by the user. To achieve that aim, two different facts will be modelled in the users' profile: (a) their personal interests, and (b) the amount of information that they are willing to read.

2.1   User Interests

A single hypermedia site may contain information about different topics. For example, one of the web sites that we have processed with our system dealt with Charles Darwin's *The Voyages of the Beagle*. It is a multi-disciplinary document in which he describes both animals and places, and the adventures he lived. It seems natural to pre-define three possible user interests for this text: biology, about animals and plants; geography, which includes all the descriptions of places; and history, which includes the fragments in which Darwin explains his adventures and other events. Other web sites have different topics predefined.

The system allows the definition of predefined interests or *stereotypes*. A user might be interested in one or several of these, or in some particular topic that had not been thought of beforehand by the designer of the web site. Therefore, it is necessary that the way in which the user's interests are encoded allows the definition of new possible topics. This section describes the design decisions that were taken in order to tailor the page contents to the user interests. The process performed consists in eliminating all the information that is considered irrelevant for each particular user, a process that can be called *topic filtering*.

In order to train the topic classifier we used the vector model, which has been used very often in Information Retrieval (IR) applications. One hundred paragraphs from each web site were classified by hand with one of the pre-defined label. Next, all the open-class words (nouns, verbs, adjectives and adverbs) appearing in those paragraphs were collected, together with their frequencies of appearance. Finally, for each stereotype, the frequencies were changed into weights indicating the support that a word gives to the decision of classifying a paragraph in each stereotype. The list of words and weights is called a *topic signature*. In our case, we weighed the words with the χ^2 metric [1], which seemed to give better results than other standard metrics such as tf·idf.

2.2   Topic Filtering

As said above, when a new user registers into the system there are two ways in which his or her interests can be specified. It is possible to select one or several stereotypes, or to ask for a user-defined profile. In the first case, the pre-defined topic signatures are copied into the new profile, and they are marked either as relevant or irrelevant. In the second case, the system will start by showing the users all the available information, and they can press small icons in the page to indicate whether a paragraph was interesting or not, so their models are updated as they browse.

While browsing a web site, for each paragraph in a hypertext page, its relevancy is calculated in the following way:

1. The paragraph's signature is formed by collecting all the open-class words.
2. The dot product is performed between that signature and each of the topic signatures in the user's profile. The metrics are normalised so they sum 1.
3. The paragraph is chosen if, for any of the topics that the user has selected as relevant, the similarity metric is above $\frac{1}{N}$, where N is the number of topics.

Note that, with this algorithm, the same paragraph may be considered relevant for different stereotypes, if it contains keywords relevant to more than one topic. The classification algorithm was evaluated with a test set that contained 58 additional paragraphs, labelled by hand. 91.38% of them were chosen as relevant for the right stereotypes.

When the user is navigating the web site, for every paragraph in the text there will be two small icons, that can be clicked to inform the system that the information in that paragraph is either very relevant or irrelevant. This information will be used to update the frequency counts in the topic signatures in the user's profile, in order to provide better information in the future.

Finally, when a user registers, all the pages in the web site are analysed and those which do not contain any relevant information are marked in the user's profile. When browsing the web site, the links to those pages will be removed.

2.3   Available Time and Reading Speed

The second aim of our adaptive site is to provide the quantity of information that the users are willing to read. A user can request different compression rates to the system by indicating the compression rate to be applied; the total number of words that the target site should contain; or the amount of time available.

The first situation is the simplest one, when the compression rate is directly provided by the user; in the second case, the rate is calculated by dividing the total number of words that the user is willing to read by the number of words in the relevant portions of the web site. The last case is somewhat more complicated. The users provide their *availability of time* as a number of hours that they intend to browse the site. Next, the users' *reading efficiency* is collected with a short test, in which the site server asks the user to read a small passage of text (∼3 minutes) and fill in a questionnaire. The *reading efficiency* is calculated as the product of the reading speed and comprehension [5], measured in words per minute. Finally, if the user interests change while browsing, the compression rate is automatically re-calculated.

The summarisation is performed with a common sentence extraction procedure [3], taking into consideration the positions of the sentences in the document, their length, and their relevancy according to the user's profile.

Table 1. Answers of the users. Each question was evaluated from 1 to 5 (very low, low, medium, high and very high).

Question	Mean	Std dev.
Easiness to register in the system	4	2.83
Did any of the stereotypes equalled your personal interests?	3.8	2.76
Did you find useful the possibility of creating new stereotypes?	4.9	0.95
The length of the summaries is appropriate	4.22	1.89
The summaries are coherent and easy to read	3.5	2.55
What is your overall opinion about the system?	4.2	1.26

3 Evaluation and Results

The evaluation has been performed with a controlled experiment, in which twelve people have used the system and provided comments. Their backgrounds are somewhat different: there were one linguist, three electrical engineers, one industrial engineer, two mathematicians and five computer scientists. The different options of the system were taught to them, and the profile of each person was collected. In general, they all had much experience using a web browser, but only some of them knew what adaptive hypermedia is; fluency reading English was very variable, as some had a high proficiency, and others could only read around 60 words per minute. Finally, few of them knew about the texts used in the experiments.

The evaluation centred on the usability of the new tool. All the users spent some time using the system, and when they felt that they had explored the different possibilities, they filled a questionnaire. The questions that concern the user model are listed in Table 1. The users considered most features of the system as highly or very highly usable (the mean score was between 4 and 5). The ones that received the lowest weights were the interest of the pre-defined stereotypes, and the coherence of the generated summaries, a fact that could be expected, as extracts are sometimes incoherent.

4 Related Work

There are several automatic algorithms to partition full-length expository text into a sequence of subtopical discussions [4], but it is also possible to partition the text in paragraphs, and to classify the paragraphs separately, considering that it is not frequent to find a topic shift in the middle of a paragraph. The problem of finding relevant topics in a text is not a new one; [6] start with a pre-defined set of topics and lists of words that are relevant for each of them, and use the lists to classify the text fragments. [7] described a supervised algorithm for which there is, initially, a set of text fragments, each one labelled with its topic, and the algorithm learns the lexical items that are useful for classifying new texts. Finally, the topics themselves can be automatically induced from the set of texts, e.g. by clustering them, or using a conceptual ontology.

Concerning adaptive hypermedia systems, there are several approaches to adapting a web site to the needs of a user using natural language processing techniques, such as those described by [8] and [9].

5   Conclusions and Future Work

A new approach has been implemented for automatically adapting a complete web site to the interests of a user. The users can specify their needs by choosing from a list of pre-defined interests, or by selecting the paragraphs that are of interest to them. Secondly, by indicating a compression rate to be performed to the pages, their contents are summarised using a sentence extraction procedure, which also takes into account the user's interests. This technique performs well for web sites that contain large amounts of text, such as those that have been generated from linear text. In this case, the system selects just the paragraphs that meet the user's interests; if a page is left empty, it is removed from the user's hyperspace, until a change in the user's profile makes it relevant again.

When used by some potential users, the system had a good acceptance. Future work includes improving the user-friendliness of the system with the suggestions gotten from the users that participated in the evaluation; and making it easier to generate new user-defined stereotypes.

References

1. E. Agirre, O. Ansa, E. Hovy, and D. Martinez. Enriching very large ontologies using the www. In *Ontology Learning Workshop, ECAI*, Berlin, Germany, 2000.
2. E. Alfonseca and P. Rodríguez. Automatically generating hypermedia documents depending on user goals. In *Workshop on Doc. Compression and Synthesis, AH-2002*, 2002.
3. H. P. Edmundson. New methods in automatic abstracting. *Journal of the Association for Computational Machinery*, 16(2):264–286, 1969.
4. M. A. Hearst. Texttiling: A quantitative approach to discourse segmentation, 1993.
5. M. D. Jackson and J. L. McClelland. Processing determinants of reading speed. *Journal of experimental psychology*, 108:151–181, 1979.
6. P. Jacobs and L. Rau. Scisor: Extracting information from on-line news. *Communications of the ACM*, 33(11):88–97, 1990.
7. B. Masand, G. Linoff, and D. Waltz. Classifying news stories using memory based reasoning. In *Proceedings of SIGIR 92*, pages 59–65, 1992.
8. M. Milosavljevic, R. Dale, S. J. Green, C. Paris, and S. Williams. Virtual museums on the information superhighway: Prospects and potholes. In *CIDOC'98*, 1998.
9. J. Oberlander, M. O'Donell, C. Mellish, and A. Knott. Conversation in the museum: experiments in dynamic hypermedia with the intelligent labeling explorer. *The new review of multimedia and hypermedia*, 4:11–32, 1998.
10. H. Wu and P. de Bra. Link-independent navigation support in web-based adaptive hypermedia. In *Proceedings of the 11th International WWW Conference*, 2002.

Declarative Specifications for Adaptive Hypermedia Based on a Semantic Web Approach

Serge Garlatti and Sébastien Iksal

Department of Artificial Intelligence and Cognitive Sciences - ENST Bretagne
Technopôle de Brest Iroise - B.P. 832, 29285 Brest Cedex, France
{serge.garlatti, sebastien.iksal}@enst-bretagne.fr

Abstract. Adaptation/personalization is one of the main issues for web services. Adaptive web applications have the ability to deal with different users' needs for enhancing usability and comprehension and for dealing with large repositories. We propose an open-ended adaptive hypermedia environment which is based on the virtual document and semantic web approaches and which is able to manage adaptive techniques at knowledge level. In this paper, we have focused on the way to specify and to manage adaptation in this environment. We propose an approach which is based on a unique evaluation principle of links/contents per document and where the author may assign user stereotypes to adaptive techniques.

Keywords. Adaptive navigation and presentation, Virtual Document, Composition Engine, Semantic Web

1 Introduction

Adaptive web applications have the ability to deal with different users' needs for enhancing usability and comprehension and for dealing with large repositories. Indeed, adaptive web services - also called Adaptive Hypermedia Systems - can provide different kinds of information, different layouts and navigation tools according to users' needs [1]. Creating and/or designing adaptive web services can be achieved by virtual documents and the Semantic Web. A virtual document is a document with no persistent state and which is at least partially generated at run time [2]. The Semantic Web is the Internet of meanings. It is a vision for making the contents of the web understandable to the machines in order to enhance reuse, sharing and exchange of resources through the web and to deal with automatic or semiautomatic services. Adaptive Hypermedia systems can be viewed as a kind of these services dealing with different users' needs and distributed resources.

We have designed an open-ended adaptive hypermedia environment which is based on the virtual document and semantic web approaches and which is able to manage adaptive techniques at knowledge level. In other words, the specification of the adaptive mechanisms is defined by semantic properties associated to a hypermedia docu-

P. Brusilovsky et al. (Eds.): UM 2003, LNAI 2702, pp. 81–85, 2003.

ment - by an author. At present, we have focused our study on the main adaptive navigation techniques. The management of these techniques is based on a unique evaluation principle of links/contents per document. It is also possible to assign user stereotypes to adaptive techniques. Then, an author can determine the relevant adaptation techniques for a given user. Indeed, some experiments have shown that it is necessary to provide the relevant adaptive methods to the current user [3].

First of all, the architecture of our adaptive hypermedia environment is introduced. Next, we focus on the management of the adaptation features. Finally, we conclude by the current state of implementation and some perspectives.

2 The Architecture

In our framework, we consider an adaptive document as an adaptive virtual document. We define it as follows: An adaptive virtual document consists of a set of information fragments, ontologies and a composition engine which is able to select the relevant information fragments and to organize them according to an overall document structure by adapting various visible aspects of the document delivered to the user.

We are interested in adaptive virtual documents for author-oriented web services. Authors have know-how which enables them to choose contents and one or more overall document structures. We propose a composition engine having an architecture based on the three different views of a digital document: semantic, logical and layout. The three views have a specific structure organizing them. The semantic structure of a document conveys the organization of the meaning of the document content. The logical structure reflects the syntactic organization of a document (for example books are organized into chapters and sections). The layout structure describes how the documents have to appear on a device. For each view our adaptive composition engine has a specific adaptation mechanism.

The composition engine is divided into three composition processes: semantic, logical and layout (cf. figure 1). The aim of the semantic composition engine is to compute on the fly an adapted document using: i) a generic document for which node contents are substituted at run time, according to user's needs, ii) an intelligent search engine, iii) semantic metadata associated with fragments, iv) a user model and v) an information space[1]. The generic document, defined by an author, is a directed graph of which nodes have a content specification according to a metadata schema and edges are semantic relationships chosen by the author. The adapted document consists of a set of selected fragments linked by semantic relationships. The logical composition engine browses the adapted document and computes for each node an XML web page with content and navigation tools. In navigation tools, links have properties for managing adaptation [4]. The layout composition engine generates an HTML page from the XML web page. Adaptation processes take place in the three engines.

---

[1] The information space can be potentially Internet/Intranet , but in our framework, it is limited by an author to ensure semantic coherence of the delivered document.

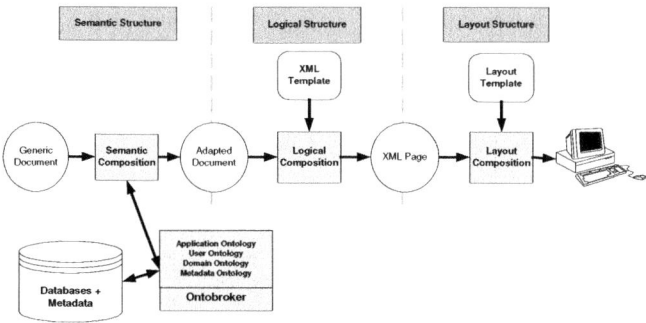

Fig. 1. The Composition Engine Architecture

This architecture relies on four ontologies [5] which are: a domain ontology for representing contents; a metadata ontology which describes the indexing structure of fragments; a user ontology for defining stereotypes and individual features; a document ontology which may represent the author's competences and know-how [6]. The domain ontology defines a shared vocabulary used in the metadata schema for the content description of data, and in the user model for the knowledge description.

3 Specification of Adaptation

The main goal of adaptation in a hypermedia document is to provide the relevant navigation tools, information units and organization. The semantic composition engine is able to manage the adaptive techniques at a knowledge level to overcome the main difficulties of the authoring task. The specification of the adaptive mechanisms is defined by semantic properties associated with a generic document by an author. Then, it can be used in various contexts which require different adaptive mechanisms. The management of the adaptive techniques is based on a unique evaluation principle of contents. An author may also specify the assignment of user stereotypes to adaptive techniques. Then, he can determine the relevant techniques for a given user.

3.1 Fragment Evaluation

In our framework, we propose to evaluate the fragments by means of a unique evaluation method for the entire document. Then, the management of adaptive techniques is made at an abstract level instead of managing them for each link or each content. Our proposal is to manage the main adaptive navigation techniques on a similar basis. Indeed, we propose to define up to five disjoint and totally ordered classes of links – at least two classes. We have chosen to have up to five classes for user comprehension. Indeed, it could be difficult for a user to deal with too many classes. Several studies have proposed up to five different classes for managing annotation but not more [1, 7].

The classification is done by an evaluation of the destination fragments of the links, that is to say the variants of fragments matching the content specification of each component. These classes are called: very good, good, average, bad, very bad. An author defines the necessary and sufficient conditions for class membership. These conditions have to be satisfied by the fragment and the user to be a member of the corresponding class. It is possible to use some computed parameters like the percentage of known concepts according to those which describe the fragment content. An example and its meaning:

```
Good = "(JOB = Fisherman) AND (PCTAGEKNOWN >= 75)"
```

The fragment is of the class "Good" if the user is a fisherman and he knows at least 75% of the domain concepts describing the semantic content of the fragment.

3.2 Stereotypes for Adaptive Navigation Techniques

An adaptive navigation technique is available for a given user whether its stereotype matches the user model. All user model features can be used to define a stereotype according to the user model ontology. According to the current adaptive navigation technique, each evaluated fragment is kept for the user or not. Then, there is a content adaptation and a modification of the semantic structure of the document. An example and its meaning:

```
ANNOTATION = "((AGE > 18) OR (JOB = Student)) AND (LOCATION IN Bretagne)"
```

annotation is for user being 18 years old or being students in Brittany.

4 Adaptive Composition

In this section, we will present how the adaptation is managed by the semantic composition process. This process falls into three sub-processes:

1. First of all, the search engine selects the relevant fragments from the information space by means of content's specifications. The outcome of this process is a set of variants of fragments. These fragments differ in a subset of the metadata schema, but have the same content description.
2. Secondly, all selected fragments are evaluated and then some semantic relationships can be suppressed or kept according to the considered adaptive navigation technique. The different classes are used by the adaptive navigation processes in order to manage the corresponding relationships.
3. Thirdly, the user model is compared to all stereotypes associated with the different adaptive navigation techniques. Those which fit the user model are kept. Among them, the user has to order them through his preferences. Author constraints have priority over user preferences in the system's choice of the technique.

For defining the links in navigation guides, logical composition engine has to browse the adaptive document and then "translates" semantic relationships into links. It has also to associate properties to links for managing annotation, hiding, partial hiding, sorting and direct guidance. This properties and a layout template are used by the layout composition engine to build an HTML page.

5 Conclusion and Perspectives

In this paper, we have presented an open-ended adaptive hypermedia environment which manages adaptive techniques at knowledge level. It is based on the virtual document and semantic web approaches. Actually, the composition engine has been implemented with the adaptive mechanisms, but the authoring tool creates only non-adaptive generic documents (adaptation has to be added by hand). Indeed, the specification of the adaptive mechanisms is defined by semantic properties associated to a hypermedia document - by an author. The management of adaptive techniques is made at an abstract level instead of managing them for each link (or content). Consequently, it is easy to change the specification and to use this environment in various contexts.

At present, we do not deal with external links and adaptive content in atomic fragments[2]. It could be done by extending the composition engines and adding metadata to external links and parts of atomic fragments to preserve our principles for adaptation. Moreover, semantic properties dedicated to adaptation mechanisms could be associated with each type of semantic relationships in a document. Consequently, adaptation would be managed at a finer level of granularity.

References

1. Brusilovsky, P., *Methods and techniques of adaptive hypermedia.* User Modeling and User-Adapted Interaction, 1996. **6**(2–3): p. 87–129.
2. Watters, C. and M. Shepherd. *Research issues for virtual documents.* in *Workshop on Virtual Document, Hypertext Functionality and the Web.* 1999. Toronto.
3. Specht, M. and A. Kobsa. *Interaction of domain expertise and interface design in adaptive educational hypermedia.* in *Second Workshop on Adaptive Systems and User Modeling on the World Wide Web.* 1999. Toronto & Banff: University of Eindhoven.
4. Brusilovsky, P., E. Schwarz, and G. Weber. *ELM-ART: An intelligent tutoring system on World Wide Web.* in *Third International Conference on Intelligent Tutoring Systems, ITS-96.* 1996. Montreal.
5. Iksal, S. and S. Garlatti, *Documents Virtuels et Composition Sémantique: Une Architecture Fondée sur des Ontologies.* NimesTic'01. 2001, Ecole des Mines d'Alès: Nimes. 91–96.
6. Iksal, S., S. Garlatti, F. Ganier, and P. Tanguy, *Semantic composition of special reports on the Web: A cognitive approach,* in *Hypertextes et Hypermédia H2PTM'01,* J.P. Balpe, et al., Editors. 2001, Hermès. p. 363–378.
7. De Bra, P. and L. Calvi, *AHA! An open Adaptive Hypermedia Architecture.* The New Review of Hypermedia and Multimedia, 1998. **4**: p. 115–139.

---

[2] An atomic fragment is not composed of other fragments.

Emotional Dialogs with an Embodied Agent

Addolorata Cavalluzzi, Berardina De Carolis, Valeria Carofiglio, and
Giuseppe Grassano

Intelligent Interfaces, Department of Informatics,
University of Bari, Italy
{cavalluzzi, carofiglio, decarolis, grassano}@di.uniba.it
http://aos2.di.uniba.it:8080/IntInt.html

Abstract. We discuss how simulating emotional dialogs with an Embodied Agent requires endowing it with ability to manifest appropriately emotions but also to exploit them in controlling behavior. We then describe a domain-independent testbed to simulate dialogs in affective domains and verify how they change when the context in which interaction occurs is varied. Emotion activation is simulated by dynamic belief networks while dialog simulation is implemented within a logical framework.

1 Introduction

We aim at implementing an Embodied Conversational Agent (ECA) that interacts with the user to provide advice in a domain that is influenced by affective factors. To behave believably, our agent should show some form of emotional intelligence, which requires the ability to *recognize and express emotions* (in self and in the hearer), *regulate them* and *utilize them to optimize the advice provided* [11]. In a first phase of our research, we focused work on emotion expression. To establish when the agent should express an emotion, which emotion and with which intensity, we developed an emotion modeling method and prototype [2]. To make the agent's mind independent of its body, we defined a XML markup language (APML) in which the *meanings* that the agent should show when uttering a sentence are specified as tags [3]. This enabled us to produce, from a discourse plan, an input to agents with different bodies: the agent could manifest emotions in addition to other *meanings* (performative types, belief relations etc), through an appropriate combination of speech and nonverbal *signals* that depended on its body.

The ability to exhibit an emotional state is, however, only a shallow form of the emotional intelligence an agent can show. Emotions have to be utilized to drive reasoning behind the dialog. This implies studying how the dialog may be affected by the emotional state of the two interlocutors and by their personalities. Again according to Picard, emotions influence learning, decision making and memory. If intelligently handled, they may help to manage information overload, regulate prioritization of activities and help in making the decision process more flexible, creative and intelligent. More in general, they motivate and bias behavior, although they do not completely determine it. Simulating affective dialogs therefore requires investigating the following problem issues:

P. Brusilovsky et al. (Eds.): UM 2003, LNAI 2702, pp. 86–95, 2003.
© Springer-Verlag Berlin Heidelberg 2003

- *which emotions arise in the agent during the dialog, as a consequence of exogenous factors (the user move);*
- *which personality factors affect emotion activation;*
- *how emotions influence the dialog course: priority of communicative goals, dialog plan, surface realization of communicative acts.*

Reaction to emotions and, more in general, their effect on the agent behavior are influenced by the social relationship with the interlocutor. Three types of relationships are envisaged, again by Picard. In situations of *friendship*, the agent tends to have *similarly valenced* emotions in response to the emotions of the interlocutor while, in situations of *animosity*, emotions with *opposite valences* are felt and shown. In situations of *empathy*, the agent temporarily substitutes the presumed goals, standards and preferences of the interlocutor for its own. Of course, empathy and animosity do not tend to go together, but empathy does not necessarily come with friendship, for instance when the agent adopts the interlocutor's goals, standards and preferences for mere convenience. We wish to go beyond the idea of simulating, in the agent, emotions that mirror or contrast those displayed by the user, to represent the cognitive bases of emotion feeling and their influence on the dialog dynamics: in this paper, we describe the results we have achieved so far.

2   A Model of Emotion Activation

In our emotion modeling method, we pay particular attention to how emotions change of intensity with time, how they mix up and how each of them prevails, in a given situation, according to the agent's personality and to the social context in which the dialog occurs. So far, we focused our attention on event-driven emotions in Ortony, Clore and Collin's (*OCC*) theory [10]. In this theory, *positive* emotions (happy-for, hope, joy, etc.) are activated by *desirable* events while *negative* emotions (sorry-for, fear, distress, etc.) arise after *undesirable* events. Events concerning the agent are in the *Well-being* category (joy, distress), events concerning other people are in the *FortuneOfOthers* category (happy-for, sorry-for, envy and gloating) while future events are in the *Prospective* category (fear, hope). In Oatley and Johnson-Laird's theory, positive and negative emotions are activated (respectively) by the belief that some goal will be achieved or will be threatened [9]. A cognitive model of emotions[1] that is built on this theory should represent the system of beliefs and goal behind emotion activation and endows the agent with the ability to *guess the reason why she feels a particular emotion and to justify it*. It includes the ingredients that enable representing *how the Agent's system of goals is revised* when emotions are felt and how this revision influences planning of subsequent dialog moves.

Our model of emotion activation is represented with a Dynamic Belief Network (*DBN*). As proposed by Nicholson and Brady [8], we use *DBN*s as a

---

[1] "We use the term cognitive to refer to psychological explanations in terms of their representation and transformation of knowledge *which may or may not be conscious*" [9]

goal monitoring system that employs the observation data in the time interval (T_i, T_{i+1}) to generate a probabilistic model of the agent's mind at time T_{i+1}, from the model that was built at time T_i. We employ this model to reason about the consequences of the observed event on the monitored goals. We calculate the intensity of emotions as a function of the *uncertainty* of the agent's beliefs that its goals will be achieved (or threatened) and of the *utility* assigned to achieving these goals. According to the utility theory, the two variables are combined to measure *the variation in the intensity of an emotion* as a product of the change in the probability to achieve a given goal, times the utility that achieving this goal takes to the agent [2]. Let us consider, for instance, the triggering of *sorry-for* that is represented in Figure 1. This is a negative emotion and the goal that is involved, in this case, is *preserving others from bad.* The agent's belief

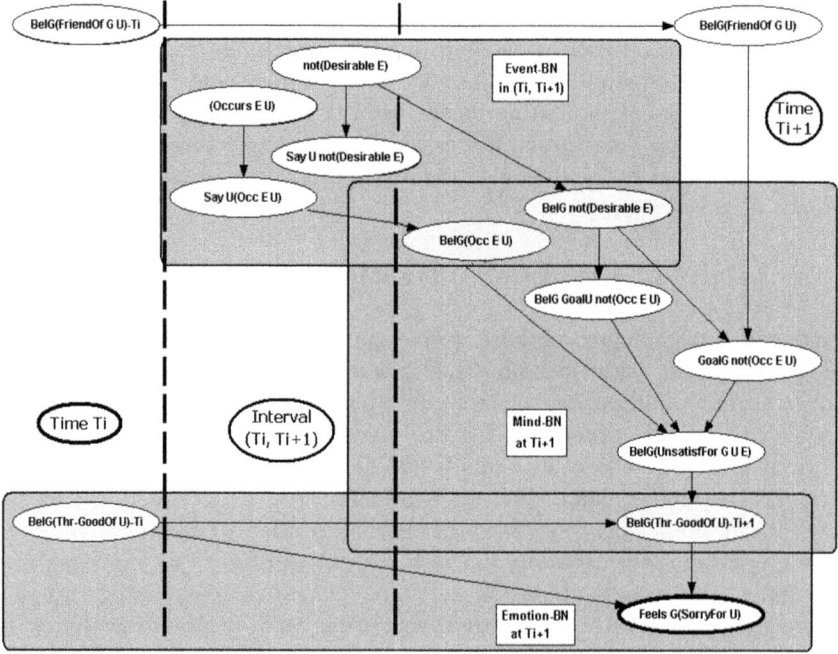

Fig. 1. A portion of the *DBN* that represents the agent's mental state.

about the probability that this goal will be threatened (Bel G (Thr-GoodOf U)) is influenced by her belief that some undesirable event E occurred to the user (BelG(Occ E U)). According to Elliott and Siegle [6], the main variables influencing this probability are the desirability of the event (Bel G not(Desirable E)) and the probability that the agent attaches to the occurrence of this event (Bel G (Occ E U)). Other factors, such as the social context (Bel G FriendOf G U)), affect the emotion intensity. The model of the agent state at time T_{i+1} is built by automatically combining several *BNs*: the main one (Mind-BN) and one or more Event-BNs and Emotion-BNs. In the Event-BNs, the user moves are interpreted as *observable* consequences of occurred events, that activate emotions through a model of the impact of this event on the agent's beliefs and goals. The strength of the link between what the user said (Say U (Occ E U)) and the *hidden* event (Occ E U) is a function of the user sincerity; the link between this observation and the agent's belief (Bel G (Occ E U)) is a function of how believable the agent considers the user to be. Therefore, the more sincere the user is and the more likely the event is a priori, the higher will be the probability that G believes in the occurrence of the event E. Similar considerations hold for the evaluation of how *desirable* the event is (Bel G (Desirable E)); these nodes are leaves of the Event-BN. They are, as well, roots of Mind-BN: they influence G's belief that U would not desire the event E to occur (Bel G Goal U ¬(Occ E U)) and (if G is in a *empathy* relationship with U and therefore adopts U's goals), its own desire that E does not occur (Goal G ¬(Occ E)). This way, they concur to increase the probability that the agent's goal of *preserving others from bad* will be threatened. Variation in the probability of this goal activates the emotion of *sorry-for* in G through the Emotion-BN. The intensity of this emotion is the product of this variation times the *weight* the agent gives to the mentioned goal. According to Carbonell, we define a personality as a cognitively plausible combination of weights the agent gives to the goals represented in the model [1].

The strength of the link between the goal-achievement (or threatening) nodes at two contiguous time instants defines the way the emotion associated with that goal decays, in absence of any event influencing it. By varying appropriately this strength, we simulate a more or less fast decay of emotion intensity. Different decays are attached to different emotion categories (positive vs. negative, FortuneOfOthers vs. Wellbeing and so on) and different temperaments are simulated, in which the *persistence* of emotions varies. The agents' affective state usually includes multiple emotions. Different emotions may coexist because an event produced several of them at the same time or because a new emotion is triggered while the previous ones did not yet decay completely. We describe in [2] how we modeled the two mentioned mixing methaphors (*microwave oven* and *tub of water*, in Picard's terminology).

3   An Example Dialog: Advice about Healthy Eating

Although Embodied Agents are seen as one of the emerging human-computer interaction metaphors, appropriate application domains have still to be found, especially for *realistic* agents. The more realistic the agent's aspect is, the more the user expects from interacting with it; this expectation still increases when the dialog considers emotional aspects. To test how incorporating affective factors may contribute to believability of the dialog, we built a domain-independent simulator. We will illustrate its principles and functioning with the test domain that we selected in the scope of the European Project *MagiCster*: advice about eating disorders. We examined some of the websites and chat-lines in this domain, to build a corpus of data that we employed in designing our simulator. Information in these sites is not tailored to the users, who cannot take the initiative to get what best suits their needs. The system cannot recognize the user problems and emotional state; as a consequence, the *empathy* it shows is quite formal. By implementing an Embodied Agent that interacts with the user, we would like to make the dialog situation-aware and more attractive, with the aim to provide a more effective advice. In the following example dialog, the agent moves are denoted with Gi and the user moves with Uj. Moves Gi are generated by our simulation program, while moves Uj are introduced in free text.

$G0$: Hi, my name is Greta! I'm here to help you in finding a healthier way of feeding yourself. What's your name?

$U0$: My name is Jana.

$G1$: What's your problem, Jana?

$U1$: I've been eating too much and badly in the past year and I feel I can't stop!

$G2$: Oh I'm sorry. That's a bad situation indeed. Which is your age?

$U2$: I'm 17.

$G3$: Well: teens are notorious for being hungry frequently, because they need to eat more to support the major growth of their bodies. Maybe you only need an appropriate diet.

$U3$: It's not a question of increased appetite! It's a serious problem that is out of my control!

$G4$: How terrible! Did you try to do something, to solve this problem?

$U4$: Yes, and I did not succeed. I now fear that stopping will not be possible to me!

$G5$: Oh no! You have to be confident in yourself! If you want to get over this, I may help you.

$U5$: What can I do?

$G6$: I have some ideas and experience on how to make a smooth, quick transition from overeating back to healthful living. If you wish, I may suggest you what to do.

$U6$: Yes, please, I want to make any possible effort to get over these problems!

$G7$: Fine! This is the way I want to see you! So, let's start, first of all, from cleansing your home from all binge foods. Whatever your current food downfalls are, get rid of them!

$U7$: But I can't stand to throw food away!

$G8$: Well, give it to someone, then! And, if your relatives insist on keeping such foods in the house, ask them to keep it away from you for a while.

In the present prototype, translation of the user move into a symbolic communicative act is quite primitive (just based on keyword analysis). For instance: *"I've been eating too much and badly in the past year and I feel I can't stop!"* is interpreted as: Say U (Occ EatingTooMuch U) and Say U not(Desirable EatingTooMuch). Symbolic communicative acts are inputs of Event-BNs and trigger building of the DBN that combines Event-BN, Mind-BN at times T_i and T_{i+1} and Emotion-BN. Figure 2 shows the dynamics of emotions that are activated in the example dialog. $U0$ does not produce any emotional reaction. $U1$ is interpreted (as we said) as an undesirable event occurring to U, that activates *sorry-for* at time T_2. $U2$ does not produce any new emotional reaction: sorry-for decays. $U3$ is interpreted as an undesirable event (*compulsive overeating*) which increases sorry-for again at T_4. $U4$ is interpreted as a risk that U stops the dialog: this undesirable (to G) prospective event provokes a light fear at T_5. $U5$ does not produce any emotional reaction: sorry-for and fear decrease. $U6$ is a desirable event to G, which activates hope at T_7. $U7$ does not produce any emotional reaction; all emotions decrease.

By changing the agent's personality and the context, we may get a sequence of emotions with different intensities. By varying parameters that define their

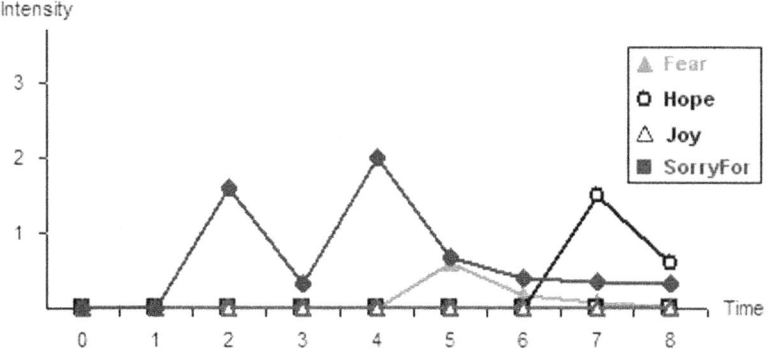

Fig. 2. Dynamics of emotions in the example dialog.

decay, we simulate a *ruminant* condition in which emotions decay slowly and an *impulsive* condition, in which they decay faster. By varying parameters defining the context, we may simulate a *neutral* or an *unfriendly* relationship. By increasing the activation threshold, we may simulate an agent who is *cold* in feeling all emotions.

4 The Effects of Emotions

A user move is a source of information and emotion to the agent. The issue the dialog manager has to solve is now the following: *how should the agent behave, after* feeling *an emotional state?* Should the agent manifest its emotion and how? How should these emotions affect the dialog dynamics?

4.1 Emotion Display

Once felt, an emotion E may be hidden or displayed. Again, this decision (although not always taken consciously) may be influenced by personality factors and by the interaction context. In [3] we describe how this aspect of the emotional behaviour of our agent can be modeled by means of rules that regulate activation of display goals. For example, the following rule:

If (Feel G E) $\land$ Is-a (E WellBeing) $\land$ (Valence E Negative) $\land$ (Adoptive G U)
then Goal G $\neg$ (Display G E)

activates the goal of hidening *fear* felt at time T_5, because the agent has an *adoptive* relashionship with the user. On the contrary, the following one:

If (Feel G E) $\land$ Is-a (E WellBeing) $\land$ (Valence E Positive) $\land$ (Adoptive G U)
then Goal G (Display G E)

activates the goal of showing *joy* felt at time T_7. When emotions have to be displayed, an *affective* tag in APML is automatically added to the agent move; this *meaning* tag is automatically translated into a combination of *signals* (in the face, the gesturing, the body movement) that depend on the character employed [5].

4.2 Behavior Control

We manipulate the *inner* aspects of the emotional response of our agent with an algorithm of activation/deactivation of its *goals* and of dynamic revision of their priorities[2]. The idea is that the agent has an initial list of goals, each with its priority, some of which are *inactive*: every goal is linked, by an *application condition*, to a plan that the agent can perform to achieve it. A presumed emotional state of the user does not influence activation and priority of goals directly. In a *reactive* framework, the agent would exhibit emotions with *similar* or *opposite* valences in response to the emotions of the user; as we said in the Introduction, our agent applies, instead, some form reasoning (or cognitive emotion appraisal) on the user move. The emotion it feels is therefore triggered by an analysis of the event that presumably produced the user's emotional state; its own emotional response depends on this event and on the context. The advantage of cognitive simulation of emotion activation over a purely reactive model is that it gives us the information we need to implement emotion-based dynamic revision of goals.

5 Knowledge Sources

The dialog manager includes three main modules. A *Deliberative* layer selects the goal with the highest priority and the plan to achieve it and stores in the agenda the actions in the plan. The *I/O Communicative layer* executes the next action in the agenda. The *Reactive layer* decides whether the goal priority should be revised, by applying reacting rules. The following knowledge sources are employed by these modules:

1. *An agent and a user model* are stored in the information state, with the interaction history. These models include two categories of factors:
   - *long-term settings* that are stable during the dialog and influence the initial priority of the agent goals and therefore its initial plan, initiative handling and behavior: agent's personality, its role, its relationship with the user;
   - *short-term settings*, that evolve during the dialog and influence goal priority change and plan revision: in particular, the emotional state of agent.

   The agent's goals can be in one of the following relations among themselves:
   - *Priority*: $g_i < g_j$: g_i is more important, to the agent, than g_j. If this relation holds and no constraints or preconditions are violated by satisfying it, g_i will be achieved before g_j.
   - *Hierarchy*: $H(g_i, (g_{i1}, g_{i2}, \ldots, g_{in}))$: the complex goal g_i may be decomposed into simpler subgoals $g_{i1}, g_{i2}, \ldots, g_{in}$, which contribute to achieving it.
   - *Causal Relation*: $Cause(g_i, g_j)$: the plan achieving the source goal g_i is a precondition for the plan achieving the destination goal g_j.

---

[2] "We suggest that the functions of emotion modes are both to enable our priority to be exchanged for another in the system of multiple goals and to maintain this priority until it is satisfied or abandoned." [9]

2. *Plans* are represented as context-adapted recipes; a recipe may be applied when some preconditions hold; its application affects the dialog state (agent's and user's mental state and interaction settings). In the eating disorder domain, our agent adopts the typical plan of intelligent advice systems:
   - *situation-assessment*, to acquire information about the user,
   - *describe-eating-disorders*, to describe eating disorders and their possible origin,
   - *suggest-solution*, to describe how eating disorders may be overcome,
   - *persuade-to stop*, to convince the users to change their eating habits.

3. *Reaction rules* implement goal-revision strategies. In 1987, Oatley and Johnson-Laird claimed that *human plans are much more flexible than those so far explored in AI* [9]: this limit was overcome by reactive planning methods. The regulation rules in Section 4.1, which activate emotion display goals, are examples of our reaction rules. Other rules regulate the goal priority revision, by formalizing the following strategies:
   - in case of *urgent events*, reduce the detail of information provided by upgrading the priority of "most relevant" subgoals and downgrading the priority of *details*;
   - in case of *desirable or undesirable events* occurred to the user, display *altruistic* social emotions (sorry-for and happy-for) by means of "full-expression" goals, that is by verbal and nonverbal means, and give them the highest priority; revise the priority of other goals; hide *egoistic* social emotions as envy and gloating;
   - in case of *desirable events* occurred to the agent, activate *surface expression* goals: use verbal and nonverbal means to express them but leave the priority of other goals unvaried;
   - in case of *undesirable events* (again occurred to the agent), activate *behavior control* goals: avoid displaying any emotional reaction by activating, at the same time, repair goals.

With these rules, we formalize a situation of *empathic reaction* in which the agent temporarily substitutes the presumed goals of the user for its own, when these goals are due to an emotional state of the user [11]. If an undesirable event occurs to the users, what they are presumed to need is to be convinced that the agent understands the situation and does its best to solve the problem. If something desirable occurs to them, they need to know that the agent shares their positive experience. If, on the contrary, the undesirable event does not concern the users, they probably want to be sure that this will not interfere negatively with the dialog. Let us continue the description of how our example dialog is generated. At move $G2$, the agent manifests its empathy by uttering the sentence *"Oh I'm sorry. That's a bad situation indeed"* with an expression of *sorry-for* and then brings over its situation-assessment plan. The same happens with the sentence in $G4$ *"How terrible!"* In this case, however, this undesirable event increases the need to understand the nature of the problem declared by the user: this goal takes the priority. At move $G5$, the agent hides its fear that the user may stop the dialog and tries to reassure and motivate her (*"Oh no!*

You have to be confident in yourself! If you want to get over this, I may help you."). Finally, at move G7 it shows its joy (*"Fine! This is the way I want to see you!"*) but does not revise the priority of the other goals. Reaction rules may produce, in general, the following effects on the dynamics of plan activation:

- *add details* when the user asks for more information;
- *reduce* details in case of urgency;
- *abandon temporarily a plan to activate a new subplan* to reassure, motivate or provide more details;
- *abandon a subplan* when its goal has been achieved: for example, when the user seems to know the information the agent is providing;
- *substitute a generic subplan with a more specific and situation-adapted one*;
- *revise the sequencing of plans, to respond to the User request of* taking the initiative. This is the most delicate situation: to be cooperative, the agent should leave aside its dialog plan and follow the user request; however, as we said, communicative goals may be linked by causal relations. Therefore, when the users show the intention to take the initiative in the dialog, the agent checks whether their goal may be activated immediately or whether some preconditions have first to be satisfied. It then satisfies these preconditions with the shortest subplan before satisfying the user request.

6   Implementation and Evaluation

This research builds on prior work on emotion modeling and dialog simulation. Our modeling method has much in common with that developed in Emile [7]. As our main hypothesis is that emotions influence dialogue initiative and planning, we need a model of initiative that adapts to the emotional state of the two interlocutors. However, emotional initiative is ruled differently from the initiatives that may occur in conversations [4]. To refine our interpretation of the user moves and the reaction rules in our dialog manager, we are collecting and analyzing a corpus of dialogs.

We implemented our emotional dialog simulator by combining different modules (emotion triggering, dialog manager and character player). The system is driven by a *Graphical Interface* which activates the various modules. Users may set the simulation conditions (agent's personality, its relationship with the user, its *body*, application domain) and input their move in natural language. The interface enables following the dialog both in natural language and with the selected Embodied Agent and shows in graphical form how the agent's emotional situation evolves. It is therefore a testbed that we employ to adjust the system components after evaluating its behavior in different situations: we calibrate parameters in the BNs, revise intepretation of user moves, upgrade the plan library and improve rendering of the agent moves by revising *APML* tags. Thanks to the mind-body independence of our system, the agent's body maybe the 3D realistic agent developed by Pelachaud [5] or a *MS − Agent*. The dialog manager is implemented with TRINDIKIT while the emotion triggering module employs a BN managing system. The main limit of the prototype is in the interpretation of the user moves. As we said, keyword analysis is a primitive method to recognize the user intentions and needs. However, rather than on the *recognition* of the emotional state of the users (which requires analysis of their verbal and nonverbal behavior), we are interested in their *interpretation*, that is in guessing the mental state components that produced this emotional state. We plan to employ, to this aim, *DBN*s of the same structure as those we employed for *generating* emotions in the agent.

An ongoing set of evaluation studies (in cooperation with the University of Reading) will suggest us how to refine this prototype. Evaluating the believability of ECAs is a research topic in itself: aspects to evaluate are strongly related to the purpose for which the agent was designed. If entertaining is the main goal, the agent's ability to be attractive should be evaluated. If the goal is to inform, the user ability to remember the information transmitted should be traced, and so on. As the goal of our agent is to advice users on what to do in a riskful situation and to persuade them to follow a *correct* line of conduct, we are evaluating how persuaded the users are after receiving the agent's suggestions and how much they remember of information received.

Acknowledgements. We owe to keen comments of our reviewers several suggestions on how to revise this paper and also some aspects of our Project.

References

1. Carbonell, J.G. Towards a process model of human personality traits. Artificial Intelligence, 15. 1980.
2. Carofiglio, V., de Rosis, F., Grassano, G.: Dynamic models of mixed emotion activation. In L. Canamero and R. Aylett (Eds). Animating Expressive Characters for Social Interaction. John Benjamins, in press.
3. De Carolis, B:, Pelachaud, C., Poggi, I. and de Rosis, F.: Behavior planning for a reflexive agent. Proceedings of IJCAI'01. 2001.
4. Core, M.G., Moore, J.D. and Zinn, C.W.: Initiative management for tutorial dialogue.
5. de Rosis, F., Pelachaud, C., Poggi, I., Carofiglio, V., De Carolis, B.: From Greta's Mind to her Face: Modeling the Dynamics of Affective States in a Conversational Embodied Agent. International Journal of Human-Computer Studies. In press.
6. Elliott, C., Siegle, G. Variables Influencing the Intensity of Simulated Affective States. In Proceedings of the AAAI Spring Symposium on Mental States '93.1993.
7. Gratch, J.: Marshalling passions in training and education. 4th Int. Conference on Autonomous Agents. 2000.
8. Nicholson, A.E. and Brady, J.M.: Dynamic belief networks for discrete monitoring. IEEE Transactions on Systems, Men and Cybernetics, 24,11. (1994) 6.
9. Oatley, K., Johnson-Laird, P.N.: Towards a cognitive theory of emotions. Cognition and Emotion. Vol. 13 pp. 29–50. (1987). 7.
10. Ortony, A., Clore, G.L., Collins, A.: The cognitive structure of emotions. Cambridge University Press, Cambridge, MA. (1988).
11. Picard, R.W.: Affective Computing. The MIT Press. (1997).
12. TRINDIKIT website: http://www.ling.gu.se/research/projects/trindi

Evaluating a Model to Disambiguate Natural Language Parses on the Basis of User Language Proficiency

Lisa N. Michaud[1] and Kathleen F. McCoy[2]

[1] Dept. of Mathematics and Computer Science, Wheaton College, Norton, MA
lmichaud@wheatoncollege.edu
[2] Dept. of Computer and Information Sciences, University of Delaware, Newark, DE
http://www.eecis.udel.edu/research/icicle
mccoy@cis.udel.edu

Abstract. This paper discusses the evaluation of an implemented user model in ICICLE, an instruction system for users writing in a second language. We show that in the task of disambiguating natural language parses, a blended model combining overlay techniques with user stereotyping representing typical linguistic acquisition sequences successfully captures user individuality while supplementing incomplete information with stereotypic reasoning.

1   Introduction: The ICICLE System

The name ICICLE represents "Interactive Computer Identification and Correction of Language Errors" and is the name of an intelligent tutoring system currently under development [5,6,7]. The system's primary long-term goal is to employ natural language processing and generation to tutor deaf students on grammatical components of their written English. ICICLE accepts as input free-written English texts and responds to the user by highlighting sentences with errors. Our system makes use of a user model to track the user's level of competence in different English syntactic structures; the development of this model is discussed in [6]. This paper addresses how we have evaluated our model within the task of disambiguating natural language parses.

1.1   User Modeling and the Disambiguation Task

ICICLE uses a CFG grammar which is descended from that described in [1], augmented with error-production rules called *mal-rules*, to parse user-written utterances. In the process of seeking a correct analysis of user errors, the ICICLE system needs to choose between multiple parses of each utterance. Some of these parses represent different structural representations of the text, and in the case of ungrammaticality, may place the "blame" for the error on different constituents. To determine which is correct, it is necessary for the system to have at its disposal a model of the student's grammatical proficiency which indicates his

P. Brusilovsky et al. (Eds.): UM 2003, LNAI 2702, pp. 96–105, 2003.

or her mastery of the language rules involved. This knowledge aids in choosing between structurally-differentiated parses by providing information on which grammatical constructs the user can be expected to use correctly or incorrectly[1].

1.2   A Model of Grammar Proficiency

The ICICLE user model, described in depth in [4,5,7], attempts to capture what we refer to as "I_i," or the user's current *Interlanguage* state. The concept of interlanguage is that a language learner is generating utterances from a hypothesized grammar I which approaches the language being learned over time [9]. At the current step in the progression, I_i, certain constructs have been mastered, others are currently being learned, and some are still beyond the user's reach.

One component of the ICICLE user model is MOGUL (Modeling Observed Grammar in the User's Language), which captures what is known about the user's interlanguage grammar I_i through an overlay representation in which individual constructs of morphology and syntax (which we refer to as Knowledge Units, or KUs) are scored according to the system's observations of the user's success in executing those KUs in the writing he or she has previously produced. This model compares the number of times the KU has appeared correctly in the user's productions against the total number of times the KU has been attempted and summarizes this information into one of three tags: *Unacquired*, meaning the user has definitely not mastered the KU, *Acquired*, meaning the user consistently uses it correctly, and *ZPD*, meaning the KU is currently being mastered by the user and is therefore exhibiting great variation in successful execution.

Incomplete knowledge in MOGUL results when the system has not yet gathered data on a specific KU. These "gaps" in the profile of the user are filled using the information provided by the second component, SLALOM (Steps of Language Acquisition in a Layered Organization Model). The current implementation of SLALOM involves a representation of three learner stereotype layers (Low, Middle, High) [4]. Each stereotype is associated with a certain level of mastery of each linguistic KU. The current MOGUL tags for a student are compared against the three stereotypes, and the system selects the stereotype profile with the greatest level of similarity to observed performance for this user. That stereotype then provides probable tags for the KUs which have not yet been observed in the user's performance.

1.3   Using the Model to "Score" a Parse

This two-component model enables ICICLE to sift through the multiple syntactic analyses provided by its parser by indicating a maximally likely candidate to represent the user's attempted syntactic structures. The algorithm to accomplish this task was implemented with the following steps:

---

[1] This is not to say that the user will not make mistakes in already-mastered material. What we wish to select is the most likely parse given the current mastery of the language.

1. Obtain all possible parses for the input sentence.
2. Score each parse tree according to how likely it is given the user's current interlanguage state I_i (as captured in the user model). This scoring process is described below.
3. Select a parse tree with maximal score, i.e. one containing the most likely nodes.

Determining a parse tree's compatibility to I_i is done as a two-step process. First, the tree is traversed so that a score for each node is determined in the following manner:

1. Determine the parsing rule used to construct the constituent represented by this node and the KU to which this rule belongs.
2. Determine the tag on this KU. This will be Unacquired, ZPD, or Acquired. If there is insufficient data in MOGUL to supply this tag, the tag is inferred using the SLALOM information on typical performance for the user's stereotype level.
3. Translate this marking into a score for this rule, giving high scores to those rules which should be in I_i given the tag on the KU, and low scores to those rules which are not expected to be in I_i.

The process of obtaining the score in Step #3 reflects an answer to the question: *Do we believe that this rule is in I_i?* If the answer is yes, the node receives a positive score of 1. If the answer is no, the node receives a negative score of -1. "Unacquired" KUs imply that rules representing correct execution of the structure are not in I_i, but rules representing malformations of the structure are. Conversely, "Acquired" KUs are represented by correct (regular) rules in I_i, not mal-rules. KUs in the ZPD represent structures realized by competing rules, both correct and incorrect, which result in the variation in ZPD-level performance; for that reason, both mal-rules and correct rules are believed to co-exist in I_i for those structures.

Once all of the node scores for a tree are determined, these scores are combined to obtain an average score to represent the likelihood of the entire tree overall.

2   Evaluating the Model

This parse scoring mechanism and the user model on which it is based have been implemented within the ICICLE system. In order to demonstrate the efficacy of the implementation, we set out to show the following:

– Parse selection based on a stereotype successfully selects parses which are the closest match to the "expected performance" depicted in the stereotype image in SLALOM.
– When a user builds up a history of performance that deviates significantly from the assigned stereotype—for instance, when the student's proficiency changes because he or she is learning—the stereotype assignment is updated to better reflect the user.

– When a user is correctly placed in a stereotype and yet has individual deviations in his or her MOGUL tags from that stereotype, representing a history
of "atypical" performance, the parse selector correctly recognizes the appropriateness of parse interpretations which are consistent with that user's
individuality.

For this evaluation, we used a corpus of sentences contained in 106 samples of
writing by deaf individuals at various levels of English proficiency.

2.1 Parse Selection Depending upon the Stereotype

The parse selection process as it operates when all decisions are based on a
selected stereotype level is consistent with the mode of operation with a new
user, and also reflects the system's ability to select parses which are consistent
with a complete performance profile. To illustrate this process, we selected a
stereotype level of "Middle" for a hypothetical user, and we parsed the following
Middle-rated sentence from our corpus:

(1) I really like wrestling.

The parser found six possible trees to span this input. Several of these parses
received low scores; they all involved a syntactic interpretation containing a
dropped copula verb[2]. This interpretation would be consistent with reading the
sentence as "I *am* really like wrestling," whose parse is similar to the standard
parse for "I am really like my mother." The parse involved dropping the copula
verb *be*, an error common for some learners in this population but inconsistent
with Middle-level performance. The mal-rule which handles dropped copulae
(-MV22>) participates in a Knowledge Unit which, according to the SLALOM
model, is in the ZPD for a Low-level learner, but is Acquired at the Middle level.
Therefore, the parses involving the dropped copula were themselves "dropped"
for involving a mal-rule reflecting an error we would not expect from this learner.
The parses receiving high scores from the parse selection mechanism were far
more consistent with the Middle-level performance profile represented by that
stereotype layer in SLALOM.

To test the stereotype aspect of our model further, we used this sentence with
a user of each of the other stereotypes. The tree scores we obtained are shown in
Table 1. The expectations generated by the Low stereotype did not penalize the
dropped copulae and, in fact, rewarded one parse (#1) which involved both the
dropped copula and a dropped determiner. In this parse, *like* was treated as a
noun without its required determiner[3]. The expectations of the High stereotype
paralleled those of the Middle stereotype, except in that the gerundive use of
"wrestling" as a noun was considered more likely at this level, raising almost
all of the scores. This also resulted in more than one parse receiving a maximal
score under the High stereotype; in Section 3, we discuss methods for empowering

---

[2] Although *wrestling* is a verb form, the gerund is used as an NP in this interpretation
and therefore does not function as a verb in this sentence.

[3] In this instance, "[a] like wrestling" was parsed as would be "a horse jumping."

Table 1. Parse Tree Scores for "I really like wrestling," All Stereotypes.

Tree	Low	Middle	High	Notes
0	0.75	0.75	**1.0**	GOOD
1	**1.0**	0.5	0.5	Dropped copula and determiner
2	0.75	0.5	0.75	Dropped copula
3	0.78	0.56	0.778	Dropped copula
4	0.78	0.56	0.778	Dropped copula
5	0.82	**0.82**	**1.0**	GOOD

the scoring procedure to make greater differentiation between parses in order to minimize this occurrence.

In sum, we see the reflections of the different stereotype expectations working as we had hoped. Given a Low level stereotype, "I like wrestling" is assumed to contain errors because a Low level user is unlikely to have acquired this use of gerunds. At the higher levels, the gerund is more likely (and the dropped copula is less likely), resulting in an error-free interpretation.

2.2   Updating the Stereotype Assignment

What if the stereotype the system has recorded for a user is wrong? Recall that we expect our user's language proficiency to be dynamic as learning progresses, and that eventually the stereotype recorded for a user at step i in his or her language acquisition will no longer be appropriate when the user is at some later step $> i$. In our next task, we sought to illustrate how the system may recognize the inappropriateness of a stereotype for a given learner and update that stereotype assignment over time[4].

We chose to create a new user for this task, again with the stereotype level Middle. We wished to design a situation in which our learner was *previously* a Middle-level English user, but has now progressed to more advanced proficiency. In this situation, we wanted to update the stereotype selection to High. We selected a batch of 20 sentences from samples in our corpus. Fifteen of these came from samples which had been scored by our judges as representing a High proficiency level, and 5 came from samples which received a Low or Middle rating, but which contained some High-level syntactic structures. Our objective was to assemble sentences which clearly exhibit structures expected primarily of a High-level learner, the new stage to which our user had progressed[5].

---

[4] There is no bias toward upward revision of the stereotype. Although we chose to illustrate a learner's upward transition in this example, the ability of the user modeling component to adjust the stereotype is the same whether it is being revised higher or lower.

[5] These sentences were extracted from the corpus through a search for specific types of error and specific levels of competence, and were screened to ensure that ICICLE was capable of parsing them with an appropriate interpretation among those parses obtained.

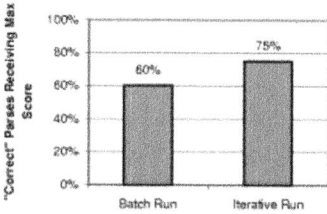 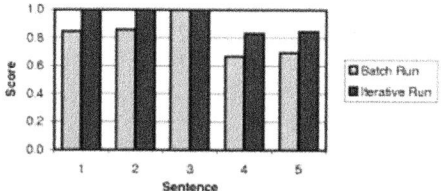

Fig. 1. Comparing the Batch and Iterative Runs.

In our first step, we fed these 20 sentences into the ICICLE analyzer (with the SLALOM-based stereotype set to Middle) together in a batch as if they were a user-written essay. This way, the parser would analyze them each in turn, but would not send data back to the user model to update it until the analysis of all 20 had finished. We sought to see how successful the suggestions of the Middle-level stereotype would be for these High-level sentences.

We compared ICICLE's parse selections against the "optimal" choices of a human judge[6]. The system gave the maximum score to an optimal parse 12 of 20 times (60%), despite having the "wrong" stereotype (Middle rather than High) on which to base these decisions[7]. We then inspected the resultant MOGUL markings to see if the system had learned something about the user in just this one sample of 20 sentences. In fact, eight Knowledge Units now bore MOGUL tags, all marking Acquired structures. Furthermore, those eight were now a closer match to a High stereotype than to a Middle one; the stereotype level of the user was therefore no longer set to Middle, but had been changed to High.

To further test the system's ability to adapt to a learning user over time, we next started with another new user (again set to "Middle") and iteratively entered these sentences one at a time, requesting an analysis (and subsequent user model update) after each sentence. The question we sought to answer here was whether the cumulative evidence provided by the earlier sentences would enable the system to make more appropriate decisions about the sentences at the end than it had in the batch run, and if the total number of correct choices would be higher, given the access to the evidence provided in the first several sentences. Despite the fact that 20 sentences provide relatively little evidence, the number of maximum-scoring optimal parses rose to 15/20 (75%). These results are compared with those of the batch run on the left in Figure 1.

---

[6] In some cases, more than one parse is considered optimal because of inconsequential syntactic differences which allow multiple parses to be acceptable. In all cases, however, the judge's choice was non-controversial; we would expect any native speaker judge to have selected the same choice.

[7] We report the "maximum score" rate here because, as mentioned above, there are cases in which the system is forced to make a random selection between parses receiving equal scores. In these situations, the system has recognized the validity of the optimal parse.

We also examined the results obtained for the last five sentences in particular. In the original batch run, only in one of these five had the optimal parse been maximally scored by the system. In the results of this iterative run, however, we observed the following:

- Before reaching the final five sentences, the stereotype had already been revised to High, so that the decisions the system made on these were already affected significantly by the input from the earlier sentences.
- In all of the sentences for which the optimal parse tree's score was originally lower than the maximum, the score increased.
- The number of maximum-scoring optimal parses rose from 1/5 to 3/5.

The differences in the two sets of scores are shown for all five sentences on the right in Figure 1.

2.3   Overriding the Stereotype

The previous two sections have illustrated how ICICLE will prefer a parse which is consistent with stereotype expectations in the absence of other information, how the system can recognize when a user deviates significantly from that stereotype (and can update the stereotype categorization accordingly), and how it can adjust its parse selection decisions to meet a user's changed acquisition status. In a final evaluation task, we explored the integration of the two facets of the user model; specifically, we tested ICICLE's ability to integrate the stereotype expectations which SLALOM provides with the specific history of parses that it records in the MOGUL model.

For this task, we chose to create a High-level user who is appropriately classified in that stereotype but in whose language mastery there exist certain fossilized structures which are executed with error in a fashion atypical of the High-level stereotype. We sought to illustrate that if the system has built up a performance history for this user illustrating these differences, it will select parses more appropriate to the user's actual interlanguage I_i even if that deviates from stereotype expectations.

We chose from the corpus 26 example sentences to represent our learner with fossilized errors. Specifically, we chose 12 sentences exhibiting Middle- and High-level structures executed correctly (as would be expected with the High-level stereotype), and 18 sentences containing Low-level errors, focusing on errors in noun pluralization, subject/verb agreement, and determiner usage.

Our first step in this test was to determine the "base case" of stereotype-based parse selection on these sentences. We therefore ran the entire set of sentences together as a single sample with only the stereotype setting of "High." We then noted in each case which parse the stereotype selected and compared it against the optimal human-selected parse. Of the 26 sentences, ICICLE gave a maximum score to the optimal parse in a total of 19 cases (73%).

We checked to see if there was a difference between those sentences which were "typical" performance for a High-level learner (and therefore true to the stereotype) and those which were "atypical." Of the 12 typical sentences, the system had given a maximum score to the optimal parse in all 12 (100%). In the atypical sentences, only 7/14 (50%) of the optimal parses received the maximum score. As may be expected, the parse selection process fared much better when the sentences were consistent with the stereotype than when the system had to go against the stereotype expectations to chose an optimal parse.

As shown in the previous section, however, the system is capable of adjusting to a user over time and the parse selection process will reflect that. To simulate an accumulated performance history, we "trained" the MOGUL model by hard-wiring the parse selector to choose the parse which was optimal according to human judgment and then running the entire set of 26 sentences through the analyzer 10 times. This recorded the rules from the optimal parse trees for each sentence 10 times into the MOGUL model.

After this history was constructed, it was inspected to see how different it was from the stereotypical MOGUL tags of a High-level learner. We noted that 44 of the 114 Knowledge Units were now marked with MOGUL tags. As expected, there were differences between these and the High-level stereotype. Most notice-ably, the KUs representing plural noun morphology, third person singular verb morphology, and determiner usage had atypical markings, the first two in the Unacquired range, and the last in the ZPD. This would not be expected in a High-level learner. We now had a MOGUL model reflecting a user who was still classified as High but who had those fossilized linguistic difficulties which were inconsistent with High-level stereotype expectations.

Following this inspection, the hard-wired parse selection was removed in order to investigate whether the acquired history would positively affect the selected parses. The sentences were given to ICICLE one final time. This time, the scoring process was not relying upon just the stereotype, but also upon this "history" we had constructed.

The difference between the choices based on the stereotype alone versus those making use of this stored performance history on MOGUL are summarized in Figure 2. The number of optimal parses receiving the maximum score rose to 81%. More specifically, although the "typical" sentences lost one in that category (as may be expected, because many of these sentences exhibit structures which this user has not fully mastered, such as noun pluralization), the percentage of atypical sentences where the optimal parse received the maximum rose from 50% to 79%. In 21/26 sentences overall, the optimal parse now received top marks.

In these results, the point is not the accuracy of the analysis (this would be an instance of testing on the training set). What we have shown is that the analysis changes in the face of the performace history. This change allows the system to begin to recognize the atypical structures that a writer at a particular stereotype level may exhibit; a history of correctly parsed atypical constituents better enables the system to correctly parse sentences containing similar atypical constituents. The user modeling component then has the ability to recognize the validity of parses whose rule usage is consistent with what it knows about the *individual*, not just expectations based on a population, using an integration of the SLALOM stereotype information and the MOGUL individual performance data.

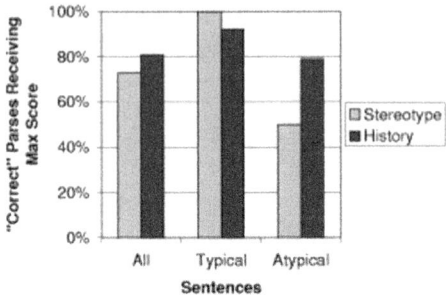

Fig. 2. Summary of ICICLE's Ability to Pick Optimal Parses Given a User History.

3   Conclusions

Explicitly-modeled errors in a parsing grammar have been used in several other systems. However, the difficulty of handling the ambiguity resulting from the application of such a grammar to parsing in an unrestricted domain is well-known, resulting in the fact that most existing CALL systems restrict their task to well-defined domains (BELLOC, [3]), the parsing of prompted translations (HyperTutor, [8]), or specific subsets of the syntactic spectrum such as pronouns (Mr. Collins, [2]). Perhaps because ICICLE is such an ambitious project with a large and broadly-defined domain, our user modeling effort is far more precise than what can be found in most comparable language instruction systems.

The evaluative runs discussed in this paper illustrate that the ICICLE parse selection mechanism scores and selects trees appropriately given a profile of expected user performance, and that the adaptive nature of the model allows it to shift to adapt to differences in user behavior. They also clearly illuminate paths toward future improvement. Because there were several instances where the system gave the maximum score to many trees, the need for even more intelligent scoring is clear. While parse node scoring on the basis of rule membership in I_i is helpful for the selection of appropriate parse trees, taken alone it does not discriminate strongly enough; in some cases, the number of trees obtaining the highest score is fairly large. In fact, rule membership in I_i is only *part* of what signifies *the most likely tree*; other factors must be taken into account. Future improvements to the system may include taking into account the likelihood of part-of-speech tags on the lexical items in the utterance.

Another future direction for this work is to show whether ICICLE can recognize correct parses for atypical constituents when they first occur (and thus create a performance history). This would involve providing a greater body of writing from a high-level learner containing some atypical errors, and then testing if, over time, the user model comes to correctly reflect the user's unique language profile and thus to correctly parse subsequent input from this user. This is planned for future analysis.

The evaluation discussed in this paper shows, however, that the design of the ICICLE user model has already found success in melding stereotypical and individual user information, creating a dynamic form which poses a novel approach to the challenge of ambiguity in the natural language task.

Acknowledgments. This work has been supported by NSF Grants #GER-9354869 and #IIS-9978021.

References

1. Allen,J.: *Natural Language Understanding.* Benjamin/Cummings, California, second edition, 1995.
2. Bull,S., Brna,P. and Pain,H.: Extending the scope of the student model. *User Modeling and User-Adapted Interaction,* 5(1):45–65, 1995.
3. Chanier,T., Pengelly,M., Twidale,M. and Self,J.: Conceptual modelling in error analysis in computer-assisted language learning systems. In M. L. Swartz and M. Yazdani, editors, *Intelligent Tutoring Systems for Second-Language Learning,* volume F80 of *NATO ASI Series,* pages 125–150. Springer-Verlag, Berlin Heidelberg, 1992.
4. Michaud,L.N.: *Modeling User Interlanguage in a Second Language Tutoring System for Deaf Users of American Sign Language.* PhD thesis, Dept. of Computer and Information Sciences, University of Delaware, 2002. Tech. Report #2002-08.
5. Michaud,L.N. and McCoy,K.F.: Error profiling: Toward a model of english acquisition for deaf learners. In *Proceedings of the 39th Annual Meeting of the Association for Computational Linguistics,* pages 386–393, Toulouse, France, July 5-11 2001. ACL.
6. Michaud,L.N. and McCoy,K.: Empirical derivation of a sequence of user stereotypes. *User Modeling and User-Adaptive Interfaces,* to appear.
7. Michaud,L.N., McCoy,K.F. and Stark,L.A.: Modeling the acquisition of English: an intelligent CALL approach. In *Proceedings of the 8th International Conference on User Modeling,* pages 14–23, Sonthofen, Germany, July 13-17 2001. Springer.
8. Schuster,E. and Burckett-Picker,J.: Interlanguage errors becoming the Target Language through student modeling. In *Proceedings of the Fifth International Conference on User Modeling,* pages 99–103, Kailua-Kona, Hawaii, January 2-5 1996. UM96, User Modeling, Inc.
9. Selinker,L.: Interlanguage. *International Review of Applied Linguistics,* 10(3):209–231, August 1972.

Incorporating a User Model into an Information Theoretic Framework for Argument Interpretation*

Ingrid Zukerman, Sarah George, and Mark George

School of Computer Science and Software Engineering
Monash University
Clayton, VICTORIA 3800, AUSTRALIA
{ingrid,sarahg}@csse.monash.edu.au, mark_thingy@yahoo.com

Abstract. We describe an argument-interpretation mechanism based on the Minimum Message Length Principle [1], and investigate the incorporation of a model of the user's beliefs into this mechanism. Our system receives as input an argument entered through a web interface, and produces an interpretation in terms of its underlying knowledge representation – a Bayesian network. This interpretation may differ from the user's argument in its structure and in its beliefs in the argument propositions. The results of our evaluation are encouraging, with the system generally producing plausible interpretations of users' arguments.

1 Introduction

Dialogue systems developed to date typically restrict users to a limited range of dialogue contributions. While this may be suitable for look-up systems, in other types of applications, e.g., tutoring systems, users would benefit from being able to present more complex responses. The discourse interpretation mechanism presented in this paper constitutes a significant step towards achieving this objective. Our mechanism interprets structured arguments presented by users in the context of an argumentation system. This research builds on our previous work on BIAS – a *Bayesian Interactive Argumentation System* which uses Bayesian networks (BNs) [2] as its knowledge representation and reasoning formalism. In previous research, BIAS interpreted single-proposition rejoinders presented by a user after reading a system's argument [3]. Here BIAS interprets user arguments of arbitrary complexity, which may differ from BIAS' beliefs and inference patterns. The basic discourse-interpretation mechanism relies on the Minimum Message Length (MML) Principle [1] to evaluate candidate discourse interpretations [4]. The main contribution of this paper is in its principled incorporation of a user model into the discourse-interpretation mechanism.

In the following section, we describe our experimental set up. Next, we outline our knowledge representation formalism, and discuss the argument interpretation process. In Section 4, we provide an overview of our Minimum Message Length approach to discourse interpretation, and describe how user modeling information is incorporated into this formalism. The results of our evaluation are reported in Section 5. We then discuss related research, followed by concluding remarks.

---

* This research was supported in part by Australian Research Council grant A49927212.

P. Brusilovsky et al. (Eds.): UM 2003, LNAI 2702, pp. 106–116, 2003.

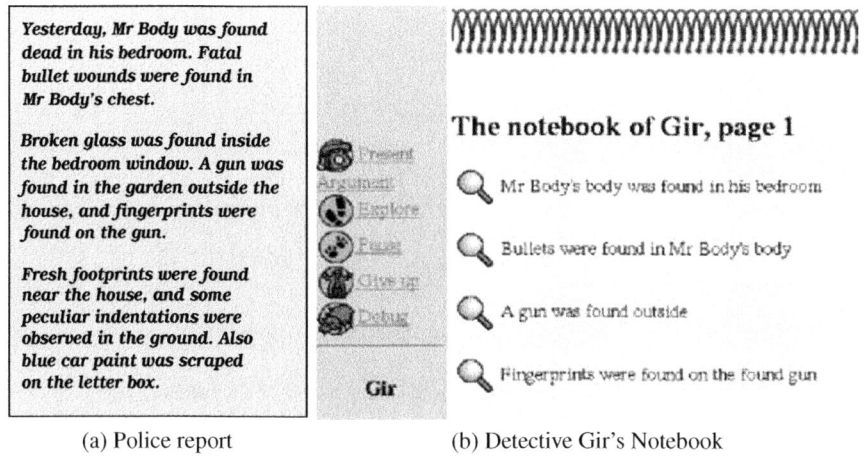

(a) Police report   (b) Detective Gir's Notebook

Fig. 1. Police report and excerpt from Notebook

2   Experimental Set Up

Our experimental set up is similar to that of the system described in [3]. The user and the system are partners in solving a murder mystery, and obtain information by investigating the murder. However, in our current set up the user is a junior detective and the system is a desk-bound boss, who knows only what the user tells him. Thus, the user does all the leg-work, navigating through a virtual crime scene, making observations and interviewing witnesses, and reports periodically to the boss. These reports consist of successively evolving arguments for the main suspect's guilt or innocence.

The interaction with BIAS starts with the presentation of a police report that describes the preliminaries of the case for a particular scenario. The user then optionally explores the virtual scenario, recording in his/her *Notebook* information s/he finds interesting (this Notebook is employed by BIAS to build the user model, Section 4.2). Figure 1(a) shows the police report presented for the scenario used in this paper, and Figure 1(b) shows an excerpt of a user's Notebook after reading the report.

Upon completion of his/her investigation, the user builds an argument composed of a sequence of implications leading to the argument goal [Mr Green Killed Mr Body]. Each implication is composed of one or more antecedents and consequents, which, in the current implementation, are obtained by copying propositions from a drop-down menu or from the user's Notebook into slots in the argument-construction interface.[1] Figure 2 shows a screen-shot of the argument-construction interface, and an argument built by a particular user after she has read the police report, seen the newspaper and spoken to the forensic experts. Figure 3 shows the interpretation generated by BIAS for the argument in Figure 2. In it the system fills in propositions and relations where the user has made inferential leaps, and points out its beliefs and the user's (the user's input has been highlighted for clarity of presentation).

---

[1] An alternative version of our system accepts Natural Language (NL) input for antecedents and consequents. However, in order to isolate the contribution of the user modeling component, we have removed the NL capability from our current version.

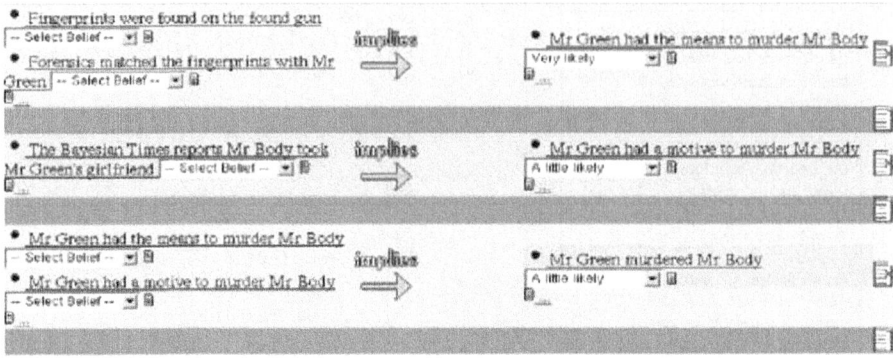

Fig. 2. Argument-construction screen and user's argument

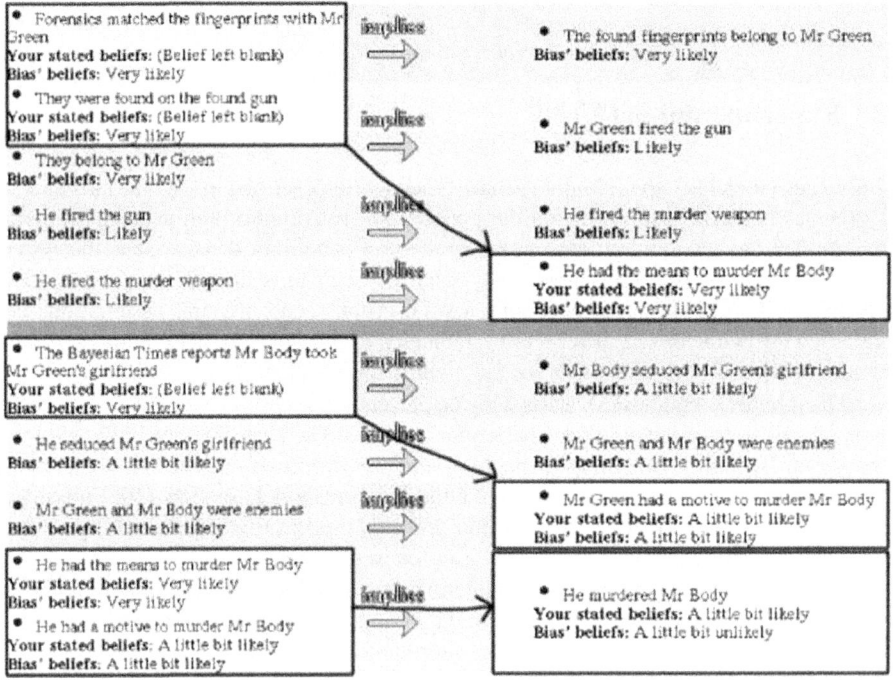

Fig. 3. BIAS' interpretation of the user's argument

In order to evaluate the discourse interpretation capabilities of the system, in this paper we restrict users' interaction with the system to a single round. That is, a user reads the police report, optionally explores the virtual scenario, and generates an argument for Mr Green's guilt or innocence. BIAS then interprets the argument, and presents its interpretation back to the user for validation. The results of this validation are discussed in Section 5. In the future, the boss will present counter-arguments, point out flaws in the user's argument or make suggestions regarding further investigations.

3   Proposing Interpretations

The domain propositions and the relationships between them are represented by means of a BN. Each BN in the system can support a variety of scenarios, depending on the instantiation of the evidence nodes. For this paper we used an 85-node BN which represents a murder mystery (this BN is similar to that used in [3]). BIAS generates an interpretation of a user's argument in terms of its own beliefs and inferences, which may differ from those in the user's argument. This may require adding propositions and relations to the argument structure proposed by the user, deleting relations from the user's argument, or postulating degrees of belief in the propositions in the user's argument which differ from those stated by the user. The procedure for proposing interpretations is described in [4]. Here we provide a brief overview, focusing on the structure of the interpretations (the beliefs in the propositions are obtained by performing Bayesian propagation).

Our system generates candidate interpretations for an argument by finding different ways of connecting the propositions in the argument – each variant being a candidate interpretation. This is done by (1) connecting the nodes in the argument, (2) removing superfluous nodes, and (3) building connected sub-graphs of the resultant graph.

Connecting nodes. This is done by retrieving from the domain BN neighbouring nodes to the nodes mentioned in the user's argument. Following [3], we perform two rounds of retrievals for each node in the user's argument. That is, we first retrieve its neighbours, and then its neighbours' neighbours from the domain BN. These retrieved neighbours are *inferred* nodes (they may have been previously added to the user model, or accessed now for the first time). We perform only two rounds of retrievals for each node in the user's argument in order to model small "inferential leaps", which the system would be expected to understand. As a result of this process, *mentioned* nodes that are separated by at most four inferred nodes in the domain BN will now be connected, but nodes that are further removed will remain unconnected. If upon completion of this process, a proposition in the user's argument is still unconnected, the system will have failed to find an interpretation (in the future, we will extend our MML-based formalism to consider interpretations that exclude one or more of the user's propositions).

Removing superfluous nodes. This is done by marginalizing out nodes that are not on a path between an evidence node and the goal node.

Building sub-graphs. BIAS derives all the interpretations for an argument by computing all the hyper-paths between two nodes (a hyper-path may comprise a single path or may be composed of more than one path between two nodes).

The Bayesian subnets generated in this manner are candidate interpretations of a user's argument in terms of BIAS' domain knowledge. However, these subnets alone do not always yield the beliefs stated by the user, as the user may have taken into account implicit assumptions that influence his/her beliefs. For instance, the argument in Figure 2 posits a belief of A Little Likely in Mr Green's guilt, while Bayesian propagation from the available evidence yields a belief of A Little **Un**likely. This discrepancy may be attributed to the user's lack of consideration of Mr Green's opportunity to murder Mr Body (her argument includes only means and motive), an erroneous assessment of

Mr Green's opportunity, or an assessment of the impact of opportunity on guilt which differs from BIAS'. In the near future, our mechanism will consider the first two factors for neighbouring nodes of an interpretation (the third factor involves learning a user's Conditional Probability Tables – a task that is outside the scope of this project).

4   Using MML to Select an Argument Interpretation

The MML criterion implements Occam's Razor, which may be stated as follows: "If you have two theories which both explain the observed facts, then you should use the simplest until more evidence comes along".[2] MML distinguishes itself from other popular model-building approaches, such as Maximum Entropy, in that it provides a theoretical criterion for evaluating the goodness of a model, while the other approaches can be validated only empirically. According to the MML criterion, we imagine sending to a receiver the shortest possible message that describes an NL argument. A message that encodes an NL argument in terms of an interpretation is composed of two parts: (1) instructions for building the interpretation from domain knowledge, and (2) instructions for rebuilding the original argument from this interpretation. These parts balance the need for a concise interpretation (Part 1) with the need for an interpretation that matches closely the original argument (Part 2). For instance, a concise interpretation yields a message with a short first part, but if this interpretation does not match well the original argument, the second part will be long. In contrast, a more complex interpretation which better matches the original argument may yield a shorter message overall. In any event, for an interpretation to be plausible, the message that encodes an NL argument in terms of this interpretation must be shorter than the message that transmits the words of the argument directly (if no such interpretation can be found, the argument is not being understood by the system).

The expectation from using the MML criterion is that in finding an interpretation that yields the shortest message for an NL argument, we will have produced a plausible interpretation, which hopefully is the intended interpretation. This interpretation is determined by comparing the message length of the candidate interpretations, which are obtained as described in Section 3.

In this section, we first review the MML encoding of an NL argument (a detailed description of this encoding appears in [4]). We then discuss the incorporation of a user model into this formalism.

4.1   MML Encoding

The MML criterion is derived from Bayes Theorem: $\Pr(D\&H) = \Pr(H) \times \Pr(D|H)$, where D is the data and H is a hypothesis which explains the data. An optimal code for an event E with probability $\Pr(E)$ has message length $\mathrm{ML}(E) = -\log_2 \Pr(E)$ (measured in bits). Hence, the message length for the data and a hypothesis is:

$$\mathrm{ML}(D\&H) = \mathrm{ML}(H) + \mathrm{ML}(D|H)$$

The hypothesis for which $\mathrm{ML}(D\&H)$ is minimal is considered the best hypothesis.

---

[2] The similarity between MML and Kolmogorov complexity, which is also an implementation of Occam's Razor, is discussed in [5].

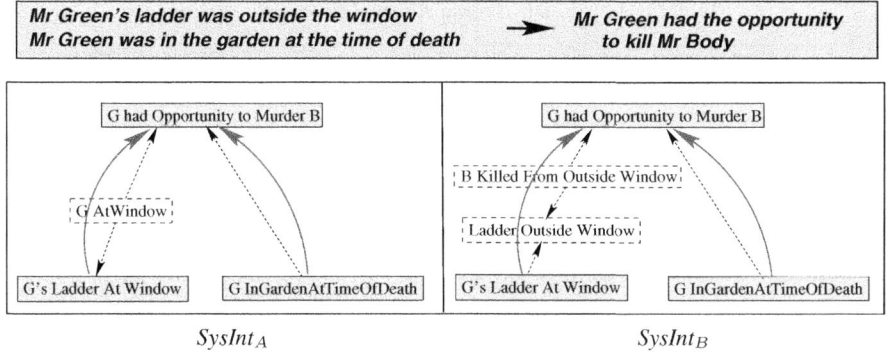

Fig. 4. Interpretation of a simple argument

In our context, the data is the argument, and the hypothesis is the interpretation. Let *Arg* be a graph representing an argument (with antecedents pointing to consequents), and *SysInt* an interpretation generated by our system. Thus, we are looking for the *SysInt* which yields the shortest message length for

$$\mathrm{ML}(Arg\&SysInt) = \mathrm{ML}(SysInt) + \mathrm{ML}(Arg|SysInt)$$

The first part of the message describes the interpretation, and the second part describes how to reconstruct the argument from the interpretation. Figure 4 illustrates the interpretation of a simple argument composed of two antecedents and one consequent. The Figure shows two *SysInt*s, with *Arg* superimposed on them (the nodes in *Arg* are shaded, and the links are curved). Since domain propositions (rather than NL sentences) are used to construct an argument, *Arg* can be directly obtained from the input.[3] *SysInt* is then derived from *Arg* by using the links and nodes in the domain BN to connect the propositions in the argument (Section 3). When the underlying representation has several ways of connecting between the nodes in *Arg*, then more than one candidate *SysInt* is generated, where each candidate has at least one *inferred* node that does not appear in the other candidates. For instance, the inferred nodes for the two interpretations in Figure 4 are [G At Window] for *SysInt_A*, and [Ladder Outside Window] and [B Killed From Outside Window] for *SysInt_B*; the inferred links are drawn with dashed lines.

After candidate interpretations have been postulated, the MML criterion is applied to select the best interpretation, i.e., the interpretation with the shortest message. The calculation of the message length takes into account (1) the size of an interpretation, and (2) the structural and belief similarity between the interpretation and the argument. These factors influence the components of the message length as follows.

– ML(*SysInt*) represents the probability of *SysInt*. According to the MML principle, concise interpretations (in terms of number of nodes and links) are more probable than more verbose interpretations.
– ML(*Arg|SysInt*) represents the probability that a user uttered *Arg* when s/he intended *SysInt*. According to this component, interpretations that are more similar to *Arg* are more probable than interpretations that are less similar to *Arg*. This probability

---

[3] This is not the case in the version of the system which takes NL input, since there may be more than one proposition that constitutes a reasonable interpretation for a sentence in an argument.

Table 1. Message length comparison of two interpretations

ML of	Factor	*SysInt*$_A$	*SysInt*$_B$	Shortest ML
SysInt	Size	4 nodes, 3 links	5 nodes, 4 links	*SysInt*$_A$
Arg|SysInt	Structural similarity	more similar	less similar	*SysInt*$_A$
	Belief similarity	farther	closer	*SysInt*$_B$

depends on the structural similarity between *SysInt* and *Arg* (which in turn depends on the operations that need to be performed to transform *SysInt* into *Arg*), and on the closeness between the beliefs in the nodes in *Arg* and the beliefs in the corresponding nodes in *SysInt* (these beliefs are obtained by performing Bayesian propagation through *SysInt*; thus, different *SysInt*s may yield different beliefs in the consequents of an argument).

Table 1 summarizes the effect of these factors on the message length for *SysInt*$_A$ and *SysInt*$_B$. *SysInt*$_A$ is simpler than *SysInt*$_B$, thus yielding a shorter message length for the first component of the message. *SysInt*$_A$ is structurally more similar to *Arg* than *SysInt*$_B$: *SysInt*$_A$ has 1 node and 2 links that are not in *Arg*, while *SysInt*$_B$ has 2 nodes and 3 links that are not in *Arg*. As a result, the structural aspect of ML($Arg|SysInt_A$) has a shorter message length. In this example, we assume that the belief in [G had Opportunity to Kill B] in *SysInt*$_B$ is stronger than that in *SysInt*$_A$, and hence closer to the asserted consequent of the argument. This yields a shorter message length for the belief component of ML($Arg|SysInt_B$). However, this is insufficient to overcome the shorter message length of *SysInt*$_A$ due to structural similarity and conciseness. Thus, although both interpretations of the user's argument are reasonable, *SysInt*$_A$ is preferred.

As can be seen from this account, the MML principle enables a discourse interpretation mechanism to weigh possibly conflicting considerations, and reach an understanding of the user's reasoning in terms of the system's domain knowledge.

4.2 Incorporating the User Model

The above formalism assumes that every proposition is equally likely to be included in an interpretation. However, this is not the case in reality. We postulate that interpretations comprising propositions familiar to the user (e.g., recently made observations, or propositions from his/her Notebook) are more probable than interpretations that include other domain propositions (although the user may still include unseen propositions of which s/he has thought independently).

In order to represent this observation in terms of the MML principle, the message that conveys *SysInt* must take into account the different probabilities associated with the domain propositions. These probabilities, which reflect the salience of propositions in the user's focus of attention, are modeled by means of two factors: (1) the type of access of a proposition, and (2) the frequency and recency of access. To derive these probabilities we need to provide numerical values for these factors.

Access type. Following [3], we distinguish between four types of access. Observations may be seen or accepted, and statements may be mentioned or inferred. Seen observations are those that the user has encountered but has not acknowledged, while accepted observations have been entered by the user in his/her Notebook. Mentioned statements have been explicitly included in the user's argument, while `inferred` statements were not mentioned by the user, but are incorporated by BIAS into an interpretation in order to connect the `mentioned` nodes (Section 3). We assign the following numerical strengths to our access categories.

$$
Str(Node) = \begin{cases} A & \text{if accepted} \\ A & \text{if mentioned} \\ \max\{\frac{A}{F_S}, \frac{A}{\#\_of\_props\_seen+1}\} & \text{if seen} \\ \frac{A}{F_I} & \text{if inferred} \end{cases} \tag{1}
$$

where A, F_S and F_I are constants obtained by testing the system. According to this formula, the strength of a `seen` proposition is inversely proportional to the number of propositions viewed concurrently (e.g., read in the same page), and is always less than the strength of `accepted` propositions. The strength of `inferred` propositions is also low, because when BIAS includes an `inferred` node in an interpretation, it is uncertain that this node is intended by the user until s/he confirms the interpretation in question.

Frequency and recency. These factors are taken into account by means of the following function, which represents the level of activation of a node.

$$
\sum_{i=1}^{n}[CurTime - TimeStmp_i + 1]^{-b} \tag{2}
$$

where n is the number of times a proposition was accessed, $b = 1$ is an empirically determined exponent, $CurTime$ is the current time, and $TimeStmp_i$ is the time of the ith access. According to this formula, the level of activation of a node decays as a function of the time elapsed since its access. In addition, when a node is accessed, activation is added to the current accumulated (and decayed) activation. That is, there is a spike in the level of activation of the node, which starts decaying from that point again.

By combining these two factors we obtain the following formula for the score of a node (where Str_i is the strength of the ith access). This formula assigns a high score to nodes that were recently accepted or mentioned by a user.

$$
Score(Node) = \sum_{i=1}^{n} Str_i(Node) \times [CurTime - TimeStmp_i + 1]^{-b} \tag{3}
$$

Probabilities for nodes. Equation 3 yields a score that reflects the salience of a node in the user's attentional focus. In order to derive a probability from this score, we normalize it as follows.

$$
Pr(Node_i) = \frac{Score(Node_i)}{\sum_{j=1}^{N} Score(Node_j)} \tag{4}
$$

where N is the number of nodes in the domain BN.

According to this formula, an `inferred` node that was not previously in the user model will have a low probability, which will incur a high message length. In contrast, an `inferred` node that was previously in the user model will have a higher score owing to previous accesses, and hence a higher probability.

To illustrate the effect of the user model on the argument interpretation process, let us reconsider the sample argument in Figure 4, and let us assume that [G At Window] is not in the user model, while [Ladder Outside Window] and [B Killed From Outside Window] are in the user model. In this case, a high score for these two propositions (obtained by accepting them recently or seeing them repeatedly) may overcome the factors in favour of $SysInt_A$, thereby making $SysInt_B$ the preferred interpretation.

5 Evaluation

The previous version of the system was evaluated by making it generate synthetic arguments, and then produce interpretations of its own arguments [4]. The results of this evaluation were encouraging, with the system generating plausible interpretations of its own arguments in 75% of the 5400 tried cases. In this paper, we report the results of a formative evaluation with a few real users (10 computer-literate staff and students from Monash University). Our evaluation was conducted as follows. We introduced the users to our system, and explained its aims. We then encouraged them to explore the scenario, and when they were ready, they built an argument using the interface shown in Figure 2. BIAS then generated an interpretation of the argument, presenting it as shown in Figure 3. The users were asked to assess BIAS' interpretation under two conditions: before and after seeing a diagram of our 85-node BN. In the initial assessment, the users were asked to give BIAS' interpretation a score between 1 (Very UNreasonable) and 5 (Very Reasonable), and to optionally provide further comments. In the second assessment, the users were asked to re-assess BIAS' interpretation in light of the domain knowledge represented in the diagram. They were also asked to trace their preferred interpretation on the diagram (on paper).

Our users found the system somewhat daunting, and indicated that the interface for entering an argument was inconvenient. We believe that this was partly due to their lack of familiarity with the available domain propositions. That is, the users were faced with 85 new propositions, which they had to scan in order to determine whether they could use these propositions to express what they had in mind. Nonetheless, the users managed to construct arguments, which ranged in size from 2 propositions to 26, and gave a generally favourable assessment of BIAS' interpretations. Overall the average score of BIAS' interpretations was 4 before seeing the BN diagram and 4.25 after seeing the diagram. This indicates that a user's understanding of the system's domain knowledge may influence his/her interaction with the system, as the domain knowledge enables a user to better understand why a particular interpretation makes sense to the system.

The main lessons learned from this preliminary evaluation pertain to two aspects: (1) the interface, and (2) the use of BNs for discourse understanding. In order to improve the usability of the interface, we will integrate it with BIAS' NL module. It is envisaged that a solution combining menus and NL input will yield the best results. Our evaluation also corroborates the insights from Section 3 regarding the difficulties of taking into account users' assumptions during the argument interpretation process. However, the results of our evaluation are encouraging with respect to the use of the MML principle for the selection of interpretations, and the consultation of a user model during the selection process. In the future, we propose to conduct a comparative evaluation with and without the user model to determine its impact more accurately.

6 Related Research

As indicated in Section 1, our research builds on work described in [3,4]. In this paper, we apply a principled approach based on the MML criterion [1] to select an interpretation for unrestricted arguments, instead of the heuristics used in [3] to select an interpretation for single-proposition rejoinders. We extend the work described in [4] in that we seamlessly incorporate a user model into the MML-based interpretation formalism. The MML principle is a model-selection technique which applies information-theoretic criteria to trade data fit against model complexity. MML has been used in a variety of applications, several of which are listed in http://www.csse.monash.edu.au/~dld/Snob.application.papers. In this paper, we demonstrate the applicability of MML to a high-level NL task.

BNs have been used in several systems that perform plan recognition, e.g., [6,7,8]. Charniak and Goldman's system [6] handled complex narratives, using a BN and marker passing for plan recognition. It automatically built and incrementally extended a BN from propositions read in a story, so that the BN represented hypotheses that became plausible as the story unfolded. Marker passing was used to restrict the nodes included in the BN. In contrast, we use domain knowledge to constrain our understanding of the propositions in a user's argument, and apply the MML principle to select a plausible interpretation. Gertner *et al.* [7] used a BN to represent the solution of a physics problem. After observing an action performed by a student, their system postulated candidate interpretations (like BIAS' *SysInt*), each comprising subsequent actions. In contrast, instead of being given one action at a time, BIAS is presented with a complete argument. Hence, it must also consider the fit between all the argument propositions and the interpretation (*Arg|SysInt*). Finally, Horvitz and Paek's system [8] handled short dialogue contributions, and used BNs at different levels of an abstraction hierarchy to infer a user's goal in information-seeking interactions with a Bayesian Receptionist. In addition, they employed decision-theoretic strategies to guide the progress of the dialogue. We expect to use such strategies when our system engages in a full dialogue with users.

7 Conclusion

We have offered a mechanism based on the MML principle that generates interpretations of extended arguments in the context of a BN. The MML principle provides a theoretically sound framework for selecting a plausible interpretation among candidate options. This framework enables us to represent structural discrepancies between the underlying, detailed domain representation and the more sparse arguments produced by people (which typically contain inferential leaps). The user modeling information incorporated into the MML framework allows the interpretation mechanism to take into account the manner of acquisition of domain propositions, and their frequency and recency of access. The results of our formative evaluation are encouraging, supporting the application of the MML principle for argument interpretation.

References

1. Wallace, C., Boulton, D.: An information measure for classification. The Computer Journal **11** (1968) 185–194

2. Pearl, J.: Probabilistic Reasoning in Intelligent Systems. Morgan Kaufmann Publishers, San Mateo, California (1988)
3. Zukerman, I.: An integrated approach for generating arguments and rebuttals and understanding rejoinders. In: UM01 – Proceedings of the Eighth International Conference on User Modeling, Sonthofen, Germany (2001) 84–94
4. Zukerman, I., George, S.: Towards a noise-tolerant, representation-independent mechanism for argument interpretation. In: COLING 2002 Proceedings – the 19th International Conference on Computational Linguistics, Taipei, Taiwan (2002) 1170–1176
5. Wallace, C., Dowe, D.: Minimum message length and Kolmogorov complexity. The Computer Journal **42** (1999) 270–283
6. Charniak, E., Goldman, R.P.: A Bayesian model of plan recognition. Artificial Intelligence **64** (1993) 50–56
7. Gertner, A., Conati, C., VanLehn, K.: Procedural help in Andes: Generating hints using a Bayesian network student model. In: AAAI98 – Proceedings of the Fifteenth National Conference on Artificial Intelligence, Madison, Wisconsin (1998) 106–111
8. Horvitz, E., Paek, T.: A computational architecture for conversation. In: UM99 – Proceedings of the Seventh International Conference on User Modeling, Banff, Canada (1999) 201–210

Using Dialogue Games to Maintain Diagnostic Interactions

Vania Dimitrova

School of Computing, Leeds University, LS2 9JT, UK
vania@comp.leeds.ac.uk

Abstract. This paper presents an approach to dynamically extract individual user models by engaging users in diagnostic interactions. A framework for maintaining diagnostic dialogues based on approaches known as dialogue games is outlined and illustrated in STyLE-OLM - an interactive student modelling system. The framework is validated in an evaluative study of STyLE-OLM, and potential improvements are sketched out.

1   Introduction

It has been acknowledged that user models (UMs) have to represent not canonical users but to capture specific aspects of each individual [7]. One of the challenges to individual user modelling is to accommodate the dynamics of users' behaviour, particularly important when dealing with students [8]. A possible approach to dynamically extract individual UMs is discussed here. We consider *intelligent computer diagnosers that interact with users and extract models of the users' cognition*, and which may be employed in a variety of applications, e.g. adaptive tutors, personal e-mentors, or adaptive e-consultants, to mention a few.

A recent stream in user/student modelling stresses the importance of involving users in diagnosis and considers approaches such as open and collaboratively constructed user models [1, 4, 6, 10]. The framework discussed here contributes to this stream and proposes an original approach for involving users in diagnosis where the focus is placed on the interaction between a computer diagnoser (denoted with c) and a human user (denoted with u) who *discuss and construct together the UM*. The diagnostic interactions modelled have the following distinctive characteristics: (1) *Diagnosis* - detecting u's intention from dialogue utterances, extracting beliefs u has committed to, discovering possible causes for u's misconceptions; (2) *Active involvement* - providing possibilities for both c and u to change their commitments and to influence the other's cognitive processes, engaging u in UM maintenance; (3) *Different views* – taking into account different views about the UM that c and u may have; (4) *Mixed initiative* – allowing both c and u to change the direction of the conversation and to take the lead in discussing the current topic, while c steers the conversation to follow specific diagnostic goals and to ensure dialogue coherence. Driven by these characteristics, we have utilised dialogue games (DGs) for

P. Brusilovsky et al. (Eds.): UM 2003, LNAI 2702, pp. 117–121, 2003.

maintaining diagnostic interactions. The remaining part of the paper discusses the dialogue maintenance model in STyLE-OLM[1] - an interactive diagnostic system in a terminology learning domain [2].

2 User Model

We assume that c has an appropriate domain expertise represented in a domain ontology and employs appropriate techniques to extract knowledge needed for maintaining dialogue focus and for reasoning about the beliefs of u. Consequently, we consider a UM structured as an enumerative bug model. The UM incorporates user's *beliefs* - domain propositions that can be correct, erroneous, and incomplete - and some possible *explanations* of what might have caused erroneous beliefs based on erroneous reasoning rules, such as *misclassification* and *misattribution*. The system's assumptions about the user's reasoning are used in the dialogue management, whilst the belief part of the UM can be open for inspection by the user.

3 Main Components of the Dialogue Framework

The framework described here combines Levin and Moore's DG theory [5] to organise dialogue episodes together with logical DGs [9] to enable the participants' symmetrical involvement and to collect their commitments.

Communicative acts (CAs) are defined as quadruples $<S, H, M, P>$, where S is the Speaker, H - Hearer, M – Move, and P - domain Proposition. The moves include: Inform, Inquire, Challenge, Disagree, Justify, Suggest, Accept, Skip.

Dialogue rules are defined as $(move_1, p_1) \vdash (move_2, p_2)$ to postulate that a CA with $move_2$ and proposition p_2 is permitted if the previous turn has included $move_1$ and proposition p_1. The rules are valid throughout the whole interaction and used by c to maintain dialogue coherence.

Commitment stores accumulate the agents' commitments disclosed throughout the interaction. The User's Commitment Store (UCS) contains the beliefs of u about the domain, while the Computer's Commitment Store (CCS) includes the beliefs of c about the beliefs of u. UCS and CCS capture respectively the views of u and c about the UM. UCS includes two types of beliefs: $B_u(p)$ (u believes the proposition p) and $\neg B_u(p)$ (u does not believe p). CCS includes: $B_c(B_u(p))$ (c believes that u believes p) and $\neg B_c(B_u(p))$ (c does not believe that u believes p). The domain beliefs of c are denoted with $B_c(p)$ or $\neg B_c(p)$, i.e. the domain ontology supports or does not support p.

Commitment rules define the effects of moves upon the agents' commitment stores. There are two operations: *adding* beliefs to the commitment stores and *removing* beliefs from the commitment stores. The commitment stores' consistency is maintained following belief revision techniques [2].

Dialogue history stores all performed CAs and is used in focus maintenance.

---

[1] STyLE-OLM has been incorporated in STyLE (Scientific Terminology Learning Environment) developed within the framework of the EU funded Larflast project which involved partners from Sofia, Manchester, Montpellier, Bucharest, Simferopol, and Leeds.

Dialogue games define interaction episodes, which correspond to certain diagnostic goals and discussion topics. Following [5], DGs are defined as triples *<Parameters, Specification, Components>*. *Parameters* represent values specific for the game and include: *Goal* of the dialogue game and *Focus_Space* - a list of domain concepts relevant to this game. *Specifications* define conditions necessary for the game to take place. Each condition is an expression that includes beliefs of the dialogue participants. *Components* determine a sequence of utterances the game generates and are represented in: *Schema* (algorithm for extracting *Relevant_Propositions* to be discussed in the game); *Game_Tactic* (CAs to be addressed in the dialogue, obtained by using the *Relevant_Propositions* and the current state of the commitment stores). Example DGs are given in Figure 1.

The DG framework is generic and can capture a variety of patterns provided that appropriate DGs are defined. STyLE-OLM incorporates three types of DG: (1) *Exploratory DGs* - collect more information about the user's knowledge on a domain topic, can be initiated by both agents; (2) *Explanatory DGs* - search for possible reasons for u's erroneous beliefs, can be initiated by c if a pattern of a misconception is recognised and appropriate schema to plan dialogue tactics exists; (3) *Negotiative DGs* - clarify agents' positions when discrepancies in their views are discovered, can be opened by both agents. The interaction in STyLE-OLM is organised as a series of DGs. At any moment of the dialogue several DGs are *open* (stored in a DG list), while one of them is *active* (on top of the DG list). Open DGs can become active in future interactions if the agents shift back to uncompleted issues.

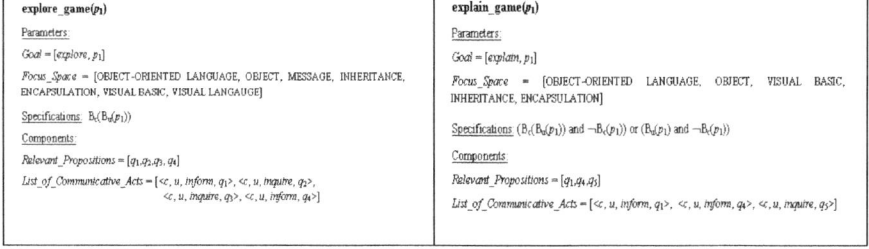

Fig. 1. Sample DGs in STyLE-OLM that can be activated when u states p_1="Visual Basic is an object-oriented language". The following propositions are extracted from the domain ontology: q_1="Object-oriented languages contain objects"; q_2="Objects pass messages between themselves"; q_3="The main characteristics of object-oriented languages are inheritance and encapsulation"; q_4="Visual Basic contains objects"; q_5="Visual Basic has inheritance and encapsulation". The exploratory DG (left) will discuss q_1, q_2, q_3, and q_4 to collect more information about the user's beliefs related to Object-Oriented Languages, while the explanatory DG (right) will seek for explanations what might have cased the user's misconception, in this case the assumption $(B_u(q_1) \wedge B_u(q_4)) \Rightarrow B_u(p_1)$ will be examined.

4   Dialogue Processing

The dialogue processing mechanism in STyLE-OLM, which is presented in Figure 2, follows [5].

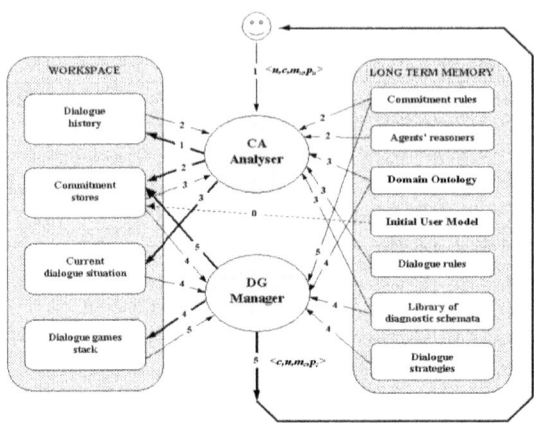

Fig. 2. Architecture of dialogue processing in STyLE-OLM

Long term memory is the knowledge the participants bring to dialogue before it starts. *Workspace* accumulates all temporary results of the dialogue. *Dialogue processors* are algorithms that modify the entities in the workspace and include: *CA analyser* that examines the user's input and updates the current dialogue situation (a structure that represents the current state of dialogue) and *DG manager* that undertakes operations upon the DG list based on the state of the dialogue situation, UCS, CCS, and DG list.

The main processes of dialogue management are: (1) The CA analyser reads the *u*'s CA and updates the dialogue history; (2) The CA analyser updates the commitment stores by applying commitment rules upon the current CA. Using agents' reasoners, *de facto* commitments are also inferred [9]. The collected participants' beliefs are deposited in UCS and CCS; (3) The CA analyser examines the current dialogue situation, compares the user's CA with the dialogue rules, calls domain inference mechanisms to assess the correctness of the user's claim, and searches for diagnostic schema when an erroneous user's belief is discovered; (4) The DG manager examines the commitment stores and the current dialogue situation and, applying dialogue strategies, performs changes in the DG list. When a new DG has to be initiated, the DG manager selects a schema in order to generate an appropriate dialogue tactic; (5) The DG manager selects the corresponding CA from the active DG and sends this act as a system's response to the user. Follows a user's turn.

When the interaction is terminated, a formal mechanism based on modal logic combines the beliefs in the commitment stores and elicits a resultant user model [2].

5   Evaluation and Future Improvements

An evaluative study of STyLE-OLM was conducted to examine the advantages of the system for learning terminology [3] and to assess the robustness of the framework STyLE-OLM is based upon. The study involved seven post graduate students from the author's department who interacted with a STyLE-OLM instantiation in a Finance domain [2,3]. The dialogue management was examined by analysing log files and asking the users and a teacher to identify interaction problems by inspecting the dialogue transcripts. In the context of this paper, the evaluation of the dialogue maintenance mechanism in STyLE-OLM is essential.

The interactions resulted in building more elaborated UMs that contained more valid users' beliefs, less invalid beliefs, and some explanations of users' misconceptions [3]. An important feature of the interaction with STyLE-OLM observed was that learners were allowed to take the initiative in maintaining the dialogue by changing the focus of conversation or initiating new dialogue games. The users found the dialogue moves useful and did not experience major interaction problems. The sessions with STyLE-OLM were classified by most of the users as discussions about their domain knowledge. The participants were not aware that two different views of the UMs were maintained but felt that they could influence the diagnosis, and, in fact, they did.

The evaluation of STyLE-OLM outlined aspects that need further investigation and ought to be addressed in an enhanced framework for interactive diagnosis.

Using shallow domain expertise. STyLE-OLM challenged inappropriately when its domain expertise did not confirm a proposition due to incompleteness of the domain ontology. Plausible DGs were not followed at times, as misconception patterns were not confirmed due to vagueness in defining misconceptions. A possible improvement may adopt clarification dialogue and uncertainty management methods.

Maintaining coherent diagnostic dialogue. There was a lack of explanation of the purpose of the system's CAs. An enhanced DG mechanism is needed which may consider complex rhetorical relations between DGs and DG nesting. More DG types need to be included, e.g. explanations, comparison, and error repair.

Acknowledgements. The author is grateful to John Self and Paul Brna who supervised her PhD studies, aspects of which are discussed in this paper.

References

[1] Bull, S., Brna, P., & Pain, H. (1995). Extending the scope of student models. *User Modeling and User-Adapted Interaction,* 5(1), 45–65.

[2] Dimitrova, V. (2002). STyLE-OLM: Interactive open learner modelling. *International Journal of AI in Education,* Vol 13, to appear.

[3] Dimitrova, V., Self, J., & Brna, P. (2001). Applying interactive open learner models to learning technical terminology. In M. Bauer, P. Gmytrasiewicz & J. Vassileva, *Proceedings of User Modelling 2001* (pp. 148–157). Springer-Verlag..

[4] Kay, J. (1995). The UM toolkit for cooperative user modelling. *User Modeling and User-Adapted Interaction,* 4, 149–196.

[5] Levin, J., & Moore, J. (1977). Dialogue games: meta-communication structures for natural language interaction. *Cognitive Science,* 1 (4), 395–420.

[6] McCalla, G., Vassileva, J., Greer, J., & Bull, S. (2000). Active learner modelling. In G. Gauthier, C. Frasson & K. VanLehn (Eds.), *Intelligent tutoring systems* (pp. 53–62). Berlin Heidelberg: Springer-Verlag.

[7] Rich, E. (1999). Users are individuals: individualizing user models. *International Journal of Human-Computer Studies,* 51, 323–338.

[8] Self, J. A. (1990). Bypassing the intractable problem of student modelling. In C. Frasson & G. Gauthier (Eds.), *Intelligent tutoring systems: At the crossroad of artificial intelligence and education.* Norwood, New Jersey: Ablex Publishing Co.

[9] Walton, D. (1984). *Logical dialogue games and fallacies.* Univ. Press, Lanham.

[10] Zapata-Rivera, J., & Greer, J. (2002) Inspecting and visualizing distributed Bayesian student models. In G. Gauthier, C. Frasson & K. VanLehn (Eds.), *Intelligent Tutoring Systems, Proceedings of ITS2002* (pp. 544–553). Berlin Heidelberg: Springer Verlag.

Extending Plan Inference Techniques to Recognize Intentions in Information Graphics*

Stephanie Elzer[1], Nancy Green[2], Sandra Carberry[1], and Kathleen McCoy[1]

[1] Department of Computer Science, University of Delaware
Newark, DE 19716 USA
[2] Computer Science Division – Department of Mathematical Sciences
University of North Carolina at Greensboro, Greensboro, NC 27402, USA

Abstract. Plan inference techniques have been used extensively to understand natural language dialogue. But as noted by Clark[5], language and communication are more than just utterances. This paper presents the problems that we have had to address and the solutions that we have devised in designing a system to recognize intentions from *information graphics*. Our work is part of a larger project to develop an interactive natural language system that provides an alternative means for individuals with sight-impairments to access the content of information graphics.

1 Introduction

The amount of information available electronically has increased dramatically over the past decade. Unfortunately, many knowledge sources are provided in a single format and thus are not accessible to everyone. For example, individuals with impaired eyesight have limited access to graphical displays, thus preventing them from fully utilizing available information resources. Although research has investigated alternative modes of presentation of graphical information for people who have visual impairments, their focus is on rendering graphical elements in an alternative medium and they have serious limitations. For example, it would be extremely difficult for a user to compare two related lines on a line graph via a soundscape[13]. The underlying hypothesis of our work is that alternative access to what the graphic looks like is not enough — the user should be provided with the message and knowledge that one would gain from viewing the graphic in order to enable effective and efficient use of this information resource.

Our overall goal is to develop an interactive natural language system that infers the intended message underlying an *information graphic* (a non-pictorial graphic such as a bar chart or a line graph),[1] provides an initial summary that includes the intended message along with notable features of the graphic, and then responds to follow-up questions from the user. Recognizing the intended message of an information graphic also has other applications. For example, as multimodal communication becomes more

---

* The work of the second author was supported by the National Science Foundation under Grant No. 0132821.

[1] *Information graphics* are distinguished from depictions of concrete entities and scientific visualizations of spatial data[4].

P. Brusilovsky et al. (Eds.): UM 2003, LNAI 2702, pp. 122–132, 2003.

prevalent, we envision users engaging in interactive communication via text and graphics; an artificial agent will need to be able to recognize the intentions that the user wants to convey via his information graphics in order to respond appropriately.

Plan recognition, a subarea of user modeling, plays a central role in our work since identifying the intended message of the graphic designer is critical. Although one might suggest relying on captions to provide the message of a graphic, Corio found in a large corpus study[6] that captions are often missing or very general. Once the intentions underlying the graphic have been inferred, they can be used 1) to construct a summary that includes the message intended by the person who constructed the graphic (when the system is serving as an alternative communication system for an individual with sight impairments), or 2) to respond appropriately to the user (when the system is an artificial agent engaged in a multimodal interaction with a user). In addition, the system should determine whether the intended message is warranted by the displayed data. Mittal[14] identified a number of strategies that are frequently employed to construct deceptive graphics, such as truncating the vertical axis of a bar chart (starting the axis at a value larger than 0), thereby magnifying differences in the heights of the bars when their actual values are proportionally quite close. A summary should call attention to such discrepancies, whereas an artificial agent should note the user's intention to be deceptive and react accordingly.

This paper focuses on the novel application of a theory of plan-based intention recognition, and presents our solutions to issues that we have had to address in extending plan inference, which has previously been applied to utterances that are part of a dialogue, to recognize the intended message underlying an information graphic.

2   Recognizing Intention from Information Graphics

Language research has posited that a speaker or writer executes a speech act whose intended meaning he expects the listener to be able to deduce, and that the listener identifies the intended meaning by reasoning about the observed signals and the mutual beliefs of author and interpreter[7,5]. But as noted by Clark[5], language is more than just words. It is any "signal" (or lack of signal when one is expected), where a signal is a deliberate action that is intended to convey a message. Although some information graphics are only intended to display data values,[2] the overwhelming majority of the graphics that we have examined (taken from newspaper, magazine, and web articles) appear to have some underlying goal, such as getting the reader to believe that a particular mutual fund has fared much better than the S&P-500 and thus that the reader should purchase the mutual fund.

Applying Clark's view of language to information graphics, it is reasonable to presume that the author of an information graphic similarly expects the viewer to deduce from the graphic the message that he intended to convey by reasoning about the graphic itself and the salience of entities in the graphic. Beginning with the seminal work of Allen[15] who developed a system for deducing the intended meaning of an indirect speech act, researchers have applied plan inference techniques to a variety of problems

---

[2] [19] used pattern recognition techniques to summarize interesting features of automatically generated graphs of time-series data from a gas turbine engine.

associated with understanding utterances, particularly utterances that are part of a dialogue. But extending plan inference techniques to the recognition of intentions from information graphics is not a straightforward task and requires that a number of issues be addressed.

In the case of information graphics, the designer has one or more high-level goals which cause him to construct a graphic that he believes will lead the viewer to perform certain perceptual and cognitive tasks[9] which, along with other knowledge, will cause the viewer to recognize the message that the designer intends the graphic to convey. By *perceptual tasks* we mean tasks that can be performed by simply viewing the graphic, such as finding the top of a bar in a bar chart; by *cognitive tasks* we mean tasks that are done via mental computations, such as computing the difference between two numbers. Section 2.1 and Section 2.2 discuss the kinds of knowledge that must be explicitly available for plan inference from information graphics. In particular, they present our approach that encodes knowledge about perceptual and cognitive tasks in plan operators and encodes knowledge about the effort required for different perceptual tasks in rules associated with primitive subgoals. These sections also describe how the operators and rules are used in plan inference.

The graphic designer has many alternative ways of designing a graphic, and the design choices facilitate some perceptual tasks more than others. Following the AutoBrief work[9] on generating graphics that fulfill communicative goals, we hypothesize that the designer chooses a design that best facilitates the tasks that are most important to conveying his intended message, subject to the constraints imposed by competing tasks. Section 2.2 presents our approach to capturing knowledge about the effort required for different perceptual tasks, as well as our approach to identifying tasks that the graphic designer intended to be salient for the viewer, and how all of this information is used as a starting point for plan inference. Section 2.3 presents our approach to guiding the search through the space of candidate plans.

2.1   Plan Operators for Information Graphics

In their work on multimedia generation, the AutoBrief group proposed that speech act theory can be extended to the generation of graphical presentations[9]. During the first phase of graphics generation in AutoBrief, media-independent communicative goals are mapped to perceptual and cognitive tasks that the graphics should support. For example, if the goal is for the viewer to believe that Company A had the highest profits of a set of companies, then it would be desirable to design a graphic that facilitates the tasks of comparing the profits of all the companies, locating the maximum profit, and identifying the company associated with the maximum. In the second phase of graphics generation, a specification of the tasks that the graphic should support, along with a description of the data, is input to an automatic graphic designer that uses constraint satisfaction, along with knowledge about the effectiveness of different design techniques for supporting different kinds of tasks, to design the graphic.

AutoBrief used algorithms to map communicative goals to partially ordered sequences of tasks and to reason about how to realize the graphic. For plan recognition we need to explicitly encode, in such a way that the plan inference system has access to it, detailed knowledge about how communicative goals decompose into perceptual

Goal: Find-value(<viewer>, <g>, <e>, <ds>, <att>, <v>)
Gloss: Given graphical element <e> in graphic <g>, <viewer> can find the value
               <v> in dataset <ds> of attribute <att> for <e>
Data-req: Dependent-variable(<att>, <ds>)
Body: 1. Perceive-dependent-value(<viewer>, <g>, <att>, <e>, <v>)

Fig. 1. Operator for achieving a goal perceptually

---

and cognitive tasks and how different perceptual tasks by the viewer can be enabled by
particular realizations of the graphic. Then we can reason backwards from the observed
graphic to hypothesize what goals might have motivated its design. Our operators decompose knowledge goals (such as getting the viewer to believe that a mutual fund has
risen substantially in value over the past decade) into tasks that the viewer must be able
to perform using the information graphic. Such tasks may be further decomposed into
a sequence of simpler tasks, which eventually decompose into perceptual or cognitive
primitives.[3] Associated with each perceptual primitive are rules that consider the various
ways that the perceptual task could be enabled and estimate the viewer effort that would
be required for each choice[4](see Section 2.2).

Our plan operators for achieving goals via information graphics consist of:

- **Goal:** the goal that the operator achieves
- **Data-req:** requirements which the data must satisfy in order for the operator to be
  applicable in a graphic planning paradigm
- **Display-const:** features that constrain how the information graphic is eventually
  constructed if this operator is part of the final plan
- **Body:** lower-level subgoals that must be accomplished in order to achieve the overall
  goal of the operator

Plan inference reasons backwards from an XML representation of an observed graphic
that is provided by a computer vision module. The display constraints are used to elim-
inate operators from consideration (i.e., if the graphic does not capture the operator's
constraints on the display, then the operator could not have been part of a plan that
produced the graphic). The data requirements are used to instantiate parameters in the
operator (i.e., the data must have had certain characteristics for the operator to have
been included in the graphic designer's plan, and these often limit how the operator's
arguments can be instantiated). Goals can often be accomplished in several different
ways. Figures 1 and 2 present two operators that can be used to achieve the goal of
enabling the viewer to find the value of an attribute for a graphical element <e> (for
example, the y-value of a point on a line graph or the y-value for the top of a bar on a
vertical bar chart). The body of the operator in Figure 1 consists of a primitive perceptual

---

[3] We are treating subgoals as *primitives* when they are simple tasks that cannot be decomposed
further with our operators. This is not to be confused with a psychological primitive.

[4] Of course, a planner would need to ensure that all of the tasks comprising the plan could be
achieved in a single graphic. In addition, it would need to decide to what degree each task would
be enabled if it was not possible to design a graphic that would enable them all to the fullest
extent.

Goal: Find-value(<viewer>, <g>, <e>, <ds>, <att>, <v>)
Gloss: Given graphical element <e> in graphic <g>, <viewer> can find the value
                    <v> in dataset <ds> of attribute <att> for <e>
Data-req: Natural-quantitative-ordering(<att>)
Display-const: Ordered-values-on-axis(<g>, <axis>, <att>)
Body: 1. Perceive-info-to-interpolate(<viewer>, <g>, <axis>, <e>, $<l_1>$,
                    $<l_2>$, <f>)
                    2. Interpolate(<viewer>, $<l_1>$, $<l_2>$, <f>, <v>)

Fig. 2. Operator that employs both perceptual and cognitive subgoals

---

task *Perceive-dependent-value*, in which the viewer simply perceives the value. Since *Perceive-dependent-value* is a primitive task, there is no operator that decomposes it further; if *Perceive-dependent-value* is a task in the final plan for the graphic, then the graphic would need to be realized so that the attribute value could be directly perceived, such as by annotating the element in the graphic with its value as is done for the bars in Figure 4. As mentioned earlier, this knowledge about how a graphic might be realized to enable a primitive perceptual task is captured in the rules discussed in Section 2.2 that compute the effort required to perform the task given different realizations. On the other hand, the operator in Figure 2 specifies how the same goal can be achieved, admittedly with more effort, using a combination of perceptual and cognitive tasks. The first subgoal, *Perceive-info-to-interpolate*, is a primitive perceptual task in which the viewer perceives the labels $<l_1>$ and $<l_2>$ immediately below and above the location on <axis> corresponding to graphical element <e> of graph <g> and the fraction <f> of the distance that this location lies between $<l_1>$ and $<l_2>$. The second subgoal, *Interpolate*, is a primitive cognitive task in which the viewer computes (via interpolation) the value <v> of attribute <att> for graphical element <e> based on $<l_1>$, $<l_2>$ and <f>. The operator in Figure 2 places constraints on the graphical display if this operator is used to construct the plan, namely that the values of the desired attribute be displayed on <axis> in ascending or descending order. The reason for this is that if the surrounding values produced by achieving the first subgoal are not from an ordered set of labels on the axis, then interpolation to get the value of <v> is not possible.

2.2   Starting Point for Plan Inference

In plan recognition, we must reason about the graphical choices that resulted in the graphic. We contend that the designer made these choices in order to make "important" tasks as easy or as salient as possible. The graphic designer can make a task easy for the viewer to perform by the choice of graphic type (for example, bar chart versus pie chart) and the organization and presentation of data. The graphic designer might also intend a task to be particularly salient, or of notable significance, to the viewer. We must have mechanisms for identifying the easiest and most salient tasks so that we can use these tasks as a starting point for the plan inference process.

Rule1: Estimate effort for task Perceive-element(<viewer>, <g>, <e>, <label>)
Graphic-type: bar-chart
Gloss: Compute effort for finding the top <e> of a bar whose label is <label> in graphic <g>
    B1-1: IF labels on the independent axis appear in sorted order,
        THEN cost=scan + 150 + 300 + 230
    B1-2: If labels on the independent axis do not appear in sorted order,
        THEN cost=scan + ((150 + 300)× number-of-preceding-items) + 150 + 300 + 230

Fig. 3. A rule for estimating effort for a primitive perceptual task

Estimating Viewer Effort. In order to estimate which primitive tasks are easy/hard (presumably the important ones are among the easiest tasks), our system uses rules that estimate the viewer effort involved in performing different primitive tasks. Our estimates of viewer effort are based on research by cognitive psychologists such as Lohse[12] who developed a cognitive model of information graphic perception that was intended to simulate human performance on graphic comprehension tasks. Figure 3 presents a rule for estimating the effort involved in finding the top <e> of a bar in a bar chart given the bar's <label>. Each rule consists of a set of condition-computation pairs, ordered so that the computations producing the lowest estimates of effort appear first. The conditions specify characteristics of the graphic which are necessary for the associated computation to be applicable. In Figure 3 the first condition-computation pair, labelled B1-1, is applicable if the labels appear in sorted order; in such cases, the effort is estimated as the cost of scanning along the x-axis until reaching the label (measured in terms of the degrees of visual arc scanned[10]), 150 units for discriminating the label (based on work by Lohse[12]), 300 units for recognizing a 6-letter word[8], and 230 units for making the saccade up to the top of the bar[17]. The second condition-computation pair, labelled B1-2, is applicable if the labels do not appear in sorted order; in this case, the costs for discrimination and recognition are charged against each label up to and including the one being sought. Often several conditions within a single rule will be satisfied; this might occur for example if the top of a bar in a vertical bar chart both falls on a tick mark and has its value annotated at the top of the bar; the easiest way to get the value represented by the top of the bar would be to read the annotated value although it could also be obtained by scanning across to the tick mark on the dependent axis. The computation associated with the first satisfied condition in a rule is used, thereby estimating the plan least effort required to perform the task.

The vision component gives the plan inference module an XML schema representing the information graphic. The effort estimates for the primitive perceptual tasks are then generated, and the least costly ones are selected. Operators containing these primitive tasks as subgoals are then used to begin the plan inference process. As bottom-up chaining suggests higher-level operators for consideration, the effort expended by the viewer to achieve the operator's goal is estimated on the basis of the effort expended to achieve the subgoals in the operator's body. This can cause a downward expansion of the operator into primitive tasks whose effort is computed.

Identifying Salient Tasks. A plan inference system should exploit all available evidence in recognizing intention. For information graphics, this entails not only reasoning about

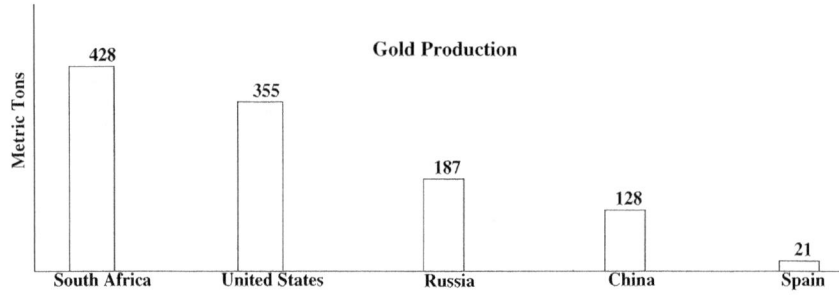

Fig. 4. A sample information graphic

Goal: Believe(<viewer>, Comparison(<g>, $<att_y>$, <ds>, $<v_1>$, $<v_2>$, $<att_x>$,
                $< rel >$))

Gloss: Viewer to believe from graphic <g> that the value of attribute $<att_y>$ for the
                element $<e_1>$ of dataset <ds> whose $<att_x>$ value is $<v_1>$ is <rel> (greater-
                than, less-than, equal-to) the value of attribute $<att_y>$ for the element $<e_2>$
                whose $<att_x>$ value is $<v_2>$

Data-req: Natural-quantitative-ordering($<att_y>$)
                Independent-variable($<att_x>$, <ds>)
                Related($<att_y>$, <ds>, $<att_x>$, $<v_1>$, $<v_2>$, <rel>)

Body: 1. Perceive-element(<viewer>, <g>, $<e_1>$, $<v_1>$)
                2. Perceive-element(<viewer>, <g>, $<e_2>$, $<v_2>$)
                3. Determine-relationship(<viewer>, <g>, $<att_y>$, $<e_1>$, $<e_2>$, <rel>)

Fig. 5. Operator for determining the relationship between two graphical elements

---

the set of perceptual tasks that are best enabled by the graphic, but also identifying any
tasks that the graphic designer intended to be salient for the viewer. We have identified
three sources of salience: captions, a model of mutual beliefs about entities of interest to
members of the viewing audience, and highlighted entities in the information graphic.

Noun phrases in captions are potentially salient to the intended message of the
graphic. For example, consider the graphic in Figure 4 and suppose that it had the
caption "United States Tops China in Gold Production". The presence of the nouns *United
States* and *China* in the caption suggests that they are relevant to the designer's intended
message. Consequently, UNITED-STATES and CHINA would be used to instantiate
<label> in two instances of the perceptual task Perceive-element(U, G, <e>, <label>),
where U and G are constants designating the particular viewer and graphic. This produces
the salient primitive perceptual tasks Perceive-element(U, G, <e>, UNITED-STATES)
and Perceive-element(U, G, <e>, CHINA) which are instantiations of subgoals in the
operator shown in Figure 5. The results of perceiving these elements would be used
to instantiate the arguments $<e_1>$ and $<e_2>$ in the operator in Figure 5 with TOP-
BAR-2 and TOP-BAR-4 from the graphic in Figure 4, and the data requirements in the
operator, along with an analysis of the graphic, would lead to the instantiation of other
arguments, thereby suggesting that part of the graphic designer's intentions might be
to get the viewer to believe that gold production in the United States exceeds that in

China. Further chaining would lead to positing higher-level goals, and other aspects of the graphic would also suggest additional inferred plans.

A model of the intended recipient of the information graphic also plays a role in the plan recognition process. In designing the information graphic, the graphic designer takes into account mutual beliefs about entities that will be particularly salient to his audience. For example, if an information graphic appears in a document targeted at residents of Pittsburgh, then both the designer and the viewer will mutually believe that entities such as Pittsburgh, its football and baseball teams, etc. will be particularly salient to the viewer. The viewer model captures these beliefs, and our approach is to treat them in a manner similar to how we handle noun phrases in captions. Verb phrases in captions also provide evidence, but they suggest particular operators of interest rather than instantiations of operators, and thus we associate verbs with particular operators in the plan library.

One might wonder why we do not deal almost exclusively with captions to infer the intentions of the information graphic. Corio[6] performed a large corpus study of information graphics and noted that captions often do not give any indication of what the information graphic conveys. Our examination of a collection of graphics supports his findings. Thus we must be able to infer the message underlying a graphic when captions are missing or of little use.

Graphic designers also use techniques to highlight particular aspects of the graphic, thus making them more salient to the viewer. Such techniques include the use of color or shading for individual elements of a graphic, annotations such as an asterisk, an arrow pointing to a particular location on the graphic, or a pie chart with a single piece "exploded." Mittal[14] discusses a variety of such design techniques in the context of distorting the message inferred from the graphic. Our working hypothesis is that if the graphic designer goes to the effort of employing such attention-getting devices, then the highlighted items are almost certainly part of the intended message. Thus we treat highlighted entities in the information graphic as suggesting instantiations of primitive perceptual tasks that produce particularly salient tasks. Suppose for example that there was no caption on the information graphic depicted in Figure 4, but that the bars for United States and for China were highlighted by shading them darker than the other bars. This suggests that these bars are particularly relevant to the intended message of the information graphic. Consequently, we use the attributes of the bars to instantiate primitive perceptual tasks and produce tasks that are hypothesized to be salient.

2.3   Guiding the Search

A plan inference system must select, from among many plausible goals, the best hypothesis about the agent's intentions. Moreover, in any reasonably sized system, it will be necessary to guide the search through the space of possible plans and goals so that only a small proportion of the plan space is examined. This has generally been done either via Bayesian approaches that estimate the probability of different hypotheses[1] or heuristics that suggest which hypotheses should be considered first[2,3,11,15]. Since we do not have available the probabilities necessary to construct a Bayesian system, we have chosen to use heuristics to guide the search. The question arises as to what features should be taken into account in heuristics that are used for plan inference from information graphics.

The evidence available for evaluating possible hypotheses includes:

- the effort expended by the viewer in carrying out the perceptual and cognitive tasks required for the message to be recognized. As higher-level goals are inferred, the effort required by the viewer to achieve those goals is computed from the effort estimates for its constituent subgoals. Since the graphic designer is assumed to be felicitous and trying to effectively convey his intended message, he is expected to construct a graphic that enables the requisite tasks so that they can be performed easily. Thus the greater the amount of effort required, the less likely it is that a candidate plan represents the designer's intentions.
- the extent to which elements of the information graphic (especially salient elements) and the perceptual tasks of least effort play a role in the inferred plan. If the graphic designer went to the effort of including particular graphical elements in the graphical display and made particular perceptual tasks easiest or salient, then it is reasonable to believe that he made these design choices in order to facilitate the viewer recognizing his intended message. Thus the percentage of such elements and tasks that play a role in a candidate plan should influence how favorably we view it as a hypothesis about the designer's intentions.
- the extent to which parameters in an inferred plan are instantiated and the basis for the particular instantiations, as discussed below.

Arguments in operators may be instantiated for a variety of reasons. Perhaps the graphic permits only one instantiation (for example, if *Recognize-maximum* is an operator that is produced during chaining and the XML representation of the graphic indicates that there is a single graphical element whose value is greater than the others in the graph). Or the instantiation may be due to highlighting in the graphic, features extracted from the caption, or the model of mutual beliefs about entities of interest. Or the parameters may be instantiated with the values that produce the lowest effort estimations.

The basis for instantiating an argument in a primitive perceptual task, and therefore in a hypothesized plan, impacts confidence about whether the plan really represents the designer's intentions. In the case of plan inference from information graphics, if only one instantiation is possible or if an instantiation is suggested by highlighting or a caption or entities that are particularly salient to the targeted audience, that partial plan should be evaluated more favorably since the designer of the graphic has provided explicit reasons for the viewer to use these instantiations in recognizing his intentions.

Moreover, the proximity compatibility principle[18] dictates that the ratings of partial plans be increased further if the plans contain operators with arguments instantiated from multiple elements of the graphic that are similarly highlighted. The proximity compatibility principle is based on perceptual proximity (how perceptually similar two elements of a display are) and processing proximity (how closely linked the two elements are in terms of completing a task). According to the proximity compatibility principle, if two elements of a graphic are to be used in the same task, then the elements should be realized so that they have close perceptual proximity. [18] showed that violating this principle increased the cost of performing tasks that used multiple elements of a graphic. For example, the points in a line graph have a higher perceptual proximity than the bars in a bar chart. (This example applies the Gestalt law of good continuation[16].) The higher perceptual proximity of the points on a line graph means that it is easier to perform integrated tasks, such as recognizing a trend, in such a graph than with the bars in a bar chart. Along the same lines, if multiple items are similarly highlighted, as in our example where the bars for the United States and China were shaded the same but darker than the other bars, then the proximity compatibility principle suggests that they were intended to be part of an integrated reasoning task and thus part of the same intention.

3   Summary

Clark[5] has argued that communication includes more than natural language utterances, and that alternative modes of communication, such as hand signals, facial gestures, and drawings, bear many commonalities with natural language communication. This paper has presented a novel use of plan inference — namely, to infer the intended message underlying an information graphic — and it has presented our solutions to issues that we have had to address in extending plan inference from natural language utterances to information graphics. Our work is part of a larger project to develop an interactive natural language system that provides an alternative means for individuals with sight-impairments to access the content of information graphics.

References

1. D. Albrecht, I. Zukerman, and A. Nicholson. Bayesian models for keyhole plan recognition in an adventure game. *User Modeling and User-Adapted Interaction*, pages 5–47, 1998.
2. L. Ardisono and D. Sestero. Using dynamic user models in the recognition of the plans of the user. *User Modeling and User-Adapted Interaction*, 5(2):157–190, 1996.
3. S. Carberry. *Plan Recognition in Natural Language Dialogue*. ACL-MIT Press Series on Natural Language Processing. MIT Press, Cambridge, Massachusetts, 1990.
4. S.K. Card, J. Mackinlay, and B. Shneiderman. *Readings in Information Visualization: Using Vision to Think*. Morgan-Kaufmann, 1999. Chapter 1.
5. H. Clark. *Using Language*. Cambridge University Press, 1996.
6. M. Corio and G. Lapalme. Generation of texts for information graphics. In *Proceedings of the 7th European Workshop on Natural Language Generation EWNLG'99*, pages 49–58, 1999.
7. H. P. Grice. Utterer's Meaning and Intentions. *Philosophical Review*, 68:147–177, 1969.
8. B. E. John and A. Newell. Toward an engineering model of stimulus response compatibility. In R. W. Gilmore and T. G. Reeve, editors, *Stimulus-response compatibility: An integrated approach*, pages 107–115. North-Holland, New York, 1990.
9. S. Kerpedjiev and S. Roth. Mapping communicative goals into conceptual tasks to generate graphics in discourse. In *Proceedings of the International Conference on Intelligent User Interfaces*, pages 60–67, 2000.
10. S. M. Kosslyn. Understanding charts and graphs. *Applied Cognitive Psychology*, 3:185–226, 1989.
11. D. Litman and J. Allen. A Plan Recognition Model for Subdialogues in Conversation. *Cognitive Science*, 11:163–200, 1987.
12. G. L. Lohse. A cognitive model for understanding graphical perception. *Human-Computer Interaction*, 8:353–388, 1993.

13. P. B. L. Meijer. An experimental system for auditory image representations. *IEEE Transactions on Biomedical Engineering*, 39(2):291–300, February 1992.

14. V. Mittal. Visual prompts and graphical design: A framework for exploring the design space of 2-D charts and graphs. In *Proceedings of the Fourteenth National Conference on Artificial Intelligence*, pages 57–63, 1997.

15. R. Perrault and J. Allen. A Plan-Based Analysis of Indirect Speech Acts. *American Journal of Computational Linguistics*, 6(3-4):167–182, 1980.

16. J. R. Pomerantz and M. Kubovy. Theoretical approaches to perceptual organization. In K. R. Boff, L. Kaufman, and J. P. Thomas, editors, *Handbook of Perception and Human Performance*, pages 36.1–36.46. Wiley, New York, 1986.

17. J. E. Russo. Adaptation of cognitive processes to eye movement systems. In J. W. Senders, D. F. Fisher, and R. A. Monty, editors, *Eye movements and higher psychological functions*, pages 89–109. Lawrence Erlbaum Associates, Inc., Hillsdale, NJ, 1978.

18. C. D. Wickens and C. M. Carswell. The proximity compatibility principle: Its psychological foundation and relevance to display design. *Human Factors*, 37(3):473–494, 1995.

19. J. Yu, J. Hunter, E. Reiter, and S. Sripada. Recognising visual patterns to communicate gas turbine time-series data. In A. Macintosh, R. Ellis, and F. Coenen, editors, *Proceedings of ES2002*, pages 105–118, 2002.

Leveraging Collaborative Effort to Infer Intent*

Joshua Introne and Richard Alterman

Department of Computer Science
Brandeis University
Waltham MA. 02454 USA
`jintrone,alterman@cs.brandeis.edu`

Abstract. We describe method for intent inference in collaborative systems, and an application that makes use of intent inference to facilitate coordination. Our approach to intent inference is unique in that we derive intent by piggybacking on coordination specific communication that occurs in collaboration. We have developed an interface component that uses the output of our inference engine to support users' awareness of eachother's activities and offload some of the individual user's work.

1 Background

To stay coordinated in any task, collaborators must be able to discover one another's intentions. In same-time, different-place groupware systems, this can be a difficult task [7]; users must be able to reason from a common understanding of the domain, remember to provide the appropriate signals to one another, and must be aware of possible signals from others [4]. One way to support users in this endeavor is to automatically infer intent and notify interested users directly. We demonstrate here a method to do this that capitalizes on work users already do to stay coordinated. In this manner, we are able to achieve better results and provide a more general method than most keyhole plan-recognition approaches.

Collaborators must actively maintain their common ground to reason about each other's intentions and plan their own activities [4] [5]. We have previously shown that this can be a significant source of error in groupware systems, and that we can reduce these errors by introducing interface components called **C**oordinating **R**epresentations (CRs) to help users manage domain information [3] [2]. In their use of a CR, users generate and maintain a dynamic external representation of their shared knowledge about the domain in a structured format.

Our underlying insight is that this structured data can be employed to significantly reduce the difficulty in building an intent inferencing system that performs well [1]. In our system, we use a Bayesian Belief Network (BN) [8] that encodes domain knowledge and heuristic information. Inference predictions are returned to the user in a shared CoWare (Collaborative Awareness) component. This component presents several of the most likely current intentions for each

---

* This research was supported by the Office of Naval Research under grants No. N00014-96-1-0440 and N66001-00-1-8965

P. Brusilovsky et al. (Eds.): UM 2003, LNAI 2702, pp. 133–137, 2003.

user in a ranked list. Users may confirm any intention in the list, and the system can generate an executable plan for any confirmed intention. The component thus performs two important functions:

- Provides, at a glance, the most likely current goals of each user.
- Provides high payoff for confirming a prediction by automating some of the routine work for the user.

2   Vesselworld

Our testbed domain, Vesselworld, is a collaborative system we have built for the purpose of developing a design methodology and adaptation techniques for collaborative systems. In Vesselworld, three participants collaborate on remote workstations to remove barrels of toxic waste from a harbor. Each participant is the captain of a ship, and their joint goal is to move all of the barrels from the harbor to a large barge without spilling any toxic waste. Each ship has geographically limited view of the harbor, and thus ships in different locations will have different directly observable domain information. There are varying types and sizes of toxic waste barrels, which entail different coordination strategies that involve two or all of the actors. Each ship has some unique capabilities, which determine the type of toxic waste it is able to remove from the harbor.

The progression of a Vesselworld session is turn based, thus every user must submit a step to be executed by the server before the server can evaluate executions and update the world on each client screen. Users may plan any number of steps in advance, but only one step is executed at a time. Communication may occur at any time, but all communication must occur through a text based chat tool or one of the special purpose CRs.

2.1   Coordinating Representations

In data obtained from experiments with an initial version of the system that offered only the chat tool for communication, we identified several classes of coordination problems. On the basis of that analysis, we developed three Coordinating Representations (CRs) that were designed explicitly to alleviate these errors.

In groupware systems, CRs can be defined as the conjunction of the following features;

- Tools that facilitate coordination.
- Tools that people will use, if given access to them.
- Tools that lend structure to information.

One of the most effective CRs developed for Vesselworld, which has been empirically shown to improve performance in the domain task and is heavily used [3], is the Object List (Figure 1). The Object List is an external representation that structures and distributes memory for information about shared domain

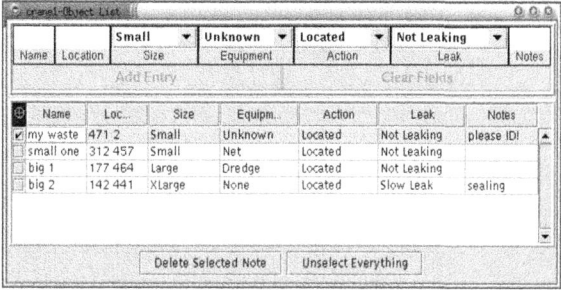

Fig. 1. The Object List.

objects; in this case, toxic waste barrels. Information is authored entirely by the users, and this is logged along with other usage data in XML format. This data includes information about the name, size, location, and required equipment for each waste.

In using the Object List, users provide us with immediate access to the their perceived state and some information that would not be otherwise available (size, equipment, and user name for each waste). The following section shows how this information is used to drive a Belief Network for intent inference.

3   The Vesselworld Belief Network

To perform intent inference, we use a BN that generates a likelihood estimate for every possible agent-waste-operator tuple, where wastes are taken directly from the Object List, and operators come from a set of high level goals we have defined. We are only concerned with relative likelihood estimates, and not absolute probabilities of each goal, and we make the assumption that goals can be evaluated independently of each other.

Figure 2 portrays a slight simplification (two interior nodes have been omitted to simplify the diagram) of the Belief Network that is currently being used in Vesselworld. Data is accumulated from the Object List, chat transcript, and plans, and posted to the unshaded nodes in the network. The interior nodes are incorporated to reduce the total number of conditional probabilities entries required by the model.

Nodes are classified into three broad categories to serve as general guidelines for building BNs in other domains that employ Coordinating Representations.

- Coordination Information: These nodes represent variables that are specific to the type of Coordinating Representation used.
- State Information: Information regarding the current state which determines the possible goals in the domain.
- Domain heuristics: These are heuristics that are not explicitly captured in the structured domain model, yet are powerful predictors of intent.

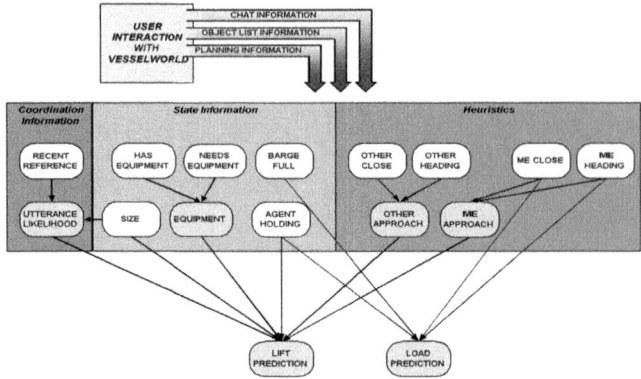

Fig. 2. The Vesselworld Belief Net.

Within Vesselworld, these categories are instantiated as follows. The "Coordination Information" nodes reflect a judgment as to how much a reference to a waste (taken directly from the Object List) that has appeared recently in chat influences the likelihood it will be lifted next. As co-referencing activities are pervasive in collaboration [6], we expect that other collaborative domains would benefit from similar CRs that provide similar referential information. The state nodes reflect information about the state, such as whether the type of equipment is is appropriate, the size of the waste (which determines how many actors must be involved with the waste), and whether the agent is holding something. Some of this information (equipment and size) is derived from the directly from the Object List. The domain specific heuristics are heading and proximity, which may be derived from the positional information of objects in the Object List, and planning information from the users.

The output of the network is a likelihood a goal will be next. The "AgentState" node functions to switch between relevant portions of a network, so that either a "LOAD" or "LIFT" goal will be returned depending on whether the agent is currently holding a waste. The output is passed to the CoWare component described in the following section.

4   CoWare

The CoWare (Collaborative Awareness) component is designed to satisfy two criteria;

- Provide useful intent awareness information to users.
- Provide individual payoff for user work.

The CoWare component is a shared WYSIWIS (what you see is what I see) component. Figure 3 displays a snapshot of the crane2's CoWare component. The top row ("Tug, Crane1, Crane2") indicates which actor each column refers

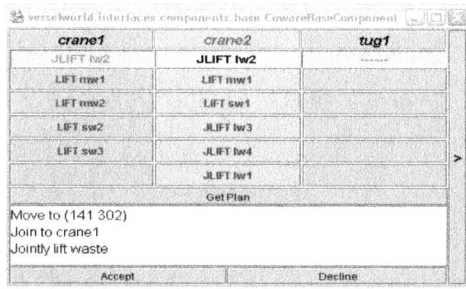

Fig. 3. CoWare component for intent inference

to. Each actor can only make modifications to her own column. The second row ("JLIFT LW2, JLIFT LW2, – – –"), indicates the currently *confirmed* intention of the user. The columns beneath the confirmed intention row display at most the five candidate goals, ranked and color coded according to the likelihood estimate from the intent inference engine.

A prediction can be chosen by the user to confirm that prediction as the next intention. Upon confirmation, a prediction is copied into the confirmed intention row. Once a confirmed, the user may request a plan for that goal. In Figure 3, crane2 has requested a plan for a joint lift, which is displayed in the lower panel of the component. The plan can than be added to the current plan.

Preliminary testing has demonstrated that the BN is good at predicting user goals. We are currently evaluating the component with user groups. We hope to find that CoWare will reduce coordination errors and reduce average clock time of user groups.

References

1. Alterman, R. Rethinking Autonomy. *Minds and Machines*, 10:1 (2000) 15–30.
2. Alterman, R., Feinman, A., Introne, J., and Landsman, S. Coordinating Representations in Computer-Mediated Joint Activities. In *Proceedings of 23rd Annual Conference of the Cognitive Science Society.* (2001)
3. Alterman, R., Feinman, A., Introne, J., Landsman, S.: Coordination of talk; Coordination of action. Technical Report CS-01-217, Department of Computer Science, Brandeis University (2001)
4. Clark, H. *Using Language.* Cambridge University Press. (1996)
5. Clark, H.H., Brennan, S.E.: Grounding in communication. In Resnick, L.B., Levine, J., Teasley, S.D., editors, *Perspectives on Socially Shared Cognition* APA Press (1991)
6. Clark, H. and Wilkes-Gibbs, D. Referring as a collaborative process. *Cognition*, 22 (1990) 1–39.
7. Dourish, P. and Belloti, V. Awareness and coordination in shared workspaces. In *Proceedings ACM Conference on Computer Supported Cooperative Work.* (1992)
8. Pearl, J. *Probabilistic Reasoning in Intelligent Systems.* San Francisco, Calif.: Morgan Kaufmann. (1988)

Plan Recognition to Aid the Visually Impaired

Marcus J. Huber[1] and Richard Simpson[2]

[1] Intelligent Reasoning Systems
4976 Lassen Drive
Oceanside, California, 92506
marcush@marcush.net
[2] Dept of Rehabilitation Science and Technology
University of Pittsburgh
Forbes Tower, Suite 5044
Pittsburgh, PA 15260
ris20@pitt.edu

Abstract. Less than half of the individuals of working age with visual impairments are employed and a significant barrier to employment is effective computer access. Screen reader applications offer some help but have limited context sensitivity and are of limited use in applications with dynamic "interfaces" like web pages. Sophisticated screen readers provide aid through application-specific scripts but their full potential is reduced by limited awareness of the scripts and the difficulty in programming and modifying scripts. Technologies such as plan recognition and automated script generation and optimization that provide a more adaptive interface for the user will significantly improve computer accessibility to the visually impaired. In this paper, we discuss the addition of probabilistic plan recognition capabilities and supporting framework to a leading screen reader in order to improve accessibility of computers to the visually impaired at work and at home.

1 Introduction

Effective access to computers is becoming increasingly crucial for academic and vocational success. It is predicted that 60 percent of U.S. jobs will require computer skills within the next five years. Currently, less than half of the individuals of working age with visual impairments are employed, and a significant barrier to employment is effective computer access. In particular, manipulating information on the WWW, our application focus, is rapidly becoming a crucial computer skill. Screen readers, applications that audibilize the text on computer screens, provide some support. However, to find relevant information on web pages, this can involve dozens if not hundreds of manual navigation actions and is very difficult to repeat. Scripts can automate such navigation tasks, but screen readers are still limited in a number of ways, including not being able to adapt their behavior to the semantic contents of specific web pages and the difficulty users have in using the scripting capabilities of screen reader.

The software developed during this project[1] has been integrated with a sophisticated screen reader with scripting capability called JAWS [2]. JAWS has been extended to do

---

[1] Funded by the National Science Foundation under grant DMI-0091590.
[2] Freedom Scientific, 11800 31st Court North, St. Petersburg, Florida 33716.

several things that other current screen readers cannot: recognize scripts to identify when the user is manually performing a task (possibly with mistakes) for which a script is available and prompt the user to make use of the script instead (saving tremendous time); know something about the goal of a set of actions and produce a script that is much shorter and more efficient than that of a simple macro recorder (simplifying and speeding script generation); and use existing scripts as the basis for recognizing scripts that can be used with minimal tailoring (also simplifying and speeding script generation). What this means to the end user is that they will be made aware of the existance of the scripts that they are performing manually, they can make errors during script generation and web page navigation, scripts automatically generated will be compact and optimized, and tailoring existing scripts will be significantly easier.

2   Enhancing a Screen Reader

One capability that provides a significant improvement in screen reader technologies is the ability to identify the user's intentions as the user is performing a task. This capability, called *plan recognition*, provides assistance to the user as well as to provide useful contextual information to our script generation and optimization extensions discussed below. Our plan recognition mechanism is based on the ASPRN (Automated Synthesis of Plan Recognition Networks) system's probabilistic modeling theories and implementation[3,4]. ASPRN takes procedures as its input, in this case scripts, and outputs specially constructed probabilistic models that we call Plan Recognition Networks (PRNs), a particular instantiation of belief networks, that models those procedures. Because PRN computations are based on probabilistic models and relationships, belief networks are well suited for dealing with uncertain, conflicting, or extraneous information, something often encountered in user interfaces. Plan recognition algorithms using probabilistic representations (e.g., [3,5]) are well suited for application to screen readers. Users will almost certainly deviate from standard task templates intentionally or unintentionally, something non-probabilistic representation schemes (e.g., [1,2]) cannot deal with in natural or pragmatic way.

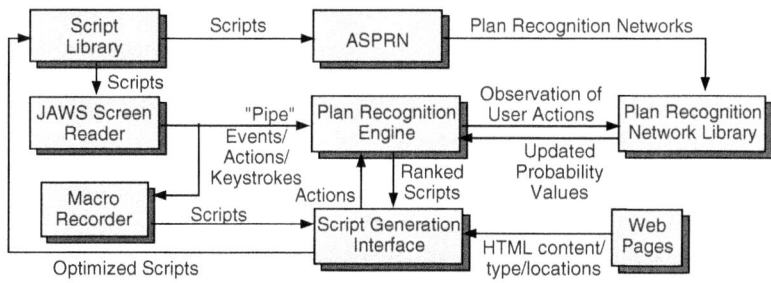

Fig. 1. Architectural diagram of our enhanced screen reader system.

Our system's design is shown in Figure 1. All of the components illustrated in Figure 1 have been implemented and are operational. The JAWS screen reader forms the basis for all of our work, providing much of the original functionality and internal representations for providing computer access to the visually impaired. The Script Library maintains all of JAWS' application-specific scripts, each of which accomplishes a specific, small task. Based on feedback from visually-impaired clients, we identified several tasks that the visually impaired frequently perform with web browsers (e.g., retrieving a weather forecast). We developed scripts for performing each of these tasks and also a number of subscripts that perform more elemental functions. These subscripts will ultimately play an important role in distinguishing between scripts when multiple strategies can be used interchangeably within a single high-level task and when multiple high-level tasks are differentiated based on which strategies can be used. Scripts within the Script Library are converted by ASPRN into PRNs and placed in the PRN Library. The Plan Recognition Engine (PRE) accesses the PRNs and uses these probabilistic models in combination with information about the user actions to determine the scripts most likely associated with the user's actions. If the user is doing something that an existing script can perform, the PRE suggests this to the user, thereby improving productivity. The Script Generation Interface (SGI) takes a recorded sequence of user actions from the Macro Recorder and, by using plan recognition and hand-coded algorithms, create an optimized script which is then placed in the Script Library for later use.

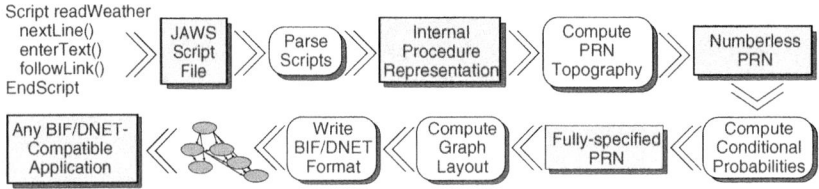

Fig. 2. The ASPRN process of taking a JAWS script and constructing a specially-designed belief network called a Plan Recognition Network (PRN).

Figure 2 shows how ASPRN parses a script into a generic (reusable) internal procedural model, computes a PRN topography based on this, computes the conditional probability values associated with the PRN instance, determines a default visual layout of the PRN for belief network visualization applications, and finally writes out the PRN for adding to the PRN Library and subsequent use by the PRE. The basic modeling theories, algorithms, and key application concepts from the original ASPRN system [3, 4] were modified to suit the specifics of the JAWS scripting language and the task of providing assistance to the visually impaired. Some redesign was necessary to account for the simpler scripting language that JAWS uses compared to the agent-based plan languages that ASPRN has thus far been applied.

Figure 3 shows how script constructs are transformed into belief networks. These belief network transformations are composable and are therefore linked together according to the script being modeled, creating a single belief network with dozens to hundreds of probabilistic nodes (depending upon the length of the script). While we cannot go into detail in this short of a paper, ASPRN supports belief network-based probabilistic modeling of the key aspects of JAWS' script constructs, including sequences of script commands, function and sub-script invocation, conditional execution, and iteration. ASPRN models a script's actions and a script's temporal, conditional, and hierarchical relationships. Each modeled low-level action also has an associated evidence node that is used to model the reliability of observations that has/has not been performed. The con-

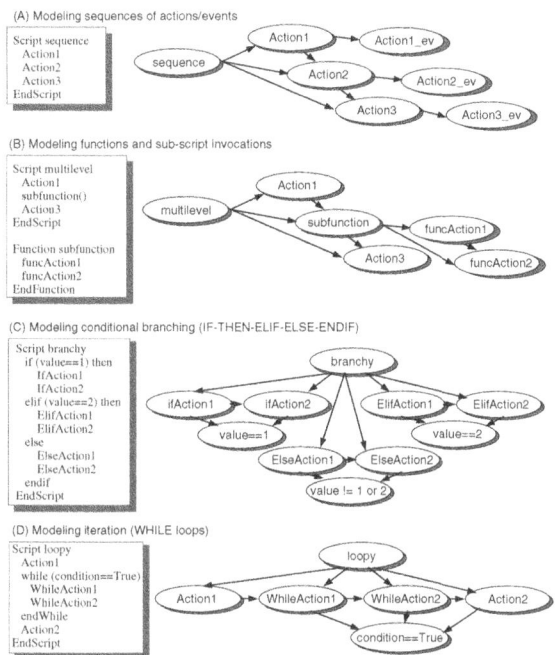

Fig. 3. PRN sub-constructs that model various JAWS script sub-constructs.

ditional probabilities within the PRNs are specified initially by case-based templates. Due to the regularity and composability with which all script components are modeled, all possible cases have been represented within ASPRN such that a completely-specified belief network is constructed. The conditional probability cases and values are based on the type of node being specified and the types of the nodes linking to it. Probability values for these generic templates were determined empirically in [3,4] to result in the natural, convex progression of posterior probabilities given correct observation sequences. Actual, in-use, statistical probabilities which will eventually be learned in future work.

The operational system works in two basic modes, one as the user is interacting normally with the system in pursuit of their task objectives, and one while the user is creating or modifying scripts. While the user is navigating between and within web pages, JAWS observes the user's actions and screen events. After each observed action, the PRE adds this information as evidence into the PRNs, performs Bayesian inferencing, and then sorts the scripts based on the subsequent posterior probabilities. Figure 4 illustrates how PRNs react to evidence of the user's actions. PRNs modeling scripts that do not quite match the evidence pattern do not react as strongly and result in lower posterior probabilities, allowing the PRE to discriminate between alternatives. Once a script has a sufficiently high likelihood of being pursued (user studies will determine an appropriate value for this), the system informs the user that a script exists that can perform their task much more efficiently, or is close but needs to be tailored slightly for the user's current task. Bayesian learning algorithms that will be added at a later stage will take the user's acceptance or rejection of this suggestion and adjust the internal PRN model appropriately to gradually adjust the PRNs to the user's preferences.

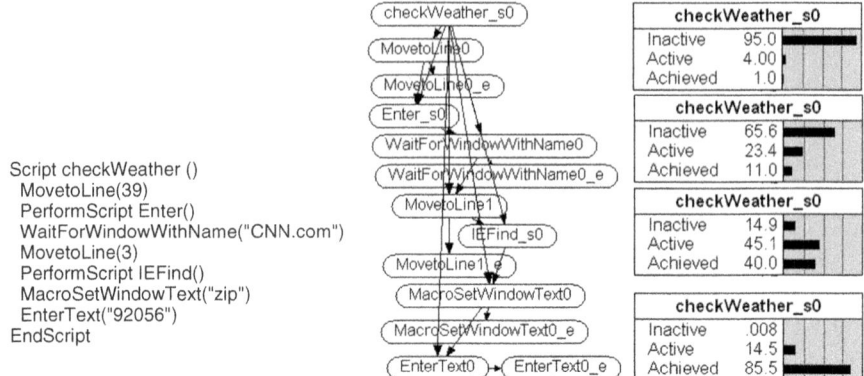

```
Script checkWeather ()
  MovetoLine(39)
  PerformScript Enter()
  WaitForWindowWithName("CNN.com")
  MovetoLine(3)
  PerformScript IEFind()
  MacroSetWindowText("zip")
  EnterText("92056")
EndScript
```

Fig. 4. Left, a segment of an actual script for reading weather at CNN.com. Center, the PRN constructed by ASPRN. Right, the probability distribution for the script being performed by the user with zero observations (i.e., priors) at top, MoveToLine observed (second), Enter observed (third), and all actions observed (bottom). Note the gradual progression from Inactive to Achieved (i.e., completed).

During generation of scripts, the user records a raw sequence of user actions using the Macro Recorder. The SGI then analyzes the sequence of actions and events and uses plan recognition and other algorithms to determine sub-sequences of the user's actions (which possibly contains mistakes) that perform the equivalent operations. If any strong matches are found then the sub-sequence is recommended as a replacement to the user (this is another possible Bayesian learning application area).

Other future work includes exploring variations and specializations of PRN topographies and probabilities, including aggressiveness and temporal accuracy. User trials are scheduled to evaluate all aspects of the system's efficacy. Our continuing work will also focus on the vocational and educational uses of the proposed software involving off-line applications.

References

1. C. Broverman, K. Huff, and V. Lesser. The Role of Plan Recognition in Design of an Intelligent User Interface. In *Proceedings of the IEEE Systems, Man, and Cybernetics Conference*, pages 863–868, 1987.
2. B. Goodman and D. Litman. Plan Recognition for Intelligent Interfaces. In *Proceedings of the Sixth Conference on Artificial Intelligence Applications*, pages 297–303, 1990.
3. M. Huber. *Plan-Based Plan Recognition Models for the Effective Coordination of Agents Through Observation*. PhD thesis, The University of Michigan, 1996.
4. M. Huber, E. Durfee, and M. Wellman. The Automated Mapping of Plans for Plan Recognition. In *Proceedings of the Tenth Conference on Uncertainty in Artificial Intelligence (UAI)*, pages 344–351, July 1994.
5. G. Kaminka, D. Pynadath, and M. Tambe. Monitoring teams by overhearing: A multiagent plan-recognition approach. *Journal of AI Research*, 2002.

Performance Evaluation of User Modeling Servers under Real-World Workload Conditions

Alfred Kobsa[1] and Josef Fink[2]

[1] School of Information and Computer Science, University of California, U.S.A.
kobsa@uci.edu
[2] Department of Mathematics and Computer Science, University of Essen, Germany
Josef-Fridolin.Fink@t-online.de

Abstract. Before user modeling servers can be deployed to real-world application environments with potentially millions of users, their runtime behavior must be experimentally verified under realistic workload conditions to ascertain their satisfactory performance in the target domain. This paper discusses performance experiments which systematically vary the number of profiles available in the user modeling server, and the frequency of page requests that simulated users submit to a hypothetical personalized website. The parameters of this simulation are based on empirical web usage research. For small to medium sized test scenarios, the processing time for a representative mix of user modeling operations was found to only degressively increase with the frequency of page requests. The distribution of the user modeling server across a network of computers additionally accelerated those operations that are amenable to parallel execution. A large-scale test with several million active user profiles and a page request rate that is representative of major websites confirmed that the user modeling performance of our server will not impose a significant overhead for a personalized website. It also corroborated our earlier finding that directories provide a superior foundation for user modeling servers than traditionally used data bases and knowledge bases.

1   Introduction

Before user modeling (UM) servers [1, 2] can be deployed to real-world application scenarios with potentially millions of users, their runtime behavior must be experimentally tested under realistic workload conditions to ascertain their satisfactory performance in the target environment. The parameters of such experiments, and specifically the workload of simulated user interactions that cause requests to the UM server, should thereby closely resemble the target domain. The few existing performance studies of UM servers [3, 4] and of directory servers [5, 6] however all employed synthetic workloads that are not based on empirical results about web usage behavior.

Unfortunately, most existing web traffic data are not very useful for empirically based workload experiments since they are based on proxy logs (e.g., [7, 8]) or web server logs (e.g., [9, 10]). Such data has limited value since it does not reflect all communication that would ordinarily take place between browsers and web servers [11]. For instance, browsers may connect to web servers via several proxies, and numerous caches may affect the amount of traffic between browsers and web servers. Most published studies are moreover based on websites of research institutions, which are not very representative for users' typical website visits[1] and presumably also not for the navigation behavior that is exhibited at more typical sites [10].

2   Web Usage Patterns

Rozanski et al. [13] recently conducted a comprehensive analysis of click-stream data collected by the audience measurement service Nielsen//NetRatings. The data was collected at the *client side* from a panel of 2,466 Internet users over several months. In a first step, the researchers identified 186,797 user sessions[2]. Subsequently, they tested a variety of session characteristics with regard to their suitability for clustering these sessions. The most differentiating session characteristics were the following:

Session length: defined as the length of a single user session on the Internet.

Time per page: denotes the time interval between two subsequent web page requests.

Category concentration: the percentage of time a user stays at websites of the same category (e.g., news, sports, entertainment, real estate).

Site familiarity: the percentage of time a user stays at familiar sites, i.e. sites she had previously visited four or more times.

Based on these characteristics, Rozanski et al. carried out a cluster analysis and distinguished the following patterns of web usage (in parentheses their relative frequency):

Quickie sessions (8%): These are short (one minute) visits to one or two familiar sites, to extract specific bits of information (e.g., stock quotes, sports results). Users visit 2.2 pages per site on average, and spend about 15 seconds on a page.

Just the Facts sessions (15%): Here users seek and evaluate specific pieces of information at related sites (e.g., compare product offers). Sessions last 9 minutes on average. Users visit 10.5 sites and 1.7 pages per site, with about 30 sec. per page.

Single Mission sessions (7%): Users focus on gathering specific information or completing concrete tasks (e.g., finding the website of a scientific conference and registering for it). They visit two websites on average, which belong to the same category (e.g., search engines or portals). Users quite carefully read the content of (frequently unfamiliar) web pages in approximately 90 seconds. The average session length is 10 minutes, and 3.3 pages per site are being visited.

Do It Again sessions (14%): These are focused on sites with which the user is familiar (e.g., online banks, chat rooms). Users spend about two minutes for each page. The average session lasts 14 minutes, with 2.1 sites and 3.3 pages per site being visited.

---

[1] E.g., [12] found that 35% of users' surfing time is spent on merely 50 (commercial) sites.

[2] A session represents the total time from when a user signs on to the Internet to when she signs off, or to the point when her activity ceases for more than an hour.

Loitering sessions (16%): Users visit familiar "sticky" sites, such as news, gaming, telecommunications/ISP, and entertainment. Sessions last 33 minutes, with 8.5 sites and 1.9 pages per site being visited (two minutes per page on average).

Information Please sessions (17%): Users gather broad information from a range of often unfamiliar websites from several categories (e.g., they collect facts about a specific car model, find a dealer, negotiate a trade-in, and arrange a loan). Users visit 19.7 websites and 1.9 pages per site. The average session length is 37 minutes, and pages are viewed for one minute on average.

Surfing sessions (23%): They appear random, with users visiting nearly 45 sites in 70 minutes on average (about one minute per page and 1.6 pages per site).

Over time, users can engage in several, if not all, session types, depending on how different their tasks are. Rozanski et al. found, e.g., that two-third engaged in five or more session types and 44 percent in all seven session types.

3   Workload Simulation

Our user modeling server comprises the following components:

Directory Component, which stores assumptions about the user in terms taken from a domain taxonomy. It utilizes the iPlanet (Sun ONE [14]) LDAP Directory Server.

User Learning Component (ULC), which learns about the user (specifically about her interests) through univariate significance analysis of her usage characteristics.

Mentor Learning Component (MLC), which learns about a user's interests via alike "mentors" found through Spearman correlation of their usage characteristics.

Domain Inference Component (DIC), which uses rules for inferences about the user.

The details of these components are not relevant for the purposes of this paper. We refer the reader to [16]. [15] additionally discusses a prototype application in mobile computing, and [17] a deployment to a major news site in Germany.

To test the performance of our UM server under different workload conditions, we simulated users' interaction with a hypothetical personalized website. Each user thereby follows one of the abovementioned session types. The content of each web page is characterized by 1-3 terms taken from the domain taxonomy. Web page requests by a user lead to add and query operations in his user profile on the UM server: the terms of the requested web page are processed and added to his interest model, and the user's interests in terms of the domain taxonomy are queried to personalize a web page that was requested by him. As a shortcut though, we omit the web server in our simulation and represent web pages by their characteristic terms only.

Our first experiment for small to medium sized personalized applications was a two-factor design with the following parameters:

- N (number of existing profiles in the UM server): 100, 500, 2,500, or 12,500[3].
- W (number of web page requests per second): 0.5, 1, 2, or 4[4].

For every factor combination, we generate a test plan with N user profiles. The behavior of currently active users of the hypothetical website is simulated by clients of our user modeling server. Clients are divided into seven classes, which represent the aforementioned session types. A class i comprises c_i clients which exhibit the web page request behavior that is characteristic for their class. The c_i clients of a class i create a total workload of w_i page requests per second. The combined workload of all clients equals the preset frequency of page requests W (i.e., 0.5, 1, 2, or 4 pages per second). We assume that w_i / W approximates the observed type frequency of class i (this assumption is corroborated by a manual count of the frequencies of Quickie and Just the Facts sessions at several German websites, such as [17]). Table 1 shows the test plan for a workload of 2 pages per second.

Table 1. Simulation environment for 2 page requests per second (* = figure rounded)

Variables / Session types	Session type characteristics		Test bed parameters	
	Relative type frequency	Interval between requests	Requests/sec. $(w_i)*$	No. of clients $(c_i)*$
Quickies	8%	15 sec	0.13	2
Just the Facts	15%	30 sec	0.30	9
Single Mission	7%	90 sec	0.14	13
Do It Again	14%	120 sec	0.28	34
Loitering	16%	120 sec	0.33	39
Information, Please	17%	60 sec	0.35	21
Surfing	23%	60 sec	0.47	28
Total	100%		2.00	146

We assume Zipf-like distributions of the frequencies in which
1. terms from the domain taxonomy become characteristic terms for web pages;
2. users engage in a new session with our hypothetical website;
3. web pages are requested by users ("page popularity").

Assumption (1) is based on the fact that term frequency distributions in documents tend to follow Zipf's law [21]. (2) is an estimate based on several studies regarding the frequency and duration of people's Internet usage (e.g., [22]). (3) is derived from the observation that web page popularity follows a Zipf-like distribution $1/i^\alpha$, where i is the popularity rank of the web page and α an adjustment for the server environment

---

[3] The corresponding user population is larger since only some users opt for personalization (5% in Yahoo and 25% in an early version of myAltaVista [18], 64% in Excite [19]).
[4] Based on data from [20], one can estimate that three of four German websites receive less than four page requests per second on average.

and the domain. [10, 23-25] recommend different values for α. We followed [10] who analyzed the MSNBC news site since their study was the most recent and their site the most similar to our own target site. The authors recommend an α between 1.4 and 1.6, hence we opted for $\alpha=1.5$ and use this value for all three distributions.

We assume further that our UM server has to process the following operations for personalizing a requested web page[5]:

- Three search operations with Zipf-distributed terms from the domain taxonomy, namely for personalizing the page header (e.g., user-tailored banner ads), the navigation section (e.g., personalized links), and the content part (e.g., personalized news). We assume one exact and two substring searches.
- One add operation for communicating the 1-3 characteristic terms of a web page as an interest event to the UM server.

For implementing our simulation environment, we took advantage of Directory Mark 1.1, a benchmark suite for LDAP servers from Mindcraft [26]. Directory Mark simulates clients that simultaneously access an LDAP server and reports a variety of performance data. For each test scenario, we generated an appropriate number of user profiles as well as transaction scripts that implement the workloads for each of the session types introduced earlier. To avoid starting a test run with all user profiles being empty, we introduced a warm-up phase during which the profiles became initially populated (lasting 10 minutes for 100 user profiles, 50 minutes for 500 profiles, etc.). During our tests, we collected and recorded 269 measures for the UM server and its components. Major results will be described below.

4   Small to Medium Scale Application Scenario

Our first series of experiments was carried out with a hardware configuration that would be typical for small web stores or news sites. In one test variant, all user modeling functionality resided on a single platform. In a second variant, we distributed the four components of our UM server across a network of four computers. In both conditions, a PC with an 800 MHz CPU, 512 MB of RAM and a 100 Mbps network card hosted the environment that simulated users submitting page requests.

4.1   Single Platform Tests

In the single platform tests, the complete UM server (i.e., Directory Component, ULC, MLC, and DIC) was running on a single PC with two 800 MHz processors, 1 GB of RAM, a RAID controller with two 18.3 GB UW-SCSI hard disks, and a 100 Mbps network card. The software used was Windows NT 4.0, iPlanet Directory Server 4.13 and VisiBroker 3.4. The learning and inference components were compiled with Java 1.2.2 and used the Java Hot Spot Server Virtual Machine 2.0.

---

[5] Note that many personalized websites do not provide personalization on all pages, which lowers the load of the UM server.

Fig. 1 shows the mean times that our UM server takes to perform the four user model operations for personalizing a page from the viewpoint of our hypothetical web application. The results for all 16 value combinations of our independent variables are charted. In general, mean times increase only degressively with the number of page requests and user profiles. In two cases (namely for 100 and 500 profiles), the times for four page requests per second are even lower than for two. This advantageous response time behavior is mainly due to database caching in the LDAP directory server. The more user model operations are being sent to the server for a given number of user profiles, the faster this cache gets filled and the more operations can therefore be directly served from cache memory. We also see that all mean times for 12,500 users are higher than those for smaller numbers of user profiles, while the mean times for 100, 500, and 2,500 user profiles appear quite similar (except for 2,500 users and four pages). We assume that this effect results mainly from a higher hit rate (i.e., probability that a specific piece of information is contained in cache memory) in those cases that have a smaller number of user profiles.

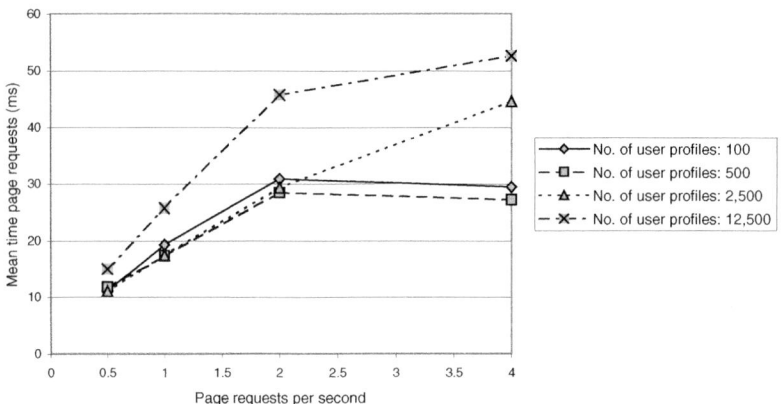

Fig. 1. Mean processing times for personalizing a web page

The overall performance and scalability of our UM server appears highly satisfactory. Even in the case of four page requests per second and 12,500 user models, the mean time to execute four user model operations and to return the results to 288 clients in parallel is smaller than 53 ms. The 99% confidence interval for the means does not exceed ± 0.24 ms due to the large sample size. The mean times plus one / two standard deviations never exceed 78 / 103 ms. A more detailed analysis shows that this graceful performance degradation occurs for both add and search operations. Since the over-head caused by the UM server is minor, web-based applications will be able to provide personalized services while responding within the desirable limit of one second and, in any case, the mandatory limit of ten seconds [27]. The moderate surge of the mean response time when the number of clients and user profiles increases does not suggest impending performance cliffs and scalability limits.

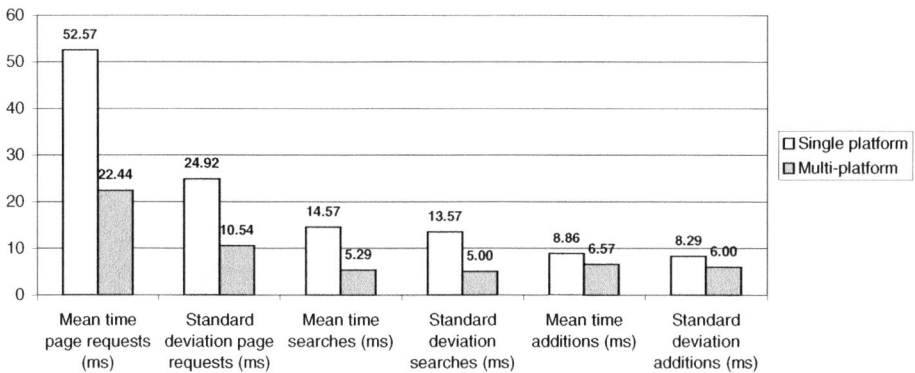

Fig. 2. Single-platform vs. multi-platform performance (12,500 profiles. 4 pages/sec)

4.2 Multiple Platform Tests

In the multi-platform scenario, only the Directory Component was running on the mentioned dual processor computer. The three other components of the UM server were each installed on a separate 600-800 MHz single processor PC with 100 Mbps network card. Fig. 2 compares several measurements for both scenarios. We see that the mean time for processing the four user model operations that personalize a web page plunges to 22.44 from 52.57 milliseconds, and its standard deviation to 10.54 from 24.92 milliseconds (i.e., nearly 60% in both cases). The single most important reason for this improvement is the considerably better search performance. The mean search time falls to 5.29 from 14.57 ms (-64%), and its σ to 5 from 13.57 ms (-63%). Less impressive is the performance gain of add operations: the mean time drops to 6.57 from 8.86 ms (-26%), and σ to 6 from 8.29 ms (-28%).

The distribution of our UM server across a network of four computers improved its performance considerably. Search operations benefit most from the relieved dual processor computer, since they can now be carried out concurrently by the directory server. Add operations with their inherent need for multi-user synchronization [16] can take less advantage of the additional hardware resources.

4.3 Evaluation of the Learning Components

So far, we discussed the performance of our UM server from the viewpoint of our hypothetical web application. Now we turn to the individual components of our server: the statistics-based User Learning Component, the similarity-based Mentor Learning Component, and the rule based Domain Inference Component. These components operate concurrently to the Directory Component. Fig. 3 shows the mean processing times of the ULC and the MLC for the single platform scenario. The performance of the DIC (which is comparable to that of the ULC) is discussed in [16].

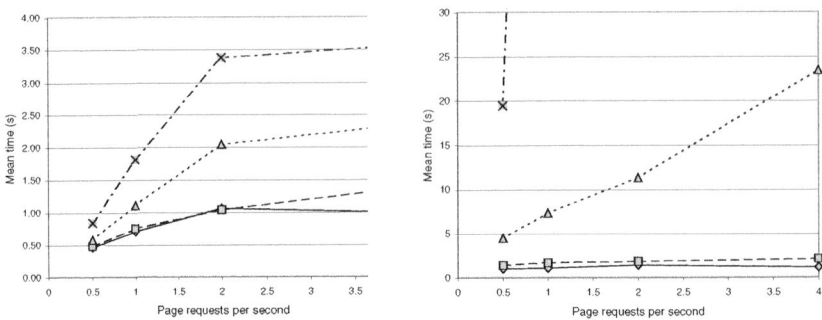

Fig. 3. Mean processing times of statistics and mentor based learning components (see Fig. 1 for legend)

For the ULC, mean times seem to mainly depend on the number of user profiles. They grow degressively with increasing page requests, which is mainly due to the queue-based architecture of the ULC (it allows for bulk processing of submitted events and for interim storage of interest probabilities in the main memory, thereby saving costly updates of the user profile). All recorded mean times are smaller than four seconds, which is highly satisfactory since it permits keeping track of users' changing interests even between consecutive page requests. The ULC fully supports this inter-request learning for all session types and workloads we tested.

The performance of the MLC is less good. For 100, 500 and 2,500 profiles, all means are below 24 seconds but grow progressively with increased page request rate. Except for Quickies, this still allows for a prediction of user interests and preferences between consecutive page requests. The response time deteriorates considerably though for 12,500 user profiles: 19 sec. for 0.5 and 141 sec. for 1 page/sec, but more than 2 hours for 2 and 4 pages/sec. In the latter two cases, the MLC presumably cannot keep pace with the stream of user arrivals and approaches its performance limits.

5   Large Scale Application Scenario

The successful simulation results for a small to medium sized user-adaptive website put us in the position to run a series of experiments on a much larger scale. The most notable one comprised eight million user profiles[6] and a workload of approximately 42 web page requests per second[7]. To realize this workload, we employed a total of 1,794 simultaneous clients in several testbeds. The UM server was installed on a Fire V880 from Sun's entry-level server segment [30] under Solaris 8, with eight 750 MHz processors, 8 MB cache per processor, 32 GB of RAM, and more than 200 GB of disk space. To take full advantage of the available hardware, we increased the cache size

---

[6] MSN had about 8 and AOL 34 million subscribers at the end of July 2002 [28].

[7] This workload roughly equals that of the largest German news portal with nearly 15 million unique users [29], which is about 15-20% the size of the top three U.S. portals.

of the Directory Component and each learning component to 2 GB. The user modeling server was implemented in version 5.1 of iPlanet Directory Server. Otherwise the design of this experiment was very comparable to the one described in Section 3.1.

The results were again very encouraging. Our UM server showed a mean response time of 35 ms for personalizing a web page (i.e., for performing three LDAP search and one add operations). This user modeling performance should easily allow a personalized application to stay well below the desirable response time limit of one second and, in any case, below the mandatory limit of ten seconds. None of the several million search and add operations that were submitted by our simulated users failed or timed out. Overall, the quality of service offered by our server seems highly satisfactory.

Another lesson from simulating the user modeling workload of real-world application environments was in terms of hardware sizing. The sizing characteristics of our server closely resemble those reported in the literature for its Directory Component. For example, [31] mentions the following rules of thumb for the number of CPUs that are necessary to process LDAP operations: "With Directory Server 4.0, search performance will scale almost linearly with the addition of up to 4 CPUs. In this range, you can expect to see 500-1,000 queries per second for each CPU. Beyond 4 CPUs, the resulting increase in performance per CPU is less but still significant".

The resource needs of the learning and inference components of our UM server depend on the number of these components (each can be present or absent, and instantiated multiple times), and several parameters that determine, e.g., the learning frequency, the size of the correlation space, etc. As far as the allocation of processor resources is concerned, we found that an even distribution between the Directory Component, and the learning and inference components, seems to be a good solution.

In conclusion, we regard our empirically founded approach of simulating the UM workload of real-world application environments as highly promising. It allows us to experimentally verify and predict the deployment characteristics of a UM server under various workload conditions. Our experience with actual installations of our UM server in commercial environments confirmed that this approach and the developed simulation testbed are an indispensable tool for real-world personalization. It also corroborated the findings in [15] (which were based on theoretical considerations and work by others) that directories provide a superior foundation for UM servers than traditionally used data bases and knowledge bases.

References

1. Kobsa, A.: Generic User Modeling Systems. User Modeling and User-Adapted Interaction **11**, (2001) 49–63. http://www.ics.uci.edu/~kobsa/papers/2001-UMUAI-kobsa.pdf
2. Fink, J. and Kobsa, A.: A Review and Analysis of Commercial User Modeling Servers for Personalization on the World Wide Web. User Modeling and User-Adapted Interaction **10**, (2000) 209–249. http://www.ics.uci.edu/~kobsa/papers/2000-UMUAI-kobsa.pdf
3. VanderMeer, D., Dutta, K., and Datta, A.: Enabling Scalable Online Personalization on the Web. 2nd ACM Conf on Electronic Commerce, Minneapolis, MN (2000) 185–196.

4. Datta, A., Dutta, K., VanderMeer, D., Ramamritham, K., Navathe, S. B.: An Architecture to Support Scalable Online Personalization on the Web. VLDB Journal **10** (2001) 104–17.
5. Keung, S. and Abbot, S.: LDAP Server Performance Report. (1998), http://www.bnelson.com/sizing/docl/ldapsPerformance.html
6. Wang, X., Schulzrinne, H., Kandlur, D., and Verma, D.: Measurement and Analysis of LDAP Performance. ACM SIGMETRICS Conference, Santa Clara, CA (2000) 156–165.
7. Duska, B. M., Marwood, D., and Feeley, M. J.: The Measured Access Characteristics of World-Wide-Web Client Proxy Caches. USENIX Symposium on Internet Technologies and Systems, Monterey, CA (1997) 23–35.
8. Gribble, S. D. and Brewer, E. A.: System Design Issues for Internet Middleware Services: Deductions from a Large Client Trace. USENIX Symposium on Internet Technologies and Systems, Monterey, CA (1997).
9. Almeida, V., Bestavros, A., Crovella, M., and Oliveira, A.: Characterizing Reference Locality in the WWW. Fourth International Conference on Parallel and Distributed Information Systems (1996) 92–103.
10. Padmanabhan, V. and Qiu, L.: The Content and Access Dynamics of a Busy Web Site: Findings and Implications. ACM SIGCOMM (2000) 111–123.
11. Fenstermacher, K. D. and Ginsburg, M.: Mining Client-Side Activity for Personalization. Fourth Workshop on Advanced Issues in Electronic Commerce and Web Information Systems (WECWIS), Newport Beach, CA (2002) 44–51.
12. 35 Percent of Surfing Time is Spent on 50 Sites. Computer Scope Ltd. (1999), http://www.nua.com/surveys/index.cgi?f=VS&art_id=905355323&rel=true
13. Rozanski, H., Bollman, G., and Lipman, M.: Seize the Occasion: Usage-based Segmentation for Internet Marketers. Booz-Allen & Hamilton, Inc. (2001), http://www.strategy-business.com/media/pdf/03-20-01_eInsight.pdf
14. Sun ONE Directory Server. Sun Microsystems (2002), http://wwws.sun.com/software/products/directory_srvr/home_directory.html
15. Fink, J. and Kobsa, A.: User Modeling in Personalized City Tours. Artificial Intelligence Review **18**, (2002) 33–74. http://www.ics.uci.edu/~kobsa/papers/2002-AIR-kobsa.pdf
16. Fink, J.: User Modeling Servers: Requirements, Design, and Evaluation. Department of Mathematics and Computer Science: University of Essen, Germany (2003).
17. Fink, J., Koenemann, J., Noller, S., and Schwab, I.: Putting Personalization into Practice. Communications of the ACM **45**, (2002) 41–42.
18. AltaVista Announcement. Compaq (1999), http://www.compaq.com/newsroom/presspaq/012699/schrock.html
19. Excite Network Online Media Kit. Excite (2002), http://www.excitenetwork.com/ advertising/index/id/Directmarket|ListRental|3|1.html
20. Online Usage Data Nov. 2001 (in German). IVW (2001), www.ivw.de/data/index.html
21. Zipf, G. K.: Human Behavior and the Principle of Least Effort. Reading: Addison (1949).
22. Patrick, A. and Black, A.: Implications of Access Methods and Frequency of Use for the National Capital Freenet. (1996) debra.dgbt.doc.ca/services-research/survey/connections/
23. Glassman, S.: A Caching Relay for the World Wide Web. First International Conference on the World-Wide Web, Geneva, Switzerland (1994).
24. Zipf Curves and Website Popularity. (1997), http://www.useit.com/alertbox/zipf.html
25. Breslau, L., Cao, P., Fan, L., Phillips, G., and Shenker, S.: Web Caching and Zipf-Like Distributions: Evidence and Implications. INFOCOM'99 (1999) 126–134.
26. DirectoryMark: The LDAP Server Benchmarking Tool. Mindcraft (2002), http://www.mindcraft.com/directorymark/index.html
27. Nielsen, J.: Usability Engineering. San Diego, CA: Academic Press (1993).

28. MSN Hits 300 Million Unique Monthly Users. Jupitermedia (2002),
    http://cyberatlas.internet.com/big_picture/traffic_patterns/article/0,,5931_1457661,00.html
29. Top 10 Web Properties for the Month of October 2002. Netratings Inc. (2002),
    http://epm.netratings.com/de/web/NRpublicreports.toppropertiesmonthly.html
30. Entry-Level Servers. Sun Microsystems (2002), http://www.sun.com/servers/entry/
31. Nelson, B.: Sizing Guide for Netscape Directory Server. (2002),
    http://www.bnelson.com/sizing/doc2/Directory4_0-SizingGuide.html

Evaluating the Inference Mechanism of Adaptive Learning Systems

Stephan Weibelzahl and Gerhard Weber

Pedagogical University Freiburg, Kunzenweg 21, 79117 Freiburg, Germany
{weibelza,webergeh}@ph-freiburg.de

Abstract. The evaluation of user modeling systems is an important though often neglected area. Evaluating the inference of user properties can help to identify failures in the user model. In this paper we propose two methods to assess the accuracy of the user model. The assumptions about the user might either be compared to an external test, or might be used to predict the users' behavior. Two studies with five adaptive learning courses demonstrate the usefulness of the approach.

1 Evaluation of Adaptive Systems

Empirical evaluations of adaptive systems are rare [1]—e.g., only a quarter of the articles published in *User Modeling and User Adapted Interaction* report significant empirical evaluations. Many of them include a simple evaluation study with small sample sizes (often $N = 1$) and without any statistical method. Several reasons for this absence of significant studies have been identified (e.g., [2] and [3]). A systematic overview of current evaluation studies can be found in EASy-D, an online database of adaptive systems and related empirical studies[1].

Recently, we proposed an evaluation framework that supports and encourages researchers to evaluate their adaptive system by separating different evaluation steps [1]: evaluation of the input data, evaluation of the inference mechanism, evaluation of the adaptation decision, and evaluation of the interaction.

In this paper we focus on the second step. The inference mechanism is the crucial part of many adaptive systems. We propose two methods that test the accuracy of a user model

- by comparing its assumptions to an external test, and
- by comparing its assumptions to the actually displayed behavior of the learners.

These two methods are applied to an adaptive learning system, called the *HTML-Tutor*, to demonstrate the usefulness of the approach.

---

[1] http://www.softwareevaluation.de

P. Brusilovsky et al. (Eds.): UM 2003, LNAI 2702, pp. 154–162, 2003.

2   Adaptive Learning Systems Built with NetCoach

Adaptive learning systems adapt their behavior to individual learner properties such as the user's current knowledge. Opposed to static learning systems that present the same material to every user in the same way and order, adaptive systems consider individual differences in terms of knowledge, experience, preferences, or learning objectives [4] and thus promise to improve the teaching process [5].

NetCoach[2] is an authoring system that enables authors to develop adaptive web-based learning courses without being required to program source code [6].

2.1   Course Structure and Adaptivity

All NetCoach courses are based on the same structure. Similar to chapters and subchapters in a book, the learning material (i.e., pages with texts, images, animations) is stored in a hierarchical tree-structure of concepts. Learners may navigate through this structure freely. However, the course adapts to each learner individually by suggesting concepts that are suitable to work on next (adaptive curriculum sequencing) and by annotating the links to other concepts (adaptive link annotation).

This functionality is based on two kinds of data: concept relations and test sets (also called test groups) that check the learners knowledge about a concept. Authors may define two kinds of relations between concepts as regards contents. First, a concept might be prerequisite to another, i.e., this concept should be learned before the second concept is presented.

Second, a concept might infer another concept, i.e., the fact that the learner knows concept A implies that she also knows concept B.

The crucial part of NetCoach to assess the learner's knowledge are the so called test sets. A test set consists of a set of weighted test items that are related to a concept. There are forced choice, multiple choice, gap filling, and ranking items. All of them are evaluated online automatically. Users receive points for answering a test item correctly. Mistakes result in a reduction of points. Items are presented randomly (not yet presented items and incorrectly answered items are preferred) until the learner reaches a critical value. Only then the related concept is assumed to be learned completely.

2.2   Inference Mechanism

Adapting to the learner's current knowledge is one of the most important features of NetCoach. If the user completed a test set successfully (either during an introductory test before the content of the concept has been presented or afterwards in a post test) the concept is marked as solved and further inferences about the user's knowledge are drawn based on the inference relations between concepts.

---

[2] http://art.ph-freiburg.de

Table 1. Possible states of a concept with a test set. The states are computed individually during interaction in dependence of the user's behavior.

state	condition	annotation
not ready	there are prerequisites for a concept (e.g., concept A has to be learned before concept B) that are not fulfilled	red ball
suggested	all prerequisites are fulfilled	green ball
solved	the learner completed the test set of this concept successfully	grey ball with tick
inferred	the learner solved a more advanced concept first and thus the current concept is inferred to be already learned as well.	orange ball with tick
known	the learner marked the concept as known without solving the test set	crossed orange ball

NetCoach summarizes the learner's current knowledge by assigning one of five states to each concept. Table 1 lists the states and describes the conditions of assignment. The current configuration of states is called a user's learning state. As it is computed on the fly for each user individually, the learning state models the idiosyncratic learning process during the interaction.

We argue that it is insufficient to assess the current knowledge by looking at the visited pages as most adaptive systems do (e.g., AHA [7] or Interbook [8]). An explicit assessment with sets of test items provides a much more reliable user model and might thus support better and adequate adaptations of the interface.

2.3   Adaptation Decision

Based on this inferred individual learning state NetCoach adapts its interface in two ways. First, links to other concepts are annotated with colored bullets that correspond to the learning state (adaptive link annotation). Table 1 gives an example of the default color configuration, however, authors are free to predefine other colors for each state.

Second, NetCoach suggests a concept that should be learned next and gives warnings if the learner visits a concept with the state *not ready* (adaptive curriculum sequencing).

Note, that for these adaptation techniques the quality of the learning state assessment is crucial. The adaptation decision will only work if the underlying assumptions about the learner are correct. Thus, the two methods to assess the accuracy of the user model are an important prerequisite to a successful adaptation.

3   Comparison of User Model to an External Test

The first proposed method to test the accuracy of a user model is to compare the assumptions in the user model to an external test. For instance, the assumption of a product recommendation system [9] about the most preferred product could be tested by actually letting the customer choose between several products. The user model of a system that adapts to the user's keyboard skills [10] might be tested by assessing the skills externally with a valid diagnostic instrument for motor disabilities. In an adaptive learning system it is possible to compare the assumed knowledge of the learner to the results of an external knowledge test that is known to have external validity. We evaluated the congruence of the user models in the *HTML-Tutor* and an extended external assessment. The HTML-Tutor is a NetCoach course that introduces to HTML and publishing on the internet. It consists of 138 concepts, 48 test sets, and 125 test items.

3.1   Method

We assessed 32 students who took part in one of three compact seminars between April 2001 and April 2002 at the Pedagogical University Freiburg. The 10 male and 22 female students had been studying for 0 to 9 semesters ($\bar{x} = 3.55$). The seminar consisted of 20 lessons on HTML and publishing in the Internet. During the seminar the students had to learn with the *HTML-Tutor* at least twice. After the seminar the students had to take part in a test. This test was designed to assess their performance as exactly as possible and consisted of three parts: first, the students had to generate an HTML page that fulfills certain conditions. Using their computer they had to produce source codes that yield a given layout and functions, e.g., clicking on the image should link to the homepage. Second, a paper and pencil test included three questions on more comprehensive knowledge, e.g., they had to explain why HTML is not very suitable to produce a specific layout. Third, they had to identify and correct errors in a given source code. For instance, the line `<a name=''page.html''>` had to be changed to `<a href=''page.html''>`.

The test was evaluated individually in regards to the concepts of the *HTML-Tutor*. Given a learner's test performance we decided which concepts are already known or unknown. That is, in a qualitative analysis for each concept we decided whether the learner has complete knowledge about it. The test collects different data types (source code generation, open question, source code correction) and it can thus be assumed to be a good estimator of the *real* domain knowledge. However, it is obviously not a perfect test which might bias the evaluation results. In fact, the proposed congruency approach can be seen as a kind of parallel test reliability. If the external test was not reliable the expected congruency would be reduced. We tried to improve the test's external validity by including different task types and by considering as much information about the learner's performance as available.

The results of this analysis were contrasted with the system's assumptions about the learners in the user model. These assumptions relied on the answers to

Table 2. Number of congruent and incongruent cases. The results of 32 participants working on a subset of 48 concepts with test sets were observed. These $32 \times 48 = 1536$ cases are categorized in terms of the assumptions about the learners' knowledge in the user model of the *HTML-Tutor* and in terms of the results of the external test. The *HTML-Tutor* assumes a concept either to be *solved* or *inferred*, otherwise there is *no information* whether the concept is known or not. The external test indicates whether a concept is *known* or *unknown*. Otherwise the case is categorized as *no information*.

		user model			
		solved	inferred	no information	Σ
	known	129	2	129	260
external test	**unknown**	9	0	23	32
	no information	601	261	382	1244
	Σ	739	263	534	1536

test items during the seminar when students were interacting with the *HTML-Tutor* and on 40 randomly selected test items that had to be completed after the external test. The user model represents a learner's knowledge but not the misconceptions. Thus, there is no direct counterpart in the user model for the unknown category in the external assessment.

3.2   Results

We found, that most assumptions were in congruence with test performance (see Table 2). 131 concepts were assumed to be either *solved* (i.e., the learner completed the test set successfully) or *inferred* (i.e., a higher concept had been solved before), while the external test also indicated that these concepts were known.

The high number of concepts that were not covered by the external test (1244 out of 1536 cases) results from the fact that the time for such a test is limited. Compared to the 20 hours of teaching one hour of testing can obviously assess only a few selected aspects.

However, we identified nine incongruencies, i.e., there were nine cases where the system assumed that a concept is already *solved*, though the external assessment indicated that the concept is *unknown* (see Figure 1). These incongruencies where caused by three out of the 11 explored concepts. For all of these three concepts we were able to show that the test set did not measure the same kind of knowledge as the external test did. The nine cases are distributed across the concepts in the following way: in five cases the external test indicated that the learners do not encode German umlauts correctly (compared to 8 congruent cases in chapter 2.5). Nevertheless they were able to respond to test items on this topic correctly. Obviously there is a mismatch between the declarative knowledge (as measured by the test items) and the displayed performance in real world settings. Similar results were found for the second concept: three students were able

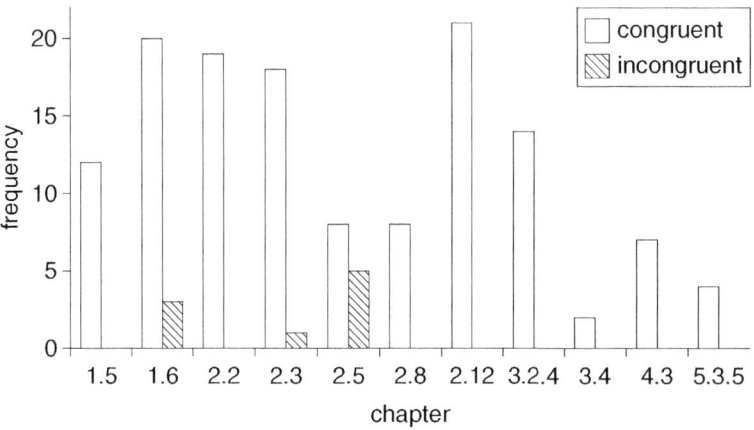

Fig. 1. Number of congruent and incongruent cases categorized by chapters

to answer test items on the structure of HTML pages (chapter 1.6), but when they had to work on their own in the test, they just skipped the header of the page which resulted in an incorrect page. Nevertheless we identified 20 congruent cases for the same concept. Finally, the third concept (chapter 2.3) with an incongruence introduces line breaks. One student encoded them correctly when answering the test items, but sometimes forgot to do so when generating a page. 18 students behaved in a congruent way in regard to this concept.

To get a quantitative measure of how close the relation of user model and external assessment is, it is possible to compute a χ^2-contingency-coefficient [11] based on the data given in table 2. A contingency measure of $C_{corr} = .24$ suggests that the two assessment methods are related, but do not measure the same. We propose to use C_{corr} for comparisons of different adaptive systems or of different versions of the same system, to estimate which system's user model is closer to the external assessment. However, from a formative evaluation perspective it is more important to know which concepts are incongruent rather than how close the assessments are related, because this provides hints for further improvements.

4   Comparison of User Model to the User Behavior

In a second evaluation study we compared the assumptions in the user model to the actual displayed behavior of the learners. The user model of NetCoach courses contains information not only about known concepts but also whether the learner is *ready* or *not ready* to work on a concept (see Table 1). Users should perform worse on concepts that have the status *not ready* in the user model.

Table 3. Comparison of user behavior in dependence of the assumed knowledge state. 3501 users (N_{users}) completed a total of $11770+1183 = 12953$ concepts in five different NetCoach courses. Learners who were prepared to work on a concept responded more often to test items correctly ($\bar{c}_{pre}$) than those who did not fulfill all prerequisites for this concept ($\bar{c}_{\neg pre}$). The number of included concepts (N_{pre} and $N_{\neg pre}$), the standard deviation (σ), and the significance (α) of the t-tests are reported. For non-significant results the test power ($1 - \beta$) is shown, respectively the effect size (d) for significant tests

course	N_{users}	$\bar{c}_{pre}$	$\bar{c}_{\neg pre}$	N_{pre}	$N_{\neg pre}$	σ_{pre}	$\sigma_{\neg pre}$	α	$1-\beta$	d
Kommunikation	172	.71	.63	1665	125	.43	.47	.04*		.18
P.-wahrnehmung	321	.69	.51	1629	132	.43	.46	.00*		.41
Piaget	1004	.59	.54	4218	169	.39	.45	.10	1.0	
Problemloesen	272	.69	.70	748	40	.43	.44	.87	.86	
HTML-Tutor	1732	.59	.52	3510	717	.41	.42	.00*		.17
Σ	3501			11770	1183					

4.1   Method

We collected data from five online courses in different domains that had been developed with the NetCoach authoring system. These courses included the *HTML-Tutor* as well as four introductory courses on psychology such as problem solving (*Problemloesen*), Piaget's developmental psychology (*Piaget*), communication (*Kommunikation*), and interpersonal perception (*Personenwahrnehmung*). 3501 users (both students and visitors from the internet) interacted at least 15 minutes with one of the courses. Everyone was free to choose which concepts to work at. For each concept, we observed both the learner's behavior and whether the learner was prepared. For each test set we specified the minimum number of items that were required to solve this set. The mean proportion of correct answers ($\bar{c}$) on these first items was computed for those who were assumed to be prepared for this concept (*pre*) (i.e, the current learning state of this concept was either *suggested* or *solved*) and for those who were assumed to have some missing prerequisites ($\neg pre$) (i.e., the current learning state of this concept was *not ready*).

4.2   Results

Table 3 reveals that learners who are supposed to be prepared for a concept performed better on the test items than those who were not fully prepared. Note that all students had the same information about the concept, the only difference between the groups is that the latter did not fulfill all prerequisites for this concept, because the learners did not follow the suggested path. For two courses (*Piaget* and *Problemloesen*) we were not able to demonstrate a statistical

Table 4. Frequency of result types for 38 concepts in *HTML-Tutor*. We expected that the proportion of correct responses should be higher if the learner was prepared to work on this concept ($\bar{c}_{pre} > \bar{c}_{\neg pre}$). While most results were conform with this hypothesis only three of them were statistically significant

	$\bar{c}_{pre} > \bar{c}_{\neg pre}$	$\bar{c}_{pre} \leq \bar{c}_{\neg pre}$	Σ
significant	3	0	3
not significant	24	11	35
Σ	27	11	38

difference between the groups. However, the statistical analysis makes obvious that the effect is not in the opposite direction. For *Problemloesen* the sample size was just too small (as indicated by the low test power).

From a statistical point of view, it would have been desirable to reduce the variance within the groups to get a clearer picture of the relevant effects. A considerable amount of variance is probably caused by varying difficulties of the test sets. While some test sets are easy to solve and therefore the mean proportion of correct answers is high, other test sets are more difficult. However, not all users worked on every concept which decreases the sample size for subsequent conceptwise tests rapidly and statistical significance becomes difficult to reach. Nevertheless, a conceptwise comparison for the *HTML-Tutor* revealed that most of the results are conform with our hypothesis (see Table 4).

In summary, the study suggests that learners who do not fulfill all prerequisites for a concept perform worse than those who were prepared for the concept. The assumed learning state predicts at least parts of the learner's performance. However, the effect sizes are rather small. But if it was possible to improve the learning process by adapting to the user's knowledge this approach should at least be considered when a new learning environment is designed. These results gain even more relevance if we consider the fact that 21,6% of the requested pages in the HTML-Tutor ($N = 40607$) are assummed to be *not ready*. As this study suggests that the learners will probably perform worse on a *not ready* page than on a *suggested* or *solved* one, it is reasonable to present a warning or to direct them to the missing prerequisite pages.

5   Conclusion

These two studies describe an approach for the evaluation of adaptive learning systems in general. Other adaptive systems might be evaluated in a similar way. For instance, there are validated tests and assessment methods for various psychological states, traits, preferences, and attitudes. For model dimensions that cannot be assessed in such a way it might be useful to observe whether the user's behavior is predicted correctly. The approach is certainly limited to explicit user models. Implicit user models as they are sometimes used by machine learning systems are excluded. Moreover, the user model is very straightforward and of low complexity. Defining external tests for complex user models might require higher efforts than the knowledge test that was used in this study.

The results show that it is possible to evaluate the accuracy of the assumptions about the learner. Such evaluations might point to possible (and otherwise indiscoverable) improvements of the inference mechanism. However, a correct user model does not guarantee a successful adaptation, because the actual adaptation decision how to adapt might still be wrong,. e.g., the interface might become confusing by the chosen way of adaptation. Nevertheless, a correct user model is an important prerequisite for the adaptation success.

References

1. Weibelzahl, S.: Evaluation of adaptive systems. In Bauer, M., Gmytrasiewicz, P.J., Vassileva, J., eds.: User Modeling: Proceedings of the Eighth International Conference, UM2001. Springer, Berlin (2001) 292–294
2. Eklund, J.: A Study of Adaptive Link Annotation in Educational Hypermedia. PhD thesis, University of Sydney (1999)
3. Höök, K.: Steps to take before intelligent user interfaces become real. Interacting With Computers **12** (2000) 409–426
4. Brusilovsky, P.: Adaptive hypermedia. User Modeling and User-Adapted Interaction **11** (2001) 87–110
5. Oppermann, R., Rashev, R., Kinshuk: Adaptability and adaptivity in learning systems. In Behrooz, A., ed.: Knowledge Transfer. Volume II. (1997) 173–179
6. Weber, G., Kuhl, H.C., Weibelzahl, S.: Developing adaptive internet based courses with the authoring system NetCoach. In Reich, S., Tzagarakis, M.M., de Bra, P., eds.: Hypermedia: Openness, Structural Awareness, and Adaptivity. Springer, Berlin (2001) 226–238
7. de Bra, P., Calvi, L.: AHA! An open adaptive hypermedia architecture. The New Review of Hypermedia and Multimedia **4** (1998) 115–139
8. Brusilovsky, P., Eklund, J., Schwarz, E.: Web-based education for all: A tool for developing adaptive courseware. In: Computer Networks and ISDN Systems. Proceedings of the Seventh International World Wide Web Conference, 14-18 April 1998. Volume 30. (1998) 291–300
9. Ardissono, L., Goy, A.: Tailoring the interaction with users in electronic shops. In Kay, J., ed.: User Modeling: Proceedings of the Seventh International Conference, UM99. Springer, Vienna, New York (1999) 35–44
10. Trewin, S., Pain, H.: Dynamic modelling of keyboard skills: Supporting users with motor disabilities. In Jameson, A., Paris, C., Tasso, C., eds.: User Modeling: Proceedings of the Sixth International Conference, UM97. Springer, Vienna, New York (1997) 135–146 Available from http://um.org.
11. Agresti, A.: An introduction to categorical data analysis. Wiley, New York (1996)

The Continuous Empirical Evaluation Approach: Evaluating Adaptive Web-Based Courses*

Alvaro Ortigosa and Rosa M. Carro

Escuela Politécnica Superior, Universidad Autónoma de Madrid
28049 Madrid, Spain
{Alvaro.Ortigosa, Rosa.Carro}@ii.uam.es

Abstract. In this paper we present the continuous empirical evaluation approach, whose goal is to improve the quality of adaptive web-based courses. The adaptive-course description, along with the users´ features and interactions with the courses, are analyzed in order to detect concrete possible fails or lacks and to propose specific solutions and actions to be performed to improve these courses. The way it is used to evaluate existing adaptive courses is also presented.

1 Motivation

Adaptive hypermedia supports the implementation of new teaching approaches based on the adaptation of multimedia materials, navigational options, teaching strategies, etc., to each user's needs. Due to the richness of adaptive course descriptions and to the fact that they are intended for different types of users, it is not easy to evaluate their quality during the design phase. Most of the existing empirical evaluations of adaptive courses focus on evaluating the benefits of adaptive versus non-adaptive versions [1]. Yet it is necessary to use specific evaluation criteria and methods to facilitate the interpretation of the observed facts. In this direction, layered evaluations of adaptive applications have been proposed [4] [6], and their benefits and limitations have also been issued [6].

On the one hand, it is important not only to understand the causes that lead to the observed results but also to detect concrete possible fails or lacks and to propose solutions to improve the quality of an adaptive course, even if it has proved to be more effective than its non-adaptive version. On the other hand, it is necessary to carry out experiments with many different real users, in order to obtain significant statistical data to analyze [3]. Provided that training is a continuous task and many adaptive courses are used for long-life learning, the evaluation of this type of courses should be ideally carried out systematically. Our goal is to support the automatic and continuous evaluation of adaptive courses in order to identify possible fails or possibilities of improvement, and to propose concrete suggestions about the possible actions to be done to improve these courses. The course components, along with the users' features, preferences, opinions and actions, are analyzed. The objective is that subsequent users interacting with the adaptive course can benefit from the improvements made after previous evaluations.

---

* This work has been partially supported by supported by the Spanish Inter-ministerial Commission of Science and Technology, projects TIC2001-0685-C02-01 and TIC2002-01948.

P. Brusilovsky et al. (Eds.): UM 2003, LNAI 2702, pp. 163–167, 2003.

2   The Continuous Empirical Evaluation Approach

The aim of the continuous empirical evaluation approach is to assist the evaluation and improvement of web-based adaptive courses, so that the needs of individual students can be better fulfilled while interacting with them. The evaluation consists on: i) analyzing the course description and the user features, interactions, behaviors, opinions and results while interacting with it, ii) detecting situations where the course does not satisfy the user needs, iii) identifying possible fails on the course design and/or possibilities of improving it, and iv) suggesting concrete actions to perform in order to implement these improvements.

The analysis process can lead to the detection of situations such as: i) the users do not learn certain topics; they fail the exercises related to the topic, ii) the users need to find and review certain topics at particular points of the course; this is detected by analyzing the course structure and the user navigation paths, iii) the users are disoriented; they go through the topics with no logical order, go back and forward and spend little time in every page, iv) the users are not motivated; their interactions with the system are not frequent and they can also express it while answering surveys, v) the users are dissatisfied; they can express it in surveys and/or leave the course prematurely, vi) etc.

These situations can be caused by problems and/or deficiencies in the course design and, in general, it is necessary to combine the available information in order to infer the right problems or lacks. Some of the deficiencies considered are: i) lack of precision or clarity of certain contents; it leads the students to the non-understanding of the topics explained, ii) lack of examples that can help the user to understand the topics involved, iii) exercises incorrectly designed; if it is the case, the assumption that the students do not learn the concepts properly can be wrong, iv) lack of summaries or reviews at certain points of the course; too many visits to previous topics can suggest the need of including summaries/reviews at certain points, v) existence of unidentified dependences between topics; when the users need to know some topics before studying others, a previous visit to the former (prerequisites) or a minimum score in the tests associated to them could be required/suggested in order to access to the later; this becomes more evident when the students that (re)visited the prerequisite topics got better results in the current topic than those who did not, vi) inappropriate organization of topics; this can be the reason why students are disoriented, do not learn the topics properly and/or need to review topics frequently, vii) inadequate adaptive guidance; a too restricted guidance may make the users to abandon the system, while a too flexible guidance can cause user disorientation, viii) and so on.

Sometimes the problems concerning a topic with prerequisites can have their origin on these prerequisites, mainly when the students that fail in the exercises related to the former did not get good results on the exercises related to the later (the required knowledge may have not been consolidated). General criteria, such as the inappropriate granularity of the information presented in each page or the excessive number of links, are also considered during the whole evaluation process. In order to offer a suggestion, lacks and flaws must be detected for a statistically significant number of users. Once they are detected, the corresponding improvement suggestions are offered. The complete evaluation process considers the user features at each time, so that suggestions can focus on specific types of students or on the whole population.

3   Application of Continuous Evaluation to Adaptive Courses

The continuous evaluation approach is being applied for the evaluation of adaptive web-based courses developed with the TANGOW [2] system. TANGOW-based courses are described by means of *Tasks*, *Rules* and *Content Fragments*. *Tasks* are the basic units in the learning process and represent topics to be learned, exercises to be done or examples to be observed. *Rules* describe the organization of tasks in the course and contain information about their execution, including the order among them (if any) or the freedom to perform them in any order, the necessity of performing all of them or only some, and the prerequisites between tasks. *Content fragments* are stored separately and associated to tasks. Adaptation is included by establishing the user features to be considered (personal features, preferences, learning styles) and/or their actions while interacting with the course, and by specifying the different tasks, rules, teaching strategies (theory-example-practice and vice-versa) and versions of content fragments for each type of student. At runtime, the TANGOW system consults the course description along with the user static and dynamic data and generates, step by step, a personalized course, adapting its components to each user at each time.

An evaluation prototype has been built to include continuous empirical evaluation in the TANGOW system [5]. The evaluation module analyzes: i) the adaptive course description, ii) the users' features, preferences and actions, including the scores obtained in self-assessment tests and the paths followed during the learning process, and iii) the student's opinion (a specific survey is generated for each student, according to his actions, to get his opinion about the difficulties detected for him). With this information, the evaluation module tries to detect possible fails in the course design and to propose changes than could improve the course quality. One of the criteria used in the evaluation consists on relating the results obtained by the students while performing a practical task to the navigational patterns followed through the course, with the aim of identifying differences between the patterns that lead to bad scores and those that lead to good scores and, according to these differences, suggesting possible changes to improve the course, if possible. In order to illustrate this process, we consider one version of a course about the HTML language, generated for a group of novice users (figure 1).

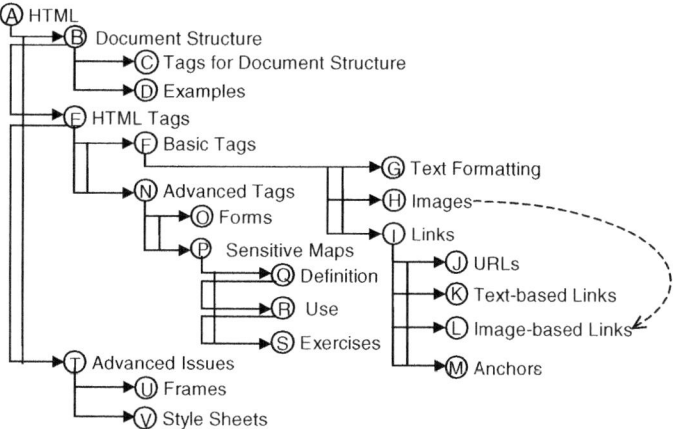

Fig. 1. Partial tree of the course structure for a given student profile

Navigation paths can be represented as sequences of task identifiers, where each identifier represents one visit to the corresponding task. Let us consider three paths followed through the course shown in figure 1, corresponding to students that obtained bad results while performing task "S":

- Case 1: [A,B,C,E,N,O,P,Q,R,S,F,G,H,I,J,K,L,M,T,U,V]
- Case 2: [A,B,C,D,E,F,G,H,I,J,K,L,M,N,O,P,Q,R,S,H,S,T,U,V]
- Case 3: [A,B,D,E,N,P,Q,R,S,O,F,G,H,I,K,J,K,L,H,L,M,T,U]

Each case corresponds to a set of students that followed the same path. The common pattern extracted, which represents what all the students that got bad scores did in common, specially before task "S", is

$$[A, B, *, E , *, N ,*, P, Q, R, \mathbf{S}, *, T, U] \qquad (1)$$

where * stands for visits to zero or more tasks. In order to determine why the students that followed these paths got bad results, these paths are compared with the cases where the students obtained good results in the same tests

- Case 4: [A,B,D,E,F,G,H,I,J,K,L,M,N,P,Q,R,S,J,S,O,T,U]
- Case 5: [A,B,C,E,F,I,J,K,M,H,N,O,P,Q,R,S,H,J,S,L,G,T,V]
- Case 6: [A,B,C,D,E,N,O,P,Q,R,S,F,I,J,K,L,M,J,S,G,H,T,V]

whose common pattern is:

$$[A, B, *, E, N, *, P, Q, R, \mathbf{S}, *, \mathbf{J}, *, \mathbf{S}, *, T, *] \qquad (2)$$

When comparing patterns (1) and (2), it can be detected that the path [S*, J, *, S] appears only in (2), that is, the students that obtained good scores in task "S" performed the task "J" ("URLs") before. Therefore, it is inferred that it can be convenient for the users to visit the "URLs" task before trying to solve "Sensitive Map Exercises". The following suggestions are made to the course designer:

- Add a prerequisite relationship between task "J" (prerequisite) and task "S" (target), so that the students are required to visit the former before the later.
- Add a review before task "S" with (part of) the contents of task "J". This is especially recommended when several topics need to be reviewed before the target task.

The pattern recognition algorithms are simplifications based on the domain knowledge. The system will propose changes only when the number of students having problems and the number of students supporting positive cases are statistically significant. A weight is associated to each case, which is used to infer a probability associated with each suggestion. In the example, some students that obtained good results also reviewed task "H", but the number of students was not significant to make a suggestion related to task "H".

Usually the problems detected can be solved in different ways. In these cases, the suggestions to be proposed are sorted according to probabilistic and heuristic criteria. If problems are detected only for certain types of students, the suggestions are related to their common features, so that the course can be improved for the corresponding students. The suggestions are strongly related to the final course generated for each student, provided that the same facts can give rise to different suggestions depending on it. For example, if the sequencing of the rule describing the decomposition of task "HTML Tags" had been AND (strict order when performing subtasks), the suggestion about creating a dependency relationship would have being pointless, because the students would already be forced to visit the required task before the target task.

The course designers can implement some of the suggestions offered by changing the course rules. For example, the guidance process can be made more free by changing the rule sequencing mode from AND to ANY or OR, and rules for different student profiles can be added to include adaptation features that had not been considered before. The effectiveness of the suggested improvements, when included, will be evaluated by the evaluation module when the next group of students access the course.

4   Conclusions and Future Work

The goal of the continuous empirical evaluation approach is to identify the possible fails or improvement possibilities in web-based adaptive courses and to propose concrete suggestions about the actions to be performed in order to improve them. It assists the course designers in the evaluation and maintenance of this type of courses, by analyzing the course description along with the user data (personal features, preferences, learning styles, actions while interacting with the course and surveys).

This approach is being applied to evaluate TANGOW-based courses. Not all the criteria proposed in section 2 have already been used; there is still work to do in this direction. The implementation of an evaluation system capable of i) combining all the available data to identify the problems than can occur in an adaptive course and ii) suggesting the best possibilities of improvements is not an easy task. Our current work concentrates on these issues. Finally, the presented approach should also be evaluated.

References

1. Calvi, L.: Formative Evaluation of Adaptive CALLware: A Case Study. In: Brusilovsky P., Stock O., Strapparava C. (eds): Adaptive Hypermedia and Adaptive Web-Based Systems. LNCS 1892. Springer-Verlag, Berlin (2000) 276–279
2. Carro, R.M., Pulido, E. and Rodríguez, P.: Developing and Accessing Adaptive Internet-based Courses. In: Jain, L.C., Howlett, R.J., Ichalkaranje, N.S., Tonfoni, G. (eds): Virtual Environments for Teaching and Learning. World Scientific Publishing (2002) 111–149
3. Chin, D.: Empirical Evaluation of User Models and User-Adapted Systems. In: User Modeling and User-Adapted Interaction, Vol. 11 (1–2). Kluwer, The Netherlands (2001) 181–194
4. Karagiannidis, C., Sampson, D.: Layered Evaluation of Adaptive Applications and Services. In: Brusilovsky P., Stock O., Strapparava C. (eds): Adaptive Hypermedia and Adaptive Web-Based Systems. LNCS 1892. Springer-Verlag, Berlin (2000) 343–346
5. Ortigosa, A., Carro, R.M.: Continuous Evaluation of Adaptive Web-based Courses. Learning Technology. IEEE Computer Society Learning Technology Task Force. Available at http://lttf.ieee.org/learn tech/issues/july2002/index.html (2002)
6. Weibelzahl, S., Weber, G.: Advantages, Opportunities, and Limits of Empirical Evaluations: Evaluating Adaptive Systems. Künstliche Intelligenz, 3/02 (2002) 17–20

Privacy Preservation Improvement by Learning Optimal Profile Generation Rate

Tsvi Kuflik[1,2], Bracha Shapira[1], Yuval Elovici[1], and Adlai Maschiach[1]

[1]Department of Information Systems Engineering,
Ben-Gurion University, Beer-Sheva Israel
{tsvikak,bshapira,elovici,mesiach}@bgumail.bgu.ac.il
[2]Department of Software Systems,
Sapir College, Israel
tsvik@makash.ac.il

Abstract. PRAW, a privacy model proposed recently, is aimed at protecting Web surfers' privacy by hiding their interests, i.e., their profiles. PRAW generates several faked transactions for each real user's transaction. The faked transactions relate to various fields of interest in order to confuse eavesdroppers attempting to derive users' profiles. They provide eavesdroppers with inconsistent data for the profile generation task. PRAW creates two profiles, a real user profile and a faked one aimed at confusing eavesdroppers. In this paper we demonstrate that the number of user transactions used for user profile generation significantly affects PRAW's ability to hide users' interests. We claim that there exists an optimal profile update rate for every user according to his surfing behavior. A system implementing PRAW needs to learn, for each specific user, the user's behavior, and dynamically adjust the optimal number of transactions that should be used to generate the user profile.

1 Introduction

The World Wide Web enables users to access easily vast amounts of information in every possible area of interest. Users searching or browsing the Web face an overflow of information, most of it irrelevant to their needs. Various Information Filtering (IF) techniques were developed aiming at building personal user profiles and representing precise users' information needs in order to filter out irrelevant information. One example is Letizia [11], a system designed to help users find relevant information while browsing the Web. Letizia builds a user profile by analyzing the content of Web pages visited and favored by the user and recommending links that could be followed. The user profile is built based on information supplied by the user. The system monitors user's behavior and infers the relevancy of Web pages for the user. For in-depth survey of user profiling techniques and systems, the reader is referred to a recent survey of the field of information filtering [9].

The same techniques that allow "Letizia" to build user profiles to support user's information needs also enable eavesdroppers to infer user needs and interests without their knowledge or approval, and to violate their privacy.

P. Brusilovsky et al. (Eds.): UM 2003, LNAI 2702, pp. 168–177, 2003.

Personal information privacy is an important challenge facing the growth and prosperity of the Internet. Many companies on the Web constantly violate the privacy of users for their own commercial benefit. Consequently users who worry about their privacy forego important Web services in order to avoid exposure. For example, an investor on the stock market might abstain from browsing stock data so as not to expose the identity of the stocks which interest him, as will a patent designer resist from browsing patents data for the same reason. Similarly, companies who wish to avoid industry espionage will prevent their staff from using certain Web services; even private users not wanting to expose their hobbies, interests, or health condition or not to be targeted by nuisance commercials, may forgo navigation.

In general, Web users leave identifiable tracks at every surfed Web site [2]. The tracks can be differentiated between information rooted in the communication infrastructure involved and explicit or implicit information rooted in the user's actions and behavior [8,10]. Various eavesdroppers observe these tracks for their own benefit; they vary between the end servers, the users' Internet Service Providers (ISP) and anyone else able and interested in listening to the communications between the user and the end server. The eavesdroppers are able to collect data about the content of the Web pages the user visited, time he spent there, frequency and duration of exchanges, and any other navigational behavior parameters. This data can be used to derive users' personal information interests and needs (i.e., profiles). The profile constructed by eavesdroppers might then be used for many purposes undesirable to the user, such as assessing the users' medical condition or industrial espionage, without the user's awareness.

The computer security community has devoted much research to improving user anonymity on the Web by hiding identifiable tracks originating from the communication infrastructure involved. The tracks are hidden by creating an anonymous channel between the user and the accessed Web site. However, hiding user identity is not an adequate solution in many situations on the Web where the user is requested to identify himself to the end server, for example when obtaining services provided to members only or when payment is made by credit card. Some of the better-known tools are:

- *Anonymizer* - [3], submits HTTP requests to the Internet on behalf of its users. By doing so, the only IP address revealed to the WEB sites is that of the *Anonymizer* but the users themselves remain anonymous. In this case users have to trust the *Anonymizer* and their own ISPs who can still observe their activities.

- *Crowds* – an anonymity agent [12,13], based on the idea of "blending into a crowd", i.e., hiding user's transactions among transactions of other users. In order to execute anonymous Web transactions using this approach, a user first joins a crowd of users. Any user's request to a Web server is passed to a random member of the crowd who can either submit the request directly to the end server or forward it to another randomly chosen member. In this case neither the end server nor any of the crowd members can determine the origin of the request.

- *Onion-Routing* [14,8] - users submit their requests in as layered encrypted data specifying the cryptographic algorithms and keys. At each pass through each onion router on the way to the recipient, one layer of encryption is removed.

All the above-mentioned tools assume that users have no need or desire to be identified. However, this is a too strong assumption for the Web today where many services require user's identification. One solution that was suggested for private identified access is originated at the Web sites and builds users trust in Internet services. The idea is that when accessing various sites users are guaranteed by the accessed sites that no data is being collected and used about them. Some initiatives exist such as *TRUSTe* [2], that are dedicated to building consumers' trust on the Internet by licensing Web sites to display a "trust-mark" on their sites meaning that a user can safely surf with no need to be concerned about his or her privacy. This trust solution depends on the good will of Web sites and limits the user's access to the licensed sites when privacy is desired.

PRAW, a new non-anonymous privacy model [6,7], allows identification of the users on one hand, and prevention of accurate derivation of users' interests on the other hand. PRAW builds a user profile, uses it to generate faked transactions to mislead a potential eavesdropper, and is able to measure the privacy level achieved. The accuracy of the user profile may impact the performance of a system based on PRAW which might be influenced by the number of user transactions being used for its generation. This study examines the impact on PRAW performance of the number of user transactions being used for profile generation. It is suggested that there is an optimal number of transactions which varies for every user that would be found by a system implementing PRAW during a training phase. The remainder of the paper is organized as follows: section 2 introduces PRAW; Section 3 presents the assumptions and hypotheses regarding the relation between number of transactions for profile generation and privacy, and describes the experiments conducted to illustrate it; section 4 concludes with future research issues.

2   PRAW Overview

2.1   Protecting User Privacy by Hiding the User Profile

We assume that preserving users' privacy requires hiding their interests from eavesdroppers, in order to prevent them from building accurate user profiles. Existing security models such as *Anonimizer* or *Crowds* [3,12,13] try to solve this problem by hiding user's identity. However, this solution is not suitable for many services on the Web where users need to identify themselves in order to receive services.

PRAW offers non-anonymous privacy where users may be identified but their interests still remain hidden. PRAW's main idea is to confuse eavesdroppers by generating additional faked transactions emanating from the user's computer. Since the user profile that eavesdroppers are able to generate is based on data collected from monitoring user's transactions, eavesdroppers see a combination of real and faked transactions but are not able to ascertain the real interests of the users.

However, if faked transactions are generated in random areas of interest, eavesdroppers might apply various techniques to distinguish between the consistent real areas of interests of the user and the faked transactions. It seems that there are two ways avoiding this situation; the first is to generate faked transactions in several distinct areas of interest and confuse the eavesdropper with several different profiles. However, this approach could still enable eavesdroppers to isolate the users' interests from other distinct areas of interest, but the probability is lower. The more distinct faked areas handled, the lower the probability of discovering the profile.

PRAW takes a second approach which generates faked transactions in the users' broader areas of interest. Thus, the general users' areas of interest are exposed, but not their exact private ones. For example, an eavesdropper might discover that a user is interested in the general area of computer security, but will not be able to discover the user's interest in specific algorithms of intrusion detection systems which is kept in private.

PRAW tracks the information accessed by the user while surfing, and generates a user profile on the local computer. In accordance with it, PRAW generates faked transactions relating to the general user's area of interest as expressed in the profile. The result is that the users' real areas of interest become blurred and this makes it impossible to an eavesdropper to generate an accurate user's profile.

To generate faked transactions the system sends queries to a search engine consisting of terms taken from the user profile and other terms randomly drawn from a glossary of terms in the user's general areas of interest. The faked transactions are the system's accesses to Web pages received as the result to those queries. In order to exhibit the user's normal behavior, the system follows links on the retrieved pages to random depth.

2.2   PRAWs Architecture

An eavesdropper is able to compute the user profile based on the information flowing from the Web to the user's computer. Hereafter we call this "external user profile" (EUP) as it is seen from outside the user's computer. The "real (or internal) user profile" (IUP) is based only on user transactions and can be monitored from inside the user's computer. The model consists of three main components: Browser Monitor, Transaction Generator and Profile Meter.

The Browser Monitor analyzes the content of all the user's transactions results (Web pages) while the user is surfing the Web. For each user transaction, the Browser Monitor generates a vector of weighted terms $v_{t^U}^U$ representing that transaction at the time it was performed (t^U).

The Transaction Generator generates faked transactions by combining random terms from an internal glossary relating to the user's general areas of interest with some relevant terms taken from the IUP. The Transaction Generator also randomly accesses selected Web pages received as a result of previous "faked queries", and follows links in depth to imitate user browsing. Each such access to a page is considered a faked transaction. For each faked transactions, the Transaction-Generator builds a vector of term weights $v_{t^T}^T$ representing the faked transaction result at the time the transaction was performed (t^T). The faked transactions vectors are sent to the Profile Meter.

The Transaction Generator generates Tr transactions *in average* for each user's transaction, but not exactly Tr transactions (Tr is the number of faked transactions generated for each user transaction). This is done to prevent eavesdroppers from discovering the regularity of faked transactions among user's transactions.

The profile meter calculates continuously two user profiles, one based on the user's transactions (IUP) and the other based on the faked transactions (FUP), and both are combined to generate the external user profile as an eavesdropper might see it (EUP). The EUP and IUP are used to calculate the privacy level achieved.

$$IUP(t^U) = \sum_{i=0}^{Pr-1} V_{t^U-i}^U$$

IUP is the Internal (real) User Profile at time t^u. It is computed by combining the current user transaction vector $V_{t^U}^U$ with former Pr-1 transaction-vectors (Pr is the number of previous transactions vectors used to form the user profile),

$$FUP(t^T) = \sum_{i=0}^{Pr \times Tr-1} V_{t^T-i}^T$$

FUP is the Faked Transaction Profile at time t^T. It is computed by combining the current faked transaction $V_{t^T}^T$ with former Pr*Tr-1 faked transactions vectors.

$$EUP(t) = IUP(t^u) + FUP(t^T)$$

EUP is the External User Profile at time t. To construct EUP(t), the Profile Meter combines IUP(t^u) and FUP(t^T).

Whenever the IUP(t^u) or the FUP(t^T) changes, the Profile Meter computes the similarity between the internal, hidden profile and the external, visible profile (IUP, EUP) by finding the cosine of the angle between the vectors. This similarity value defines the privacy level achieved at time t.

3   Number of Transactions Included in Profile Generation and Privacy

3.1   Hypothesis

PRAW builds the real user profile from a number of previous user transactions denoted by Pr. Thus, the profile represents the user interests as reflected by the content of the Pr last Web pages he surfed. Some of the most important terms of this profile are used by the Transaction Generator to form faked query to generate the faked transactions. Intuitively, it can be expected, that a higher number of user transactions included in the generation of the profile may result in a more accurate user profile. However, if the user changes his interests within the Pr transactions, the profile reflects a combination of the user's old and new interests.

In this study we examined the impact of the number of user transactions (Pr) used to generate the user profile on PRAW performance. In particular we asked the following research questions:
1. Does the Pr value affect privacy? Moreover, is there a certain Pr value that results in an optimal user profile providing the highest possible privacy level?
2. Is there a fixed Pr value for the optimal profile that is right for all users all the time, or is it that the optimal Pr value is user dependent or time dependent?
   Our hypothesis was that the Pr value affects privacy and that for different users, different Pr values are optimal. We also suspected that the optimal Pr value is not constant even for a user, and might change over time according to user activities.

In order to check our hypothesis a set of experiments were conducted using a special prototype system developed to implement the PRAW model.

3.2 Experiments and Results

Five experienced computer users were asked to surf the Web (search and navigate in computers related pages). Each user accessed about 200 sites and his transactions were recorded. The recorded transactions served as input to a Web surfing simulation system that was used to evaluate the PRAW model. Using the recorded transactions, the simulation browser component imitated the users surfing. It submitted the users' queries to the search engine, accessed the search results, followed the links and spent the same time on a Web page as recorded for the real user transactions. In parallel to simulating "real" transactions, PRAW agent ran and generated faked transactions intended to hide the real user profile. During a simulation session that simulated about 200 user transactions, based on a predefined Pr value, dynamic user profile was generated each time from the previous Pr user transactions. The profile served as the source for terms for the faked transactions. The simulation process was repeated for Pr values of 5, 10, 15, 20, 25, 30, 35, 40, 45 and 50. The process was performed with different Tr values (number of faked transaction for every user's transaction) ranging between 1 and 10. Hence every Pr value was checked with ten different Tr values. In order to evaluate PRAW, the IUP (Internal User Profile), and EUP (External User Profile) were recorded at every transaction for future analysis.

The simulation yielded transactions logs for every Pr value. For each user transaction, the similarity between the IUP and the EUP was calculated. This similarity value represents the degree of privacy achieved, where smaller similarity means higher privacy.

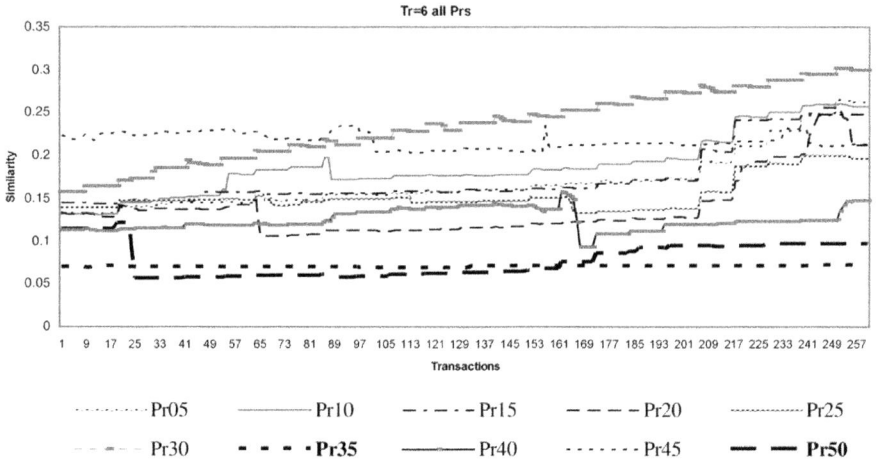

Fig. 1. Privacy level achieved for various Pr values

Figure 1 presents the similarity between IUP and EUP for one user, for all possible Pr values 5, 10, 15...50. Each curve presents the similarity at $Tr = 6$ (6 faked transactions for every real user transaction). The similarity level is presented as a function of the number of transactions performed (also referred to as the time). The results shown by the graph were sampled after the first 50 real user transactions performed in order to assure that a complete profile was built even for the highest Pr

value (*Pr*=50). The graph shows plots of 24 consecutive user's real transactions combined with 240 faked transactions.

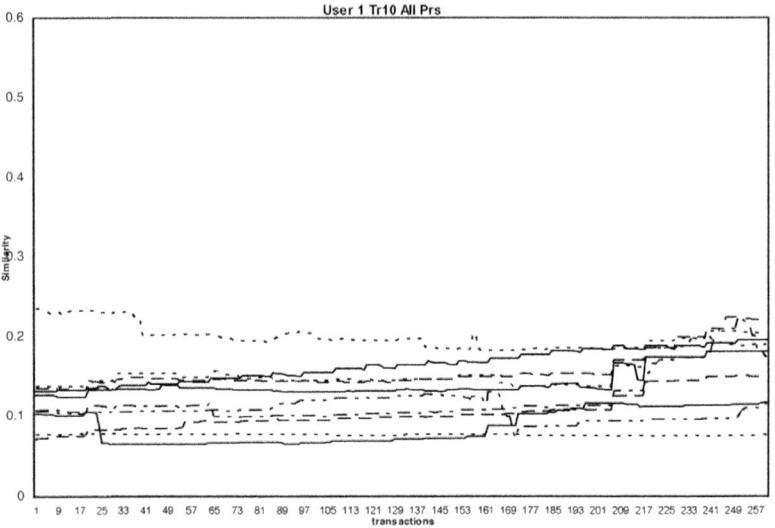

Fig. 2. User 1 Tr=10

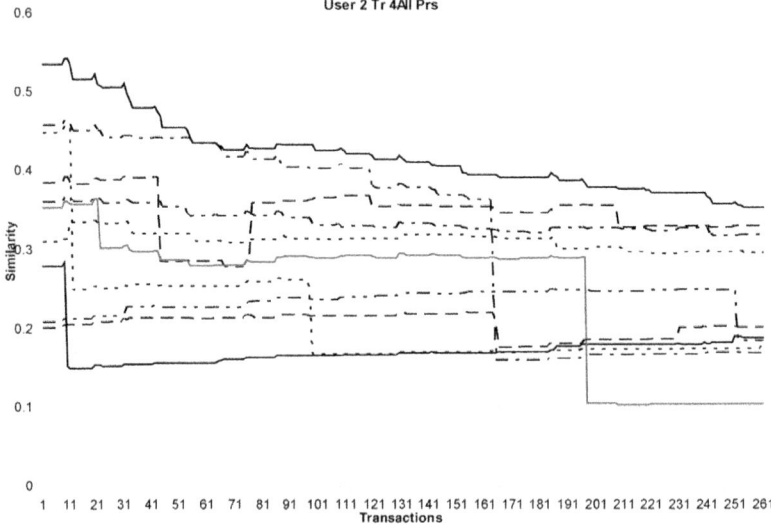

Fig. 3. User 2 Tr=4

Looking at Figure1 it can be seen that at different times different *Pr* values provide the highest privacy, i.e., the lowest similarity between IUP and EUP. For example, for the first 25 transactions, *Pr*=35 (i.e., user profile generated from 35 user transactions) provides the best privacy level. For transactions 26-165 *Pr*=50 provides the best privacy level, and for transactions 166-260 the highest privacy level is achieved, again at *Pr*=35. We observe a consistent behavior for this session and for this user, on which *Pr*=35, and *Pr*=50 provide the best privacy level (*Pr*=35, and *Pr*=50 appear in bold at Figure 1).

The same result was observed for *Pr*-privacy relations for all users and for all *Tr* values. For example, Figure 2 presents the results for *Tr*=10 of the same user observed at figure 1. Figure 3 presents the results for *Tr*=4 for another user. Additional results are not presented here due to space limitation.

It can be seen that the privacy level is not randomly distributed for different *Pr* values. Rather, for each user, and for a particular surfing session, there exists a *Pr* value that provides a noticeable better privacy level. Thus, based on the above observation, it seems that there is not one fixed optimal *Pr* that can be predicted for all users, nor for surfing sessions of a specific user. Rather, it seems that the best privacy level can be achieved by different *Pr* values for different users at different times. *A method to approximate the optimal Pr value for a user and for a session is required.*

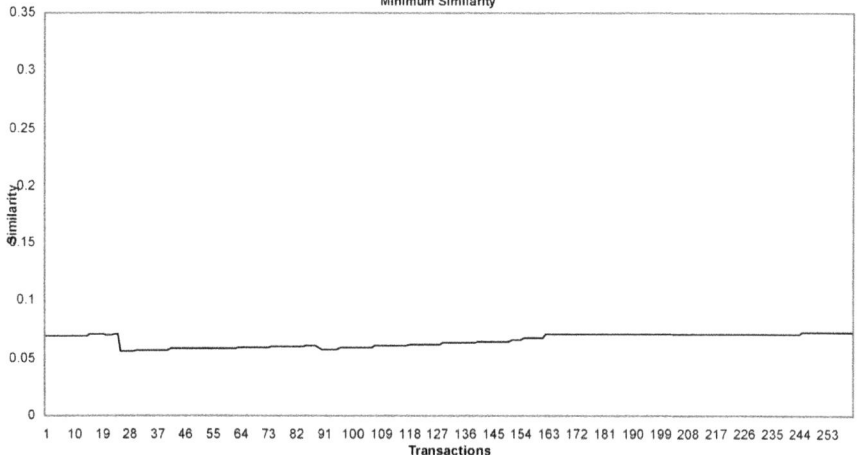

Fig. 4. Minimal similarity (best privacy) during the entire user session

The graph in Figure 4 shows the same user observed on Figure 1 and the same ~260 transactions session. However, on Figure 4 we combine the best privacy achieved by optimal *Pr*s throughout the session. The curve shows the privacy level that might have been achieved by the system if the optimal *Pr* values could have been found and applied throughout the session for the sampled user. It is easy to see that the privacy level that could have been obtained for the optimal *Pr* at each step is very high: similarity[1] for the entire session is ~0.07 compared to similarity levels above 0.25 for certain Prs at several points of time in Figure 1 and even higher in Figures 2 and 3.

Theoretically, to achieve the best privacy level during a session, a system needs to generate candidate profiles for all possible *Pr*s, examine the privacy level achieved by using each of the *Pr*s, and select the best *Pr* for the user in each period of time.

---

[1] High privacy=low similarity

However, this is not feasible because applying more than one Pr results in an impractical traffic load, as explained below.

The Pr controls the number of real user transactions considered for the generation for the user's profile. Different Prs result in different user profiles. Different user profiles result in different faked queries. Different faked queries result in different retrieved sets of Web pages that the system needs to access to form the faked transactions. Thus, different Pr values actually result in different faked transactions to be performed. However, if for example the system would generate ten transactions ($Tr=10$) for each of the Pr values in order to find the best Pr value, traffic would be overloaded and slow.

We suggest that a practical method would be to learn an initial Pr value for every user from a training set by a batch learning process similar to the experiment described in this paper. During the batch learning, privacy levels should be calculated for each user and for all Pr values, and for a set of a few hundred users transactions recorded by the system. Then, a Pr value providing on average the best results is selected for every user, and applied later by the system in real user sessions.

However, this solution is still not complete as it is not adaptive to changes in user's surfing behavior that might necessitate a change in the Pr value. We suggest constantly monitoring privacy level, so that when it gets below a certain threshold it triggers a new batch learning process that will be applied on the latest transactions as the training set. This of course requires continuous recording of the latest transactions performed by the user.

4   Conclusions and Future Research

This study has demonstrated that the optimal level of privacy that can be achieved by PRAW is user and time dependent. PRAW suggests adjusting the Pr parameter controlling the number of previous user transactions being used as input to the profile generation process. We have confirmed the importance of setting the optimal Pr and demonstrated experimentally that there exists an optimal value of Pr that can optimize PRAW performance i.e., maximize privacy levels achieved.

We have found that the optimal value of Pr is different for each user and is relatively stable, but not constant during a user session. Thus, we suggest adding to PRAW a learning component that finds the optimal values of Pr using examples provided by the user as training data.

The learning component should be activated periodically in order to adapt PRAW to changes in the user surfing behavior. In addition the privacy level should be constantly monitored for each user so that a low level of privacy triggers the learning process.

Monitoring the privacy level and using different values of Pr accordingly does not change the complexity of PRAW, hence dynamic selection of the Pr value can improve the performance of the system without additional major overhead.

Further studies are required in order to explore the possibilities of the suggested model and the impact of users' behavior on the level of privacy they might achieve. Better knowledge about users' behavior may enable dynamic prediction of Pr values and thus enable the system to provide a privacy level closer to the optimal privacy possible.

References

1. Balabanovic', M., and Shoham, Y. Fab: Content-Based, Collaborative Recommendation. Communications of the ACM 40(3), (1997) pp. 66–72.
2. Benassi, P.: TRUSTe: An online privacy seal program. Communication of the ACM, 42(2) (1999) 56–59
3. Claessens, J., Preneel, B., Vandewalle, J.: Solutions for anonymous communication on the Internet. Proceedings of the 1999 IEEE International Carnahan Conference on Security Technology 487 (1999) 298–303
4. Claypool, M., Le, P.,Wased, M.,Brown, D. Implicit Interest Indicators. Proceedings of IUI 2001 2001 International Conference on Intelligent User Interfaces (2001) 33–40.
5. Crossen, A., Budzik, J., Warner, M., Birnbaum, L., Hammond, K. J. XLibris: An Automated Library Research assistant. Proceedings of IUI 2001 2001 International Conference on Intelligent User Interfaces (2001) 49–53.
6. Elovici, Y. , Shapira,B., Mashiach, A,: A New Privacy Model for Hiding Group Interests while Accessing the Web., In Proceedinsg of The ACM Workshop in Electronic Society, at The 9th ACM Conference on Computer and Communication Security, November 2002.
7. Elovici, Y., Shapira, B., Maschiach, A, : A New Privacy Model for Web Surfing. NGITS (2002) (Lecture Notes): 45–57
8. Goldschlag, D. M., Reed, M. G., Syverson, P. F.: Hiding Routing Information, Information Hiding, R. Anderson (editor), Springer-Verlag LLNCS 1174 (1996) 137–150
9. Hanani, U., Shapira, B. and Shoval, P. Information Filtering: Overview of issues, research and systems. User Modelling and User Adapted Interaction 11(3), (2001) 203–259.
10. Grabber, E., Gibbons, P.B., Matias, Y., Mayer, A.: How to Make Personalized Web Browsing Simple, Secure, and Anonymous. Proceedings of Financial Cryptography (1997)
11. Lieberman, H., Autonomous Interface agents. Proceedings of the ACM Conference on Computers and Human Interfaces, CHI 97, Atlanta, Georgia (1997).
12. Reiter, M.K., Rubin, A.D.: Crowds: Anonymity for Web Transactions, ACM Transactions on Information and System Security, 1(1) (1998) 66–92
13. Reiter, M.K., Rubin, A.D.: Anonymous Web Transactions with Crowds, Communications of the ACM 42(2) (1999) 32–38
14. Syverson, P. F., Goldschlag, D. M., & Reed, M. G. (1997). Anonymous Connections and Onion Routing, Proceedings of the 18th Annual Symposium on Security and Privacy, IEEE CS Press, Oakland, CA, 44–54

Interfaces for Eliciting New User Preferences in Recommender Systems

Sean M. McNee, Shyong K. Lam, Joseph A. Konstan, and John Riedl

GroupLens Research Project
Department of Computer Science and Engineering
University of Minnesota–Twin Cities
Minneapolis, MN, 55455 USA
{mcnee, lam, konstan, riedl}@cs.umn.edu

Abstract. Recommender systems build user models to help users find the items they will find most interesting from among many available items. One way to build such a model is to ask the user to rate a selection of items. The choice of items selected affects the quality of the user model generated. In this paper, we explore the effects of letting the user participate in choosing the items that are used to develop the model. We compared three interfaces to elicit information from new users: having the system choose items for users to rate, asking the users to choose items themselves, and a mixed-initiative interface that combines the other two methods. We found that the two pure interfaces both produced accurate user models, but that directly asking users for items to rate increases user loyalty in the system. Ironically, this increased loyalty comes despite a lengthier signup process. The mixed-initiative interface is not a reasonable compromise as it created less accurate user models with no increase in loyalty.

1 Introduction

Recommender systems help users sort through the vast quantities of information deluging them every day. These systems build user models based on users' stated preferences for items in a domain (e.g., ratings of movies) and use these models to generate personalized recommendations for the user.

All of these systems share a common problem: generating recommendations for new users of the system. One solution is to make non-personalized recommendations at first, dynamically learning the user's preferences and incrementally adjusting the user model. Brusilovsky, however, claims that this approach will not learn accurate enough models, and suggests that the system will still need to elicit information from the user [3].

In this paper, we explore the question of how to elicit user preference information in the context of recommender systems. We contrast system-controlled approaches, where the system decides which items the user can rate, with methods that allow the user to specify some or all of the items to be rated.

P. Brusilovsky et al. (Eds.): UM 2003, LNAI 2702, pp. 178–187, 2003.
© Springer-Verlag Berlin Heidelberg 2003

2   Eliciting New User Preferences

There are several effective strategies for creating user models in recommender systems. One common strategy is to use the text of items a user likes to build a keyword profile and then recommend new items that match the profile. These content-based filtering systems work well when the content of items is amenable to machine processing. Other effective strategies for building models include the use of Bayesian networks [2], adaptive decision trees [13], and rule-based systems [5].

An alternative family of strategies, called collaborative filtering (CF), works directly with users' preferences to build a user model [11]. Typically, CF systems generate recommendations for a target user by generating a "neighborhood" of other like-minded users. The preferences found in the neighborhood are then used to create personalized recommendations for the target user.

CF systems can make recommendations in any domain and are more likely than content-based systems to recommend serendipitous items, items to which users may never have been exposed but may like. However, CF systems are particularly afflicted by the new user problem [11] as they typically require several ratings from a new user before they can find similar users with which to make personalized recommendations.

The obvious solution: ask new users to rate items. But how should the system select items to ask the users about that are both useful to the system and will not bore or alienate new users? Asking a user to rate the movie "The Godfather" doesn't help a movie recommender, since most people have seen "The Godfather" and enjoyed it. Asking the user to rate the movie "Grand Exit" from 1935 is equally useless, since the odds that the user has seen the movie are quite low–regardless of how much the system would gain from knowing the user's rating of that movie. Therefore, a solution to this problem should attempt to balance cost to the new user, in terms of frustration, time, and effort spent, with the amount of information the system would gain from each rating.

Pennock et al. proposed that information-theoretic calculations might prove useful for solving this new user problem in a CF-based recommender [9]. Rashid et al. showed that choosing items with a high score on a metric that combined an entropy calculation with a measure of the item's popularity reduced users' rating effort while maintaining high recommendation quality [10]. This metric is simple to calculate and was more effective than other metrics that personalized the items presented to the users.

Brusilovsky discusses three approaches to collaborative user modeling in building personalized hypermedia systems [3]. The first approach automatically updates the user model based on user-provided information. This is implicit in collaborative filtering since the user model is based on user-provided ratings. The entropy calculations from Rashid et al. employ the second of these approaches: to directly ask the user for data the system needs to update the model. Brusilovsky's last approach allows users to make direct changes to their model. In the context of the new user problem, this translates into allowing the users to directly specify what items they are interested in, instead of having the system question them.

3   New Interfaces: Who's in Charge?

In order to effectively test how these different methods of creating user models compare to each other in a recommender system, we created user interfaces to reflect these different model-building approaches. We then compared these alternative interfaces for new users to enter preference information in a CF-based recommender system.

Conventional user interfaces fall into a spectrum of use from user-controlled interfaces (such as a word processor) to system-controlled interfaces (such as an ATM) [1,12]. Splitting the difference between the two extremes are mixed-initiative interfaces [1,5,8,14]. These interfaces are usually viewed as a dialogue between the system and the user with each side contributing to the interaction. Mixed-initiative interfaces can take many forms from augmented flight control systems where the computer monitors and maintains various aspects of controlling the plane reporting potential problems to the pilot, to 'smart' CAD programs that recommend modifications to various building structures for compliance with safety and fire codes [6].

The entropy-based calculations from Rashid et al. are an example of a system-controlled interface for soliciting new user preference information. Using interfaces of this type the system can efficiently gather information it needs to create high quality user models. Intelligently choosing which items to ask a new user is very important, but it limits the user to choose only from the items the system selects.

Instead of prompting the user to rate particular items, a user-controlled interface allows users to tell the system which items they want to rate. Interfaces of this type may be more difficult for new users since the users will be required to remember items with no context or prompting. At the same time, this interface will allow users to more fully express their interests across the entire universe of items and create a profile that they feel more accurately reflects who they are.

Lately, mixed-initiative interfaces have focused on the interaction of multiple system agents and one human user making decisions together [1,8]. We instead will focus on the idea of a mixed-initiative interface as providing a choice to the user of a system. Thus, our mixed-initiative interface is a composite of the system-controlled and user-controlled interfaces (Figure 1). As such, it should provide the benefits of both interfaces by generating high quality user models that the users believe accurately reflect their tasks and opinions.

In summary, we hypothesize that human-controlled interfaces will have higher user satisfaction, whereas system-controlled interfaces will generate better user models. The mixed-initiative interface should perform better than both of the other interfaces, i.e., have the highest user satisfaction and generate the best user models.

4   Experiment

We performed a study using new users of MovieLens (www.movielens.org), an online collaborative filtering-based movie recommender system. New users registering for a MovieLens account were asked to volunteer for an experiment

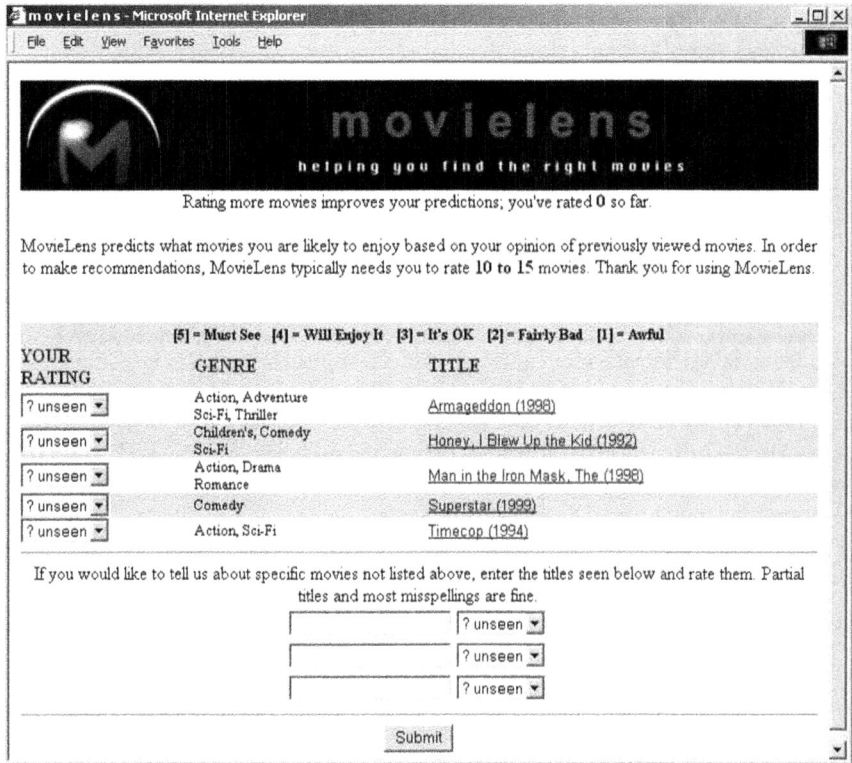

Fig. 1. The mixed-initiative interface includes elements from the system-controlled (top half) and user-controlled (bottom half) interfaces

concerning alternative interfaces for rating movies. The signup process requires new users to rate a minimum number of movies, typically 10 to 15, on a 5-star scale before being allowed to receive personalized recommendations.

Users agreeing to participate were randomly placed into one of three groups: a group that received a system-controlled rating interface, one that received a user-controlled rating interface, and one that received a mixed-initiative rating interface.

The system-controlled interface is based on the log(popularity) * entropy movie selection metric presented in [10]. The system presented ten titles at a time, randomly chosen from the top 250 titles as scored by the metric. This interface is similar to the current signup method used in MovieLens, and is represented in the top half of Figure 1.

The user-controlled interface presented the user with five empty text fields per page. The user is asked to enter the titles of movies to rate. Upon submission, the user confirmed her entries by selecting her choice from a list of possible title matches as generated by a nearest edit distance algorithm. The page gave no hints or suggestions as to what movies should be rated and is similar to the bottom half of Figure 1.

The mixed-initiative interface is a hybrid of the system and user-controlled interfaces and is shown in Figure 1. Five system-selected movies and three text fields are shown on each page. The user can choose to rate the presented movies, enter titles of her own choice, or both. Since this interface both presented movies to rate and provided open text boxes, the presented movies could have acted as hints for items to rate via the textbox interface.

4.1   Experimental Method

Users were asked to rate movies using the given interface until they had rated 12 movies. They were then given the opportunity to continue rating movies using their assigned interface or to end the signup process and start receiving recommendations. Once the user finished rating items, they were asked to complete a brief survey before entering MovieLens. The survey consisted of the following five questions, each asked on a 5-point scale.

1. How well did you understand this signup process? Answers ranged from "Did Not Understand" to "Completely Understood".

2. How hard was it for you to find/enter movies that you have seen? Answers ranged from "Easy" to "Difficult".

3. How much time did it take you to complete this signup process? Answers ranged from "Short Period" to "Long Period".

4. How would you describe this interface for entering movie ratings? Answers ranged from "Simple" to "Complex".

5. How well do the movies you rated represent your movie tastes? Answers ranged from "Not At All" to "Perfectly".

4.2   Results

A total of 225 new users participated in the experiment. 192 users successfully completed the signup process and 163 completed the survey.

For each group, Table 1 shows the percentage of users who completed the signup process, the average number of ratings provided, and the average time required for each user to provide 12 ratings. Mixed-initiative users had the highest completion rate while system-controlled users rated the most items on average. Users receiving the user-controlled interface took far more time to complete the process and did not provide as many ratings as users in the mixed-initiative or system-controlled groups.

We used Mean Absolute Error (MAE), a common measure of recommendation accuracy [7], to measure the quality of the user models for each interface. MAE is the average absolute difference in actual rating for an item compared to the prediction the system would have generated for that item. Thus, a high quality user model would have low MAE.

The "30 based on 12" and "30 based on N" MAE calculations were run by taking either the first 12 or all N ratings from the signup process as the user's model and then generating predictions for 30 randomly selected ratings the user

Table 1. Statistics on the Completion of the Signup Process

	User	Mixed	System
Percentage of Users Finishing Signup	80%	92%	88%
Mean Number of Ratings	14	30	36
Mean Time to 12 Ratings	565 sec	382 sec	286 sec

entered into the system after finishing signup. For the "All But One" calculation [2], one of the first 12 user ratings was removed and a prediction was generated for it using the other 11 ratings as the user model. This was repeated for each of the first 12 ratings. In all cases, we computed the MAE for each individual user, and averaged the per-user MAE's to compute an overall measure of quality.

Table 2 shows the MAE results. At odds with our hypotheses, the user-controlled interface had the best MAE, followed closely by the system-controlled interface. The mixed-initiative interface generated the worst user models. Using either the first 12 ratings or all ratings users provided during the startup process made no difference. The "All But One" condition has higher MAEs across the board and shows a difference between the user-controlled interface and the other interfaces.

Table 2. Mean Absolute Error (MAE) calculations for the three signup interfaces, based on a 5-star rating scale. Lower is better

	User	Mixed	System
30 based on original 12	0.79	0.88	0.81
30 based on all of signup (N)	0.78	0.88	0.81
"All But One" on first 12	0.90	0.99	1.03

Table 3 shows the survey results. Users understood the signup process and felt the interface was not complex. Even though the user-controlled group took twice as long to finish, most reported that the signup process took a short amount of time to complete. In agreement with our hypotheses, the user-controlled group also felt that the items they entered more accurately represented their tastes than those entered by the other two groups. Finally, the system-controlled interface was voted to be the hardest to locate and rate items that the user had already seen.

Although Table 2 showed that the user-controlled group had the lowest percentage of users finishing the signup process, the longevity statistics in Table 4 show that these users had the highest number of logins, highest percentage of active users (defined as users who gave at least 10 ratings after signup), and the highest number of total ratings provided in the system after signup was completed. In contrast, the mixed-initiative group had the most users finish the

Table 3. Percentage of users giving positive responses to survey questions

	User	Mixed	System
Understood signup process	95%	96%	93%
Easy to find items to rate	59%	67%	40%
Short amount of time to complete	70%	75%	69%
User interface was not complex	77%	88%	88%
Preferences reflect tastes	63%	30%	19%

signup process, but tied for the lowest percentage continue to use MovieLens and provided fewer ratings than the user-controlled group.

Table 4. Statistics about longevity of users from the different interfaces. Longevity was measured as active use in the system after 25 days

	User	Mixed	System
Percentage of active users	35%	21%	21%
Mean ratings entered post signup	225	159	125
Mean number of user logins, post signup	5.1	3.8	3.2

5   Discussion

Even though the user-controlled group did not feel they were spending a long time in the signup process, compared to users from the other two groups, they in fact spent nearly twice as long (9.4 vs. 5.6 minutes on average). Because they received no prompting or hints for movie titles, it took time to recall items to rate. We believe that users in the user-controlled group did not notice the effort because asking them to recall titles created focus and engagement with the system. These users are the most likely to keep returning to the system and provide more ratings. They also thought the system best understood their tastes. In some sense of the word, we could say these users were more "loyal" to the system.

The fact that the user-controlled group had the best MAE results is surprising and very intriguing. To confirm our results, we re-ran the MAE calculations against another CF-based recommender engine. This second engine produced uniformly higher MAEs but still maintained the relative ordering of the interfaces for all three experiments. These results confirm that users who directly choose items can do as good of a job defining their user models as a system probing users for the information. Users know what is good for them.

The difference in MAE for the system-controlled interface between the "All But One" test and the "Predict 30" tests also requires investigation. The items rated in the system-controlled interface were taken from the log(popularity) * entropy metric. Further analysis shows that high entropy movies are harder to make accurate predictions on; these items have a higher MAE for all users. That is, even though high entropy items lead to good user models, even the best user model will have trouble making predictions for these items. Because of this property, we expect the "All But One" metric to have higher MAEs for both the system-controlled and mixed-initiative interfaces, and this is exactly what we see in Table 2.

While this may explain the high MAE for the mixed-initiative interface in the "All But One" test, it does not explain its poor performance for the other two conditions. Just as the mixed-initiative interface can be split into two halves, the ratings gathered from users in this group can be split into two distributions: a system-controlled part and a user-controlled part. Each distribution looks similar to the distributions found for its respective parent interface. More importantly, each half has different MAE scores: for example, in "30 Based on N", the system-controlled interface had an MAE of 0.90 and the user-controlled interface had an MAE of 0.64.

We theorize the two interfaces interacted with each other; by explictly listing titles, the system-controlled half provided movie hints that could have been used by users to generate titles for the user-controlled half. Seeing this, users internally renormalized their ratings, rating items in the user-controlled half higher and items in the system-controlled half of the interface lower than the users from the respective parent interfaces. This interaction is important as it altered the makeup and lowered the quality of the user model the interface generated. As system designers, we need to be aware of how subtle interactions in interface elements can profoundly affect the user models our systems generate.

Although the mixed-initiative interface produced the worst models, its users voted the interface high in terms of ease of rating items they had seen. Moreover, users rated this interface as taking the shortest amount of time to complete the signup process, even though it took longer for users to complete than the system-controlled interface. Again this can be traced to higher user engagement with the system. Mixed-initiative users, while not as loyal as the user-controlled, provided more ratings than either of the other groups, and felt the system understood their tastes better than the system-controlled group. They did not, however, come back as often.

6 Conclusion

Both system- and user-controlled interfaces generate high quality user models. New users tended to take a longer period of time to complete the signup process when using a user-controlled interface when compared to a system-controlled interface. Moreover, these users did not notice the extra time required to complete the signup process and also felt that the system better understood their tastes. This comes at a price, however. Only 80 percent of users in the user-controlled group finished the signup process, compared to 92 percent for mixed-initiative and 88 percent for system-controlled. Of those that finished the signup process, there was a 15 percent higher user retention rate from the user-controlled group than the other two groups.

We theorize these users were more enagaged and focused when using the system because of the higher burden and extra control associated with the user-controlled interface. The economic theory of reciprocity suggests in part that users who put forth more effort into a system will expect more from the system in return [4]. Thus, by creating a signup process with higher burden and extra control, those users who complete the process are more likely to be loyal users.

A hybrid mixed-initiative interface does not provide a sensible alternative to the two other interfaces. Users of this interface were the least likely to return and had the worst user models. We also believe that the components of a hybrid interface may interact with each other in unexpected ways, affecting the quality of the user model the system generates for users of the interface.

It appears that there will often be a tradeoff between giving users control and increasing their workload. Depending on the goals of the application being built, system designers need to decide whether low user burden or high user loyalty is more important and choose an interface to elicit user preferences and generate user models appropriately.

Acknowledgements. We would like to thank Dan Cosley and Istvan Albert for their suggestions and comments on early drafts of this paper. This work is supported by grants from the NSF (DGE 95-54517, IIS 96-13960, IIS 97-34442, IIS 99-78717, and IIS 01-02229), and by Net Perceptions, Inc.

References

1. Allen, J. (1999) Mixed Initiative Interaction. Proceedings IEEE Intelligent Systems. 14 (6), pp. 18–23.
2. Breese, J., Heckerman, D. and Kadie, C. (1998) Empirical Analysis of Predictive Algorithms for Collaborative Filtering. Proceedings of UAI 1998. Pp. 43–52.
3. Brusilovsky, P. (1996) Methods and techniques of adaptive hypermedia. User Modeling and User-Adapted Interaction. 6 (2–3), pp. 87–129.
4. Fehr, E. and Gächter, S. (2000) Fairness and Retaliation: The Economics of Reciprocity. Journal of Economic Perspectives. 14(3), pp. 159–181.
5. Flemming, M. and Cohen, R. (1999) User Modeling in the Design of Interactive Interface Agents. Proceedings of User Modeling 1999. Pp. 67–76.
6. Fu, M. C., Hayes, C. C., and East, E. W. (1997) SEDAR: Expert Critiquing System for Flat and Low Slope Roof Design and Review. Journal of Computing in Civil Engineering. 11(1), pp. 60–69.
7. Herlocker, J., Konstan J, A., Borchers, A., and Riedl, J. (1999) An Algorithmic Framework for Performing Collaborative Filtering. Proceedings of SIGIR 1999. Pp. 230–237.
8. Horvitz, E. (1999) Principles of Mixed-Initiative User Interfaces. Proceedings of CHI 1999. Pp. 159–166.
9. Pennock, D., and Horvitz, E. (2000) Collaborative Filtering by Personality Diagnosis: A Hybrid Memory- and Model-based Approach. Proceedings of UAI 2000. Pp. 473–480.

10. Rashid, A. M., Albert, I., Cosley, D., Lam, S. K., McNee, S. M., Konstan, J. A., and Riedl, J. (2002) Getting to Know You: Learning New User Preferences in Recommender Systems. Proceedings of IUI 2002. Pp. 127–134.
11. Resnick, P., Iacovou, N., Sushak, M., Bergstrom, P., and Riedl, J. (1994) GroupLens: An Open Architecture for Collaborative Filtering of Netnews. Proceedings of CSCW 94. Pp. 175–186.
12. Shneiderman, B. (1998) Designing the User Interface, third edition. Reading, MA: Addison Wesley.
13. Stolze, M. and Strobel, M. (2001) Utility-Based Decision Tree Optimization: A Framework for Adaptive Interviewing. Proceedings of User Modeling 2001. Pp. 105–116.
14. Terveen, L. G. (1993) Intelligent Systems as Cooperative Systems. International Journal of Intelligent Systems. 3, 2–4, pp. 217–250.

Modeling Multitasking Users

Malcolm Slaney, Jayashree Subrahmonia, and Paul Maglio

IBM Almaden Research Center
650 Harry Road, San Jose, CA 95120
malcolm@ieee.org, jays@us.ibm.com, pmaglio@almaden.ibm.com

Abstract. This paper describes an algorithm to cluster and segment sequences of low-level user actions into sequences of distinct high-level user tasks. The algorithm uses text contained in interface windows as evidence of the state of user–computer interaction. Window text is summarized using latent semantic indexing (LSI). Hierarchical models are built using expectation–maximization to represent users as macro models. User actions for each task are modeled with a micro model based on a Gaussian mixture model to represent the LSI space. The algorithm's performance is demonstrated in a test of web-browsing behavior, which also demonstrates the value of the temporal constraint provided by the macro model.

1 Problem Statement

To design interfaces that effectively support human-computer interaction, we must first understand the complex behavior computer users exhibit when carrying out their jobs. Apple Computer, for example, popularized an approach to interaction design based on observing users as they perform their work and then analyzing how users interact with specific software components [8]. This type of interaction design optimizes interfaces for individual users performing individual tasks. Our approach, by contrast, supposes individual users constantly shift among tasks, seamlessly interleaving low-level activities in the pursuit of high-level goals [3]. Here, we describe a method for modeling users engaged in a sequence of many different tasks.

Models of multitasking users can be used by adaptive or attentive user interfaces [2, 10, 11], which monitor user behavior in order to anticipate user needs. These sorts of systems aim to automatically provide users with additional information just when it would be most helpful. By relying on a user model that keeps very close tabs on users shifting tasks, such systems can potentially provide very precisely targeted information.

Our approach of modeling multitasking users has applications beyond the creation or adaptation of individual user interfaces. For instance, a corporation might want to understand the behavior of a computer system used by large number of employees, as they use a number of applications to perform their tasks, and optimize overall system cost. This sort of large-scale interface optimization requires understanding the behavior of a large number of users as they move from task to task during the day.

In this paper, we describe a method for discovering and building a hierarchical model of user activities from unlabeled data. Given a trace of user activities, we segment the user data and learn multiple micro models, each corresponding to a separate "task." Each task is defined by a set of actions that are represented as a single micro

P. Brusilovsky et al. (Eds.): UM 2003, LNAI 2702, pp. 188–197, 2003.
© Springer-Verlag Berlin Heidelberg 2003

model. A macro model controls switching between micro models of individual tasks. These models can take many forms, including discrete Markov chains and continuous hidden Markov models (HMM) [7]. We demonstrate the time-series clustering algorithm with a simple web-browsing example.

2   Related Work

Work in user modeling has focused mainly on building a single model of a user's activities. For instance, Davison and Hirsch [4] describe a system called IPAM that builds a table which predicts the next command given a list of past commands. At any point in time, they predict the most likely next command by indexing into a table with the last N commands (where N is between 0 and 5). The table is updated in real-time as the user enters new commands and the correct Unix command is predicted upwards of 70% of the time. In our approach, each micro model makes the same type of predictions as IPAM, but our macro model captures the relationship between a set of tasks with different probabilities.

Horvitz and his colleagues [6] describe a system that uses a Bayesian model to infer a software user's goals. They developed a language to link the user's and computer's actions to elemental features that can be used by the inference engine. In this work, we use the text showing in an active window to judge the state of the interactive system.

Westphal and Syeda-Mahmood [14] learn a model of user's behavioral state as they interact with a video browser. Given a sequence of low-level events such as "fast forward" or "play" the system learns user's states such as "aimless browse" or "found something interesting". Their approach is supervised; they train the system with a small set of labeled data. The user states their goal and the system then learns the corresponding pattern of low-level events. Our approach on the other hand is completely unsupervised. (Although in a real application somebody would probably look at the micro models and assign them names.)

Our work builds on the hidden Markov experts ideas proposed by Weigend 13.. His goal was to automatically cluster the time-series data and build models that predict different portions of the data with different experts. Our goal is to simply label the data and we extend Weigend's work by using a novel text feature to capture the user's state.

3   Hierarchical Segmentation Algorithm

We cluster time-series data with a hierarchy of models. Figure 1 illustrates the basic model. In this work, a set of high-level models with three states (S_i) determines the high-level behavior of the signal. For instance, each macro state (S_i) might correspond to one speaker in a speaker-segmentation task, one user task in a user-interface interaction recognition task, or one type of multimedia content. We assume that the system can move from one macro state to another at any time, under control of transition probabilities that are assumed or learned from the data. Each macro state controls execution of its own micro model, which outputs feature vectors based on its own transition and output probabilities. The macro state of the system is hidden, except for the change in feature output probabilities captured by the different micro models. Each macro state controls a micro

190   M. Slaney, J. Subrahmonia, and P. Maglio

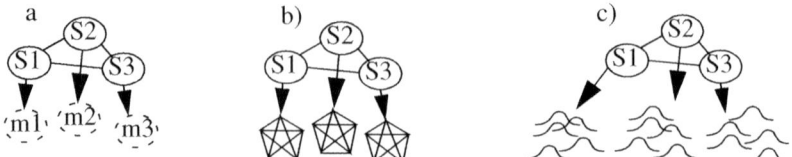

Fig. 1. A hierarchy of models. a) The general model is a macro model with states Si, each macro state has its own micro model (mi) of arbitrary complexity to generate output data. b) A specific form of hierarchical model with micro models implemented using five-state fully-connected Markov models. c) A continuos model where each micro model is implemented using Gaussian mixture models (GMM). This is the form described in this paper.

model that generates features we can observe. These micro models can take many different forms.

A discrete hierarchical model is shown in Figure 1b. In this case, we are interested, for example, in modeling a user's interaction with a computer interface using a discrete set of features. When a user is performing the "create a database" task, he or she will step through particular dialog boxes and tabbed windows. When in the "file open" dialog box, the probability that the user will go to the "name database" dialog box will depend on whether the "create a database" macro model is active. We model the system with a set of (hidden) macro states described by a Markov model. Each micro model is represented by its own Markov model, where the micro-state output is equal to the state label. The model in Figure 1b generates signals that switch between models. When described this way, the model is not a simple hidden Markov model.

Figure 1c shows the model structure described in this paper. In this case the macro states of the system are described with a Markov model, each macro state controlling a single micro model implemented with Gaussian mixture models (GMM). A GMM micro model corresponds to the output probabilities in a conventional HMM. This type of model is good for data with little structure and continuous features such as for speaker segmentation and for modeling and labeling multimedia data.

Figure 2 shows an overview of the hierarchical segmentation algorithm we use to cluster, segment and summarize the user's actions. We use the text on the user's screen at each point in time as input to this algorithm. Latent semantic indexing (LSI), described in Section 3.1, encodes the interface's text as a multidimensional feature vector as a function of time. The best segmentation of the user signal and the parameters of the micro model are estimated using the expectation–maximization (EM) algorithm as described in Section 3.2.

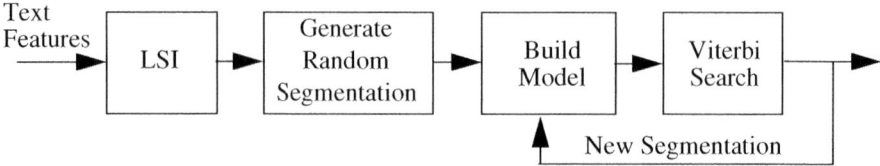

Fig. 2. Block diagram of the hierarchical clustering and segmentation algorithm.

3.1   Text Features via LSI

Actions need to be encoded in a manner that allows us to associate probabilities with the user's events. In this work we consider the text on the screen, due to the user's actions, as a good indication of what the user is trying to do. A "Print" dialog box contains words about printing, while a help page gives information about the options a user has. There are many ways to describe an action. One application might use the words "open document" while another might use "open file." Latent semantic indexing (LSI) gives us a feature set that spans these differences [5].

We use LSI to form a feature vector that summarizes the text contained in each window displayed to the user. LSI is often used in information retrieval to cluster documents and for determining the similarity between a document and a semantic query. LSI creates a bag-of-words model for each document. A term-frequency histogram is formed by counting how many times each word occurs in each document, regardless of what words precede or follow each word. This data is then used as input to a singular-value decomposition (SVD) that finds a low dimensional sub-space that approximates the original histogram space.

A feature space based on LSI solves two difficult problems associated with semantic information retrieval: synonyms and polysemy. Often, two or more words have the same meaning—synonyms. For information retrieval, we want to use any synonym to retrieve the same information. Conversely, many words have multiple meanings—polysemy. For example, apple in a story about a grocery store is likely to have a different meaning from Apple in a story about a computer store.

Changes in semantic space are based on angles, rather than on distance. A simple "sentence" such as "Yes!" has the same semantic content as "Yes, yes!" Yet the second sentence contains twice as many words, and, in semantic space, it will have a vector magnitude that is twice as large. After computing the SVD and projecting the raw histogram data into a low-dimensional subspace, we normalize[1] each document vector so it has a vector length of 1. This normalized vector is a semantic feature that describes what we know about the user's actions at each point in time.

In this work, we use GMMs to form the micro models that describe each task. A GMM models the probability distribution of semantic events that form one task using a sum of N_m Gaussian "bumps" 7.. This is a simple model since any one topic (represented by one Gaussian) can follow any other topic (another Gaussian) with equal probability. Richer micro models are also possible.

3.2   Training

We use the EM algorithm to train a hierarchy of models. Given an initial set of models, we compute the best macro- and micro-level models. All the data corresponding to a macro state are used to train the micro model corresponding to the macro state. We re-

---

[1] Note, normalizing all document vectors so they have unit length does not make the pattern discrimination easier—we lose information when this is done. But the resulting vectors all lie on the unit sphere and are a better match for the diagonal-covariance GMMs we use to model their distribution.

peat the procedure until we reach a stable solution. Training the micro model involves estimating the output probabilities of the GMM.

The segmentation training algorithm is a straightforward application of EM. We describe the approach by segmenting a discrete signal with N multidimensional points and finding N_c clusters with N_m states in each micro model. The topology is shown in Figure 1c. More details on this class of algorithms is in Weigend's paper 13..

Assumption: We assume that the macro model has N_c states, with a self-loop probability of $1 - \varepsilon$ and a probability of a transition to any other state of $\varepsilon/(N_c - 1)$. This simple model encourages temporal continuity on the macro-state sequence. It is equivalent to saying that on average a user spends $1/(1 - \varepsilon)$ time steps performing each task, and any one task is equally likely to follow any other task. Richer models, as represented by different Markov macro models, do not change the algorithm shown below.

Initialization: Choose $N_c - 1$ points in the region $(1, N)$. These points define an initial segmentation. If any segment has too few points, choose a new segmentation. For each segment, build a micro model (m_i) which captures the transition probabilities. These are the initial m_i models. See Section 3.3 for more details.

E-step: Given the models, use the Viterbi algorithm [7] to find the path through the lattice that has the maximum likelihood. We can use this path to decode the signal and decide the macro and micro states that are most likely to generate each portion of the signal.

Termination test: Exit this loop when (a) the signal's temporal cluster assignments do not change or (b) after 10 iterations.

Degenerate check: Make sure that all models are used to cluster some portion of the signal. If there is no data assigned to one model (M_i) then find the cluster (M_j) with the largest temporal support. Concatenate all the segments assigned to M_j and split this signal at a random point. Model M_i is relearned from the portion of the signal before the split point; Model M_j is relearned from the portion of the signal after the split point. See Section 3.4

M-step: For each cluster (M_i) concatenate all the chosen portions of the signal. Build a new model (m_i) which captures the transition and output probabilities of the data at this state. Return to the E-step.

The micro model, m_i, used in the E-step and trained in the M-step can take many forms. It can be a time-varying Markov model or a simple GMM as we describe in the rest of this paper.

In practice, the performance of this algorithm depends on how the models are initialized and what happens when a model becomes degenerate because it no longer wins any of the time-series data in the E-step.

3.3   Initialization

Clusters with a k-means algorithm [7] are often initialized with a random data point from the data set. The temporal micro models are more complicated so we need to use more data. We had the best success segmenting the initial training data into N_c non-overlapping random-length segments and using each segment to train one of the N_c macro models that describe the data clusters. Initializing the models with random transition probabilities did not work since the space of random models is so large and often one model is much closer to the data than the rest and wins all the data points in the initial (E-step) segmentation.

3.4   Degenerate Models

Occasionally we saw cases were one (macro) model captures none of the data in the time series. There is no data to retrain the model so it needs to be reassigned. We tried several approaches to address this problem.

1) Look at each segment and its winning model. For each segment calculate the negative log-likelihood (NLL) of the data given its assigned model. We normalize each NLL by the number of data points so we can compare different sized segments. Choose the segment with the highest NLL (the worst fit to the data) and assign it to the missing cluster.

2) Split the model with the largest support by perturbing this model in two different directions. This is a common approach in data clustering, and is relatively easy to perform since one can do the perturbation along the major axis of the modeled data and effectively split the cluster into two along its major axis. We chose to perturb the transition matrix by a small random amount.

3) Find the cluster with the largest support (most data points) and split it at a random point in time. Train a new model for the original cluster with the first section of the data, and train a model for the missing cluster using the second half.

The last approach was the most successful, perhaps because the random segment sizes never came up with the same answer twice. Often the first attempt, in all the approaches above, fails and one model remains degenerate. The random segmentation approach often finds its way out of a locally degenerate situation.

3.5   Learning the Model Structure

There are two common means to build the necessary number of models and to decide how many models or clusters are necessary. Often in k-means a single model is learned from all the data. One model or cluster is added at each stage by splitting the largest cluster and retraining all models using the procedures described in Section 3.2. Alternatively, one can start with N random models and learn the right number of models all at once.

Meignier [11] suggests an approach where a single global model is split by removing a small portion of the data that best fits the model. This small portion is used to train a new model and the original model is trained on the remaining data. If the data is closely clustered then each iteration picks out the centroid of the data and builds the new model and leaves the remainder of the data to be modelled more poorly with the global model. This approach did not work well in our simulations compared to the random-segment approach.

3.6   Performance Evaluation

The approach described in this report is completely unsupervised; there is no reason that the (macro) model labels generated by our learned models should agree with the macro labels used when generating the test data. We want to compare the structure of the learned model with the labeled data. There are information-theoretic approaches to finding the optimal mapping, but for small numbers of states we can use a brute-force approach to enumerate all possible label permutations and choose the one which gives the smallest decoding error.

4   Illustrative Example

In practice, we expect that the text content of all windows and dialog boxes displayed to the user will form the input signal for this work, but we have not instrumented our systems to capture this data yet. Instead, we illustrate the behavior of our algorithm using a multi-tasking web-browsing example. Using the log from a web proxy [9], we collected a sequence of uniform-resource locators (URLs) as a user looked for information on a series of three different topics: (1) PERL hash, (2) molecular biology hmm, (3) sudden oak disease. We used Google [1] to find appropriate pages on these topics. About 20 pages were selected from each topic in order, and then the three topics were revisited in order again.

For each URL that was logged, we used a text-only web browser to gather the contents of the page. We used simple heuristics based on the file suffix to remove uninteresting URLs (such as images and code) and then used simple heuristics based on the average distance between space characters to decide if the URL pointed to a web page containing text. The text on each web page is a single document for LSI analysis. In this experiment, the user visited a total of 155 web pages.

We used LSI to reduce the semantic feature vector from 8009 dimensions (the total number of distinct words, after removing stop words, in all documents) to a three-dimensional space. The resulting feature vectors are shown in Figure 3. Note the three clusters are distinguishable by drawing lines between the clusters, although there would be some errors with simple discriminators such as GMMs.

We modeled the data assuming a fully-connected three-state Markov model. We expected the model to use one state per semantic topic and properly segment the web-browsing data by topic. Each micro model was implemented using a two-component GMM. Each GMM estimates the probability that a (3D) point in semantic space is seen in this macro state.

Figure 4 shows the original and the reconstructed segmentation and macro-state sequences. The EM algorithm converged to the correct answer; each portion of the signal was assigned to the correct model although the labels are permuted. This reconstruction converged—reached a stable segmentation—after three iterations. Figure 5 summarizes the learned GMM micro models.

The macro model provides an important temporal constraint. In its simplest form, the self-loop probability suggests that a user stays in one task for a number of time steps before moving to a new task. Without this constraint, the model makes a locally optimal decision and is free to predict that at each time step the user jumps to a different task.

The time-series constraint is important because it smooths out noisy data. A user might visit a web page that is independent of task (i.e. the Google home page) or see a

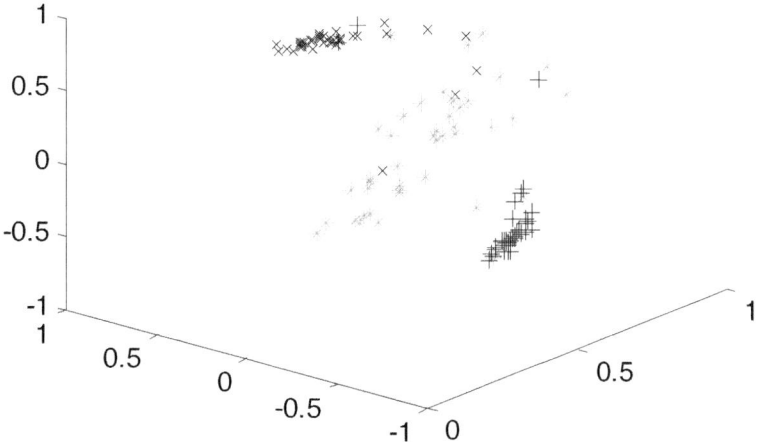

Fig. 3. Raw data in a 3D LSI feature space for the experiment described in Section 4. The data marked by 'x' represents PERL pages, '*' represents molecular biology, and "+" represents oak disease. Note the classes are not separable with simple decision surfaces.

dialog box that is common to all tasks (i.e. a print dialog). We want to ignore these common, information-free windows since they do not tell us anything about the task.

Figure 6 shows a typical segmentation learned by the hierarchical EM algorithm with no temporal constraint. The self-loop probability was set to 0.33 so that each state had a 33% probability of being used. In this example, the state labels match the original labels, but there are many single point errors. About 25% of these labels are incorrect when using the simple 2-component GMMs to represent each cluster probability. A more sophisticated model can make the proper distinctions and discriminate between these data. In this switching-task model of user behavior the macro model constrains the solution and allows a simple GMM to perform without errors (See Figure 4). The dif-

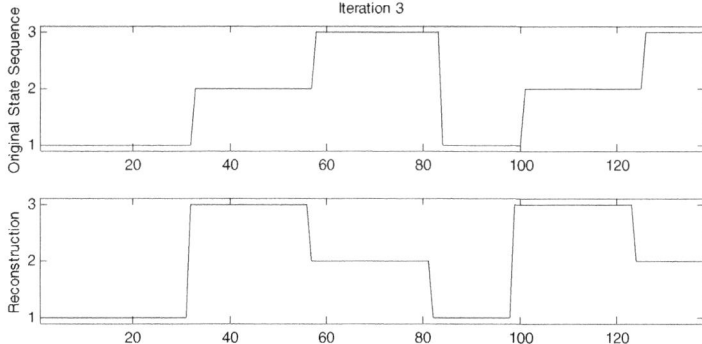

Fig. 4. The original and reconstructed sequence of user states. In the original data, the 3 different topics were encoded as: 1 is PERL, 2 is molecular biology, 3 is oak disease. The labels on the reconstructed state sequence are arbitrary, and can be permuted as they are in this example. With the ideal permutation, the reconstructed sequence matches the original exactly.

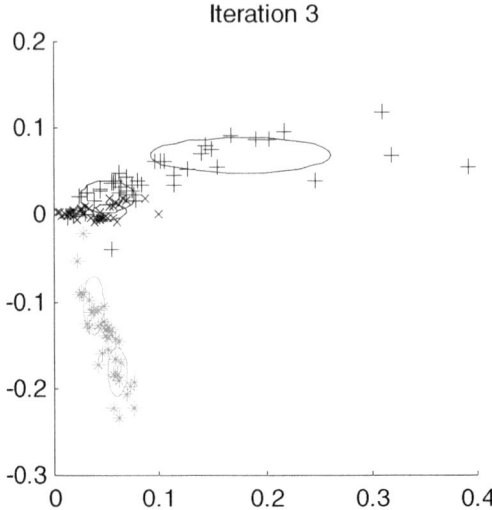

Fig. 5. Each of the three micro models are implemented with 2-component, 3-dimensional GMMs, which are summarized by the ellipses shown above. (Only the two of the three most important LSI directions are shown in this plot.)

ferences in the results shown in Figures 4 and 6 are due to the power of a global decision versus a local decision.

5   Future Work

In this paper, we reported simulation results for a single type of hierarchical model. Much more remains to be done. A thorough test and evaluation requires collecting more data of web browsing and ordinary computer use to try to characterize realistic user tasks. Attentive user interfaces (e.g., [10]) can be built around this sort of complex mul-

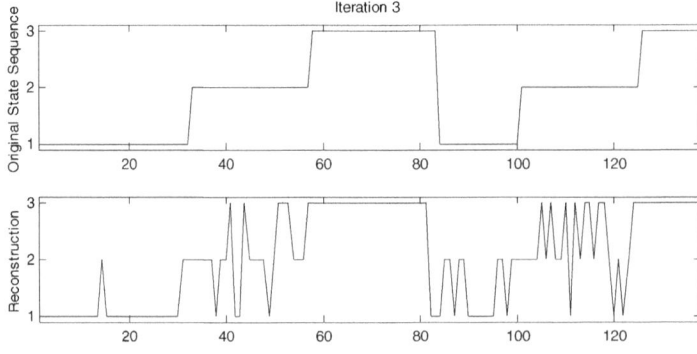

Fig. 6. Reconstrctured state sequence without the temporal constraint. This is equivalent to clustering the raw data into three clusters and thus the actions at many points in time are misclassified.

titasking user model, and can be evaluated in comparison to simpler text-based user models. Data from large numbers of computer users in large corporations can be aggregated and analyzed to begin to understand how people really spend their time, possibly informing the design of corporate applications and systems. By capturing user behavior in models that take account of multitasking, we can finally develop tools that support how people naturally work.

Acknowledgments. We appreciate the support we received from Myron Flickner, Daniel Russell and the anonymous reviewers.

References

1. S. Brin and L. Page. The anatomy of a large-scale hypertextual web search engine. In *Proceedings of the Seventh World-Wide Web Conference*, 1998.
2. J. Budzik and K. J. Hammond. User interactions with everyday applications as context for just-in-time information access. In *Proceedings of the 5th international conference on Intelligent user interfaces*, New Orleans, pp. 44–51, 2000.
3. A. Cypher. The Structure of Users' Activities. In Norman D. and Draper S. eds., *User Centered System Design*, Lawrence Erlbaum Associates, Hillsdale, New Jersey, 1986, pp. 243–263.
4. B. D. Davison and H. Hirsh. Predicting Sequences of User Actions. In *Proceedings of the AAAI/ICML 1998 Workshop on Predicting the Future: AI Approaches to Time-Series Analysis 1*, AAAI Press, pp. 5–12, 1998.
5. S. C. Deerwester, S. T. Dumais, T. K. Landauer, G. W. Furnas, and R. A. Harshman. Indexing by latent semantic analysis. *JASIS*, 41(6), pp. 391–407, 1990.
6. E. Horvitz, et al. The Lumiere project: Bayesian user modeling for inferring the goals and needs of software users. In *Proc. of the 14th Conf. on Uncertainty in AI*, Madison, WI, pp. 256–265, 1998.
7. F. Jelinek. *Statistical Methods for Speech Recognition*. MIT Press, Cambridge, MA, 1998.
8. B. Laurel, editor. *The Art of Human Computer Interface Design*. Addison-Wesley, 1990.
9. P. P. Maglio and R. Barrett. Intermediaries personalize information streams. *Communications of the ACM*, 43(8), pp.96–101, 2000.
10. P. P. Maglio, C. S. Campbell, R. Barrett, T. Selker. An architecture for developing attentive information systems. *Knowledge-Based Systems* 14, pp. 103–110, 2000.
11. S. Meignier, Jean-Francois Bonastre and S. Igounet. E-HMM approach for learning and adapting sound models for speaker indexing. *2001: A Speaker Odyssey*, Crete, Greece, June 2001.
12. B. J. Rhodes. Margin notes: building a contextually aware associative memory. In *Proceedings of the 5th international conference on Intelligent user interfaces*, New Orleans, pp. 219–224, 2000.
13. S. Shi and A. S. Weigend. Markov gated experts for time series analysis: Beyond regression. In *Proceedings of IEEE International Conference on Neural Networks*, Houston, TX pp. 2039–2044.
14. B. Westphal, T. Syeda-Mahmood. On learning video browsing behavior from user interactions. *Proceedings of the Eleventh International World Wide Web Conference*, Honolulu, Hawaii, USA, 2002.

VlUM, a Web-Based Visualisation of Large User Models

James Uther and Judy Kay

School of Information Technologies,
The University of Sydney,
N.S.W 2006, Australia
{jimu,judy}@it.usyd.edu.au
http://www.it.usyd.edu.au/

Abstract. This paper describes *VlUM*, a new tool for visualising large user models. It is intended to help users gain both an overview of the system's model of a user as well as the ability to find interesting parts of the model. In particular, it is intended to enable users to quickly identify outlier or interesting parts of the model.

1   Introduction

There is a growing appreciation of the need to make user models accessible to the user. This is partly due to the nature of user models as a form of personal information about a user. It also appears to be particularly valuable to make a user model available in teaching systems as advocated by Self [11]. This has been explored by several researchers, for example [3,2,9,14,15].

As a user model represents larger numbers of elements, it becomes increasingly difficult for the user to get an overview of the model, or to find useful data, and even more difficult to find patterns or surprising data. Previous work on interfaces that give an overview of a user model, such as [5] was limited to modest sized models with no more than 100 knowledge elements represented. Even this aimed to collapse parts of the model so that far less than this number of elements were actually displayed at once. In other work, such as Zapata-Rivera and Greer [13,14,15], the interface shows just a small part of the detailed elements of a Bayesian Net model.

This paper describes a *visualisation* [1,4] tool for user models. It was designed expressly to give users an overview of their model. In particular, this paper describes the support for users to determine what the system models as true, what it models as false and how the beliefs are related, if there is a relationship between them.

Since many practical user models are likely to be large, the tool helps the user to find this information by allowing the user to:

- get an overview of the whole model
- get a clearer overview of a subset of related beliefs in the model
- adjust the sensitivity of the display so that the user can decide what strength should be treated as true.

P. Brusilovsky et al. (Eds.): UM 2003, LNAI 2702, pp. 198–202, 2003.

The model itself is structured as a graph of related concepts. Each concept may contain a title, a 'score' value between 0.0 and 1.0, and a 'certainty' value of the same range, that indicates how strongly the evidence for the model supports the 'score' value. This model is encoded in RDF [7] format.

2   The Visualisation

We designed *VlUM* so that the user model might be explored in conjunction with an associated activity. Accordingly, the *VlUM* visualisation exists in a vertical segment of the screen about 350×600 pixels in size, leaving room for a web page to be displayed in full to its right.

While a user may wish to focus on the attributes of a single component of the user model, they will often wish to still see the 'context', including related

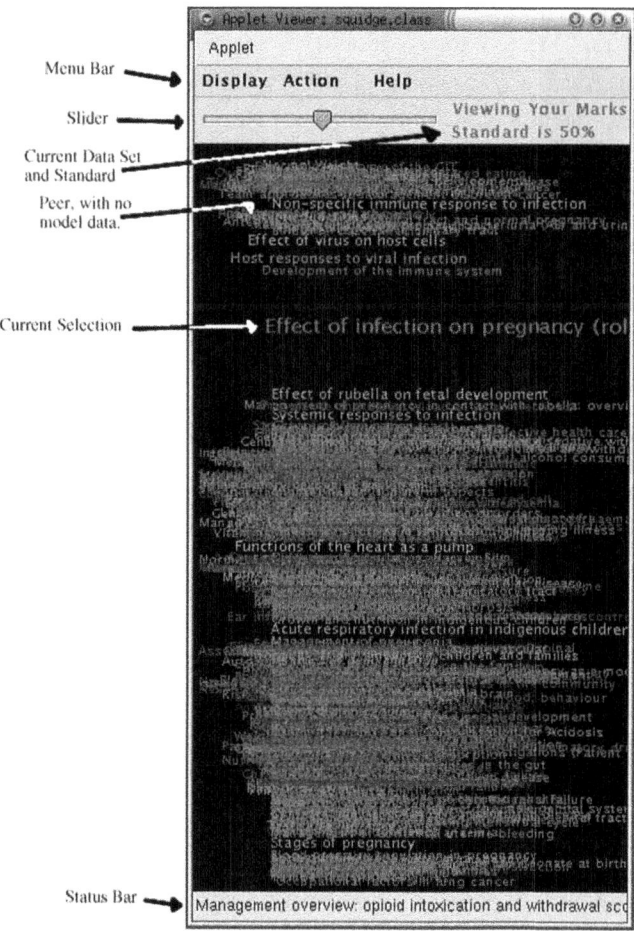

Fig. 1. The visualisation in *VlUM*.

components. *VlUM* takes this to an extreme, showing all components at all times, but with emphasis on the current component of interest and its peers, a visualisation technique known as 'focus+context' [8,6,10].

For example, in Figure 1, which shows a user model from a medical domain, the currently selected component is *Effect of infection on pregnancy (role of placenta)*. This title is in a larger font, and has more space around it. Related titles, which are peers of the current selection in the model graph, are shown in a slightly smaller font and with less space. An example would be *Functions of the heart as a pump*. This regression in font size and spacing continues through the graph, and so the topics most distant from the current selection are crowded together and small.

A slider above the main pane enables the user to set the standard required to assess a component of the model as true. In the spirit of user control, this means users can determine the boundary between the classification of a component as true (displayed as green) or false (red). The saturation of the colour indicates degree. The current selection in Figure 1 is very red, indicating that the user is not doing well in that topic.

We considered it important that a user have the means to adjust this standard for assessing the data in a user model. For instance, in a medical course, a student should have the freedom to define their pass standard at a high standard if they wish. In that case, a component would appear in green only if the system had strong evidence that the user knew that aspect. Equally interestingly, the user could set the standard very low. In that case, the only red components would be those for which the system had strong evidence that the user did not know the aspect. These would indicate areas the student might work on first. Similarly, where the model is displaying predicted user preferences, the user should be able to set a high standard in order to see just the most highly recommended components.

The 'certainty' attribute of a component is shown by the x offset of the title from the left of the display. The user model value for the current selection in Figure 1 is not certain. If a component has no data, it is coloured yellow.

If a user is given *VlUM* in the state shown in Figure 1, and clicks on *Effect of virus on host cells* which is slightly above *Effect of infection on pregnancy (role of placenta)*, *VlUM* will change (with animation) to the state shown in the right image of Figure 2. The graph now has *Effect of virus on host cells* at the root, and *Effect of infection on pregnancy (role of placenta)* at a lower depth. Since the distance between the topics in the graph has not changed, the sizes of the two components are essentially swapped. However, the relative positions of the components on the display will change to reflect the new spanning tree of the graph. Titles are not fixed to any particular position, but move as the spanning tree causes 'warping' of the display surface, but as already mentioned, the components are always displayed in the order they appear in the model file.

There are three menus. These enable a range of functions which are irrelevant for this paper.

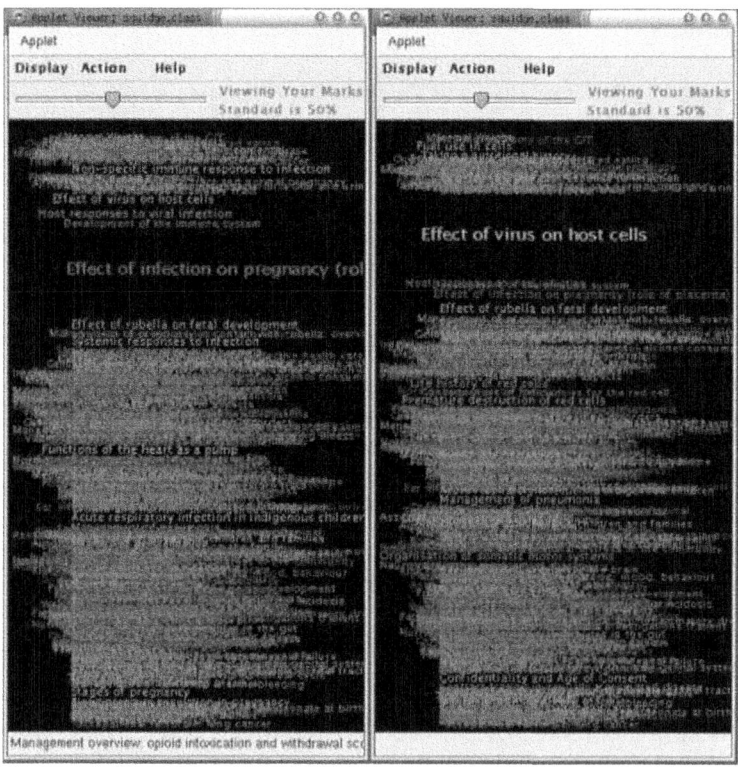

Fig. 2. Two steps in use of the model visualisation. The viewer starts as seen on the left. The focus component is *Effect of infection in pregnancy*. Topics which most closely related to this have more space around them and so are more visible. For example, slightly above it is *Effect of virus on host cells*. Clicking on it alters the display to that on the right.

3 Summary and Conclusion

There are strong reasons for offering an overview of a user model. *VlUM* is a new visualisation, which was developed for the purpose of providing such an overview. It aims to allow a user to find interesting features of a large model. It exploits relationships between the components of a user model to control the parts which are most visible at any point in time. It enables users to identify the true components within a large model, since these can be seen as the green strings in the display. Similarly, it enables users to see the false components, as the red strings in the visualisation. We have performed an extensive evaluation [12] which indicates that it enables users to navigate and scrutinise user models with up to 700 components.

References

1. J. Bertin. *Graphics and Graphic Information Processing*, pages 62–81. 1981.
2. S. Bull and P. Brna. What does Susan know that Paul doesn't? (and vice-versa): contributing to each other's student model. In B de Boulay and R Mizoguchi, editors, *International Conference on Artificial Intelligence in Education*, pages 568–570. IOS Press, 1997.
3. S. Bull, P. Brna, and H. Pain. Extending the scope of the student model. *User Modeling and User-Adapted Interaction*, 5(1):44–65, 1995.
4. I. Herman, G. Melançon, and M. S. Marshall. Graph visualisation and navigation in information visualisation, 1999.
5. J. Kay. *A scrutable user modelling shell for user-adapted interaction*. PhD thesis, University of Sydney, 1999.
6. J. Lamping and R. Rao. The hyperbolic browser: A focus + context technique for visualizing large heirarchies. *Journal of Visual Languages and Computing*, 7(1):33–55, 1996.
7. O. Lassila and R. Swick. Resource description framework (RDF) model and syntax specification, 1999.
8. Y. K. Leung and M. D. Apperley. A review and taxonomy of distortion-orientation presentation techniques. *ACM Transactions on Computer-Human Interaction*, 1:126–160, 1994.
9. A. Paiva, J. Self, and R. Hartley. Externalising learner models. In J. Greer, editor, *Proceedings of the World Conference on Artificial Intelligence in Education*, Washington DC, U.S.A.. 1995. AACE.
10. R. Rao and Stewart K. Card. The table lens: Merging graphical and symbolic representations in an interactive focus + context visualization for tabular information. In *Proceedings CHI'94*, pages 318–332, 1994.
11. J. Self. Bypassing the intractable problem of student modelling: Invited paper. In *Proceedings of the 1st International Conference on Intelligent Tutoring Systems*, pages 18–24, Montreal, 1988.
12. J. Uther. *On the visualisation of large user models in web based systems*. PhD thesis, University of Sydney, 2001.
13. J. D. Zapata-Rivera and J. Greer. Inspecting and visualizing distributed bayesian student models. In G Gauthier, C Frasson, and K VanLehn, editors, *Intelligent Tutoring Systems ITS 2000*, pages 544–553, Montreal, June 2000.
14. J. D. Zapata-Rivera and J. Greer. Externalising learner modelling representations. In *Proceedings of the Workshop on External representations in AIED: Multiple forms and multiple roles, held with the 10th International Conference on Artificial Intelligence in Education (AI-ED)*, 2001.
15. J. D. Zapata-Rivera and J Greer. Exploring various guidance mechanisms to support interaction with inspectable learner models. *Intelligent Tutoring Systems*, pages 442–452, 2002.

A Multiagent Approach to Obtain Open and Flexible User Models in Adaptive Learning Communities

Felix Hernandez, Elena Gaudioso, and Jesus G. Boticario

Dpto. de Inteligencia Artificial
Universidad Nacional de Educacion a Distancia
Senda del Rey 9, Madrid, Spain
{felixh,elena,jgb}@dia.uned.es

Abstract. Nowadays, many user-modeling systems are applied to web-based adaptive systems. The large number of very different users using these systems make user model construction difficult. The solution is to use machine learning techniques that dynamically update the models by monitoring user behavior. However, the design of machine learning tasks for user modeling is static. This poses a problem in adaptive learning environments based on virtual communities. Each virtual community has its own administrators, and each administrator may prefer to include some more information on the user model. Another problem in the application of machine learning techniques for user model construction is the need to retrain the machine learning algorithms when new user interaction data become available. To face these problems, in this paper we present a multiagent adaptive module set in an adaptive learning collaborative environment. Our goal is two fold: (i) we want each administrator to be able to define new machine learning attributes in the user model (ii) we want to provide a mechanism to dynamically retrain the algorithms.

1 Introduction

Distance learning has been one of the fields that has benefited most from Internet development. And a new way to group students and lecturers to work and learn together has emerged by means of *Web-based learning communities* [2].

So as to achieve effective learning communities, we make use of a group *administrator* or moderator. In addition, in order to facilitate access to aimed information and cooperation, an adapted response should be provided to each user [5].

For this purpose, we apply user modeling techniques which exploits a combination of predefined rules with machine learning techniques [5]. The last is due to the large number of very different users using the system.

However, in order to improve personalization, each administrator must have control of the information the system has on each user. Thus, they must be able to include new information in the user model. For instance, if an administrator

P. Brusilovsky et al. (Eds.): UM 2003, LNAI 2702, pp. 203–207, 2003.

add a new service (i.e. a chat) to the community, she/he should be able to add a new machine learning attribute related to that service (i.e. chat activity level) that was not required before.

In this paper we present a combination of a multiagent approach [8] and machine learning techniques [9] in order to achieve two main goals: (i) let administrators add new machine learning attributes dynamically in the user model, and (ii), an autonomous retrain of the algorithms.

We will start first by giving a general overview of the whole system.

2   A Multiagent Adaptive Module in a Web-Based Collaborative Environment

In order to support the learning communities mentioned in section 1, we have chosen a web-based collaborative environment called aLF.

aLF (active Learning Framework)[5] is based on a web server, a set of scripts and a database. It dynamically constructs pages from the data stored in the database. Both the contents to be presented and user personal and interaction data are stored in the aLF database so as to have a clean and efficient access to these data.

The adaptive module is connected to aLF via the database. This module will be in charge of the personalization in the system. An example can be found when the system suggests not enough *active* users to increase their interaction with the community, where *activity level* is a machine learning attribute in the user model.

A multiagent architecture is used in the adaptive module (see a more detailed description in [3]). Here, an agent called *User Model Agent* is in charge of the user model. Inside of the adaptive module, a subset of agents called *User Modeling Subsystem* are in charge of the machine learning part of the user model. We will only focus on this last subset of agents.

One of the problems that we solve with the User Modeling Subsystem is the dynamic extension of the user model by an administrator. In order to facilitate communication between the User Modeling Subsystem and the administrator we use a repository common to all of them: a *blackboard*. This blackboard is implemented as a set of tables in the system database.

The other problem consist of choosing dynamically the best machine learning algorithm for each dataset. We will see how we solved it in the following section, where we will show *User Modeling Subsystem* in more detail.

3   User Modeling Subsystem

In this section we will show (section 3.1) the problem of choosing dynamically the best machine learning algorithm for a given machine learning task. Afterwards (section 3.2), we will see how we can use it to the more general problem of adding *dynamically* machine learning features in the user model.

3.1   An Efficient Response for Any Learning Task from the Dynamic Combination of Several Classifiers

It is well known that no machine learning algorithm can be the best choice for all possible tasks. Each algorithm contains an explicit or implicit bias [7] that leads it to prefer certain generalizations to others.

Thus, for each learning task we must do a search for the machine learning algorithm that offers the best result for this task. Some solutions to this problem have been given by the so-called *ensemble of classifiers* [4].

The basic objective of the ensembles is to combine the responses given by several classifiers in an attempt to reduce the error that each of them make.

The autonomy and dynamism of multiagent systems [8] can improve response performance from a static combination of classifiers in environments where an efficient response has to be offered to all the different tasks, with the additional problem that these tasks may change with time.

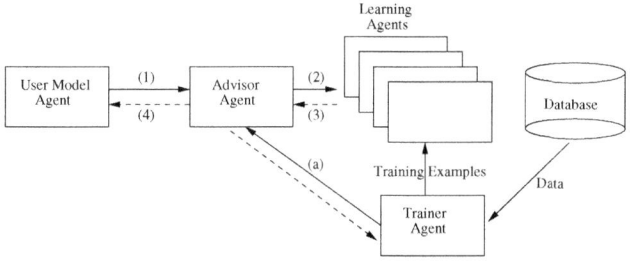

Fig. 1. Basic architecture for the user modeling subsystem.

In our user modeling subsystem (see figure 1) we try to achieve the right dynamic combination of algorithms for any learning task using a multiagent system consisting of:

- Several *learning agents* with an inherent machine learning algorithm. After each classifier has been constructed by each agent, it can respond to the classification tasks that it is asked.
- An *advisor agent* with the function of responding out the User Modeling Subsystem with a response combining all the responses received from the learning agents. Using the results offered by earlier works as a basis [6] we propose a combination of responses from a reinforcement algorithm based on the number of correct responses given by each learning agent.
- A *trainer agent*, which creates training examples and ask the learning agents to construct new classifiers with these examples. It has sufficient autonomy to decide, using the advises of the advisor agent, the best moment to train each learning agent from new user interaction data.

Each request to the modeling subsystem of a machine learning attribute value will be solved by the advisor agent. These external requests come from an agent out of the User Modeling Subsystem called *user model agent* (see section 2). When this agent needs a machine learning attribute value, it will send the question to the *advisor agent*.

The stages that correspond to the steps after a request to the user modeling subsystem are: (1) the advisor agent receives an external request that consists of solving the value of one of the learning attributes, (2) the advisor agent *processes* the external request to obtain the value of the predictive attributes corresponding to the learning task in question (which depends on the learning attribute being queried) and it transmits the processing result to all the learning agents, (3) the learning agents respond to the advisor agent using their pre-learnt classifiers, (4) the advisor agent considers all the responses using its *reinforcement table* and finally responds to the external request.

To prove the advisor agent chooses the most efficient response for each machine learning task, we carried out a preliminary evaluation over 4 domain related datasets from the UCI repository [1]. We used two learning agents with c4.5 and Naive Bayes learning algorithms. The results showed that our actual advisor agent chooses the most efficient response when there is enough difference between learning agents or when the learning agents response is efficient enough, even though there is no much difference between them.

3.2 Extension of the Model and Autonomous Retraining of the User Modeling Subsystem

We will focus first on extending the model by adding new learning attributes.

After identifying the need of new learning attributes, the administrator must communicate these to the modeling subsystem. For this we will use the blackboard mentioned in the previous section.

For each new attribute, the administrator must add new information on the blackboard using a web form designed for this purpose. The agents, after reading this blackboard information, will perceive the new attributes and act accordingly.

The information that the administrator has to communicate to the modeling subsystem for each new learning attribute is as follows:

1. The observable, inferred or learnt attributes that will be used as *predictive attributes* (see section 1) in this new learning task. For example, on adding the new learning attribute chatActivityLevel the administrator must communicate to the subsystem the predictive attributes num-mesgs-chat (number of messages sent to the chat), Num-conx-day (the number of chat connections per day), etc.
2. The labels used afterwards by the trainer agent to create the training examples. For example, in the case of a new attribute chatActivityLevel, we would have to add for some users the labels Low, Medium or High depending on the level of activity in the chat of the corresponding user.

After this information has been brought to the blackboard, the trainer agent will be able to create the training examples necessary for training the learning agents. Thanks to the autonomy of the training agent, the administrator does not have to deal with this task. The trainer agent will decide when to do it. This decision will be taken according to the system existing restrictions, for example, that there are sufficient labels available or a sufficient downloading of the system.

The same will occur for the retraining of the learning agents. The trainer agent will do this retraining always bearing in mind the advisor agent indications, considering only the updating of the learning tasks and for the learning agents that the advisor agent considers no longer give a sufficiently efficient response.

4   Future Work

Regarding the work presented, two main directions lie ahead for future work that will allow us to improve it. On the one hand, in order to improve the response of the system, we will work with other algorithms into the advisor agent. On the other hand, we will evaluate usability aspects as, for instance, how easy is, for each administrator, to enter the information needed to revise the user models by themselves. All these objectives are included in a recent European funding project called ALFANET[1].

References

1. C.L. Blake and C.J. Merz. UCI repository of machine learning databases, 1998.
2. J. G. Boticario and E. Gaudioso. An internet distance-learning operating model. *Computers and Education in the 21st Century*, pages 101–109, 2000.
3. J.G. Boticario, E. Gaudioso, and F. Hernandez. Adaptive navigation support and adaptive collaboration support in webdl. In *Adaptive Hypermedia and Adaptive Web-based Systems*, volume 1892 of *LNCS*, pages 51–61, 2000.
4. J. P. Gama. *Combining Classification Algorithms*. PhD thesis, Facultade de Ci ncias da Universidade do Porto, 1999.
5. E. Gaudioso and J. G. Boticario. Supporting personalization in virtual communities in distance education. *Virtual Environments for Teaching and Learning*, 2002. http://www.ia.uned.es/personal/elena/egvjgbkes02.pdf.
6. J. I. Giraldez and D. Borrajo. Distributed reinforcement learning in multi-agent decision systems. In *Progress in Artificial Intelligence, Iberamia 98*, number 1484 in LNAI, pages 148–159, 1998.
7. T. Mitchell. *Machine Learning*. McGraw Hill, 1997.
8. K. P. Sycara. Multiagent systems. *AI Magazine 19*, 2:79–92, 1998.
9. G. I. Webb, M. J. Pazzani, and D. Billsus. Machine learning for user modeling. *User Modeling and User-Adapted Interaction*, 11:19–29, 2001.

---

[1] ALFANET (Adaptive Learning For Adaptive interNET) IST-2001-33288. http://www.rtd.softwareag.es/alfanet/

A Model for Integrating an Adaptive Information Filter Utilizing Biosensor Data to Assess Cognitive Load

Curtis S. Ikehara, David N. Chin, and Martha E. Crosby

Univ. of Hawaii, 1680 East-West Road POST 317, Honolulu, HI 96822, USA
Phone: 808-956-3581, fax: 808-956-3548
{cikehara, chin, crosby}@hawaii.edu

Abstract. Information filtering is an effective tool for improving performance but requires real-time information about the user's changing cognitive states to determine the optimal amount of filtering for each individual at any given time. Current research at the Adaptive Multimodal Interactive Laboratory assesses the user's cognitive ability and cognitive load from physiological measures including: eye tracking, heart rate, skin temperature, electrodermal activity, and the pressures applied to a computer mouse during task performance. A model of adaptive information filtering is proposed that would improve learning and task performance by optimizing the human-computer interface based on real-time information of the user's cognitive state obtained from these passive physiological measures.

Keywords: Physiological sensor, biosensor, information filter, cognitive load

1 Introduction

Users can vary greatly in cognitive capabilities depending on their expertise and aptitude while the cognitive ability of all users are affected by stress, fatigue, injuries, attention lapses, and distractions. Information filtering is an effective method of enhancing performance on cognitive tasks, but can be suboptimal when it does not respond to changes in the user's cognitive ability. Subsequent sections will discuss a potential solution using a suite of real-time passive physiological sensors to assess the cognitive ability of the user and control an adaptive information filter.

2 Experimental Methodology

The goal of the research at the AMI laboratory is to create a methodology to improve learning and task performance by optimizing the human-computer interface based on the user's cognitive state, which is obtain from passive physiological measures. The desired learning improvements are to increase the rate of learning, comprehension and retention while maintaining user satisfaction. The desired task performance improvements are for the user to be more accurate, faster and make strategic decisions (i.e., situationally appropriate). "Augmented cognition" is the name of the research area that encompasses the methodologies used to achieve these goals.

P. Brusilovsky et al. (Eds.): UM 2003, LNAI 2702, pp. 208–212, 2003.

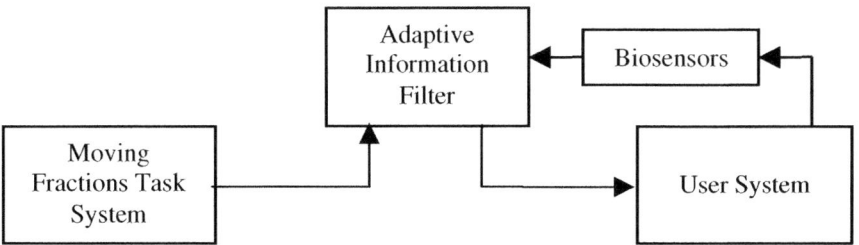

Fig. 1. Model of how the Adaptive Information Filter changes the display of the Moving Target Fractions (MTF) task when biosensor information indicates excessive cognitive load.

2.1 Adaptive Information Filter Model

Figure 1 shows the system model used for augmented cognition research. The user, Moving Target Fractions (MTF) task and adaptive information filter are subsystems of the testbed system. What makes this system model unique is that there are biosensors (i.e., passive physiological sensors) that monitor the user and provides input to the adaptive information filter.

Research is underway to determine which sensor or combination of sensor data will be necessary to assess the user's cognitive states listed in Table 1. Once the cognitive state of the user is assessed, presentation changes are made by an adaptive information filter to improve task performance.

2.2 Testbed Software Description – Moving Targets Fraction Task

The testbed software, MTF (Moving Targets Fractions), presents a controlled cognitive load task to the user and adapts the presentation by adjusting the degree of information filtering based on what the biosensors indicate is the instantaneous cognitive load of the user. The MTF task presents on a computer screen a fixed number of oval targets containing fractions. These fractions float across the screen from left to right (see Figure 2). The primary goal of the user is to maximize the score by selecting the correct fractions before they reach the right edge of the screen. Cognitive load is controlled by adjusting fraction values, speed of the fractions across the screen and the number of fractions presented. Adaptive information filtering provides incomplete but helpful information to the user and the degree of filtering is modified based on the user's cognitive state.

2.3 Maximizing the Score – Goal and Subgoals

For the user to obtain the highest score, the user must select all fractions greater than the critical value of 1/3 before they touch the right edge of the screen. The goal of the user is to maximize the score by achieving four subgoals before taking action.

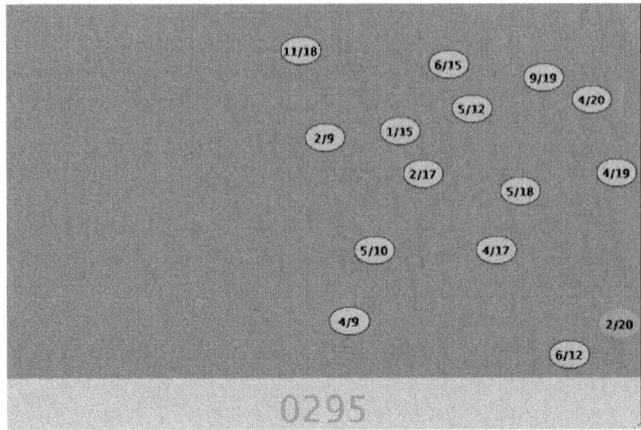

Fig. 2. Screen capture of the Moving Targets Fraction (MTF) task.

Subgoals include evaluating difficulty, fraction relationships, score and timing. The subgoals can take on different priorities depending on task variables such as the difficulty of evaluating the fraction, the value of the fraction, how close the fraction is to the right side of the screen and the number of fractions presented. The priorities of the subgoals can also be affected by user factors such as arousal, stress and motivation.

2.4   Biosensors

The first column of Table 1 lists all the physiological sensors currently being used (i.e., biosensors). Secondary measures (column 2) can be extracted from the primary physiological measures and are needed to derive some of the potential cognitive and affective states. Column 3 lists several potential cognitive measures.

2.5   Cognitive Load

In the MTF task, cognitive load is affected by fraction values, movement speed of the fractions and the number of fractions presented. Numeric computation and visual/spatial cognitive abilities are of specific interest.

A measure of the user's cognitive load can be inferred from the cognitive measures and mental states detected with the biosensors (see Table 1). The biosensors may be able to provide both computational and visual/spatial load assessments in real-time. Computational load could be extracted from blink rate, blink duration, stress levels, and arousal state. Visual/spatial load could be extracted from gaze locations, search patterns and eye fixations.

In Figure 3, Cognitive Load #1 (Computation) has a graded vertical scale. The top of that scale represents the maximum cognitive ability. When the user is performing the MTF task, each subgoal (i.e., "S#1, S#2, S#3 & S#4") increases the total computational cognitive load (i.e., "Load #1"). The solid arrow next to Load #1 shows the current computational cognitive load. The dashed arrow indicates a desired cognitive load value. The desired computational cognitive load range is denoted by the two-headed arrow. The figure shows the computational cognitive load is currently above the desired range. In the same figure, Cognitive Load #2 (Visual/Spatial) shows the visual/spatial cognitive load to be less than the desired range. The adaptive information filter shifts cognitive load from computational to visual to maintain the computational cognitive load within the desired range.

Table 1. Measures from the Biosensor and Potential Cognitive States

Physiological Measures	Secondary Measures	Potential Cognitive Measures
Eye Position Tracking	Gaze Position, Fixation Number, Fixation Duration, Repeat Fixations, Search Pattern	Difficulty, Attention, Stress, Relaxation, Problem Solving, Successful Learner [1][2]
Pupil Size	Blink Rate, Blink Duration	Fatigue, Difficulty, Interest, Novelty, Mental Activity, Information Processing Speed [1]
Skin Conductivity	Tonic and Phasic Changes	Arousal [1]
Finger, Wrist and Ambient Temperature		Negative Affect (Decrease) [4], Relaxation (Increase) [1]
Relative Blood Flow	Heart Rate and Beat to Beat Heart Flow Change	Stress, Emotion Intensity [1]
Mouse Pressure Sensors (Left/ Right Buttons and Case)		Stress [3], Certainty of Response
Mouse Position	Speed of mouse motion	Arousal, Stress, Difficulty

2.6   Adaptive Information Filtering

Adaptive information filtering can be presented to the user by a combination of three methods: emphasis, de-emphasis and deletion.   Information filtering using de-emphasis is the preferred method since it will allow an incremental change in the task difficulty changing the number of filtered targets based on the user's computational cognitive load. Cognitive load is shifted from computation to visual/spatial load.

3   Conclusion

The augmented cognition research at the AMI laboratory collects biosensor information from the user so that the adaptive information filtering program can in real-time optimize the presentation of information. The MTF task requires the user to elicit several important abilities including: hand-eye coordination, visual search, mathematical computation, fraction estimation, strategy selection, learning, memory and motivation.   Manipulation of the presentation to the user is designed to optimize the user's cognitive ability to achieve the short term goal of maximum performance and the long term goal of maintaining a high level of cognitive ability.

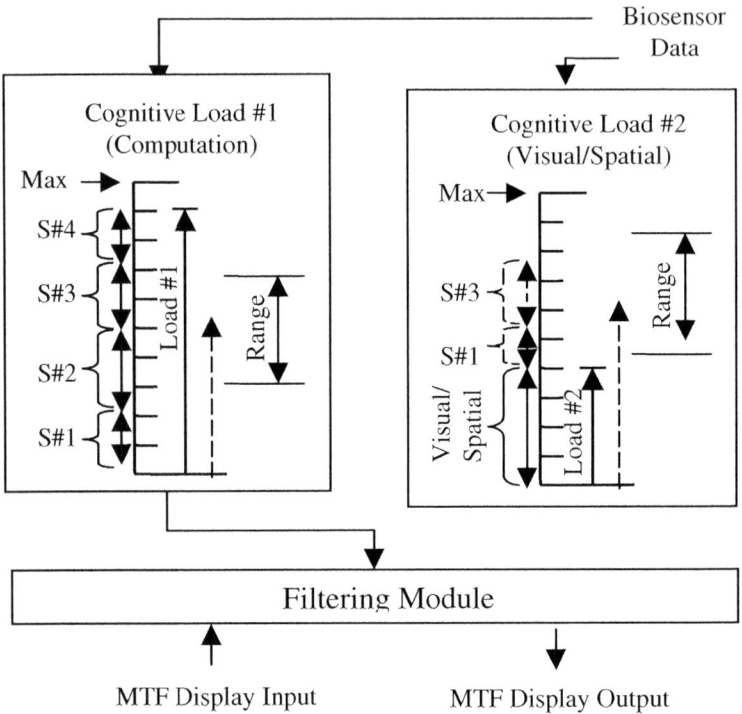

Fig. 3. The adaptive information filter changes the MTF display depending on the computational cognitive load derived from the biosensors. The adaptive filter shifts cognitive load from computation to visual/spatial.

This research was supported in part by the Office of Naval Research grants no. N000149710578 and N000140310135 and DARPA grant no. NBCH1020004.

References

1. Andreassi, J. L.: *Psychophysiology: Human Behavior and Physiological Response*, Third Edition. Hillsdale, NJ: Lawrence Erlbaum, (1995).
2. Crosby, M. E., Idling, M. K. and Chin, D. N., *Visual search and background complexity: does the forest hide the trees?*, In: Bauer, M., Gmytrasiewicz, P. J., and Vassileva, J. (eds.): User Modeling 2001Springer-Verlag, Berlin Heidelberg New York (2001)
3. Lange-Küüttner, C.: *Perceptual and Motor Skills*, 86 (3 Pt 2), (1998) 1299-310.
4. Sheldon, E.: *Virtual Agent Interactions*, Doctoral Dissertation, Orlando: University of Central Florida, (2001).

Ontology-Based User Modeling for Knowledge Management Systems

Liana Razmerita, Albert Angehrn[1], and Alexander Maedche[2]

[1]INSEAD, CALT-Centre of Advanced Learning Technologies, 77300 Fontainebleau, France
liana.razmerita@ugal.ro, albert.angehrn@insead.edu

[2] FZI Research Center for Information Technologies, 76131 Karlsruhe, Germany
http://www.fzi.de/wim
maedche@fzi.de

Abstract. This paper is presenting a generic ontology-based user modeling architecture, (OntobUM), applied in the context of a Knowledge Management System (KMS). Due to their powerful knowledge representation formalism and associated inference mechanisms, ontology-based systems are emerging as a natural choice for the next generation of KMSs operating in organizational, interorganizational as well as community contexts. User models, often addressed as user profiles, have been included in KMSs mainly as simple ways of capturing the user preferences and/or competencies. We extend this view by including other characteristics of the users relevant in the KM context and we explain the reason for doing this. The proposed user modeling system relies on a user ontology, using Semantic Web technologies, based on the IMS LIP specifications, and it is integrated in an ontology-based KMS called Ontologging. We are presenting a generic framework for implicit and explicit ontology-based user modeling.

1 Introduction

The knowledge-based theory of the firm suggests that knowledge is the organizational asset that enables sustainable competitive advantage in very dynamic and competitive markets. Knowledge is considered the most important asset for organizations and the effective management of knowledge has become an important issue. KMSs refer to a class of information systems applied to managing organizational knowledge [1]. Knowledge in the context of KMSs consists of experience, know-how and expertise of people (tacit knowledge) as well as different information artifacts, knowledge assets and data stored in documents, reports available within the organization and outside the organization (explicit knowledge).

Knowledge Management Systems are designed to allow users to access and utilize the rich sources of data, information and knowledge stored in different forms, but also to support knowledge creation, knowledge transfer and continuous learning for the knowledge workers. Recently KMSs, unlike databases, have aimed at going beyond the mere administration of electronic information; they now aim at fostering learning

P. Brusilovsky et al. (Eds.): UM 2003, LNAI 2702, pp. 213–217, 2003.

processes, knowledge sharing, collaboration between knowledge workers irrespective of their location, etc. KMSs tend to become complex in order to support the tasks mentioned above as they are not limited to providing easy access to knowledge assets and they address different categories of users with different needs, roles and preferences. Research on user modeling is motivated by two reasons: 1) differences in individual users' needs and 2) heterogeneity between different groups of users. Moreover user models and user modeling are the key element for personalized inter-action and adaptive feature integration, two very important steps in developing ad-vanced information systems.

The paper is organized as follows: section 2 provides an introduction of the overall ontology-based user modeling architecture. Subsequently, we provide details about explicit and implicit user modeling. In section 3 we discuss implementation details and in section 4 we conclude.

2   Ontology-Based User Modeling Architecture

This section introduces the overall ontology-based user modeling (OntobUM) archi-tecture. The overall user model for a specific user is based on an explicit definition provided by the user through the user profile editor (UPE) and by an implicit part maintained by intelligent services, as represented in Figure 1.

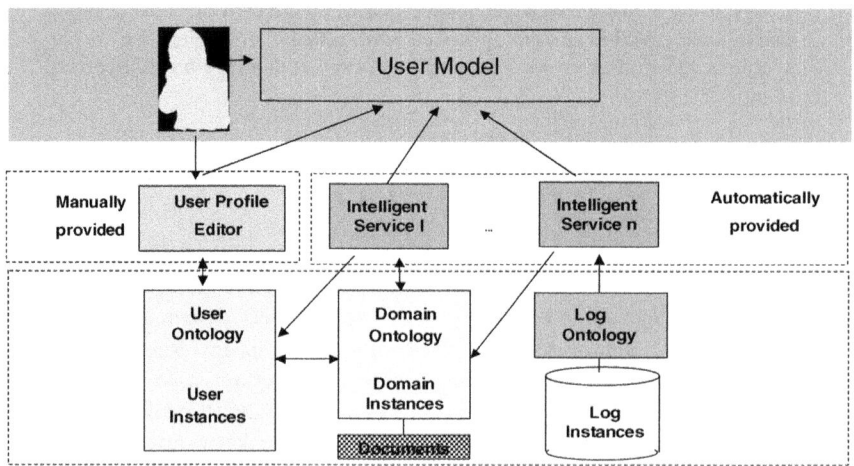

Fig. 1. An ontology-based user modeling system

The intelligent services have two main roles in the system: (1) to update and maintain the user model on the basis of usage data through the application of a number of heu-ristics, (2) to provide personalized services based on the characteristics of the users (e.g. personalized views are generated and presented to the user based on the user's interests, background and role; notification agents announce new entries relevant to the user, etc). The system's general architecture enables one to add incrementally such intelligent services. The architecture of the ontology-based user modeling system integrates three different ontologies, as represented in Figure 1:

- The **User Ontology** structures the different characteristics of users and their relationships.
- The **Domain Ontology** defines the domain and application specific concepts and their relationships.
- The **Log Ontology** defines the semantics of the user interaction with the system.

The log instances, or usage data, are generated by monitoring the user interaction with the system. Based on this usage data the system updates the user model and derives a user related behavior as described in section 2.2.

2.1   The Explicit Part of the User Model

The user profile editor UPE is a specialized ontology editor for user models. The UPE enables the user to enter user data but also to visualize them, revise them and update them afterwards. The definition of the user ontology captures rich metadata about the employee's profile including characteristics such as: identity, email, address, competencies, cognitive style, preferences, etc. but also a "behavioral profile" as described in the next section.

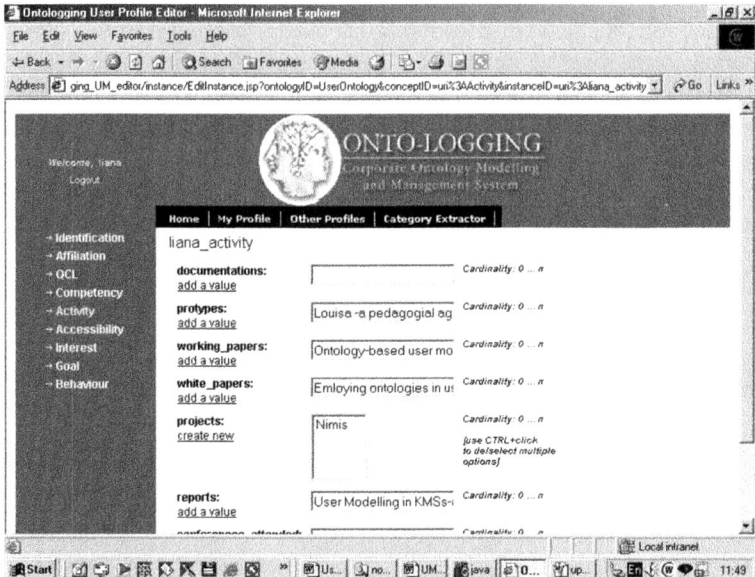

Fig. 2. User profile editor

The proposed user model is structured according to Information Management Systems Learner Information Package specifications (IMS LIP). The IMS LIP package [2] is structured in eleven groupings including: Identification, Goal, QCL (Qualifications, Certification and Licenses), Accessibility, Activity, Competence, Interest, Affiliation,

Security Key and Relationship. Figure 2 shows a screenshot of the OntobUM's UPE, representing the Activity concept and its properties in the editing mode. UPE enables to switch from an edit mode to a view mode.

2.2   The Implicit Part of the User Model

KMSs need to encourage people to codify their experience, to share their knowledge and to develop an "active" attitude towards using the system. For this purpose we have extended the IMS LIP groupings with the Behavior concept. The Behavior concept and its subconcepts were introduced to "measure" two processes that are important for the effectiveness of a KMS, namely knowledge sharing and knowledge creation. The Behavior concept describes characteristics of users interacting with a KMS such as: level_of_activity, type_of_activity, level_of_knowledge_sharing, etc. Based on their activity in the system, namely the number of contributions to the system and the number of the documents read, OntobUM classifies the users into three stereotypes: readers, writers or lurkers. These categories are properties of the type_of_activity concept. The level_of_activity comprises four attributes that can be associated with the users: very active, active, passive or inactive. The classification of the users according to the type_of_activity or level_of_activity is based on heuristics. For example a lurker is defined as somebody who doesn't contribute and who reads/accesses very few knowledge assets in the system. Several heuristics are dedicated to capture the interest areas and the level of expertise of the users. Through the level_of_knowledge_sharing we are capturing the level of adoption of knowledge sharing practices. The user states in relation to the level of knowledge sharing are defined as: unaware, aware, interested, trial and adopter using Roger's terminology related to the attitude of people towards innovation (see [3]). Based on the identified characteristics, the system provides feedback, virtual reward or adapted interventions for a behavioural change (e.g. for adoption of knowledge sharing behaviour). In Razmerita et al. [4] we elaborate on how user models and user modeling can enhance the support in KMSs. We show how user models can be applied for: personalization, expertise discovery, networking, collaboration and learning.

3   Implementation and Related Work

In the area of user modeling, (Kay [5]; Chen and Mizoguchi, [6]) have already pointed out the advantage of using ontologies for learner/user models. Kay emphasizes the fact that a user model "needs an agreed ontology and representation so it can be used by different application programs".

OntobUM is a user-modeling server, which stores data in a RDF/RDFS format. Unlike other existing user modeling servers analyzed by Kobsa [7], OntobUM integrates Semantic Web technology. The system has been implemented as a web application using Java 2 (jdk 1.4). We have used the KAON - Karlsruhe Ontology and Semantic Web [8] framework as an API for managing ontologies. As a web ontology language, KAON extends RDF/RDFS, so the user ontology is RDF/RDFS compatible.

4 Conclusions

In this paper we address aspects of ontology-based user modeling and we present a generic architecture for modeling users based on ontologies. The main contribution of the paper consists in: (1) identifying aspects of user modeling relevant to KMSs, (2) integrating them in a generic framework based on ontologies. We give a concrete example of the use of the OntobUM framework in an ontology-based KMS, but this framework can be adapted to different ontology-aware environments. The user ontology is implemented using Semantic Web technology and it is structured on extended IMS LIP specifications. We have identified characteristics of the users that are relevant for a KMS under the Behaviour concept, but the largest part of the user ontology is generic and it could be reused in other application domains.

Acknowledgment. Research for this paper was partially financed by the EU in the IST-2000-28293 project Ontologging. We thank our Ontologging project partners for their contributions and their collaboration to this research work.

References

1. Leidner, D., Alavi, M., Review: knowledge management and knowledge management systems: conceptual foundations and research, *INSEAD-MIS Quarterly*, vol. 25 (no. 1), pp. 107–136, 2001.
2. IMS LIP, IMS Learner Information Package http://www.imsproject.org/aboutims.html, 2001
3. Angehrn, A., Nabeth, T., Leveraging Emerging Technologies in Management-Education: Research and Experiences, *European Management Journal*, Elsevier, 15, pp. 275–285, 1997.
4. Razmerita, L., Angehrn A., Nabeth, T., On the role of user models and user modeling in Knowledge Management Systems, *in Proceedings of HCI International*, Greece, to appear 2003.
5. Kay, J., Ontologies for reusable and scrutable student model, position paper, *In Proceedings of AIED99 Workshop on Ontologies for Intelligent Educational Systems,* 1999.
6. Chen, W. and Mizoguchi, R., Communication Content Ontology for Learner Model Agent in Multi-Agent Architecture, *Proceedings of AIED99 Workshop on Ontologies for Intelligent Educational Systems,* 1999.
7. Kobsa, A., Generic User Modeling Systems, in *User Modeling and User-Adapted Interaction,* 11(1–2), pp 49–63, 2001.
8. Maedche, A., Motik, B., Stojanovic, L., Studer, R. and Volz, R., Ontologies for Enterprise Knowledge Management, *IEEE Intelligent Systems*, November/December, 2002.

Motivating Cooperation on Peer to Peer Networks[*]

Helen Bretzke[1] and Julita Vassileva[2]

[1] Computer Science Department, University of Toronto
bretzke@trinity.toronto.edu
[2]Computer Science Department, University of Saskatchewan
jiv@cs.usask.ca

Abstract. This paper addresses the problem of free riding on peer-to-peer re-
source-sharing networks and explores methods for motivating more cooperative
user behaviour via an adaptive interface. The paper argues that the free-riding
problem is not so much an economic issue as a socio-psychological one due to a
paradigm shift the user community is undergoing. Users do not yet understand
that they, and all of their peers, are both clients and servers and must therefore
be taught new behaviour. Our method stimulates community awareness and
highlights the cause and effect relationship between user behaviour and performance (QoS) consequences. Modeling the user's interests, attitude and relationships with other users enables the interface to adapt to the individual's cooperativeness bias and give feedback on current community structure and activity. Feedback is delivered in the form of graphs, animations and informative
text.

1 Introduction

Peer-to-peer (P2P) applications have become popular over the last three years, especially with music-swapping applications like Napster, AudioGalaxy or KaZaA and the
related copyright lawsuits. P2P systems consist of networked applications "servents"
that act as both *serv*ers (producers) and *clients* (consumers) of resources. Shared
resources can be files (most often music or video), computation cycles (e.g. the
SETI@home project), or human time and effort (e.g. the I-Help system [8]). A servent built on the open-source Gnutella protocol is characterized by a completely decentralized architecture and by the anonymity of its users [17].
  A free rider is a user who consumes far more resources than s/he offers. According
to the study conducted by Adar and Huberman [1] "almost 70% of Gnutella users
share no files, and nearly 50% of all responses are returned by the top 1% of sharing
hosts". In the context of file sharing, free-riding is not necessarily harmful [18], provided that the users continue to share the replicated files and that they keep their servents running so that they can provide messaging and routing of queries. Therefore
most file-sharing P2P applications use servents that are difficult to shut down, are set
to share downloaded files by default and cleverly hide the options to turn these features off. However, free riding is pernicious in a service-sharing network, like the I-
Help system [8], where there are costs associated with the resources shared (e.g. time

---

[*] This work has been supported by Canadian NSERC and CRA-Women Peer Mentor Grants.

P. Brusilovsky et al. (Eds.): UM 2003, LNAI 2702, pp. 218–227, 2003.

and effort to give help). The few peers who contribute can quickly become saturated with requests, thereby consuming all of their shared resource e.g. bandwidth. In this type of network, Quality of Service (QoS) – the time to find and download a file – degrades as a result of free riding and the system is at risk of collapse.

The free rider in file-sharing P2P applications, like KaZaA, isolated by the asynchronous and anonymous nature of the P2P network, operates under the misconception that s/he is taking resources from some wealthy corporate central server. From the perspective of a single user with a single task, benefiting from a service is simply what a traditional client expects. This user is accustomed to being served and is lagging behind a paradigm shift: s/he is no longer just a client, but in the P2P realm, is a server as well. For the service to persist, everyone needs to make a contribution. The problem that needs to be addressed is creating a perception in the user of the P2P network as a community of volunteers.

This paper proposes to cultivate greater user understanding of his/her role in this community. Through the user interface of a P2P file-sharing client, users are exposed to attractive and informative views of their community and are taught cooperative behaviour through feedback (text messages and reward in terms of better QoS). Modeling the user's level of cooperativeness and relationships with other user enables the interface to take into account individual differences in user interests and cooperative attitude.

COMTELLA (COMmunity GnuTELLA) is a Gnutella-based P2P application, that enables research or study groups of students to share resources, e.g. to exchange both services (e.g. help each other) and files (e.g. research papers, annotations, or stored previous help-sessions). Such an application is needed in an active research group, since maintaining a set of shared bookmarks or links to papers by a dedicated person is difficult and internet links get quickly useless since the target-files (papers) get moved, renamed, or impose access control. The members of the group while performing Internet searches to satisfy their own interests can save interesting papers in an efficient and natural manner. The files (mostly PDF and PS) are stored locally at the group member machines and can be shared with other members using COMTELLA. To be successful, the application requires active involvement of the users. Therefore, it is important to ensure user participation and to encourage the following cooperative behaviours:

- finding, annotating and sharing files; offering services (help)
- staying connected to relay queries and to allow uploads to successfully complete.

The following uncooperative behaviours have to be discouraged:

- sharing very few or no files, not offering any services
- interrupting uploads or services by disconnecting from the network
- searching, receiving services or downloading files and promptly disconnecting.

2   Previous Work

Various approaches have attempted to control free-riding through the imposition of micro-payments [6] or through banning of uncooperative clients. Mojo Nation (www.mojonation.net) [16] attempted to introduce an electronic currency and micro-payments (i.e. payment for each download) to provide economic incentives to sharing. However, this approach failed to stimulate users to contribute, since the extra expenditure of user cognitive resources to decide whether to start a download when s/he has to pay for it acts as a disincentive [19].

"Direct Connect (http://www.neo-modus.com/) ... survives because of its strong community. The community makes people feel responsibility for the network and leave the program running to help it. It also helps to keep freeloading down"[5]. The trouble with Direct Connect, however, lies in the exclusivity of its community. It forces users to share a minimum of 3 GB and bans them from the network if they do not comply. This method does not encourage cooperation because clearly banned users are not available to be influenced. Limewire (www.limewire.com) has a user-controlled free-rider policy that quietly denies access to those who do not share the required minimum number of files. While this policy allows altruists to support free-riders and is more inclusive than Direct Connect's approach, it relies on default preference settings that can be changed by the user. However, Limewire does not give any feedback to the user to effect a change in user attitudes or behaviours.

Only one P2P application, Kazaa Lite v.2, has recently attempted to model user participation and to reward it by better QoS. The servent maintains a numeric participation level for each node and adjusts the speed of downloads based on this value. The participation level of a user seems to be a function of the difference of how much (what amount of MB) other people have uploaded from the user and how much the user has downloaded. Therefore, participation level and QoS of users offering many files can deteriorate quickly, if no one happens to download from them at a time when they need to download more. This leads to unexplainable for the user fluctuations in the his/her participation level, resulting in frustration and feeling of unfairness [13].

None of the above-mentioned applications employs effective methods to promote cooperative behaviour and inhibit uncooperative behaviour in the users. None have intentionally built a community structure. Successful applications such as Napster and Direct Connect can, however, attribute their success largely to the sense of community that has emerged from the common interests of their users. Napster attracted users with a shared interest in exchange of music files, a popular goal that ensured a critical mass of user participation. Direct Connect attracts an exclusive group of like-minded people (those who enjoy visibility and abhor free-riding). Our approach intentionally strives to create and promote a strong sense of community.

Based on our experience with I-Help [8] we found four strategies of motivating users to participate in a community [21].
1. by trying to influence the user's feelings to stimulate altruism in the community,
2. by rewarding the user with visibility / reputation depending on his/her contribution,
3. by allowing the user to develop relationships with other users in the community (one would do a favour to a friend, but not to anonymous people),
4. by providing a tangible incentive for user contribution in terms of better QoS: (priority in queues, more bandwidth for download).

It seems that to successfully apply these methods, one needs to know whether the user tends to be selfish or altruistic, what are his/her areas of interest and who else shares these interests (since users behave differently in different communities of interest), whether s/he is socially motivated by status, reputation, or by maintaining a large set of friends. COMTELLA employs user modeling to capture the first two types of features. Modeling the individual social motivation factors of the user has not yet been implemented in COMTELLA. To our best knowledge, apart from modeling user interests, there have been no approaches to modeling these user characteristics.

3 COMTELLA: An Adaptive P2P Servent

The COMTELLA servent uses an open-source Gnutella v.06 servent (jTella) that has been extended to perform user modeling, advanced searches, transfers and logging of experimental data. The servent is equipped with a personalized motivational interface.

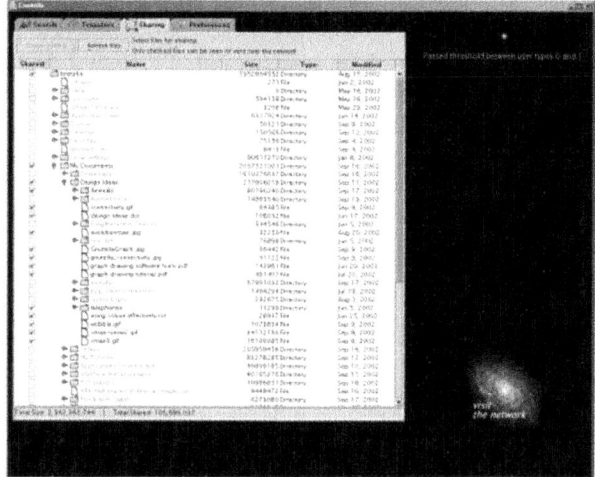

Fig. 1. The COMTELLA Interface

The interface (see Figure 1) provides the user with a "Tasks" area consisting of a tabbed set of four panels. The 'Search', 'Transfers', and 'Options' panels offer functionality similar to that found in the interfaces of all file-sharing servents. The 'Sharing' panel is hierarchical file-management tree / table in which shared files are indicated in bold font with a tick mark. Shared files are displayed in the context of all files and directories to provide users with a clear picture of which files and directories are visible to the network and which are private [7].

To the right of the tasks area is a rectangular frame reserved for displaying motivational text. In the lower right of this frame a spiral galaxy icon invites the user to visit the community. The icon is intended to arouse user curiosity and when clicked, toggles between the tasks window and the community view.   The community view and the motivational text comprise the persuasive aspects [4] of the interface and adapt to changes in user behaviour. The graphs shown in the community view and the motivational text are generated based on the user model. The COMTELLA servent models three types of user characteristics: the user interests, relationships and level of cooperativeness. The next three sections discuss these models in more detail.

3.1 Modeling User Interests

The servent models the user's interests through reinforcement learning with evidence coming from the user's queries. To form an ontological model of user interest groups, a hierarchy of search categories and subcategories was created for the domain of computer science extending the ACM classification system. The user's strength of interest S in an area a is calculated based on how frequently and how recently the user has searched in this area.

$$S^a(e_t, t) = i * S^a(e_{t-1}, t-1) + (1 - i) * e_t \qquad (1)$$

where the new (at time t) evidence of interest $e_t \in [0, 1]$ is calculated as $e_t = 1/d$, and $d = 1 + the\_distance$ between the level of the sub-area of the query and the level of the area a in the ontology hierarchy. Currently, the ontology hierarchy has only 2 levels, corresponding to the list of categories and subject descriptors of ACM. Therefore, d can be only 1 or 2. In a more complex ontology hierarchy, there can be more subtle evidence of user interest for categories on higher levels in the hierarchy.

The parameter $i \in [0.5, 1]$ is an inflation rate used to model the fact that older experiences become less important over time. It can be fixed at a given value, say 0.5, giving equal weights to old and new evidence or be computed as a function of the time elapsed since the last evidence of interest in this area, which better captures the current tendency in user interests.

3.2 Modeling User Relationships

The agent also models the servent's relationships with each peer with whom it has a history of file sharing or service usage in areas of shared interests. The agent uses reinforcement learning to update the strength of each relationship within a certain context (area of interest) and computes the balance (reciprocity) of relationships over all contexts.

The success of each download or service is used to update the *strength of the relationship* between the users through a reinforcement learning formula similar to (1). Servents searching for files / services offered by the user, who choose to download files or use the services offered by the user, are also added to the list of "relationships" of the user for the particular area of interest. The area of interest is dependent on the query used for the search. Thus relationships are indexed with respect to areas of interest.

Also a *general ranked list of relationships* is maintained. The same two users X and Y can be involved in different relationships R_{a1}^{XY}, R_{a2}^{XY}, R_{a3}^{XY} in different areas of interest $a1$, $a2$, $a3$. A high *general strength of relationship* $R^{XY} = \Sigma_i (R_{ai}^{XY})$ between X and Y means an overlap of interests between the users, so they are considered as "friends". The general ranked list contains the relationships in which the user is involved, sorted with respect to "general strength".

In addition to the relationship's strength and context, the servent keeps track of the general *balance (reciprocity)* of each relationship. The servent of user X calculates the balance of its relationship with the servent of user Y as:

$$B^{XY} = (N^{X \leftarrow Y} - N^{Y \leftarrow X}) / (N^{X \leftarrow Y} + N^{Y \leftarrow X}) \qquad (2)$$

i.e. the difference between the number of times when the user X has downloaded files from Y ($N^{X \leftarrow Y}$) and the number of times when user Y has downloaded files from X ($N^{Y \leftarrow X}$). If the balance is negative, the user X "owes" user Y.

The sum of the balances of all relationships of a user defines how much s/he has contributed to the community and how much s/he has consumed. This measure seems similar to the participation level computed by KaZaA Lite v.2. However, keeping a balance of each relationship allows us to maintain a model of the user's contribution to individual users, to every interest group in which s/he participates and to the network as a whole. The servent uses the model of user relationships to create a visualization of the community, as will be explained in the section 4.

3.3 Modeling User Cooperativeness Level

The user cooperativeness model is based on a three-way classification of user type: *altruistic, reciprocal* and *selfish* [22]. Altruists contribute more than they take. Selfish users take but do not give. Reciprocal users consume in proportion with how they contribute. The user type is initialized as *reciprocal*, since it can be assumed that most users are rational and will behave fairly given sufficient incentive.

When the user performs an action that gives evidence of her cooperativeness, the model is updated accordingly. Altruistic actions include selecting files for sharing, setting the program shutdown options to either allow all transfers to complete before exiting, to complete all uploads or only uploads to friends. Selfish actions include revoking sharing privileges for files, stopping and/or cancelling uploads, setting shutdown options to terminate all transfers and exit immediately or to complete downloads only. Let $w \in [-1,0) \cup (0,1]$ represent the weight of evidence, where $w < 0$ is a selfish act while $w > 0$ is an altruistic act. The measure of user cooperativeness at time t is then

$$C(w_t, t) = i * C(w_{t-1}, t-1) + (1 - i) * w_t, \tag{3}$$

Let B^{XY} be as defined in (2) and n represent the total number of users Y with whom user X has formed relationships.

$$overallBalance = (1/n)*\Sigma_Y(B^{XY}) \tag{4}$$

$$userType = (C(w_t, t) + overallBalance) /2 \tag{5}$$

If *userType* is in [-1, -0.5) then user is *selfish*, if it is in [-0.5) $\cup$ (0.5] then user is *reciprocal*, and if it is in (0.5, 1] then user is *altruistic*. A larger interval is defined for reciprocal users and smaller, but equal intervals for both extremes since altruists and selfish users are assumed to be more rare. Although empirical studies [1] indicate that most participants on P2P file-sharing networks are selfish, it is more likely that they are reciprocal users who haven't yet learned the rules or simply haven't been offered sufficient incentive to cooperate.

3.4 Adaptation

Adaptation in COMTELLA has two aspects:
1) rewarding with higher QoS the users who have many strong relationships in a given community of shared area of interests, and
2) selection of appropriate motivational strategies to encourage higher levels of participation.

Since the focus of this paper is on 2), the remainder of this section only briefly sketches the approach for achieving 1). More details are available in [20].

Better QoS i.e. faster finding of higher quality files and services is achieved by:

- Adaptively selecting the servents that form the neighbourhood among those involved in strong positive relationships with the user in the area of search.
- Prioritizing transfers according to the balance of relationship with the user requesting the file.
- Not decrementing the time to live of the 5-6 best friends' queries, which leads to increase in their search horizon.

Since the success of searches and transfers is based on the user's relationships, users who are cooperative and create strong positive relationships, i.e. who contribute a lot of high quality resources that are in demand in their areas of interest will be rewarded with a higher QoS. The remainder of the paper focuses on the second part of the adaptation process - the selection of appropriate motivational strategies to promote higher levels of participation and cooperativeness in the user.

4 Persuasion Strategies for Participation and Cooperativeness

Persuading the user to participate in a P2P environment is similar to teaching him/her to be a good net citizen. Cultivating greater user understanding of his/her role in the sharing community is approached in two ways:

- exposing users to attractive and informative visualizations of their community, and
- using visual cues and runtime feedback to teach cooperative behaviour.

Modeling of the user's level of cooperativeness enables the servent to adapt the interface to the individual user.

4.1 Stimulating Community Awareness

A P2P network community can be likened to a large city, where anti-social behaviour flourishes in its complexity and anonymity. Strong neighbourhoods and cities emerge from the "constant procession of eyes" on city sidewalks. This is because sidewalks "provide both the right kind and the right number of local interactions" among its citizens [11]. The P2P interface can provide analogous feedback to stimulate community awareness and promote understanding of the user's role in a sharing community.

To provide "the right kind and the right number of local interactions", the COMTELLA servent extracts a cognitively manageable set of events from the potentially overwhelming amount of network traffic and runtime events. Pertinent events include uploads to friends, uploads to freeloaders, interrupted downloads and queries received in areas of high interest.

Feedback is triggered both by interesting network events and by changes in the user cooperativeness model [4]. Cues are delivered in the persuasive panel as subtle animations coupled with explanatory text. The animations and text target the user's low and high level cognitive processes respectively. The animations depict shooting stars, galaxy formation and other astronomical phenomena.

When evidence of (un)cooperativeness is detected, the text explains the cause and effect relationship between user behavior and QoS. For example, when a user of type "selfish" acts altruistically, s/he is informed of future improvement in e.g. search results and download speed. It is permissible for users to consciously ignore the text. It will continue to serve as a cue, targeting the low-level cognitive processes of the user and long-term memory storage [9].

The community views are revealed by clicking on the galaxy icon. These views are also visualized according to an astronomical metaphor using stars and galaxies. Radio buttons offer a choice of three views of the network community, organized by connectivity, rank and interest clusters.

The connectivity view shows the hop-graph of the current network architecture [12]. Each node represents a peer that is currently reachable from the servent. This view targets the user's need for current information [4] by adapting to the changing topology of network.

The rank view organizes peers according to balance (reciprocity) and strength of relationship (as discussed in 3.2). Peers are represented as stars of differing size and intensity. Brighter stars indicate that a peer has been a strong contributor (i.e. the user "owes" the peer). Size indicates the general strength of the relationship (i.e. large stars imply a large R^{XY}). Position indicates overall rank: top-ranking peers are placed at the top of the view. Using these visual semantics, rank view (presented in Figure 2) shows the peers who have been of greatest utility to the user as the most prominent stars.

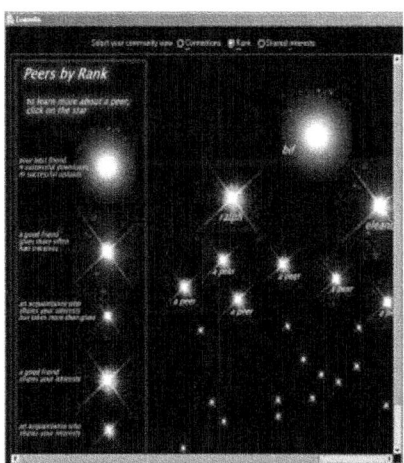 

Fig. 2. Rank visualization   **Fig. 3.** Interest clusters

The ranking views are targeted at reputation-motivated and socially motivated users: reputation-aware users to gain visibility on the community stage, and socially motivated users to build up and maintain relationships, for example, by not interrupting transfers of friends or by serving help requests.

Figure 3 shows the peers grouped by shared interests. Clusters of peers with strong interest in different areas are represented as galaxies from the Hubble heritage collection [10]. Each cluster represents a single interest category, so peers can appear in more than one context. When the mouse is hovered over a galaxy icon, the full name of the interest category and the number of members is displayed. When clicked on, each galaxy icon explodes to show a detailed cluster of the stars / peers in that group.

The visualization of interest clusters targets altruistic users, who tend to be motivated by a common cause. In each of the views, the user can click on a star to access information about the represented peer.

5 Evaluation

COMTELLA can be run with or without the persuasive interface. When the persuasion is turned off, the interface only shows the tasks panel. The user models are constructed in both modes. COMTELLA will be run in the MADMUC and ARIES labs at the University of Saskatchewan with 24 graduate students for 3 months starting in April 2003; half of the students will use the program with the persuasive elements turned on, while the remaining students will use the non-persuasive version. A central "spy" server is added to the decentralized Gnutella network. This server will be running for the duration of the experiment and will collect statistics from servents about their cooperativeness measures, overall balance of relationships, as well as login/logout times, number of files and disk space shared, number of completed downloads, speed of transfers.

To demonstrate the effectiveness of our approach, COMTELLA's motivational interface will be evaluated to answer the following questions:

- Does average uptime (users leaving their servents running) increase?
- Does membership stabilize at a critical mass with persuasion turned on?
- Does QoS (speed of finding and downloading acquiring files) improve?
- Are users satisfied with the functionality of the system?

The evaluation has to look for changes over time in each user, because of effects resulting from the complexity of the system [11]. For example, altruists may be turned off by the interface, but other users could be stimulated to participate more, thus free riding may remain the same globally, but different users may be involved.

6 Conclusions

Free riding, while perhaps not disastrous in P2P systems for sharing replicable resources (files), is a serious problem for bootstrapping a system especially when there are costs associated with sharing, e.g. in P2P systems for sharing services such as processor cycles or bandwidth. This paper proposes applying user modeling and adaptation techniques in the area of P2P systems and is the first one to suggest modeling the user cooperativeness and relationships with other users. User modeling and social persuasion cues are utilized to help users realize their role in the community. At the time of writing of this paper, it still remains to experimentally evaluate this approach to assess its effectiveness with respect to stimulating participation, improving QoS and ensuring user satisfaction. We hope that most collaborative multi-user networked environments can benefit from this approach.

References

1. Adar, E. & Huberman, B.A., (2000). Free Riding on Gnutella. Available online at http://www.firstmonday.dk/issues/issue5_10/adar/
2. Bornstein Pittman, R.S. (1992). Perception Without Awareness, New York, Guilford Press.
3. Erwin, P. (2001). Attitudes and Persuasion, Philadelphia, Psychology Press.
4. Fogg, B.J. (2000). Persuasive Technologies and Netsmart Devices in: Bergman, E. (ed.) Information Appliances and Beyond, Chapter 11, Morgan Kaufman.
5. Gnutella Developer Forum, http://groups.yahoo.com/group/the_gdf/
6. Golle, Ph., Leyton-Brown, K., Mironov, I. (2001) Incentives for Sharing in Peer-to-Peer Networks. Proc. EC'01, October 12–17, 2001, Tampa, Florida, ACM Press, 264–267.
7. Good, N.S., Krekelberg, A. Usability and privacy: a study of Kazaa P2P file-sharing. http://www.hpl.hp.com/shl/papers/kazaa/KazaaUsability.pdf
8. Greer J., McCalla G., Vassileva J., Deters R., Bull S., Kettel L. (2001) Lessons Learned in Deploying a Multi-Agent Learning Support System: The I-Help Experience, Proc. AI in Education AIED'2001, San Antonio, IOS Press: Amsterdam, 410–421.
9. Heath, R. (2001). The Hidden Power of Advertising, Oxfordshire, Publications.
10. Hubble Heritage Collection. Available online at http://heritage.stsci.edu/
11. Johnson, S. (2001). Emergence: The Connected Lives of Ants, Brains, Cities, and Software. New York: Scribner.
12. Jovanovic, M. (2001) Modeling Large Scale Peer-to-Peer Networks, M.Sc. Thesis, University of Cincinatti, http://www.ececs.uc.edu/~mjovanov/Research/gnutella.html
13. Kazaa Lite Version 2 http://www.fasttrackmovies.com/forum/topic.asp?TOPIC_ID=298
14. Khaslavsky, J. and Shedroff, N. (1999). Seductive Computing. Available online at http://captology.stanford.edu/Key_Concepts/Papers/CACMseduction.pdf
15. Maddock (2000). Motigraphics: The Analysis and Measurement of Human Motivations in Marketing, Wesport CT, Quorum Books.
16. MojoNation. Available on line at: www.mojonation.net
17. Shirky C., K. Truelove, R. Dornfest, L. Gonze. (2001) The Emergent Platform of Presence, Identity, and Edge Resources. O'Reilly 2001 Networking Overview, O'Reilly Online Catalog, Available at http://www.oreilly.com/catalog/p2presearch/chapter/ch01.html
18. Shirky, C. (2000). In Praise of Freeriders.
Available online at http://www.openp2p.com/pub/a//2000/12/01/shirky_freeloading.html
19. Shirky, C. (2000). Peers not Pareto.
Available online at http://www.openp2p.com/lpt/a/p2p/2000/12/15/pareto.html
20. Vassileva, J. (2002) Motivating Participation in Peer to Peer Communities, Proc. ESAW02, Madrid.
http://www.ai.univie.ac.at/%7Epaolo/conf/esaw02/esaw02accpapers.html.
21. Vassileva J. (2002) Motivating Participation in Virtual Communities, Proc. 12th International Conference of Women in Engineering and Science, ICWES'12, 28 July-2 August, Ottawa, Canada. Available at: http://julita.usask.ca/Texte/ICWES12.pdf
22. Voss, J.L. (2001) "Minds, Cultures, the Environment and Altruism: a meta-model using Particle Swarm + Agent Based Modeling" in Proc. Particle Swarm Optimization Workshop, Purdue University, Indianapolis. McGraw (2001).

Discourse Analysis Techniques for Modeling Group Interaction*

Alexander Feinman and Richard Alterman

Computer Science Department, Brandeis University MS018,
415 South St., Waltham MA 02454
{afeinman,alterman}@cs.brandeis.edu

Abstract. This paper presents discourse analysis techniques that model
the interaction of a small group of users engaged in same-place/different-
time interaction. We analyzed data from *VesselWorld*, our experimental
testbed, and formulated a modeling technique based on the recurrence
of coordination problems and the structure that users create to handle these problems. Subsequent experiments revealed that our original
analysis had failed to capture issues with the cognitive load required to
maintain common ground. By tracking references users make to both
domain and conversational objects, we were able to extract patterns of
information access and model the cognitive load incurred to maintain
common ground. The improved model of user interaction was successful
in explaining systems designed to support interaction.

1 Introduction

Groupware applications for supporting interaction can be very hard to use, sometimes impairing the work they are built to support. Design of successful groupware applications is challenging, for reasons ranging from technical concerns to
sociological issues of introducing groupware into an existing interaction. Ideally,
a software system is built to support the emergent practice of work for a community of users. For groupware systems, this requires modeling the interaction
of users as they perform their work.

This paper presents discourse analysis techniques that model group interaction, and analyzes results based on data collected using our groupware testbed,
VesselWorld [9]. Initially, we analyzed experimental data from VesselWorld to
model recurrent issues of coordination and investigate the conversational structure that users created. This analysis indicated that we needed to model the
cognitive load of maintaining common ground. By building a model of how users
publish, access, and modify information, we can determine how a system should
mediate that information to improve performance. In particular, the length of
time that a topic is relevant, the frequency of reference to the topic over that
time, and the pattern of access to the information all serve as useful indicators of

---

* This research was supported by the Office of Naval Research under grants No.
N00014-96-1-0440 and N66001-00-1-8965

P. Brusilovsky et al. (Eds.): UM 2003, LNAI 2702, pp. 228–237, 2003.

cognitive load and indicate how to present and store information. This method of modeling user interaction explains observed results from the VesselWorld experimental data, and can be used to create systems that properly support the way users exchange information or adapt existing systems to improve such support.

2   Modeling Recurrence in Coordination

To study issues in same-time/different-place coordination [5], our lab constructed the VesselWorld groupware system. Three users conduct a simulated clean up of a harbor via a graphical interface. The harbor contains toxic waste that must be cleared safely to a large garbage barge. As the users interact, the system logs all actions and communication for later analysis. This makes VesselWorld ideal for exploring issues of group interaction. At this time, we have collected over 250 hours of data from 18 groups using various versions of VesselWorld.

   Each of the three users acts as the captain of a ship navigating the harbor: two users pilot ships with waste-retrieval cranes attached (referred to as crane1 and crane2), allowing them to lift and load barrels of toxic waste; the other user pilots a tugboat (referred to as tug1), and is able to move small barges around the harbor, identify waste, and seal the leaks caused by mishandling of waste. The harbor is cleared in a turn-based fashion, with each user explicitly planning actions for each turn before submitting them to the system for evaluation. During a session, the users are physically separated, but are able to communicate freely via a textual chat facility built into the VesselWorld system.

235. `crane2: ok, then XLD right?`	proposes lifting a waste
⌈ 236. `crane2: sub Lift`	initiates lift adjacency pair
237. `tug1: yep`	(acknowledges plan to lift waste)
⌊ 238. `crane1: k`	completes lift adjacency pair
⌈ 239. `crane2: sub load`	initiates load adjacency pair
⌊ 240. `crane1: k`	completes load adjacency pair

Fig. 1. Adjacency pairs in dialogue from the VesselWorld system.

   Despite the simplicity of the harbor-clearing task, users of the VesselWorld system had extensive problems staying coordinated. Problems with maintaining common ground, communicating intentions, and managing information appear throughout the data. To handle these issues, users created conversational structure. For example, to lift and load a large barrel of waste, the two cranes must submit a `lift` and `load` commands in synchronization. This led the users to create discourse structure, such as adjacency pairs seen in Figure 1, to help them stay coordinated.

   We turned to discourse analysis to help make sense of the dialog. We made use of theories about rules governing conversational flow [10] and grounding in communication [3] to understand how and why users were constructing conversational structure. We developed an analytic method that built on this research, searching the discourse for three indicators of areas of potential improvement:

1. Recurring patterns of coordination.
2. Recurring errors in coordination.
3. Development of conversational structure by the users to organize recurrent problems of coordination.

Recurrent patterns of coordination and repeating errors are situations in which the users might introduce conversational structure to better organize activity so as to improve performance. The last indicator goes a step further; in this case, the users have determined a potential area of improvement, and have also devised structure to simplify their conversation about the situation and thereby improve it. Examples of structure generated by users include the invention of notational conventions, like specialized jargon ("XLD" meaning an extra-large waste, dredge equipment required), and conversational procedures that support the coordination of activities, like adjacency pairs.

Of the three indicators, the third seems to be the surest bet for the analyst; the users have added corroborating evidence for a particular analysis of the situation. There are problems, however, with an analysis strategy that relies exclusively on the third indicator. The data would have to be very extensive so the users would have time to generate all the most useful secondary structures. The users might identify a coordination problem they would like to fix, but lack the means to fix the problem; there is some evidence for this in our data. Finally, there is no guarantee that organizational structure users might add would improve the situation at all.

2.1   Applying the Model

Based on analysis of data generated in our VesselWorld pilot study, three *coordinating representations* (CRs) — software tools for simplifying context sharing — were introduced into VesselWorld: the *shared planning* window, the *object list*, and the *high-level planning* window. These representations were aimed at capturing specific forms of information being passed between the users: fine-grained timing issues in shared planning, coarse-grained planning and ordering issues in high-level planning, and object references in the object list.

One of these, the object list, is pictured in Figure 2. It presents information about barrels of toxic waste in the harbor in a concise tabular format. A user adds an entry to the object list by entering details about it in the entry fields at the top and clicking "Add Entry". The entry then appears in the list of objects, which is visible to all users. Entries can be modified by anyone by clicking on the cells of the table; updates are sent to all users.

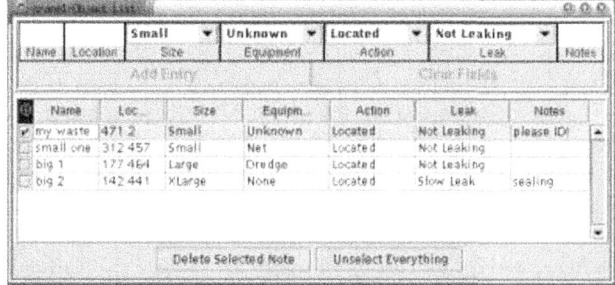

Fig. 2. A coordinating representation: the object list.

2.2   Results

To evaluate the coordinating representations we ran the *VW3* experiment, completed in early 2001. The experiment was a single-variable study conducted to test the utility of these coordinating representations. Six groups of three people were paid to use VesselWorld for 12 hours each, including training time. We examined only the data from the last five hours for each group, in an effort to avoid interference from the effects of having novice users. Three groups used the base (*non-CR*) version of Vesselworld, and could only communicate via textual chat. The other three groups used a version that included the three CRs. Differences were dramatic; users of the CR system completed similar problems in 49% of the clock time that users of the non-CR system required, and committed 61% fewer errors. A complete summary of experimental results can be found in [1].

Significantly, users did not make full use of the provided CRs. The "Action" column of the object list, dealing with the status of the waste was rarely used, and one of the three CRs, the high-level planning window, was not used at all. To figure out what had gone wrong, we developed an analytic method based on discourse analysis that examined the referential structure of the users' discourse.

3   Modeling Cognitive Load

We noted that many of the issues we saw with the existing CRs could be attributed to imbalance in the collaborative effort required to them. For example, using the high-level planning CR seemed to require a lot of effort on the part of the author, while providing only a minimal return on investment. To examine these issues, we created an analysis method centered around the sharing of information between users. In a shared environment like VesselWorld, users interact by negotiating over both domain objects and conversational objects. The initial analysis indicated that tracking these exchanges of information would be useful.

Preliminary analysis of information exchange in the VesselWorld data showed that information of different categories was handled quite differently. Information relating to wastes and other objects in the domain tended to have a long lifetime of relevance (time between first mention and last mention), and the users accessed this information infrequently but steadily during that time. Plans, on the other hand, dominated conversation while they were being discussed, but rarely were reused or referred to once agreed upon unless an error occurred. Repairs, where users attempted to fix mismatches in common ground, correct errors in the interaction, or disambiguate misunderstandings, dominated conversation until corrected: only occasionally would another message find its way into the thread of conversation while a repair was underway.

In VesselWorld, information usually has a simple life cycle. Information is reported by a user, either in the chat window, or (in the CR groups) via the object list or shared planning window; it may then be noted by other users; it again becomes relevant at some point and must be retrieved. Information that is relevant over a long span of time may be updated, modified, or otherwise accessed before it is finally rendered irrelevant and forgotten. While information may reside in the short-term memory of the users, storing complex information there can put an unreasonable cognitive burden on the user; distributing the information into the environment [8] yields superior results. However, presenting too much information can lead to information overload. It is important, therefore, to determine what information is worth supporting by constructing CRs. We formed two hypotheses:

1. Information with a *long period of relevance* is worth recording in a external representation
2. Information which is *accessed frequently* by the users is worth recording in an external representation

These hypotheses serve as general indicators of when adapting the system may simplify coordination. In the first case, information that is relevant over a long period is very likely to be irrelevant for some subsection of that period. During this time, it represents an unnecessary burden on the user's short-term memory, and in a complex situation with many such items, the burden can easily outstrip the user's ability to memorize. In the second situation, the information is used frequently, and hence needs to be readily available to the users. However, there may be too much information for the user to keep it all in short-term memory. Hence, it needs to be easily and continuously accessible to users as they perform their tasks.

3.1   Identifying Referential Structure

In order to highlight information falling into the above categories, an analyst must track the referents users refer to by thorough examination of the discourse. Past work has looked at reference-tracking to help with the difficult problem of reference resolution ([11]). DeCristofaro et al.'s program REFEREE [4] allowed an analyst to manually tag each reference and attempt to thereby resolve references. Our tool works similarly, with the added functionality of providing tools for statistical analysis of analyst-generated data.

Our scheme focuses on identifying the information that users share and following its subsequent use within the system. To avoid the tongue-twister "references to referents", we will call these referents "iotas". An iota represents a simple conversational item that the users refer to. Examples include: a barrel of toxic waste in the VesselWorld domain; a plan to clear a barrel of waste; a repair of differences between common ground between two users; a conventional procedure for handling a particular situation. In general, any sort of information that the users refer to qualifies. To make this clear, let us follow through an example taken from a non-CR group in their final VesselWorld session.

```
  :
  :
 7. tug1: mX at 400 125                          [IOTA-7 waste: mx@400,125]
 8. crane1: medium at 392 127                    [IOTA-8 waste: m?@392,127]
 9. crane1: that's got to be the same one        [IOTA-9 repair: IOTA-8 same as IOTA-7]
10. tug1: yep                                     IOTA-9
11. tug1: that's an mX                            [IOTA-7 waste: mx@392,127]
```

Fig. 3. Analysis of discourse from a non-CR VesselWorld session

In Figure 3, the users have encountered a few wastes, and are sharing what they see so that they can plan how to clean up the harbor. First, in line 7, the user operating the tug reports information about a nearby waste, using an established shorthand: "mX at 400 125". Here, mX indicates that the tug is talking about a waste of medium size (m) that requires no special equipment (X) to handle safely. The tug indicates that the waste can be found at the location (400, 125) in the harbor. To create a waste iota for this referent, the analyst generates a unique name based on the current line of discourse (IOTA-7), puts the iota in square brackets to indicate that this is a new or modified reference, denotes the type of the iota as "waste", and lists all information available about that waste.

In line 8, crane1 simultaneously reports on a waste nearby. The analyst again creates an iota to track it. Here, the type of equipment needed is unknown to the user, as only the tug can ascertain equipment needs. The user indicates this by omission; the analyst instead uses a question mark in the iota definition. In line 9, crane1 notes the similarities between the two waste reports: both wastes are medium-sized, and they are located very close to each other. The reports of equipment (unknown vs. none) are not contradictory. Also, crane1 can likely see the area the tug is referring to, and does not see a waste there. The users have run into this situation before, and so crane1 quickly proposes (in line 9) a need for repair of common ground. The analyst notes the repair as an iota of type "repair", and makes sure to mention the iotas that are involved.

The tug, who can also see both locations (400,125 and 392,127), and is able to refer to the info window to get the exact coordinates for the waste, implicitly agrees to (and therefore refers to) the repair in line 10. It appears that the tug estimated the original specification of the waste location (400,125), rounding to the grid intervals visible on the user's display. The analyst notes the agreement to the repair, and refers to the already-instantiated iota IOTA-9 by naming it without square brackets. In line 11, the tug reviews relevant information about the waste. This acts as evidence supporting the repair (that the two references refer to the same waste). The analyst updates IOTA-7's expansion (again using square brackets, this time to indicate that the contents of the iota are being modified), and chooses the earlier of the two names for the waste (IOTA-7 and IOTA-8) to disambiguate further references to the waste.

3.2 Results

A great deal of information can be gleaned about group interaction and the passing of information from identifying iotas in the discourse. However, in a long session, it is hard to keep track of the large number of iotas that are generated. To help with the task of interpreting the data we developed a number of special-purpose visualization tools. The access pattern for each iota, that is, when and how it is referred to, can be visualized using a program that extracts the iotas from the analysis, summarizes information about the iotas, and graphically represents the access pattern for each iota as a timeline, greatly aiding interpretation.

Iota type	Mentions	Lifetime	Density
Vessel	3.1	183.6	1.7%
Waste	6.6	168.7	3.9%
Location	2.6	62.6	4.2%
Convention	5.5	109.5	5.0%
Barge	11.9	294.0	5.6%
Plan	3.4	12.0	28.5%
Repair	3.0	4.8	62.5%

Fig. 4. Selected results from analysis of the VW3 experimental data.

Some results from analyzing the VW3 data are summarized Figure 4. *Mentions* counts the average number of times an iota is mentioned in any user utterance; for example, in Figure 3, IOTA-8 is mentioned twice. *Lifetime* is the average number, inclusive, of utterances between first and last mention; for IOTA-8, two. *Density* is the ratio of these two numbers, and represents the percent of utterances over the life of an iota that refer to that iota; as IOTA-8 dominates conversation over its short life, its density is 100%. These measures are calculated for each iota, and the average for each type is calculated.

Raw data about lifetime of relevance, frequency of reference, and density of reference can be represented in a scatter plot, to highlight clusters of iotas with similar access patterns. In the semi-log plot shown in Figure 5, the domination of longer lifetimes by waste iotas is clearly visible. Iotas in the upper-left quadrant represent those that by their nature will dominate conversation, and are unlikely to require a persistent representation. In contrast, those in the lower-right quadrant of the scatter plot (i.e., wastes) require the most long-term coordination

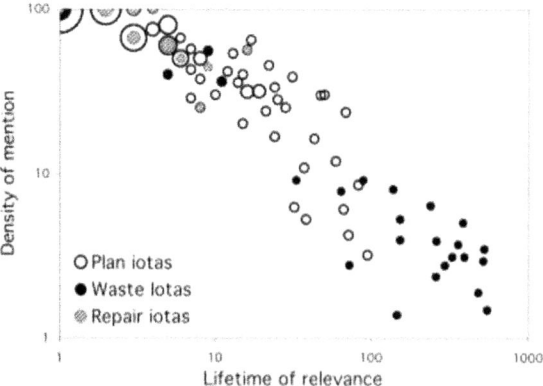

Fig. 5. Distribution of iotas for a non-CR group (larger bubbles indicate multiple iotas)

work. From this data we drew conclusions about the workload required to stay coordinated over each sort of information. Here we present results for the most frequent types of iotas used by users in the VW3 experiment, plans and wastes, which together comprised over 80% of the iotas seen.

Plans. As can be seen in Figure 5, plan iotas generally have a short lifetime: 85% of plans seen lasted 6 or fewer utterances. During this lifetime they had a high frequency of mention, with 50% or higher density for 70% of the plans seen. Only in about 10% of the cases will a plan drag on for some time, generally when it is postponed in favor of another plan; it then shows a pattern resembling two plans strung together, one starting at the initial negotiation, and one starting at the (postponed) re-negotiation.

This distribution of most plans leads us to conclude that, while negotiation of a plan is crucial, their short lifetime means that users will be unlikely to want to put any effort into constructing a shared external representation of their plan. In addition, because a small number of plans co-exist at any one time, and they tend to dominate conversation while they are being discussed, users are probably storing them in short-term memory and using the recent chat for reference. Hence, while an external representation of a plan may serve to ground the plan for multiple users, it is unlikely that users would require persistent storage of plans.

This prediction agrees with the experimental evidence produced by the VW3 experiment. Despite extensive training in its use users refused to use the high-level planning window, which required significant user effort to create and share a representation of plans, but allowed persistent storage of these plans. The features offered by high-level planning (persistent plan storage, visible plan commitments) were not of sufficient worth to users to outweigh the cost of reporting their plans via the window. However, they fully embraced the shared planning window, which allowed a low-impact (if less general-purpose) method for sharing near-term intentions. Because it provided good visibility of current intentions, coupled with a low cost to communicate those intentions, shared planning matched the short-term, non-persistent usage pattern of plans.

Shared domain objects. The most common type of shared domain object, wastes, have a quite long lifetime of relevance: anywhere from 50 to 500 utterances, depending on session length, complexity, and the order in which the users clear the wastes. In addition, there are short periods of intense activity relating to the wastes, separated by long stretches of up to 40% of the lifetime where they are not discussed at all. This periodic distribution imposes a heavy load on short term memory for the long stretches where the waste information is not relevant. Also, because of the long lifetime, multiple wastes are often relevant simultaneously; hence, when retrieving information about wastes, users will first need to choose a waste. Storing waste information therefore requires a persistent representation providing easy access and modification capabilities.

In the non-CR system, we provided two methods for discussing wastes: chat history and private markers. As waste is discovered, users generally announce their discovery in chat. Other users could access waste information in the history of their chat, but this was difficult, as it was interleaved with all other communication. Most users used the private markers instead. These allowed a user to annotate his or her map view with a simple note, akin to a sticky note. They were used extensively by most users to keep track of the waste. But markers had a number of problems. First, they effectively tripled the amount of group work needed to stay coordinated, by making each user place a marker in their own private environment. Second, placing a marker required the user to take information from chat, process it correctly, and place a marker in the appropriate position on the map. These complications were a source of great error in non-CR groups. Users often discovered mismatches in their sets of markers, prompting one group to introduce the "marker check", a complex conversational structure, to synchronize these private representations.

The object list, which consolidates information about wastes and other domain objects, addresses these issues. To support the periodic distribution characteristic of waste iotas it is important to construct a persistent and easy-to-access shared representation. The object list gives such a shared, persistent representation. Despite the relatively high cost of formulating an object in the object list (generally 15-30 seconds of interface work, mixed between mouse and keyboard), users willingly performed the task, perhaps sensing a return on the time investment: times for retrieving waste information were as high as a minute when the user had to scan through the chat history, in comparison to a few seconds required to scan of the object list. By providing an authoritative shared source of waste information, mismatches in common ground were reduced. Overall collaborative effort was therefore greatly reduced.

4   Future Work

We are working on quantifying the costs associated with communication for maintaining common ground. Users follow a path of least collaborative effort

([3], [7]) when deciding what medium to communicate information; therefore, modeling the exact costs with using a particular tool for communication will allow a designer to compare them directly. We saw evidence of this tendency in the object list: despite a high cost of formulating utterances in the object list, groups universally used it, due to the reduction in group effort to maintain common ground thereafter.

Finally, the methods here are presented as methods by which an analyst can adapt and redesign a system off-line. However, improvements in live tagging of natural language discourse (as demonstrated by systems such as TRIPS-98 [6]) may allow automatic extraction and tracking of iotas, which would lead to a system that could continuously reassess use of information. By building continuously-updated models of user information use, the system could track live information use and adapt its interface dynamically to present the information in a more favorable or easy-to-use fashion.

References

1. Alterman, R., Feinman, A., Introne, J., Landsman, S.: Coordinating Representations in Computer-Mediated Joint Activities. Proceedings of 23rd Annual Conference of the Cognitive Science Society (2001)
2. Carpenter, T., Alterman, R.: A Taxonomy for Planned Reading. 16th Annual Conference of the Cognitive Science Society (1994)
3. Clark, H.H., Brennan, S.E.: Grounding in communication. In Resnick, L.B., Levine, J., Teasley, S.D., editors, *Perspectives on Socially Shared Cognition* APA Press (1991)
4. DeCristofaro, J., Strube, M., McCoy, K.: Building a Tool for Annotating Reference in Discourse. Proceedings of the Workshop on the Relation of Discourse/Dialogue Structure and Reference, ACL'99 (1999)
5. Ellis, C.A., Gibbs, S.J., Rein, G.L.: Groupware: some issues and experiences. Communications of the ACM **34** (1991)
6. Ferguson, G., Allen, J.: TRIPS: An Intelligent Integrated Problem-Solving Assistant. Proceedings of the 15th National Conference on Artificial Intelligence (1998)
7. Gray, W., Fu, W.: Ignoring perfect knowledge in-the-world for imperfect knowledge in-the-head: implications of rational analysis for interface design. CHI Letters **3** (2001)
8. Hutchins, E.: Cognition in the Wild. Cambridge: MIT Press (1995)
9. Landsman, S., Alterman, R., Feinman, A., Introne, J.: VesselWorld and ADAPTIVE. Technical Report TR-01-213, Department of Computer Science, Brandeis University (2001). Presented as a demonstration at *CSCW-2000*
   http://group.cs.brandeis.edu/group/papers/CSCWDemo.pdf
10. Sacks, H., Schegloff,, E., Jefferson, G.: A simplest systematics for the organisation of turn-taking for conversation. Language **50** (1974)
11. Seville, H., Ramsay, A.: Reference-based Discourse Structure for Reference Resolution. Proceedings of the Workshop on the Relation of Discourse/Dialogue Structure and Reference, ACL'99 (1999)

Group Decision Making through Mediated Discussions

Daniel Kudenko[1], Mathias Bauer[2], and Dietmar Dengler[2]

[1] Department of Computer Science, University of York
Heslington, York, YO10 5DD, UK
kudenko@cs.york.ac.uk
[2] German Research Center for AI
Stuhlsatzenhausweg 3, 66123 Saarbruecken, Germany
{bauer,dengler}@dfki.de

Abstract. To date, product recommendation systems have mainly been looked at from a single-agent perspective, where only the interests of a single user are taken into account. We extend this scenario and consider the case where multiple users are planning a joint purchase, and therefore many (potentially conflicting) interests have to be considered.

In this paper we present an overview of a system that assists a group of users to reach a joint decision on an online catalogue purchase. This is done by acquiring individual user models and using these models to mediate a kind of group discussion with the goal to arrive at a compromise that is acceptable to all group members.

1 Introduction

Consider the following scenario. A family is planning to purchase a car via catalogue. Each family member has certain preferences and these have to be taken into account in the decision process. Furthermore, the preferences of some individuals have higher priority than others. For example, the parents may have more of a say than the children.

Using current online catalogue technology, each family member would need to browse the catalogue individually to find his or her optimal choice, and then the family members would have to go through a (potentially lengthy and cumbersome) negotiation process with frequent references to the catalogue to reach a decision.

In this paper we propose a system that will assist a group of users in a joint catalogue purchase and help them to efficiently reach a decision by acquiring user models and simulating a negotiation that is fair and acceptable to all. Users can question individual negotiation steps and the system will subsequently present an explanation of the step based on the user models and the argumentation techniques involved. Users may update their preference models at any time, which accounts for the possibility that a user changes his mind when presented with mediation results. While joint catalogue purchases are a focus domain in

P. Brusilovsky et al. (Eds.): UM 2003, LNAI 2702, pp. 238–247, 2003.

this paper, our proposed mediation system can be applied to any domain where a group of users need to make a joint decision.

The paper is organized as follows. First, we present a general overview of the system and its architecture. We then continue with a more detailed description of the two main components: the user modeling component, and the mediator. Finally, related and future work is discussed.

2   The MIAU System

Figure 1 depicts the overall architecture of the MIAU system. In a first phase, each of the users asynchronously interacts with the electronic catalog using a Web-based search interface. The system observes this interaction and derives a user model capturing the essential aspects of the user's preferences w.r.t. the catalog entries. Once this session is complete, the user models so generated are handed over to the Mediator. It identifies negotiable aspects as well as in-surmountable differences between the various users' preferences and—using a number of conflict resolution strategies—suggests seemingly acceptable compromises. Each user can accept or reject these suggestions which leads to an update of her respective preference model. This process is repeated until a compromise has been found that is accepted by all group members.

In the rest of this section we will introduce the representation of the preference models and describe in some detail the various stages of the compromising process.

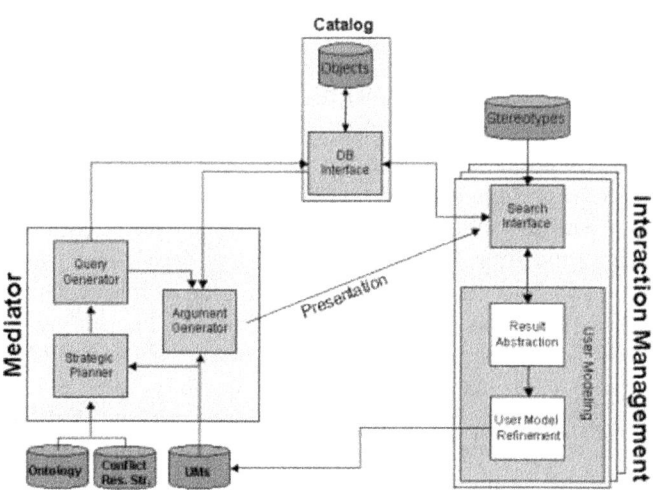

Fig. 1. System overview

3   User Model Representation, Generation, and Maintenance

The items in a catalogue are described by a number of attributes or *dimensions*. In our case, the cars are described in terms of their price, maximum speed, fuel consumption etc. Users, however, typically do not consider these attributes in isolation, but rather assess the appropriateness of a car using more abstract value dimensions. These include the sportiness of car, its environmental friendliness or its suitability as a family car. The various attributes and their concrete values contribute more or less strongly in a positive or negative way to the user's assessment of a car with respect to these dimensions. While a strong engine positively contributes to a car being perceived as sporty, the same value will have a negative influence on the assessment of its environmental friendliness which indicates that value dimensions are frequently in conflict with each other such that acceptable trade-offs are required.

In order to formalize a user's preferences in such a multi-dimensional setting, we use the multi-attribute utility theory (MAUT) [3] value functions to quantify the acceptability (or utility) of various attribute values (e.g. a low fuel consumption will have a higher value than a high consumption). Similarly, numerical values indicate how strongly an attribute influences the assessment of a car along a particular dimension and how important a dimension is to the user. While e.g. the size of the trunk has a strong impact on the car's suitability as a family car, it has little to do with its environmental friendliness. The latter, in turn, might be much more important to the user than its sportiness.

Given such a user model and the concrete values of the various attributes describing a car, a numerical value reflecting its overall utility can be computed, thus allowing allowing a rank order to be computed for all catalogue entries.

The atomic and abstract dimensions are normally specified in advance by a domain expert, but can also be defined by the user.

The richness of the MAUT formalism that allows the user's preferences to be described in a very detailed way has to be bought by a lengthy acquisition process as a large number of parameters has to be determined. To shorten this process, missing values are usually filled with default values taken from *stereotypical* user models capturing typical preferences of e.g. "sporty drivers" or "family men".

In our scenario the individual user models are derived from the user's interaction with the electronic catalog. To shorten the dialog, the user can compose an initial user profile by combining predefined stereotypes such as those mentioned above to formulate a first catalog query. The user can then react to the search result using a variety of means including candidate critique (see [5]), ordering items according to their appropriateness etc. from which a new, refined query to the catalog is derived. Eventually this process will converge and a corresponding preference model is derived from the properties of the top rated catalog entries.[1]

In many cases a user's preferences cannot be captured by a single preference model. Instead there exist more or less disjoint classes of products that are

---

[1] A detailed description of the interaction is beyond the scope of this paper.

preferred in certain situations. In the car scenario, for example, a user might in general be interested in cars with high transportation capacity (e.g. a station wagon) in which case she prefers an inexpensive model. If, however, discussion turns around a more sporty car, she tends towards a convertible and is much less interested in the price.[2]

As a consequence, each *user model* U_i for a user u_i in the MIAU system consists of a number of *preference models* P_{ij} represented by one value tree each and capturing one of the abovementioned distinct interest areas:

$$U_i = \{P_{i1}, ..., P_{in_i}\}. \tag{1}$$

To simplify the following discussion, we will nevertheless assume the existence of just one preference model per user. In the complete model the mediator has the additional task of selecting the appropriate preference model among those available for each user.

4   Finding a Compromise

The negotiation simulation process is controlled by a central mediator module based on the individual user models. The mediation process takes place in three stages: the choice of the negotiation target, individual trade-offs, and the choice of the negotiation operators and their order (i.e., the actual negotiation simulation).

4.1   Choice of Negotiation Target

At first, the mediator computes the optimal choice for each user and an equilibrium point in the catalogue that is used as the target point of the negotiation (i.e., the choice that is the outcome of the negotiation). The equilibrium point is computed according to the following criteria:

- The utility loss of moving from the optimal choice to the equilibrium point is roughly equal for all users. Note that it is often impossible to find an ideal compromise within the catalogue for which all users would have exactly the same utility loss.
- The sum of the utility losses of all users is minimal (or within a certain range of this minimum).

In addition to the above criteria, each user may select personal criteria that further restrict the choice of equilibrium point, such as:

- Prefer small utility losses on a large number of dimensions.
- Prefer larger utility losses on fewer dimensions.

---

[2] In the current version the user explicitly indicates such an interest shift while interaction with the search interface. Future work includes the development of a machine learning approach for the automatic detection of such product classes.

– Prefer fewer utility losses on more important dimensions to more utility losses on less important dimensions.

Preferences like these may also be derived from previous interactions of the user with the mediator.

Of course, there are cases where not all user preferences can be satisfied completely, at which point the closest possible approximation is chosen.

4.2   Individual Trade-Offs

For an individual user, changing the choice from the optimum to the equilibrium point does not necessarily mean a loss of utility on all dimensions. Some dimension values may even yield a higher utility, if taken separately. In return for receiving benefits along one dimension, a user may be willing to make compromises on others. For example, a user purchasing a car may be willing to pay more for a faster car.

In the individual trade-off phase, for each dimension that yields a utility increase when changing the choice to the equilibrium point, another dimension with a utility decrease is chosen and a trade-off is performed. While the latter dimension is currently chosen at random, it would be useful to make it dependent on user preferences. For example, from past negotiations it could be derived that a user prefers individual trade-offs on dimensions with higher weight.

If a user has no specific preference between the current value of a dimension and the target value (e.g., because the dimension weight is 0, or the user model specifies no utility decrease), the respective dimension value is changed during the individual trade-off phase.

4.3   Negotiation Simulation

Once an equilibrium point has been chosen and individual trade-offs have been executed, a group negotiation is simulated that leads to the choice of the target item. While the negotiation target is fixed (due to the need for fairness), there are potentially many ways to reach the target in the negotiation. The goal of the negotiation simulation is to convince the users of the validity of the proposed purchase (i.e., the equilibrium point).

A negotiation simulation consists of a sequence of negotiation operators. The following negotiation operators are included in the system:

– *Offer trade-off:* A user offers to reduce his utility by changing the value of one or more dimensions in order to move closer to the negotiation target. Once a user (or rather the mediator) makes such an offer, other users must follow up and offer dimension changes to move closer to the target as well. In order to ensure a fair negotiation, the utility loss for these replies has to be equal to the loss for the original proposal.[3]

---

[3] A user may also *conditionally accept* a trade-off ("I accept this, provided we also have that."). Internally, this corresponds to a modification of this user's preference model.

– *Refer to precedent:* This operator is used in combination with a trade-off and strengthens the choice of a dimension value by referring to one or more precedents (e.g., "we always bought a Dodge"). This operator modifies the utility functions for the respective dimension.

The choice, instantiation, and order of negotiation operators is based on heuristics that are designed to make the process of reaching an agreement more efficient and the negotiation more convincing. For example, executing trade-offs on more important dimensions early in the negotiation, may allow a user to detect crucial mistakes in the user model earlier. Also, reply offers to trade-offs should (wherever possible) be on dimensions that are equally important to all users involved.

The negotiation simulation algorithm is defined as follows:

1. All users announce their optimal (i.e., maximum utility) choice from the catalogue. The current choice of each user is set to the respective optimal choice.
2. A user and dimension are chosen and the user proposes to change the value of this dimension from the current choice to the negotiation target value. The current choice is modified accordingly. Note that the current choice does not necessarily represent existing catalogue items.
3. All other users match this offer, i.e., propose changes in dimension value(s) from their respective optimal choice to the current choice. The sum of utility losses for these changes must match the utility loss of the initial proposal in step 2. The current choices are modified accordingly.
4. If there are still one or more users whose current choice is not equal to the negotiation target, go to step 2.

For example, an iteration step of the above negotiation loop may look as follows:[4]

```
Son: I am willing to change SPEED from 200.0 to 100.0.
          What can you offer me in return?
Father: I am willing to change GSM from 8.0 to 10.0.
Mother: I am willing to change BHP from 40.0 to 70.0.
Daughter: I am willing to change SPEED from 150.0 to 100.0.
```

The selection of the user who makes the initial trade-off proposal (in step 2) is arbitrary, but in order to give the impression of a balanced negotiation a different user is chosen in each iteration. Of course, only a user whose current choice is different from the negotiation target may be selected.

The choice of dimensions in steps 2 and 3 are based on heuristics. In our system dimensions with the highest weights in the respective user models are selected first for trade-offs, in order to catch potential problems early in the negotiation. Nevertheless, other heuristics are possible, e.g., based on previous interactions with the users.

---

[4] BHP = horse power; GSM = gas mileage.

4.4   Extensions

The negotiation simulation procedure outlined above can be extended to take account of social ranks and group pressure. These extensions are modular, and can also be used in combination.

Group Pressure. If all but one user in the group want a blue car, but one user wants a red one, it clearly wouldn't be fair if all users would have to suffer the same utility loss as the one user who disagrees with the rest of the group. In order to model this, we introduce a modifier for the utility loss that takes group pressure into account and penalizes the single disagreeing user.

Formally, let $\delta(v_1, v_2, D) \in [0, 1]$ be the degree of difference between the two values v_1 and v_2 of dimension D. The function δ has to be defined individually for each dimension.

Let v_i be the value of dimension D of the current choice of user U_i.

Assume that user U_j is offering a trade-off on dimension D. The modifier on the utility loss of the trade-off is

$$\omega_j := \frac{\sum_{i \neq j} \delta(v_i, v_j, D)}{(n - 1)}$$

ω_j is in $[0, 1]$ and is used as a factor in the computation of the utility loss for the trade-off offered by U_j. ωj is closer to 0 the more v_j differs from the other v_i's.

Note that it only makes sense to introduce this modifier if the number of users is significantly larger than 2.

Social Ranks. Computed utility losses may be modified due to social relationships between the users. For example, in the family car purchase utility losses of the parents may count more than utility losses of the children.

Formally, a numerical rank r_i between 1 and n is assigned to each of the n users (1 being the highest and n the lowest rank). Note that it is possible that two users have the same rank and thus the lowest rank is less than n.

Assume that user U_j is offering a trade-off on dimension D. The modifier on the utility loss of the trade-off is

$$\rho_j := \frac{\sum_{i \neq j} R(r_i, r_j)}{(n - 1)}$$

where $R(ri, r_j)$ is a function that denotes the rank difference between U_i and U_j as a number between 0 and 1. $R(ri, r_j)$ is equal to 1 if r_j is greater than r_i and closer to 0 the lower the rank of U_j is relative to U_i.

ρ_j is in $[0, 1]$ and is used as a factor in the computation of the utility loss for the trade-off offered by U_j. ρj converges to 0 the lower the rank of U_j is relative to the other users.

4.5   Explaining Negotiation Steps

Since the acquired user models can't be guaranteed to be correct, there may be negotiation steps with which a user does not agree. In that case, it is possible for the user to inspect the reasons behind a specific negotiation step.

If a user disagrees with an offer that the mediator chose for him, he can inspect his user model and decide on appropriate modifications. If, on the other hand, a user believes that another user's reply offer has been inappropriate or unfair he can request an explanation that refer to the user model and utility functions of the other user. For example, for a user who doesn't care about money, a compromise on the price may look like an inappropriate reply. Nevertheless, once he sees that the other user cares a lot about money this opinion may change.

Rather than present a user with pure numbers, the explanation component translates numerical utility values and weights into qualitative descriptions that denote pre-defined intervals (e.g., high, medium, low).

Given a trade-off announcement of the form

> *User i:* I am wiling to change dimension D from v_1 to v_2.

a user may request an explanation that, for example, could look as follows:

> Dimension D has *high* importance to user i. Changing his current choice from value v_1 to v_2 will make a *medium* difference to him.

Words in italics are qualitative statements denoting specific intervals. "High importance" denotes the weight that the user model assigns to dimension D, while "medium difference" denotes the level of utility loss (for dimension D only).

Should the social components such as group pressure and rank be activated, the explanation will include information about this as well, for example:

> Furthermore, there have been *many* users whose preferences are *very* different to v_2 and they exerted group pressure on user i.

> Also, users $j_1, \ldots, j_k$ have *significantly* different preferences on dimension D than user i, but higher rank.

The social explanation component is only activated if the respective social modifier is above a given threshold.

5   Related Work

Finding a compromise using negotiation has long been a topic of interest in the multi-agent community. Zlotkin and Rosenschein, for example, present solutions in state, task, and worth oriented domains (see [8] for an overview). One of the main differences to our approach is the fact that agents negotiate over a goal state to be reached and there will be a joint plan to be carried out by all agents involved to reach this state. Taking a role in such a plan, however, induces costs for agent that reduce the benefit of actually reaching the goal. The notion of a plan does not play a role in our approach, and the costs incurred are due to utility losses as a consequence of trade-offs. Additionally, the utility function quantifying the desirability of a goal is assumed to be fully specified and fixed whereas in our case the incremental refinement and modification as a reaction on other persons' behavior is a central aspect.

Argumentation-based negotiation is described, e.g. [7]. There both arguments supporting a suggestion and the user's beliefs are explicitly represented in a logical language. Rejection or acceptance of an argument—and the induced change of the user's beliefs—mainly depend upon the respective social ranks. While this supports negotiation among software agents, we decided not to follow this approach for our scenario that involves human decision making as it would be impossible to capture all the possible motivations for a user to change her mind in a logical theory. So we concentrate on offering decision support by guiding the discussion into a hopefully reasonable direction and limit belief revision to the update of the underlying quantitative preference models. In the next version of our system, we will also support a kind of informal "justification" of decisions. The users will be allowed to annotate e.g. the rejection of a proposal with a short description of her personal motivation (e.g. "I need a large transportation capacity for my sports gear.") that will be accessible to the other group members without begin integrated into the formal reasoning process.

Static group preference models are applied, e.g. by the collaborative browsing agent "Let's Browse" [4]. A simple linear combination of individual user interest profiles is used to determine potentially interesting Web pages for a group of users. While there exist no formally verified results of how successful this approach is, this method has the disadvantage of requiring completely specified preference models in advance. In contrast to this, our approach dynamically modifies the individual preference models, thus filling in missing pieces of information and possibly modifying aspects where an acceptable compromise has already been found.

[2] applies a formal representation similar to ours to the problem of finding a consensus between the members of a group. However, to come to a joint solution, they reduce the users' preference models to the corresponding rank orders of all catalog entries. Discussion then proceeds by checking one item at a time and making those users change their minds whose opinion deviates most from the group average. This process, however, causes significant loss of information because all the details of the preference model are projected onto one single value.

[6] describes a system that enables a group of users to find a movie to watch together. The movie choice (i.e., the arbitration mechanism) is based on "mimimizing the misery" of the individual group members. This is much simpler than our arbitration mechanism, and did not perform well in the evaluations of the system.

6   Conclusions and Outlook

We presented an overview of an automatic assistant for mediated discussions that supports the finding of a compromise that is fair and acceptable to all users. One of the advantages of this approach is the fact that the various users' preference models do not have to be completely specified in advance. Rather, they are refined and completed during the process of finding a compromise when personal interests have to be "defended" and contrasted against other persons' preferences.

The system supports a kind of "asynchronous discussions" as not all the group members have to be present at the same time to find an acceptable compromise. Furthermore it can provide arguments supporting suggested solutions by either reasoning about the product properties as listed in the catalog or searching for additional information on the Web.

The system as depicted in Figure 1 has been fully implemented except for the integration with presentation agent teams [1]. Once this is accomplished user studies will be carried out to evaluate the system's effectiveness.

References

1. E. André and T. Rist. Presenting Through Performing: On the Use of Multiple Lifelike Characters in Knowledge-Based Presentation Systems. *Knowledge-Based Systems*, 14((1–2)):3–13, 2001.
2. E. Herrera-Viedma, F. Herrera, and F. Chiclana. A Feedback Process to Model the Consensus in Multiperson Decision Making with Different Preference Representations. In *Eighth International Conference on Information Processing and Management of Uncertainty in Knowledge-Bases Systems (IPMU 2000)*, 2000.
3. A. Jameson, R. Schäfer, J. Simons, and T. Weis. Adaptive Provision of Evaluation-Oriented Information: Tasks and Techniques. In *IJCAI*, pages 1886–1895, 1995.
4. H. Lieberman, N. Van Dyke, and A. Vivacqua. Lets Browse: A Collaborative Browsing Agent. In *Proceedings of the International Conference on Intelligent User Interfaces, Los Angeles, January 1999 (IUI99)*, pages 65–68, 1999.
5. G. Linden, S. Hanks, and N. Lesh. Interactive assessment of user preference models: The automated travel assistant. In *Proceedings, User Modeling '97*, 1997.
6. M. O'Connor, D. Cosley, J.A. Konstan, and J. Riedl. PolyLens: A Recommender System for Groups of Users. In *Proceedings of the European Conference on Computer Supported Cooperative Work*, 2001.
7. C. Sierra, N. R. Jennings, P. Noriega, and S. Parsons. A Framework for Argumentation-Based Negotiation. In *ATAL-97*, volume 1365, pages 167–182, 1997.
8. G. Zlotkin and J.S. Rosenschein. Compromise in negotiation: exploiting worth functions over states. *Artificial Intelligence*, 84:151–176, 1996.

Modeling Task-Oriented Discussion Groups

Roy Wilson*

University of Pittsburgh
rwilson@pitt.edu

Abstract. Several recent studies present complementary mathematical models of actor behavior in small, task-oriented, groups. This paper describes both models, which share the Markov property, discusses their strengths and limitations, and suggests that user modeling researchers and small group process researchers might benefit from collaboration. Several possibilities for model-based collaboration are suggested in connection with Computer Supported Collaborative Learning.

1 Introduction

The literature on small group behavior is vast [1]; the literature on mathematical models of small group behavior less so [2]. Moreno used a matrix to depict the interactive preferences of each group member [3]. Benne and Sheets [4] observed group dynamics and offered generalizations that are still influential [5]. The theoretically-driven technique of interactive process analysis introduced by Bales [6] influenced subsequent attempts to *model* the behavior of individuals in small, task-oriented, groups. James Coleman, a figure later influential in the history of education in the United States, used a Markov chain to model the behavior of individuals and to identify emergent, but stable, patterns of behavior in groups [7].

User modeling researchers have also suggested modeling social relationships between persons. Two systems [8,9] have been informed by the framework for conceptualizing adaptive, interactive, human-computer environments laid out by Vassileva [10]. The relevance of that framework for Computer Supported Collaborative Learning is perhaps clearest in [11], where it is envisioned that goal-based, autonomous, social agents teach persons how to use a distributed working/learning environment. In keeping with a spirit of formal integration [12], this paper explores possible synergies and limitations [13] between user modeling research and small group process research in the area of Computer-Supported Collaborative Learning (CSCL).

A particular concept of group cohesion animates the particular small group process model presented here. In the 'Limitations' section, I briefly review that concept, the scope restrictions that result, and suggest how the analysis of small group behavior and large-scale communities of users might be complementary. In the final section, I suggest several possibilities for model-based collaboration between user modeling researchers and small group process researchers.

---

* I owe thanks to each reviewer. The remaining flaws are, of course, solely mine.

P. Brusilovsky et al. (Eds.): UM 2003, LNAI 2702, pp. 248–257, 2003.

2   Markov Models, Markov Chains

A system has the Markov property if the probability of the next state of the system depends only on the current state [14, p. 107]. Suppose we have a model of a process and that model generates a sequence of symbols, each representing an outcome of the process being modeled. If the probability of the next output of the model depends only on the current state of the model, we have a Markov Model (MM). Each sequence of outputs of a MM is associated with a sequence of states occupied by the Markov chain (as defined in the appendix) that underlies the MM. As described below, MMs can be differentiated on the basis of how they are related to their underlying Markov Chain (MC).

Suppose that each output of a MM is a *deterministic* function of the state of the underlying MC. Because the state of the underlying MC can be directly inferred from the MM output, the model is said to be a Visible Markov Model (VMM). Given a sequence of VMM outputs, the probability of that sequence is calculated as the product of the probabilities of a corresponding sequence of states of the underlying MC.

Suppose that each output of a MM is a *stochastic* function of the state of the underlying MC: that is, the model output depends on both the underlying MC and an intermediate stochastic process (as defined in the appendix). Because the state of the underlying MC cannot be directly inferred from the model output, we have a Hidden Markov Model (HMM). The Viterbi algorithm can be used to efficiently determine the most likely sequence of states in the underlying MC, given a sequence of HMM outputs [15].

3   Using the Markov Property to Model Interaction

This section describes two studies of task-oriented discusssion groups. The first study used a HMM to characterize sequences of task-oriented interaction between users of a CSCL system [16]. The second study analyzed data on individual rates of participation [2] in order to test a MC model of participation in task-oriented discussion groups. In the following section, the possibility of further work that draws on the strengths of each formal modeling approach is entertained.

Soller and Lesgold intend, like others [17], to build a pedagogical software agent. That agent is intended to intelligently coach collaborative learners on the basis of having itself learned to distinguish effective from ineffective knowledge sharing episodes. Soller and Lesgold have developed a CSCL system named Comet that allows users to collaborate, but does it not yet include an agent.

Each communicative act is initiated by a Comet user selecting a sentence opener from a menu and then completing the interaction by entering free text. Comet logs each communicative act, showing the initiator, the sentence opener employed, and the free text generated. From the data logged by Comet, Soller and Lesgold hope to learn to identify knowledge sharers and recipients since they see such identification as critical for distinguishing effective from ineffective knowledge sharing episodes.

For Soller and Lesgold,

> Understanding and analyzing the collaborative learning process requires a fine-grained sequential analysis of the group interaction in the context of the learning goals.

Since Comet logs communicative acts, a human coder working offline can subsequently identify and code the knowledge sharer in a sequence of such acts. These data serve as training examples for machine learning [18].

Soller and Lesgold use a HMM to model the training examples. Given a sequence of previously unseen communicative acts, the trained HMM predicts the knowledge sharer. Although the examples could be modeled using a VMM, the authors chose a HMM since, according to sources cited by them, VMMs do not generalize well, even when trained with a large amount of data. Although the trained HMM performs relatively well at identifying the knowledge sharers using previously unseen test data, Soller and Lesgold note that

> [t]he difficulties encountered in analyzing the process of collaborative learning can be attributed to the complex nature of group interaction, ..., and the coupling of task-based and social elements that factor into collaborative activities.

The remainder of this section describes a complementary modeling approach that explicitly addresses the coupling of task-based and social elements.

A recent study analyzes data on individual rates of participation in task-oriented discussion groups [2]. The data were obtained from videotaped observations of 61 groups, each of size four. The purpose of the study was to test a discrete parameter, finite-state, time-independent, MC model previously developed by Skvoretz and Fararo [19] (hereafter designated as the SFMC model).

A number of mathematical models have succeeded in reproducing the long-observed outcome in task-oriented discussion groups that status and participation rates are positively correlated. Few models of small group behavior have been able to explain the fact that low status individuals sometimes have higher rates of participation than high status members. The SFMC model attempts to help explain why differences in rates of participation often, but not invariably, follow differences in status.

The SFMC model is, according to the distinction made in the previous section, most closely related to a VMM. Since each ouput of a VMM is a *deterministic* function of the state of an underlying MC, and VMMs do not generalize well in a machine learning context, one might infer that the SFMC model is likely to perform poorly. Of course, whether a model performs well in the context of a particular purpose is an empirical question. The purpose of the SFMC model is not to model *sequences* of interaction as such, but rather the interactions of which they are composed and the social networks that such interactions generate.

The SFMC model is based on the body of social psychological research associated with Expectation States Theory (EST), which

... holds that actors' behavior toward others depends on the performance expectations they hold for themselves and for others [and that] ... expectations refer to unobservable states of relational orientation to ... others. [2]

Put otherwise, the members of a task-oriented discussion group need not have cognitive awareness of relational orientations. Despite the importance it accords to unobservables, EST has generated a number of specific, experimentally verified, behavioral predictions [20, p. 6]. EST has also been applied to the classroom, yielding a set of guidelines for status-related interventions in small groups [21].

The SFMC model describes a cycle: shared expectation states constrain the task-related behavior of members; task-related behaviors (probabilistically) induce binary social relations R between group members; and binary social relations determine future shared expectation states. If the social relation R forms between members x and y, denoted by xRy, it is said that xRy holds. For example, if member x comes to consistently defer to y in matters related to the completion of a well-defined, shared, task, then xRy designates deference. The set of social relations that hold at time n is described by a social network. Over time, interactions (and their observation) cause the social network to change according to the axioms summarized in the appendix. The SFMC model is described below in greater detail.

The small group social network at time n is defined by a $k \times k$ matrix M, where k is the size of group and the value in the xy entry of M at time n is determined by whether xRy holds at time n. If xRy holds, then the xy entry of M is equal to 1, otherwise it is equal to 0. By Axiom 1, each entry of M is initially equal to 0. Once xRy holds at time n, Axiom 2 implies that the value in the xy entry of M is, and remains, equal to 1. This is, of course, a simplification of social relations. Axioms 3 and 4 describe the formation of xRy. If x addresses y, designated as xAy, Axiom 3 states that the possible formation of xRy depends stochastically on *either* a status difference between x and y or on the behavior of x toward y. According to Axiom 4, relations can also form that involve x, y and the bystanders z who observe xAy or yAx.

One strength of the SFMC model is that it gives an account of how stable social orders emerge within task-oriented groups, in turn shaping the distribution of opportunities for group members to contribute to, and benefit from, group discussion. A more detailed formulation of Axiom 5 would indicate that the probability that xAy at each time n is non-zero, for each x and y. Axioms 3 and 4 imply that each interaction in the group raises the possibility that one or more social relations will form. Hence, given enough interactions, either xRy or yRx will hold for each pair of members x and y. When either xRy or yRx hold for each pair of members x and y, the social network is said to have reached *an* equilibrium state. Axiom 5 implies that the shared expectation states cannot change, so that the pattern of subsequent interaction between group members is stable except for random variation[1].

---

[1] Although the social network M changes over time, at least until it reaches an equilibrium, the transition probabilities from one social network state to another do not. The probability that the system transitions from state M at time n to state M' at

It is possible, assuming a particular equilibrium state, to calculate the expected number of times xAy, for each pair of members x and y. Since the observational data collected by Skvoretz and colleagues counts the actual number of times xAy for all members of each group, it is possible to test the hypothesis that a set of observational data is consistent with a particular equilibrium social network state. Such hypotheses can be tested using the log-likelihood ratio statistic, as done with "quite favorable" results [2].

4   A Potential Payoff for the Study of CSCL

In their study of CSCL, Soller and Lesgold advocate fine grained analyses of sequences of interaction. Skvoretz and Fararo, on the other hand, regard the individual interaction as central it has the potential to constrain subsequent interactions. For the purpose of modeling and explaining outcomes associated with CSCL, however, the HMM and SFMC modeling approaches may be complementary, as suggested by the following.

Soller and Lesgold cite the need for models of CSCL that can explain *why* new knowledge is not effectively conveyed and *why* new knowledge is not effectively assimilated. McDermott has noted that if the receiver of a message interprets it as also carrying an assertion of superiority by the sender, the receiver may reject the informational content of the message [22]. In the SFMC model, the meaning of a communicative act depends on the state of the social network: if xAy and neither xRy nor yRx has formed, y interprets xAy as x's *claim* to superiority.[2] Put simply, y interprets xAy differently depending on the relative status of x and y. Based on McDermott's application of communication theory to the classroom, y may reject the informational content of x's communicative act, thus resulting in a breakdown in knowledge sharing. The mere fact that the SFMC model is grounded in EST and its associated experimental tradition does not warrant the claim that it can explain such breakdowns, but it does suggest the possibility that such a model can contribute to the formulation of a *principled*, perhaps causal, explanation.

5   Synergy

The above example suggests that the benefits from a collaboration between user modeling researchers and small group process researchers might flow only in one direction. This is not the case. As described below, both sides stand to benefit from model-based collaborations.

---

time $n + 1$ is equal, in the simplest case, to the probability that xRy forms at time n for some x and y. The latter probability is entirely determined, via expectation states, by the value of M at time n. Hence, state transition probabilities in the SFMC model are independent of time.

[2] In the SFMC model, R is the relation of status superiority concerning the quality of one's expected contribution toward the successful completion of a well-defined, shared, task. Group members x and y may interact without the relation xRy having previously formed and without necessarily forming as a result of an interaction.

One difficulty in empirical studies involving SFMC models concerns data collection. Although the data analyzed by Skvoretz and colleagues came from a partially automated system for annotating videotape, it was necessary for analysts working offline to segment the video stream into speech acts. If two speech acts by the same group member were separated by a pause of less than 1.5 seconds, then the two acts were counted as one. Because Comet captures and classifies conversational acts, the data collected could be used to ease some of the measurement difficulties associated with SFMC models. This is not to suggest, however, that the role of user modeling is simply to help resolve some of the data collection difficulties encountered by small group process researchers.

In principle, there is no reason why data obtained by Comet could not also be modeled using an SFMC model. For example, a conversational act described by Soller and Lesgold as a Request-Opinion skill-attribute pair might be interpreted as an act xAy involving the two members x and y. Doing so would make it possible to model the social network on-line, representing an emerging social structure and *predicting* its status-related effects on subsequent communication. If a social network associated with ineffective knowledge sharing developed, or was likely to develop, an intelligent coach might make a status-related intervention along the lines suggested in [21]. Hence, SFMC modeling might augment the HMM approach to CSCL.

6   Limitations

Despite the possibility of mutual benefits from model-based collaboration, difficulties remain, as illustrated by the case of CSCL. The SFMC model assumes that it is possible to determine the sender and receiver(s) of each communicative act. Comet, however, appears to log only the sender of each communicative act. In order to acquire the data needed by the SFMC, Comet software would need to be augmented to identify the recipient of each logged communicative act (as done in [23]). In addition, it is necessary at a minimum to establish a mapping between the meaning of xAy in an SFMC model and the subskill-attribute schema used by Soller and Lesgold. Using the SFMC model to help identify potentially unhelpful patterns of communication faces another roadblock. From a history of interactions within a small, task-oriented, group it would be desirable to identify the most likely equilibrium state toward which the social network of the group is evolving. It is an empirical question whether the equilibrium identification task could best be handled via a log-likelihood [2] or some other approach. In addition to these technical obstacles, conceptual difficulties must be addressed.

The SFMC model is derived from EST. By design, the scope of EST is limited by a set of assumptions. One such assumption is that user interaction is face-to-face. Although it is not clear whether Comet and similar systems provide an interface sufficient to satisfy this requirement in a practical sense, it seems reasonable to assume that they approximate it. The following assumptions concerning group cohesion are more important: members share a common definition of the task situation and task success; and task success requires members to take into account each others task-related contributions. The potential explanatory power of the SFMC model is paid for by a restriction in the scope of its applicability.

As noted by one reviewer, the modeling of group interaction is of growing importance to the user modeling community. Much of that interest focuses on peer-to-peer systems such as those described by Vassileva and colleagues [9]. Peer-to-peer communities are not necessarily cohesive groups in the sense required by the scope limitations inherited by the SFMC model. According to Vassileva, the I-Help peer-to-peer system lacked the proper economic system to motivate enough user participation in order to attract the "critical mass" of users needed for its success [8]. It may also be that the community of I-Help users did not constitute a small, cohesive, group. There seems no reason, however, why certain interactions within a large user community might not sometimes be fruitfully (though incompletely) analyzed as interactions occuring within the small, cohesive, groups (as the case of CSCL) that come to be and pass away.

7 Collaborative Tasks for the Future

Whether the potential payoff of collaboration between user modeling researchers and small group process researchers can be realized in the context of CSCL studies is an empirical question. Several paths toward its resolution are described below.

First, a post-hoc analysis of the data already obtained by Soller and Lesgold might reveal whether the use of social network information increases the ability to predict the knowledge sharer in group interactions. The group members would be assumed to be equals on measures of external status. To classify the equilibrium social network of each group, a log-likelihood analysis of Comet data could be carried out. This classification could then be used, along with probabilities from the HMM, to predict the knowledge sharer.

Second, in order to avoid or postpone the logistical difficulties associated with the first path, a simulation based on the SFMC model might be developed that focuses on the relationship between the social network and knowledge sharing. The SFMC model is rooted in a tradition that represents the task-oriented situation as "a bundle of mental relations among cognitive units" [24, p. 593]: this is not to say that each participant in the situation is *reducible* to such units, but that how each one defines the situation can be *modeled* in terms of such a bundle of relations involving such units. On this premise, it seems entirely reasonable to turn to "computational models which provide a mechanistic description [see [25]] and the means for testing the sufficiency of those explanations." [26, p. 1]. In a study based on the the axiomatic framework that supports the SFMC model, Wilson [27] simulated a small group of semi-autonomous agents interacting in real-time: Work is underway to extend that simulation to take knowledge sharing into account.[3]

---

[3] That study explored the effects of concurrency in the underlying computational model on the simulation model outcomes. Conversational acts as understood by Soler and Lesgold are not modeled, so the results of that study have no direct bearing on modeling CSCL.

8   Appendix

8.1   Some Mathematical Distinctions

The formal distinction between a stochastic process and a Markov chain, given below, makes possible a relatively precise distinction between a Markov chain, a Visible Markov Model and a Hidden Markov Model. The following definitions are taken from [14]

Definition. A discrete parameter, finite-state, *stochastic process*

$$X = \{X_n; n \in N\} \tag{1}$$

is a collection of random variables all defined on the same probability space (which includes a probability measure P) and taking values in the state space $E = \{1, \dots, M\}$. Note that, in the case of the SFMC model (as described above), each value in E refers to a particular matrix describing a social network.

In the definitions that follow, it is assumed that X is a discrete parameter, finite-state, stochastic process.

Definition. X is a *Markov chain* provided that

$$P\{X_{n+1} = j \mid X_0, \dots, X_n\} = P\{X_{n+1} = j \mid X_n\} \tag{2}$$

for all $j \in E$. This is the Markov property, which means that the probability of the next state of the process depends only on the current state. Note that, although every Markov chain is a stochastic process, a stochastic process need not be a Markov chain.

Definition. A Markov chain X is *time-independent* if, for all $i, j \in E$,

$$P\{X_{n+1} = j \mid X_n = i\} \tag{3}$$

does not vary with n.

Definition. A Markov chain X can be described by the *state transition matrix* α defined as follows:

$$\alpha(i, j) = P\{X_{n+1} = j \mid X_n = i\} \tag{4}$$

for all $i, j \in E$; and

$$\sum_{j=1}^{M} \alpha(i, j) = 1, \tag{5}$$

for all $i \in E$.

8.2   Axioms Concerning the Emergence of Status Orders

The following axioms are not, of course, to be taken as statements of fact. Rather, they provide a basis for a particular style of social-psychological theorizing. The reader interested in a fuller account and a more precise formulation should consult [19].

Axiom 1. (Initial state) Each task is relatively unique, so at the start of interaction xNy for all pairs of members x and y: that is, neither xRy nor yRx.

Axiom 2. (Relational stability). If xRy forms between members x and y at time n, then xRy holds at each subsequent time.

Axiom 3. (Interaction). If x addresses y, denoted xAy, the probability that xRy forms depends on the relative status of x and y and the following: η, the probability that a status difference will structure the formation of xRy; π, the probability that task-relevant behavior will structure the formation of xRy.

Axiom 4. (Observation of interaction). If bystander z observes xAy, any and all of the following four social relations may form: xRz, zRx, zRy, or yRz. The probability that any one of them forms depends on: whether xRy, xNy, or yRx; the relative status of x and z or of y and z; and the probabilities η and π.

Axiom 5. (Behavior). The probability that xAy, for any x and y, depends on the expectation states of all group members. The expectation state for each member at time n is determined by the social relations R that exist at time n.

References

1. Johnson, D.W., Johnson, F.P.: Joining together: Group theory and group skills. Allyn and Bacon, Boston (1994)
2. Skvoretz, J., Webster, M., Whitmeyer, J.: Status orders in task discussion groups. Advances in Group Processes **16** (1999) 199–218
3. Moreno, J.L.: Who shall survive? Nervous and Mental Diseases Publishing, Washington, D.C (1953)
4. Benne, K.D., Sheets, P.: Functional roles of group members. Journal of Social Issues **4** (1948) 41–49
5. Goodman, B., Hitzeman, J., Ross, H.: Intelligent agents for collaborative learning: Predicting the roles of dialogue participants. Manuscript in preparation (2001)
6. Bales, R.F., Strodtbeck, F., Mills, T.M., Rosenbrough, M.E.: Channels of communication in small groups. American Sociological Review **16** (1951) 461–468
7. Coleman, J.S.: The mathematical study of small groups. In Solomon, H., ed.: Mathematical thinking in the measurement of behavior. Free Press (1960)
8. Vassileva, J.: Motivating participation in peer-to-peer communities. In: Proceedings of the Workshop on Emergent Societies in the Agent World, ESAW'02, Madrid, Spain (2002)
9. Vassileva, J., Greer, J., McCalla, G., Deters, R., Zapata, D., Mugdal, C., Grant, S.: A multi-agent approach to the design of peer-help environments. In: Proceedings of AIED'99, Le Mans, France (1999) 38–45
10. Vassileva, J.: A new view on interactive human-computer environments. In: Proceedings of UM'97. Springer-Verlag, New York, NY (1997) 433–435
11. Vassileva, J.: Goal-based autonomous social agents supporting adaptation and teaching in a distributed environment. In: Intelligent Tutoring Systems, Proceedings of ITS'98. Springer-Verlag, Berlin (1998) 564–573
12. Fararo, T.J.: Social action. Praeger, Westport, CT (2001)
13. Zukerman, I., Litman, D.: Natural language processing and user modeling: Synergies and limitations. User Modeling and User-Adapted Interaction **11** (2001) 129–158

14. Cinlar, E.: Introduction to stochastic processes. Prentice Hall (1975)
15. Manning, C., Schutze, H.: Foundations of statistical natural language processing. MIT Press, Cambridge, MA (1999)
16. Soller, A., Lesgold, A.: Modeling the process of collaborative learning. In: Proceedings of the International Workshop on New Technologies in Collaborative Learning, Awaji-Yumebutai (2000)
17. Lester, J.C., Stone, B.A., Stelling, G.D.: Lifelike pedagogical agents for mixed-initiative problem solving in constructivist learning environments. User Modeling and User-Adapted Interaction **9** (1999) 1–44
18. Mitchell, T.M.: Machine Learning. McGraw-Hill (1997)
19. Skvoretz, J., Fararo, T.J.: Status and participation in task groups: A dynamic network model. American Journal of Sociology **101** (1996) 1366–1414
20. Berger, J., Murray Webster, J., Ridgeway, C., Rosenholtz, S.J.: Status cues, expectations, and behavior. In Lawler, E.J., Markovsky, B., eds.: Social psychology of groups: A reader. JAI Press (1993)
21. Cohen, E.G., Lotan, R., eds.: Working for equity in heterogeneous classrooms: Sociological theory in practice. Prentice Hall (1997)
22. McDermott, R.P.: Achieving school failure: An anthropological approach to illiteracy and social stratification. In Spindler, G.D., ed.: Education and cultural process in modern societies. Holt, Rinehart and Winston, New York, NY (1974)
23. Isbell, C.L., Kearns, M., Kormann, D., Singh, S., Stone, P.: Cobot in lambdamoo: A social statistics agent. In Goettl, B., Halff, H., Redfield, C., Shute, V., eds.: AAAI/IAAI. (2000) 36–41
24. Fararo, T.J., Skvoretz, J.: E-state structuralism: A theoretical method. American Sociological Review **51** (1986) 591–602
25. Hedstrom, P., Swedberg, R., eds.: Social mechanisms: An analytical approach to social theory. Cambridge University Press (1998)
26. Schunn, C.D., Gray, W.D.: Introduction to the special issue on computational cognitive modeling. Cognitive Systems Research **3** (2002) 1–3
27. Wilson, R.: Simulating classroom interaction using communicating process architecture. In: Proceedings of the 2001 International Conference on Parallel and Distributed Processing Techniques and Applications, Las Vegas, NV (2001)

Modeling the Multiple People That Are Me

Judith Masthoff

University of Brighton, UK
Judith.Masthoff@brighton.ac.uk

Abstract. A new approach is outlined in which group modeling techniques are used to model an individual user. This helps to reduce cold-start problems, and allows aggregating multiple criteria.

1   Background

Interactive television offers the possibility of personalized viewing experiences. Different domains have been identified in which this personalization would have a great impact, such as education, news, advertising, and electronic program guides [1,2]. As watching television tends to be a social activity, adaptation needs to be to groups rather than individuals. In [3,4] we have explored this issue of group adaptation, in particular group modeling. We have empirically explored how *humans* select a sequence of items for a group to watch based on data about the individuals' preferences, and compared their behavior with twelve strategies (inspired by Social Choice Theory). The results show that humans care about fairness and avoiding individual misery. In a second experiment, we have investigated how satisfied people believe they would be with sequences chosen by the different strategies, and how their satisfaction corresponds with that predicted by a number of satisfaction functions [4]. The results show that subjects use normalization, deduct misery, and use the ratings in a non-linear way. A Multiplicative Utilitarian strategy produced most satisfaction for all individuals in the group.

This paper focuses on the applicability of group modeling strategies to the modeling of *individual* users. The idea is that even an individual user in a sense represents a group: multiple personalities hide within the user. There are different reasons for having these multiple personalities: one is the multiple perspectives somebody can have of something (see Section 1.1), another is the uncertainty we may –in particular initially- have of the kind of user we are dealing with (see Section 1.2).

1.1   Multiple Contributing Factors

Multiple factors can contribute to a recommender's prediction of the user's opinion of an item. For instance, [5] *adds* the rankings produced by content-based filtering, collaborative filtering, and demographic filtering. [6] uses a *weighted addition* of attributes describing a movie: director, casting, genre, star rating and running time.

P. Brusilovsky et al. (Eds.): UM 2003, LNAI 2702, pp. 258–262, 2003.
© Springer-Verlag Berlin Heidelberg 2003

Though stressing the importance of aggregating ratings, neither discusses why they have chosen their particular *additive* aggregation function, nor (in the case of [6]) how to determine the weights. Clearly, this area could benefit from the group modeling results.

1.2   Cold Start Problem

Recommender systems tend to suffer from the *cold start* problem: before the system can recommend anything to users, it needs to get to know them. Various methods have been proposed to solve this problem (e.g. [6], [7], [8]). There is one main problem with these methods: they require initial contributions by the user (either rating items, or answering questions), a threshold not every user will want to overcome. Besides, even with the user cooperating, the accurateness of the predictions is not flawless. For some domains, such as interactive television, it is important that users are presented with items they like (or at least not hate) *from the start*. If there is a set of other users, or a set of stereotypes, and the system does not yet know which of them the user resembles, then one way to ensure enjoyment is to present items that the other users (or stereotypes) would enjoy as a *group*.

2   Proposed Rating Combination Algorithm

2.1   Multiplication Rather than Addition

Our empirical research has shown that "avoiding misery" is important in group modeling, and that a Multiplicative Utilitarian strategy therefore works better than an Additive one [3,4]. When modeling an *individual* user, avoiding misery means avoiding that one criterion has a very low rating but is ignored because of high ratings for the others. For example, suppose the user needs a recommendation for a restaurant. Assume we have ratings for restaurants on "geographical location", "food type", "budget", "food quality", and "atmosphere", each being between 1 (awful) and 5 (excellent). A restaurant with ratings of 5-1-5-5-5 would lead to an additive rating of 21 and would be recommended above a restaurant with ratings of 4-3-4-4-4 (additive rating of 19). So, you might end up eating at a high class, low cost, close to home restaurant that only serves the kind of food that you really hate. Multiplication of the ratings, rather than addition, suffers less from this problem. For instance, in the example above, the multiplicative rating of
5-1-5-5-5 is 625, and is beaten by the multiplicative rating of 4-3-4-4-4 (728).

If the contributing ratings represent other users (or stereotypes) rather than criteria, then misery should also be avoided. After all, misery for one of those users (or stereotypes) could lead to misery for our user, as we do not know yet whom our user resembles. So, we propose to combine the individual ratings by:

$$GR = \prod_{1} r_i$$ Where GR stands for group rating, and the item with highest GR will be shown (or recommended) to the user.

2.2   Using Weights

Not all criteria have to be equally important. For instance, in the restaurant example above, "food quality" might be regarded as more important than "atmosphere". To express difference in importance, weights can be used. We can, however, not multiply our ratings with weights. After all, it would not make a difference to our multiplicative function whether the weight for one factor is twice as large as the weight for another or the other way around. We propose to use the weights as exponents, leading to:

$$GR = \prod_i r_i^{w_i}$$

Note that this means that the closer the weight is to zero, the less influence the rating has on the outcome of the multiplication.

If the contributing ratings represent other users (or stereotypes) rather than criteria, the weights express how similar the user is to the other users (or stereotypes). A weight close to zero then expresses complete dissimilarity, and a high weight expresses similarity.[1]

2.3   Learning Weights

Weights are likely to be user dependent. This is obviously the case when the contributing ratings represent other users (or stereotypes), but also when they represent criteria. For instance, in the restaurant example above, while some users would emphasize "budget", others might not mind "budget" as much but mind more about "food quality". Users could be asked for weights, for instance, "express how important on a scale from 1 to 5 budget is for you", or "express how much you are like this person whose ratings you see". However, this requires user effort, and becomes unfeasible when the number of contributing factors is high (as likely when they represent other users). Additionally, users might not be consciously aware of the importance they place on different factors. So, it would be better if the system could learn the weights automatically.

For the system to learn the weights, it needs to get feedback on its recommendations. Feedback could be obtained explicitly (by letting the user rate the recommendation) or implicitly (by observing the time the user spends on the item). Feedback will be compared with the ratings of the individual contributing factors. Weights can be seen as similar to confidence. If a factor's prediction is close to the feedback then it gains in weight, if it is far off then it loses. This leaves the question of what is "close", and what is "far off". We assume that the feedback is given on the same scale as the rating of the contributing factors[2]. We propose the following learning algorithm: For individual ratings r, weights w, and overall feedback f,

$$\text{If } r_i = f \text{ then } w_i := 2*w_i \qquad \text{If } r_i \neq f \text{ then } w_i := \frac{w_i}{|r_i - f|}$$

---

[1] If we would like to model the fact that a user might be the *opposite* of another user, we could do so by adding an extra "opposite" rater for each rater.

[2] If the contributing factors use different scales, then for the formula the feedback will need to be normalized to the scale of each contributing factor before calculating the impact.

Note: if the difference between r_i and f is only 1 then no changes in weighting happen. For example, assume initial weights for contributing factors of 1:

	Food type	Budget	Food quality	Atmosphere	Geographical location
Rating	4	1	5	3	4
Feedback	5				
New Weight	1	0.25	2	0.5	1

3   A Small MovieLens-Data Based Evaluative Example

For our example, we have used the MovieLens data set of the GroupLens project[3], focusing on the movies with ids 1 to 5, and the twelve users who have rated each of these five movies. We have selected ten of these users as predictors for the other two. As test subjects, we have chosen the two users with highest id that had at least one rating of 2 or lower, namely users 435 and 880.

UserID	1	130	276	280	293	303	393	682	886	916	Product
ItemID 1	5	5	5	4	2	5	3	4	4	4	960000
2	3	4	4	3	3	3	4	3	4	3	186624
3	4	5	3	2	2	3	3	3	3	3	58320
4	3	2	4	3	4	4	4	3	3	4	165888
5	3	4	3	4	3	2	3	3	3	3	69984

So, the first item recommended would be item 1, followed by 2–4–5–3. Comparing this with the ratings we have for the other two users (435 and 880):

UserID	435	880	
ItemID 1	5	4	Best-liked movie for both users, so good to show first.
2	4	3	Second best for user 435, but user 880 would have preferred movie 4 (though not disliking this movie)
4	4	4	
5	2	3	
3	3	1	Strongly disliked by user 880, so it is good that it is shown last.

We have ignored changes in weights. When weights are learned, user 435 would be shown 1-2-3 first (in contrast with the above, where 3 is the last item shown). As shown below, after showing 1-2-3, weights start to reflect similarity: in particular the low weight for 293 shows its dissimilarity to user 435, and the weights of 276 and 303 are starting to reflect their similarity to user 435.

UserID	1	130	276	280	293	303	393	682	886	916
Weights	2	2	8	1	0.33	4	2	2	4	2

---

[3] http://www.cs.umn.edu/Research/GroupLens/ - the dataset consists of 100,000 ratings, 943 users and 1682 movies.

Some issues raised by the example:

- When a contributing factor (in the example, another user) has no predicted rating for a particular item, it seems most sensible to use the average rating of that factor[4]. The weight of that factor should remain unchanged.
- When using other users as contributing factors, it is important to use a range of different users. We have taken them more or less at random. It is better, of course, to determine prototypical users (stereotypes) mathematically.

4 Conclusions

We have described and illustrated how strategies from group modeling can be applied to the modeling of individual users. We have limited the discussion to Multiplicative Utilitarianism, which we have extended by adding weights and an algorithm for learning the weights. We based the choice for this algorithm on our group modeling experiments. It would be worthwhile to revisit the other algorithms mentioned in [4] to see what their contribution could be in this domain.

Acknowledgement. The author is supported by Nuffield grant NAL/00258/G. We thank the GroupLens project at the university of Minnesota for making the MovieLens dataset publicly available.

References

1. Masthoff J. and Luckin, R. (Eds.) (2002). Proceedings of the workshop Future TV: Adaptive instruction in your living room, San Sebastian.
2. Ardissono, L., and Faihe Y. (Eds.). (2001). Proceedings of the first workshop on Personalization in Future TV, Sonthofen.
3. Masthoff J. (2002). Modeling a group of television viewers. In [1], pp. 34–42.
4. Masthoff, J. (2002). Group modeling: Selecting a sequence of television items to suit a group of viewers. Unpublished manuscript submitted to journal.
5. Pazzani, M.J. (1999). A framework for collaborative, content-based and demographic filtering. Artificial Intelligence Review, 13, pp. 393–408.
6. Nguyen, H., and Haddawy, P. (1998). The decision-theoretic video advisor. Proceedings of AAAI Workshop on Recommender Systems. pp. 76–80.
7. Rashid, A.M., Albert, I., Cosley, D., Lam, S.K., McNee, S.M., Konstan, J.A., and Riedl, J. (2002). Getting to know you: Learning new user preferences in recommender systems. Proceedings of the Intelligent User Interface conference. pp. 127–134.
8. Gena, C. and Ardissono, L. (2001). On the construction of TV viewer stereotypes starting from lifestyle surveys. In [2].

---

[4] In the example, of course, a predicted rating could be used for that person using content-based or collaborative filtering, but such a method could not apply for all multiple criteria cases.

Iems: Helping Users Manage Email

Eric McCreath[1] and Judy Kay[2]

[1] Department of Computer Science,
The Australian National University,
ACT 0200 Australia
ericm@cs.anu.edu.au
[2] School of Information Technologies,
The University of Sydney,
NSW 2006 Australia
judy@it.usyd.edu.au

Abstract. This paper reports our work to build an email interface which can learn how to predict a user's email classifications at the same time as ensuring user control over the process. We report our exploration to answer the question: does the classifier work well enough to be effective? There has been considerable work to automate classification of email. Yet, it does not give a good sense of how well we are able to model user's classification of email. This paper reports the results of our own evaluations, including a stark observation that evaluation of this class of adaptive system needs to take account of the fact that the user can be expected to adapt to the system. This is important for the long term evaluation of such systems since we may find that this effect means that our systems may be performing better than classic evaluations might suggest.

1 Introduction

As people need to cope with increasing amounts of email, there is a corresponding growth in the need to support users in organising mail and attending to it more effectively. This paper describes the i-ems (Intelligent-Electronic Mail Sorter) project which has the broad goal of improving our understanding of how to build systems which can assist users in managing email.

A good foundation for this work comes from the studies of the ways that people manage email within current email clients. Mail folders would seem to offer a useful organisational structure for email. Yet these facilities appear to be of limited value for many users. For example, in one study of 20 workers [1], the average inbox had 2482 items, with an average of 858 filed. Some users kept most of their email in the inbox. When users do classify email, Ducheneaut and Bellotti [2] report that this is commonly based on quite simple criteria: sender name or organisation, project or personal interests.

Most mail clients allow users to write rules which will automatically sort email into folders. This has limited value for many users. Generally, users avoid customizing software [3,2] and many users avoid such rules, as they are too difficult to create.

P. Brusilovsky et al. (Eds.): UM 2003, LNAI 2702, pp. 263–272, 2003.

There has been considerable work in the use of machine learning to automatically classify email. An interesting subproblem is the identification of junk mail. This has been explored with a variety of machine learning techniques, for example, Naive Bayes [4,5,6], Bayesian approaches [7], genetic approaches [8], keyword approaches [5], a memory-based approach similar to K-Nearest Neighbour [9], the RIPPER algorithm [6]. These typically report precision and accuracy measures around 95% or better and recall values of 70-80%.

Broader classification has, as one would expect, achieved less success. Cohen [10] used RIPPER, achieving 87%- 94% accuracy and TF-IDF (85%-94%). A Naive Bayes classifier [11] gave 89% accuracy. Brutlag and Meek [12] compared a Linear Support Vector Machine (70% to 90% correct), the Unigram Language Model (65% to 90%) and TF-IDF (67% to 95%) with the range due to different email sets. As a body, these results are encouraging. In spite of the non-comparability of these studies, they give an overall indication that a variety of approaches can achieve average accuracy of 70-90% and a lesser level of recall.

Central to our i-ems project is the ability to measure the effectiveness of approaches that are currently available as well as those we create. The email classification domain has some special evaluation challenges. Notably, there is the issue of user consistency. This has been been observed, for example, in the case of human classifiers of the Reuters data [13]. The work listed above tends to report accuracy, precision and recall. All appears to have been tested by taking a set of preclassified email, testing on part of it and then evaluating on the remainder. If some of that was actually misclassified, it is harder to assess the actual effectiveness of an approach.

A different and interesting approach to both the classification of email and evaluation of effectiveness was taken in *MailCat* [14]. This interface provides three buttons showing the three best predicted mail folders for the current message. This approach increased the chance of offering a correct folder. It is interesting in that this design of the interface ensures a modest cost for incorrect classifications. Moreover, they have reported both the accuracy and user's affective assessment: their earlier single button design, with 20% to 40% error rates was considered unacceptable while users were satisfied with the three-button interface. A repeat study [15] supported the claim of user satisfaction. Our approach takes a similar philosophy, with a focus on the interface and the role of user involvement in evaluation processes.

In Section 2, we describe the i-ems interface. Then, in Section 3, we describe experiments which evaluate the relative power of hand crafted mail classification rules, rules learnt automatically and a combination of these. We also report an unexpected observation, the effect of the system's recommended classification affecting the user's classification of messages. In the final section, we discuss the findings, especially the matter of performance metrics for such systems.

2   IEMS – The Electronic Mail Sorter

The i-ems approach sorts each message in the *inbox* according to its predicted classification. Figure 1 shows an example of an i-ems screen. The long left panel lists the user's folders. To the right of this, there are two main parts to the screen.

The upper part shows the messages in the folder that is currently selected. In the figure, this is the inbox. This shows each message under its predicted folder category or under the category *Unknown* if no prediction has been made. For example, the messages sent from Judy Kay have been predicted to belong in the *crc* folder. Each appears as a single line with the sender and the subject. The user has currently selected one of these messages from Judy Kay. This message is displayed in the lower right-hand window.

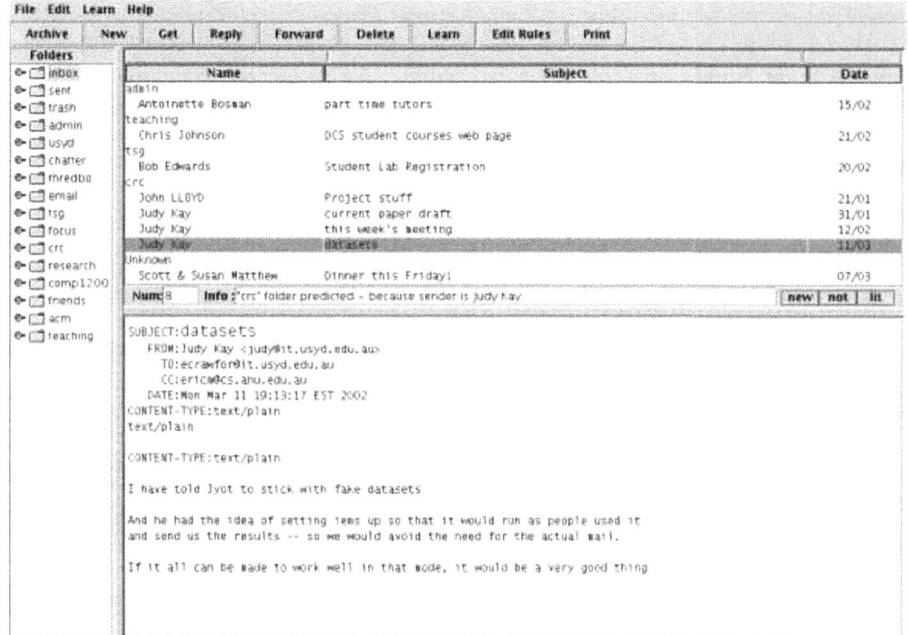

Fig. 1. A screen shot of the i-ems interface.

Once a user has read a message, there are two possible courses of action. If they are happy with the classification, they can simply click on the *Archive* button at the top left of the screen. In the case of the current message shown in Figure 1, the *Archive* button would move it to the *crc* folder.

The other possible case is that the user is not happy with the recommendation. In this case, the user can simply drag and drop the message into the desired folder. This is much the same amount of effort required for a user to archive messages in a standard email manager.

At times, a user may wish to direct and assist these recommendations. This is especially the case when the user knows that particular class of messages will be filed into a particular folder. For example a user may know that all messages with "[seminar]" in the subject with be filed into the "research" folder. The user may simply add such a rule by doing the following: highlighting the "[seminar]" keyword in the subject of a message, clicking on the "new" button to the right of the information text field, and selecting the "research" folder in the dialog box that appears. This is shown in Figure 2. In a similar way, the user may refine existing rules by using the "not" and "lit" button. These respectively add negated and ordinary literals to a rule. As hand crafted rules tend to be more precise, they are given priority in classifying new messages over the learnt rules. Hence, the learnt rules are only used when the hand crafted rules do not make any classification.

Another important aspect of our approach is that i-ems allows the user to scrutinise the classifier. The interface shows the user the reason email was classified into a particular folder. When the user clicks on an email, it is displayed along with the reason for the classification. The explanation is displayed in the middle right hand panel (as seen in Figure 1). The learner that generates the hypothesis is given the task of generating these explanations. If the classification resulted from a hand crafted rule then this rule is simply appears here.

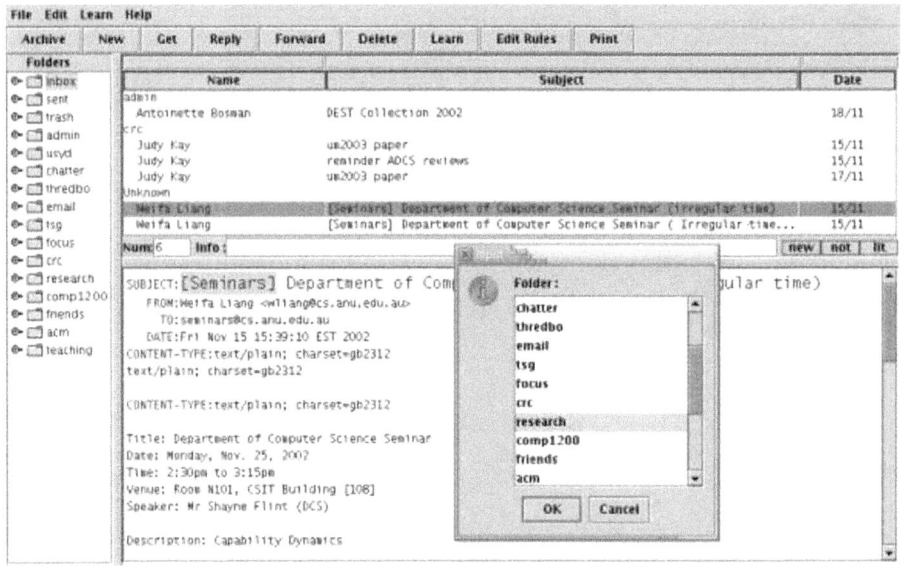

Fig. 2. A screen shot of adding a new rule with the i-ems interface.

The user is thus able to both scrutinize why the recommendations are made and refine, augment, and control these recommendations. This gives the user a sense of control over their email manager while still aiding them.

3   Empirical Results

We now describe our experiments which show two characteristics of the email system. First, we show how the combination of hand crafted and learnt rules can be more effective than either approach working alone. Second, we see how the use of a particular learning approach within the email manages influences the way the user classifies messages. However, before we look at these results we describe: the learners, the testing, and the dataset used.

The i-ems system uses an abstract class that allows different learning approaches to be considered. In previous work, [16,17] we evaluated a number of learners. However, within this study just two learners are considered:

- **Sender** : This learns rules to predict the folder for a new message based solely on the sender. For each sender, a rule is created to filter new messages into the folder that the sender most commonly goes into. Mail from new senders is classified as "unknown". We realised this was a very simplistic and limited approach. However, it has shown to be effective [17].
- **Keyword** : The keyword approach induces a set of clauses in a similar way to Quinlan and Cameron-Jones' FOIL [18]. The literals considered are whether a particular word is contained in one of the : sender, to, subject, or body fields. This operates somewhat like Cohen's Ripper [10] in that it induces rules for the smallest folder first, progressing to larger ones.

A cross validation testing approach would be inappropriate given the temporal nature of email. A sequence of email messages will often contain threads of discussions relating to particular topics. If cross validation were used, the training data may always contain messages from these threads, hence simplifying induction. When an email manager is used it will have an initial sequence of messages and must predict the classification of future messages. We reflect this in our evaluation approach. A sequence of messages is presented to the learner chronologically ordered and then we test on the subsequent collection of messages. This process is repeated giving a "sliding window" tester where the testing window is moved across the examples and all the messages prior to the window are provided for training. This testing approach has the merit of reflecting the way a learner within a mail client would operate.

We wanted to test on a substantial corpus of mail. We also wanted a complete set. This meant that all mail should be kept and classified. In the case of mail that the user would have normally deleted, we wanted that mail classified into a folder. Other than this, we wanted the user to choose the folder names and associated concepts as they wished. So, for example, in some of our experiments, users have created a "deleted" folder for mail they would have deleted. Others made folders called "readndelete" to indicate what that person did with those messages.

Our previous work involved five users who were willing to classify mail as required [16,17]. For this experiment, we collected a much larger data set over a longer period. This was for a single user, who had participated in the earlier work.

The large corpus of messages contains 5100 messages spanning approximately 3 months of email activity. The user has 21 folders and 70 hand crafted rules giving the system a nontrivial real world test. By conducting the empirical study only on one user, we limit the generality of any conclusions we can make. However, as seen in previous studies[16, user 1][2], the way the user archives messages is characteristic of at least a sub-group of users. Hence, we argue that our results are valid for at least a subgroup of users.

The testing window contains 100 messages and is moved in steps of 100 messages. The "error" is calculated as the percentage of the messages within the testing window that are incorrectly classified. This shows the percentage, over all the messages, where the rules make a definite classification and this classification is incorrect. We also calculate "precision" which is the percentage of messages correctly labeled that were not labeled "unknown". Also the percentage of messages the learner labels "unknown" is given. [1] The results of these tests are shown in Figures 3 to 5.

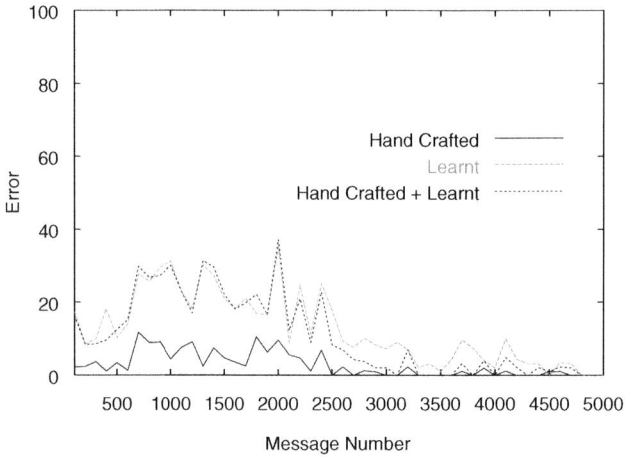

Fig. 3. Sliding window test results showing error.

Figure 3 shows the error rate for the three approaches, with the hand-crafted rules performing best. Figure 5 shows that the hand crafted rules are consistently more precise than the learnt rules. However, as seen in Figure 4, the hand crafted rules classify more messages as "unknown". The combination of the learnt and handcrafted rule always has a lower level of "unknown" messages, this is because the learnt rules attempt to guess the classification of the messages the hand crafted rules considered "unknown". So by combining the two approaches the number of messages classified as "unknown" is reduced while still maintaining a similar precision and overall error. This result is also reflected in the Table 1 which shows the average performance on the first half of the corpus, split equally between training and test set. If a user's primary criteria is reducing the error rate, then hand crafted rules are best. However, the hand crafted rules alone are

---

[1] "Error", "precision", and "unknown" are defined as follows: **error** $= 100 \times \frac{i}{u+c+i}$, **precision** $= 100 \times \frac{c}{c+i}$, **unknown** $= 100 \times \frac{u}{u+c+i}$, where i is the number of message incorrectly classified, u is the number of messages classified as "unknown", and c is the number of messages correctly classified.

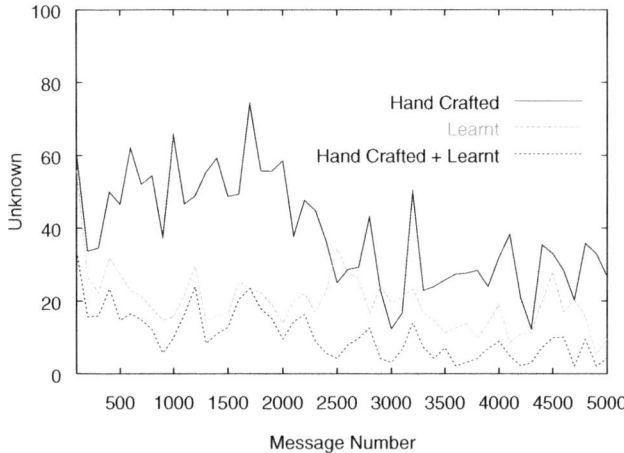

Fig. 4. Sliding window results showing unknown.

less useful as they make considerably less predications, so many of the messages that come into the users inbox would be labeled "unknown". We argue that by combining the approaches, with a small cost in error rate, the number of unknown messages can be considerably reduced. This would be more useful for many users.

One striking and interesting aspect of these graphs is the sharp improvement in performance of the system after about 2500 messages. This is because the first 2500 messages were collect and archived simply using the drag and drop facility, whereas, the archiving of the second 2500 messages was aided by the sorting of the inbox using a combination of the hand crafted and learnt rules (using the sender approach). Clearly the use of such a system influences the way in which a user will archive messages. Hence, the utility of measuring the performance of a particular system in isolation is questionable, as recommendations provided by the system will influence the archiving of messages. This is particularly the case in email sorting, as often folders will have blurred and overlapping intentions. So when a system recommends a particular folder it may not be the folder the user would have used without such a recommendation. However, it may be 'close enough', in which case the user will archive it directly into the recommended folder rather than dragging and dropping it into another folder. It may even

Table 1. Comparison of combining learnt and hand crafted rules using the Sender learner training on messages 0–1249 and testing on messages 1250–2499.

Rules used	Error	Unknown	Precision
Hand crafted	7.1%	52.4%	85.0%
Learnt only	20.2%	29.1%	71.5%
Hand crafted + learnt	22.5%	20.0%	71.9%

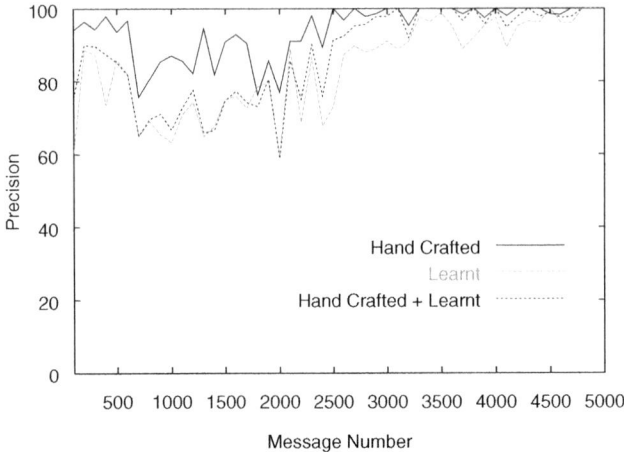

Fig. 5. Sliding window results showing precision.

be that the user would be inconsistent in their classification and that i-ems is helping them to maintain consistency. This is clearly reflect in Table 2 where we use the 'sender' approach (combined with the hand crafted rules) and the system trains on the first 2500 messages and we test on the next 2500 message the overall error is reduced to 2.7% and the unknown percentage is only 9.3%.

Note that, as the 'sender' approach was used in aiding the sorting of messages, the sorting of messages is particularly biased toward this learner. When we train and test the systems prior to the user being aided by the sorting of messages within the inbox the 'sender' and 'keyword' approaches both produce very similar results. However, when we expand the test into the region where the user is aided by the sorting of messages within the inbox the difference between the sender and the keyword approach is stark. These results are shown in Table 2.

4   Discussion and Conclusion

The i-ems project explores a range of approaches to support users in managing email information overload. This has many of the elements that are common to

Table 2. A comparison of the sender and keyword approaches when they are incorporated into the system.

Training/Testing messages	Learner Used	Error	Unknown	Precision
Training 0–1249/	Sender	22.5%	20.0%	71.9%
Testing 1250-2499	Keyword	22.1%	22.8%	71.3%
Training 0–2499/	Sender	2.7%	9.3%	97.0%
Testing 2500-4999	Keyword	16.2%	5.4%	82.8%

emerging areas for personalisation. It should improve our understanding of the potential for a range of approaches to building individualised and automated text classification tools that users can readily understand and control.

The design of the i-ems interface was driven by the need to operate with flawed classifiers. It ensures a modest cost in the case of misclassification. It also has several levels at which it ensures a real sense of user control: the user can create classification rules; the user can see the reason for the classification of each mail item; and the user can refine and augment classification rules, including those learnt by the system. We have achieved important additional functionality. When i-ems organises the inbox according to the categories, it effectively groups related mail. This means that the user can maintain focus on the context represented by the items of one folder, while the mail is still in the inbox.

This paper reported an extensive experiment with over 5000 email items. It has reported evaluations with two classifiers and the potential for combining automated machine learning and user constructed rules. The generality of our claims is limited by the fact that this work was restricted to a study of one user's mail management. We note, however, that our previous work [16,17] and broader studies of users [2] suggests that this has considerable generality.

Our evaluation strongly suggests that when the user was presented with an inbox, organised into classes predicted by i-ems, they were influenced by this classification. This has important implications for the evaluation of such systems. We believe that an important direction for future evaluations of such systems should include field tests similar to that we have reported. This approach takes account of the known problem of inconsistent classification by the user [13]. Indeed, in personalised document classification, this is apt to be a significant factor. It also measures success in terms of the individual judgement of the user: an item need only be regarded as misclassified if the user takes the trouble to correct it. Like the *MailCat* [14,15] evaluations, it essentially has an affective evaluation built in. While it may seem more rigorous to train and test classifiers on preclassified email, we believe that a field test such as we have reported should also be used to give a better answer to our core question: how effective is this classifier and interface for this user?

Acknowledgments. We would like to thank the Smart Internet Technology - Corporate Research Center for their support of this research. We thank the reviewers for their valuable recommendations. Also thanks to Daren Ler for help in proof reading this document.

References

[1] Whittaker, S., Sidner, C.L.: Email overload: Exploring personal information management of email. In: CHI. (1996) 276–283

[2] Ducheneaut, N., Bellotti, V.: E-mail as habitat: an exploration of embedded personal information management. Interactions **8** (2001) 30–38

[3] Mackay, W.: Triggers and barriers to customizing software. In: CHI'91 Conference on Human Factors in Computing Systems, New Orleans, Louisiana (1991) 153–160

[4] Pantel, P., Lin, D.: Spamcop: A spam classification & organization program. In: Proceedings of AAAI-98 Workshop on Learning for Text Categorization. (1998) 95–98

[5] Androutsopoulos, I., Koutsias, J., Chandrinos, K., Spyropoulos, C.: An experimental comparison of naive bayesian and keyword-based anit-spam filtering with personal e-mail messages. In: Proceedings of the 23rd annual international ACM SIGIR conference on Research and development in information retrieval. (2000) 160–167

[6] Provost, J.: Naive-bayes vs. rule-learning in classification of email. Technical Report AI-TR-99-284, University of Texas at Austin, AI Lab (1999)

[7] Sahami, M., Dumais, S., Heckerman, D., Horvitz, E.: A bayesian approach to filtering junk e-mail. In: AAAI-98 Workshop on Learning for Text Categorization. (1998)

[8] Katirai, H.: Filtering junk e-mail: A performance comparison between genetic programming & naive bayes (1999)

[9] Androutsopoulos, I., Paliouras, G., Karkaletsis, V., Sakkis, G., Spyropoulos, C., Stamatopoulos, P.: Learning to filter spam e-mail: A comparison of a naive bayesian and a memory-based approach. In: Proceedings of the Machine Learning and Textual Information Access Workshop of the 4th European Conference on Principles and Practice of Knowledge Discovery in Databases PKDD. (2000)

[10] Cohen, W.: Learning rules that classify e-mail. In: Papers from the AAAI Spring Symposium on Machine Learning in Information Access. (1996) 18–25

[11] Rennie, J.: ifile: An application of machine learning to e-mail filtering. In: KDD-2000 Text Mining Workshop, Boston. (2000)

[12] Brutlag, J. Meek, C.: Challenges of the email domain for text classification. In: Seventeenth International Conference on Machine Learning. (2000)

[13] Apte, C., Damerau, F., Weiss, S.M.: Automated learning of decision rules for text categorization. Information Systems 12 (1994) 233–251

[14] Segal, R., Kephart, M.: Mailcat: An intelligent assistant for organizing e-mail. In: Proceedings of the Third International Conference on Autonomous Agents, Seattle, WA (1999) 276–282

[15] Ruvini, J.D., Gabriel, J.M.: Do users tolerate errors from their assistant?: experiments with an e-mail classifier. In: Proceedings of the 7th international conference on Intelligent user interfaces, ACM Press (2002) 216–217

[16] Crawford, E., Kay, J., McCreath, E.: Automatic induction of rules for e-mail classification. In: In Proceedings of the Sixth Australiasian Document Computing Symposium, Coffs Harbour, Australia. (2001)

[17] Crawford, E., Kay, J., McCreath, E.: Iems - the intelligent email sorter. In: In Proceedings of the Nineteenth International Conference on Machine Learning, 2002, Sydney, Australia. (2002)

[18] Cameron-Jones, R., Quinlan, J.: Efficient top-down induction of logic programs. SIGART Bulletin 5 (1994) 33–42

Modelling Reputation in Agent-Based Marketplaces to Improve the Performance of Buying Agents

Thomas Tran and Robin Cohen

School of Computer Science
University of Waterloo
Waterloo, ON, N2L 3G1, Canada
{tt5tran, rcohen}@math.uwaterloo.ca

Abstract. We propose a reputation oriented reinforcement learning algorithm for buying agents in electronic market environments. We take into account the fact the quality of a good offered by different selling agents may not be the same, and a selling agent may alter the quality of its goods. In our approach, buying agents learn to avoid the risk of purchasing low quality goods and to maximize their expected value of goods by dynamically maintaining sets of reputable and disreputable sellers. Modelling the reputation of sellers allows buying agents to focus on those sellers with whom a certain degree of trust has been established. We also include the ability for buying agents to explore the marketplace in order to discover new reputable sellers. In this paper, we focus on presenting the experimental results that confirm the improved satisfaction for buying agents that model reputation according to our algorithm.

1   Introduction

The problem of how to develop algorithms that guide the behaviour of personal, intelligent agents participating in electronic marketplaces is a subject of increasing interest from both the academic and industrial research communities [1,7]. Since a multi-agent electronic market environment is, by its very nature, open (agents can enter or leave the environment at will), dynamic (information such as prices, product quality etc. may be altered), and unpredictable (agents lack perfect knowledge of one another), it is very important that participant agents are equipped with effective and feasible learning algorithms to accomplish their delegated tasks or achieve their delegated goals. In this paper, we propose a reputation-oriented reinforcement learning based algorithm for buying agents in electronic marketplaces and demonstrate its value through experimentation.

We model the agent environment as an open marketplace populated with economic agents. The nature of an open marketplace allows economic agents, which we classify as *buyers* and *sellers*, to freely enter or leave the market. Buyers and sellers are self-interested agents whose goal is to maximize their own benefit.

P. Brusilovsky et al. (Eds.): UM 2003, LNAI 2702, pp. 273–282, 2003.

Our market environment is rooted in an information delivery infrastructure such as the Internet, which provides agents with virtually direct and free access to all other agents. The process of buying and selling goods is realized via a *contract-net* like mechanism [3], which consists of three elementary phrases: *(i)* A buyer announces its request for a good. *(ii)* Sellers submit bids for delivering such goods. *(iii)* The buyer evaluates the submitted bids and selects a suitable seller. The buyer then pays the chosen seller and receives the good from that seller. Thus, the buying and selling process can be viewed as an *auction* where a seller is said to be *winning the auction* if it is able to sell its good to the buyer.

We assume that the quality of a good offered by different sellers may not be the same, and a seller may alter the quality of its goods. We also assume that a buyer can examine the quality of the good it purchases only after it receives that good from the selected seller. Each buyer has some way to evaluate the good it purchases, based on the price and the quality of the good received. Thus, in our market environment a buyer tries to find those sellers whose goods best meet its expected value of goods, while a seller tries to maximize its expected profit by setting suitable prices for and providing more customized value to its goods, in order to satisfy the buyers' needs.

In our proposed algorithm, buyers are designed to be reputation-oriented to avoid the risk of purchasing low quality goods. They each dynamically maintain sets of reputable and disreputable sellers, and learn to maximize their expected value of goods by selecting appropriate sellers among the reputable sellers while avoiding the disreputable ones. This paper focuses on demonstrating the advantages of modelling reputation for buyers in electronic marketplaces, an important extension to the design of buying agents using reinforcement learning in market environments, such as [6].

2   The Proposed Learning Algorithm

This section proposes a reputation-oriented reinforcement learning algorithm for buyers in electronic marketplaces. The algorithm is aimed at maximizing the expected values of goods and avoiding the risk of purchasing low quality goods for buyers[1].

Consider the scenario where a buyer b requests for some good g. Let G, P, and S be finite sets of goods, prices, and sellers in the market, respectively.

Buyer b maintains reputation ratings for sellers using function $r^b : S \mapsto (-1, 1)$, called the *reputation function* of b. Initially, buyer b sets $r^b(s) = 0$ for every seller $s \in S$. After each transaction with a seller s, buyer b will update $r^b(s)$ depending on whether or not s satisfies b. A seller s is considered *reputable* by buyer b if $r^b(s) \geq \Theta$, where Θ is buyer b's *reputation threshold* $(0 < \Theta < 1)$. A seller s is considered *disreputable* by buyer b if $r^b(s) \leq \theta$, where θ is buyer b's *disreputation threshold* $(-1 < \theta < 0)$. A seller s with $\theta < r^b(s) < \Theta$ is neither reputable nor disreputable to buyer b. In other words, b does not have enough information to decide on the reputation of s.

---

[1] This model includes important extensions to the algorithm presented in [5].

Let S_r^b and S_{dr}^b be the sets of reputable and disreputable sellers to buyer b respectively, i.e.,

$$S_r^b = \{s \in S \mid r^b(s) \geq \Theta\} \text{ and } S_{dr}^b = \{s \in S \mid r^b(s) \leq \theta\}. \tag{1}$$

Buyer b will focus its business on the reputable sellers and stay away from the disreputable ones.

Buyer b estimates the expected value of the goods it purchases using the *expected value function* $f^b : G \times P \times S \mapsto \mathbb{R}$. Hence, the real number $f^b(g, p, s)$ represents buyer b's expected value of buying good g at price p from seller s.

Since different sellers may offer good g with different qualities and a seller may alter the quality of its goods, buyer b puts more trust in the sellers with good reputation. Thus, it chooses among the reputable sellers in S_r^b a seller $\hat{s}$ that offers good g at price p with maximum expected value:

$$\hat{s} = \arg\max_{s \in S_r^b} f^b(g, p, s) \tag{2}$$

where arg is an operator such that $\arg f^b(g, p, s)$ returns s.

If no sellers in S_r^b submit bids for delivering g or if $S_r^b = \emptyset$, then buyer b will have to choose a seller $\hat{s}$ from the non-reputable sellers provided that $\hat{s}$ is not a disreputable seller.

In addition, with a small probability ρ, buyer b chooses to explore (rather than exploit) the marketplace by randomly selecting a seller $\hat{s} \in (S - S_{dr}^b)$. This gives buyer b an opportunity to discover new reputable sellers. Initially, the value of ρ should be set to 1, then decreased over time to some fixed minimum value determined by b.

After paying seller $\hat{s}$ and receiving good g, buyer b can examine the quality $q \in Q$ of good g, where Q is a finite set of real values representing product qualities. It then calculates the true value of good g using the *true product value function* $v^b : G \times P \times Q \mapsto \mathbb{R}$. For instance, if buyer b considers the quality of good g to be twice more important than its price, it may set $v^b(g, p, q) = 2q - p$.

The expected value function f^b is now incrementally learned in a reinforcement learning framework:

$$f^b(g, p, \hat{s}) \leftarrow f^b(g, p, \hat{s}) + \alpha(v^b(g, p, q) - f^b(g, p, \hat{s})) \tag{3}$$

where α is called the *learning rate* $(0 \leq \alpha \leq 1)$. The learning rate should be initially set to 1 and, similar to ρ, be reduced over time to a fixed minimum value chosen by b.

Thus, if $\Delta = v^b(g, p, q) - f^b(g, p, \hat{s}) \geq 0$ then $f^b(g, p, \hat{s})$ is updated with the same or a greater value than before. This means that seller $\hat{s}$ has a good chance to be chosen by buyer b again if it continues offering good g at price p in the next auction. Conversely, if $\Delta < 0$ then $f^b(g, p, \hat{s})$ is updated with a smaller value than before. So, seller $\hat{s}$ may not be selected by buyer b in the next auction if it continues selling good g at price p.

In addition to updating the expected value function, the reputation rating $r^b(\hat{s})$ of seller $\hat{s}$ also needs to be updated. Let $\vartheta^b(g) \in \mathbb{R}$ be the product value that buyer b demands for good g. We use a reputation updating scheme motivated by that proposed in [8] as follows:

If $\delta = v^b(g, p, q) - \vartheta^b(g) \geq 0$, that is, if seller $\hat{s}$ offers good g with value greater than or equal to the value demanded by buyer b, then its reputation rating $r^b(\hat{s})$ is increased by

$$r^b(\hat{s}) \leftarrow \begin{cases} r^b(\hat{s}) + \mu(1 - r^b(\hat{s})) \text{ if } r^b(\hat{s}) \geq 0 \\ r^b(\hat{s}) + \mu(1 + r^b(\hat{s})) \text{ if } r^b(\hat{s}) < 0 \end{cases} \tag{4}$$

where μ is a positive factor called the *cooperation factor*[2] $(0 < \mu < 1)$.

Otherwise, if $\delta < 0$, that is, if seller $\hat{s}$ sells good g with value less than that demanded by buyer b, then its reputation rating $r^b(\hat{s})$ is decreased by

$$r^b(\hat{s}) \leftarrow \begin{cases} r^b(\hat{s}) + \nu(1 - r^b(\hat{s})) \text{ if } r^b(\hat{s}) \geq 0 \\ r^b(\hat{s}) + \nu(1 + r^b(\hat{s})) \text{ if } r^b(\hat{s}) < 0 \end{cases} \tag{5}$$

where ν is a negative factor called the *non-cooperation factor* $(-1 < \nu < 0)$.

To protect itself from dishonest sellers, buyer b may require $|\nu| > |\mu|$ to implement the traditional idea that reputation should be difficult to build up, but easy to tear down. Moreover, buyer b may vary μ and ν as increasing functions of v^b to reflect the common idea that a transaction with higher value should be more appreciated than a lower one (i.e., the reputation rating of a seller that offers higher true product value should be better increased).

The set of reputable sellers to buyer b now needs to be updated based on the new reputation rating $r^b(\hat{s})$, as in one of the following two cases:

- If $(\hat{s} \in S_r^b)$ and $(r^b(\hat{s}) < \Theta)$ then buyer b no longer considers $\hat{s}$ as a reputable seller, i.e., $S_r^b \leftarrow S_r^b - \{\hat{s}\}$.
- If $(\hat{s} \notin S_r^b)$ and $(r^b(\hat{s}) \geq \Theta)$ then buyer b now considers $\hat{s}$ as a reputable seller, i.e., $S_r^b \leftarrow S_r^b \cup \{\hat{s}\}$.

Similarly, the set of disreputable sellers also needs to be updated. If $(\hat{s} \notin S_{dr}^b)$ and $(r^b(\hat{s}) \leq \theta)$ then buyer b now rates $\hat{s}$ a disreputable seller, i.e., $S_{dr}^b \leftarrow S_{dr}^b \cup \{\hat{s}\}$.

We have also designed a learning algorithm for sellers in electronic marketplaces in which sellers learn to maximize their expected profits by adjusting product prices and by optionally altering the quality of their goods. The proposed selling algorithm, however, is not presented due to the page limit of the paper.

3   Experimentation

We have performed a number of experiments to measure the value of our model on the microscopic and macroscopic levels. On the micro level, we were interested in examining the individual benefit of agents, particularly their level of

---

[2] Buyer b will consider seller $\hat{s}$ as being *cooperative* if the good $\hat{s}$ sells to b has value greater than or equal to that demanded by b.

satisfaction. Our experimental results confirm that in both modest and large-sized marketplaces, a buyer will obtain higher true product values (therefore better satisfaction) if it models sellers' reputation, and a seller will have more opportunities to win an auction (hence greater satisfaction) if it considers improving the quality of its goods, according to the proposed algorithm. On the macro level, we studied how a market populated with our buyers and sellers would behave as a whole. The experimental results show that such a market can reach an equilibrium state where the agent population remains stable (as some sellers who repeatedly fail to sell their goods will decide to leave the market), and this equilibrium is optimal for the participant agents.

Because of the page limit of the paper, we report in this section only the modest-sized marketplace experiments that confirm the satisfaction of buyers following the proposed algorithm. In particular, we would like to show that in a marketplace where there are sellers altering the quality of their goods, buyers following the proposed algorithm should obtain better satisfaction, compared to those buyers following a simplified version where they do not model sellers' reputation.

We simulate a marketplace populated with 8 sellers and 4 buyers using Java 2. Among the four buyers, buyers b_0 and b_1 use the simplified version while buyers b_2 and b_3 follow our proposed algorithm. Of the eight sellers, the first half (namely sellers s_0, s_1, s_2, and s_3) offers fixed-quality goods while the second half (namely sellers s_4, s_5, s_6, and s_7) offers goods with quality altered. We consider two cases in which a seller may alter the quality of its goods:

(i) *Quality Chosen Randomly:* For each auction, the quality is chosen randomly from the interval $[low\_Q, high\_Q]$, where low_Q and $high\_Q$ are seller specific constants.

(ii) *Quality Switched Between Two Values:* The quality is switched between a high value and a very low one. This strategy is used by dishonest sellers who try to attract buyers with a high quality good first and then cheat them with a really low one.

The following parameters are used in our experiments:

- The learning rate α and the exploration probability ρ are both set to 1 initially, and then decreased over time (by factor 0.995) down to $\alpha_{min} = 0.1$ and $\rho_{min} = 0.1$.
- The quality q of a good is chosen to be equal to the cost for producing that good. This supports the common assumption that it costs more to produce high quality goods.
- The true product value function $v^b(p, q) = 3.5q - p$, where p and q represent the price and quality of the good, respectively.
- The reputation threshold $\Theta = 0.5$, and the disreputation threshold $\theta = -0.9$.
- The demanded product value $\vartheta^b(g) = 102$. Thus, even when a seller has to sell at cost, it must offer goods with quality of at least 40.8 in order to meet the buyers' demand [3].

---

[3] Because $v^b(p, q) = 3.5q - p$ and $3.5(40.8) - 40.8 = 102$.

– If $v^b - \vartheta^b \geq 0$, we define the cooperation factor μ as

$$\mu = \begin{cases} \dfrac{v^b - \vartheta^b}{v^b_{max} - v^b_{min}} & \text{if} \quad \frac{v^b - \vartheta^b}{v^b_{max} - v^b_{min}} > \mu_{min} \\ \mu_{min} & \text{otherwise} \end{cases} \qquad (6)$$

where $\mu_{min} = 0.005$, $v^b_{max} = 3.5q_{max} - p_{min}$, $v^b_{min} = 3.5q_{min} - p_{max}$, $q_{max} = p_{max} = 49.0$, and $q_{min} = p_{min} = 1.0$. We vary μ as an increasing function of v^b to reflect the idea that the reputation rating of a seller that offers goods with higher value should be better increased. We also prevent μ from becoming zero when $v^b = \vartheta^b$ by using the value of μ_{min}.

– If $v^b - \vartheta^b < 0$, we define the noncooperation factor ν as

$$\nu = \begin{cases} \lambda(\dfrac{v^b - \vartheta^b}{v^b_{max} - v^b_{min}}) & \text{if} \quad \lambda(\frac{v^b - \vartheta^b}{v^b_{max} - v^b_{min}}) > \nu_{min} \\ \nu_{min} & \text{otherwise} \end{cases} \qquad (7)$$

where $\nu_{min} = -0.9$ and $\lambda = 3$. In this definition ν is also varied as an increasing function of v^b to support the idea that the lower product value a seller offers, the more its reputation rating should be decreased. The use of factor $\lambda > 1$ indicates that a buyer will penalize a non-cooperative seller λ times greater than it will award a cooperative seller, thus implementing the traditional assumption that reputation should be difficult to build up but easy to tear down. We prevent ν from moving out of the required lower bound -1 by using the value ν_{min}.

The experimental results presented in this section are based on the average of 100 runs, each of which has 5000 auctions.

3.1   Quality Chosen Randomly

For this first case we let sellers s_0, s_1, s_2, and s_3 offer goods with fixed qualities of 32.0, 36.0, 40.0, and 44.0, respectively; while sellers s_4, s_5, s_6, and s_7 alter the quality of their goods by, for each auction, choosing at random a quality value in the interval $[32.0, 48.0]$. It should be obvious from the settings that a buyer would achieve greater satisfaction by making as many purchases as possible from seller s_3 (who offers the highest fixed product quality) instead of purchasing from those sellers that randomly change the quality of their goods.

Table 1 shows the average number of purchases made from each seller by buyer b_2 and b_3 - the buyers that follow the proposed buying algorithm (labelled as $b_{2,3}$), and by buyer b_0 and b_1 - the buyers using the simplified version (labelled as $b_{0,1}$). Indeed, buyer $b_{2,3}$ made 1086 more purchases from s_3, which is approximately 28.8% of the number of purchases made from s_3 by $b_{0,1}$. Buyer $b_{2,3}$ also made about 684 fewer purchases from those sellers that randomly alter the quality of their goods, which is about 85.8% of the number of purchases made by $b_{0,1}$ from the sellers altering the quality of their goods.

Table 1. Number of purchases made from different sellers by a buyer not modelling sellers' reputation ($b_{0,1}$), and by a buyer following the proposed buying algorithm ($b_{2,3}$).

Seller	s_0	s_1	s_2	s_3	s_4	s_5	s_6	s_7
$b_{0,1}$	134.5	142.5	160.7	3765.2	195.8	205.4	195.3	200.6
$b_{2,3}$	4.5	7.9	23.3	4851.2	27.6	28.6	27.9	28.9

Alternatively, Fig. 1(a) and (b) present the histograms of true product values obtained by a buyer not modelling sellers' reputation and by a buyer following the proposed algorithm, respectively. We notice that the number of purchases in Fig. 1(b) where the true product values are in the high interval $[107, 109]$ is almost 4000, while that in Fig. 1(a) is just a few. The number of purchases in Fig. 1(b) where the true product values are in lower intervals such as $[105, 107]$ is about 1600 purchases less (or 62.7% less) than that in Fig. 1(a). This indicates that the buyer following the proposed algorithm obtains more goods with higher value and fewer goods with lower value, therefore achieving better satisfaction.

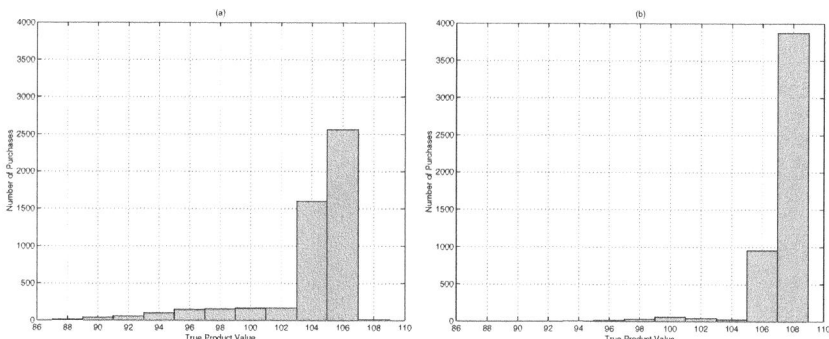

Fig. 1. Histograms of true product values obtained by a buyer not modelling sellers' reputation (a), and by a buyer following the proposed algorithm (b).

3.2 Quality Switched between Two Values

For this second case we let sellers s_0, s_1, s_2, and s_3 offer goods with fixed quality 38.0, 40.0, 42.0, and 44.0, respectively; while sellers s_4, s_5, s_6, and s_7 are made dishonest sellers who offer goods with quality switched between 45.0 and 1.0. Again, it should be clear that a successful buyer will make as many purchases as possible from seller s_3 and stay away from the dishonest sellers.

Table 2 indeed shows that the buyer following the proposed algorithm ($b_{2,3}$) makes more purchases from seller s_3 but fewer purchases from the dishonest sellers, in comparison with the buyer not modelling the reputation of sellers ($b_{0,1}$). In particular, buyer $b_{2,3}$ made approximately 12.3% more purchases from seller s_3 and about 95.1% fewer purchases from the dishonest sellers, compared to the numbers of purchases buyer $b_{0,1}$ makes from s_3 and from the dishonest sellers, respectively.

Table 2. Number of purchases made from different sellers by a buyer not modelling sellers' reputation ($b_{0,1}$), and by a buyer following the proposed buying algorithm ($b_{2,3}$).

Seller	s_0	s_1	s_2	s_3	s_4	s_5	s_6	s_7
$b_{0,1}$	118.1	138.0	151.4	4263.3	88.3	79.9	78.3	82.8
$b_{2,3}$	11.9	23.5	162.9	4785.7	4.0	4.0	4.0	4.0

Alternatively, Fig. 2 displays graphs of true product values obtained by a buyer not modelling sellers' reputation (graph (i)) and by a buyer following the proposed buying algorithm (graph (ii)), respectively. The figure confirms that the buyer following the proposed algorithm receives higher product values and therefore better satisfaction. Particularly, our calculation shows that the mean product value obtained by the buyer not modelling sellers' reputation is 101.49, while that obtained by the buyer following the proposed algorithm is 106.27, which is 4.7% higher.

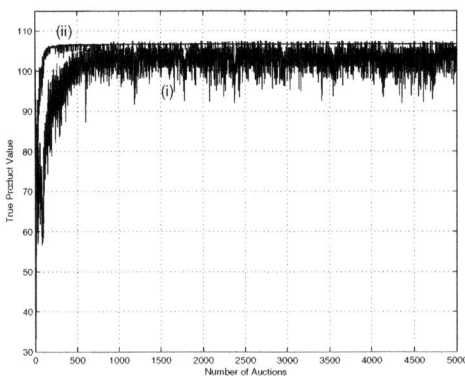

Fig. 2. Comparison of the true product values obtained by a buyer not modelling sellers' reputation (graph (i)), and by a buyer following the proposed algorithm (graph (ii)).

4　Discussion and Conclusions

This paper discusses the application of user modelling techniques in the area of electronic commerce. In particular, it proposes a feasible, reputation based and reinforcement learning algorithm for buying agents in electronic marketplaces. According to this algorithm, buying agents learn to optimize their expected product values by selecting appropriate sellers to do business with among the reputable sellers and avoiding the disreputable ones. We show how to adjust the reputation model of a seller, based on its performance in the market. Our proposed solution assigns appropriate adjustments, allowing for reputation to be easy to tear down but difficult to build up, and providing strict disreputable ratings for sellers with significantly disappointing performance. We also discuss how reputation models of entirely new sellers can be initiated. Our experimental results confirm the value of the proposed buying algorithm, providing better satisfaction for buyers than cases where reputation of sellers is not modelled.

Our work is motivated by [6]. This research, however, focuses on the question of when an agent benefits from having deeper models of others, resorting to recursive modelling of other agents in the marketplace. In contrast, we use a reputation mechanism to shield buyers from being cheated by malicious sellers, instead of having agents deal with the computational costs of maintaining recursive models of others. Moreover, reputation of sellers is an important factor that buyers can exploit to reduce the risk of purchasing low quality goods, and so should be included in the buying algorithm.

Other researchers have investigated the modelling of reputation. Yu and Singh [8] develop a general model for trust, focusing on acquiring information from other agents in an agent community. They use specific values to update the trust ratings of agents. In contrast, we have variable cooperative and non-cooperative factors, to allow for agents who greatly disappoint to be more seriously penalized. We also outline specifically the strategies for adjusting the model of reputation within a setting of electronic marketplaces.

Other researchers, such as Sabater and Sierra [4], do not elaborate on strategies for initiating and updating reputation models, but do offer more extensive representations for reputation. They consider the reputation of an agent not as a single and abstract concept, but rather a multi-facet concept. This idea may be useful to implement our algorithm with deeper models of quality in which the quality of a product can be judged according to a combination of various factors such as the physical product characteristics, whether the product is distributed on time, whether the product is supported after purchase, etc.

Modelling reputation in electronic marketplaces is also related to the topic of modelling trust to optimize coalitions in agent societies. Breban and Vassileva [2] have examined the use of trust models to determine coalition formation for improved buying activities. We offer a distinct algorithm for adjusting the reputation ratings of agents, but for future work it would be useful to examine coalitions of agents working together to improve their performance. In this case, a model of the trust of other buyers in the marketplace would be important.

For future research, we plan to investigate more sophisticated learning algorithms for agents in electronic markets that allow agents to cooperate with other agents and/or take advantage of their knowledge about other agents to maximize their local utility. One interesting case to consider is allowing buyers in the market to form neighborhoods as in [8], such that within a neighborhood they inform one another of their knowledge about sellers. These buyers can then use their own knowledge combined with the informed knowledge to make decisions about which sellers to select. We predict that this form of transferring knowledge may be beneficial to new buyers, who can use the experience of existing buyers to make satisfactory purchase decisions without having to undergo several trials to build up enough experience for themselves.

In fact, it would be useful to conduct experiments to characterize whether it is more beneficial for buying agents to acquire knowledge about selling agents from other buyers in the community, rather than only using their own personalized models of reputation. The ultimate aim of this research would be to provide some general guidelines for AI-systems designers in building effective economic agents and desirable market environments. On the whole, our work aims to confirm the value of introducing the modelling of reputation into algorithms for buying agents in electronic marketplaces.

References

1. A. Chavez, and P. Maes. Kasbah: An Agent Marketplace for Buying and Selling Goods. In *Proceedings of the First International Conference on the Practical Application of Intelligent Agents and Multi-Agent Technology*, 1996.
2. S. Breban, and J. Vassileva. Using Inter-agent Trust Relationships for Efficient Coalition Formation. In *Proceedings of the Fifteenth Conference of the Canadian Society for Computational Studies of Intelligence*, pages 221–236, May 2002.
3. R. Davis, and R. G. Smith. Negotiation as a Metaphor for Distributed Problem Solving. In *Artificial Intelligence*, 20(1): 63–109, January 1983.
4. J. Sabater, and C. Sierra. REGRET: A Reputation Model for Gregarious Societies. In *Papers from the Fifth International Conference on Autonomous Agents Workshop on Deception, Fraud and Trust in Agent Societies*, pages 61–69, 2001.
5. T. Tran, and R. Cohen. A Reputation-Oriented Reinforcement Learning Strategy for Agents in Electronic Marketplaces. In *Computational Intelligence Journal, Special Issue on Agent Technology for Electronic Commerce*, to appear in November 2002.
6. J. M. Vidal, and E. H. Durfee. The Impact of Nested Agent Models in an Information Economy. In *Proceedings of the Second International Conference on Multi-Agent Systems*, pages 377–384, 1996.
7. P. R. Wurman, M. P. Wellman, and W. E. Wash. The Michigan Internet Auction-Bot: A Configurable Auction Server for Humans and Software Agents. In *Proceedings of the Second International Conference on Autonomous Agents*, pages 301–308, 1998.
8. B. Yu, and M. P. Singh. A Social Mechanism of Reputation Management in Electronic Communities. In M. Klusch and L. Kerschberg, editors, *Cooperative Information Agents IV*, Lecture Notes in Artificial Intelligence, Vol. 1860, pages 154–165. Springer-Verlag, Berlin, 2000.

Customising the Interaction with Configuration Systems

Liliana Ardissono[1], Anna Goy[1], Matt Holland[2], Giovanna Petrone[1], and
Ralph Schäfer[3]

[1] Dipartimento di Informatica, Università di Torino, Italy
{liliana, goy, giovanna}@di.unito.it
[2] BTExact Technologies, UK
matthew.holland@bt.com
[3] DFKI. Germany
Ralph.Schaefer@r77.de

Abstract. This paper presents an intelligent user interface for the management
of personalised configuration in business-oriented domains. The proposed system
fills the gap between the technical interaction style adopted by current configuration systems and the user's needs, by assisting the user during the selection of the
features of the items to be configured and by customising the presentation of the
solutions.

1 Introduction

The techniques currently applied in recommender systems [4] do not support the configuration of items, which is essential to comply with the customer's requirements when
purchasing complex products, or registering for services. Indeed, efficient configuration systems have been developed, e.g., see [5], but they require that the user knows all
the details about the items to be configured. One way to enhance the usability of such
systems is to extend them with *user-adaptive interfaces* guiding the user through the
configuration process.

Within the CAWICOMS project, we developed an intelligent user interface (the
CAWICOMS frontend) which mediates the interaction between configuration systems
and their users by assisting the user during the specification of the features of the items to
be configured and by presenting the solutions in accordance with the user's interests and
expertise [2]. This paper presents the CAWICOMS frontend and describes its exploitation
in the configuration of IP-based Virtual Private Networks (IP-VPNs).

In order to suitably design the system, we have taken into account a set of requirements which we have collected by interviewing people regularly using the configuration
systems available to a telecommunication company and occasional users of on-line configuration systems. In particular, such users complained that the configuration process
may require the specification of a large set of data and that this task may be difficult
for the non-expert user. Moreover, they pointed out that the configuration of items and
the presentation of solutions should be organised by taking the structure of the items
into account, and by focusing on the most interesting features for the user, instead of
being specified as a flat feature list, as most configuration systems do. The users also had
interaction requirements concerning the possibility to postpone configuration decisions
and to trigger the automatic configuration of items.[1]

---

[1] We will not address such issues in the present paper, for space reasons.

P. Brusilovsky et al. (Eds.): UM 2003, LNAI 2702, pp. 283–287, 2003.
© Springer-Verlag Berlin Heidelberg 2003

2   Adaptive User Interaction

The CAWICOMS frontend manages the interaction with the user as a dynamically generated sequence of configuration steps, where the user is asked to set the features of the item to be configured. The configuration solutions are presented by focusing the descriptions on the features fitting the user's interests and expertise.[2] The generation of the user interface is tailored to the user's expertise and interests and relies on an explicit representation of the knowledge about configurable items, on the management of a dynamic user model describing the end-user's features, and on the application of adaptive hypermedia techniques [1].

2.1   Representation of Knowledge about Products and Services

The representation of the knowledge about products and services relies on the *component-port* approach for configuration described in [5]. To support a user-oriented management of the configuration process, we have extended this representation in various ways. For instance, we enriched the representation of features with an explanation of their meaning and the specification of the type of information they convey (e.g., technical, economic, general information). Moreover, we specified a complexity level representing an estimate of the degree of expertise required to understand the meaning of the feature. Furthermore, we specified a criticality level, needed to identify features whose values should be acknowledged by the user (important features, from the configuration, or business point of view). We also introduced the representation of properties aimed at evaluating the items from a qualitative point of view. In the IP-VPN domain, we defined properties such as the performance and the reliability of the networks. The impact of the technical features on the evaluation of the item properties is represented by defining evaluation functions that map property values onto the feature values as defined by Multiattribute Utility Theory [7].

2.2   Management of the User Model

An individual user model stores explicit and implicit information about the user. The explicit portion of the user model stores the user's characteristics, such as the nationality and the type of company she represents. The implicit portion describes the system's estimates about the user's interests in the properties of the configurable items (e.g., reliability and economy) and the estimates of the user's knowledge about the features of the configurable items.[3]

The user's knowledge and interests are estimated by combining stereotypical information about the classes of users of the system (e.g., technical engineers, managers, end-customers) with user modeling acquisition techniques, based on the interpretation of the user's interaction behaviour. In particular, the system estimates the user's interests

---

[2] The ILOG JConfigurator engine is used to generate the configuration solutions.

[3] As the estimates of the user's interests and expertise are uncertain, they are represented as probability distributions on the values of variables associated to the knowledge of items and to the properties.

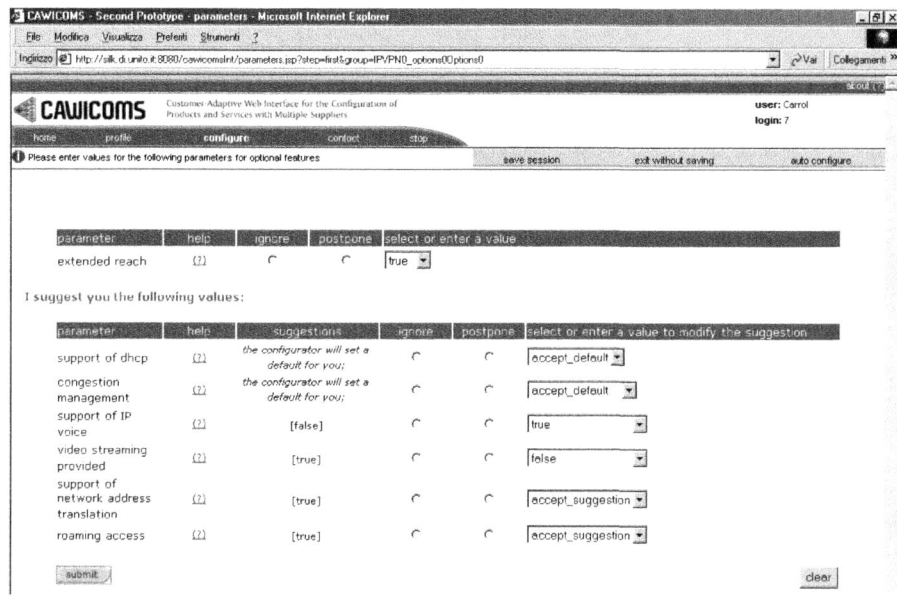

Fig. 1. A step in the configuration of an IP-VPN.

in the properties of products and services by ascribing her a model for the evaluation of items based on the Multiattribute Utility Theory. This model defines the evaluation of items as a function of the evaluation of their properties, given the user's interests in such properties. The exploitation of this theory enables the system to interpret the acceptance or the rejection of a specific configuration solution as a sign that the user's evaluation of the item is good/bad. In turn, this information is relevant to assess the user's interests in the item properties. As the interpretation of the user's actions is affected by uncertainty, we use Bayesian Networks to perform this task [6]. Finally, the user's expertise is estimated by applying the approach described in [3].

2.3   Elicitation of the User's Requirements

The system employs the estimates on the user's current interests in the item's properties, such as its reliability, to steer the configuration process by proposing feature values and components that maximise the user's expected evaluation of the solution. In this way, the number of features she has to set is dramatically reduced. The system also uses other personalisation strategies. For example, features can be set by applying personalised defaults describing business rules based on the customer's characteristics.

The personalisation strategies are represented as declarative rules with priority. Given a feature to be set, a rule-based engine selects the strategy to be applied by evaluating the alternative rules according to their priority and by choosing the first one matching the current situation in a satisfactory way. The evaluation is performed by taking into account, on the one hand, the complexity and the criticality of the feature, and, on

Fig. 2. Elicitation of user requirements about a property of IP-VPNs.

the other hand, the user's expertise and interests in the item properties. The following strategies are defined:
1) Very critical features have to be set by the user.
2) If a personalised default matching the user's characteristics is available for the feature and the suggested values are consistent with the current domain of the feature, suggest the default values.
3) If the feature is related to some properties for which the user's estimated interest is low, set a default value consistent with the domain of the feature.
4) If the user's estimated expertise is sufficient to choose a value for the feature, ask her to set the preferred value, given the current domain.

As asking the user is the last resort, whenever possible, the system suggests the values to be set. Figure 1 shows a page generated during the configuration of the optional services of an IP-VPN. The system asks the user to specify whether the company (a Web Design one) wants the extended reach to Eastern countries. Moreover, the system suggests to set some features in a standard way (support of dhcp, congestion management protocol). Furthermore, personalised defaults are suggested for the support of IP voice, the provision of video streaming, the support for network address translation, and the roaming access. The suggestions can be overridden, as the user did with the IP voice and video streaming. As shown in Figure 2, the system may also elicit the required information in an indirect way, by asking the user about her preferences for properties of an IP-VPN related to the features to be set. Given the answer, the most suitable settings to achieve such properties are determined.

3 Evaluation

The prototype system was evaluated a number of times throughout the development process. This evaluation was used to guide the further development of the prototype. In order to test features of the adaptive interface, we used role-playing exercises involving a small number of users with different levels of expertise. Some of them were familiar with existing configuration systems, but not necessarily IP-VPN, some were familiar with the domain, some completely new to this area of technology. These users gave feedback in the form of a questionnaire.

We performed tests using two sets of scenarios: One for the Telecommunications Switches domain and one for the IP-VPN domain. Here, we concentrate on the IP-VPN domain, which was used for the final evaluation. Our IP-VPN test scenarios involved a fictitious company named WooCorp. WooCorp are a fast growing technology start-up company with offices across Europe and need to purchase a VPN to replace their existing collection of ad-hoc communications links. They have decided to go to a reseller (Network Global Services) who employ a CAWICOMS configuration system. We developed a number of different test scripts within this scenario going from the initial specification of a small network to connect WooCorp's major sites, then adding in more complexity such as further sites and dial-up access for mobile users.

The results of this evaluation were quite satisfactory. The total number of questionnaires analysed was 30. Approximately half of the test subjects were novices, with 10% in the "Intermediate" bracket. Our test users particularly liked the features designed to help novice users: 55% liked the suggestion functionality and 35% explicitly praised the auto-configure feature. This feature was equally liked by novice and expert users. 70% of users felt that the adaptive features of the system improved the user experience. As for future development of the system, it was suggested that the adaptive features could go even further: expert users thought that explanations of why particular values were suggested would aid them.

4   Conclusions

We have presented the intelligent user interface employed in the CAWICOMS configuration system to assist the user during the configuration of complex services. This user interface is based on the dynamic generation of the Web pages, which are personalised by taking the user's expertise and interests into account.

CAWICOMS is the acronym for "Customer-Adaptive Web Interface for the Configuration of Products and Services with Multiple Suppliers"; see http://www.cawicoms.org. This work was funded by the EU through the IST Programme under contract IST-1999-10688. We thank the other project partners (Telecom Italia Lab, ETIS, ILOG SA, University of Klagenfurt) for their contribution to the design and development of CAWICOMS.

References

1. The adaptive Web. *Communications of the ACM*, 45(5), 2002.
2. L. Ardissono, A. Felfernig, G. Friedrich, A. Goy, D. Jannach, M. Meyer, G. Petrone, R. Schäfer, W. Schütz, and M. Zanker. Personalising on-line configuration of products and services. In *Proc. 15th Conf. ECAI*, pages 225–229, Lyon, 2002.
3. A. Jameson. *Knowing What Others Know: Studies in Intuitive Psychometrics*. PhD thesis, University of Amsterdam, 1990.
4. A. Kobsa, J. Koenemann, and W. Pohl. Personalized hypermedia presentation techniques for improving online customer relationships. *The Knowledge Engineering Review*, 16(2):111–155, 2001.
5. D. Mailharro. A classification and constraint-based framework for configuration. *AI in Engineering, Design and Manucturing*, 12:383–397, 1998.
6. W. Schütz and R. Schäfer. Bayesian networks for estimating the user's interests in the context of a configuration task. In R. Schäfer, M. E. Müller, and S. A. Macskassy, editors, *Proc. UM2001 Workshop on Machine Learning for User Modeling*, pages 23–36, July 2001.
7. D. von Winterfeldt and W. Edwards. *Decision Analysis and Behavioral Research*. Cambridge University Press, Cambridge, UK, 1986.

Does Adapted Information Help Patients with Cancer?

Diana Bental[1], Alison Cawsey[1], Janne Pearson[2], and Ray Jones[2]

[1] Department of Mathematics and Computer Science
Heriot-Watt University, Riccarton, Edinburgh EH14 4AS, UK
{d.bental, a.cawsey}@hw.ac.uk
http://www.macs.hw.ac.uk/~diana/paccit/index.html
[2] Department of Public Health, University of Glasgow, Glasgow UK

Abstract. Models of patients' information needs have great potential in improving health information. Such models can adapt information to patients' medical circumstances, educational level and psychological needs. However, building these models and the information systems based on them can be difficult and costly, and it is difficult to assess the benefits of such systems for the patients. We describe a study to compare the psychological effects for cancer patients of tailored information against information that has not been tailored.

1   Background

Patient information systems can help patients identify what is most relevant and helpful in the vast amount of available information. They can adapt to patients' specific medical circumstances, educational level and psychological needs. However, the costs of producing effective personalised material must be assessed against the benefits.

Many personalised patient information systems have been developed over the last 10 years (reviewed in [1]), with a number of studies as to their efficacy. These systems include both online information systems and systems to generate tailored leaflets and letters.

The results of the studies have been somewhat unclear. In two different studies of personalised "stop smoking" letters, for example, one [5] concluded that the personalised system had a positive effect, and one [3] failed to demonstrate any such effect. Reiter discusses the problems of such studies in [4]. In our own previous work we have undertaken a large randomised trial of (online) tailored information for cancer patients [2] and observed a statistically significant preference for the tailored system. We also observed a small difference in the anxiety levels of patients receiving personalised information. However, what is missing from this work and similar studies was an explanation *why* (and therefore, in what circumstances) the personalised information brings benefits. In our current study we therefore measure how patients use the information provided, including how they discuss it with family and friends. One of our hypotheses is that patients are more likely to discuss the personalised information.

P. Brusilovsky et al. (Eds.): UM 2003, LNAI 2702, pp. 288–291, 2003.

2   An Architecture for Adapted Patient Information

We have developed PaTXML (Personalised and Tailored XML), an architecture in which we can create on-line displays and printed documents which are automatically adapted using information from an online patient record. PaTXML includes a simple XML-based document markup-language, motivated by the need to allow the material to be created and edited by someone with only limited knowledge of the underlying technologies.

```
<subheading>Grade <field>Grade</field> Breast Cancer</subheading>
Breast cancer is divided into three grades: grade 1, grade 2 and
grade 3. Grade 1 is most like normal tissue and least likely to
spread. Your breast cancer was a grade <field>Grade</field>
<if><field>Invasive</field>
    <value>yes</value>
    <then>, invasive</then>
</if>
<field>Type</field>.
```

Grade 3 Breast Cancer
Breast cancer is divided into three grades: grade 1, grade 2 and grade 3. Grade 1 is most like normal tissue and least likely to spread. Your breast cancer was a grade 3, invasive carcinoma.

Fig. 1. A fragment of text marked up with PaTXML, and generated text

PaTXML is the core representation for the patient data and for the pages of information about cancer. Using the PaTXML mark-up language, we have created a range of cancer information booklets which may either be standardised or adapted. PaTXML selects information topics for the adapted booklets according to whether it is likely to be relevant to this patient, and the adapted texts may include personal information from the patient's record (Figure 1). PaTXML also offers an online interface through which patients may select the information topics for their booklet. The list of topics may be standardised or it may be tailored to the patient.

We are using PaTXML to offer both tailored and generic information for patients with cancer, so as to compare the effects of these different types of information.

3   The Study

Our present study is a randomized controlled trial which compares the effects of different kinds of booklets and how the booklets are created:

– Whether patients choose the information for themselves, or if the contents of the booklet are chosen for them;

- Whether the booklet is tailored to include personal information from their own medical records and to include only the most relevant information, or whether it contains just general information about a given type of cancer;
- Whether it includes specific advice on the management of anxiety.

We use a range of questionnaires to measure baseline data at recruitment and outcome measures three months later, including:

- psychological measures of depression and anxiety
- social support and negative interactions
- patients' satisfaction with the information received;
- how patients used the reports and how the reports influenced the patient's interactions with families and friends.

The patients in the study attend an outpatient cancer clinic. Patients in the self-selection arm of the study used a workstation with the choice of a mouse or touch screen to choose the information to be included in their booklet. The target number of 400 patients have now been recruited. A preliminary analysis of more than 300 patients (not comparing the intervention groups, but characterising the population) showed that the patients in the study are not highly computer literate; 44% of the patients recruited had not used a computer before. Almost one third had already used information obtained from the Internet, but more than half of this group had not used the Internet themselves; instead someone else had obtained the information for them. The majority (72%) of patients recruited were female. Information was developed for a range of cancers, but most patients recruited had either breast or prostate cancer. The majority chose to use a touch screen rather than a mouse.

Before beginning our main study we undertook two small pilot studies, one to test the questionnaires and one to test and revise the PaTXML implementation. Nine patients used the pilot version of PaTXML. During the pilot, the researcher stayed with the patients while they used the computer, observed how they used the computer and any difficulties they encountered, and answered any queries they had. Text had to be enlarged and links had to be clearly separated to make navigation easier on the touch screen. We also found it was helpful to allow patients to see a checklist of all the topics they had selected so far, and let them add to or delete items from the list.

We had originally intended that patients in the self-selection arm of the study would view all the information for their booklet online, while making their selection. However, during the pilot study we found that this was not realistic due to the amount of information available to each patient (up to 100 printed pages). Patients did not have time to read all this material online, and the quantity of text presented difficulties for attention and navigation. Scrolling windows and deeply nested menu structures were both found to be very difficult for patients to manage, especially when using the touch screen. The usability requirements identified during the pilot most resembled a kiosk, that is: small amounts of text on screen in a large font; no scrolling; a few large, clear buttons; a simple navigation structure. It was extremely difficult to reconcile these requirements with topics that consisted of several printed pages (and many more screenfuls) of text and graphics. As a result, for the main study patients were shown instead brief summaries of each topic online, which they used to select materials for their booklet.

We are also seeking feedback on the study via the Web. We have created a web page which describes the study, provides a link to an online demonstration, and offers a questionnaire asking the reader's expectations of our results; whether they expect that self-selection, tailoring or anxiety information will have the greatest effect on patients. We have advertised the web site mainly in electronic mailing lists used by health information scientists, and these have formed the majority of respondents so far. Self-selection and tailoring of information were judged roughly equally in terms of how likely patients were to feel satisfied with the information and whether they were likely to discuss the information with others. Despite this, tailoring of information was judged likely to have a greater effect than self-selection on the patients' anxiety levels, and information tailoring was expected to be as helpful as specific information on anxiety reduction in reducing patients' anxiety. We await completion of the main study to see whether these expectations are fulfilled.

References

1. Bental, D., Cawsey, A., Jones, R.: Patient Information Systems that Tailor to the Individual. Patient Education and Counselling **36** (1999) 171–180.
2. Cawsey, A., Jones, R., Pearson, J.: The Evaluation of a Personalised Information System for Patients with Cancer. User Modeling and User-Adapted Interaction **10** (2000) 47–72.
3. Lennox, A., Osman, L., Reiter, E., Robertson, R., Friend, J, McCann, I., Skatun, D., Donnan, P.: The Cost-Effectiveness of Computer-Tailored and Non-Tailored Smoking Cessation Letters in General Practice: A Controlled Trial. British Medical Journal **322** (2001) 1396–1400.
4. Reiter, E., Roberston, R., Osman, L.: Lessons from a Failure: Generating Tailored Smoking Cessation Letters. Artificial Intelligence **144** (2003) 41–58.
5. Strecher, V., Kreuter, M., Den Boer, D.J., Kospers, S., Hospers, H., Skinner, C.: The Effects of Computer-Tailored Smoking Cessation Materials in Family Practice Setting. The Journal of Family Practice **39** (1994) 262–271.

Empirical Evaluation of Adaptive User Modeling in a Medical Information Retrieval Application

Eugene Santos, Hien Nguyen, Qunhua Zhao, and Erik Pukinskis

Computer Science and Engineering Department
University of Connecticut
191 Auditorium Road, U-155, Storrs, CT 06269-3155
{eugene,hien,qzhao,erik}@cse.uconn.edu

Abstract. A comprehensive methodology for evaluating a user model presents challenges in choosing metrics and in assessing usefulness from both user and system perspectives. In this paper, we describe such a methodology and use it to assess the effectiveness of an adaptive user model embedded in a medical information retrieval. We demonstrate that the user model helps to improve the retrieval quality without degrading the system performance and identify usability problems overlooked in the user model architecture. Empirical data help us in analyzing drawbacks in our user model and develop solutions.

1 Introduction

Empirical evaluation of a user model's effectiveness is useful for both the user modeling community and the researchers in the area of the target application. Without a comprehensive methodology, the usefulness of an embedded user model can not be properly analyzed. Worse yet, researchers can be misled by the idea that adding a user model will improve system performance and reduce the users' workload when it actually degrades the system's performance resulting in important information needed by the users to be omitted. Unfortunately, empirical evaluation often has been overlooked even in the user modeling community itself. As pointed out in [2], only a third of the papers from the User Modelling and User-Adapted Interaction journal (1990 - 1999) included any type of evaluation. In particular, in information retrieval (IR), the usability of the applications enhanced by user models has been overlooked even though standard metrics have been well-established for retrieval performance [3]. While valuable in many respects, these metrics are not enough for assessing systems in which the primary goal is not to only maximize the quality of the retrieval process, but also maximize the quality of the user experience. Recently, the evaluation methods have shifted towards more concerns for the end users, including friendliness and responsiveness. Most of the existing methods which included usability evaluation focused solely on the appraisal of the interactions between users and graphical user interfaces (GUI) while ignoring the interactions between users and the information retrieved [1,5]. In summary, the existing evaluation methods for IR applications which use user models, focused either just on the accuracy of

P. Brusilovsky et al. (Eds.): UM 2003, LNAI 2702, pp. 292–296, 2003.

the retrieval process or just on the user interaction with a GUI. As such, they do not reflect the overall effectiveness of the user model and do not take into account the entire user experience with the system.

Here, we describe our methodology for evaluating the effectiveness of the user model in a medical IR application called Kavanah. The goal of the user model used in Kavanah is to accurately capture user intent and adapt the retrieval process by modifying the search query correspondingly [7].

We assess the effectiveness of the user model with regard to the target application in terms of its influence on system response time, accuracy and usability. We argue that by doing so, we obtain a more complete picture of the effectiveness of the user model from both user and system perspectives. The system response time assessment addresses our concern of whether the user model may degrade system performance. The accuracy assessment uses two common metrics, precision and recall [8], and ensures the user model improve retrieval quality while offering the benefits of easy comparison against other IR applications. Finally, our usability assessment combines both qualitative and quantitative metrics to evaluate the user's experiences with a GUI and the information retrieved.

2   User Model Architecture in Kavanah

The goal of the user model is to accurately capture and represent a user's intent. We partition user's intent into three formative components: Interests, Preferences and Context. The Interests component captures the focus of the user's attention. The Preferences component describes the actions that can be used to achieve the goals and is stored in a preference network (Figure 1c). The Context provides insight into the user's knowledge behind the goals upon which the user is focused. It is stored in the user context network (Figure 1b).

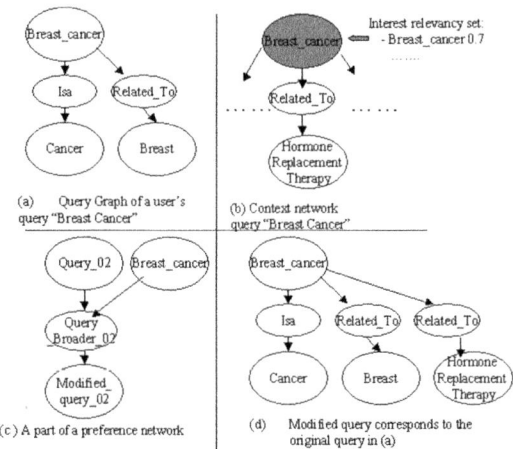

Fig. 1. Query graph,context,preference networks and modified query graph

Kavanah first accepts a natural language query from the user and converts it to a query graph (Figure 1a). The user model modifies the query graph based on the user's interests, preferences and context having been captured (Figure 1d). The modified query graph is matched against each document graph and returns documents where the similarity is greater than a user-defined threshold. Note that each document is represented as a document graph which contains concept nodes (e.g Cancer) and relation nodes (e.g Isa). The user relevance feedback is used to update three components of the user model accordingly. For a more detailed information, please see [7].

3   Methodology and Experimental Execution

Kavanah is implemented as a web-based application. We started with a small database of 521 records to evaluate our methodology before scaling to a larger one.

Effects of the user model on system response time. Our hypothesis is that the user model will not significantly degrade system performance. We take 15 seconds as an acceptable delay time [9]. We test this hypothesis by assessing the response time of Kavanah with and without the user model. The user model is constructed on-the-fly based on the relevance feedbacks collected during this test. The response time is defined as follows: $responsetime = T_{end} - T_{begin}$ in which T_{end} and T_{begin} are the time at displaying the results and the time at issuing the query, respectively. We ran this test with 2 query sets, each set contains 50 natural language queries on some randomly chosen medical topics. We denote the values of response time for Kavanah running with a user model as $a_1..a_n$ and those without as $b_1..b_n$ (n=50). We then compute the slowdown rate for each test set as $slowdownrate = \frac{\sum (b_i - a_i)}{n}$. In this experiment, the average slowdown rate of these two test sets is 0.65 which means that by adding the user model, the system slows down by 0.65 seconds. Note that the average response time for Kavanah without a user model is 40.65 seconds. This experiment demonstrated that adding a user model does not impact performance significantly.

Effects of the user model on system accuracy. Our hypothesis is that the user model in Kavanah will improve the accuracy of the retrieval process. We ran the system over a set of 35 queries with and without the user model. This set of queries is built around the topics such as cancer, diabetes, and infection on which our database has a lot of information. We set the threshold to filter out irrelevant documents to be low to maximize the retrieval of relevant documents available in the database. In our experiments, the precision and recall of the retrieval algorithm with a user model are at least as good as without a user model and improve as the user model learns from the user interactions. For example, by query 34 " Breast cancer risks for the elderly", without a user model, the retrieved results contained a lot of documents on breast cancer in general. With a user model, the system eliminated these documents and returned those documents focusing on breast cancer risks for women with hormone replacement therapy which reflected the user's goals in the query set. An important observation here is that the normal tradeoff of improved precision with decreased recall did not occur in our case. With our user model, we are able to increase the precision, though small, while keeping the recall the same or even increasing. This trend opens a window of opportunity to fill in the gap to improve both precision and recall simultaneously through user modeling.

Usability evaluation. Our hypothesis is that the user model will not add extra workload to the users and will eventually reduce it.To measure the usability of Kavanah, we have adapted the framework laid out in [6]. We asked 16 undergraduate pre-med and pharmacy students to perform an extensive search on two topics, taking notes and providing feedback about relevant documents as they went. Our measure of usability has two components: objective task efficiency which is the ratio of task completion to task time, and subjective user efficiency which is the ratio of user effectiveness to user effort. Task completion was calculated from the number of relevant documents the user identified and the number of topics they covered in their notes. Subjective user effectiveness and user effort were captured by a simple effectiveness questionnaire and the NASA Task Load Index [4], respectively.

After carrying out this experiment, we were unable to find a significant effect of the user model on efficiency, $t(15)=.560$, $p=.585$, or task efficiency, $t(15)=.047$, $p=.963$. There are several factors that may have contributed to this. Because of the small size of the database, participants were not motivated to issue many queries, which meant that Kavanah didn't have enough feedback to react to the user's behavior before they finished their task. Second, Kavanah's behavior is largely opaque to the user. It is our hypothesis that making the query expansion more interactive and more visible to the user will allow Kavanah to realize the usability potential that the AUI paradigm provides. Further research in this area is necessary.

4 Discussion and Summary

The unified framework of our evaluation methodology enabled us to jointly analyze the effects of the user model on the system and users, which may not have been possible if each evaluation is conducted in isolation.

In Figure 2, we show some possible outcomes of experiments and provide possible analyses of the effects of the user model on the system and user behaviors. We assume that the outcome of each experiment can be good (G) or bad (B) and denote effects on system response time, accuracy and usability tests as RT,A,U respectively. Outcomes of task efficiency and user efficiency are denoted as TE and UE respectively. Based on this table, we can determine if the user model has an overall bad or good effect on the system and users. Even better, we can use the real numbers obtained from these tests to analyze further about the actual causes of any effects and make decisions for possible solutions for the next design iteration. This analysis gives us a better understanding rather than looking at the outcomes of each test in isolation because it incorporates more information from different perspectives. Due to space limitations, we focus on cases where the effect on system response time is good. The possible analyses are similar for the other outcome.

RT	A	U	Possible Analysis
G	B	TE: B, UE:B	The user model degraded system accuracy. Thus, the users spent a lot of effort with little success.
G	B	TE: G, UE: B	The user model degraded system accuracy but the user who knows the domain well managed to complete the tasks at the expense of extra effort.
G	B	TE: B, UE: G	The user model degraded system accuracy but the user did not know the domain as well as he thought.
G	B	TE: G, UE: G	The user model degraded system accuracy but the user who has a different domain view from the experts involved in system development still could find right information fast enough because he knows the domain well.
G	G	TE:B,UE:B	The user model did not help the expert user who has different domain knowledge from the experts involved in system development. Thus, he was frustrated for not finding any right information despite his knowledge. If the user is a novice, he might not know enough to complete the task in the given allotted time.
G	G	TE: G,UE: B	The user model helped the user who knows the domain well to retrieve the right information at the expense of extra effort because he and the experts involved in system development have different domain views.
G	G	TE: B,UE: G	The user model did not help the user, who thought he found the right information. In fact, he may not know the domain well enough to finish the tasks.
G	G	TE: G,UE: G	The user model supports users well.

Fig. 2. Possible analyses of influence on response time, accuracy and usability.

In summary, we have not only demonstrated that the evaluations actually address our concerns about whether the user model would delay the system or decrease the accuracy of the retrieval process, but we also pointed out how these empirical measures actually helped us identify the potential problems with the current architecture of the user model and with the target system.

References

1. Brajnik G.; Mizzaro S.; and Tasso C. 1996. Evaluating User Interfaces to Information Retrieval Systems. In *Proceedings of SIGIR 96*.128–136.
2. Chin N. David. 2001. Empirical Evaluation of User Models and User-Adapted Systems. In *User Modeling and User-Adapted Interaction*. Vol 11. 181–194.
3. Harter S. P.; and Hert C. A. 1997. Evaluation of Information Retrieval Systems: Approaches, Issues and Methods. In *Annual Review of Information Science and Technology*. Vol 32. 3–94.
4. Hart, S. G.; and Staveland, L. E. 1988.Development of the NASA-TLX (Task Load Index): Results of Empirical and Theoretical Research. In*Human Mental Workload, Hancock, P. and Meshkati, N. (Ed.)*. North Holland B.V., Amsterdam. 139–183
5. Koenemann, J.; and Belkin, N. 1996. A case for interaction: a study of interactive information retrieval behavior and effectiveness. In *Proceedings of CHI 96*.205–212.
6. McLeod, M.; Bowden, R., Bevan, N. 1997. The MUSiC Performance Measurement Method. Behaviour and Information Technology. Volume 16(4). 279–293.
7. Santos E. Jr.; Nguyen H.; and Brown M.S. 2001.Kavanah: An active user interface Information Retrieval Application. In *Proceedings of 2nd Asia-Pacific Conference on Intelligent Agent Technology*.412–423.
8. Salton, G.; and McGill, M. 1983. *Introduction to Modern Information Retrieval*. McGraw-Hill Book Company.
9. Shneiderman, B. 1998. *Designing the User Interface: Strategies for Effective Human-Computer Interaction*. Addison-Wesley.

Multivariate Preference Models and Decision Making with the MAUT Machine

Christian Schmitt, Dietmar Dengler, and Mathias Bauer

DFKI, Stuhlsatzenhausweg 3, 66123 Saarbrücken, Germany
Firstname.Lastname@dfki.de

Abstract. With the advent of e-commerce, systems supporting the user in finding just the right product in an electronic catalog have gained increasing attention. While *collaborative* recommender systems (RS) derive their suggestions from other users' opinions, *structure-based* systems assess a product according to how well its properties satisfy a user's preferences. This paper presents the MAUT Machine, a system implementing the basic machinery to be used by a structure-based RS to elicit and maintain complex user preference models and evaluate the entries of an electronic catalog according to their appropriateness for a given user or group of users.

1 Introduction

With the advent of e-commerce, systems supporting the user in complex decision-making situations, e.g. when trying to decide for a suitable product from an electronic catalog, have gained increasing attention. These *recommender systems* typically fall into one of two classes, depending on how they arrive at their suggestions. *Collaborative* recommender systems combine the opinions of other users with similar purchasing history to generate a product recommendation. *Content-* or *structure-based* systems, on the other hand, consider structural properties of an item and try to find the best match between user preferences—expressed in terms of item attributes—and items available.

The *MAUT Machine* (MM) that we will describe in the following provides the basic machinery for structure-based recommendation in that it provides means for the acquisition and maintenance of complex, multivariate preference models and the evaluation of alternatives using flexibly configurable quantifiers and scoring rules. The latter is important for the development of user-friendly interfaces in which the user can specify her preferences in a most natural way.

The rest of this paper is organized as follows. In Section 2 the theoretical foundations for structure based decision making and its implementation in MM are explained. Section 3 gives a brief overview of the current prototype before Section 4 discusses related work. Section 5 summarizes this paper and gives an outlook on future work.

P. Brusilovsky et al. (Eds.): UM 2003, LNAI 2702, pp. 297–302, 2003.

2   Theoretical Foundations

This section reviews Multi-Attribute Utility Theory (MAUT) as a formalism for capturing multivariate user preferences and assessing item alternatives. It forms the basis for the Analytic Hierarchy Process (AHP) to be described in Section 2.2, a systematic decision-making procedure that incrementally elicits preferences at various abstraction levels and combines them to compute scores for all alternatives under consideration. Finally, Section 2.3 will introduce alternative ways to aggregate preferences and how these are realized in MM.

2.1   Multi-attribute Utility Theory

Multi-Attribute Utility Theory is an evaluation scheme used when the decision maker has to take several competing objectives (or requirements) into account. It is a normative/prescriptive method in that it indicates what *should* be done by a perfectly rational decision maker. Each item is described in terms on n attributes $A_1, ..., A_n$ which can assume values from the domains $V_1, ..., V_n$. A concrete item o can be represented as a tuple $o = \langle x_1, ..., x_n \rangle \in V_1 \times ... \times V_n$. The overall utility for an item o is defined by

$$U(o) = \sum_{i=1}^{n} w_i \cdot u_i(x_i) \quad \text{with } \sum_{i=1}^{n} w_i = 1, \tag{1}$$

where x_i is o's concrete value for the ith attribute A_i, w_i is the *importance weight* of A_i as compared to the other attributes, and u_i is a value function representing the respective utility values of the various possible instantiations of A_i. That is, while the various w_i quantify the impact of an attribute on the user's overall evaluation of an object, the functions u_i represent the user's preferences regarding instantiations of object attributes.

Remark: MAUT also allows the definition of more abstract value dimensions as weighted combinations of basic attributes, similar to the abstract criteria as discussed in the next section in the context of AHP. For a good introduction to MAUT the reader is referred to [3].

(1) is a *scoring rule* (a special kind of evaluation function in the sense of [2], see also Section 2.3) as it assigns a numerical score to each tuple. The most significant extension of our implementation of MAUT is the ability to use a variety of alternative scoring rules. This will be discussed in detail in Section 2.3.

2.2   The Analytic Hierarchy Process

The Analytic Hierarchy Process (AHP) [5] is a decision-making method that tries to find the candidate out of a set of alternatives that best satisfies a set of criteria. The criteria may be divided into sub-criteria and so on, thus forming a hierarchical criteria tree. A leaf criterion is typically the specification of a desired property the candidate should have (in form of an assignment of a desired value to a candidate's attribute) and parent criteria are more abstract criteria that cannot be represented by a single attribute. Instead of performing a potentially large number of pairwise comparisons—as is typically being done to elicit the importance weights of the various criteria—it is also possible to

- try and find direct estimations of the various importance weights,
- model the weights as random variables with corresponding distributions,
- have a domain expert provide generally accepted default values, or
- apply heuristics such as the *candidate-critique approach* [4] to focus on relevant comparisons only.

AHP uses the MAUT evaluation function (1) to rate the candidates. The utilities indicate how well a candidate fulfills the criteria and the weights quantify the respective impact of each criterion on the overall evaluation. AHP is therefore a compensatory decision methodology because alternatives that are deficient with respect to one criterion can compensate by their good performance with respect to other criteria. One aspect that makes this approach particularly attractive is the fact that the preference elicitation dialog with the user can be conducted just at the appropriate level of detail.

2.3   Scoring Rules as Evaluation Functions

The standard version of AHP uses the additive value function (1) to compute the overall utility of the alternatives which limits the expressiveness w.r.t. user preferences. As wil be discussed below, MM allows all sorts of generalized logical connectives and (fuzzy) quantifiers like "most" or "at least" and even more exotic functions to be used to aggregate intermediary results.

OWA operators. *Ordered weighted averaging operators* have been introduced by Ronald R. Yager in [6]. This family of operators allows for the representation of virtually any (fuzzy) logical connective. Besides expressing "and" and "or" by "min" and "max" functions, also graded versions are representable. For example, an operator "max'" can be constructed that not only considers the maximum value, but also the second largest to a somewhat smaller degree. In general, an OWA operator of dimension n has an associated vector $A = \langle a_1, ..., a_n \rangle$ such that $\sum_i a_i = 1$ and a mapping function $\Omega : I\!\!R^n \to I\!\!R$ defined by $\Omega(x_1, ..., x_n) = \sum_{i=1}^n a_i \cdot x'_i$, where $X' = \langle x'_1, ..., x'_n \rangle$ is the vector obtained by sorting vector $X = \langle x_1, ..., x_n \rangle$ by decreasing order. That is, x'_i is the ith largest element of the set $\{x_1, ..., x_n\}$.

Examples for OWA operators are $\langle 1, 0, ..., 0 \rangle$ (which corresponds to "max" as only the first element is taken into account), $\langle 0, ..., 0, 1 \rangle$ (representing "min") and $\langle 0.9, 0.1, ..., 0 \rangle$ (which is one implementation for "max'" mentioned above).

Weighted Scoring Rules. Operators like maximum and minimum are not readily applicable in cases where the various arguments are weighted as is the case with evaluation criteria in AHP. For example, what is min(0.2, 0.5) when the former has a weight of 0.9, the latter of 0.1? In [2] a transformation formula is

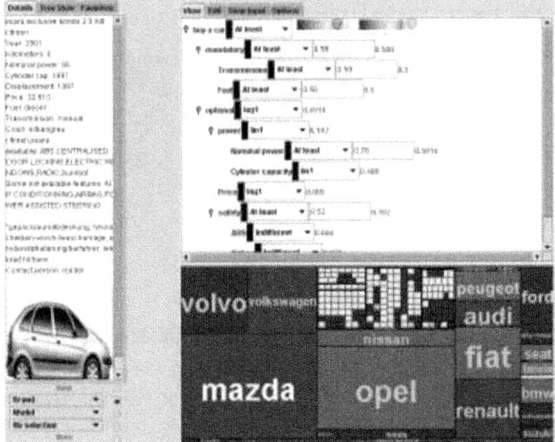

Fig. 1. A screenshot of MAUT Machine.

introduced that allows every unweighted *scoring rule* (i.e. aggregation function) to be transformed into a weighted variant that preserves its essential character.

For the MAUT Machine, we restricted ourselves to transformations of OWA operators. To compute the overall score of an item, the transformation formula is applied to every criteria node (each node having its own scoring rule). As a side effect, the classical MAUT aggregation function (1) can be obtained as the transformation of the "mean" operator.

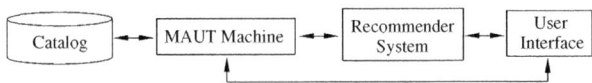

Fig. 2. MAUT Machine in a complete recommender-system configuration.

3   The MAUT Machine Prototype

The MAUT Machine is not intended as a stand-alone decision-support system. Instead it is meant to be integrated in a configuration like the one depicted in Figure 2 where it is complemented by a user-friendly interface to conduct the preference elicitation dialog and a recommender system that can make use of the scores determined by MM. In an expert mode a knowledge engineer can define operators, quantifiers, and connectives that form the input vocabulary to be used in the user interface to express a user's preferences. The flexibility of the formal approach taken (see Section 2.3) allows the support of a very natural style for the user to specify her interests, likes, and dislikes. In the expert mode, the knowledge engineer can also define the abstract criteria to be used to describe and categorize the catalog entries as well as all default settings for value functions and importance weights. For technical details of the prototype and an on-line demo the reader is referred to http://www2.dfki.de:8080/mautmachine/html.

4   Related Work

In [1] a combination of treemaps and AHP has been suggested. The goal was to demonstrate the effectiveness of treemaps for displaying the AHP criteria tree. The user could change the importance of criteria dynamically on the two-dimensional treemap and immediately see the impact on the outcome of the decision. The approach taken with MM is slightly different in that we use a treemap-like display to present the distribution of scores over the catalog entries and for visual data mining guided by the scores assigned on the basis of the user's preferences. Some advanced e-commerce sites allow the user to specify her preferences using a simple natural-language interface. Examples include the "International Porsche Locator" (ucl.porsche.de/ucl/plsql/uk/pages.search_car) where the user can input a text similar to a classified ad to express her search criteria. Using MM, such a system could be extended such as to also allow expressions with fuzzy quantifiers ("at least" etc.) that could then be mapped onto the corresponding function specified in the expert mode.

5   Conclusion

This paper presented the MAUT Machine, a tool implementing a basic decision-support engine based on MAUT and the Analytic Hierarchy Process AHP. Enabling the free specification of quantifiers and aggregation functions to be used during decision making, MM provides the basis for the development of user interfaces that allow a user to specify her preferences in a most natural and flexible way. The fieldmap visualization of the distribution of scores over the complete catalog of products or alternatives (see lower right part of Figure 1) enables the user to visually search for appropriate items by zooming in and out of the data. Additionally, MM supports group decision making by aggregating the preference models of all users involved. Currently, MM is being integrated into the overall prototype of the MIAU project, a group decision support system in the context of an e-commerce application. Future work will investigate means for data reduction which is particularly useful for very large catalogs that will have to be considered at various abstraction levels.

References

1. T. Asahi, D. Turo, and B. Shneiderman. Using treemaps to visualize the analytic hierarchy process. *Information Systems Research*, 6(4):357–375, 1995.
2. R. Fagin and E. Wimmers. A formula for incorporating weights into scoring rules. In *Proc. of the International Conference on Database Theory*, pages 247–261, 1997.

3. A. Jameson, R. Schafer, J. Simons, and T. Weis. Adaptive provision of evaluation-oriented information: Tasks and techniques. In *IJCAI*, pages 1886–1895, 1995.
4. G. Linden, S. Hanks, and N. Lesh. Interactive assessment of user preference models: The automated travel assistant. In *User Modeling 97*, 1997.
5. T.L. Saaty. *The Analytic Hierarchy Process.* McGraw-Hill, 1980.
6. R. Yager. On ordered weighted averaging aggregation operators in multi-criteria decision making. *IEEE Transactions On Systems, Man and Cybernetics*, 18:183–190, 1988.

Predicting Student Help-Request Behavior in an Intelligent Tutor for Reading

Joseph E. Beck, Peng Jia, June Sison, and Jack Mostow

Project LISTEN
School of Computer Science
Carnegie Mellon University
Pittsburgh, PA 15213. USA
joseph.beck@cmu.edu
http://www.cs.cmu.edu/~listen

Abstract. This paper describes our efforts at constructing a fine-grained student model in Project LISTEN's intelligent tutor for reading. Reading is different from most domains that have been studied in the intelligent tutoring community, and presents unique challenges. Constructing a model of the user from voice input and mouse clicks is difficult, as is constructing a model when there is not a well-defined domain model. We use a database describing student interactions with our tutor to train a classifier that predicts whether students will click on a particular word for help with 83.2% accuracy. We have augmented the classifier with features describing properties of the word's individual graphemes, and discuss how such knowledge can be used to assess student skills that cannot be directly measured.

1 Introduction and Motivation

Project LISTEN's Reading Tutor [10] is an intelligent tutor that listens to students read aloud with the goal of helping them learn how to read English. Target users are students in first through fourth grades (approximately 6- through 9-year olds). Students take turns with the Reading Tutor picking stories to read. Students are shown one sentence at a time, and the Reading Tutor uses speech recognition technology to (try to) determine which words the student has read incorrectly [13]. The student can also request help on words about which he is uncertain; types of help include sounding out the word, pronouncing the word, and providing rhyming hints.

The Reading Tutor is more effective at helping children learn to read than simply letting children read books on their own [11]. Much of the Reading Tutor's power comes from allowing children to request help and from detecting some mistakes that students make while reading. It does not have the strong reasoning about the user that distinguishes a classic intelligent tutoring system, although it does base some decisions, such as picking a story at an appropriate level of challenge, on the student's reading proficiency.

Our goal is to strengthen the Reading Tutor's user model and determine which user characteristics are predictive of student behavior. If we can predict how students behave while using the Reading Tutor, we can use such knowledge to help adapt the

P. Brusilovsky et al. (Eds.): UM 2003, LNAI 2702, pp. 303–312, 2003.

tutor's behavior, assess students, and we will have discovered useful features for understanding students using the tutor. Given our current lack of knowledge of good features for student modeling within the Reading Tutor, learning how to describe students is a worthwhile goal. We take the approach of observing users and trying to learn patterns from their behavior. Being able to validate hypotheses about how users behave against already logged data also simplifies experimental design: it is not necessary to run a new study to evaluate the accuracy of the student model.

2 Approach

In this section we discuss how we collected data from students, what aspect of the students we choose to model, how to approach the problem as a classification task, and various architectures for training the classifier.

2.1 Data Collected

In the 2000-2001 school year, 88 students in two schools used the Reading Tutor as part of a controlled study. Students used the Reading Tutor from the end of October 2000 until the beginning of June 2001. On average, students used the Reading Tutor for approximately 18 hours.

The Reading Tutor logged when students started reading a story, when a new sentence was displayed, when a student read each word in the sentence, and when the student clicked on a word for help. These data were parsed and used to construct an SQL database [12]. Across the 88 students, students saw a total of 2.4 million words over the year, which amounts to students seeing 25 words per minute while using the Reading Tutor (about one-tenth of the average adult reading rate).

Students requested help on a word from the Reading Tutor 229,000 times over the course of the year. We know what word the student clicked on and when he clicked.

Unfortunately, the logging was incomplete. We are not able to extract from the logs what type of help the Reading Tutor provided to the student. Since many students would continue to click until the Reading Tutor read the word (the Reading Tutor randomly selects which type of help to give each time the student clicks), it is difficult to interpret what multiple requests for help mean: the student could be very confused or simply holding out until the RT read the word.

Another area where logging was incomplete was when the Reading Tutor decided to provide help to the student. The Reading Tutor gives help to students before they start reading a sentence on words that it thinks are difficult. The rationale for this help is that if a student gets practice reading a word incorrectly it will be harder to teach him later the correct way of reading the word [4]. Therefore, the Reading Tutor gives help on words the student is likely to have difficulties with. Unfortunately, whether the Reading Tutor gave preemptive assistance was logged, but the actual word for which the tutor provided assistance was not recorded in an easily analyzable form.

2.2 Modeling Problem: What to Predict?

Predicting student behavior is a means of adapting instruction. If the tutor knows when the student will, for example, require assistance, it can provide help before the student becomes stuck. There are a variety of student behaviors we could predict: whether the student will speak a word correctly, the delay before a student begins to pronounce a word [6, 9], whether the student clicks on a word for help, etc. Speech recognition is a far from perfect technology, so to simplify our task we concentrate on predicting whether the student will click for help on a word.

We treat predicting whether the student asks for help as a binary prediction task. One use for such a model is to determine when the Reading Tutor should provide preemptive assistance before the student attempts to read the sentence. Currently, preemptive assistance is biased towards giving help on longer words and on words the student has read poorly in the past. This approach is somewhat lacking as it does not consider the length of time since the student saw the word, whether the student has previously asked for help on this word, etc. A model of help requests is also a model of relative word difficulty: words that a student is likely to click for help on are harder than words for which the student does not need help. Such a model of word difficulty could be used to select stories that are appropriate for the student, or to provide additional information to speech recognizer. In particular, if a student is likely to need help on a word (and does not receive help) the prior probability that he will read the word correctly should be lowered.

We examined student help request patterns on common and uncommon words. Dolch words [3] are 220 high-frequency words that children should learn by sight. Students tend to have few help requests on Dolch words, so we do not consider them in our analysis. Fig. 1 shows student help request patterns on non-Dolch words. The x-axis is how many times the student has seen this word previously in the Reading Tutor. The y-axis is the probability he will request help on a word. Each line on the curve represents a group of students who scored similarly on the Woodcock Reading Mastery's Word Identification test [15]. The Word Identification (WI) test reports student's ability to read words correctly in English. A score of 2.3 means that a student reads at a level comparable to a student in the 3rd month of the 2nd grade. Students were pre-tested in October before using the Reading Tutor and post-tested in late March. We define a student's *grade level* as the average of pre- and post-test scores on the WI test. This figure excludes students who had grade levels of 4, 5, or 6 for clarity (their help request rate was lower than students at grade level 3).

Fig. 1 shows a strong effect for students' reading ability; students at higher grade level ask for help less often. Students initially ask for help on words fairly often, but after being exposed to words ask for help less often. For example, someone with an average Grade level of 1 asks for help about 20% of the time on a word he has seen only once. After seeing a word 10 times, students ask for help only ≈6% of the time on average. We have marked the region of Fig. 1 that we have chosen to try to model. We are focusing on an "interesting" region of the space. For students at higher grade levels, it is easy to predict accurately whether the student will ask for help: simply predicting "no" does an excellent job. Since one use of our model of student help requests is to decide when to give preemptive assistance, focusing on students who need assistance is a good first step. Therefore, we concentrate on students whose grade level is 1 or 2.

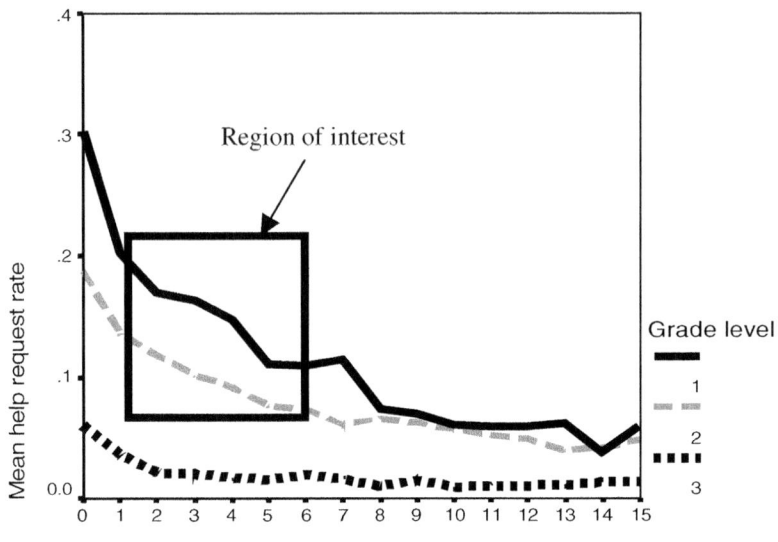

Number of previous encounters of word

Fig. 1. Learning curves showing students decreasing help request rate

The first time a student sees a word, preemptive assistance is almost always provided. Since we do not know whether the Reading Tutor gave assistance on a word, it is difficult to predict whether the student will click on the word (presumably if the Reading Tutor provides help the student will not also click for help). Therefore, we ignore first encounters of a word. After a student has seen a word 6 times the chances of asking for help become rather low. Therefore, we focus on words that have only been seen 6 or fewer times.

This screening procedure reduces our sample of students from 88 to 53, and the number of word encounters from 2.4 million to 555,818.

2.3 Casting the Problem as a Classification Task

Since our goal is to determine whether the student will click for help on a word, and we know which words the student clicked or did not click for help, we need to find some method of describing words that will allow us to predict into which category a particular word falls. We consider information that is static for a particular encounter of a word, such as the student's reading proficiency and past history with reading and asking for help on this word.

For each word, we computed **static properties** such as its length and its frequency of occurrence in children's stories. We also computed word properties that are not-static, but are **constant for a particular sentence** such as the word's position in the sentence. Features about position were encoded both as an absolute and as a percentage of the length of the sentence (i.e. a word at position 3 in a 12 word sentence would be 0.25).

We used **properties about the student**, including gender and grade. We also use the student's current WI score for the day when he encountered each word. We estimate his WI score by assuming that it increases linearly between the pre- and post-tests. For a coarse measure on a grade equivalent scale, linear growth is a reasonable assumption. Linear growth is not a reasonable assumption for a more specialized skill such as solving a linear equation. For this research we used the linearly interpolated WI score provided by the paper tests; a deployed Reading Tutor would obviously not have access to the student's posttest score, so would have to use its estimates of the student's WI level [1, 6]. Another feature we used is the student's overall rate of clicking for help on words.

We also used the **student's history of reading this word** as a source of information for features. Information extracted from the log files includes how many days have passed since the student last encountered this word, the average latency [9] (delay before pronouncing a word) in past encounters, how many previous encounters the student has had with this word, and how many times the speech recognizer heard the student read this word.

The student's **help request behavior on this word** is also important. Features include whether the student has ever asked for help on this word, whether he has asked for help on this word today, and if the student asked for help the first time he saw this word.

We generated an exhaustive list of 60 features from the above sources. Knowledge of which features were likely to be redundant trimmed this list down to 20 features.

Our goal is to use these features to predict whether a student will ask for help on a particular word. We now turn to constructing a model to make such predictions.

2.4 Group vs. Individual Modeling: How to Construct Models

We use the term "group modeling" to refer to user models that are constructed from a group of users and applied to a new user, and the term "individual modeling" to refer to user models constructed with a user's own data. Some researchers use the terms "collaborative" and "feature-based" [16] respectively to describe such models. "Collaborative" is already an overused term in education circles, and "feature-based" is similarly misleading since many group models are feature-based.

Given that we have a series of labeled instances, features describing words and students, and information about which words the student clicked on for help, how can we construct a classifier to make predictions? We do not have sufficient training data to build a model for each word in the English language. Therefore, we collapse across words and rely on the features describing them (length and frequency) to describe meaningful differences.

We have a similar option for whether to build a separate classifier for each student [14] (individual modeling) or whether to aggregate the data for all of the students together to construct a group model [2, 5]. Advantages of aggregating the data together include more training instances than for any individual student. Having more data tends to result in more accurate models. Another advantage is that we can tune the classifier's performance and once it is satisfactory, we can deploy it in the Reading Tutor.

Advantages of building a separate model for each student include possibly higher accuracy. If the features do poorly at describing students, or if some students differ dramatically, then constructing a model for each student might do a better job. We compare both group and separate models as means for constructing a classifier.

To evaluate the classifiers, we used a different penalty for different types of mistakes. A classifier can make two types of mistakes: it can predict that a student wishes to receive help when he doesn't, or it can predict that a student does not need help when in fact he does. We believe that the second mistake is more important to avoid. If a student needs help, he might not realize it and proceed to read the word incorrectly (young children often do not have strong meta-cognitive skills [8]). The Reading Tutor does not do a good job at detecting misread words. Also, due to occasionally mishearing correctly read words, the Reading Tutor permits the student to advance to the next sentence after reading at least 50% of the words in the sentence correctly. Therefore, it is possible for a student to complete a sentence without knowing how to read a particular word. If a student gets practice at incorrectly reading the word, then correcting him later will be more difficult. Table 1 shows how we penalize the classifier for various types of mistakes.

Table 1. Penalty matrix for classifier

	Classifier predicts help requested	Classifier predicts no help requested
Student clicks for help	0	5
Student does not click for help	1	0

3 Results

We now compare the results of grouped and individual modeling, and then discuss adding phonemic features to the classifier.

3.1 First Experiment: Group vs. Individual Modeling

To evaluate the performance of a group modeling agent, it is necessary to aggregate the data from multiple students to train the classifier. To test the classifier, we planned to evaluate its accuracy using a leave-one-out approach by constructing the classifier with the data from N-1 students, testing on the Nth student, and repeating the process for each student. However, we built the classifier with data from only 25% of the other students since using more of the data crashed the computer.

For individual modeling, we are trying to determine how our classifier performs if it were trained on the data from an individual student. One approach is to load **all** of he student's data, and perform a cross-validation to determine the model's accuracy. Such an approach is not appropriate since the data are temporally dependent on each other. For example, imagine the third time a student encounters the word "telephone" is in the training set, and we know that he asked for help on both prior encounters. If the second time the student saw the word "telephone" is in the test set we can predict with perfect accuracy that he must have asked for help. Therefore, we incrementally add instances to the training data.

Fig. 2 shows our approach for training an individual's model. The student's data are first sorted by time, and then the first item is presented to the classifier. The classifier makes a prediction for this one item, which is then added to the training data. This iterative process continues, such that over time the classifier's training data grows and is used to make a prediction for the next word encountered by the student.

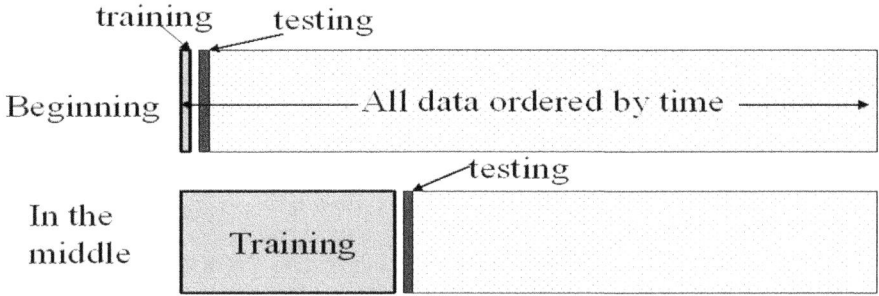

Fig. 2. Individual modeling approach

We used Weka, a public domain data mining package written in Java, to perform these analyses. Specifically, we used Weka's J48 (a version of C4.5) and naïve Bayesian classifier (NBC) methods for performing the classifications.

For group modeling, J48 was correct on 71% of its predictions and NBC was correct on 75% of its predictions. For individual modeling, 81% of J48's predictions were correct and 75% of NBC's predictions were correct.

These results are somewhat surprising. Naïve Bayesian classifiers tend to outperform decision trees when there is a small amount of training data [7]. However, we found that decision trees work better for predicting on the basis of data from one student, while NBCs work better with data from multiple students.

Overall, individual modeling with J48 gave the best result, with an accuracy of 81%. One way to improve on this result is to use the model trained from a group of students until enough data are collected to construct a model from the current student's data. Another approach is to combine data from the current student with the data from the population to improve the model's predictions [2, 5].

3.2 Second Experiment: Adding Phonemic Information

Another goal of student modeling in the Reading Tutor is to assess "hidden skills." That is, skills that are not directly measured but that must be performed to solve a task. For reading, an example is the grapheme *ph* makes the sound /f/ in the word "phone." There are many letter to sound mappings in English, and testing the student on each of them would disrupt the natural process of reading.

As a first step towards this goal, we provide our classifier with information about the graphemes (letters and groups of letters) and grapheme to phoneme (the sound that a grapheme makes) mappings that make up each word. A grapheme→phoneme mapping (abbreviated as "g→p mapping") is simply the grapheme and phoneme for a particular word paired together. E.g. the word date contains *D*→/D/, *A*→/EY/, and *TE*→/T/ as g→p mappings.

If such features are useful in helping to predict on which words students request help, then we can reason backwards and infer that students are having difficulties reading words with those particular hidden skills. This approach of adding information about the components that make up a word generalizes to other predictive tasks. For example, if we are predicting whether a student will read a word correctly, determining whether students make mistakes on words that contain rare graphemes will aid in drawing conclusions about a student's ability on these hidden skills.

We added phonemic features to the already existing features. Specifically, we added features about how likely various grapheme$\rightarrow$phoneme mappings are in the English language. $P(g\rightarrow p)$ is defined as the word frequency weighted probability of a word containing this g$\rightarrow$p mapping. Specific features were:

1. Average probability of all g$\rightarrow$p mappings in the word
2. Probability of the first g$\rightarrow$p mapping in the word
3. Probability of the rarest g$\rightarrow$p mapping in the word

The first feature describes the overall unusualness in the word's pronunciation. The second feature accounts for the fact that students often try to read the first portion of a word and guess at the remainder of the word. The last feature models the most difficult part of the word. If the word is hard overall (feature #1), or if the student cannot get started in reading the word (feature #2), or if the student encounters a very rare mapping (feature #3), then we expect the student is more likely to ask for help.

We also added features about how likely it is for a grapheme to make a particular sound. That is, what is $P(p|g)$. If a word contains a rare g$\rightarrow$p mapping, such as in *CH* making the sound /k/ as in "chord," then we could expect students to have difficulties reading this word. For each word, we added the following features:

1. Average of $P(p|g)$ for all graphemes in the word
2. $P(p|g)$ for the first grapheme in the word
3. $P(p|g)$ of the rarest grapheme in the word

Unfortunately, we did not have g$\rightarrow$p mappings for all the words in our dataset. We had g$\rightarrow$p mappings for only 2,460 out of 4,169 distinct words.

To run experiments, we first screened out words for which we did not have g$\rightarrow$p mappings. Since constructing models for individual students outperformed building models from groups of students, we constructed a model for each student using J48. On the subset of words for which we had g$\rightarrow$p mappings, our classifier had an accuracy of 82.5%.

Adding the six features described above gave an average accuracy of 83.2%. This marginal gain was statistically reliable at $P=0.013$ (paired samples t-test). Improvements in performance were not distributed randomly across students. There was a correlation of -0.46 between the classifier's performance with the original set of features and gain from adding phonemic information. I.e. for students who were already well-modeled, there was little gain from additional information.

We have demonstrated that information about the phonemic properties of words can help predict whether students will click for help on a word. This result suggests that a word's phonemic information affects whether students believe they know a word and ask for help. Therefore, help request patterns are an avenue for assessing these hidden skills. If students request help on a word containing a set of g$\rightarrow$p mappings, we can update the tutor's estimate of the student's proficiency on those skills. Fine-grained assessment of a student's knowledge is helpful for predicting what types of mistakes he is likely to make. For example, if a student can pronounce "chord," it is probable that he can also pronounce "chords," and will have a better chance at pronouncing "chaos" than a student who cannot read the word "chord." The common factor in all of these words is the initial grapheme /CH/ making the sound "k." Being able to assess student knowledge at the grapheme level would be a large improvement in the Reading Tutor's capabilities.

4   Conclusions and Future Work

Logging student interactions with the tutor in an easily analyzable form is a powerful strategy for constructing user models. We have used a database constructed from logged information to construct a student model capable of predicting whether the learner will click on a word for help. Such user models can be used to adapt the tutor's behavior by, for example, determining when to give the student help preemptively. Analyzing predictive user models can also be a means for assessing a student's proficiency at "hidden skills."

Our first attempt at adding phonemic features met with mixed success. Although the improvements in performance were significant statistically, they may not be meaningful. Finding a stronger set of features would benefit both predicting student help requests and relating a student's actions to his underlying knowledge of English words. One possibility for better features is to consider the student's history for each $g \rightarrow p$ mapping. E.g. what percentage of words containing this $g \rightarrow p$ mapping does the student read correctly? What percentage of words containing this $g \rightarrow p$ mapping does the student ask for help on? Such historical information was useful at the word level for predicting a student's help requests, so it is likely historical information at the grapheme level will also have predictive power.

One possibility is not all students are decoding words, but are instead recognizing them as whole words (or guessing). One way to determine which strategy students are using is to use the inter-word latency [9]. Presumably a decoding approach will result in a larger latency. We are exploring such approaches.

Acknowledgements. This work was supported in part by the National Science Foundation under Grant No. REC-9979894. Any opinions, findings, conclusions, or recommendations expressed in this publication are those of the authors and do not necessarily reflect the views of the National Science Foundation or the official policies, either expressed or implied, of the sponsors or of the United States Government. We thank members of Project LISTEN who contributed to this work, especially Susan Rossbach for conducting the field studies, and Andrew Cuneo for constructing the database from the logfiles.

References

(see www.cs.cmu.edu/~listen for LISTEN publications)

1. Beck, J.E., Jia, P. and Mostow, J., Assessing Student Proficiency in a Reading Tutor that Listens. Proceedings of the *Ninth International Conference on User Modeling*. 2003
2. Beck, J.E. and Woolf, B.P., Using a Learning Agent with a Student Model. Proceedings of the *Fourth International Conference on Intelligent Tutoring Systems*. p. 6–15. 1998

3. Dolch, E., A basic sight vocabulary. *Elementary School Journal*, 1936. **36**: p. 456–460.

4. Hebb, D.O., *The Organization of Behavior*. 1949, New York: Wiley.

5. Jameson, A. and Wittig, F., Leveraging Data About Users in General in the Learning of Individual User Models. Proceedings of the *Seventeenth International Joint Conference on Artificial Intelligence*. p. 1185–1192. 2001

6. Jia, P., Beck, J.E. and Mostow, J., Can a Reading Tutor that Listens use Inter-word Latency to (better) Assess a Student's Reading Ability? Proceedings of the *ITS 2002 Workshop on Creating Valid Diagnostic Assessments*. 2002

7. Langley, P., Iba, W. and Thompson, K., An Analysis of Bayesian Classifiers. Proceedings of the *National Conference on Artificial Intelligence*. p. 223–228. 1992

8. Lundberg, I. and Olofsson, A., Can computer speech support reading comprehension? *Computers in Human Behaviour*, 1993. **9**(2–3): p. 283–293.

9. Mostow, J. and Aist, G., The Sounds of Silence: Towards Automated Evaluation of Student Learning in a Reading Tutor that Listens. Proceedings of the *Fourteenth National Conference on Artificial Intelligence (AAAI-97)*. p. 355–361. 1997

10. Mostow, J. and Aist, G., Evaluating tutors that listen: An overview of Project LISTEN, in *Smart Machines in Education*, K. Forbus and P. Feltovich, Editors. 2001. Menlo Park, CA: AAAI. p. 169–234.

11. Mostow, J., Aist, G., Bey, J., Burkhead, P., Cuneo, A., Junker, B., Rossbach, S., Tobin, B., Valeri, J. and Wilson, S., Independent practice versus computer-guided oral reading: Equal-time comparison of sustained silent reading to an automated reading tutor that listens. Proceedings of the *Ninth Annual Meeting of the Society for the Scientific Study of Reading*. 2002

12. Mostow, J., Beck, J., Chalasani, R., Cuneo, A. and Jia, P., Viewing and Analyzing Multimodal Human-computer Tutorial Dialogue: A Database Approach. Proceedings of the *Fourth IEEE International Conference on Multimodal Interfaces (ICMI 2002)*. p. 129–134. 2002

13. Mostow, J., Roth, S.F., Hauptmann, A.G. and Kane, M., A prototype reading coach that listens [AAAI-94 Outstanding Paper Award]. Proceedings of the *Twelfth National Conference on Artificial Intelligence*. p. 785–792. 1994

14. Webb, G.I. and Kuzmycz, M., Feature Based Modelling: A methodology for producing coherent, consistent, dynamically changing models of agents' competencies. *User Modeling and User Adapted Interaction*, 1996. **8**: p. 97–115.

15. Woodcock, R.W., *Woodcock Reading Mastery Tests - Revised (WRMT-R/NU)*. 1998, Circle Pines, Minnesota: American Guidance Service.

16. Zukerman, I. and Albrecht, D.W., Predictive Statistical Models for User Modeling. *User Modeling and User Adapted Interaction*, 2001. **11**(1–2): p. 5–18.

A Comparative Analysis of Cognitive Tutoring and Constraint-Based Modeling

Antonija Mitrovic[1], Kenneth R. Koedinger[2], and Brent Martin[1]

[1]Intelligent Computer Tutoring Group,
University of Canterbury, Christchurch, New Zealand
{tanja, brent}@cosc.canterbury.ac.nz
[2]Human-Computer Interaction Institute, Carnegie Mellon University
koedinger@cmu.edu

Abstract. Numerous approaches to student modeling have been proposed since the inception of the field more than three decades ago. What the field is lacking completely is comparative analyses of different student modeling approaches. In this paper we compare Cognitive Tutoring to Constraint-Based Modeling (CBM). We present our experiences in implementing a database design tutor using both methodologies and highlight their strengths and weaknesses. We compare their characteristics and argue the differences are often more apparent than real: for specific domains one approach may be favoured over the other, making them viable complementary methods for supporting learning.

1 Introduction

Student modeling is one of the crucial components of Intelligent Tutoring Systems (ITS). Numerous modeling approaches have been devised over the years, such as overlay modeling, enumerative bug modeling, generative and reconstructive modeling, and constraint-based modeling [4]. Early ITS projects focused on the development of student modeling approaches, and rarely evaluated the methods properly. Although the percentage of papers that include evaluation results has been growing steadily, they always relate to a single student modeling approach in isolation. For the maturation of the field, it is of critical importance to perform comparative analyses of various approaches. Unfortunately, such comparative evaluations are extremely difficult; it is a major undertaking to develop any ITS, let alone two for the same domain.

In this paper we explore the student modeling approaches used in cognitive tutors and constraint-based tutors. We report on an initial case study in which reimplemented part of an existing constraint-based tutor as a cognitive tutor to compare and contrast the various features of these two approaches. We briefly overview cognitive tutors and constraint-based tutors. In section 4 we present the case study, followed by a comparative analysis of the two approaches. We give the conclusions in the final section.

P. Brusilovsky et al. (Eds.): UM 2003, LNAI 2702, pp. 313–322, 2003.
© Springer-Verlag Berlin Heidelberg 2003

2 Cognitive Tutors

Cognitive Tutors [5] are some of the most successful ITS today. They have been developed for a number of domains including algebra, geometry and LISP. Cognitive Tutors are based on the ACT-R theory of cognition [2], which claims that there are two long-term memory stores: declarative and procedural. The theory explains human learning as going through several phases. The first involves learning declarative knowledge, including factual knowledge (such as theorems in a mathematical domain), which is represented as *chunks*. Declarative knowledge is later turned into procedural knowledge, which is goal-oriented and therefore more efficient to use. Procedural knowledge is represented in the form of production rules. In the last phase, the production rules are further optimised when the student becomes an expert. The fundamental assumption of ACT-R is that cognitive skills are realised by production rules. In order to support students to learn a specific task, that is, to learn a specific set of production rules that will enable students to perform the tasks correctly, cognitive tutors organize instruction around the underlying production rules.

A generic student model is produced and used in a process called *model tracing*, while a student-specific model is produced by *knowledge tracing*. A cognitive tutor is based on a cognitive model of the domain expertise, represented by production rules, which describes the domain knowledge needed to perform tasks like good (and perhaps poor) students. Cognitive tutors generate immediate feedback, i.e. they react to each step the student makes while solving a problem. An error is detected either when a student step does not match any rule, or it does match one of the *buggy rules,* which represent typical mistakes. Model tracing thus checks whether or not the student is performing correctly by comparing each student's step directly with one or more correct or incorrect steps generated dynamically by the production system.

To illustrate, consider a set of production rules for finding the angles in geometry problems like the one shown at the top of Figure 1. The first two production rules can be used in sequence to first find angle B (because angles opposite equal sides are equal) and then to find angle C (because the sum of the angles in a triangle is 180). Once the first rule fires and finds the value for angle B, it is possible for the next rule to fire and find angle C (note that the angle label names are arbitrary: these rules apply to a triangle with any point labels.) The last rule in Figure 1 is an example of a buggy rule used to detect particular common mistakes. In geometry, students often over-generalize from common orientations of figures. This buggy production represents the shallow inference that the angles at the bottom of an isosceles triangle are always equal.

3 Constraint-Based Tutors

Constraint-Based Modeling (CBM) is an approach proposed by Ohlsson [11] as a way of overcoming the intractable nature of student modeling [14]. CBM arises from Ohlsson's theory of learning from performance errors [12], which proposes that we often make mistakes when performing a task, even when we have been taught the correct way to do it. According to this theory, we make mistakes because the declarative knowledge we have learned has not been internalized in our procedural

Angle A is 65.
What is angle C?

Two correct production rules:

IF goal is to find an angle in an isosceles triangle ABC and AC = AB
  and angle A is known
THEN set the value of angle B to A.

IF goal is to find an angle in a triangle ABC and angles A and B are known
THEN set the value of C to 180-A-B

Buggy production rule:

IF goal is to find an angle in an isosceles triangle ABC
  and angle A and C are at the bottom of the triangle and angle A is known
THEN set the value of angle C to A.

Fig. 1. Three production rules for computing the size of an angle

knowledge, and so the number of decisions we must make while performing the procedure is sufficiently large that we make mistakes. However, by practicing the task and catching ourselves (or being caught by a mentor) making mistakes, we modify our procedure to incorporate the appropriate rule that we have violated. Over time we internalize all of the declarative knowledge about the task and so the number of mistakes we make is reduced. Ohlsson describes the process of learning from errors as consisting of two phases: *error recognition* and *error correction*. After detection, an error can be corrected so that the solution used is applicable only in situations in which it is appropriate. A student needs declarative knowledge to detect an error. If the student does not possess such declarative knowledge, an ITS may play the role of a mentor and inform the student of the mistake. A carefully designed sequence of feedback messages that reflects the action of a human teacher helps the student to overcome problems in his/her knowledge.

The starting point for CBM is that correct solutions are similar to each other in that they satisfy all the general principles of the domain. No correct solution can be arrived at by traversing a problem state that violates a fundamental principle of the domain. In CBM, we are not interested in what the student has done, but in what *state* they are currently in. As long as the student never reaches a state that is known to be wrong, they are free to perform whatever actions they please.

Constraints define equivalence classes of problem states. An equivalence class triggers the same instructional action; hence all states in a class are pedagogically equivalent. It is therefore possible to attach feedback messages directly to constraints. The domain model is therefore a collection of state descriptions of the form:

  "If <relevance condition> is true,
  then <satisfaction condition> had better also be true,
  otherwise something has gone wrong."

In other words, if the student solution falls into the state defined by the relevance condition, it must also be in the state defined by the satisfaction condition. A violated constraint signals an error, which translates to incomplete or incorrect knowledge.

Consider the same example of calculating angles of a triangle, used in Section 2. Figure 2 illustrates the constraints that can be used to diagnose students' solutions. The first two constraints jointly define that (only) the two base angles in an isosceles triangle have the same size. The third constraint is equivalent to the second rule in Figure 1. Constraint 2 catches the same error as the buggy rule from Figure 1.

First, all relevance patterns are matched against the problem state. Then, the satisfaction components of constraints that matched the problem state in the first step (i.e., the relevant constraints) are tested. If a satisfaction pattern matches the state, the constraint is satisfied. Otherwise, it is violated. The short-term student model consists of all violated constraints.

We believe that CBM is neutral with respect to the domain. Within the ICTG group, we have developed SQL-Tutor, a tutor for teaching the declarative language SQL [10], CAPIT, a system that teaches the rules of punctuation and capitalization in English [8], KERMIT, a system for database design [15], and NORMIT [9], an ITS that teaches the procedural task of data normalization. We have experienced no problems expressing the knowledge in these domains in terms of constraints.

CBM, as proposed in [11] is a method for diagnosing students' solutions. The approach identifies errors, which is extremely important for students lacking declarative knowledge, because they are unable to detect errors themselves. We have also shown that CBM can be extended to allow for long-term modeling of students' knowledge, and alternatives for generation of pedagogical actions [7].

4   Case Study: Teaching Database Design

In this case study we re-implemented a part of the KERMIT tutor using the cognitive tutors methodology. This allows us to compare the two approaches. We start by briefly introducing KERMIT, the context of the study, and then present our experiences.

C_{r1}: A base angle of an isosceles triangle is known (θ_1),
      And the student has calculated the size of the other base angle θ_2
C_{s1}: The size of θ_2 is θ_1

C_{r2}: A base angle of an isosceles triangle is known (θ_1),
      And the student has calculated that the size of another angle θ_2 that equals θ_1.
C_{s2}: θ_2 is a base angle

C_{r3}: Two angles of a triangle are known (θ_1 and θ_2),
      And the student has calculated the size of the third angle θ_3
C_{s3}: The size of θ_3 is $(180-\theta_1-\theta_2)$

Fig. 2. Three constraints that check whether the size of an angle is correct

4.1   KERMIT: A Constraint-Based Tutor for Database Design

KERMIT (Knowledge-based Entity Relationship Modeling Intelligent Tutor) is an ITS for teaching database design that was developed at the ICTG group. One of the goals of the system was to test the ICTG's methodology for building ITS, because database design is a domain whose characteristics are different from those of the domains previously worked on. Database design is a particularly open-ended task: although there is an outcome defined in abstract terms, there is no single "correct" procedure to obtain that outcome. For a detailed discussion of the system, see [15]. KERMIT is a problem-solving environment in which students practice database design using the Entity Relationship (ER) data model.

KERMIT consists of an interface, a pedagogical module that determines the timing and content of pedagogical actions, and a constraint-based modeller, which analyses student answers and generates student models. The interface displays the current problem and provides controls for stepping between problems, submitting a solution and selecting the level of feedback. It also contains the main working area, in which the student draws the ER diagram. Feedback is presented on request. KERMIT contains a set of problems and the ideal solutions to them, but has no problem solver.

In order to check the correctness of the student's solution, KERMIT compares it to the correct solution using domain knowledge represented in the form of more than 90 constraints. The constraints cover both syntactic and semantic knowledge. The syntactic constraints are concerned with syntactic details in a student's solution. An example of such a constraint is "A regular entity must have at least one key attribute." Semantic constraints relate the student's solution to the system's ideal solution. For example, there are constraints that check for equivalent, but not identical, ways of modeling a database in the student's and ideal solution.

4.2   Re-implementing KERMIT as a Model-Tracing Tutor

To compare these two approaches, we implemented a subset of KERMIT using model tracing. We refer to this implementation as KERMIT-MT. Table 1 summarizes the differences between the two implementations. In the following discussion we will use this ER modelling problem: *"Some students live in student halls. Each hall has a unique name, and each student has a unique number."*

Table 1. A comparison of the two implementations

Feature	KERMIT-MT	KERMIT
Problem representation	Text + chunks (words + world knowledge)	Text + tags
Ideal solution	Not stored	Entity and relationship lists
Domain knowledge	Production rules:	Matching constraints:
	Entities: 2	Entities: 5
	Attributes: 4	Attributes: 9
	Relationships: 14	Relationships: 9
	Done: 5	

Beginning with problem representation, KERMIT requires the problem text to be stored together with tags that identify phrases corresponding to the constructs in the ideal solution. For example, the word *"student"* would have a tag that identifies it as corresponding to an entity type in the ideal solution. The ideal solution and the student's solution are represented in the same way. There is also a list of entities, where each entity is described in terms of its name, type and a list of attributes. Similarly, there is a list of relationships, containing the name of each relationship, its type, the names of participating entities and possibly a list of attributes.

KERMIT-MT, on the other hand, requires the problem text plus additional structures that represent what such a system might output for this problem. In addition, the problem author specifies declarative chunks to represent the semantics of all relevant words (nouns, verbs, or modifiers) appearing in the problem text. Interestingly, the text of an ER problem often does not contain everything the student needs to know in order to solve the problem: some chunks come from the student's world knowledge. In KERMIT-MT, such elements were specified explicitly in order to enhance the ability to give advice. In contrast, this difference between what a student can infer from the text and what they must know is not represented in KERMIT, and thus it cannot provide specific instruction on the difference, or diagnose a student with difficulties with one kind of inference but not the other.

KERMIT requires an ideal solution to be stored, while there is no such requirement in KERMIT-MT. However, it is easier to create a representation of the ideal solution than to specify all the chunks needed in KERMIT-MT. On the other hand, the solution representation has less information and thus less to draw on when creating meaningful advice for students.

The domain knowledge in KERMIT-MT covers only a part of the domain covered by KERMIT, so in Table 1 we include only the relevant part of the domain model (KERMIT currently contains over 90 constraints, but covers the complete ER domain). KERMIT-MT has 25 production rules, which cover simple and key attributes, regular entities and regular binary relationships only. These were written by Koedinger in about 20 hours and could be refined to fewer rules with more time. There are 23 constraints in KERMIT that correspond to KERMIT-MT's rules. However, these constraints are more general, in that they deal with all kinds of attributes (including composite and multi-valued) so they cover more of the domain than the rules in KERMIT-MT. Further, KERMIT-MT uses buggy rules to generate error-specific feedback to students, while KERMIT does not. On the other hand, KERMIT only provides error feedback, whereas KERMIT-MT can provide hints when a student is stuck about the thinking process to pursue to perform the next step.

5 Discussion

Table 2 summarizes the main differences between MT and CBM. The learning theories that underlie these approaches—ACT-R (MT) and "learning from performance errors" (CBM)—are both based on the distinction between declarative and procedural knowledge, and the view that learning consists of two main phases: in the first, declarative knowledge is encoded; in the second phase, this declarative knowledge is turned into more efficient procedural knowledge. The difference between the theories is in the amount of effort that is assumed in each phase, and also in the focus of instruction based on each theory. ACT-R assumes that the encoding of declarative knowledge is a straightforward process, where experiences are stored in an unchanged form, e.g. examples, successes and failures of attempts. Therefore, efforts are needed in the second phase, when declarative knowledge is proceduralized. In contrast, Ohlsson [11,12] claims that we make mistakes if we do not have sufficient declarative knowledge to detect errors. Consequently, cognitive tutors tend

Table 2. Comparative analysis of CBM and MT

Property	Model Tracing	Constraint-Based Modeling
Knowledge representation	Production rules (procedural)	Constraints (declarative)
Cognitive fidelity	Tends to be higher	Tends to be lower
What is evaluated	Action	Problem state
Problem solving strategy	Implemented ones	Flexible to any strategy
Solutions	Tend to be computed, but can be stored	One correct solution stored, but can be computed
Feedback	Tends to be immediate, but can be delayed	Tends to be delayed, but can be immediate
Problem-solving hints	Yes	Only on missing elements, but not strategy
Problem solved	'Done' productions	No violated constraints
Diagnosis if no match	Solution is incorrect	Solution is correct
Bugs represented	Yes	No
Implementation effort	Tends to be harder, but can be made easier with loss of other advantages	Tends to be easier, but can be made harder to gain other advantages

to focus on generative knowledge (production rules), while constraint-based tutors teach evaluative knowledge (constraints). However, more recent cognitive tutors have successfully addressed evaluative knowledge [6] and declarative knowledge more generally [1]. Other researchers also stress the importance of declarative knowledge. For example, Chi et al [3] see performance in problem solving as largely determined by the completeness of declarative knowledge, rather than the efficiency of procedural knowledge.

MT tutors represent domain knowledge as production rules. This knowledge has high cognitive fidelity, because it is an explicit model of the reasoning that the learner must acquire. High cognitive fidelity is a strong advantage of Cognitive Tutors. In contrast, CBM tutors represent domain knowledge in a declarative form. It is interesting to note similarities between constraints and the inference rules Chi and colleagues discuss in [3]: they find that students who engage in self-explanation learn better, as a consequence of forming inference rules. Chi states that inference rules are more operational than general principles conveyed in traditional instruction, because the conditions are more specific, and inference rules are more decomposed than the general principles. The same reasoning applies to constraints: it takes a number of constraints to equal a general principle of a domain.

Model tracing tutors have been criticised for being too rigid, in that they force students to follow a fixed set of desirable approaches to solving problems [16]. For example, the Lisp tutor requires that the top-down approach be used for writing functions. One might speculate that this may be more beneficial to novices and less so for more knowledgable students, however evaluations of the LISP tutor have tended to show fairly uniform learning improvements for students at all levels. In other words, the evidence suggests the LISP tutor does work well both for novice and more knowledgable students. On the other hand, CBM neither imposes nor supports any particular strategy, since it evaluates the current state in problem solving (as opposed to the current action which is evaluated in Cognitive Tutors). By ignoring the procedures used to solve problems, CBM allows for inconsistencies in problem-solving strategies. The downside is that CBM systems typically are not capable of giving strategic planning advice.

Typical CBM-based systems generate instructional actions without being able to solve problems, by comparing the ideal solution (specified by the human teacher) to the student's solution. If there are alternative solutions, they are recognized as such by constraints that check for the necessary elements in the solution. We have developed an extension to CBM that allows problems to be solved (and student solution errors to be corrected) directly from the constraint set, and implemented it for SQL-Tutor [7]. However, it requires that the constraint set be more complete, otherwise erroneous solutions may be generated, but has the benefit of being optional. In contrast, Cognitive Tutors typically are able to solve problems, and having some simulation of problem solving is important for providing planning advice. However, it is also possible for Cognitive Tutors, like CBM, to store solutions (or approximations thereof) and write rules that work from them. In both cases, an incremental development strategy is possible whereby one starts by implementing the ITS using stored solutions and then adds problem solving capabilities as needed (ideally driven by student usage data).

Cognitive Tutors typically offer immediate feedback (usually only implicitly by "flagging" an error when it occurs), while constraint-based tutors provide feedback on demand. However, both approaches are capable of providing the other type of feedback, so this difference is somewhat superficial. Further, Cognitive Tutors can offer strategic problem-solving hints in terms of the next step to perform in a plan. These hints are typically provided on demand or after the student has made more errors on a goal than a teacher-set error threshold. Hints are generated by running the production set. Constraint-based tutors are, in general, not able to solve problems, but they can provide feedback on missing elements of the solution.

Another important issue is the completeness of the knowledge base. It is widely accepted that the quality of the knowledge base is the determining factor for the quality of instruction and diagnosis. In model tracing, an incomplete knowledge base may mean that there are some correct or buggy rules missing. When a student performs a step that matches neither a correct or buggy rule, that step is assumed to be incorrect. While the system cannot explain why (because there is no buggy rule), it is able to point to the particular step in the whole solution that is in error. Cognitive Tutor developers work hard to avoid it, but it is possible that a correct rule is missing in such a case, and that the student's step is actually correct. Thus, it is possible in Cognitive Tutors that a correct solution is rejected. In CBM, the default no-match diagnosis is that the student's solution is *correct*, even though this may be false. The default behaviour is therefore "*innocent until proven guilty*", versus "*guilty until proven innocent*" for Cognitive Tutors. In both cases, it is important to perform careful engineering and iterative student testing to prevent such situations.

Although the approach of modeling all possible solutions works well for well-defined domains such as mathematics, it may not be a realistic solution when the domain is ill defined. However, as discussed above, this purported difference between CBM and Cognitive Tutors is more apparent than real. The task of composing a collection of buggy rules is also a major undertaking. Studies have shown that bug libraries do not transfer well to new population of students; if a bug library is developed for a certain group of students, it may not cover the bugs that another group of students may make [13]. Neither Cognitive Tutors nor CBM require studies of student bugs, but both can benefit from such study. Whereas student bugs are represented directly in Cognitive Tutors, in CBM they can be used to help determine the pedagogical states to represent.

6 Conclusions

This paper presented a comparative analysis of two student modeling approaches: model tracing and constraint-based modeling. We discussed the characteristics and the underlying learning theories of these two approaches, and presented a case study where two tutors were developed for the same domain. We also analysed the two approaches in terms of their main attributes. Creating constraint-based modeling systems tends to require less time and effort, but the result tends to be less comprehensive in terms of specific advice-giving capabilities. Creating model-tracing tutors tends to require more time and effort, but this results in more specific advice-giving capabilities. This is apparent from the case study where it was arguably harder to develop a model-tracing tutor for database design than a constraint-based system. On the other hand, the model-tracing tutor has capabilities to give planning hints and advice expressed more in terms of what a student needs to think to generate a part of the answer than in terms of the desired features of that part of the answer. We emphasize that the stated differences are tendencies and are not hard and fast. It is possible to write constraint-based systems that generate solutions [7] and thus can be used to provide planning advice. Of course, doing so takes more time and effort. Conversely, it is possible to more quickly and easily build a model-tracing tutor by writing production rules in a diagnostic mode that focus more on whether student steps are correct or not and less on how to generate those steps. But, again, such a change does not come without cost: the resulting cognitive tutor will not be able to provide planning advice.

   We conclude that both approaches have their strengths and weaknesses. Model tracing is an excellent choice for domains where appropriate problem solving strategies are well-defined, and where comprehensive feedback on them is desirable. On the other hand, CBM offers a workable alternative when such strategies are not available or appropriate, or there is too little time or resources to build a model-tracing knowledge base. CBM and model-tracing are viable, complementary approaches to building real-world tutors.

Acknowledgments. KERMIT was developed by Pramuditha Suraweera. The authors thank the Erskine fund of the University of Canterbury for funding the visit of Kenneth Koedinger to New Zealand. The work presented here was supported by the University of Canterbury research grant U6430. This research could not have been done without the support of past and present members of HCII and ICTG.

References

1. Aleven, V., Koedinger, K.: An Effective Metacognitive Strategy: Learning by Doing and Explaining with a Computer-based Cognitive Tutor. Cognitive Science 26 (2002) 147–179
2. Anderson, J. R., Lebiere, C.: The Atomic Components of Thought. Mahwah, NJ: Erlbaum (1998)
3. Chi, M. T. H., Bassok, M., Lewis, W., Reimann, P., Glaser, R.: Self-Explanations: How Students Study and Use Examples in Learning to Solve Problems. Cognitive Science, 13 (1989) 145–182
4. Holt, P., Dubs, S., Jones, M., Greer, J.E.: The State of Student Modeling. In: Greer, J.E., McCalla, G.I. (eds.): Student Modeling: the Key to Individualized Knowledge-based Instruction. NATO ASI Series, Vol. 125. Springer (1994) 3–35
5. Koedinger, K. R., Anderson, J. R., Hadley, W. H., Mark, M. A.: Intelligent Tutoring Goes to School in the Big City. Int. J. Artificial Intelligence in Education, 8 (1997) 30–43
6. Mathan, S., Koedinger, K.: An Empirical Assessment of Comprehension Fostering Features in an Intelligent Tutoring System. In: S. Cerri, G. Gouarderes, F. Paraguacu (eds.) Proc. ITS 2002, LNCS Vol. 2363 Springer-Verlag, (2002) 330–343
7. Martin, B, Mitrovic, A.: Tailoring Feedback by Correcting Student Answers. Proc. ITS'2000, LNCS Vol. 1839, Springer-Verlag, (2000) 383–392
8. Mayo, M., Mitrovic, A.: Optimising ITS Behavior with Bayesian Networks and Decision Theory. Int. J. Artificial Intelligence in Education, 12 (2001) 124–153
9. Mitrovic, A.: NORMIT, a Web-enabled Tutor for Database Normalization. Kinshuk, R. Lewis, K. Akahori, R. Kemp, T. Okamoto, L. Henderson, C-H Lee (eds.) Proc. ICCE 2002 (2002) 1276–1280
10. Mitrovic, A., Ohlsson, S.: Evaluation of a Constraint-Based Tutor for a Database Language. Int. J. on Artificial Intelligence in Education 10 (3–4) (1999) 238–256
11. Ohlsson, S.: Constraint-based Student Modeling. In Student Modeling: the Key to Individualized Knowledge-based Instruction. Springer (1994) 167–189
12. Ohlsson, S.: Learning from Performance Errors. Psychological Review 103 (1996) 241–262
13. Payne, S., Squibb, H.: Algebra Mal-rules and Cognitive Accounts of Errors. Cognitive Science, 14 (1990) 445–481
14. Self, J. A.: Bypassing the Intractable Problem of Student Modeling. In: C. Frasson and G. Gauthier (eds.), Intelligent Tutoring Systems: at the Crossroads of Artificial Intelligence and Education. Norwood: Ablex (1990) 107–123
15. Suraweera, P., Mitrovic, A.: KERMIT: a Constraint-based Tutor for Database Modeling. In: S. Cerri, G. Gouarderes, F. Paraguacu (eds.) Proc. ITS 2002, LNCS Vol. 2363 Springer-Verlag, (2002) 377–387
16. VanLehn, K. et al.: Fading and Deepening: the Next Steps for Andes and other Model-Tracing Tutors. In: Proc. ITS'2000, LNCS Vol. 1839, Springer-Verlag, (2000) 474–483

Assessing Student Proficiency in a Reading Tutor That Listens

Joseph E. Beck, Peng Jia, and Jack Mostow

Project LISTEN
School of Computer Science
Carnegie Mellon University
Pittsburgh, PA 15213. USA
joseph.beck@cmu.edu
http://www.cs.cmu.edu/~listen

Abstract. This paper reports results on using data mining to extract useful variables from a database that contains interactions between the student and Project LISTEN's Reading Tutor. Our approach is to find variables we believe to be useful in the information logged by the tutor, and then to derive models that relate those variables to student's scores on external, paper-based tests of reading proficiency. Once the relationship between the recorded variables and the paper tests is discovered, it is possible to use information recorded by the tutor to assess the student's current level of proficiency. The major results of this work were the discovery of useful features available to the Reading Tutor that describe students, and a strong predictive model of external tests that correlates with actual test scores at 0.88.

1 Introduction and Motivation

Project LISTEN's Reading Tutor is an intelligent tutor that listens to students read aloud and helps them learn how to read. Target users are students in first through fourth grades (approximately 6- through 9-year olds). The Reading Tutor uses speech recognition technology to (try to) determine which words the student has read incorrectly and provide help.

Constructing a student model for the Reading Tutor is a challenging task. Most student models are structured according to the domain content or a model of how students solve procedural problems [1]. Previous work at constructing student models in computer tutors for language learning has focused on understanding students' typed input [5]. Although the Reading Tutor uses mouse for some input, requiring typing would not work well since non-readers cannot write.

Our goal with this work is to use fine-grained data generated by student-Reading Tutor interactions to provide assessment of students' reading performance that rely on empirical knowledge that we can derive from data. Previous work [3] has used external tests to validate the accuracy of a user model. This prior work used the student model's estimates of the student's proficiencies to predict what his score would be on an exam. Correlations between predicted and actual scores reached 0.81. We are instead starting with student data and using external tests to *derive* a student

P. Brusilovsky et al. (Eds.): UM 2003, LNAI 2702, pp. 323–327, 2003.
© Springer-Verlag Berlin Heidelberg 2003

model. If we can accurately predict how a student would perform on a paper test, we can use that prediction to direct the tutor's decision making. Such automated assessments can be used to help adapt the Reading Tutor's functionality by selecting stories for the student at an appropriate level of difficulty.

2 Approach

In the 2000-2001 school year, 88 students in grades one through four (i.e. 6- through 9-year olds) used the Reading Tutor from late October through early June. There were 37 first graders, 18 second graders, 17 third graders, and 16 fourth graders.

We tested students individually 4 times. In October and April, students were measured for fluency and the Woodcock Reading Mastery Test (WRMT) [7]. We also tested students' fluency in January and May. We measured fluency by having each student read 3 grade-level passages and counting the number read correctly, and then taking the median of those 3 numbers. The WRMT is a battery of tests designed to assess the student's reading proficiency across a broad spectrum.

In this paper, we use these test scores to relate student interaction data logged by the Reading Tutor to the paper tests for purposes of automatically assessing the student. Specifically, we predict student fluency and Word Identification (WI) from the WRMT. WI measures the student's skill at correctly reading words in English. A 2.4 means a student demonstrates word identifications skills at the level of 4 months into the second grade.

The Reading Tutor logs when a student reads a story, a sentence, and a particular word. It also logs when students request help on a word. From this information we can define a series of measures that describe how students are performing while using the Reading Tutor. One measure is the interword latency [6], defined as the time from when a student finishes speaking the $i-1$th word in the sentence until he begins to **correctly** pronounce the ith word. Note that some words do not have defined latencies. If a student never reads word $i-1$ in the sentence, then word i does not have a latency.

We defined several features based on latency:
1. Total percentage of words having a defined latency
2. Percentage of words read fluently (latency of 10ms)
3. Percentage of words read disfluently (latency >5000ms)
4. Median of all latencies
5. Mean of all latencies

We also defined features based on the student's help request behavior
1. Percentage of sentences for which the student requested sentence help
2. Percentage of words about which the student requested help

The features about latency and help requests were defined for all words the student encountered. We also computed those features just for words that are on the Dolch list [4] of 220 frequent words. We then computed those features just for words that are not on the Dolch list. We also used as features each student's grade and gender, and the percentage of words the student read the Reading Tutor accepted as correct.

Since the Reading Tutor's logs were designed primarily for debugging rather than educational data mining, certain types of interactions were not logged in a parseable form. See [2] for a description of problems with the logging procedure. In spite of relatively minor warts with the logging (which have been fixed in later versions of the Reading Tutor), we were able to define and extract many potentially useful descriptors of student performance from our database. We now turn to using these data to predict scores on the WRMT and fluency tests.

We only consider data about student performance in the Reading Tutor from within a window of time before a paper-test is administered. We experimented with a variety of window sizes: 1 week, 2 weeks, 4 weeks, 8 weeks, 12 weeks, and all data before the test was administered to explore tradeoffs between timeliness of data and noisiness of estimate. Data that are more recent better describe a student's changing state of knowledge. However, if the window is too small, then we our estimates of the parameters may be noisy (i.e. a version of bias-variance tradeoff). Once we have a specified window size, we collect data on all of the student measures from within that window and use those data to construct a set of features representing the student's performance within the Reading Tutor.

Each training instance consists of one paper test score and 62 features computed from student performance during its associated time window.

We aggregated the data for all 4 fluency tests and for both WI tests together. Since there are 88 students and 4 fluency tests, combining the data together provides 352 instances to train a model of fluency. With only 2 WI tests, there are 176 instances for training a model of the WI component of the WRMT. Due to students missing some tests and our losing low-level Reading Tutor data from one student, we only had 344 fluency and 173 WI test scores to serve as labels.

We conducted experiments using Weka, a public domain set of datamining tools written in Java, and used its model tree and linear regression algorithms to make predictions. Model trees are a combination of decision trees and linear regression: first the training data are partitioned as in a decision tree, but the leaf nodes contain a linear model for making predictions. Model trees handle non-linearities in data by splitting the data into regions that can be better modeled with linear techniques. For both techniques we used the default settings in Weka.

3 Results

We now relate our model's predictions to how students actually performed on the paper-based tests. These results are from a 10-fold cross validation of 87 students. We used window sizes of 1 week, 2 weeks, 4 weeks, 8 weeks, 12 weeks, and all data before the test. The best result for predicting fluency was a correlation of 0.86 from using a model tree with a 12 week window. Model trees did better than linear regression for all window sizes except for 1 week.

For Word Identification, the pattern between window size and performance was less clear. Model trees outperform Weka's linear regression, and performance improves somewhat as window size increases. Using an 8-week window, the model tree's predictions correlate at 0.87 with the actual test scores while Weka's linear regression correlates at 0.82.

A truism in datamining and machine learning is to start with simple models first, and then see if using more complex models is needed and justified. However, we have found that which software you use for your simple models can make a noticeable difference. We performed the majority of our work in Weka since it is free and the source code is available. Having source code is a great advantage for researchers since it simplifies conducting experiments that software designers may not have thought of. However, we have found that Weka and SPSS disagree on how well linear models fit our data.

Fig. 1 shows how SPSS and Weka compare in model accuracy. SPSS gives a maximum correlation of 0.88 with the actual test scores, compared to 0.87 with Weka's model trees. This difference in correlations is negligible; however, models generated by SPSS are relatively insensitive to window size, which is a good feature. This difference in performance between regression techniques is linked to Weka's default behavior that first prunes variables before building its linear models. For regression it is easy to disable this pruning. For model trees, turning off the pruning requires a source code modification that we have not yet completed.

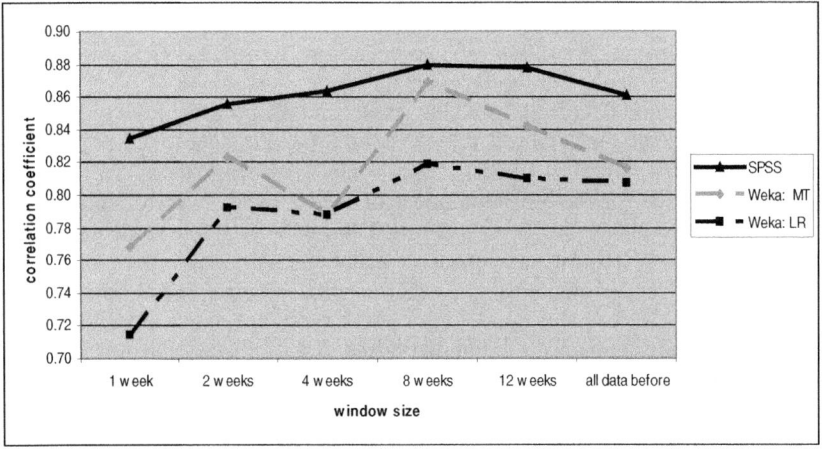

Fig. 1. Performance at predicting word identification test

4 Conclusions

The approach of constructing a user model by relating fine-grained features to existing, external measures is a promising one. It makes sense to bootstrap from the extensive effort that has been spent psychometrically validating instruments such as the WRMT. For domains such as reading, where it can be difficult to determine which student performance measures are important, and it is impractical to make the user interface transparent to show the student's "problem-solving steps," constructing a student model in this manner is a sensible procedure. However, this approach would not be practical for modeling finer-grained aspects of student-knowledge (e.g. whether a student knows *ph* makes the sound /f/ in the word "phone").

We have determined which variables are important in assessing student knowledge at a coarse level. Viewing the variables as broad categories, both latency and help request features provided useful information for predicting a student's level of reading ability. Both variables combined did better than either one alone.

The most useful single variable was the percentage of words that had a latency defined. This feature is somewhat different from, and outperformed, the percentage of words the speech recognizer heard the student say correctly. Since latency is only defined for 2 successive words read correctly [6], it is not defined for the first word of the sentence or for isolated words read correctly. Thus, the student's ability to string multiple words in a row together seems to have some predictive power above and beyond just saying those words correctly in isolation.

Acknowledgements. This work was supported in part by the National Science Foundation under Grant No. REC-9979894. Any opinions, findings, conclusions, or recommendations expressed in this publication are those of the authors and do not necessarily reflect the views of the National Science Foundation or the official policies, either expressed or implied, of the sponsors or of the United States Government. We thank members of Project LISTEN who contributed to this work, especially Susan Rossbach for conducting the field studies, Andrew Cuneo for constructing the database from the logfiles, and June Sison for commenting on a draft of this paper.

References

(see www.cs.cmu.edu/~listen for LISTEN publications)

1. Anderson, J.R., *Rules of the Mind.* 1993, Lawrence Erlbaum Assoc.
2. Beck, J.E., Jia, P., Sison, J. and Mostow, J., Predicting student help-request behavior in an intelligent tutor for reading. Proceedings of the *Ninth International Conference on User Modeling.* 2003
3. Corbett, A.T. and Bhatnagar, A., Student Modeling in the ACT Programming Tutor: Adjusting a Procedural Learning Model With Declarative Knowledge. Proceedings of the *Sixth International Conference on User Modeling.* 1997
4. Dolch, E., A basic sight vocabulary. *Elementary School Journal*, 1936. **36**: p. 456–460.
5. Michaud, L.N., McCoy, K.F. and Stark, L.A., Modeling the Acquisition of English: an Intelligent CALL Approach". Proceedings of the *Eighth International Conference on User Modeling.* 2001
6. Mostow, J. and Aist, G., The Sounds of Silence: Towards Automated Evaluation of Student Learning in a Reading Tutor that Listens. Proceedings of the *Proceedings of the Fourteenth National Conference on Artificial Intelligence.* p. 355–361. 1997
7. Woodcock, R.W., *Woodcock Reading Mastery Tests - Revised (WRMT-R/NU).* 1998, Circle Pines, Minnesota: American Guidance Service.

Adaptive Bayes for a Student Modeling Prediction Task Based on Learning Styles

Gladys Castillo[1,2], João Gama[2], and Ana M. Breda[1]

[1] Department of Mathematics / R&D Unit "Mathematics and Applications"
University of Aveiro, 3810 Aveiro, Portugal
{gladys, ambreda}@mat.ua.pt

[2] LIACC – University of Porto, Rua Campo Alegre, 823,
4150 Porto, Portugal
jgama@liacc.up.pt

Abstract. We present Adaptive Bayes, an adaptive incremental version of Naïve Bayes, to model a prediction task based on *learning styles* in the context of an Adaptive Hypermedia Educational System. Since the student's preferences can change over time, this task is related to a problem known as *concept drift* in the machine learning community. For this class of problems an *adaptive predictive model*, able to adapt quickly to the user's changes, is desirable. The results from conducted experiments show that Adaptive Bayes seems to be a fine and simple choice for this kind of prediction task in user modeling.

1 Introduction

Over the past few years, there has been an increasing interest to include assumptions about the *learning style* into the student model. *Learning style* can be defined as the different ways a person collects, processes and organizes information. This kind of information helps more effectively adaptive systems to decide how to adapt its navigation and its presentation, thus enhancing the student learning. As usual, the systems modeling *learning styles* acquire this information explicitly inquiring the students through one of the existing psychometric instruments. In most of them, these acquired assumptions are no longer updated during the future interactions between the student and the system. By matching a *learning style* with some relevant characteristics of *learning resources*, these systems [e.g. 1] can determine what type of resources are more appropriate to the student, hence adapting their contents. In general, the rules defined in their decision models never change. However, it is a fact that the student preferences of certain types of *multimedia resources* or *learning activities* can change over time. So, this prediction task, which consists in determining what kind of *learning resources* are more appropriate to a *learning style*, can be related with a problem known as *concept drift*. This problem has been discussed in several works about the use of machine learning for user modeling [4, 5]. In *concept drift* scenarios, the most

P. Brusilovsky et al. (Eds.): UM 2003, LNAI 2702, pp. 328–332, 2003.
© Springer-Verlag Berlin Heidelberg 2003

recent observations become more important for the learning algorithms. Therefore, an *adaptive predictive model* is desirable.

In this paper we show that Adaptive Bayes, an incremental adaptive version of the Naïve Bayes, can be used in this student-modeling task. The main difference between the incremental Naïve Bayes and this new adaptive approach is that it includes an *updating scheme*, making it possible to adapt the current model to new data. Experiments with simulated *concept drift* scenarios in this context compare Adaptive Bayes with its non-adaptive version. These experiments were conducted using artificial datasets, which were generated to simulate the changes in the student's preferences.

2   The GIAS's System

GIAS evolved from a non-adaptive web-based tutorial in Plane Geometry that was planned for math students of the University of Aveiro. First we begin to investigate its conversion into an *adaptive tutorial system*. Since the creation of these systems requires a lot of effort we decided to design GIAS as an *authoring-tool* to support learning and teaching. The authors can make use of the existing online *learning resources* to enhance the learning processes of their students. The adaptation techniques are focused on the appropriate selection of the *course's topics* and *learning resources* based on the student's *goals, knowledge level, learning style* and *preferences*.

GIAS has three main components: the *Domain Model*, the *Student Model* and the *Instructional Module*. The *Domain Model* is composed by the *cognitive model* for knowledge representation and by *the course model* for course representation. The latter is organized into three-layers: *goal layer* (the course's goals), *topic layer* (the course's topics) and the *resource layer* (a set of *learning resources* associated to each topic). A *learning resource* can be defined as the implementation of a *learning activity* (e.g. Historical Review) in a *multimedia support* (e.g. HTML text). The *learning resources* are discriminated according to its *difficulty level*. The *Student Model* is composed by three components: *the student profile* (stores information such as *name, age, learning style,* etc), *the cognitive overlay* (records the system's *beliefs* of the student's knowledge) and *the course overlay* (stores information about the student's interaction with the system). To model the *student's learning style* we have adopted the Felder-Sylverman model. It classifies students in five dimensions: *visual/verbal, sensing/intuitive, sequential/global, inductive/deductive, active/reflective* (we use only the first three dimensions). To acquire the *student's learning style* we use the *Index of Learning Styles Questionnaire* (ILSQ) [2]. It helps us to classify the preference for one or the other category as *mild, moderate* or *strong*. Finally, the *Instructional Module* includes three main processes: *course generation, topic generation* and *test generation*. These processes implement the adaptive algorithms based on the information stored in the *student model* and in the *domain model*.

3 The Prediction Task Based on Learning Styles

In this paper we focus on the *topic generation* decision process. The choice of the suitable *learning resources* for a topic depends on the resource's *characteristics* and on the student's *knowledge level, learning style* and *preferences*. This process is performed in three steps: 1) *selection*: using *'if-then-else'* rules, the *learning resources* are filtered according to the matching between the *resource's difficulty level* and the *student's knowledge level*; 2) *prediction*: using the actual *predictive model*, each selected resource is classified into two classes: *'appropriate'* or *'not appropriate'* based on the *resource's characteristics* and the *student's learning style;* 3) *decision*: decisions about how to adapt are taken based on these predictions.

We propose to employ Adaptive Bayes, an incremental version of Naïve Bayes, as our *predictive model*. It includes an *updating scheme*, making possible to adapt the current model to new data. After seeing each example, the model is updated according to the discrepancy between the *predicted class* and the *correct class* with the aim to increase the confidence on this last one. In a previous work [3] we have evaluated Adaptive Bayes in both, an *incremental* and an *on-line framework* using 23 problems from the UCI repository. In both frameworks, the obtained results showed significant gains in accuracy in comparison with its non-adaptive versions.

The examples are described through 5 attributes*: the first three* characterizing the *student's learning style* and *the last two* characterizing the *learning resource*. The possible values for each attribute are presented in the Table 1.

Table 1. Establishing attributes and their possible values

Attributes	Values
Characterizing the student's learning style	
VisualVerbal	VV_i, $VV \in \{Visual, Verbal\}$, $i \in \{mild, moderate, strong\}$
SensingConceptual	SC_i, $SC \in \{Sensing, Conceptual\}$, $i \in \{mild, moderate, strong\}$
GlobalSequential	GS_i, $GS \in \{Global, Sequential\}$, $i \in \{mild, moderate, strong\}$
Characterizing the learning resource	
Learning Activity (LA)	*Lesson objectives/Explanation/Example/Conceptual Map/Synthesis Diagram/ Glossary / Summary /Bibliography /HistoricalReview /Inter.Activity*
Resource Type (RT)	*Text/HTML Text/Picture/Animated Picture/ Animated Picture with Voice/ Audio /Video /Software*

For each student his/her *predictive model* is maintained. The topic generation process is executed whenever a student requests the contents of a topic. During this process his/her actual *predictive model* is used to classify the available resources. Since the classifier returns probabilities, all the resources of a same class can be ranked according to these probabilities. As a result, a HTML page is sent to the student including two separated ranked lists with the resource's links: a *'resources suggested for study'* list with the links for those resources classified as *'appropriate'* and *'other resources for study'* list for those resources classified as *'not appropriate'*. Whenever possible, the *correct class* is obtained based on the observations about the *user's choice of links*: visited links are taken as '*appropriate*' (positive examples). Obtaining a relevant set of negative examples is more difficult. To obtain more examples we suggest to the students to rate the resources explicitly. The obtained examples are used to update the *student's predictive model*.

4   Experiments

In order to compare the performance of Adaptive Bayes against its non-adaptive version we have conducted experiments simulating *concept drift* scenarios in the context of the described prediction task using *artificial datasets*. These datasets were generated to simulate the changes in the user's preferences, a fact that really exists in this context. To simplify the model we don't discriminate the preferences for a *learning style* category. Hence, the number of different *learning styles* is equal to 2^3, which corresponds to the number of datasets evaluated for each algorithm. For each *learning style*, examples were *randomly* generated and classified according to the current concept. After N examples the current concept changes. With this aim, a sequence of rules "*if-then-else*" (R1-R2-R3-R4) was defined. By matching a student *learning style* with the resource's characteristics, these rules allow to determine whether a *learning resource* is *appropriate* for the student. The basic idea enclosing in this simulation is: for instance, a *verbal student* should feel more comfortable with a kind of learning resources that *matches* with his/her *learning style* (e.g. a *learning resource* implementing a *learning activity* "*Historical Review*" in a support "*HTML Text*" should be *appropriate* for a *Verbal student*). We can define the following rule:

```
IF LearningStyle Is Verbal AND
   (ResourceLearningActivity OR ResourceType) matches Verbal
   THEN Resource is Appropriate
```

But during the interaction with the system the student, over time, can change the preferences for another kind of *learning resource* that doesn't match with his/her *learning style*. We can change the previous rule to another one, like this:

```
IF LearningStyle Is Verbal AND
   (ResourceLearningActivity OR ResourceType) matches Visual
THEN Resource is Appropriate
```

We have evaluated three approaches of the incremental Naïve Bayes: *without adaptation*, Adaptive Bayes and this last one using *fading factors*. Each model is incrementally built from a *training set* and then it is used to classify a *test set*. Training sets with 400 and 800 examples respectively, and its corresponding test sets with 200 and 400 examples were generated. For the training (test) sets the concept changes after every 200(100) examples. Each batch of 100 test examples was evaluated in the learning epoch corresponding to the current concept. The evaluation statistic is the percentage of *misclassified examples* in the test set. For each learning style the results were averaged over 10 runs and then the obtained results were averaged for each algorithm. The final results are shown in the table 2. They provide evidence of the advantage of using adaptive techniques to take concept drift into account.

Table 2. Comparison between incremental Naïve Bayes and Adaptive Bayes

# Training Examples	# Test Examples	Algorithm	Fading Factor	Error Rate
400 200 R1+200 R2	200 100 R1+100 R2	No Adaptation		27.16 ± 12.4
		Adaptive Bayes		13.31 ± 5.9
		Adaptive Bayes	0.95	14.24 ± 6.1
		Adaptive Bayes	0.90	**12.44 ± 7.7**
		Adaptive Bayes	0.85	13.08 ± 9.7
800 200 R1+200 R2 + 200 R3+200 R4 +	400 100 R1+100 R2 + 100 R3+100 R4 +	No Adaptation		27.16 ± 12.4
		Adaptive Bayes		17.98 ± 4.4
		Adaptive Bayes	0.95	11.78 ± 2.7
		Adaptive Bayes	0.90	**10.61 ± 3.0**
		Adaptive Bayes	0.85	12.11 ± 3.98

5   Conclusions and Future Work

In this paper we have presented Adaptive Bayes to model a prediction task based on *learning styles*. The results obtained in conducted experiments show that Adaptive Bayes seems to be a good and simple choice for *concept drift* scenarios in user modeling. In the near future we plan to compare this approach against other learning methods using weighted examples and/or time windows. We also plan to model this task using Bayesian Networks and infer the *learning style*, based on the observations during interactions of the student with the system. We are going to investigate similar adaptive learning approaches for these networks.

Acknowledgments. Gratitude is expressed to the financial support given by the ALES project (POSI/39770/SRI/2001).

References

1. Carver, C.A., Howard, R.A., Lane, W.D.: Enhancing Student Learning Trough Hypermedia Courseware and Incorporation of Student Learning Styles. IEEE Transactions on Education, vol 42, n° 1 (1999) 33:38
2. Felder, R.M., Soloman, B.A.: Index of Learning Style Questionnaire, available online at http://www2.ncsu.edu/unity/lockers/users/f/felder/public/ILSdir/ilsweb.html
3. Gama, J., Castillo, G.: Adaptive Bayes for User Modeling. Advances in Artificial Intelligence - IBERAMIA 2002, LNAI 2527, Springer Verlag (2002) 765:774
4. Koychev, I., Schwab, I.: Adaptation to Drifting User's Interests. In Proceedings of ECML2000 Workshop: Machine Learning in New Information Age, Spain (2000)
5. Webb, G., Pazzani, M., Billsus, D.: Machine Learning for User Modeling. User Modeling and User-Adapted Interaction, 11 (2001) 19:29

User Modeling and Problem-Space Representation in the Tutor Runtime Engine

Steven Ritter, Stephen Blessing, and Leslie Wheeler

Carnegie Learning
{sritter, sblessing, leslie}@carnegielearning.com

Abstract. Our efforts to commercialize Cognitive Tutors have led us to a runtime representation that is significantly different from the production system representation used in the Tutor Development Kit. This paper describes our new representation, which we call the Tutor Runtime Environment (TRE).

1   Introduction

Cognitive Tutors [1] based on Anderson's ACT-R theory [2] have typically been developed and deployed using the Tutor Development Kit (TDK) [3]. As these tutors have proceeded through commercialization, several factors have driven us to reconsider using the TDK for deployment.

This paper describes a new deployment system, referred to as the Tutor Runtime Engine that uses a different technique for modeling the task and user abilities than the TDK, while retaining its abilities and providing better performance, advantages in testing and efficiencies in development.

2   Two TRE Tutor Implementations

You are strongly encouraged to use LaTeX2e for the preparation of your camera-ready manuscript together with the corresponding Springer class file llncs.cls; see Sect. 3. Only if you use LaTeX2e can hyperlinks be generated in the online version of your manuscript.

We discuss two of the tutors that are currently using the TRE. The Algebra Word Problem Tutor [4] was originally developed in the TDK and we ported it over to the TRE representation. The Algebraic Transformation Tool depicted in Figure 1 is a more recent tutor that was developed from the start using the TRE.

3   Cognitive Tutor Functions

Cognitive Tutors use several general techniques to provide appropriate assistance and instruction to students. Among these are "model tracing," "knowledge tracing" and context-based feedback.

P. Brusilovsky ct al. (Eds.): UM 2003, LNAI 2702, pp. 333–336, 2003.

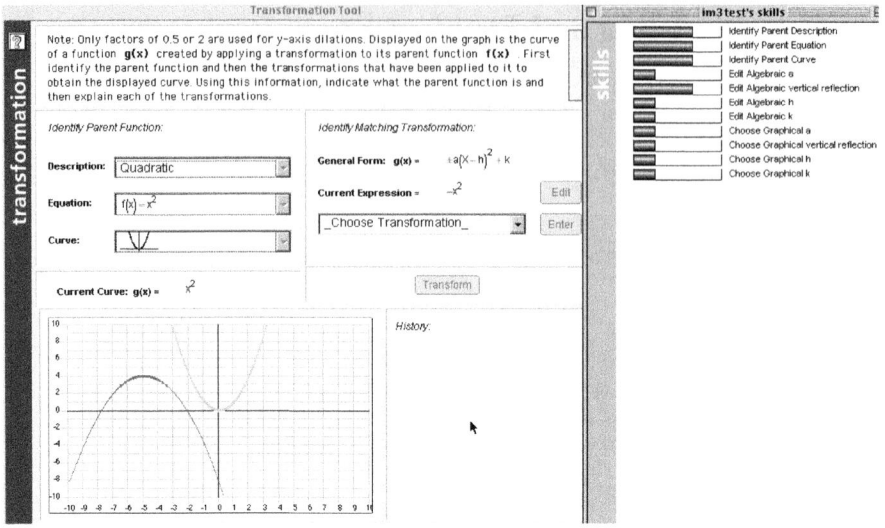

Fig. 1. The Algebraic Transformation Tool

3.1 Model Tracing

In a typical task, students have choices about how to proceed. Some of these choices represent fundamentally different strategies for solving problems.

In most cases, the student's own actions disambiguate strategies. For example, there are two major strategies for entering an expression for the dependent variable in terms of the independent variable in the Algebra I Cognitive Tutor [5]. A student might look at the text, aim to understand it in terms of an initial value and a rate of change and use that understanding to construct an algebraic expression. Alternatively, the student might use concrete, situational reasoning to solve specific instances within the problem situation and then use induction to move from those instances to the general expression. Generally, the student's strategy can be determined reasonably well from the student's actions.

A TDK-based tutor uses a set of production rules to model the student's actions. If such a set can be found, then the student's strategy can be identified. If no such set can be found, the tutor might also match the student's action against a set of production rules representing some known "buggy" strategy. If the tutor still cannot model the student's action, the action is considered wrong and the student must correct it.

3.2 Knowledge Tracing

Knowledge tracing provides a way for the tutor to track the growth of individual students' knowledge over time and use that knowledge to target instruction to individual students. Through model tracing, the cognitive model identifies each student action with a set of production rules. Each production rule represents a skill.

Since the model knows which skills the student has successfully executed (and which the student has attempted unsuccessfully), it can estimate the student's proficiency on each skill included in the curriculum.

3.3   Hints and Feedback

In TDK-based tutors, production rules (or more accurately, sets of production rules) are associated with hint templates. The tutor is able to give students advice on how to proceed by using a process similar to model tracing. At any point in the problem, the tutor is able to identify a set of production rules that implement the "preferred" strategy to use at this point in the problem, and it uses the hint templates associated with that strategy to present hints to the student.

4   Implementation in a TDK-Based Tutor

A TDK-based system essentially has two types of representations: production rules and working memory elements (WMEs). We have discussed the role of production rules, but it is worthwhile to consider the role of the WMEs. The WMEs are the data in the system. They are called WMEs because, in a cognitive model, they represent elements in the student's working memory.

In fact, WMEs represent two kinds of information. First, they represent aspects of the problem situation. That is, working memory elements need to represent aspects of the problem that are initially evident to the student. Second, they represent information that the student has created about the problem. Production system models may or may not explicitly represent problem initial state and student-created representations differently. In the TRE, these types of representation are inherently different.

5   The TRE Implementation

The TRE's primary representation is a problem space representation. In contrast to the TDK representation, subgoals are explicitly represented. Information that the TRE needs to implement model tracing, knowledge tracing and hints is associated with each subgoal.

In addition, information about state changes is explicitly represented. Similar to the role of working memory elements that represent student-specific information, this state information represents elements of the problem state that are determined by student actions.

This representation is subordinate to the problem space representation. This amounts to a strong claim that the majority of reasoning in the cognitive model has to do with the problem, not with the way that the student chooses to solve the problem. This has been the case in the Cognitive Tutors we have implemented and, as Simon's famous "ant on the beach" example illustrates [6], we should expect this to be true in most cases. That is, a student's apparent complex behavior is due to the environment (problem) they find themselves in, and the space of that problem is known at the time the problem is authored.

In fact, the assumption that most complexity is in the problem rather than the student has a profound effect on the TRE functioning. In a production system model, the goal of the production system is to model all problem solving in problems of a certain type. Since most complexity is contained in the problem itself, most of the production system modeling amounts to making decisions about the problem itself. For example, in giving a hint about entering an expression in the Algebra Word Problem Tutor, the production system model differentiates at run time between problems whose intercept is zero and problems where this is not the case. In the TRE representation, a production system is built in to the authoring tool, so that these decisions can be made at problem authoring time. The runtime problem space is specific to the problem being solved. The result is that, at run time, the TRE system needs only make decisions that are related to aspects of the state that the student has created, which greatly simplifies the runtime processing.

References

1. Anderson, J. R., Corbett, A. T., Koedinger, K. R., & Pelletier, R. (1995). Cognitive tutors: Lessons learned. The Journal of the Learning Sciences, 4 (2) 167–207.
2. Anderson, J. R. & Lebière, C. (1998). *The atomic components of thought.* Mahwah, NJ: Erlbaum.
3. Anderson, J. R., & Pelletier, R. (1991). A development system for model–tracing tutors. In L. Birnbaum (Ed.), *Proceedings of the International Conference of the Learning Sciences* (pp. 1–8). Charlottesville, VA: Association for the Advancement of Computing in Education.
4. Koedinger, K. R., Anderson, J. R.., Hadley, W. H.., & Mark, M. A. (1997). Intelligent tutoring goes to school in the big city. *International Journal of Artificial Intelligence in Education,* 8.
5. Koedinger, K. R., & Anderson, J. R. (1998). Illustrating principled design: The early evolution of a cognitive tutor for algebra symbolization. *Interactive Learning Environments,* 5, 161–180.
6. Simon, H. (1981/1992). *The Sciences of the Artificial.* Cambridge: MIT Press.

A Neuro-fuzzy Approach in Student Modeling

Regina Stathacopoulou[1], Maria Grigoriadou[1], George D. Magoulas[2], and Denis Mitropoulos[1]

[1] Department of Informatics and Telecommunications, University of Athens, Panepistimiopolis, GR-15784 Athens, Greece,
{sreg,gregor,dmitro}@di.uoa.gr
[2] Department of Information Systems and Computing, Brunel University, Uxbridge UB8 3PH, United Kingdom,
George.Magoulas@brunel.ac.uk

Abstract. In this paper, a neural network-based fuzzy modeling approach to assess student knowledge is presented. Fuzzy logic is used to handle the subjective judgments of human tutors with respect to student observable behavior and their characterizations of student knowledge. Student knowledge is decomposed into pieces and assessed by combining fuzzy evidences, each one contributing to some degree to the final assessment. The neuro-fuzzy synergism helps to represent teacher experience in an interpretable way, and allows capturing teacher subjectivity. The proposed approach was used to assess knowledge and misconceptions of simulated students interacting with the exploratory learning environment "Vectors in Physics and Mathematics", which is used by high school pupils to learn about vectors. In our experiments, this approach provided significant improvement in student diagnosis compared with previous attempts.

1 Introduction

The educational software "Vectors in Physics and Mathematics" is an exploratory learning environment that has been designed and developed according to constructivist theory of learning [4]. Within this framework, the design is based on a series of principles, which emphasize the student's active involvement in authentic activities, which correspond to real world processes (situated/anchored learning) [2],[11]. Moreover, the software supports students' creative activities that simulate phenomena and actions happening in real world. In order to design the software and to choose its thematic units, we took into account the conceptual difficulties secondary students develop during the learning of mathematical and physical entities represented by vectors.

In order to collect the best available information for student's diagnosis, we allow for a close monitoring of student's actions over time, where each response such as keystroke, mouse move or drag can be timed and recorded. However, the nature of the available evidence about student's behavior provided by the student's inputs to an ITS contains a good deal of uncertainty [6]. Bayesian networks have been proposed [10] to relate, in a probabilistic way, a particular piece of student's knowledge with student's observable behavior.

P. Brusilovsky et al. (Eds.): UM 2003, LNAI 2702, pp. 337–341, 2003.

Another approach to handle the inherent uncertainty in student's behavior and to achieve a human description of knowledge is to use fuzzy logic. Fuzzy logic techniques have been proposed in a variety of user and student modeling approaches [6]. In student modeling, fuzzy logic has been originally proposed as a flexible and realistic method to easily capture the way human tutors might evaluate a student [5].

Neural networks have been proposed in a variety of user and student modeling approaches [9],[12], due to there abilities to learn from noisy or incomplete patterns of users behavior [12]. A problem which is coming up when trying to apply a neural network in modeling a human behavior is knowledge representation [12], since the weights learned are often difficult for humans to interpret. To alleviate this situation, a neural network approach where each node and connection has symbolic meaning has been proposed in TAPS [9].

Along this line, this paper investigates a neural network-based fuzzy logic approach for student modeling. This approach allows handling uncertainty of student behavior, by expressing teacher's qualitative knowledge in a clearly interpretable way with the use of fuzzy logic, and at the same time offers the possibility for adaptation to teacher's personal evaluation style and criteria by employing a neural network implementation of the student model.

2   The Neural-Network Based Fuzzy Modeling Approach

2.1   A Scheme for Fuzzy Knowledge Representation

Fuzzy logic is used to describe teacher's subjective linguistic description of student's behavior (e.g. s/he draws a vector after a *long* time, s/he answered *enough* questions in the pre-test). This is achieved by transforming numerical data describing student's behavior pattern $X = \{x_1, x_2, ..., x_k\}$ into membership degrees of linguistic terms that describe student's behavior variables. Student's behavior patterns contain k elements. The set $B = \{B_1, B_2, ..., B_k\}$, where $B_1, B_2, ..., B_k$ are words or sentences describing elements of the behavior pattern (e.g. time needed to draw a vector, number of questions answered in the pre-test), describes linguistically the aspects of student's observable behavior that will serve as inputs to the diagnostic process. Each element B_i is treated as a linguistic variable [13] that takes f linguistic values. $T(B_i) = \{V_{i1}, V_{i2}, ..., V_{if}\}$ is the term set of B_i. set. For example, let us consider the linguistic variable $B_i = $ "time on task". The corresponding term set could be T(time on task)={Very Short, Short, Normal, Long, Very Long}. To each linguistic value V_{if} correspond a membership functions $y_{if}(x_i)$ in [0,1] that calculate the degree of membership of each element x_i $(i=1,..k)$ of an input pattern into the term sets of B_i that use linguistic values V_{if}.

Student's knowledge K is decomposed into L pieces $K_1, K_2, ..., K_L$ that refer to concepts, relations or facts associated with the teaching subject. An approximation of If-THEN rules is performed that represent teacher's reasoning in the qualitative evaluation of student's knowledge. For example, *If student's prior knowledge is insufficient and large number of trial and error attempts have been made to find the correct answer then the student probably does not understand the third Newton's law.*

The qualitative description of student's knowledge level is provided by considering student's knowledge level regarding K_L as a linguistic variable with m linguistic values, $T(K_L)=\{K_{L1}, K_{L2}, \ldots, K_{Lm}\}$ being the term set. For example, if we treat the linguistic variable "student's knowledge about vectors addition" using four linguistic values, then the term set could be: T(student's knowledge about vectors addition)= {Good, Almost good, Rather bad, Bad}. In this way, a mode of qualitative reasoning [13], in which the preconditions and the consequents of the IF-THEN rules involve fuzzy variables, is used to provide an imprecise description of teacher's reasoning:

"IF B_1 is V_{1l} AND B_2 is V_{2l} ...AND B_k is V_{kl} THEN K_1 is K_{1j} AND K_2 is K_{2j}...
AND K_L is K_{Lj}.",   where $l=1,2,\ldots,f$, $j=1,2,\ldots m$.

2.2 Neural-Network Implementation of the Fuzzy Model

The process has three stages (Fig. 1). At the first stage, we have adopted an approach that simplifies the implementation by approximating the membership functions using a library of regular shapes and implementing the fuzzifiers as fixed weight neural networks that calculate such regular shapes. Thus, for a behavior pattern X, the fuzzifier calculates the output $Y=\{(y_{11}, y_{12},\ldots y_{1f}), (y_{21},y_{22},\ldots,y_{2f}), \ldots, (y_{k1},y_{k2},\ldots ,y_{kf})\}$of numeric values in [0,1] based on the input vectors $X =\{x_1, x_2, \ldots, x_k\}$.

At the second stage a layer with n nodes process all possible cases n in the preconditions in order to obtain logical AND between the linguistic values. The output of this layer is the numerical truth-value p_n of the precondition. Thus, student's current behavior is described by a vector $P = [p_1, p_2, \ldots, p_n]$, where $p_1, p_2, \ldots, p_n$ are in the interval [0,1], representing degrees of fulfillment of preconditions.

The third stage consists of a set of backpropagation networks. Each network receives the input P from the precondition layer and provides at its output a characterization for a particular piece of student's knowledge K_L. In particular, each neural network has n input nodes, m output nodes , and a hidden layer. Weights have been defined though learning by examples. To this end, the BPVS [7] algorithm has been used to train the networks with labeled pattern of student's behavior in order to encode teacher's knowledge.

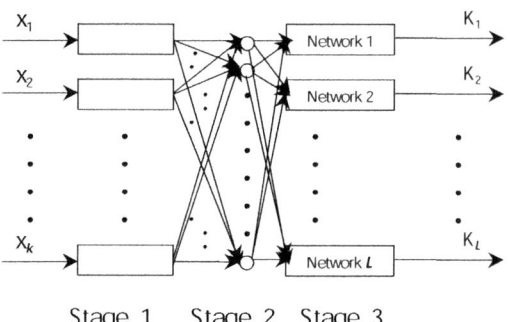

Stage 1   Stage 2   Stage 3

Fig. 1. Schematic of the connectionist implementation

3 The Experiment

The neuro-fuzzy model was tested in the scenario "bodies in equilibrium" (Fig 2). The environment resembles a simple mechanics-laboratory. The students can drag and drop objects and compose an equilibrium experiment. Students' knowledge errors and misconceptions associated with this scenario were found from several studies [1],[3] and summarized as the following knowledge pieces: lack of motion implies no force, unfamiliar with contact forces, unfamiliar with gravitational force, confusing gravitational with contact forces. Each student's action is timed and recorder in a log file.

In Figure 2, an example activity with two boxes on the table is shown. The student draws the forces acting on the top box, according to his ideas. In this way a student is allowed to give their own Newtonian model for the equilibrium of this box. Students can then use the "test" button to observe the behavior of their models. For example, if the resultant force is not equal to zero, the box will move towards the direction of this force. Students can also click the "reality" button, in order to observe the scientific model, i.e. the representation of the correct forces acting on the box.

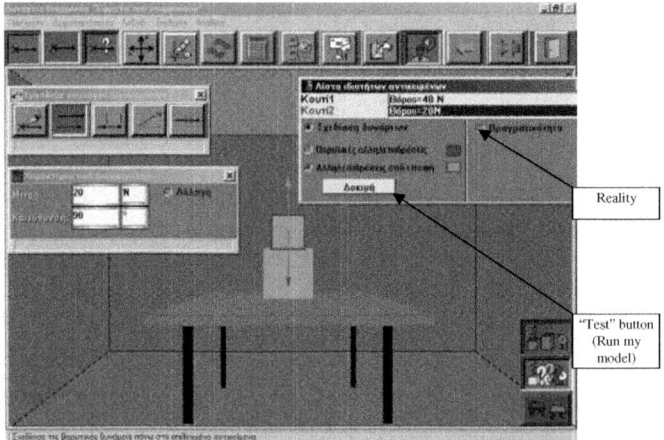

Fig. 2. Activity with two boxes on the table

Diagnosis of student's knowledge is related to the kind (gravitational-contact forces), the number and the direction of the forces acting on the object that the student chooses to draw. A first estimation of student's knowledge level is provided by comparing the kind and the direction of these forces with the respective parameters of the scientific model. For example, if the student does not draw the contact forces we can first assume that he is unfamiliar with contact forces. Final diagnosis is realized from detailed information of student's behavior while he carries out the task.

A set of simulated students was created with the assistance of a teacher, representing patterns of student's behavior and a human teacher labeled these patterns classifying them into different knowledge level categories. Preliminary results where promising, since the test data proved a diagnostic success of 87% for the proposed method, in comparison with 82% for the pure neural-network approach [8].

4 Conclusions

The problem of inferring student's level of knowledge from their interactions with an exploratory learning environment has been investigated using a synergistic approach. Student behavior has been analyzed through a set of fuzzy models. The inference of these models that categorize student's knowledge from student's actions is implemented with a combination of fixed weight and backpropagation neural networks. The neuro-fuzzy synergism exploits the advantages of both fuzzy logic and neural network training to encode teacher's experience in assessing student's knowledge from student's observable behavior. The preliminary testing of the proposed approach in the learning environment "Vectors in Physics and Mathematics" used a construction of simulated students with the assistance of a teacher. The results were encouraging but further experimentation with simulated students based on the behavior of real students is necessary to fully explore the potential of this approach to evaluate students working in exploratory/discovery learning environments.

References

1. Arons A. B. (1990) A guide to introductory physics teaching. Washington : John Wiley & Sons, Inc.
2. Brown J. S., Collins A., Duguid P. (1989) Situated cognition and the culture of learning. Educational researcher 18 32–34.
3. Driver R. (1983) The pupil as a scientist? Milton Keynes: Open University Press.
4. Grigoriadou M., Mitropoulos D., Samarakou M., Solomonidou C., Stavridou E. (1999). Methodology for the Design of Educational Software in Mathematics and Physics for Secondary Education. Computer Based Learning in Science, Conf. Proc. 1999 pB3.
5. Hawkes, L. W., Derry, S. J. & Rundensteiner. E. A. (1990) Individualized tutoring using an intelligent fuzzy temporal relational database. International Journal of Man-Machines Studies, 33,pp 409–429
6. Jameson A.,(1996) Numerical Uncertainty Management In User and Student Modeling: An Overview of Systems and Issues. User Modeling and User-Adapted Interaction, 5, p. 193–251.
7. Magoulas G.D., Vrahatis M.N., and Androulakis G.S. (1997). Effective back-propagation training with variable stepsize. Neural Networks, 10, pp. 69–82.
8. Mitchell T. M. Machine learning (1997), McGraw-Hill, cp.4, pp. 81–117.
9. Posey C. L., Hawkes L. W. (1996). Neural Networks Applied to Knowledge Acquisition in the Student Model. Information Science 88, p. 275–298.
10. Vanlehn K., Niu Z. (2001). Bayesian student modeling, user interfaces and feedback: A sensitivity analysis. Inter. Journal of Artificial Intelligence in Education 12 154–184.
11. Vosniadou S. (1994) From cognitive theory to educational technology. In: Vosniadou S., De Corte E., Mandl H. (Ed), Technology-Based Learning Environments, Psychological and Educational Foundations. NATO ASI Series. F, vol. 137, 11–17. Berlin: Springer-Verlag.
12. Yasdi R.(2000). A Litetature Syrvey on Applications of Neural Networks for Human-Computer Interaction. Neural Computing & Applications, 9, p.245 258.
13. Zadeh L.A.(1989). Knowledge Representation in Fuzzy Logic. In Fuzzy Sets, Fuzzy Logic, and Fuzzy Systems Advances in Fuzzy Systems-Application and Theory, Vol 6. Editors G.J. Klir & B.Yuan.

Student Modeling for an Intelligent Agent in a Collaborative Learning Environment

F. Linton, B. Goodman, R. Gaimari, J. Zarrella, and H. Ross

The MITRE Corporation, 202 Burlington Rd., Bedford MA 01730, USA
{linton, bgoodman, rgaimari, jzarrella, hross}@mitre.org

Abstract. We present an application of student modeling in support of individual learning and group collaboration. The design is based on an empirical analysis of collaborative dialogs collected in earlier work. During use, student modeling data will be acquired not only from learners' graphical user interface actions but also from their text chat by using keywords and speech acts. An agent in the collaborative learning environment will promote deliberative discussion and individual learning based on these group and student models.

1 Introduction

Collaborative learning environments and intelligent tutoring systems; each of these instructional technologies has its strengths and limitations. This research is investigating the extent to which it might be possible to combine them such that their combined strengths outweigh their combined limitations. Intelligent tutoring systems strive to emulate the main advantage of human tutors, namely instruction proceeds at an optimal pace and manner for each student. However, intelligent tutoring systems (ITS) trade off many of the social qualities of human-human interaction in exchange for a limited set of student actions that are fully interpretable by the system.

Collaborative learning environments, in contrast, provide not only tools and resources for learning but also fellow students who supply alternative solutions that must be judiciously evaluated, provide the chance to explain and justify one's own solutions, and engage in other activities known to enhance learning. However, collaborative learning environments (CLE) add the overhead of small group interaction, and the pooled knowledge of the learners may, at times, be insufficient for problem-solving.

The architecture for this research extends the collaborative learning environment described in [1] wherein three learners collaborate in a distributed learning environment consisting of a solution-construction tool – a shared whiteboard with drawing tools specialized for the task of Object-oriented Analysis and Design, a text-chat tool for verbal communication, and an agenda for learners to track their tasks. The architectural extensions will add ITS capabilities in the form of domain expertise and instructional skills; these capabilities are built upon an expert system shell, JESS (http://herzberg.ca.sandia.gov/jess/) and a knowledge representation system, Protégé (http://protege.stanford.edu/index.html). The implementation is described further in

P. Brusilovsky et al. (Eds.): UM 2003, LNAI 2702, pp. 342–351, 2003.
© Springer-Verlag Berlin Heidelberg 2003

[2]. The artificially intelligent agent will act as facilitator, interacting with learners through the whiteboard and chat tools.

Using the original collaborative learning environment, we obtained data from ten groups of three learners solving an object-oriented analysis and design problem using object modeling technique in 90 minute sessions. We logged the learner's chat sessions and their use of the drawing and agenda tools. Based on an analysis of these session logs, we believe it may be possible to draw inferences from learner and group behaviors to build student and group models and perform instructional interventions. We present the rationale and the analysis in this paper.

The question becomes, can the skills of an ITS be applied in a CLE to optimize individual learning, given that it will now have the added task of facilitating and perhaps teaching small group interaction, and that it will now have an added limitation on its ability to interpret student actions, namely it will have an incomplete understanding of student-student natural language interaction [3, 4]?

In particular, the agent will need to understand which part of the problem the learners are discussing, i.e., the topic of discussion, and it will need to determine whether each portion of the solution is correct or not. Also, it will need to gauge the extent to which the learners are having a productive or deliberative discussion, and finally it will need to estimate each learner's grasp of each topic and his or her ability to apply that knowledge. The following sections will discuss each of these items further, and the means we use for determining them.

In this work we accept the theoretical perspectives on learning that are summarized in [5], namely that learning is a process of meaning making, rather than knowledge transmission, and that meaning making is a social-dialogical process of deliberation among participants as they engage with the artifacts (conceptual, physical, or otherwise) of a domain, guided by their intentions and reflections.

One of the potential strengths of this design is that the agent can direct the learners to engage in supportive behavior, for example, if one learner seems not to understand a topic while another does, the agent might elicit an explanation from the more knowledgeable student, thereby modeling the desired behavior (of asking for an explanation) while perhaps starting a discussion on the topic. More precisely, the intelligent agent will prompt, scaffold, and provide feedback for the self-construction and the co-construction of knowledge [6].

2   Topic Identification

When an agent is observing a group of learners in problem-solving mode with the goal of intervening as necessary to facilitate learning, the agent must be able to observe and interpret the learners' conversation and problem-solving actions to some extent. In fact, the agent can intervene productively only to the extent it can observe and interpret the learners' actions.

In contrast to intelligent tutors for individuals, where the individual's interactions with the system are constrained to interface gestures that are, by design, interpretable by the tutor, tutoring a group of learners who are allowed to chat among themselves in natural language introduces the difficulties of natural language understanding. Simply determining the topic of a chat conversational turn is a difficult natural language research problem. In this paper we use *topic* to mean one main concept of the Object-oriented Analysis and Design (OOA&D) task such as defining classes, or giving them attributes, creating associations among classes, defining the multiplicities of the associations, etc. A complete OOA&D exercise is expected to address each of these topics at some level of complexity.

In this research we explored the potential of keywords to reveal the topic of the conversational turns [7]. For the domain of object-oriented analysis and design, we found learners use around 20 keywords; example keywords are *class, attribute, association, multiplicity*, etc. Most turns contain one keyword, however, some turns contain no keywords, some contain keywords pertaining to two distinct topics, and sometimes the keyword used is not the topic of the turn. While using keywords to detect the topic of the conversation has its weaknesses, we believe the method, with the refinements discussed below, will provide 'good enough' data for an agent to make limited instructional interventions such as prompts. For example, the agent might intervene to encourage further discussion on a topic when the learners are about to go on to another topic and the current topic is incomplete or incorrect.

3   Complete and Correct Solutions

One of the tutor agent's goals is that the students' work on a topic should be complete and correct for reasons discussed in [8]. In the case of OOA&D, a domain knowledge module can determine the extent to which a topic is currently complete and correct by interpreting the diagram of the solution as the learners are constructing it on the whiteboard drawing tool and comparing the learners' partial solutions to the answers stored in its knowledge base using model tracing [9]. Implementing model tracing in the architecture described above has been fairly straightforward for limited OOA&D. Both the tutoring agent and the student modeling component will use the model tracing results.

Obtaining a correct and complete solution is only an enabling goal in service of a second, more important, goal for the learners of mastering the skills and knowledge they are attempting to acquire with respect to OOA&D. The agent will use its assessment of the completeness and correctness of the solution together with other measures to determine its interventions to promote mastery. For example, if a topic has just been correctly completed on the whiteboard, and one learner's student model indicates she or he does not yet have a good understanding of the topic, the agent might prompt that learner for an explanation as to why that solution was chosen.

The student modeling component will use model tracing results as well, along with an analysis of each learner's participation and contribution to the topic, to update each individual's student model.

4   Deliberative Discussion

The process by which learners arrive at a complete and correct solution merits as much attention as the solution itself. We believe this process should be a deliberative one. The knowledge that learners bring to the discussion is, at least temporarily, uncertain and incomplete. For this reason, we desire their discussions to be *deliberations* rather than *debates* or *negotiations* wherein participants enter with their positions fully formed and aim to achieve a balance of competing preferences. Deliberations are instead characterized by an attitude of social cooperation, a willingness to share information, openness to persuasion by reason, a good faith exchange of views, and decisions made by a pooling of judgements; all of which should lead to substantively better learning outcomes [10]. To put it briefly, the tutoring agent should foster an environment in which participants are willing and able to learn from each other by interacting with one another. To do so, the ideal tutor agent would ensure that all relevant questions and objections are reasonably addressed, all perspectives have a voice, and that all decisions are free from domination and coercion.

It is expected and desirable that learners propose several alternatives at each step of the solution process. Disagreements should not be treated as problems but as opportunities to explore alternatives, to examine the strengths and weaknesses of various ideas and to evaluate them and their consequences. However, the learners should arrive at a design decision by deliberation, not by one learner imposing his or her solution on the others by decree or by seizing control of the drawing tool. A deliberative discussion will encourage reflection, explanation, examples, etc., and ultimately result in better, more deeply engrained knowledge [6]. Thus, the student model component must examine the collaborative dialog for indicators of deliberative discussion and the tutoring agent must foster its occurrence.

Fostering deliberative discussion is a non-trivial task for a human tutor and it is not one we expect a tutor agent to do well. Nevertheless, deliberative dialogs may have distinguishing characteristics that are detectable with little natural language understanding and to which the agent could respond.

To get at the underlying thrust of learners' utterances without using natural language understanding, we have elected to use a chat tool with *sentence openers*. Sentence openers are phrases that comprise the first few words of a sentence [11]. To enter an utterance in the chat tool, learners must first select the most suitable sentence opener; they may then input the remainder of the utterance in their own words. The sentence opener reveals the speaker's intention or *speech act* [12]. It is these speech acts which we correlate with deliberative discussion and with individual understanding of the subject matter. The set of speech acts and their corresponding sentence openers that we use were determined empirically in earlier work reported elsewhere [1]. In a later section we will discuss our process of coding dialogs for deliberative discussion and the correlation of deliberative discussion with specific speech acts. We suspect, from observations during data gathering, that learner activity on the whiteboard will also indicate the presence of multiple possible solutions under discussion, as well as their eventual resolution.

5   Individual Understanding

As the group engages in deliberative problem-solving, individuals are simultaneously internalizing the domain knowledge to enhance their individual understanding. Until they have achieved this understanding they may be expected to be confused. Learners may go through several rounds of confusion and (apparent) understanding before internalizing a topic thoroughly. For example, one may arrive at an apparently clear understanding of a concept, then be stymied in ones' first attempt to apply the concept when problem solving. Again, one may successfully apply a concept several times and then be unable to see how it applies in different or more complex circumstances.

One task of the student model module is to observe each learner and estimate his or her degree of understanding with respect to each topic. At present we are examining four indicators of learner understanding for possible incorporation into the student modeling component.

First is the pure volume of the learner's contribution to a topic. There is evidence that both self-explanations and co-constructed explanations deepen understanding [6]. Simply put, the activity of talking and explaining significantly improves learning.

A second indicator of understanding is response latency, or the amount of thinking time required to generate an utterance. The less one must think before generating a response, the more skilled one is at applying the knowledge [13].

A third indicator of learner understanding, or lack of understanding, is the use of specific speech acts, e.g., "I'm not so sure…" The correlation of specific speech acts with the expression of propositional domain knowledge is discussed further below.

The fourth indicator is the learner's use of the whiteboard tool to design portions of the solution to the domain exercises, as with conventional intelligent tutoring systems.

The main value of these indicators is that they are observable. We have some way to go in developing a student model from them. While there is a theoretical rationale and experimental evidence for each of them, it is not clear that the learning rates reported in the literature would apply in this case. Furthermore we do not yet have an empirical or theoretical basis for combining them into a single student model. Nevertheless, the presence of so many observable factors in a collaborative learning environment, even without natural language understanding, is grounds for optimism.

6   Analysis and Discussion

In this section we present the data to support the material in the previous sections. We begin with an analysis of using keywords found in the text chat to determine the topic of discussion.

6.1   Using Keywords to Determine Topic of Discussion

The introduction to object-oriented analysis and design (OOA&D) that we use in this work has five subtopics: General OOA&D, classes, attributes, associations, and multiplicities. When the learners are using the agenda tool or the OOA&D whiteboard, their topic of discussion is explicit, however, when learners are chatting, the topic of discussion may or may not be explicitly referred to. In the vocabulary of the learners' dialogs, about 20 distinct keywords pertaining to the five topics appear. We hypothesized that a student modeling module could determine the current subject of a conversation by listening solely for the domain keywords.

To perform the analysis we selected a conversation log for one set of subjects on the exercise, searched it for keywords, and marked the turns where the keywords occurred. We labeled each turn with its keyword related topic. If more than one keyword occurred in the turn, we used the more specific topic mentioned as the label. We then manually reviewed the text of the conversation and again labeled the utterances, this time with the actual topic of the conversation. In comparing the keyword-based 'automated' topic labels with the experimenter-determined topic labels we made the following observations. The automated process made errors of commission and errors of omission; the former are rare, the latter are of several types. Errors of commission are when the system thinks learners are talking about object modeling technique (OMT) but they are not. Typically they are talking about process or procedure instead, as in "Let's put the association links in next." Errors of omission are when learners are talking about OMT but are not using any OMT keywords. Here are some examples:

1. Vocabulary is limited to the terms in the exercise, e.g., "A bank has a loan"

2. A phrase refers to someone else's action or statement, e.g., "I agree"

3. Pronominal reference, e.g., "I'm reasonably sure you have it correct"

4. A comment that refers explicitly to a previous line, e.g., "{Re line 43} ..."

5. Misspellings, e.g., "asociation"

6. Idiosyncratic domain vocabulary, e.g., referring to OMT multiplicity balls as "dots"

The agent's understanding of the topic of conversation will improve as these errors are reduced or eliminated. For example, to address the first type of error, exercise-specific vocabulary can be introduced as the materials are authored, and mapped to the domain vocabulary. For errors of the second and third type, statements such as "I agree" and "I'm reasonably sure you have it correct" may reasonably be assumed to refer to the current topic, and comments that reference a previously typed line of dialog can be assumed to have that line's topic. Based on the initial keyword analysis without these improvements, errors of commission account for about 6% of the total, errors of omission account for 29%, and 65% of the time topic identification was correct. This is almost good enough for the tutoring agent to use as is, and we are confident that either a more refined keyword analysis or the insertion of a natural language processing tool such as MITRE's Alembic (http://www.mitre.org) will yield topic identification sufficiently adequate for use by the tutoring agent.

Figure 1 graphs the topics of discussion over the duration of one conversation. The actions graphed include text chat, whiteboard drawing, and agenda setting. The essence of the learner's exercise was to modify a given software design, replacing certain attributes with a discriminator. Discussion of the discriminator is charted under Gen OMT. When charted in this manner, it is easy to observe that certain topics dominated the conversation at certain times, yet no topic was left undiscussed for long. The topic of classes tended to be discussed more heavily early in the conversation and the topic of associations (among classes) to be discussed later. Attributes are discussed in the context of classes, but they are taken up last and dropped first. The learners clearly do not exhaust one topic before going on to another, each topic is revisited many times in the course of the conversation. Similar charts reveal patterns of learner participation, tool use, learner-by-topic contribution, etc.

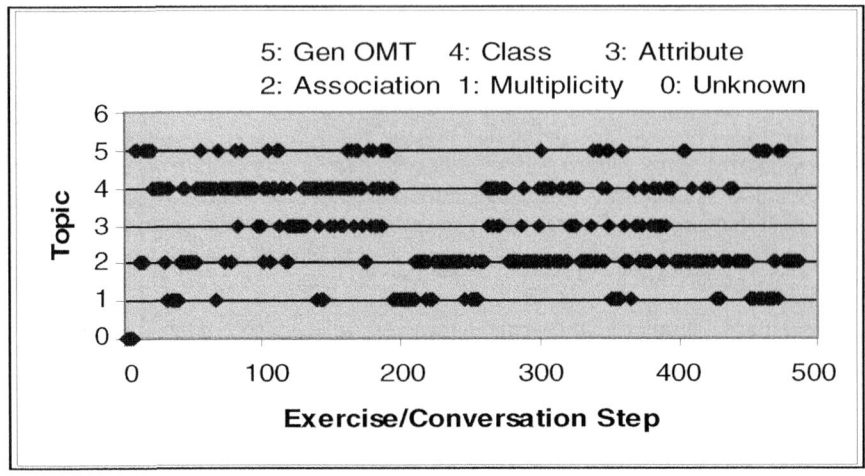

Fig. 1. The topic of conversation varies over the course of a conversation.

6.2 Using Speech Acts to Determine Deliberative Discussion, and Individual Understanding and Confusion

To test our hypotheses that a) speech acts are indicators of deliberative discussion, and, that b) speech acts are indicators of learner understanding, several steps are required. The first step is to develop a coding system that captures the desired information about learner activity and code the dialogs along these measures, then correlate codes with speech acts to ensure that speech acts do indicate the presence of that activity, and finally determine the predictive validity of the speech acts using cross-validation. As we coded the dialogs, we noticed that the set of sentences containing evidence of understanding and the set of sentences containing evidence of deliberative discussion overlapped somewhat.

We coded each line of five dialogs on two dimensions; first we coded for evidence of individual understanding or individual confusion. For example, any statement that proposed a potential solution step, or that elaborated upon, or agreed or disagreed with, or posed an alternative to a postulated solution step, was taken as an indication that the learner had some understanding of the content pertaining to the topic. Statements that requested explanations or explicitly expressed lack of understanding were treated as indicators that the learner did not yet understand the topic. Apart from attempting to determine the topic of each sentence, the propositional content of the dialogs was ignored.

Besides learner understanding, we also coded indicators of deliberative discussion. As a starting point, we took any statement that proposed a potential solution step, that continued another's proposal, or posed an alternative to a postulated solution step, and statements that explicitly agreed or disagreed with someone, as evidence of deliberative discussion. Learners proposed more than one potential solution to many topics, so the system could note the presence or absence of multiple potential solutions, but none of the groups exhibited the undesirable discussion techniques of debate or negotiation of fixed competing preferences, so we cannot yet compare the characteristics of deliberative discussion with these.

The coding standard was developed and refined iteratively. We first defined a tentative standard; two coders independently coded a dialog using it, then compared the codings, jointly refined the coding standard to address the uncertainties and discrepancies in interpretation, and recoded the dialog. After two iterations on each of several log files the standard settled down and the coders concurred on more than 95% of the codings. However, we would expect that the dialog codings of independent coders using the final standard, without any joint review, to have a somewhat lower correlation.

The next step was to correlate codings with speech acts, since the goal is to use speech acts as indicators of learner behavior for building student models. The overall correlation of speech acts to the codings for each line of dialog was 75%. However, many speech acts occur relatively infrequently, so that their occurrence predicts a coding with 100% accuracy. The more frequently occurring speech acts are used in a wider variety of contexts and their correlation to specific codings is correspondingly less, at 68%. This correlation could perhaps be improved by replacing frequently used speech acts with more finely-grained ones to more precisely discern the speaker's intent.

Once we knew that speech acts were potentially suitable indicators of the coded behaviors, the next step was to evaluate the generality of the correlations. For this we used cross-validation, that is, we iteratively combined the data from all the conversations but one and compared the combined result to the remaining conversation. The average correlation for these comparisons was 0.74, from which we may conclude that the relationship of speech acts to codings is relatively consistent across groups, so that the values determined by experiment from some groups will be valid for others.

7   Future Work: The Student Model and the Intelligent Agent

We tentatively assume that there are two equally important domains of knowledge, OOA&D and deliberative discussion, and that the student model consists of a long term part and a short term part. The long term student model of domain knowledge consists of some sort of scoring mechanism on each element of the domain knowledge and the domain knowledge is organized in hierarchical fashion, with nodes higher in the tree representing topics and summarizing student knowledge of the lower, more elemental nodes.

The short term model consists of the state of the solution of the current exercise and each student's contribution to it. The collaboration model will track each student's collaborative contribution to each topic and to the exercise as a whole. Upon completion of each exercise, students' scores on both types of knowledge will be used to update the long-term model.

The agent will combine its knowledge of the completeness and correctness of each topic of the current exercise with its assessment of the learners' deliberation processes around that topic to make intervention decisions regarding the quality of the solution and the nature of the learners' small group interactions.

The agent will also combine its knowledge of the completeness and correctness of each topic of the exercise with its assessment of each individual learner's capability to perform that step to make intervention decisions either to further improve the learner's skill in that topic (either in the current exercise or in a later one) or to move on to another topic.

Briefly, the automated tutor will

- Attempt to keep the conversation coherent, focusing one topic at a time, and keeping all learners on the same topic, while still permitting learner control and flexibility in terms of topic selection,
- Help the learners reach a complete correct solution by encouraging further discussion of incomplete or incorrect topics,
- Encourage deliberative discussion to produce high-quality knowledge, deeply embedded in learners' cognitive structures,
- Encourage each learner to increase their knowledge of each topic by measuring their degree of understanding and coaching them to interact with their peers to increase their knowledge.

8   Concluding Remarks

The presence of a chat tool in a CLE permits learner-learner interaction that is not formalized and therefore is beyond the capability of the student modeling module to interpret. Nevertheless, topic detection by means of keywords and speech act detection by means of sentence openers, as well as speaker and timing information, provide information that allows the student modeling module to make useful inferences.

These results are preliminary and any conclusions must be tentative, however it appears that even without high-quality natural language understanding, it is possible to extract sufficient meaning from text chat to infer the topic of discussion, the deliberative nature of learners' interactions, and the level of individual learner's understanding. When these data are combined with data from GUI events where learners' actions are constrained and interpretable as with conventional intelligent tutoring systems, it appears that detailed student models can be developed and an intelligent agent can be activated.

References

1.   Soller, A., Goodman, B., Linton, F., and Gaimari, R. (1998). Promoting effective peer interaction in an intelligent collaborative learning environment. Proceedings of the Fourth International Conference on Intelligent Tutoring Systems (ITS 98), San Antonio, TX, 186–195.
2.   Goodman, B., Hitzeman, J., Linton, F., and Ross, H. (Manuscript in preparation). Towards Intelligent Agents for Collaborative Learning: Recognizing the Roles of Dialogue Participants.
3.   Lesgold, A., Katz, S., Greenberg, L., Hughes, E., and Eggan, G. (1992). Extensions of intelligent tutoring paradigms to support collaborative learning. In S. Dijkstra, H. Krammer, J. van Merrienboer (Eds.), Instructional Models in Computer-Based Learning Environments. Berlin: Springer-Verlag, 291–311.

4. Mühlenbrock, M., Tewissen, F., and Hoppe, H. U. (1998). A Framework System for Intelligent Support in Open Distributed Learning Environments. International Journal of Artificial Intelligence in Education, 9, pp. 256–274.
5. Jonassen, D., and Land, S. (2000). Theoretical Foundations of Learning Environments. Mahwah, NJ: Erlbaum.
6. Chi, M. (1996). Constructing Self-Explanations and Scaffolded Explanations in Tutoring. Applied Cognitive Psychology, Vol. 10, S33–S49.
7. Waibel, A., Bett, M., Finke, M., and Stiefelhagen, R. (1998). Meeting browser: Tracking and summarizing meetings. In D. E. M. Penrose (Ed.) Proceedings of the Broadcast News Transcription and Understanding Workshop (Lansdowne, Virginia, Feb. 1998). San Francisco: Morgan Kaufmann, pp. 281–28.
8. Corbett, A.T. and Anderson, J.R. (1989). Feedback timing and student control in the LISP Intelligent Tutoring System. Proceedings of the Fourth International Conference on AI and Education, 64–72.
9. Anderson, J. R., Boyle, C. F., Corbett, A., and Lewis, M. (1990). Cognitive modeling and intelligent tutoring. Artificial Intelligence, 42, 7–49.
10. Rehg, W., McBurney, P. and Parsons, S. (2001): Computer decision support systems for public argumentation: criteria for assessment. In H. V. Hansen, C. W. Tindale, J. A. Blair and R. H. Johnson (Eds.), Argumentation and its Applications. Proceedings of the Fourth Biennial Conference of the Ontario Society for the Study of Argumentation (OSSA 2001).
11. McManus, M. and Aiken, R. (1995). Monitoring computer-based problem solving. Journal of Artificial Intelligence in Education, 6(4), 307–336.
12. Searle, J. (1996). A Taxonomy of Illocutionary Acts. Reprinted in A. Martinich (Ed.) The Philosophy of Language. New York: Oxford University Press, (3rd edition).
13. Anderson, J. R. (1990). The Adaptive Character of Thought. Mahwah, NJ: Erlbaum.

A Teaching Model Exploiting Cognitive Conflict Driven by a Bayesian Network

K. Stacey, E. Sonenberg, A. Nicholson, T. Boneh, and V. Steinle

The University of Melbourne, Parkville, 3010, Australia
l.sonenberg@unimelb.edu.au

Abstract. This paper describes the design and construction of a teaching model in an adaptive tutoring system designed to supplement normal instruction and aimed at changing students' conceptions of decimal numbers. The teaching model exploits cognitive conflict, incorporating a model of student misconceptions and task performance, represented by a Bayesian network. Preliminary evaluation of the implemented system shows that the misconception diagnosis and performance prediction performed by the BN reasoning engine supports the item sequencing and help presentation strategies required for teaching based on cognitive conflict. Field trials indicate the system provokes good long term learning in students who would otherwise be likely to retain misconceptions.

1   Introduction

This paper describes the design and construction of the teaching model in an adaptive tutoring system designed to diagnose and modify students' conceptions of decimal numbers. The approach is of interest because it is designed primarily to bring about conceptual change, rather than teach new facts or procedural skills. In general terms, the teaching strategy is designed to provide an individual student with a sequence of tasks that (a) engage their interest (hence the use of computer games), (b) expose them to a wide range of topic specific task types (so fully exploring their domain understanding), and (c) vary in difficulty – with "difficulty" individualised to the student (by exploiting the rich model of student misconceptions). Difficulty is varied to raise a student's awareness that they have something to learn (by including tasks they are likely to get wrong) while keeping the student involved (by ensuring a student is not exposed to too many tasks they are likely to get wrong).

When students come to realise that there is something wrong with their existing interpretation of a situation, *cognitive conflict* occurs, and creating such conflict in the learner is one strategy that has been recommended for situations where students need to move from one way of thinking to another [1,2]. Bell and colleagues [1,3] conducted a series of studies examining teaching where conceptual change is required, one of which also involved the decimals domain, and showed that classroom teaching generating cognitive conflict was much more effective than "positive-only" teaching (which focuses on presentation of correct information only), especially when measured over the long term.

P. Brusilovsky et al. (Eds.): UM 2003, LNAI 2702, pp. 352–362, 2003.

Despite its promise, this teaching method has not been adopted as normal teaching practice, at least partly because of the difficulty of reliably generating usefully wrong answers. Our machine-based system can ensure that student errors are sufficiently frequent to make them realise there is something to be learned, by posing questions that, based on the system's current student model, the student is likely to get wrong. Further, the immediate feedback and the putative authority of the computer make it likely that students will take notice of wrong answers in a computer game. These factors should ensure the system avoids a common problem with educational games [4], whereby they often do not generate the constructive reasoning required for learning.

Our teaching model incorporates a model of student misconception and task performance, represented by a Bayesian network (BN). BNs have previous success in intelligent tutoring applications [5,6,7,8]. They offer an intuitive graphical representation with efficient probabilistic algorithms for updating beliefs in the light of new evidence. In our case, the beliefs are the estimates of the probabilities that a given student has a particular misconception or will demonstrate certain knowledge when playing the games. Others have shown that user modelling with this technology can be very effective in domains where domain knowledge can be decomposed into small observable components with known interdependencies, e.g. [9]. We use a BN to model the interactions between a student's misconceptions, their game playing abilities and their performance on a range of test items. Building the student model from misconceptions (c.f. [10]) rather than in terms of gaps in correct pieces of domain knowledge, (c.f. [5]), is only viable because of the nature of the domain and the extensive research on student understanding in the domain. The information provided by the BN reasoning engine is used for diagnosis, assessment and control of the teaching.

In Section 2 we explain some important features of the domain and describe the extensive research on student thinking about the domain that provides the basis of a well-structured student model. The creation of the adaptive system has required developing a teaching model, described in Section 3, that draws upon diagnosis of student (mis)conceptions, presents students with tasks that make them aware of their lack of knowledge and provides information to assist them in constructing correct and integrated understanding. Selecting the frequency of items to get right and to get wrong is part of the teaching model. Results from field trials of the system are given in Section 4, which indicate good success with children who have developed misconceptions through normal school instruction.

2   The Teaching Context

To understand the meaning and size of numbers written using a decimal point includes knowing about place value columns, the ordering of numbers by size and the value of digits. Although this is a topic plagued by misconceptions, very often students don't know they harbour them. A prime task of any teaching strategy is therefore to make sure that students know whether or not they do really understand. Our data on students' thinking has been gathered by researchers in the classroom from carefully planned and conducted interviews; within the classroom, a teacher is rarely able to gather such information. The system has the potential to diagnose and target an individual's wrong way of thinking about decimals, providing a invaluable tool for the classroom teacher.

Students' understanding of decimal numeration has been mapped using a short test, the Decimal Comparison Test (DCT), where the student is asked to choose the larger number from each of 24 pairs of decimals [11]. The pairs of decimals are carefully chosen so that from the patterns of responses, students' (mis)understanding can be diagnosed as belonging to one of a number of classifications. These classifications have been identified manually, based on extensive research [11,12,13,14]. The crucial aspects are that misconceptions are prevalent, that students' behaviour is very often highly consistent, and that misconceptions can be identified from patterns amongst simples clues.

We describe the task of comparing two decimal numbers as a conceptual task, rather than a procedural task even though there are two apparently simple algorithms for it. One can compare digits from left to right, or add zeros to equalize length and then compare as whole numbers. For students who use either of these procedures, systematic errors can arise as explained by Van Lehn's repair theory [15]. However, some students with certain misconceptions do not try to apply either procedure. Instead they conceptualise the decimal part of a number in a quite different way and so they apply procedures for other mathematical entities (e.g. fractions). For this reason, we say that the decimal comparison task tests conceptual rather than procedural knowledge.

About a dozen misconceptions have been identified [11]. Table 1 shows the rules the domain experts originally used to classify students based on their response to 6 types of DCT test items: H = High number correct (e.g. 4 or 5 out of 5), L = Low number correct (e.g. 0 or 1 out of 5), with '.' indicating that any performance level is observable for that item type by that student class other than the combinations seen above. Most misconceptions are based on false analogies, which are sometimes embellished by isolated learned facts. For example, many younger students think 0.4 is smaller than 0.35 because there are 4 parts (of unspecified size, for these students) in the first number and 35 parts in the second. However, these 'whole number thinkers' (LWH, Table 1) get many questions right, e.g. 5.736 compared with 5.62, with the same erroneous thinking. So-called 'reciprocal thinking' students (SRN, Table 1) choose 0.4 as greater than 0.35 but for the wrong reason, as they draw an analogy between fractions and decimals and use knowledge that 1/4 is greater than 1/35.

The key to designing the DCT was the identification of "item types". An item type is a set of items which a student with any misconception should answer consistently (either all right or all wrong). The definition of item types depends on both the mathematical properties of the item and the psychology of the learners. In practice, the definition is also pragmatic – the number of theoretically different item types can be very large, but the extent to which diagnostic information should be squeezed from them is a matter of judgement. We note that the fine misconception classifications have been "grouped" by the experts into a coarse

Table 1. Response patterns expected from students with different misconceptions.

Coarse Class	Fine Class	Item type (with sample item)					
		1	2	3	4	5	6
		0.4	5.736	4.7	0.452	0.4	0.42
		0.35	5.62	4.08	0.45	0.3	0.35
A	ATE	H	H	H	H	H	H
	AMO	H	H	H	L	H	H
	AU	H	H	.	.	.	.
L	LWH	L	H	L	H	H	H
	LZE	L	H	H	H	H	H
	LRV	L	H	L	H	H	L
	LU	L	H	.	.	.	.
S	SDF	H	L	H	L	H	H
	SRN	H	L	H	L	L	L
	SU	H	L	.	.	.	.
U	MIS	L	L	L	L	L	L
	UN	.	.	.	.	.	.

classification – L (think longer decimals are larger numbers), S (shorter is larger), A (correct on straightforward items (Types 1 & 2)) and U (other). The LU, SU and AU "catch-all" classifications for students who on their answers on Type 1 and 2 items behave like others in their coarse classification, but differ on other item types. These and the UNs may be students behaving consistently according to an unknown misconception, or students who are not following any consistent interpretation.

The computer game genre was chosen to provide children with an experience different from, but complementary to, normal classroom instruction and to appeal across the target age range (Grades 5 to 10). Each game focuses on one aspect of decimal numeration, thinly disguised by a story line. In the "Hidden Numbers" game students are confronted with two decimal numbers with digits hidden behind closed doors; the task is to find which number is the larger by opening as few doors as possible. Requiring similar knowledge to that required for success on the DCT, the game also highlights the place value property that the most significant digits are those to the left. The game "Flying Photographer" requires students to "photograph" an animal by clicking when an "aeroplane" passes a specified number on a numberline. This task also requires understanding of decimal numeration and can be used to contribute to diagnosis of misconceptions. These games, together with two other games Decimaliens and Number-Between (see [16] for details), address several of the different tasks required of an integrated knowledge of decimal numeration based on the principles of place value. It is possible for a student to be good at one game or the diagnostic test, but not good at another; emerging knowledge is often compartmentalised.

3   The Teaching Model

The high-level architecture of our system is shown in Figure 1. The BN is initialised with a generic model of student understanding of decimal numeration constructed using the DCT results from a large sample of students [17]. The network can also be tailored to an individual student using their age or results from a short online DCT. During a student's use of the system, the BN is given information about the correctness of the student's answers to different item types encountered in the computer games. The student's responses are used as evidence to perform ongoing diagnosis of student misconceptions, to predict the student's performance on other item types, and to assess which item type answers will be most useful in improving on the current diagnosis. This information is, in turn, used by a controller module, together with the specified sequencing tactics (see below), to select items to present to the student, to decide whether additional help presentation is required, or to decide when the user has reached expertise and should move to another game. The controller module also makes a current assessment of the student available to the teacher, and reports on the overall effectiveness of the adaptive system.

The BN representing the student model was constructed through a combination of elicitation from the domain experts and automated methods. [18] gives a detailed description of the construction process, the alternative network structures and parameters considered, and the qualitative and quantitative network validation and evaluation undertaken. Here we shall describe briefly the BN being used in the deployed ITS (more details are given in [16]).

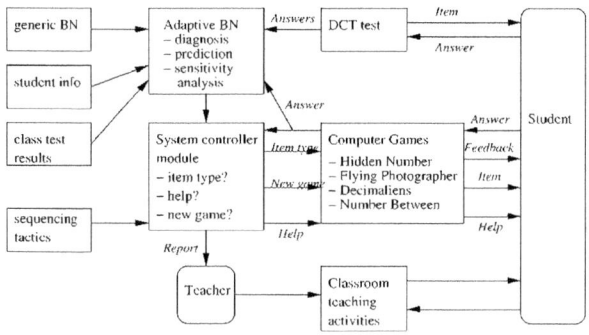

Fig. 1. Intelligent Tutoring System Architecture

The network structure for the DCT, together with the Hidden Number and Flying Photographer games, is shown in Figure 2. Student misconceptions are represented on two levels, by two variables. The coarseClass and fineClass nodes can take as values the misconception types identified by the domain expert (see Table 1, columns 1 and 2). Each DCT item type has a corresponding variable in the BN, representing student performance (correct or incorrect answer) on items of that type. These type nodes are observation nodes, where entering evidence for a type node should update the posterior probability of a student having a particular misconception. An arc was added from the fineClass node to each of the `type` nodes, showing qualitatively that a student's answer will depend on their misconception. A conditional probability table associated with each node specifies this influence quantitatively. No connections were added between any of the `type` nodes, reflecting the experts' intuition that a student's answers for different item types are independent, given the fine classification. The "HN" nodes relate to the Hidden Numbers game, with evidence entered for the number of doors opened before an answer was given (`HN_nod`), and a measure of the "goodness of order" in opening doors (`HN_gos`). The root node for the Hidden Number game subnet reflects a player's game ability – in this case door opening "efficiency" (`HN_eff`). The "FPH" nodes relate to the Flying Photographer game. The node `FPH_ls` records evidence when students have to place a long number, which is small in size, such as 0.23456. As noted above, LWH students are likely to make an error on this task, but the SRN students are likely to be correct. The other nodes perform similar functions, with the root node `FPH_pa` reflecting overall game playing ability. BNs for the other two games are constructed according to similar principles.

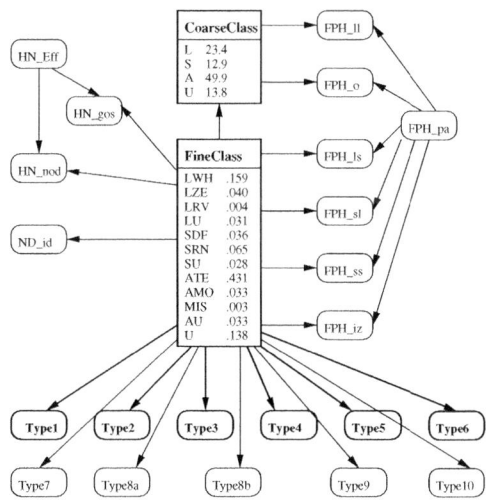

Fig. 2. BN representation of the student model.

A well recognised obstacle to using numerical measures of uncertainty is the identification of appropriate prior and conditional probabilities to be used in the model. Our BN priors are available from extensive longitudinal data [11]. Estimates for the required conditional probabilities were based on the classification rules in Table 1. A student with a particular misconception may not always behave precisely in the predicted manner. We model this uncertainty by allowing a small probability of a careless mistake on any one item. More difficult is to model situations where the experts do not know how a student will behave (i.e. where the experts specified '.' for the classifications LU, SU, AU and UN in Table 1).

We modelled this by using 0.5 in the conditional probability table, representing 50/50 that a student in the classification will get that item correct.

Given the model, and given evidence about answers to one or more item types, the Bayesian belief updating algorithm then performs diagnosis; it calculates the reverse probabilities, that is, that a student with these behaviours has a particular misconception. Changes in the beliefs in the various misconceptions are in turn propagated within the network to perform prediction; the updating algorithm calculates the new probabilities of a student getting other item types right or wrong. After each set of evidence is added and belief updating performed, the student model stored within the network is updated, by changing the misconception node priors. Updating the network in this way as the student plays the game (or games) allows changes in students' thinking and skills to be tracked. The identification of the misconception with the highest probability provides the best estimation of the students' current understanding.

The major proactive task of the system controller module is to decide which item types the user should be presented with next in the game and whether the student should try the item with or without help. The algorithm for item type selection incorporates several features of the teaching model described earlier. For example, users are presented with examples of all item types at some stage during each session. After the network has been initialised with the results of the short diagnostic test, students meeting a new game can be presented with items which they will be very likely to get correct by using the predictive capacity of the Bayesian updating algorithm described above; this is to ensure they have understood the rules and purposes of the game. If the probabilities of competing hypotheses about the student's misconception classification are close, the system gives priority to diagnosis and proposes a further item to be given to the user. By employing the value of information measures provided by the Netica BN software,[1] the user can be presented with an item that is most likely to distinguish between competing hypotheses. Perhaps the most interesting proactive use of the network is to select subsequent items in an appropriate sequence for the learner. Human teachers generally select questions for students beginning with "easy" items and progressing to harder items, while a teaching strategy that aimed to maximise cognitive conflict might use items that the student is predicted to get wrong. Alternatively, perhaps to keep motivation higher by ensuring some success, the sequence may alternate easy and hard items. The current implementation of the system allows comparison of different sequencing tactics: presenting the hard items first, presenting the easy items first, and presenting easy and hard items alternatively.

In addition to raising the student's awareness that they may have something to learn, we also incorporated two forms of teaching into the games: clear feedback and visual scaffolding. For example, in the Flying Photographer, where students have to place numbers on number lines, feedback is given after each placement: if the position is incorrect a sad red face appears at the point, whereas the correct position is (finally) marked by a happy green face. In this game, the

---

[1] www.norsys.com.au, Netica's "sensitivity to findings" function.

visual scaffolding marks intermediate numbers on the interval, for example, when a student has twice failed to place a number correctly on the interval [0,1], the intermediate values 0.1, 0.2, 0.3, ..., 0.9 appear for this and the next item.

4   Evaluation

All components of the complete system have now been field-tested. The games have been trialed with individual students holding known misconceptions and their responses and learning have been tracked [19]. This has refined the design of the games and of the visual scaffolding and led to the decision to provide the visual scaffolding automatically. Initial trials indicate that this is a satisfactory approach, although students do not always look at the help provided or understand what it means without teacher intervention. Feedback to the students' own answers seems generally to be examined closely and so the games provide this in all cases. There is clearly some conflict between wishing to diagnose a students' thinking and wishing to teach, but in most circumstances, the latter takes priority so help and feedback should be offered.

The BN structure for misconception diagnosis and the conditional probabilities assigned to each event have been tested by comparing the results of by-hand diagnosis according to Table 1 with the diagnosis by the system on the results of 2432 students who had completed the DCT. The results showed from 80-90% agreement between the network and the by-hand classification, depending on the particular parameter setting (see [18] for details). It is important to note here that the by-hand classification is only a best-guess of what a student is thinking – it is not possible to be certain of the "truth" in a short timeframe.

The complete system has also been field tested with 25 students in Grades 5 and 6, who had persistent misconceptions after normal school instruction (see [16] for details). Students worked with a partner (almost always with the same misconception) for up to 30 minutes, without adult intervention. The observer recorded their conversations, which were linked to computer results and analysed to see where students learned or missed learning opportunities and how cognitive conflict was involved. Long term conceptual change was measured by re-administering the DCT about three weeks later. Students played in pairs so that the observer could, without intervention, monitor their thinking as revealed by their conversations as they played the games.

Ten students tested as experts on the delayed post-test, indicating significant progress. Seven students demonstrated improvement while eight retained their original misconception. There were some instances where students learned from the visual scaffolding of the help screens, but active teacher intervention seems required for most students to benefit fully from these. Very frequently, students learned by observing and discussing with their partners, but they did not always learn the same things at the same time. This means that the computer diagnosis was not necessarily meaningful for both students so that the item type selection may not perform as designed for either student. This disadvantage needs to be weighed against the benefits of working with a partner.

Feedback provided by the games provoked learning in two ways. In some instances students added new information to their conceptual field, without addressing misconceptions (e.g. learned that 0 in the tenths column makes a number small, without really changing basic whole number thinking). In other instances the feedback provoked cognitive conflict and sometimes this was resolved within the session, resulting in a significant change from a misconception to expertise, maintained at the delayed post-test. The item type selection was set to alternate between "easy" and "hard" items for these field trials but this experiment indicated that it gave too many easy items. Following up an error with another hard item of the same and other types may be more effective. The real-time updated diagnosis by the system of the student's thinking patterns was (generally) consistent with the observer's opinion. Discrepancies between classifications and the delayed post-test were tracked to known limitations of the DCT, which could not diagnose an unusual misconception prevalent in that class.

On balance, the system seems to be a useful supplement to class instruction. By providing a wide range of item types, students' understanding is probed in a way which teachers cannot do without extremely detailed planning. Making mistakes in the games does provoke cognitive conflict in students and this can be partially resolved within the games. The system, however, does not provide the thorough instruction in place value that is necessary to produce real understanding; this has to come from a teacher for young students.

5   Conclusions

We have described the considerations behind the design of the teaching model for a system to supplement classroom instruction in the domain of decimal numeration – an important topic, not well grasped by significant numbers of students. Distinctive features of the teaching model reflect particular aspects of the domain – student misconceptions abound, there is new body of research expertise surrounding the types of misconceptions and their identification, and teaching is aimed at conceptual change.

The teaching model, based around the stimulation and resolution of cognitive conflict, includes four purpose built computer games and a diagnostic test based on the research literature. It uses a Bayesian network to identify when to provide feedback and what activities to select next. The detailed design of the teaching model draws heavily on research into student misconceptions in this domain. The keys to exploiting this research are that item types can be identified fairly simply and one can introduce item sequencing tactics, and the ability to thoroughly explore a student's understanding by use of the full range of item types. Further, relationships between student behaviour on particular item types and their domain understanding can be embedded in the teaching model. So, as the student interacts with it, the system can adapt its presentation to the perceived needs of the individual student. Exploiting this research in a teaching approach accessible in the classroom, is arguably only feasible in a machine-delivered format because of the fine-grained pedagogical content knowledge required, and yet is likely to be best suited as a supplement to conventional instruction because of the limitations of current machine-based teaching methods.

From a modelling perspective, we found that using a Bayesian network as the underlying reasoning engine has a number of advantages. The availability of priors from longitudinal studies ensures the system starts with a usable generic student model. The incremental incorporation of a student's answers is achieved by adding evidence and performing belief updating. This updating provides misconception diagnosis information, as well as predictions of the student's performance on other items required for sequencing strategies. The BN structure was based around fragments for the different games, which facilitated the incremental construction and testing of the model, and confirms that the technology can be used for user modelling in bigger domains, as long as the domain knowledge can be decomposed into tractable fragments with known inter-dependencies [9].

Further empirical evaluation of individual design decisions and modifying the sequencing tactics is planned. We hope that further work with the system will also shed light on generic questions concerning provision of support and feedback, and other broad issues in the design of intelligent systems for education.

Acknowledgements. Thanks to Elise Dettmann for early work on the architecture, Jenny Flynn and Sally Helm for conducting field trials, and to Brent Boerlage for help with Netica. The project has been supported by grants from the Australian Research Council.

References

1. Bell, A.: Principles for the design of teaching. Educational Studies in Mathematics **24** (1993) 5–34
2. Light, P., Glachan, M.: Facilitation of individual problem solving through peer interaction. Educational Psychology **5** (1985) 217–225
3. Swan, M.: Teaching Decimal Place Value: A Comparative Study of 'Conflict' and 'Positive Only' Approaches. Shell Centre for Mathematical Ed., Nott. Univ. (1983)
4. Klawe, M.: When does the use of computer games and other interactive multimedia software help students learn mathematics? In: NCTM Standards 2000 Technology Conference. (1998)
5. Conati, C., Gertner, A., VanLehn, K., Druzdzel, M.: On-line student modeling for coached problem solving using Bayesian Networks. In: UM97 – Proc. of the 6th Int. Conf. on User Modeling. (1997) 231–242
6. Conati, C., Gertner, A., VanLehn, K.: Using Bayesian Networks to manage uncertainty in student modeling. User Modeling and User-Adapted Interaction **12** (2002) 371–417
7. Mayo, M., Mitrovic, A.: Optimising ITS behaviour with Bayesian networks and decision theory. Int. Journal of AI in Education **12** (2001) 124–153
8. VanLehn, V., Niu, Z.: Bayesian student modelling, user interfaces and feedback: a sensitivity analysis. Int. Journal of AI in Education **12** (2001) 154–184
9. Horvitz, E., Breese, J., Heckerman, D., Hovel, D., Rommelse, K.: The Lumiere project: Bayesian user modeling for inferring the goals and needs of software users. In: Proc. of the 14th Conf. on Uncertainty in AI. (1998) 256–265

10. Sleeman, D.: Mis-generalisation: an explanation of observed mal-rules. In: Proc. of the 6th Annual Conf. of the Cognitive Science Society. (1984) 51–56
11. Stacey, K., Steinle, V.: A longitudinal study of childen's thinking about decimals: a preliminary analysis. In Zaslavsky, O., ed.: Proc. of the 23rd Conf. of the Int. Group for the Psych. of Math. Education. Volume 4., Haifa, PME (1999) 233–241
12. Resnick, L.B., Nesher, P., Leonard, F., Magone, M., Omanson, S., Peled, I.: Conceptual bases of arithmetic errors: The case of decimal fractions. Journal for Research in Mathematics Education **20** (1989) 8–27
13. Sackur-Grisvard, C., Leonard, F.: Intermediate cognitive organization in the process of learning a mathematical concept: The order of positive decimal numbers. Cognition and Instruction **2** (1985) 157–174
14. Stacey, K., Steinle, V.: Refining the classification of students' interpretations of decimal notation. Hiroshima Journal of Mathematics Education **6** (1998) 49–69
15. Brown, J., van Lehn, K.: Repair theory: A generative theory of bugs in procedural skills. Cognitive Science **4** (1980) 379–426
16. Boneh, T., Nicholson, A., Sonenberg, L., Stacey, K., Steinle, V.: Decsys: An intelligent tutoring system for decimal numeration. Technical Report 134, School of CSSE, Monash University, Australia (2003)
17. Steinle, V., Stacey, K.: The incidence of misconceptions of decimal notation amongst students in grades 5 to 10. In Kanes, C., Goos, M., Warren, E., eds.: Teaching Mathematics in New Times, MERGA 21. MERGA (1998) 548–555
18. Nicholson, A., Boneh, T., Wilkin, T., Stacey, K., L.Sonenberg, Steinle, V.: A case study in knowledge discovery and elicitation in an intelligent tutoring application. In: Proc. of the 17th Conf. on Uncertainty in AI, Seattle (2001) 386–394
19. McIntosh, J., Stacey, K., Tromp, C., Lightfoot, D.: Designing constructivist computer games for teaching about decimal numbers. In Bana, J., Chapman, A., eds.: Mathematics Education Beyond 2000. Proc. of the 23rd Annual Conf. of the Mathematics Education Research Group of Australasia, Freemantle (2000) 409–416

Towards Intelligent Agents for Collaborative Learning: Recognizing the Roles of Dialogue Participants

Bradley Goodman, Janet Hitzeman, Frank Linton, and Helen Ross

The MITRE Corporation, 202 Burlington Road, Bedford, MA 01730 USA
{bgoodman, hitz, linton, hross}@mitre.org

Abstract. Our goal is to build and evaluate a web-based, collaborative distance-learning system that will allow groups of students to interact with each other remotely and with an intelligent agent that will aid them in their learning. The agent will follow the discussion and interact when it detects learning trouble of some sort, such as confusion about the problem they are working on or a participant who is dominating the discussion or not interacting with the other participants. In order to recognize problems in the dialogue, we are first examining the role that a participant is playing as the dialogue progresses. In this paper we discuss group interaction during collaborative learning, our representation of participant roles, and the statistical model we are using to determine the role being played by a participant at any point in the dialogue.

1 Introduction

Classroom learning improves considerably when students participate in structured learning activities with small groups of peers [2]. Peers can encourage each other to reflect on what they are learning and to articulate their thinking, which enhances the learning process. When students try to learn a topic outside a small-group oriented classroom, they lose the opportunity to interact with other students, which can impede learning. The educational value of student collaboration has led to the development of computer-supported collaborative learning tools [5, 6]. These tools enrich learning in a setting that encourages students to communicate with their peers while solving problems on-line. In previous work on distance learning, either a student is given an electronic agent to interact with as a peer [3], or is allowed to work with students in other locations through a collaborative system [4]. Our current work combines these approaches by allowing students to work both with a collaborative system and with an electronic peer. The overall goal is to provide an electronic peer that can co-exist in cyberspace with human collaborators and interact as a partner to promote effective collaborative learning and problem solving. This approach not only allows for collaboration at a distance, but also avoids the potential problem of learning being inhibited because no one is taking a directive role, encouraging participation, or asking questions to get the others to think. The peer monitors the discussion and interacts with the participants when it detects learning trouble of some sort, such as confusion about the problem they are working on, or a participant who is dominating the discussion or not interacting with the other participants. When a problem is

P. Brusilovsky et al. (Eds.): UM 2003, LNAI 2702, pp. 363–367, 2003.

encountered, the peer puts forth a question or comment intended to facilitate learning or to improve the interaction and help steer the group back on track.

The current focus of our work is on automatically detecting such learning problems. The actions of participants, with respect to chat and workspace tools, provide an initial indicator of discussion and progress towards completing an assigned task or dealing with an obstacle. The roles of participants can provide a secondary indicator. We will discuss our use of participant roles as indicators of group activity, how we determine them statistically, and our plans for moving on to the next step.

2 Research Approach

Our work is an outgrowth of research in both the intelligent tutoring system (ITS) and computer-supported collaborative learning (CSCL) communities [4, 5]. We first developed a simulated learning companion capable of acting as a peer in an intelligent tutoring system [3]. The presence of the learning companion can help ensure the availability of a capable collaborator to enrich learning through the promotion of reflection and articulation in the human student. A learning companion can help a student reflect on thinking by critiquing, questioning, or evaluating particular problem-solving steps. Similarly, the student and learning companion may articulate those steps through further explanation or elaboration.

Our research in learning companions also motivated us to investigate collaborative learning among students more closely. We studied the dynamics of collaborative learning groups by observing students working together to solve a common problem in software design using the Object Modeling Technique (OMT) methodology. We found that students learning in small groups encourage each other to ask questions, explain and justify their opinions, articulate their reasoning, and elaborate and reflect upon their knowledge, thereby motivating and improving learning. These benefits, however, are only achieved by active and well-functioning learning teams. Placing students in a group and assigning them a task does not guarantee that the students will engage in effective collaborative learning behavior. While some peer groups seem to interact productively, others struggle to maintain a balance of participation, leadership, understanding, and encouragement. We also observed students stepping in and out of particular instructional roles that helped the group move forward towards solving the problem. These roles, such as Questioner or Facilitator, fit in well with research in group dynamics [1].

We followed our initial study with the development of a collaborative learning environment for OMT. Our goal was to provide a web-based environment that would permit us to analyze peer-to-peer dialogue and tool actions in an attempt to identify the strength and weaknesses of a group's interaction. The collaborative environment, shown in Figure 1, employed a sentence opener-based chat interface and a shared OMT workspace tool. The sentence-opener interface allowed the conversational act underlying each student utterance to be logged; the shared OMT workspace tool permitted student tool actions to be recorded. We ran an experiment in which groups of three subjects used our collaborative environment to solve a software design problem with OMT. The results of our experiment demonstrate the potential of conversational acts to identify, for example, the distinction between a balanced, supportive group and an unbalanced, unsupportive group.

Soller and Lesgold [7] extend our initial research. They point out that supporting group learning requires understanding the process of collaborative learning. This understanding entails a fine-grained sequential analysis of the group activity and conversation. Conversational acts provided the representation for communication between collaborators. They discuss the merits of applying different computational approaches for modeling collaborative learning activities such as the transfer of new knowledge between collaborators. We adopted their revised version of our CSCL software but focused on a different aspect of collaboration and chose a different modeling technique for our research.

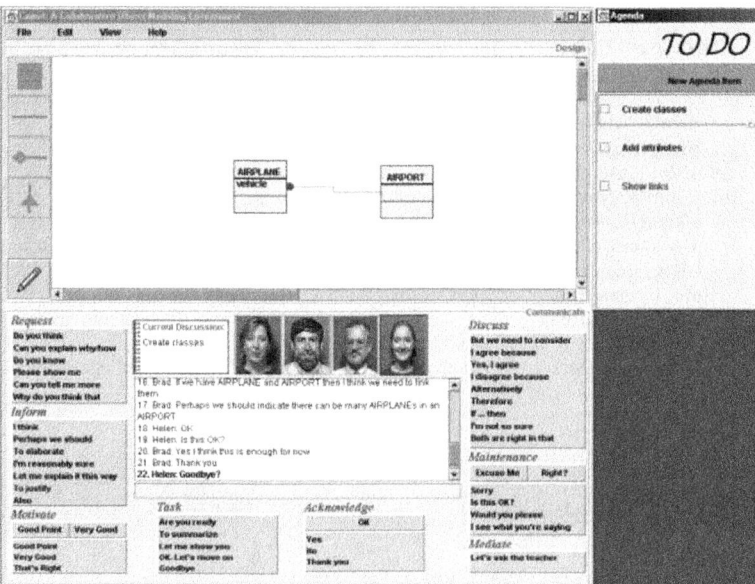

Fig. 1. Collaborative object modeling technique environment

3   Research Method

Our goal in this research was to conduct an experiment to reveal the ways participants in a collaborative learning task interact and the factors that govern those interactions. We wanted to see if (1) the instructional roles played by members of the group could be deduced from machine-inferable factors about the collaboration and (2) whether the presence or absence of particular instructional roles indicated the effectiveness of the learning. Our hypothesis is that the presence or absence of particular roles is a powerful indicator of the status of the on-going learning process. The work we describe here outlines the data we are collecting on the collaboration and the role identification model we are constructing.

The CSCL system, shown in Figure 1, provides a sentence-opener chat interface, an OMT workspace, and a new agenda tool. The agenda tool lists high-level goals to be achieved. Dialogues were collected at the University of Pittsburgh and the MITRE Corporation to provide a corpus for study. Our goal is to identify problem-solving roles portrayed by the group members during the session to see if they might indicate progress or lack thereof towards successfully completing the exercise. This undertaking entails examining the relationship between conversational acts and problem-solving roles. The conversational acts underlying the subjects' chats are automatically collected by the sentence opener interface. The participant roles required hand-coding by the experimenters.

We chose a set of roles developed by Benne and Sheats [1], and modified them slightly to suit the type of dialogues the system elicits, i.e., dialogues involving the use of a whiteboard and a problem-solving task. A subset is shown in Table 1.

Table 1. Group Problem-Solving Roles

Participant Roles	Description
Init (initiator)	Proposing goals, plans of action, or activities. These must be new goals rather than subgoals or elaborations of goals.
Eval (evaluator)	Expressing judgments on a plan or a statement
Sugg (suggester)	Suggesting a procedure for carrying out a plan.
Infog (information-giver)	Offering facts and information, giving an opinion.
Infos (information-seeker)	Asking others for facts and information.
Elab (elaborator)	Explaining, developing an idea.
Cons (consulter)	Asking if the group has reached a decision acceptable to all.
Rec (recorder)	Keeping the records.
Summ (summarizer)	Reviewing what has been said or done.
Coord (coordinator)	A suggestion in which the speaker tells another person what to do.
Supp (supporter)	Supporting a participant's proposal or belief. Showing solidarity.
Draw (drawer)	Draws on the whiteboard.

4   Research Results

We examined the problem-solving data from five groups of subjects. Each group had three subjects. The subjects were paid undergraduates and MITRE employees. We coded the data with participant roles. We describe next our approach towards automatically detecting underlying participant roles. In particular, we present here a discussion of classification and regression tree (CART) models for recognizing roles.

CART models are binary decision trees that can build statistical models from feature values. They take a series of input feature values and use them to predict another feature value. We use a set of features that describe the utterances in our dialogues to predict the role that the participants are playing. We chose a series of input feature values that were either captured by the system or derived from some shallow processing on the utterances. The features we find most useful for predicting roles at this stage store information concerning the general category of each utterance (a high-level conversational act), the specific subcategory into which the utterance falls (a more specific conversational act) and the person who made the utterance. For example, the general utterance category includes *Request*, which includes subcategories such as *Request-Attention* and *Request-Action*, and the category *Motivate*, which includes subcategories such as *Encourage* and *Agree*.

We are using 4-fold cross-validation with the Festival CART-model building program, **wagon** (http://www.cstr.ed.ac.uk/projects/festival/), to determine the parameters for the CART model which best predict the participants' roles. At the moment, we do not have a large enough corpus of dialogues to decide which CART model we will ultimately use in our system. While we continue to code dialogues, we are using these models to give us an initial indication of whether we can predict roles. The indicators look good: Our ability to predict roles on unseen data is 81.5%.

5 Conclusions and Future Directions

We believe recognizing and modeling the roles taken by participants in the collaborative problem-solving activity and contrasting them to patterns of effective collaborative interchange can provide the fuel for an electronic peer to promote effective learning. Our experiment provided us with a potential recognition algorithm for instructional roles. We are in the process of verifying the validity of the model through our experimental data. Initial results with the CART model are promising.

The next step is to build a classifier that predicts group interaction problems in the dialogue, which means annotating the dialogues for different types of problems and using the role and conversational act information to predict the occurrence of a problem. The classifier must have information concerning sequences of roles played by an individual and series of consecutive roles played by all the participants. An initial classifier has been developed using a rule-based reasoning engine and trainable analysis tools. It is still being tuned but has shown some limited success so far.

References

1. Benne, K. & Sheats, P. (1948). Functional Roles of Group Members. *Journal of Social Issues*, 4:41–49.
2. Brown, A. & Palincsar, A. (1989). Guided, Cooperative Learning and Individual Knowledge Acquisition. In Lauren B. Resnick (Ed.), *Knowledge, Learning and Instruction*. Hillsdale, NJ: Lawrence Erlbaum.
3. Goodman, B., Soller, A., Linton, F., & Gaimari, R. (1998) Encouraging Student Reflection and Articulation using a Learning Companion. *International Journal of Artificial Intelligence in Education*, 9(3–4).
4. Lesgold, A., Katz, S., Greenberg, L., Hughes, E., & Eggan, G. (1992). Extensions of intelligent tutoring paradigms to support collaborative learning. In S. Dijkstra, H. Krammer, J. van Merrienboer (Eds.), *Instructional Models in Computer-Based Learning Environments*. Berlin: Springer-Verlag, 291–311.
5. Lund, K., Baker, M, and Baron, M. (1996). Modeling Dialogue and Beliefs as a Basis for Generating Guidance in a CSCL Environment. In *Proceedings of the ITS-96 Conference*, Montreal, 206–214.
6. McManus, M, & Aiken, R. (1995). Monitoring computer-based problem solving, *Journal of Artificial Intelligence in Education*, 6(4), 307–336.
7. Soller, A., & Lesgold, A. (2000). Modeling the Process of Collaborative Learning. International Workshop on New Technologies in Collaborative Learning, Awaji-Yumebutai, Japan.

Modeling Student Performance to Enhance the Pedagogy of AutoTutor

Tanner Jackson[1], Eric Mathews[1], King-Ip Lin[2], Andrew Olney [1], and Art Graesser[1]

[1]Department of Psychology
[2]Department of Computer Science
University of Memphis
Memphis, TN 38152, USA
{gtjacksn, emathews, davidlin, aolney,
a-graesser}@memphis.edu

Abstract. The Tutoring Research Group from the University of Memphis has developed a pedagogically effective Intelligent Tutoring System (ITS), called AutoTutor, that implements conversational dialog as a tutoring strategy for conceptual physics. Latent Semantic Analysis (LSA) is used to evaluate the quality of student contributions and determine what dialog moves AutoTutor gives. By modeling the students' knowledge in this fashion, AutoTutor successfully adapted its pedagogy to match the ideal strategy for students' ability.

1 Introduction

Recent educational technologies attempt to engage users in the learning process in an active manner and to simultaneously address the needs of the user through interactive displays and discourse. Tutorial dialog systems are interactive, conversing directly with the user by providing hints, corrections, and support throughout the entire learning process. The advantages of such an educational technology tool are numerous, but one of the foremost advantages lies in the fact that the educational tool can be personalized and tailored to the needs of the individuals, who vary in ability, background, and learning styles.

Research continually points to the fact that "Designers of collaborative HCI face the formidable task of writing software for millions of users, at design time, while making it work as if it were designed for each individual, at use time" [2]. Once emerging educational technologies can intelligently adapt to the need of the user, the learning process presumably can be optimized to achieve the greatest learning gains in the shortest amounts of time.

This paper outlines our efforts at the University of Memphis to build an adaptive educational technology that optimizes the learning process. We provide a brief overview of our system, AutoTutor, its user modeling, and evaluation data.

P. Brusilovsky et al. (Eds.): UM 2003, LNAI 2702, pp. 368–372, 2003.

2 Overview of AutoTutor

From a large amount of research on human-human tutoring conducted by our group and others, we have determined the underlying principles of tutoring that are found in our intelligent tutoring system called AutoTutor [4], [9], [11], [12]. AutoTutor engages the learner in a conversation while simulating the dialog moves of human tutors. The user and AutoTutor collaboratively improve the quality of the student's contributions to problems and questions while participating in a mixed-initiative dialog, distinguishing it from mere information delivery systems. During the conversation, AutoTutor implements a constructivist-based tutoring strategy. That is, in order for AutoTutor to believe that a student knows something, the student must actually state it during the conversation.

AutoTutor has recently been developed to help college students learn Newtonian conceptual physics (previous versions handled computer literacy). AutoTutor has been described in several previous publications, so it will not be detailed here (See [3], [5], [8], [10], [13]).

AutoTutor's dialog moves lead the student towards the correct ideas in answering the question, all the while trying to let the student provide as much of the information as possible. The types of dialog moves used by AutoTutor vary on a continuum of specificity from the student supplying information (pumps and hints), to information delivery on the part of AutoTutor (prompts and assertions). Within AutoTutor, pumps are the least specific form of dialog elicitation and they provide the least amount of information delivery (e.g., "Tell me more", "What else?"). In contrast, assertions have the highest amount of information delivery because the correct piece of the answer is directly expressed.

2.1 Tailoring the Tutoring within AutoTutor

Developers of intelligent tutoring systems continually make use of discourse planning models that adapt to the user's ability [1], [2], [6], [7], [14]. AutoTutor is no different in this respect, for it tailors its tutoring to the student in two specific ways: pedagogical feedback and dialog move selection. Without properly modeling the ability of the user within AutoTutor, the task of tailoring tutoring would be impossible. If AutoTutor operated on the assumption that all users were the same, we would find one of two things happening: (1) High ability students being frustrated and bored by AutoTutor being pedantic or (2) Low ability students being overly challenged and frustrated by getting nothing correct.

Additionally, feedback is a necessary component of tutoring; without it the user cannot engage in needed metacognitive analyses to determine whether they are providing good or bad material. In AutoTutor, we should find that higher ability students receive more positive feedback (positive correlation with ability) and less negative feedback (negative correlation with ability), in contrast to lower ability students where we should find the opposite to be true.

AutoTutor needs to be able to adapt the conversation at various levels of specificity, accommodating student ability. For instance, high ability users should receive less content delivery and more general requests for information, which require active knowledge construction. Hence, in AutoTutor we should find that high ability users receive more pumps and hints, but fewer assertions.

3 The Experiment

The learners were 24 undergraduate students recruited from the University of Memphis, University of Pittsburgh, Christian Brothers University, and Rhodes College. Each participant was given a pre- and a post-test consisting of 4 different essay questions (8 total) and 40 different selected items from the Force Concept Inventory (80 total from FCI). The Force Concept Inventory is an established multiple-choice test in physics, from which we selected questions addressing Newtonian physics. Though the pre- and post-tests were administered for each participant, they are not factored into the user modeling in AutoTutor.

The focus of this study is on the actual tutoring sessions of AutoTutor, during which students completed the 10 conceptual physics dialog. The 10 problems were split into two sessions, one week apart, for approximately 3 hours total. During the first session, each participant took a pre-test and then spent the rest of their time (approximately 70 min.) going through the first five conceptual physics problems with AutoTutor. At the second session, each participant spent about the same amount of time working with AutoTutor through the second five conceptual physics problems, and then took a post-test.

4 Determining Student Ability

To determine student ability from this experiment we examined the participants' pretest scores. Specifically we looked at their FCI pretest ability. We used a median split to distinguish between high and low ability. For all further analyses, high ability students are those who had a proportion of correct answers higher than .63, while low ability students are those who had a proportion of correct answers lower than .63.

5 Experimental Results and Discussion

We examined the application of AutoTutor's user modeling capabilities by analyzing correlations between student ability and the proportions of various dialog moves. Specifically, we examined the distribution of dialog moves (pumps, hints, prompts, and assertions) and the proportions of positive and negative feedback.

An analysis of the dialog moves was performed that correlated student ability with each dialog move proportion. As briefly mentioned earlier, we expected the following ordering of proportions for high ability students, to the extent that the student is supplying information, as opposed to the tutor: pumps > hints > prompts > assertions. The analysis resulted in the following correlations: pumps ($r = .49$), hints ($r = .24$), prompts ($r = -.19$), and assertions ($r = -.40$). As you can see, AutoTutor tended to deliver pumps and hints to high ability students, but was forced to deliver prompts and assertions to low ability students. In this sense, AutoTutor's user modeling components are valid. There was also a significant positive correlation ($r = .38$) between positive feedback and objective physics knowledge, FCI score, and a negative correlation in the case of negative feedback ($r = -.37$).

The correlation of r = .49, p= .016, between student ability and the proportion of pumps demonstrates that the high ability students receive more pumps than anything else. The fact that pumps are correlated with ability demonstrates that AutoTutor's user modeling properly tracks a good student's behavior and ability and then properly adapts by 1) using less specific dialog moves and 2) moving faster through the material instead of exhausting all possible dialog moves for a particular piece of information.

Similarly, the marginally significant negative correlation between student ability and the proportion of assertions, r= -0.40, p= .055, demonstrates that low ability students require a higher proportion of assertions. This means that AutoTutor was able to correctly identify those students who could not actively construct the knowledge on their own, and who needed more of the information to be provided for them. These correlations between the pretest ability and the proportion of dialog moves show us that AutoTutor is doing an appropriate job of modeling user ability.

The results from the short feedback analysis follow the same trend as the dialog moves. We found that the high ability students received a higher proportion of positive feedback from AutoTutor, while the low ability students received more negative feedback. This means that AutoTutor did an adequate job of discriminating the contributions from low versus high ability students, and was able to respond with appropriate levels of pedagogical feedback.

6   Concluding Remarks

These analyses of student ability correlated with dialog move and short feedback proportions provide evidence of effective user modeling within AutoTutor. This recent analysis of AutoTutor supports the claim that it does an effective job of modeling user ability, and adapting accordingly with appropriate pedagogical strategies. Although some of these phenomena are often easily implemented within computer systems, it is not so easily implemented within natural language dialog. The unique contribution of this work is the fact that we have a natural language system that extracts semantic intent and properly models the user.

Acknowledgements. The Tutoring Research Group (TRG) is an interdisciplinary research team comprised of approximately 35 researchers from psychology, computer science, physics, and education (Visit http://www.autotutor.org). This research conducted by the authors and the TRG was done in collaboration with members of the CIRCLE Group at the University of Pittsburgh, and was supported by grants from the National Science Foundation (SBR 9720314 and REC 0106965) and the Department of Defense Multidisciplinary University Research Initiative (MURI) administered by the Office of Naval Research under grant N00014-00-1-0600. Any opinions, findings, and conclusions or recommendations expressed in this material are those of the authors and do not necessarily reflect the views of ONR or NSF.

References

1. Anderson, J. R., Corbett, A. T., Koedinger, K. R., & Pelletier, R. (1995). Cognitive tutors: Lessons learned. *The Journal of the Learning Sciences, 4*, 167–207.
2. Fischer, G. (2001). User modeling in human-computer interaction. *User-Modeling-and-User-Adapted-Interaction, 11(1-2)*: pp 65–86.
3. Foltz, P.W. (1996). Latent semantic analysis for text-based research. *Behavior Research Methods, Instruments, and Computers, 28*, 197–202.
4. Graesser, A. C., Person, N. K., & Magliano, J. P. (1995). Collaborative dialog patterns in naturalistic one-on-one tutoring. *Applied Cognitive Psychology, 9*, 359–387.
5. Landauer, T. K., Foltz, P. W., & Laham, D. (1998). An introduction to latent semantic analysis. *Discourse Processes, 25*, 259–284.
6. Lepper, M. R., Woolverton, M., Mumme, D.L., & Gurtner, J.L. (1991). Motivational techniques of expert human tutors: Lessons for the design of computer-based tutors. In S.P. Lajoie & S.J. Derry (Eds.), *Computers as cognitive tools* (pp. 75–105). Hillsdale, NJ: Erbaum.
7. Merrill, D. C., Reiser, B. J., Ranney, M., & Trafton, J. G. (1992). Effective tutoring techniques: A comparison of human tutors and intelligent tutoring systems. *The Journal of the Learning Sciences, 2*, 277–305.
8. Person, N. K., Graesser, A. C., Kreuz, R. J., Pomeroy, V. & the Tutoring Research Group. (2000). *Simulating human tutor dialog moves in AutoTutor.* Submitted to *International Journal of Artificial Intelligence in Education.*
9. Person, N. K., Graesser, A. C., Magliano, J. P., & Kreuz, R. J. (1994). Inferring what the student knows in one-to-one tutoring: The role of student questions and answers. *Learning and Individual Differences, 6*, 205–29.
10. Person, N. K., Klettke, B., Link, K., Kreuz, R. J., & the Tutoring Research Group (1999). The integration of affective responses into AutoTutor. *Proceeding of the International Workshop on Affect in Interactions* (pp. 167–178). Siena, Italy.
11. Person, N. K., Kreuz, R. J., Zwaan, R., & Graesser, A. C. (1995). Pragmatics and pedagogy: Conversational rules and politeness strategies may inhibit effective tutoring. *Cognition and Instruction, 13*, 161–188.
12. Putnam, R. T. (1987). Structuring and adjusting content for students: A study of live and simulated tutoring of addition. *American Educational Research Journal, 24*, 13–48.
13. Wiemer-Hastings, P., Graesser, A. C., Harter, D., & the Tutoring Research Group (1998). The foundations and architecture of AutoTutor. *Proceedings of the 4th International Conference on Intelligent Tutoring Systems* (pp. 334–343). Berlin, Germany: Springer-Verlag.
14. Zukerman, I. & McConachy, R. (2001) WISHFUL: A discourse planning system that considers a user's inferences. Computational Intelligence. 17(1): 1–61

Modeling Hinting Strategies for Geometry Theorem Proving

Noboru Matsuda[1] and Kurt VanLehn

Intelligent Systems Program
University of Pittsburgh
mazda@pitt.edu, vanlehn@cs.pitt.edu

Abstract. This study characterizes hinting strategies used by a human tutor to help students learn geometry theorem proving. Current tutoring systems for theorem proving provide hints that encourage (or force) the student to follow a fixed forward and/or backward chaining strategy. In order to find out if human tutors observed a similar constraint, a study was conducted with students proving geometry theorems individually with a human tutor. When working successfully (without hints), students did not consistently follow the forward and/or backward chaining strategy. Moreover, the human tutor hinted steps that were seldom ones that would be picked by such tutoring systems. Lastly, we discovered a simple categorization of hints that covered 97% of the hints given by the human tutor.

1 Introduction

As a first step in designing an improved intelligent tutoring system for geometry theorem proving, we sought to characterize the hints given by a human tutor to students trying to prove geometry theorems. Little is known about the mechanism of effective hinting strategy [1, 2], but current tutoring systems have relatively simple, inflexible hinting policies. Some tutoring systems demand that the students follow a prescribed problem solving strategy, such as forward or backward chaining [3], so their hints are always aimed at the next step taken by the prescribed strategy. Other tutoring systems accept any correct inference even if it is not on an ideal solution path [4], but when a student reaches an impasse, the tutor provides a hint on the next step that is a strict backward or forward inference no matter what assertions the student has made so far. Not only are the steps targeted by hints often quite inflexibly chosen, the hints themselves are usually a simple human-authored sequence that proceeds from general hints to specific hints, and usually culminates in a "bottom out" hint that describes exactly what the student should enter. We hypothesize that human tutors have less rigid hinting policies, and this might cause increased learning. This paper tests the first conjecture by characterizing the hinting strategy of a single human tutor.

---

[1] This research was supported by NSF Grant 9720359.

P. Brusilovsky et al. (Eds.): UM 2003, LNAI 2702, pp. 373–377, 2003.
© Springer-Verlag Berlin Heidelberg 2003

2 The Study

Nine students were randomly selected from a Japanese middle school. Three geometry proof-problems were used. Two problems were construction problems, which require students to draw additional lines by compasses and straightedges to complete a proof. Each student solved problems individually while thinking out aloud. The tutor was asked to provide hints only when the students could not otherwise proceed. The sessions were videotaped and transcribed. The students' utterances were segmented so that a single segment corresponds to a proof step or a response to the tutor's assistance. The tutor's utterances were segmented so that a single segment corresponds to a hint. The following sections present an analysis of these protocol data.

3 Students' Problem Solving Strategies

In order to determine whether students followed the forward and/or backward chaining strategies prescribed by tutoring system for theorem proving, we located individual students' utterances in a proof tree and observed a pattern of progress in their proof. As an example, Fig. 1 shows a chronological progress of a student's reasoning. The goal to be proven is shown at the top of the tree, with the givens at the bottom. A branching link shows a conjunctive justification. Nodes with a rectangle show the propositions that this student asserted. The numbers on their shoulder show the order of assertion. Since the proposition Bx//AP is a premise for both $\angle$BxM=$\angle$APM and $\angle$PAM=$\angle$MBx, the first assertion is located on two places.

As shown in the figure, this student built up a proof neither in a strict forward chaining nor in a strict backward chaining manner. Rather she seems to assert facts (i.e., propositions) that were eventually recognized. This opportunistic ordering is not peculiar to this particular student. All students participating in our study showed the same behavior.

4 Topics of Hint Events

We observed 31 hint events, each consisting of a sequence of hints on the same topic. They were categorized into 4 types of hint events; (a) 10 hint events for a next step, (b) 14 hint events for a justification of proposition that the student had just mentioned, (c) 3 hint events for a geometry construction, (d) 1 hint event to get started on a proof, and (e) 3 hint events that do not fall under any of these types. Because tutoring systems often follow rigid policies when selecting the target step for a next-step hint, we analyzed the 10 next-step hint events in more detail.

If we define a *step* to be applying a postulate to some premises and producing a conclusion, then the human tutor always provided a next-step hint on a single step (as opposed to discussing a generic strategy and no steps). Steps can be categorized by which elements (premises, conclusions) have been mentioned already by the student or tutor. In particular, let us use the first two letters of the classification to show whether the conclusion is asserted (C1) or not asserted (C0), and the second two letters for whether all the premises are asserted (Pa), none are asserted (P0), only some of the premises are asserted (Ps), or all but one premises are asserted (P1). Table 1 shows the results of applying this classification to the protocol data. It indicates the number of times a step was chosen as target (first row) and the number of steps available at the time a next-step help event began (second row).

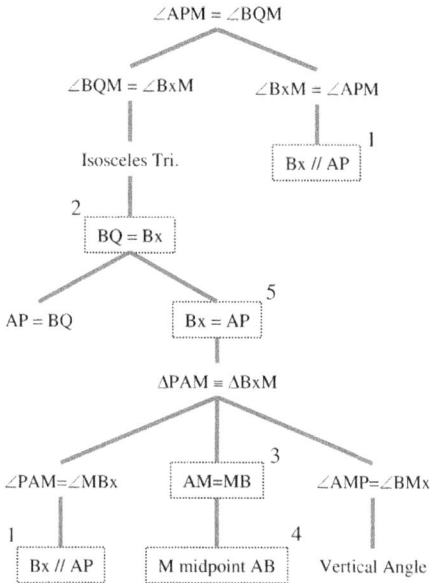

Fig. 1. A typical progress of student's input over a proof tree

The human tutor always chose either C0Pa or C0P1 as a target of a next-step hint event. Several existing tutoring systems, such as GPT [3], ANGLE [4], and CPT [5], choose target steps that would be picked by forward or backward chaining, which means either C0Pa or C1P0. Clearly, the human tutor's target steps seldom agreed with those that would be chosen by these tutoring systems.

Table 1. Frequency of motivation of hinting in the 'next step' hint events

	State of assertions for a step					
	C0Pa	C0P1	C1Pa	C0Ps	C1P1	C1P0
Choice	2	8	0	0	0	0
Occurence	10	14	4	1	3	3

5 A Classification of Hints

So far, we have discussed only hint events and their targets, but not the hints that comprise hint events. In order to understand the structure of human tutoring better, this section categorizes the hints from the hint-events for justifications, next-steps, and the first step of the proof. There were 90 hints observed in these 25 hint events.

The individual hints were organized into a Cartesian product with respect to the focus and format of the hint. There are four categories regarding the *focus* of hint: (1) a hint on a whole application of a postulate (e.g., "Remember if two sides of triangle are equal, then the base angles are also equal"), (2) a hint on a premise of a postulate application (e.g., "If you want to prove these two angles are equal, what should be true among these two segments?"), (3) a hint on a conclusion of a postulate application (e.g., "What can you conclude about the base angles in a triangle with two equal sides?"), and (4) a hint on a proposition apparently involved in a postulate application but not mentioning it explicitly (e.g., "Can you say anything about these two segments?").

We observed five different *forms* of hint; (1) a direct exhibition, (2) a question asking a whole postulate/proposition, (3) a question asking about a relationship in the proposition, (4) a question asking about the elements involved in a proposition, and (5) mentioning or pointing to a related configuration in the problem figure.

As an illustration of this Cartesian product categorization, Table 2 shows all possible hints for a proof step that invokes the theorem of isosceles triangle (i.e., if two sides of a triangle are equal, then the base angles are also equal).

We could classify 87 hints (out of 90; 97%) with the coding schema shown in Table 2. The parenthesized numbers in Table 2 shows the number of hints in each category.

Table 2. The type of hints for a next-step hint

Focus \ Form	Exhibit	Question — Whole proposition	Question — Relation	Question — Element	Pointing
Whole application	(3) If AB=AC, then <ABC=<ACB	(0) What can you do now?	(0) Can you say anything about segments AB and AC, and angles <ABC and <ACB?	(0) -	(16) Look at this triangle
Premise of application	(2) It is sufficient to show AB=AC to conclude <ABC=<ACB	(4) What should you prove when you want to conclude <ABC = <ACB?	(0) You want to conclude <ABC=<ACB. Now, what should be true among AB and AC?	(2) Which two segments must be equal to conclude <ABC=<ACB?	(0) -
Conclusion of application	(1) Given that AB=AC, <ABC and <ACB are equal	(6) What can you conclude when AB and AC are equal?	(5) We know AB=AC. So, what can we conclude with <ABC and <ACB?	(0) We know AB=AC. So, which two angles can you conclude to be equal?	(0) -
Proposition	(21) AB and AC are equal	(0) What is known?	(24) can you say anything about AB and AC?	(0) Which segment is equal to AB?	(3) Look at AB and AC

6   Conclusion

The analysis of protocol data gathered from students in middle school has shown several aspects of hinting in a learning context where the tutor acts as a helper for students to overcome an impasse.

We found that students tend to make opportunistic assertions that follow neither a strict forward nor backward chaining order.

Accepting their reasoning style might be beneficial for students, but it requires that the tutoring system be more complex so that it can provide an appropriate hint depending on the students' reasoning. We discovered that human tutors prefer to hint steps where one or more premises have been mentioned, although not necessarily recently, and the conclusion has not been mentioned. It is not clear yet how the tutor decides which step to pick when there are several that meet this criterion. The human tutor's policy for choosing target steps does not correspond to the policies of existing tutoring systems for theorem proving, but it might be easy to modify such systems to follow the human tutor's policy.

Moreover, 97% of the hints observed in our study fell into a simple Cartesian product categorization. This categorization appears amenable to incorporation in the hint generation module of a tutoring system.

References

1. Hume, G., J. Michael, A. Rovick, and M. Evens, Hinting as a tactic in one-on-one tutoring. Journal of the Learning Sciences, 1996. **5**(1): p. 23–47.
2. DiPaolo, R.E., A.C. Graesser, D.J. Hacker, and H.A. White, Hints in Human and Computer Tutoring, in The impact of media on technology of instruction, M. Rabinowitz, Editor. 2002, Erlbaum: Mahwah, NJ.
3. Anderson, J.R., C.F. Boyle, and G. Yost, The geometry tutor. Proceedings of the International Joint Conference on Artificial Intelligence, 1985: p. 1–7.
4. Koedinger, K.R. and J.R. Anderson, Reifying implicit planning in geometry: Guidelines for model-based intelligent tutoring system design, in Computers as cognitive tools, S.P. Lajoie and S.J. Derry, Editors. 1993, Lawrence Erlbaum Associates: Hillsdale, NJ. p. 15–45.
5. Scheines, R. and W. Sieg, Computer Environments for Proof Construction. Interactive Learning Environments, 1994. **4**(2): p. 159–169.

User Modelling in the Car

Niels Ole Bernsen

Natural Interactive Systems Laboratory, University of Southern Denmark,
DK 5230, Odense, Denmark
nob@nis.sdu.dk
http://www.nis.sdu.dk

Abstract. The paper presents work on user modelling of car drivers. The paper
presents an implemented solution to user modelling in the car, which includes
an aspect of location-based user modelling.

1 Introduction

The proliferation of mobile systems in the future offers new challenges for user
model-based adaptation technologies. Mobile systems will communicate with their
users in an increasing number of modalities [1], such as input/output speech, in addition to the customary GUI input/output modalities. Mobile systems may offer location-based and situation-based information. Coupled with the user-awareness provided
by user model-based adaptation, opportunities are huge indeed.

This paper describes work on user model-based adaptation in a large mobile system
under development. The system is called VICO or Virtual Intelligent CO-driver. Section 2 describes the system's functionality. Section 3 presents some findings on generic system tasks for user modelling, user identification, user modelling information,
and criteria for selecting the information to model. Section 4 and 5 describe the VICO
user modelling module. Section 6 describes the next step in our work.

2 The VICO System

Spoken language dialogue systems (SLDSs) are migrating into mobile environments,
such as the car. VICO is such a system, addressing some next-step challenges in the
context of supporting car drivers whilst driving [2]. In brief, the challenges include:
(1) ease of use by a large and heterogeneous user population; (2) processing of fully
spontaneous spoken input, English, German, and Italian; (3) multiple-task assistance:
with navigation to addresses and points of interest in Italy, hotel reservation, restaurant
reservation, and VICO system information; (4) confidence-score adaptive dialogue;
(5) GPS-based location-awareness; (6) multimodal interaction through push-to-talk
button and spoken input, and spoken and display (text) output; and (7) integration of
adaptive user models built on-line.

P. Brusilovsky et al. (Eds.): UM 2003, LNAI 2702, pp. 378–382, 2003.
© Springer-Verlag Berlin Heidelberg 2003

3   General Findings

At the start of VICO, we analysed the scope of user modelling for in-car use, taking into account the particular tasks of VICO (see Sect. 2).

3.1   Generic System Tasks

VICO's *generic* UM-related tasks are [3]: (1) identify the present driver; (2) retrieve the present driver's user model; (3) optionally: create a new user model UM(Dx) for a new driver, Dx; (4) make appropriate on-line use of the present driver's user model during the driver's dialogue with VICO; (5) collect new information on the driver during the driver's dialogue with VICO; (6) update the present driver's user model with the new information gathered; and (7) store the user model whenever it has been updated with new information.

3.2   Driver Identification

VICO must determine the car's current driver since cars often have several different drivers. Driver identification must be made with *near-certainty*. If it is uncertain that VICO has correctly identified the driver, misidentification will happen too often. In such cases, the driver is likely to be "mistreated" because VICO will adapt to the driver based on a wrong user model. Similarly, the modelled behaviour of the mis-identified driver will tend to fudge up the misallocated user model with misleading information. Since the driver's user model cannot be invoked before identification, VICO must identify the driver *up front,* i.e. as soon as that driver starts the dialogue. Later identification means less support for the driver, and the updated user model runs the risk of having missed to collect important information on the driver's behaviour.

In SLDSs, driver identification design is a non-trivial problem. We have considered (a) voice identification, (b) a driver's code, however input to VICO, (c) driver's spelled first name, and (d) combinations of (a) through (c). We prefer to use voice identification-cum-spelling of their first names by first-time users. This combines the unobtrusive elegance of voice identification with (non-coded) first-name feedback and avoids having to remember and use a code or spell one's name on each occasion of use. This option also allows passengers to speak to the system without being registered in the UM database – passengers just have to avoid giving the system their first names.

3.3   Which Type(s) of Information to Model?

Based on analysis of some 25-30 candidate kinds of information about driver behaviour which VICO might collect and use adaptively, we distinguish between: (T1) information on the driver's task objectives due to task goals, preferences, habits, etc.; (T2) information on the driver's communication with VICO; and (T3) information on the driver's experience of various kinds. This information typology helps generate a structured space of candidates for observation-based adaptive user modelling, each generic type of information subsuming several specific information types, such as the driver's: preferences for hotels, restaurants, points of interest, petrol brands, or address locations; native language, communication difficulties due to strong accent or dialect, speech disorders, extreme talkativeness, elaborate politeness, frequent cross-talk with passengers, unusual speaking style, etc.; and experience in using VICO itself.

We identified a set of criteria which should be satisfied by the driver information to be modelled. These are: (C1) *universality:* unless other factors advocate in their favour, the chosen information should be top quality in terms of usefulness to all or most drivers; (C2) *quality:* the information should provide genuine driver adaptivity without significant drawbacks; (C3) *feasibility:* the functionality should be implementable without extreme or unpredictable effort, the latter being due to, e.g., a needed research breakthrough; and (C4) *verifiability:* the functionality must be based on clearly verifiable information about the driver.

An example of T1 in the information typology is: store the driver's past hotel preferences, such as number of stars, price, location (city centre, countryside), hotel chain, etc. Even if not presently told about them by the driver, VICO could offer to use those constraints as selection criteria when looking for a suitable hotel.

Let us evaluate the hotel preferences user modelling functionality using the selection criteria C1 through C4. C4 is met because the driver's hotel preferences become apparent during dialogue with VICO and they do not appear to have any significant drawbacks (C2). The functionality can be implemented without extreme or unpredictable effort (C3). Whether C1 is met depends on, at least, (i) how many users of VICO will need to book hotels, (ii) how many users will do so *en route,* and (iii) how many users have systematic hotel preferences. We do not know the answers at this point.

It is harder to identify suitable T2 information candidates. An example is a system which adapts its dialogue to drivers having a strong dialect or accent. A major problem is that any solution may be at risk as long as we do not have efficient ways of diagnosing different *possible causes* of recognition problems. Low confidence scores, many out-of-vocabulary words, or multiple error corrections, for instance, cannot tell if the cause of repeated recognition problems is a strong dialect or accent or something different, such as a driver who regularly talks to passengers during dialogue (C3, C4). T2 solutions might well satisfy C2. And even if not benefiting all or most drivers, they might benefit large fractions of those drivers who have great difficulty using spoken language dialogue systems at all, illustrating the exception clause in C1.

T3 information includes at least one obvious candidate, i.e. the driver's experience with VICO itself. The idea is to offer up-front information on VICO to all new drivers independently of whether or not a new driver asks for it. Provision of this information would seem to rather easily meet C1 through C4.

Guided by the above analysis, we have implemented a general-purpose UM module which currently facilitates drivers' hotel selection dialogue through knowledge of their hotel preferences in the past.

4 Location-Dependent and Location-Independent Adaptivity

The following driver hotel preference behaviour feature-value pairs are collected and used by the UM:
- type [VALUE = HOTEL]
- hotel name [VALUE = NAME]
- hotel address [VALUES = ADDRESS ITEMS]
- number of stars [VALUES = 1, 2, 3, 4, 5]
- hotel chain [VALUE = NAME]
- hotel location [VALUES = TOWN, OUTTOWN, COUNTRYSIDE]
- max. prices for single (S)/double (D) rooms [VALUES = S: X and D: Y Euros]
- restaurant in hotel [VALUE = TRUE, FALSE]
- protected parking [VALUE = TRUE, FALSE]

These attribute-value pairs are of two very different kinds, i.e. the generic hotel properties 1, 4, 5, 6, 7, 8, and 9, and the specific hotel properties 2 and 3. *Generic* hotel properties may belong to any particular hotel. *Specific* hotel properties imply all properties of a particular hotel: once you choose a *particular* hotel, e.g. by its name, you choose all its properties. The UM thus cannot use specific hotel properties to support the driver's hotel selection task independently of where the driver happens to be. Only generic hotel properties can be used for *location-independent* user model-based driver support. Thus, the hotel selection UM has two distinct adaptive functionalities. The first, *location-independent,* functionality offers hotels having the generic properties of hotels which the driver has preferred in the past. The second, *location-dependent,* functionality offers the specific hotels which were preferred in the past if and only if the driver is in the area in which those hotels are located.

5 User Model Update and Use

A crucial design issue is how to *update* the UM with new information. If, e.g., the update algorithm averages over the past, and if there is a long UM record of staying in inexpensive hotels, then the UM may never fully realise that the driver has changed hotel preferences. As they are, our update algorithms for *generic* hotel properties take the two latest hotel reservations into account. As for the driver's previous choices of *specific* named hotel/location pairs, the VICO UM preserves and uses all of them, no matter how long ago it was when the driver stayed in a particular hotel.

The context of use of the hotel selection UM is that the driver asks VICO to help book a hotel, possibly adding some selection constraints, saying, e.g., "VICO, please find a three-star hotel." At this point, the hotel preferences UM is being applied.

VICO UM application raises several design issues likely to strongly affect user acceptance. Firstly, it seems clear that the UM should never override the driver's stated hotel selection constraints. Thus, if the three-star constraint in the example above conflicts with the UM, the former prevails by applying conflict resolution. By implication, if the driver's stated selection constraints suffice for uniquely identifying a hotel through querying the hotels database, the UM is not applied. Secondly, when UM hotel selection constraints are being applied in querying the database, possibly as complements to the driver-provided selection constraints and following conflict resolution, the driver is informed that the returned hotel suggestions are the results of UM application. This allows the driver to decide whether the suggestions match current preferences. Adaptation should be made behind the driver's back.

In the case of *location-based* selection support, the UM provides a list of past selected hotel/location pairs. If the driver provides a location corresponding to a location on the list, s/he is offered the corresponding hotel(s). If no location is provided, VICO assumes that the driver wants a local hotel. If the car's current location matches a location in the hotel/location pairs list, the driver is offered the corresponding hotel(s).

VICO's historical UM consists of a managing module, a reasoning module for updating the user model of each driver, and a database. Only the reasoning module is UM task-specific. The database has (i) a record of the drivers known to VICO, (ii) a record of all observed, UM-relevant past driver behaviour organised per driver and sub-divided into the different UM tasks performed by VICO, and (iii) a record of updated UMs per driver, sub-divided into the UM tasks performed by the system.

6   Conclusion and Future Work

The VICO UM module has been integrated into the hotel reservation task domain agent module. Our next task is to test with real users in order to evaluate the UM's update algorithms and the principles behind its on-line use.

Acknowledgement. The VICO support by the EU HLT Programme is gratefully acknowledged. I would like to thank Aziz Joumady and Dymitro Kupkin who implemented the VICO UM module, and Laila Dybkjær who specified the hotel reservation task.

References

1. Bernsen, N.O.: Multimodality in Language and Speech Systems - from Theory to Design Support Tool. In: Granström, B., House, D., Karlsson, I. (eds.): Multimodality in Language and Speech Systems. Dordrecht: Kluwer Academic Publishers (2002a) 93–148.
2. Bernsen, N.O., Dybkjær, L.: A Multimodal Virtual Co-Driver's Problems with the Driver. In: Dybkjær, L., André, E., Minker, W., Heisterkamp, P. (eds.): CD-ROM Proceedings of the ISCA Tutorial and Research Workshop on Spoken Dialogue in Mobile Environments, Irsee, Germany. Bonn, Germany: International Speech Communication Association (2002).
3. Bernsen, N.O.: Report on User Clusters and Characteristics. VICO report D10, NISLab, August (2002b).

User Modelling and Mobile Learning

Susan Bull

Educational Technology Research Group, Electronic, Electrical and Computer Engineering,
University of Birmingham, Edgbaston, Birmingham B15 2TT, UK.
s.bull@bham.ac.uk

Abstract. This paper describes a study investigating the potential for two user modelling systems: a location-aware user modelling system providing easy access to applications, files and course materials commonly used by an individual student in different locations; and a mobile open learner model for consultation by a student away from the intelligent tutoring system in which the learner model was generated.

1 Introduction

Educational institutions are starting to introduce mobile learning into courses. In line with this technological development, the Electronic, Electrical and Computer Engineering (EECE) building at the University of Birmingham has had wireless LAN installed. Members of the 2002 intake of the MSc in Human Centred Systems have been loaned a Compaq iPAQ Pocket PC and wireless LAN card. With the purpose of further supporting future students, a study is being undertaken to observe current students' use of their Pocket PCs. In accordance with Jameson's call for combining research in context-awareness and user modelling [1], the study aims to identify whether there are sufficient patterns and differences in Pocket PC use with reference to activity and location, to suggest a role for user modelling in this setting.

A second investigation is students' desire for a mobile open learner model which can be consulted away from the tutoring system in which it was generated. The educational benefit of open learner models to promote reflection has been suggested in the desktop PC context [2,3,4,5], but has not yet been considered for mobile learning. In a mobile environment an open learner model may be even more useful as, similar to the way in which mobile learning materials may be used for brief periods at convenient times and locations, learners may access a mobile learner model to examine their misconceptions for short periods between their main computer sessions.

2 User Study

The study investigated the potential for two user modelling systems to assist students in their learning: (1) a location-aware system to offer easy access to the applications, files and course materials commonly used by an individual in each of their frequently visited locations; (2) a mobile open learner model for consultation by a student after an interaction with the learning environment in which the model was created.

P. Brusilovsky et al. (Eds.): UM 2003, LNAI 2702, pp. 383–387, 2003.

17 students taking an MSc in Human Centred Systems took part. 8 had taken an MSc module in User Modelling. All had Pocket PCs. 10 undergraduate students taking a degree in Computer Interactive Systems, who had completed undergraduate modules on Personalisation and Adaptive Systems and Interactive Learning Environments, voluntarily took part. Data was obtained by anonymous questionnaire from all subjects, and anonymous logbooks on Pocket PC use over 6 weeks from MSc students. Due to the low numbers it is inappropriate to perform a statistical analysis of the results: the aim is to discover if initial data indicates further work to be valuable.

2.1 Results

Location-Aware User Modelling System. Logbook data shows the most common location of Pocket PC use to be at home, followed by various rooms in EECE. Some students also used their Pocket PC in other parts of the campus and elsewhere. Results of 3 typical users are presented in Table 1, as an example of similarities and differences between Pocket PC use. 10 of the generally common activities are listed: reading, email, web browsing, notes, calendar, computer assisted learning, word processing, calculator, music, games. Each user also performed a few additional tasks in other categories, not shown (e.g. MSN Messenger, Excel, viewing lecture slides).

Table 1. Activities and location of use of Pocket PC by 3 students

	Location	read	mail	web	note	cal	CAL	WP	calc	mus	game
S1	home	1	2		5	4	2	2	1	7	1
	EECE G16	1	2	1	4	1			1		
	EECE 337		1	1		1			1	2	
	EECE 421	1		1						1	
	EECE 435			2					2		
	EECE CR	1	3	3							
	EECE lib		3	1		1			1		
	main lib			3	1		1				
	shop				4			1			
S2	home	1	4	3	1	4	2	2		7	3
	other home		1		1			1	1		
	EECE 123		1	1							
	EECE 337		5						1		
	EECE 522				1	1					
	EECE CR		1								
	EECE lib							1			
	EECE rec	1	2								
	campus		1			1					
	restaurant		1			1			1		
	train		3							1	1
S3	home	1	1		20	4	2			4	8
	EECE 225		1	2							
	EECE 337			2							
	EECE 421	1	1	1	9					1	1
	learn centre			1	1						

Several tasks and activities were common, for example: using the calendar at home. There were also individual differences: S3 made many more notes, and also played more games at home. S2 was the only student to view web pages at home. The students also used their Pocket PC in EECE. However, they used these in different locations within the building - the only common location (apart from home) was EECE 337 (a lab). Their individual activities in this location differed.

S1 and S2 had a larger spread of locations of use, in addition to home and the university: S1 in shops; S2 in someone else's home, restaurants and trains. S3 used the Pocket PC only at home and the university. Tasks undertaken varied to some extent - S3 had heavy use of notes, but this was restricted mainly to two locations (home and EECE 421 - a lab). S1 also used notes quite frequently (at home, in EECE G16 - a lecture theatre, and while shopping). S2 only used notes twice. Games were played frequently by S3; to a lesser extent by S2; and infrequently by S1. Only S1 used the calculator, in four locations. Other activities were performed by all students, such as using the calendar, with S1 and S2 using it in various locations, but mostly at home. S3 used it exclusively at home. Listening to music was common to all, with a preference for this activity at home. All students used a computer assisted learning package at home (and S1 also once in the main library). S1 and S2 used email frequently in many locations, with S2 showing greater preference for some locations. S2 used the web at home 3 times, and once in EECE (123 - a seminar room), and S1 and S3 used it mainly in various locations in EECE, but also elsewhere on campus. In summary: there were both similarities and differences in Pocket PC use across users.

Mobile Open Learner Model. In the second part of the study, MSc and undergraduate students were asked by questionnaire about the potential utility of a mobile open learner model, and the features that they would like included, from the following: (1) a statement of known topics; (2) a statement of problematic topics; (3) a discussion of probable reasons for difficulties; (4) a comparison of student beliefs and domain information; (5) suggestions of areas to revise; (6) tailored revision material. The results are shown in Table 2.

Table 2. Perceived utility of a mobile open learner model

	very useful	useful	possibly useful	probably not useful	not useful	don't know
Known topics	3	15	8	1		
Problematic topics	13	9	5			
Reasons for difficulties	11	10	5	1		
Comparison	6	9	9	3		
Revision requirements	14	12	1			
Revision material	15	7	5			

Results were mainly positive, for each component of the mobile open learner model.

2.2 Discussion

Location-Aware User Modelling System. Data from the MSc students' logbooks suggests that a location-aware user modelling system could be beneficial. Several activities were common to many, for example: email, web browsing, notes and music; though the locations differed. There was greater variation in the frequency of other activities, e.g. MSN Messenger and viewing lecture slides. Some of these may fluctuate at different stages of the course, for example viewing lecture slides might be most common at the time of lectures, when writing assignments, and revising before exams. This will become apparent as the study progresses. It may be possible to set up stereotypes for course module attributes of the learner model, used to make initial predictions about users' needs, and then evolve into individual models where appropriate. However, at this stage it seems less likely that stereotypes will be useful for the location aspect of the user model, as there appears to be less overlap between location and task, amongst users. For some individuals a pattern for some activities and locations is emerging. Therefore, in contrast to many location-aware systems, the approach will be to combine information about location and individual behaviour.

A more detailed analysis of the logbook data is still required, in particular to discover whether usage levels and patterns change over time. Initial results suggest further investigation to be warranted in our setting, and the results may be applicable to similar contexts. A context-aware user model that, in its context information included an awareness of location and course information, together with data on individual user behaviour, would seem useful. Work is beginning on such a system. We will not be relying entirely on automatic detection of location: outside the EECE building users will need to select their location from a menu. The extent to which a user's location in EECE can be accurately detected automatically is at this stage undetermined. It is likely that users will have to select their precise location from a menu at least in some EECE locations. Nevertheless, even broader location recognition can be used to predict some of a user's needs, for example: when S2 is on the 3rd floor, they are probably in lab 337, and hence most likely to want to use email.

Mobile Open Learner Model. To complement the work on location-awareness, MSc and undergraduate students were asked about the likely utility of an open learner model that could be decoupled from the intelligent tutoring system in which it was generated, and used as a learning resource away from the main system. The results were unexpectedly positive. Although it is not possible to accurately assess the utility of an environment based on a description of proposed software, the positive response does indicate that it might be worth investigating further. An intelligent tutoring system is therefore being designed (see [6] for an early version). Users will be able to interact with teaching materials followed by diagnostic multiple choice tests, the results of which will be used to update the learner model. Two approaches are being investigated: the first is a system that can be used either on a desktop PC or Pocket PC (with appropriate presentation according to the device), with a learner model that can be viewed on either device; the second is a system where the main interaction takes place on a desktop PC, but where the learner model is designed primarily for viewing on the Pocket PC after the main learning session is completed. In both versions, based on the questionnaire responses in Table 2, the learner model will hold representations of a student's knowledge and misconceptions, and will display these attributes in as much detail as is required by the student, using the categories: known topics, problematic topics. It will be able to state probable reasons for difficulties based on common misconceptions, and be able to offer a comparison of a student's beliefs (knowledge and misconceptions) with the target domain. Furthermore, the system will suggest areas for revision and offer tailored revision or new material based on the learner model. Users will be able to edit their learner model to update the contents. This has the educational benefit of promoting learner reflection as learners will have to think about their understanding before making changes to their model. These are major benefits of open learner models that are just as important in mobile learning as in the more traditional intelligent tutoring contexts. Indeed, as learning may take place on either a PC or Pocket PC, and the learner may switch devices before synchronising their learner model, the ability to edit the model is essential in this mobile context.

Conclusions. Early results of investigations into the likely utility of the two mobile environments have been quite positive. Of course, it is likely that students taking a degree in Human Centred Systems (MSc) or Computer Interactive Systems (undergraduates), will be more open to this approach. Nevertheless, the fact that data from students in this environment is positive suggests that this is a useful undertaking. The results may generalise to similar settings. Further work will be required to determine the extent to which the results are applicable in non-technological courses.

3 Summary

This paper has presented a study to assess the likely utility of 2 user modelling systems: (1) a context-aware user modelling system to provide easy access to the applications, files and course materials often used by a student in their commonly visited locations; (2) a mobile open learner model for consultation by a student following the interaction during which the learner model was generated. Results of a questionnaire survey and logbook analysis suggest both to be fruitful areas for further work, which is now being undertaken.

References

1. Jameson, A. (2001). Modelling Both the Context and User, *Personal Technologies* 5(1), 1–4.
2. Bull, S. & Pain, H. (1995). 'Did I Say What I Think I Said, And Do You Agree With Me?': Inspecting and Questioning the Student Model, J. Greer (ed), *Proceedings of World Conference on Artificial Intelligence and Education*, AACE, Charlottesville VA, 501–508.
3. Dimitrova, V., Self, J. & Brna, P. (2001). Applying Interactive Open Learner Models to Learning Technical Terminology, M. Bauer, P.J. Gmytrasiewicz & J. Vassileva (eds), *User Modeling: 8th International Conference*, Springer-Verlag, Berlin Heidelberg, 148–157.
4. Kay, J. (1997). Learner Know Thyself, *Proceedings of International Conference on Computers in Education*, Kuching, Malaysia.
5. Mitrovic, A. & Martin, B. (2002). Evaluating the Effects of Open Student Models on Learning, P. De Bra, P. Brusilovsky & R. Conejo (eds), *Proceedings of Adaptive Hypermedia and Adaptive Web-Based Systems*, Springer, Berlin Heidelberg, 296–305.
6. Bull, S. & McEvoy, A.T. (2003). An Intelligent Learning Environment with an Open Learner Model for the Desktop PC and Pocket PC, to appear in *Proceedings of International Conference on Artificial Intelligence in Education 2003*, IOS Press, Amsterdam.

D-ME: Personal Interaction in Smart Environments

Berardina De Carolis, Sebastiano Pizzutilo, and Ignazio Palmisano

Intelligent Interfaces, Department of Informatics,
University of Bari, Italy
{decarolis, pizzutilo}@di.uniba.it

Abstract. Ubiquitous access to information services in active environments depends on the user and on the situation in which interaction occurs. We propose a multiagent architecture in which users and environments are represented by agents that negotiate tasks execution and generate results according to *user in context* features.

1 Introduction

With the evolution of devices and connection technologies towards wireless devices and active objects, access to services is enabled from everywhere and simultaneously with other activities [14]. Personalization then requires considering not only user features, but also the interaction context [1,9]. Context has been defined as information that describes the situation in which interaction occurs, with emphasis on time, place, people and things [3]: this information is dynamic, as relevant features may change while interaction evolves. In particular, context features related to the **user** (location, activity, emotional state, device employed) may be distinguished from those related to the **environment** (spatial information, date and time, weather conditions, noise and light level, temperature and available resources). The relation between these two entities (user and environment) is a key factor in a system that is aimed at supporting ubiquitous interaction between users and smart environments. Systems of this type should match the tasks the user wants to perform with the services the environment can provide. By building on research about Intelligent Interface Agents [11,13], we developed a MultiAgent System in which mobile users interact with ubiquitous services through agents (digital "alter ego") that represent them in the environment. The agent, that we call D-Me (Digital-Me), perceives the presence of a smart environment and controls adaptation of tasks to the user needs and the context. Our approach is focused on the concept of task: we therefore implemented a context-aware To-Do-List application that reminds tasks to the user by considering the situational context [1,4] and we added to this functionality the ability to perform tasks, entirely or in part, on the user behalf. In this paper, we outline the main features of D-Me by focusing on its personalization component.

P. Brusilovsky et al. (Eds.): UM 2003, LNAI 2702, pp. 388–392, 2003.

2   The Architecture of D-ME

The idea of delegating complex or tedious tasks to an agent is the core of Intelligent Interface Agents research. In ubiquitous computing, a user may benefit of a context-aware agent for the proactive execution of tasks scheduled, for instance, in a To-Do-List [3]. In this case, the user lists the task to be performed in different contexts and environments and gives to a personal agent the autonomy to perform them entirely or in part. When the user is in a particular situation (environment, time, location, emotional state, etc.) that triggers one of these tasks, her/his agent requests its personalized execution on the user behalf, by transferring to the environment the needed information. When the task has been performed, the agent communicates results to the user: these may be of various nature, according to the performed service, and can be adapted to *user in context* features. The architectural model of D-Me is based on this vision. It includes two interacting entities: a **D-Me Agent**, representing the user, and the **Environment**, a physical or logical place in which various services are available. The D-Me Agent: i) knows the tasks in the To-Do-List and how to perform them in a given context; ii) manages the *Mobile User Profile* (**MUP**) with its privacy requirements; iii) requests execution of services and iv) presents messages appropriately. The environment is "active" [12]: it is populated by several D-Me Agents and by **Service Agents** which execute various tasks. While the number of Service Agents depends on how many tasks the environment supports, there is only one **Keeper Agent** that knows which (D-Me and Service) agents exist in the environment. It therefore provides to D-Me environment-related information and the list of agents which could accomplish the required service. Users may interact with services in a remote way or by being physically in the environment. We adopted a distributed approach to personalization [10]: on one side, D-Me knows its user and how to perform delegated tasks; on the other side, the environment can provide adapted service execution. Both entities need to sense and elaborate context information. We implemented personalization by means of specialized agents: the **UMAgent** and the **ContextAgent** which manage, respectively, user and context modeling; the **D-Me Agent**, which manages user and task related data, and the **Interface Agent**, whose role is to communicate user-adapted results. The D-Me architecture has been developed using the JADE toolkit [7] which is FIPA [6] compliant.

3   User, Context, and Tasks

In the model described above, adaptation to "user in context" features can be applied at different levels: by triggering user tasks, by asking specialized services in the environment to execute these tasks and by exchanging messages with the user: for instance, remind messages or information presentation. To show how D-Me deals with personalization, we will use a simple example that we developed in our first prototype: MY-DIB. In this prototype, the Department of Informatics in Bari (DIB) is the Environment while the users are students with different levels of experience, teachers and staff members. These users can be represented by D-Me agents. Let us assume that the To-Do-List includes the two following tasks: *"Give back to the library the book on Operating Systems"* (with low priority) and *"Find documentation for the Web Programming exam"* (with high priority). When the user comes close to the library, D-Me generates a reminder for giving back the book; it also proactively asks the library Service Agent whether Web Programming books are available and displays information received according to students rating. Let's see how our MAS deals with this situation.

- **Environment Modeling**: an environment is made 'active' by giving to agents which populate it the capability to understand its features: that is, by modeling it. In MY-DIB, the user needs for services may belong to the following scopes: learning, social relations, leisure, food-services and administration. Every scope identifies a set of specialized services. For instance, the 'learning' family includes the following services: register for an exam, get information on how to prepare it, collect learning material and so on. As we said, scopes are used to identify the user and context features that are relevant for performing a task. The physical features of the environment have also to be described. For instance, the library has 'learning' as a scope and is a 'public' place. In the library there is a PC, identified by an ID and an address, that can be used to communicate results. Therefore, all the tasks in the To-Do-List that are enabled in the library and have 'learning' as a scope will be proactively activated when the user is in it or passes nearby.

- **User Modeling**: in the present prototype, data in the MUP are collected in two ways:the user can input information through a graphical interface, while other information (i.e. temporary interests) can be derived from tasks scheduled in the To-Do-List. The XML fragment in Tab. 1 shows the MUP of a female second-year student. The XML structure reflects the user profile ontology used in D-Me and includes four main sections: IDENTITY (with identification data such as the user name, sex, id, password, and email), MIND (background knowledge, interests and know-how), BODY (disabilities or preferences in using a body part during interaction) and PERSONALITY (personality traits and habits). Every slot in the MUP can be protected by giving a 'scope' validity to the corresponding XML tag and can be made 'not public' by setting the 'publicly' attribute to 'false'. For instance, in the example in Tab. 1 the student interest towards web programming can be shared with other agents only in the 'DIB', while her interest in pop music is always public. When users access some environment service through their D-Me Agents, data that are relevant to adapt service execution are passed to their UMAgents, which start the modeling process. In the considered example, when the user is in the DIB, her identification data, interest in web programming and pop music will be considered, together with the preferred interaction modalities (visual interaction). When interaction ends, the environment sends back to D-Me a portion of the model, updated according to what has been inferred: D-Me stores this data in the MUP as 'inferred'. We did not consider consistency issues so far; however, since we provided the D-Me model with an infrastructure able to support federation of environments, we are considering how they could exchange information about the user. Communication between the agents that interact to accomplish the user modeling task is based on ontology sharing. This enables us to overcome problems due to agents using different representations for user profiles [8].

Table 1. An example of XML file representing a MUP.

```
<UserIdentify slotName="userIdentity" login="lpam" password="miky75" publicly="false"/>
<classIdentity slotName="Identity" surname="leone" telephone="33232" email=""
name="pam" job="" sex="F" cYear="II" resident="no" publicly="true"/ >
<Interest slotName="Interest">
<UserConcept slotName="music" confidence="high" topic="pop" publicly="true">
<EnvScope nameScope="All"/></UserConcept>
<UserConcept slotName="study" confidence="high" topic="web programming"
publicly="true"><EnvScope nameScope="DIB"/ >< /UserConcept>
—
< /Interest>
<Body slotName="Body"><classBody use="true" part="Eye" publicly="true"/ >
<classBody use="true" part="Hear" publicly="false"/ >
.....
< /Body>
<Personality slotName="Personality">
<UserConcept confidence="high" topic="sociality" publicly="true"
slotName="userConcept"><EnvScope nameScope="FreeTime"/ >< /UserConcept>
< /Personality>
.....
```

- **Context Modeling**: in D-Me, context is grounded on the concept of 'tasks executable in an environment'. Given a task in the To-Do-List, its execution and results may be influenced by the context in which interaction occurs. In particular: i) *environment-related* features (scope, noise and light level); ii) dynamic *user-related* features that identify the physical and social surroundings of the user (emotional state, location, activity the user is performing, time and weather conditions); iii) *device* employed and its state at the considered time (battery, connection, and so on.). These factors are sensed and controlled by dedicated **Sensors Agents**, which communicate relevant changes to the **Context Agent**. In the previous example, the Sensor Agent controlling the user location detects the user presence in the DIB and in particular her relative position to key places such as the library. The Sensor Agent controlling the device detects that the user has got a PDA. The context situation relevant at time ti is represented in an XML structure compliant to the context ontology.

- **Task Modeling**: D-Me may execute tasks in the To-Do-List that are enabled in the given context. To model the 'task-user-context' relation, we employed an extension of Petri Nets which was developed by our research group in a previous project [5]. For instance, in the previously described situation the first task in the To-Do-List corresponds to the D-Me goal *Remind(U, Do(Task, env, Cti))*, where U denotes relevant user features, $Task$ denotes the task in the To-Do-List, env denotes the environment and Cti the context at time ti. In this case, when the user comes close to the library, D-Me generates a reminder for giving back the book that is presented appropriately by the Interface Agent. The second task in the To-Do-List activates another D-Me goal *Search(D-Me, News(U, Task, env, Cti))*. In the current context, for achieving this goal, D-Me asks the library Service Agent whether Web Programming books are available and displays information according to student ratings.

- **Interaction Modeling**: The *Interface Agent*interacts with the user and is responsible for communicating results of tasks or for asking information or confirmation required for task execution. In the To-Do-List application, we consider the following families of communication tasks: *request* for input or for confirmation, *notification, remind messages* and *information provision*. Communication with users is adapted to their preferences and features, activity, location in the environment, emotional state and device. To this aim, the Interface Agent implements two typical behaviors of Natural Language Generation systems: *Content Generation* and *Surface Generation*. The first one decides how to communicate results provided by ServiceAgents as XML structures, according to the selected communication strategy. The second one displays the content according to factors influencing personalization [2], by applying XSL transformation rules.

Acknowledgements. We thank Fiorella de Rosis for her comments and the students who cooperated in the implementation of the prototype in the scope of their dissertation work.

References

1. Byun, H.E., and Cheverst.,K.:Exploiting User Models and Context-Awareness to Support Personal Daily Activities, Workshop in UM2001 on User Modelling for Context-Aware Applications, Sonthofen, Germany (2001).
2. De Carolis, B., de Rosis, F., and Pizzutilo, S.: Adapting Information Presentation to the "User in Context". IJCAI Workshop on AI in Mobile Systems, Seattle (2001).
3. Dey, A.K.: Understanding and Using Context. Personal and Ubiquitous Computing **5** (2001) 4–7.
4. Dey, A.K., and Abowd, G.D.: CyberMinder: A Context-Aware System for Supporting Reminders. Proceedings of International Symposium on Handheld and Ubiquitous Computing (1999).
5. de Rosis F., Pizzutilo S., and De Carolis, B.: Formal description and evaluation of user adapted interfaces. Int. Journal of Human-Computer Studies **49** (1998) 95–120.
6. http://www.fipa.org.
7. http://sharon.cselt.it/projects/jade/
8. Heckmann,D.: Ubiquitous User Modeling for Situated Interaction. In: Proceedings of the 8th Int. Conf. on User Modeling.LNCS, Vol. 2109. Springer (2001) 280–282
9. Jameson, A.: Modeling Both the Context and the User. Personal and Ubiquitous Computing. **5**. Nr 1. 29–33 (2001).
10. Kobsa A.: Generic User Modeling Systems.UMUAI. Vol. II. nos.1-2,Kluwer Academic Publisher (2001) 49–63
11. Maes, P.: Agents that Reduce Work and Information Overload, Communications of the ACM, **37-7**, ACM Press (1994).
12. McCarthy, J.F.: Active Environments: Sensing and Responding to Groups of People. Journal of Personal and Ubiquitous Computing, **5**, No. 1 (2001).
13. Lieberman H. and Selker T. Out of Context:Computer Systems That Adapt To, and Learn From, Context.IBM Systems Journal **39** n.3-4 (2000) 617–631,.
14. Weiser M.: The Computer for the 21st Century. Scientific American, September (1991).

A User Modeling Markup Language (UserML) for Ubiquitous Computing

Dominik Heckmann[1] and Antonio Krueger[2]

[1] European Post-Graduate College "Cognitive Systems and Speech Technology"
http://www.coli.uni-sb.de/egk
heckmann@dfki.de

[2] Saarland University, Germany
http://w5.cs.uni-sb.de/
krueger@dfki.de

Abstract. Ubiquitous computing offers new chances and challenges to the field of user modeling. With the markup language UserML, we try to contribute a platform for the communication about partial user models in a ubiquitous computing environment, where all different kinds of systems work together to satisfy the user's needs. We also present an implementation architecture of a general user model editor which is based on UserML. The keywords are ubiquitous computing, distributed user modeling and markup languages.

1 Introduction

Ubiquitous computing [1] is a paradigm shift where technology becomes virtually invisible in our lives. Instead of only using mobile devices or desktop computing devices, the technology will be embedded in the objects of our daily life. In 1995, Jon Orwant already claimed in his Doppelgänger [2] project that *We need a protocol for encoding information about users, any given user modeling system should be able to benefit from others and that user models should follow you around.* If we look at ubiquitous computing through the eyes of user modeling and decide to enable the interaction to be uniformly user-adaptive, a need for extended user model communication becomes obvious. In this paper, the ideas of ubiquitous computing are used as a justification for the development of UserML.

2 The User Modeling Markup Language UserML

Using XML as knowledge representation language has the advantage that it can be used directly in the Internet environment. For UserML we have chosen to take a modularized approach in which several modules will be connected via identifiers (IDs) and references to identifiers (IDREFs). With this method, the tree structure of XML can be extended to represent graph structures. In this paper we focus on the content level, to say "which" information will be send

P. Brusilovsky et al. (Eds.): UM 2003, LNAI 2702, pp. 393–397, 2003.

and not "how" the information will be send. The level of "how to send XML messages" between different user model applications, sensors, smart objects and so on, will be solved by the *Web Service Architecture* of the World Wide Web Consortium, where the interaction between so called *services requestors* and *service providers* will be defined, (see i.e. `http://www.webservices.org`). The UserML documents will be embedded in SOAP envelopes.

The content of a `UserML` document will be divided into `MetaData`, `UserModel`, `InferenceExplanations` as well as `ContextModel` and `EnvironmentModel`. The main focus in this poster presentation lays on the UserModel and the Inference-Explanations, but however, in order to explain inferred user model entries, the instrumented environment and the context (see i.e. [3]) of the interaction process need to be represented or referred to as well.

2.1   Example: A User-Adaptive Airport Navigation System

In this subsection we present an example of a user-adaptive airport navigation system, which is currently under development in the integrating scenario of the *German Collaborative Research Center on Resource-Adaptive Cognitive Processes, SFB378, in the projects READY and REAL.*

How can we represent for example the following derived user property together with the description of the situation? *A system at an airport detects that a person is currently under high time pressure because she has a flight ticket for a flight, which boarding time will probably close in 10 minutes and the user still has to navigate to the gate.*

2.2   UserML Syntax: An Example and It's DTD

The approach that we suggest separates between two different levels. On the first level, we offer a simple XML structure for all entries of the partial user model. These `UserData` elements consist of the elements: `category`, `range` and `value`. On the second level, we find the ontology that defines the categories. The advantage of this approach is that different ontologies can be used with the same UserML tools. Thus different user modeling applications could use the same framework and keep their individual user model elements.

Example of a partial user model which uses categories from the ontology "UserOL"

```
<UserModel>

    <UserData id="231">
        <category>userproperty.timepressure</category>
        <range>low-medium-high</range>
        <value>high</value>
        <ontology>"http://www.u2m.org/UserOL/"</ontology>
    </UserData>
```

```
<UserData id="224">
    <category>userproperty.walkingspeed</category>
    <range>slow-normal-fast</range>
    <value>fast</value>
    <ontology>"http://www.u2m.org/UserOL/"</ontology>
</UserData>

<UserData id="122">
    <category>usercontext.location</category>
    <range>airport.location</range>
    <value>X35Y12</value>
    <ontology>"http://www.u2m.org/UserOL/"</ontology>
</UserData>
```

```
</UserModel>
```

The UserModel consists of an unbounded list of UserData entries. Each one defines the category, the range and the value. The reference to the ontology can also be set by default in the UserModel element. The alternative approach would have been to encode the user modeling knowledge into the XML elements like `<timepressure>`, `<psychologycal-states>`, `<typing-behaviour>`. Confidence values, a notion of time and the references to the inference explanations will be added with the next step.

Preliminary DTD for the Element "UserModel"

```
<!ELEMENT  UserModel (UserData)*>
<!ELEMENT  UserData (category, range, value, ontology?)>
<!ATTLIST  UserData id ID>
<!ELEMENT  category (#PCDATA)>
<!ELEMENT  range (#PCDATA)>
<!ELEMENT  value (#PCDATA)>
<!ELEMENT  ontology (#PCDATA)>
```

Remark. The user model ontology "UserOL" is still under construction. It will be presented at the webpage http://www.u2m.org/UserOL/. The current syntax definition of UserML can be found at the webpage http://www.u2m.org/UserML/.

3 Implementing a General User Model Editor Which Is Based on UserML

If an interaction system or an intelligent environment collects data about a user, this person should have the possibility to inspect and edit this model in a human readable format. A private (not necessarily mobile) device seems to be a good choice to serve as an editing tool for user models of different user-adaptive systems. Especially in ubiquitous computing not every user-adaptive system will

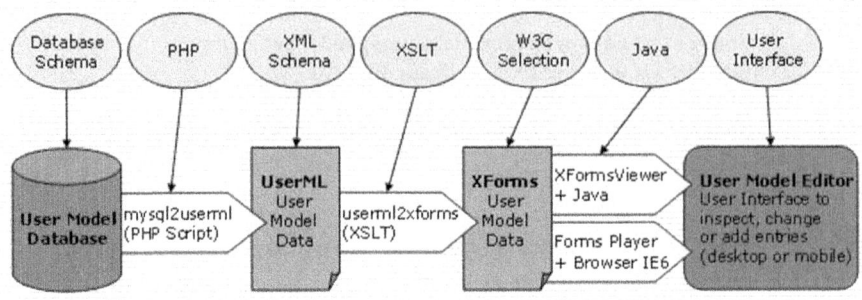

Fig. 1. A general user modeling editing tool based on UserML

have a user interface. With the help of UserML the information and the user model editor could be send to the nearest user interface.

The current implementation of this editing tool transforms UserML into the W3C Candidate Recommendation "XForms" (see [5]) with XSLT. XForms documents can be interpreted by web browsers or on mobile devices with a java vm. UserML can also be generated from a database.

Conclusion

We think that ubiquitous computing will have a great influence on user modeling. The development of a markup language for user modeling within the new paradigm of ubiquitous computing is important. The main idea of UserML is to enable communication about partial user models via the Internet. In this paper, we put the focus on the aspect of representing partial user models with inference explanations. This work is under progress.

References

1. Weiser, M.: "The Computer for the 21st Century". Scientific American, 265(3) (1991)
2. Orwant, J.: "Heterogeneous Learning in the Doppelgänger User Modeling System", User Modeling and User-Adapted Interaction **4** (1995)
3. Jameson, A.: "Modeling Both the Context and the User", Personal Technologies, **5** (2001)
4. Heckmann, D.: "Ubiquitous User Modeling for Situated Interaction", UM2001
5. W3C: "XForms Candidate Recommendation", http://www.w3.org/TR/xforms/

Appendix

An experimental representation of the the airport scenario example

```
<InferenceExplanations>
    <inference id="002">
        <inferred>
            <userplan>goto.airport-location-X34</userplan>
            <userproperty>timpressure.high</userproperty>
        </inferred>
        <inferred-from>
            <evidence>user.has-flight-ticket</evidence>
            <evidence>user.airport-location-X20</evidence>
            <evidence>boarding-time.flight</evidence>
        </inferred-from>
        <inferred-by>
            <device>334</device>
        </inferred-by>
    </inference>
</InferenceExplanations>
```

A preliminary DTD for the Element "InferenceExplanations"

```
<!ELEMENT  InferenceExplanations (inference)*>
<!ELEMENT  inference (inferred, inferred-from, inferred-by)>
<!ATTLIST  inference id ID>
<!ELEMENT  inferred (UserData | ContextData)+>
<!ELEMENT  inferred-from (evidence)*>
<!ELEMENT  evidence (UserData | ContextData)+>
<!ELEMENT  inferred-by (device)*>
```

A preliminary DTD for the Element "UserML"

```
<!ELEMENT  UserML (MetaData, UserModel, InferenceExplanations)>
<!ELEMENT  MetaData %metadata;>
<!ELEMENT  UserModel %usermodel;>
<!ELEMENT  InferenceExplanations %inferenceexplanations;>
```

A preliminary DTD for the Element "ContextML"

```
<!ELEMENT  ContextML (ContextModel, EnvironmentModel)>
<!ELEMENT  ContextModel %contextmodel;>
<!ELEMENT  EnvironmentModel %environmentmodel;>
```

Purpose-Based User Modelling in a Multi-agent Portfolio Management System

Xiaolin Niu, Gordon McCalla, and Julita Vassileva[1]

Department of Computer Science
University of Saskatchewan
Saskatoon, Saskatchewan, S7N 5A9 Canada
{xin978, mccalla, jiv}@mail.usask.ca

Abstract. This poster outlines a new approach for decentralized user modelling using a taxonomy of *purposes* that define a variety of context-dependent user modelling processes rather than creating and maintaining a single centralized user modelling server. This approach can be useful in distributed environments where autonomous agents develop user models independently and do not necessarily adhere to a common representation scheme.

1 Introduction

Traditionally user modelling has focused on creating and maintaining a single global description of the user used internally in an application for some purpose defined at design time [1]. Knowledge representation is a key issue in this kind of traditional user modelling. With the emergence of networked applications, user modelling servers have been proposed [3]. User modelling servers provide a centralized solution: even if the user data comes from and serves various applications, the representation of the user model follows a particular centralized schema, which is known in advance to the applications.

However, in a multi-agent based software environment, a single user model is typically replaced by user model fragments, developed for particular purposes and contexts by the various autonomous software agents populating the environment [7, 9]. These fragments cannot be expected to share the same representation scheme (the same problem arises in distributed databases, see [4]). Therefore the focus of user modelling shifts from the collection at one place of as many data about a user as possible to collecting on demand whatever user information is available at this moment from various agents and interpreting it for a particular purpose. This is called *active* user modelling [7].

Our goal is to develop a methodology for active user modeling and a library of purpose clichés for active user modelling. The representation of each purpose is procedural and contains a description of the context in which the procedure can be applied to achieve the purpose. The purposes are retrieved and executed by distributed

---

[1] This work is supported by the Natural Sciences and Engineering Research Council of Canada.

P. Brusilovsky et al. (Eds.): UM 2003, LNAI 2702, pp. 398–402, 2003.

autonomous agents to compute user models "just in time" [6] as they are needed. Similarly to developing a full ontology of a domain, envisaging all possible purposes for user modelling in all possible contexts is an impossible task. Therefore, the effort of the designer should focus on creating a library of important, reusable purpose clichés.

2 Purposes in a Multi-agent Portfolio Management System

A multi-agent portfolio management system [8] serves as a domain for our investigations into purpose clichés. There are two kinds of agents: personal agents (PA) represent investors who need advice, and expert agents (EA) who provide that advice. A main purpose for a PA is to find an appropriate EA for a given investor, and for this models of both the investor and the EA are needed. There are many other typical purposes in this domain.

Each purpose consists of inputs, functions and outputs. The inputs denote the type of raw data that is relevant to the given purpose. The functions are algorithms used to compute the desired outputs using the inputs within context-specific resource constraints. The outputs are the result of this computation, and can be considered to be context-specific partial user/agent models. These partial models can also form input to other purposes. The purposes can be organized into *hierarchies* with respect to *generalization* and *aggregation* (similar to plans produced using hierarchical planning [2]).

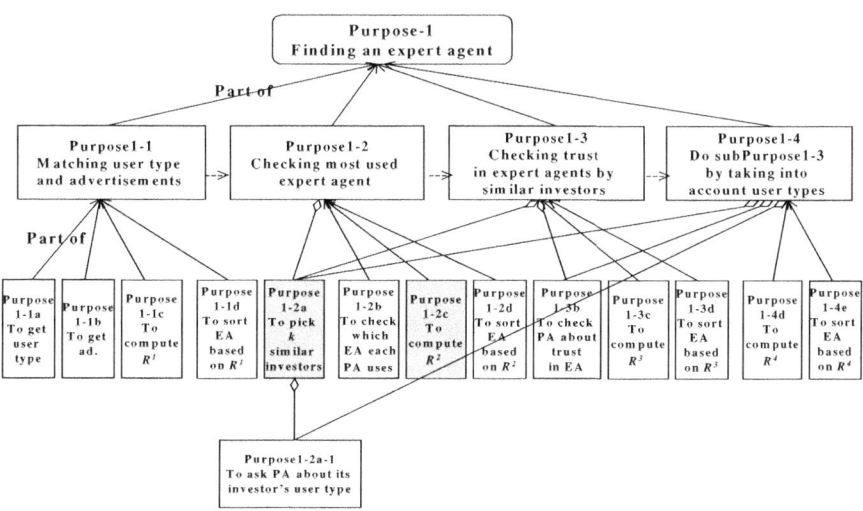

Fig. 1. The aggregation hierarchy for *purpose-1*, finding an expert agent

In a generalization hierarchy, the specific purposes inherit information and procedures from more general purposes in the hierarchy. For example, one specific purpose in the stock investment domain is *Purpose-1*, which is to select an appropriate expert agent for an investor. The higher-level purpose might be to select an agent (not necessarily an expert agent) to match the needs of a person (not necessarily an investor). Two more specific purposes might be to find an expert agent for an investor who is already retired and to find an expert agent for an investor who is a student.

Purposes can also aggregate sub-purposes, resulting in aggregation hierarchies where some sub-purposes can be part of several super purposes. The way sub-purposes are aggregated can be defined by the functions of the super purpose. For example, *Purpose-1* matches the model of the investor and the EA by gradually integrating user/agent model fragments by consecutively aggregating the results of 4 sub-purposes (as shown in Fig.1). The 4 sub-purposes of *Purpose-1* can be called in one by one depending on resource and time availability. The algorithm in *Purpose-1* can be stopped at any time and will generate the best answer so far (depending on which of the sub-purposes were executed). However, the sub-purposes of *Purpose1-1* (and the other second level purposes) do not have this anytime aspect, since they require fully completing each sub-purpose.

Consider one of the sub-purposes of *Purpose1-2*, **Purpose1-2c**: to calculate the rating R^2 of each expert agent. This purpose calculates the rating of each expert agent based on what proportion of a given group of personal agents uses the expert agent. Let's denote with $\beta_E \in [0,1]$ the evidence of usage. For example, if EA_1 (Expert Agent 1) is used by 75% of the personal agents, then β_1 is 0.75. Therefore, the rating R^2 for each expert agent so far can be derived using the rating computed by *Purpose1-1* (*Purpose1-1* computes the rating of each expert agent based on the difference between the advertisement of the expert agent and user type of the investor), i.e. R'_E and the new evidence β_E. The simple reinforcement learning formula is:

$$R^2_E = \varepsilon\, R'_E + (1 - \varepsilon)\, \beta_E$$

where $0 \le \varepsilon \le 1$ is a coefficient which denotes how much the agent values the new evidence β_E. The output from *Purpose1-2c* is a vector $[R^2_1 \ldots R^2_n]$, where R^2_i denotes the rating of the ith expert agent.

3   Purpose Re-use

A library of purposes forms a repository of clichés, which can be plugged into any application where there is a correspondence between the application's needs and the reuse purposes. There are several ways to reuse the purposes:

- *Generalization*: A purpose can be generalized into a higher-level purpose, which can be used in different domains.
- *Specialization*: A purpose can be specialized into a more specific purpose by specifying more constraints in additional sources of information that can be used in a specific context.
- *Modification*: A purpose can be modified in order to adapt to a new domain where the available input data are of different types. For example, *Purpose-1* could be

adapted for the domain of peer help [5] to choose a helper for a student who needs some help.

- *Sharing a purpose*: A sub-purpose can be shared in aggregation by several super purposes. For example, *Purpose1-2a* is to pick the personal agents of investors who are of similar user type. This purpose can be re-used by three super purposes. Once this purpose is created, designer effort is saved when other super purposes re-use this sub-purpose.

Purpose re-use is valuable from a software engineering point of view and critical to the active user modelling approach. The basic motivation of re-using purposes is to save time and effort. If an existing solution can be reused, this saves time that would otherwise be spent on the creation of similar or identical software components. Another motivation is flexibility in response to new requirements. Purposes can be selected and tailored to the designer's needs by changing some parameters, such as inputs and context information, etc. A library of purposes could thus be designed to provide the clichés that makes the engineering of a new system much easier.

4   Possible Multi-agent System Architectures

There are several options to place the purpose hierarchies within a multi-agent system architecture:

- *On board of each agent.* This, however, can result in complex and "fat" agents leading to scalability and performance issues.
- *On a centralized "server".* When an agent needs a particular purpose, it fetches it from the server. This contrasts with centralized user modelling where the server collects and computes the user modelling data and the applications are clients, which receive and use the data. In this case, the data is kept by the personal agents. Each agent retrieves from the server the purpose that is relevant to its user modelling need at the moment and uses it to compute the new user model data. The computation and data are distributed, only a library of purposes is centralized.
- *On specialized user modeling (UM) agents associated with each purpose.* Distributed application agents subcontract UM tasks to be done by specifically-tasked UM purpose agents. Each of these specialized UM purpose agents is like a UM server, but strongly specialized. Such agents don't store any data, but perform computation upon request.

Which of these options is chosen depends on the application and the designer. Important criteria are how complex the purpose hierarchies are, how often computation is needed, how much communication is involved (influencing network traffic, performance, response time), and how important is privacy.

5   Conclusions and Future Work

We are currently implementing a comprehensive purpose hierarchy to support active user modelling in the portfolio management system. The quality of decisions made by the agents will be evaluated with simulated users. However, demonstrating that user modelling helps achieve better decisions, is only a "proof of solution existence", and doesn't show the advantages of active user modelling versus centralized modeling. The strongest argument for the active approach is that it implies less constraint on the agents (with respect to shared representation scheme, reliance on a connection to a server etc.) and is more robust (no central point of failure). We feel that the weakest point for the active approach is the practicality of developing comprehensive reusable purpose hierarchies. Our hope is that in the future, much as ontology research is leading to comprehensive shared vocabularies for many domains, over time a set of overlapping user modelling purpose cliché hierarchies will be devised for many domains and will be used to carry out active user modelling by heterogeneous software agents.

References

1. Browne, D., Totterdell, P., Norman, M.: Adaptive user interfaces. Academic Press Ltd., London, UK, 1990
2. Corkill, D.: Hierarchical Planning in a Distributed Environment. In Proceedings of the Sixth International Joint Conference on Artificial Intelligence, (1979), 168–175
3. Fink, J., and Kobsa, A.: A Review and Analysis of Commercial User Modeling Servers for Personalization on the World Wide Web. User Modeling and User-Adapted Interaction, 10 (3-4) (2000), 209–249
4. Giunchiglia, F., Zaihrayeu, I.: Making peer databases interact - a vision for an architecture supporting data coordination. Technical Report # DIT-02-0012. Also to appear in Proc. Cooperative Information Agents (CIA 2002), Madrid, September 2002
5. Greer, J., McCalla, G., Cooke, J., Collins, J., Kumar, V., Bishop, A. and Vassileva, J.: The Intelligent HelpDesk: Supporting Peer Help in a University Course. In Proc. ITS'98, San Antonio, Texas, LNCS No1452, Springer (1998), 494–503
6. Kay, J.: A scrutable user modeling shell for user-adapted interaction. Ph.D. Thesis. Baser Department of Computer Science, University of Sydney, Sydney, Australia. (1999)
7. McCalla, G., Vassileva, J., Greer, J. and Bull, S.: Active Learner Modeling. Proc. ITS2000, Springer LNCS 1839, (2000) 53–62
8. Tang, T., Winoto, P. & Niu, X.: Who Can I Trust? Investigating Trust between Users and Agents in a Multi-agent Portfolio Management System. In AAAI-2002 Workshop on Autonomy, Delegation, and Control: From Inter-agent to Groups. Edmonton, Canada, July 28, 2002
9. Vassileva, J., McCalla, G., Greer, J.: Multi-Agent Multi-User Modelling. To appear in User Modelling and User-Adapted Interaction, (2003), 28 pp manuscript

User Modeling in Adaptive Audio-Augmented Museum Environments

Andreas Zimmermann, Andreas Lorenz, and Marcus Specht

Fraunhofer Institut for Applied Information Technology
Schloß Birlinghoven
53754 Sankt Augustin, Germany
{Andreas.Zimmermann, Andreas.Lorenz,
Marcus.Specht}@fit.fraunhofer.de

Abstract. The paper illustrates approaches for making audio-augmented museum environments adaptive. Based on well-known user modeling techniques we present a combination of suitable components that adapt audio information to the interests, preferences and motion of a museum's visitor. The underlying environment, i.e. the carrier and transmitter of information, is provided by the LISTEN system, which enables the augmentation of everyday environments with audio information.

1   Introduction

The European founded LISTEN project of the Fraunhofer Institute and its partners deals with the audio augmentation of real and virtual environments [1]. The users of this system move in space wearing headphones and listen to audio sequences emitted by virtual sound sources placed in the environment. The audio pieces vary according to the user's spatial position and orientation of his/her head.

A first LISTEN prototype is intended to be applied to an art exhibition at the Kunstmuseum in Bonn [6]. The visitors of the museum experience personalized audio information about exhibits through their headphones. The audio presentation takes into account the visitor's profile. Besides presentation, the system provides recommendations to the visitor regarding to his/her context. Recommended exhibition objects attract the visitor's attention by emitting sounds from its position.

This environment offers the ability to adapt the order of audio pieces, their content, and sound source to the visitor's focus in the exhibition and his/her position. In order to provide a personalized adaptation of the audio-augmented environment according to the visitor's interests, preferences, and motion, the LISTEN system builds and maintains a user model. In our approach this user model is composed of six major parts, each fulfilling a certain role within the adaptation process. In this paper we describe the system's architecture and the user modeling components that have been employed for the personalization of the LISTEN system.

P. Brusilovsky et al. (Eds.): UM 2003, LNAI 2702, pp. 403–407, 2003.

2   The LISTEN System Architecture

In the LISTEN system, a tracking system observes the movements of the user and delivers his/her current physical position and orientation to the several modules of the LISTEN system. Since the only user interface in LISTEN is the user's motion, the tracking data has to relate to a space model. For this purpose, a virtual environment is overlaid on the physical one in order to connect real world objects with virtual objects. Figure 1 introduces the overall architecture of the LISTEN system: The AVANGO application [5], which encapsulates the space modeling and tracking modules, and the LISTEN Lounge containing the user modeling components.

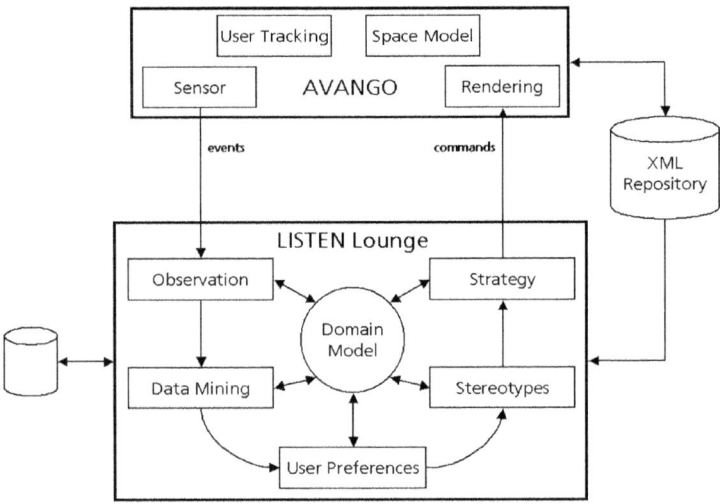

Fig. 1. The LISTEN Architecture

2.1   The AVANGO System

As shown in Figure 1, AVANGO serves as an *information collector* and *rendering engine* for the LISTEN Lounge. In the role of an information collector the AVANGO's sensor component delivers events that are filtered and semantically enriched in order to build a user model. Due to the short time intervals the user is being tracked a large set of events has to be processed.

In the role of a rendering engine, AVANGO receives and interprets commands assembled by the LISTEN Lounge in order to control its behavior for adapting the presentation of the sound items. Thus, different sequences of commands lead to different kinds of augmentation of the environment by an audio stream.

3   User Modeling in the LISTEN Application

On this *control level* of the LISTEN system, the LISTEN Lounge converts the information held in the user model into real world actions. According to the user's interests, preferences, and motion AVANGO adjusts variable properties of the user's environment based on the retrieved control information. The LISTEN Lounge control mechanisms affect the following domain properties:

- Presentation style (e.g. music, spoken text, sound effects)
- Content of the presented sound (e.g. facts, emotions, overview)
- Length and Volume of the sound item
- Sound source (i.e. the direction of the sound)

Motion of the sound source (e.g. for realizing a moving sound)
In order to realize user modeling on a high level, the LISTEN Lounge implements the six major components, which are described in the next subsections in more detail.

Domain Model
Without any connection to a domain model a valuable adaptation process according to the user's interests and preferences cannot be performed. That is why a domain model plays a central role in every adaptive system. User specific attributes like age, sex, etc. can be applied in several domains but some attributes like interest in arts are essential in specialized domains. From the central XML repository the LISTEN Lounge extracts parts of the domain model that are relevant for its operation, such as descriptions of the sound items (length, language, meta-data, …), sound source identifiers and location, or meta-data about visual objects.

Observation
The observation module of the LISTEN Lounge receives all incoming events sent by AVANGO. Thus, an event history for every user is saved and an *implicit user profile* is recorded. By the means of statistical models this implicit user profile already allows the deduction of valuable information that can be used for standard adaptation activity. For example, the more time a visitor spends in front of an art exhibit the more s/he might like it. It is planned to gain more significant information relating to the behavior of the user by implementing different machine learning and data mining algorithms to extract semantically enriched information.

Data Mining
In the LISTEN application, the only user interface is the user's motion. Once the user has started his/her walk through the environment, s/he does not carry any device except the headphones. Thus, the system will not get any explicit feedback from the user during the user's tour but needs to infer information from the user's behavior by some data mining process (e.g. for clustering and detecting stereotypes). The basis for this inference process is the data delivered by the observation component: *Time* (i.c. timestamps, delays, time sequences), *position* (i.e. position in the physical and virtual environment), and *focus* (i.e. name of the object the user is looking at).

User Preferences

In our user modeling approach for a museum environment we chose to employ an adapted information-brokering tool for modeling user preferences (cf. [7]), because the information items to be brokered are composed of sound items. By requesting user preferences, different user profiles can be built up that facilitate the filtering of information according to the users' needs, preferences *and* position [3].

Stereotypes

With the aid of stereotypes, the LISTEN Lounge defines the user 's observation type and thus, the system is able to accordingly adapt the scenery and cause a different sound presentation. In a museum environment it is not trivial to predefine meaningful stereotypes. Some easy to identify stereotypes are for example adults and children. To create more expressional stereotypes, we have subdivided the adult category into three stereotypes: Fact-oriented (the presentation is mainly composed of spoken text), emotional (music pieces and effects) and overview (short sound items).

Adaptive Methods and Strategy

Based on a meaningful user model, this control component takes a decision between several high-level adaptive methods and different strategies for presenting objects in the user's environment. For example, when a user enters a room the system can either follow in a more passive mode and pace the visitor's exploration of the space or actively give auditive cues to guide him/her on a strictly predefined or context-aware adapted tour (Prompting).

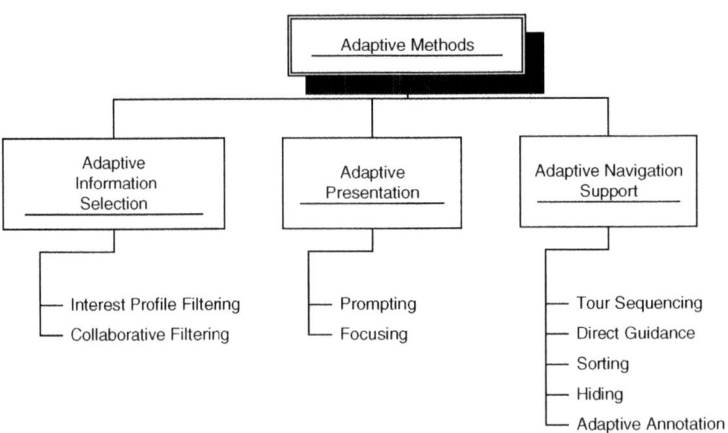

Fig. 2. Structure of adaptive Methods

For the LISTEN principle we adjusted several adaptive strategies from the field of adaptive hypermedia (cf. Figure 2) that are suited to tailor information selection and presentation to the individual user.

4   Conclusion and Future Work

In this paper we presented an approach for adapting the sound presentation in an audio augmented environment. The technology for this sound augmentation is provided by the LISTEN system, into which the user modeling component LISTEN Lounge was embedded. The LISTEN Lounge assembles a bunch of well-known user modeling techniques for adapting the audio presentation regarding to the users' preferences, interests, and motion. We discussed the application of these techniques in our special environment and described suitable realizations.

We expect that one of the drawbacks of the LISTEN system will be *the lack of explicit user feedback* we have to cope with. Computer users are known for providing little feedback to rate the quality of items recommended to them. The lack of explicit feedback causes difficulties in clearly distinguishing between interesting and non-interesting objects. In these situations, some systems use heuristics to determine positive and negative evidence of the user's information interest (i.e. unselected objects are negative examples [2]). Another approach developed in [4] uses significant analysis aiming at selecting those features that are extraordinarily important to the user for identifying relevant objects.

In addition, we have to approach the fact that in the LISTEN system the *human-computer interaction only lasts a short time period*. Therefore, the system needs to preprocess a sufficient amount of past users' data in order to build a meaningful user model. Since such adequate information opulence is not accessible by now, we are forced to develop learning algorithms that can infer from a small set of data.

References

1. Eckel, G. (2001), LISTEN – Augmenting Everyday Environments with Interactive Soundscapes. In: Proceedings of the I3 Spring Days Workshop "Moving between the physical and the digital: exploring and developing new forms of mixed reality user experience", Porto, Portugal 2001.
2. Mladenic D. Personal WebWatcher (1996), Implementation and Design. Technical Report IJS-DP-7472, Department of Intelligent Systems, J. Stefan Institute, Slovenia, 1996.
3. Pazzani M. J. and Billsus D. (1997), Learning and Revising User Profiles: The Identification of Interesting Web Sites. In: Machine Learning 27, pp. 313–331.
4. Schwab, I., Pohl, W. and Koychev, I. (2000), Learning to Recommend from Positive Evidence, In: Proceedings of Intelligent User Interfaces, ACM Press 2000, pp.241–247.
5. Tramberend, H. (1999), Avango: A Distributed Virtual Reality Framework. In: Proceedings of the IEEE Virtual Reality '99 Conference, Houston,Texas, USA, 1999
6. Unnützer, P. (2001), LISTEN im Kunstmuseum Bonn, KUNSTFORUM International, Vol. 155, June/July 2001, pp. 469/70.
7. Zimmermann, A., Lorenz, A. and Specht, M. (2003), The Use of an Information Brokering Tool in an Electronic Museum Environment. To appear in: Proceedings of the Museums and the Web (MW2003), Charlotte, North Carolina, 2003

MAPS: Dynamic Scaffolding for Independence for Persons with Cognitive Impairments

Stefan Carmien

Center for LifeLong Learning and Design, University of Colorado at Boulder
carmien@cs.colorado.edu
http://www.cs.colorado.edu/~carmien

Abstract. Individuals with cognitive disabilities are often unable to live independently due to their inability to perform daily tasks. Computationally enhanced dynamic prompting systems can mitigate this inability. Poor user interfaces, however, drive high levels of assistive technology abandonment by this population. To address this issue, MAPS (**M**emory **A**iding **P**rompting **S**ystem) provides an effective prompting system with an intuitive interface for configuration. User modeling techniques facilitate simple and effective prompting scripts for individual user needs.

1 Background

Cognitively impaired individuals are often unable to live on their own due to deficiencies in memory, attention, and executive functionalities. These deficits can result in an inability to consistently perform normal domestic tasks, which then forces these persons to require ongoing support, often in assisted-living homes. A common way of transitioning from assisted living to independent or semi-independent living is through the use of prompting systems. A prompting system is produced by breaking down a task into constituent steps; a set of steps constitute a prompting script. Each step or prompt is made up of a visual and a verbal component. Traditional prompting systems, however, provide only pre-task generated scripts, ignoring changing environments, dynamic situations, and evolving user needs.

Caregivers report that difficulties in producing and modifying configurations in assistive technology often lead to abandonment. Some experts estimate that as much as 75% of all assistive technology devices and systems are abandoned [8].

These deficits in prompting and reasons for abandonment are addressed in the prompting system MAPS (**M**emory **A**iding **P**rompting **S**ystem). The target populations for MAPS are cognitively disabled individuals in the "trainable Mentally Handicapped" (IQ 55-72) range and in the upper range of "Severely Mentally Handicapped" (IQ < 55); as well as their caregivers with basic computer skills.

2 Related Research

Prompting studies provide a background for the design and study of computationally based prompting systems. A small body of literature, including the work of King

P. Brusilovsky et al. (Eds.): UM 2003, LNAI 2702, pp. 408–410, 2003.

[7] and Beukelman [3], addresses design and implementation issues for assistive technology and augmentative and alternative communication devices. Existing PC- [2] and PDA- [1] based prompting systems provide information to base design and theoretical inferences.

MAPS provides a mobile prompting platform that provides context-sensitive prompts. MAPS approaches the configuration and script generation tasks as a second user interface, acknowledging the dual user interface requirements in assistive technology design. My research with MAPS is based on several topics from the larger UM (**U**ser **M**odeling) and HCI (**H**uman-**C**omputer **I**nteraction) communities. The design of MAPS context sensitivity, error detection, and error correction functions are informed by various studies of distributed cognition [9]. User modeling studies shape the design of the script editor application and error trapping and correction modules of the MAPS system [4].

3 Design

MAPS comprises a PDA prompter and a PC-based script editor tool. Functional requirements include a simple way to backtrack, or start over, to allow for mistakes during task completion; appropriate wireless connectivity for dynamic, context-based prompt generation; and "panic button" functionality.

The MAPS caregiver interface, a PC-based application, provides tools for script creation, previewing, modification, and sharing via a repository of scripts. The script editor and system configuration software must be simple enough to allow immediate use as well as deep enough to allow many different types of tasks to be scripted. User categorization models [6] provide support for *critic*-style aid in composing scripts, as well as automatic generation of error trapping and appropriate corrective actions.

A MAPS script may have several points at which the timing and content of the next required step depends on the context of the user, the user's capabilities, and the state of the environment. For instance, on a bus trip, the user may need to wait at the bus stop *until* the correct bus arrives, and when the right bus arrives, a prompt must be displayed instructing the user to board *that* bus. By interfacing the MAPS prompter with a server coordinating GPS (**G**lobal **P**ositioning **S**ystem) data from the bus, the running of a typical bus trip script can interact with the real-time events on the streets, prompting the user to wait and proceed when appropriate.

One of the advantages of computationally enhanced prompting systems is the ability to track and repair errors. This dynamic adaptivity affords great gains in useful functionality and reliability, but at a cost in configurational complexity. Because every script is, by design, unique to the user and situation, the number of potential error states and sets of error-trapping flags can become unmanageably big if configured individually. By generating a user model in the MAPS caregiver script editor/creator setup, error situations at typical stages of a given type of script can be populated by uniform *templates* of correction (which will be then instantiated with the appropriate contextual data). This combined user-needs model (user specifics and generic task/segment error correction template) affords almost automatic error flag pattern trapping as well as appropriate dynamic prompt generation.

4 Open Issues and Next Steps

The full scope of my research, beyond the implementation and evaluation of the prompter and script editor, includes utilizing and evaluating user modeling techniques to create individual "templates" for script design, error detection, and error correction for specific task domains, such as using public transportation or shopping. A rough framework and preliminary design of database schema for user modeling templates, generic script types, and script error type segmentation has been developed.

Implementing and evaluating context-sensitive wireless dynamic prompt generation, such as in the case of a bus delay or missed connection, constitutes the second challenge in my research. Issues of data format standardization and intercommunication need to be addressed and solved due to the designed reliance on, and the tight integration of, the MAPS prompter system and several other CLever projects [5],

Acknowledgments. I thank the members of the CLever research team, Leysia Palen, and my advisor, Gerhard Fischer, who gave comments on previous versions of this document. The Coleman Foundation provided financial support for this research.

References

1. http://www.ablelinktech.com and. http://www.brainaid.com
2. http://www.thevisionssystem.com
3. Beukelman, D., Mirenda, P.; *Augmentative and Alternative Communication* (second edition), Brookes, 1998
4. Fischer, G.; *User Modeling in Human–Computer Interaction,* User Modeling and User-Adapted Interaction 11 (1-2): 65–86, 2001
5. Gorman, A , Sullivan, J (2003) http://www.cs.colorado.edu/~l3d/clever/projects
6. Helander, M., Landauer, T., Prabhu, P. (eds.); *Handbook of Human-Computer Interaction*: 49 63, North-Holland, 1997
7. King, T.; *Assistive Technology Essential Human Factors-*, Allyn & Bacon, 1999
8. Reimer-Reiss, M.; *Assistive Technology Discontinuance*, Technology and Persons with Disabilities Conference, Los Angeles CA. 2000
9. Salomon, G. (ed.); *Distributed Cognitions: Psychological and Educational Considerations*, Cambridge University Press, Cambridge, United Kingdom, 1993

Adaptations of Multimodal Content in Dialog Systems Targeting Heterogeneous Devices

Songsak Channarukul

University of Wisconsin-Milwaukee
songsak@uwm.edu

Abstract. Dialog systems that adapt to different user needs and preferences appropriately have been shown to achieve higher levels of user satisfaction [1]. However, it is also important that dialog systems be able to adapt to the user's computing environment, because people can access computer systems using different devices. Existing research has focused on either user-centered adaptations or device-centered adaptations. To my knowledge, no work has been done on integrating and coordinating both types of adaptation interdependently. In this thesis, I aim to investigate how multimodal dialog systems can adapt their content and style of interaction to individual users and their current device. The primary contribution of this thesis will be a framework that extends and combines both types of multimodal content adaptations that should occur in dialog systems.

1 Problem Statement

Dialog systems that adapt to different user needs and preferences appropriately have been shown to achieve higher levels of user satisfaction [1]. However, it is also important that dialog systems be able to adapt to the user's computing environment, because people are able to access computer systems using different kinds of devices such as desktop computers, personal digital assistants, and cellular telephones. Each of these devices has a distinct set of physical capabilities, as well as a distinct set of functions for which it is typically used.

Existing research on adaptation in both hypermedia and dialog systems has focused on how to customize content based on user models [1,2] and interaction history. Some researchers have also investigated device-centered adaptations that range from low-level adaptations such as conversion of multimedia objects [3] (*e.g.,* video to images, audio to text, image size reduction) to higher-level adaptations based on multimedia document models [4] and frameworks for combining output modalities [5]. However, to my knowledge, no work has been done on integrating and coordinating both types of adaptation interdependently.

The primary problem I would like to address in this thesis is how multimodal dialog systems can adapt their content and style of interaction, taking the user, the device, and the dependency between them into account. Two main aspects of adaptability that my thesis considers are: (1) adaptability in content presentation and communication and (2) adaptability in computational strategies used to achieve system's and user's goals.

P. Brusilovsky et al. (Eds.): UM 2003, LNAI 2702, pp. 411–413, 2003.

1.1   Adaptability in Content Presentation and Communication

Multimodal dialog systems must be able to customize their content and determine the appropriate modality based on individual users and the computing environment. For example, if the user is using a desktop computer with high bandwidth Internet, the system can opt for heavy uses of video and audio. However, if the bandwidth is low, a video might be substituted by pictures with captions.

In some situations, a handheld computer is more appropriate for the user. For example, in the tutoring domain, users might want to review their past lessons while commuting, or need a summary of some procedures while practicing in the real-world. The device and the intended purpose of accessing the system will also affect the style of the presented information that might range from a declarative format (textual and lengthy) to a procedural format (more precise and imperative).

Both user and device models must be taken into consideration in order to achieve well-customized content and presentation. Beside general user modeling questions such as how to acquire information about the user and construct a user model, this thesis also considers the following issues:

– How can the system employ user and device models to adapt the content and determine the right combination of modalities effectively?
– How can one model the characteristics and constraints of devices?

1.2   Adaptability in Computational Strategies Used to Achieve System's and User's Goals

The system must be able to choose the best possible way to proceed adaptively, so that each user will be treated differently given the goals they want to achieve, past interactions, and also the system's goals. The primary issue related to computational strategies is how a planning module in a dialog system makes use of its knowledge about the user, and plan its strategies and interactions accordingly.

2   Proposed Solution

I will build a multimodal dialog system that employs a uniform, declarative, knowledge-based representation [6] to represent domain knowledge and information about users and devices. The system will keep track of information about individual users and the device they are using. Some techniques such as stereotyping [7] will be adopted to create an initial user model. A device model will be developed to represent characteristics of different device types such that appropriate modalities can be determined. A goal-based planning technique will be used to determine how the system can customize the interaction to the users' needs and to the characteristics and likely purpose of their devices.

Separate modules for text and multimodal content generation will be used to realize content into appropriate forms. I have developed a text realization module, YAG [8], that employs a template-based approach to generate texts from a domain-independent input structure or from a knowledge representation. An extension to YAG that allows multimodal content presentation generation (using SMIL[1]) is being developed.

3 Tentative Plan

First, I will investigate and develop device models and complete the extension of YAG that allows multimodal generation. Then, content-independent decision methods for customizing the interaction to users and their devices will be developed using existing knowledge representation and planning system such as SNePS [9]. Finally, I will investigate and extend some evaluation schemes such as PROMISE [10] to validate the effectiveness and usefulness of the system when it interacts with users across heterogeneous devices.

References

[1] Stent, A., Walker, M., Whittaker, S., Maloor, P.: User-Tailored Generation for Spoken Dialogue: An Experiment. In: Proceedings of ICSLP 2002. (2002) 1281–84
[2] De Bra, P., Brusilovsky, P., Houben, G.J.: Adaptive Hypermedia: From Systems to Framework. ACM Computing Surveys (CSUR) **31** (1999) 1–6
[3] Vetro, A., Sun, H.: Media conversions to support mobile users. In: Proceedings of The IEEE Canadian Conference on Electrical and Computer Engineering (CCECE). (2001) 607–612
[4] Boll, S., Klas, W., Westermann, U.: A comparison of multimedia document models concerning advanced requirements. Technical Report 99-01, Ulmer Informatik-Berichte, University of Ulm, Germany (1999)
[5] Vernier, F., Nigay, L.: A framework for the combination and characterization of output modalities. In: Proceedings of DSV-IS2000, Lecture Notes in Computer Science, Springer-Verlag (2000) 32–48
[6] McRoy, S., Haller, S., Ali, S.: Uniform Knowledge Representation for NLP in the B2 System. Natural Language Engineering **3** (1997) 123–145
[7] Rich, E.: User Modeling via Stereotypes. Cognitive Science **3** (1979) 355–366
[8] McRoy, S., Channarukul, S., Ali, S.: An Augmented Template-Based Approach to Text Realization. Natural Language Engineering (2003) To Appear.
[9] Shapiro, S.C., Group, T.S.I.: SNePS 2.4 User's Manual. Department of Computer Science, SUNY at Buffalo. (1998)
[10] Beringer, N., Kartal, U., Louka, K., Schiel, F., Turk, U.: PROMISE - A Procedure for Multimodal Interactive System Evaluation. In: Proceedings of The LREC Workshop on Multimodal Resources and Multimodal System Evaluation, Las Palmas, Spain (2002)

---

[1] http://www.w3c.org/AudioVideo

Learning Knowledge Rich User Models from the Semantic Web

Gunnar Astrand Grimnes[*]

Dept. of Computing Science, University of Aberdeen
Aberdeen, AB24 5UE, Scotland
ggrimnes@csd.abdn.ac.uk

1   Introduction

The Semantic Web [2] is a vision in which today's Web will be extended with machine readable content, and where every resource will be marked-up using machine readable metadata. The intention is that documents on the Semantic Web will convey real meaning by using structured data-formats and by referring to common ontologies.

In our research we wish to explore the impact such a Semantic Web would have on personalisation and user modelling. We investigate how a language with a well-defined semantic data model could be used for describing instances for learning user preferences, how this affects the learning process, and also how it could be used for describing the learned user models.

2   Research Problems

Techniques for acquiring user models from World Wide Web content have traditionally used keyword based approaches and keyword weighting such as TF/IDF [9] in combination with statistical machine learning algorithms, e.g. Naïve Bayes [7]. With the introduction of the Semantic Web we suggest that a more knowledge intensive approach to the acquisition of user models is needed. Learning from data represented according to the principles of the Semantic Web should have several advantages:

1. The additional structure should increase the accuracy of the learned model [3].
2. The use of ontologies should allow generalisations that would not be possible with plain keyword matching, i.e. this user likes *Hobgoblin* and *Flowers*, both of which are subclasses of *Real Ale*, so we can deduce that the user likes *Real Ale*.
3. Ideally the use of a language with well-defined semantics for input to the learning algorithm should allow the learned model to be expressed in the same language. The semantic data model should then make the learned outcome easier to understand and should allow re-use of the knowledge outside the original scenario. For example in [6] it is shown how a profile based on a certain ontology can be generated by one application and applied in another.

---

[*] The work described is supervised by Dr P. Edwards and Dr A. Preece, both of the Department of Computing Science.

P. Brusilovsky et al. (Eds.): UM 2003, LNAI 2702, pp. 414–416, 2003.

3 Contributions to the Field of User Modelling

3.1 Contrasting Statistical and Knowledge-Intensive Approaches to Model Acquisition

In our initial work we conducted an empirical investigation which compared the performance of learning user models from two different instance representations, one encoded using a semantic mark-up language, the other encoded using plain-text [4].

We used a range of different machine learning algorithms, as well as different ways of exploiting the semantic structures. The most interesting results where acquired using the Inductive Logic Programming system Progol [8], which created rules that we felt represented re-usable knowledge, see Figure 1.

Our initial hypothesis was that learning from the instances marked up with RDF should outperform learning from the plain-text versions; unfortunately this was not fully supported by our results, as the plain-text method performed at least as well as, or better than the RDF methods. The only *positive* result was the decrease in computational complexity when learning from RDF. We suspect that the reason for the unsatisfactory results was the shallow nature of the RDF data used. By "shallow" here we mean that our data was lacking ontological support, and did not express any relations between instances, only simple attribute-value pairs.

3.2 Granite Nights – A Framework for Semantic Personalisation

Granite Nights[1] is an open, standards based multi-agent application, allowing a user to schedule an evening out in Aberdeen (aka *The Granite City*).

Figure 2 shows the agents that makes up the Granite Nights architecture. The application knows about several activities available in Aberdeen: public houses, restaurants and cinemas. The profile agent is responsible for managing models of Granite Nights users; these models contain static user information, such as name and email address, and preferences for the events, such as *"I prefer pubs serving Orkney Skullsplitter Ale"*.

RDF is used consistently throughout the application for message passing, ontologies, information agent data and for user models. All the agents are FIPA[2] compatible. The motivation for developing Granite Nights emerged out of the lack of a Semantic Web application as a framework for our experiments. With this framework now in place we can begin to consider how knowledge-intensive profiling techniques can be employed.

4 Future Work

Our immediate plans are to experiment with a number of knowledge intensive machine learning algorithms in the context of Granite Nights framework. Initially we intend to investigate Explanation Based Generalisation [10] and Case-Based Reasoning [1]. We will look more into the advantages of expressing learned models in a Semantic Web language. As mentioned, this should allow re-use of the acquired knowledge about the

---

416   G.A. Grimnes

```
Machine Learning:
inClass(A) :-
  publisher(A,'Morgan Kaufmann'),
  booktitleword(A, learning).
inClass(A) :-
  titleword(A,based),
  titleword(A,case).
```

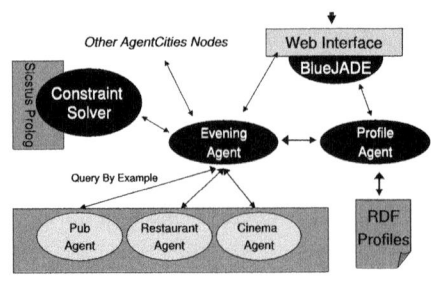

Fig. 1. Excerpt of Progol Results when attempting to classify papers from the citeseer dataset.

Fig. 2. Granite Nights - Architecture Diagram.

user. For example, a Granite Nights user-model containing information about a user's film preferences could be used in a recommendation system for an online video retailer.

A longer-term objective is to investigate the scope of user models in Granite Nights; moving away from the current model which simply captures preference information to a richer model which also includes information on a user's roles, responsibilities, commitments and relationships to other agents. We will also investigate to what extent this information can be learned. This information could, for example, enable personal agents to automatically negotiate contracts for users [5].

References

1. A. Agnar and P. Enric. Case-based reasoning : Foundational issues, methodological variations,and system approaches. *AI Communications*, 7:39–59, 1994.
2. T. Berners-Lee, J. Hendler, and O. Lassila. The semantic web. *Scientific American*, May 2001.
3. P. Edwards, D. Bayer, C. Green, and T. Payne. Experience with learning agents which manage internet-based information. In *AAAI Stanford Spring Symposium on Machine Learning in Information Access*, pages 31–40, 1996.
4. P. Edwards, G. A. Grimnes, and A. Preece. An empirical investigation of learning from the semantic web. In *ECML/PKDD, Semantic Web Mining Workshop*, 2002.
5. M. Kollingbaum and T. Norman. Supervised interaction - create a web of trust for contracting agents in electronic environments. In *Proc. of the First International Joint Conference on Autonomous Agents and Multi-Agent Systems*, pages 272–279. ACM Press, 2002.
6. S. Middleton, H. Alani, N. Shadbolt, and D. De Roure. Exploiting synergy between ontologies and recommender systems. In *11th International WWW Conference*, 2002.
7. T. Mitchell. *Bayesian Learning*, pages 154–200. McGraw-Hill, 1997.
8. S. Muggleton. Inverse entailment and Progol. *New Generation Computing, Special issue on Inductive Logic Programming*, 13(3-4):245–286, 1995.
9. G. Salton and C. Buckley. Term-weighting approaches in automatic text retrieval. *Information Processing and Management*, 24:513–523, 1988.
10. F. van Harmelen and A. Bundy. Explanation based generalisation = partial evaluation. *AI*, 36:401–412, 1988.

Modeling User Navigation

Eelco Herder

Department of Computer Science, University of Twente
P.O. Box 217, 7500 AE, Enschede, The Netherlands
herder@cs.utwente.nl

Abstract. For providing users with navigation aids that best serve their needs, user models for adaptive hypermedia should include user navigation patterns. This paper describes elements needed and how these elements can be gathered.

1 Navigation Strategies and Lostness in Hyperspace

One of the most common problems in the field of hypermedia is that users tend to become *disoriented*: they lose one's sense of location and direction in non-linear documents. This problem is aggravated by the fact that users need to maintain track of their tasks, their previous actions and their current context. This additional effort has been given the term *cognitive overhead*. Both disorientation and cognitive overhead may lead users to get 'lost in hyperspace' [7].

Despite several attempts to infer lostness from users' navigation patterns (e.g. [9]), no clear measure has been found yet. This is mainly due to the fact that users who are *exploring* a document can be rated as disoriented, even though they may be experiencing no disorientation [1]. As users may display various navigation strategies, varying from goal-directed to explorative [3], it is hard to tell from their actions whether or not they feel lost. The document structure has impact on user navigation as well, as one cannot follow non-existing links. For example, densely linked hyperspaces with many cross-references provide more freedom for exploration than hierarchically structured hyperspaces do [5].

Navigation support that is adapted to user goals, preferences and knowledge, and to the context of use, is seen as a proper way of providing adequate navigation support for varying user needs [2]. Equally important to selecting the *right* navigation suggestions, is the *number* of suggestions that should be given to the user and the *way* they should be presented [5]. However, various types of navigation strategies call for different types of navigation assistance [3]. Therefore, user navigation strategy is an indispensable part of a user model for adaptive hypermedia.

2 Navigation Support That Matches User Needs

Hypermedia links may or may not be embedded in the content regions. Links within the text are usually *associative links*, which interlink semantically related concepts. Links that are not embedded in the text – such as menus, indexes, and site maps –

P. Brusilovsky et al. (Eds.): UM 2003, LNAI 2702, pp. 417–419, 2003.

expose a document's primary structure [6] and therewith function as *contextual navigation aids* [8]. Both types of links can be adapted to the user needs. Disabling, removing or annotating associative links [2] can help users to find relevant items more easily, but does not provide the context information needed to prevent disorientation or cognitive overload. Therefore, many research projects have focused on adaptive contextual navigation aids. These projects can be categorized as either focused on the user's local or global *spatial context* or on the user's *temporal context*.

Strategies found in the former category include personalizing or adding textual or graphical views of relevant parts of the document structure [2]. Site maps, contextual menus, direct guiding and recommendations help users to decide where to go. Most strategies in the latter category concentrate on various visualizations of previously visited pages. Several examples are mentioned in [10]. As 58% of user navigation involves revisits [10], users highly profit from reminders where they have been.

Each form of navigation support addresses one or more user needs with respect to ease of navigation. Unfortunately, one cannot provide users with all contextual information at once: even if sufficient screen space is available, users will most likely be overwhelmed by the quantity of navigation suggestions. Therefore, the best approach is to provide users with only those associative, spatial or temporal navigation aids that match their navigation strategies and address the problems they are experiencing. These issues can be derived from a user navigation model.

3   Elements of a User Navigation Model

A user navigation model should be able to recognize user navigation strategies and to predict future navigation strategies. Moreover, it should be able to predict future user problems. It is unlikely that navigation strategies and problems related to lostness can be captured by a single measure. Otter [7] suggests that we could make use of a 'battery of measures', which correlate well with one another and which have been shown to measure lostness to some degree. Since – as argued in the first section – user navigation is highly dependent on a document's structure, observed navigation patterns need to be compared to this structure. Quantitative measures based on the document structure and user navigation paths have shown to be very useful for this purpose [4].

Interesting features of a document's structure include its size, link density, linearity, distances and clustering. Characteristics of user navigation include path length, the amount of backtracking, revisitation patterns and path linearity. Metrics for these features can be derived from adaptive hypermedia literature as well as from graph theory. For an overview of these metrics we refer to [4] and [5]. It is expected that user navigation strategies will be reflected in these quantitative measures of navigation patterns through a hypermedia document. As users may display various navigation strategies, a user navigation model should contain various patterns as observed in different hypermedia structures and in different user contexts. We hypothesize that deviations from these patterns can be regarded as indicators for disorientation.

4   Current and Future Work

In order to make the user navigation model useful for adaptive hypermedia purposes, the metrics, as mentioned before, need to be gathered in real-time. We are implementing these metrics in Scone, a proxy-based programmable framework that provides methods for access tracking, site crawling and page modification [11].

An experiment is planned to provide us with qualitative and quantitative data on user navigation patterns, usability problems as perceived by the user and success measures. We are interested in relations between site structure and navigation strategies, and relations between navigation patterns and perceived lostness. The results will be used for further developing the user navigation model, and for developing suitable adaptation strategies.

Acknowledgements. This research is part of the PALS project (Personal Assistant for onLine Services). The project is supported by the Dutch Innovative Research Program IOP-MMI. Our research partners are TNO Human Factors and the University of Utrecht.

References

1.   Ahuja, J.S. & Webster, J.: Perceived disorientation: an examination of a new measure to assess web design effectiveness. *Interacting with Computers 14 (1)* (2001) pp. 15–29
2.   Brusilovsky, P.: Adaptive Hypermedia. *User Modeling and User-Adapted Interaction 11* (2001) pp. 87–110
3.   Catledge, L.D. & Pitkow, J.E.: Characterizing Browsing Strategies in the World-Wide Web. *Computer Networks and ISDN Systems 27 (6)* (1995) pp. 1065–1073
4.   Herder, E.: Metrics for the Adaptation of Site Structure. *Proc. of the German Workshop on Adaptivity and User Modeling in Interactive Systems*, ABIS02, Hannover (2002) pp. 22–26
5.   Herder, E. & Van Dijk, B.: From Browsing Behavior to Usability Matters. *Workshop on Human Information Processing and Web Navigation, HCI 2003*, Crete (to appear)
6.   Miles-Board, T., Carr, L. & Hall, W. Looking for Linking: Associative Links on the Web. *Proc. 13th ACM Conference on Hypertext and Hypermedia (HT'02)*, Maryland USA (2002) pp. 76–77
7.   Otter, M. & Johnson, H.: Lost in hyperspace: metrics and mental models. *Interacting with Computers 13 (1)* (2001) pp. 1–40
8.   Park, J. & Kim, J.: Contextual Navigation Aids for Two World Wide Web Systems. *International Journal of Human-Computer Interaction 12 (2)* (2000) pp. 193–217
9.   Smith, P.A.: Towards a practical measure of hypertext usability. *Interacting with Computers 8 (4)* (1996) pp. 365–381
10. Tauscher, L. & Greenberg, S.: How people revisit web pages: empirical findings and implications for the design of history systems. *International Journal of Human-Computer Studies 47* (1997) pp. 97–137.
11. Weinrich, H., Buchmann, V., Lamersdorf, W.: Scone: Ein Framework zur evaluativen Realisierung von Erweiterungen des Webs. *Tagungsband Kommunikation in Verteilten Systemen - KiVS* (2003) pp. 12

A Longitudinal, Naturalistic Study of Information Search & Use Behavior as Implicit Feedback for User Model Construction & Maintenance[1]

Diane Kelly

Rutgers University,
4 Huntington Street, New Brunswick, NJ, 08901, USA
diane@scils.rutgers.edu

Abstract. A longitudinal, naturalistic study of the online information search and use behavior of seven users is being conducted during a four-month period to understand how behavior can be used as implicit sources of evidence for user model construction and maintenance. Users are provided with laptops and printers, and their activities are monitored with logging software, paper instruments and weekly interviews. The goal of the study is to develop methods for using online search and use behaviors to predict document usefulness in order to unobtrusively build and maintain a model of the user's interests.

1 Introduction

Each time a user engages in information search and use activities, a large quantity of potentially useful data is produced. This data has the potential to tailor retrieval and personalize interactions through the disambiguation of term usage and the creation of topic models. The behaviors produced during these interactions have been used to understand and model users' interests, intentions and interactions [1,2].

This work has contributed much to what is known about using behavior as implicit sources of evidence, but such studies are limited in many ways. Studies based solely on the analysis of log data are limited because often little is known about individual users, needs and intentions. While laboratory studies attempt to understand and measure attributes of users, needs and intentions, they are limited because the information tasks, environments, and small sample sizes restrict the results. These studies are further limited because they often assume that all users exhibit the same or similar behaviors and that this behavior is not subject to change with respect to cognitive states and contextual factors.

Using a longitudinal, naturalistic approach, the work reported in this paper seeks to understand how an individual's online information behavior can be used as implicit evidence for the construction and maintenance of a personalized user model for that individual, and how this behavior changes with respect to contextual factors such as task and topic, and characteristics of each of these factors.

---

[1] This work was funded in part by NSF Grant #99-11942.

P. Brusilovsky et al. (Eds.): UM 2003, LNAI 2702, pp. 420–422, 2003.

2   Purpose of Participation in UM 2003 Doctoral Consortium

At the time of the UM 2003 Doctoral Consortium, much of the work described in this paper will have been completed. My purposes for participating in the Consortium are to obtain assistance with identifying possible approaches to analysis. I am interested in a thorough critique of the method of the study including feedback about how the method may limit the study findings and how it might be improved for future studies.

3   Method

Seven graduate students, from seven academic departments, are participating in the four-month study. At the beginning of the study, each user is provided with a Gateway Solo 1450 laptop equipped with the Windows XP operating system and standard utilities, and an Epson Stylus Printer. Users are allowed to keep these items as compensation upon completion of the study. All users have had previous experience with the Windows operating system and standard Microsoft Office tools.

The laptops are equipped with the WinWhatWhere[2] client-side logger that monitors and records users' interactions with the operating system and all other applications. The monitoring software is launched automatically each time the machine is started, executes in stealth mode while the machine is in operation and records information such as applications used, URLs visited, start, finish and elapsed times for interactions, and all keystrokes. Users are made aware of this software in a consent form that they are required to sign and are unable to access the software during the study. A proxy server captures all pages that the user views while online.

An Entry Questionnaire eliciting background information from the user, such as education and search experience, is administered at the beginning of the study, along with a Task and Topic Questionnaire that elicits the tasks and topics the user will be engaged with during the study. Users are asked to think about their online activities in terms of tasks and topics. For example, a task might be *shopping* and the topic of this task might be *clothing*, or *guitars*. Another example task might be *writing a research paper*; the topic of this task might be *political ecology* and *West Africa*. While it is not always easy for users to make these distinctions, results from several pilot tests demonstrated that users could do this consistently. Users are further asked to characterize each task according to endurance, frequency and stage of completion, and each topic according to persistence and familiarity (see Table 1).

Users participate in weekly one-hour meetings with the investigator, where a Task and Topic Update Questionnaire is administered that presents users with their previously identified tasks and topics and asks them to update the list through additions and/or deletions and re-characterize each task and topic according to the attributes identified above. Users are also shown the documents viewed up to that time and asked to classify the documents according to the tasks and topics previously identified, evaluate the *usefulness* of the document, and indicate their *confidence* in the evaluation (see Table 1). Users can also add new tasks and topics at this time.

---

[2] http://www.winwhatwhere.com

Table 1. Description of task, topic and document variables

Variable	Definition	Scale	Anchors
Task Endurance	Length of time the user expects to be working with a task	8	[One Day] ... [Several Years]
Frequency	How often the user expects to conduct activities related to the task	7	[Once or twice a day] ... [Yearly]
Stage	Stage the user is in with regard to completing the task	7	[Starting] ... [Finished]
Topic Persistence	Length of time the user expect to be interested in the topic	8	[One Day] ... [Several Years]
Topic Familiarity	How familiar the user is with the topic	7	[Unfamiliar] ... [Familiar]
Usefulness	How useful the user found the document	7	[Not useful] ... [Useful]
Confidence	User's confidence in evaluation	7	[Low] ... [High]

4 Approaches to Analysis

This study will yield several pieces of document level data: a usefulness score, a task and topic and one or more behaviors. Further, each task and topic is described by several characteristics. The goal of the analysis is to relate variables such as usefulness, familiarity and stage, to explicit behaviors such as reading time, printing and saving, and to evaluate the predictive power of these behaviors. Basic statistical techniques will be used to evaluate the relationship between variables and regression analysis will be used as the initial method for deriving the prediction model. Analysis techniques such as sequential data analysis, and techniques from data mining and machine learning, are also under consideration, as are time-series approaches for understanding how behavior changes over time.

5 Contribution to UM Research

The work described in this paper contributes to UM research by attempting to determine empirically, what characteristics of behavior are significant for the development and maintenance of user models in the domain of online information seeking. The results from the study can provide evidence of how behavior changes over time and with respect to contextual factors, such as specific task. Finally, this work seeks to determine how one might create a personalized user model based on the behavior of a single individual instead of stereotypes or groups.

References

1. Claypool, M., Le, P., Waseda, M., Brown, D. Implicit interest indicators. Proceedings of *IUI '02*, Santa Fe, NM, USA, 2001.
2. Heer, J., Chi, E.H. Separating the swarm: Categorization methods for user sessions on the web. Proceedings of *CHI '02*, Minneapolis, MN, USA, 2002.

Facilitating the Comprehension of Online Learning Courses with Adaptivity

Stefan Lippitsch

University of Education, Kunzenweg 21, 79117 Freiburg, Germany
lippitsc@ph-freiburg.de

Abstract. Knowledge acquisition with texts is assumed to be a process of building a mental model of the specific subject. For readers with more prior knowledge, the building of an accurate mental model is easier because they do not have to establish a new structure. Readers with less or no prior knowledge might build an inadequate mental model of a subject. In a hypertext learning environment this could be prevented by several adaptive features that support the user with additional information. We plan to examine the effectiveness and efficiency of such adaptive features within an online course by assessing the user's acquired domain knowledge, the user's satisfaction, and achievement of the user's objectives.

1 Text Comprehension in Hypertext

As a first step towards improving the user's comprehension of hypertext learning courses, one has to analyze reading comprehension processes. According to Storrer [1], an author of learning courses has to design them especially to facilitate the user's comprehension. For an integrating theory, Storrer suggests a model of Schnotz [2], which she stated to be especially adaptable for the use in knowledge transfer with hypertext, although it is designed for linear text only. It assumes the building of a mental model to be the central element of the comprehension process. The user's mental model of the learning object is built through an interaction between the already acquired knowledge and the actual text information.

In contrast to linear text, one of the main features of hypertext is to provide the user with opportunities to jump to different anchors or pages even within another context. Due to this distributed nature of hypertext, following links may confuse the user about the contextual linkage between pages. Thus, the level of prior knowledge may be crucial for text comprehension: when a novice user jumps to advanced pages, he or she is in danger of building a mental model in a way the author did not intend to. In our approach, the user's knowledge acquired within the course will be taken into account to limit this effect by providing him or her with hint texts, representing brief summaries of and links to background concepts the user does not have sufficient knowledge about. With this help, users with less or no prior knowledge should be able to build a more coherent mental model of the course subject.

P. Brusilovsky et al. (Eds.): UM 2003, LNAI 2702, pp. 423–425, 2003.

2 Project Description

The project aims to examine different ways of facilitating the user's comprehension of online learning courses. All approaches are based on the adaptation of the page presentation to the user's prior knowledge, acquired either within the course or beforehand. Here, we use the expression 'prior knowledge' for the knowledge state on prerequisite pages within the course. In contrast, 'background knowledge' is the topic related knowledge at the beginning of the course.

Our first attempt to comprehension enhancement is the presentation of adaptive coherence information to users who did not learn prerequisite pages within the course. Coherence means the connectivity between the pages regarding the overall topic. As a future option, the user may mark the referred pages manually as already learned outside of the course. The system may then update the user model and would no longer present hint texts of these pages.

Second, there may be differences in the usage of an online learning course regarding the user's goals of information retrieval. One user may use the course as a reference, just to look up some currently important detail, while another user may want to learn the whole course. The system may present the course differently to these user groups by focusing on either the search features or the text coherence features.

Finally, a decision between the presentation of more detailed or more brief texts to novice users may be made by presenting long or short text fragments to novice users experimentally. Theoretically, both methods are reasonable.

3 First Step: Adaptive Coherence with Hint Texts

Our first approach to comprehension facilitation is to add coherence to a hypertext learning course. This was first realized by Foltz [3]. He introduced a system that presented some additional but non-adaptive coherence information if the user followed a link that lead far away from the actual page. His additional coherence information consisted of short summaries of those pages the user just skipped. The summaries were presented on top of the page the user jumped to. That means, there were no summaries presented on pages closely related to the one he or she just left (e.g., parents, children, siblings).

As Foltz mentioned himself, one complication in his study may have been that many users went through the course in a coherent way, just rarely producing any summaries at all. The reason for this user behavior may have been their lack of background knowledge at the beginning of the course. To have even novice users navigating through a course in a non-coherent way, we chose to use an existing HTML-course. A pilot study demonstrated that a not inconsiderable fraction of users jump between pages in a non-coherent way.

However, in contrast to Foltz, hint texts should only be presented to users with less course knowledge, because users with a higher level of course knowledge may get distracted by additional information (e.g., [4]). Therefore, we propose to present the hint texts individually, depending on the knowledge about prerequisite concepts from within the course.

In NetCoach [5], which we use as underlying authoring system and online server, the domain model consists of prerequisites and inferences. One page (A) is called a prerequisite for another page (B), if page A has to be learned before page B is visited. The user model consists of the knowledge states of all course pages.

We want to provide the user with additional coherence information about important (i.e., prerequisite) pages he or she does not yet have knowledge about. This is accomplished by presenting additional hint texts and links on top of the requested page. Each hint text is a short sentence on the basic topic of one not yet learned prerequisite page. These additional texts are not meant to substitute the original pages, but to hint to important reference pages. Thus, next to these texts a link is arranged to access the referred page. As a further step, we are planning to use a pretest to take into account the background knowledge biasing the knowledge states in the user model.

In summary, the system improves the coherence of the text flow by presenting hint texts and links to pages which could provide the necessary knowledge for sufficient comprehension of the current page.

4   Experimental Evaluation

We expect that users will profit from the additional coherence information resulting in a better exercise performance and better satisfaction and achievement of objectives than those users without the additional information.

We are planning an evaluation of the new coherence feature in several subsequent steps. The first step will be to assess the use of the hint texts in general, i.e. whether users actually follow the additional links. The second step will be a field experiment in which the users would be assigned to different conditions randomly. The user's exercise performance and the satisfaction will be assessed and compared between these groups. We expect to find a better performance and satisfaction in the group with the hint texts. The third step will be an offline laboratory experiment. The advantage of such a setting will be the reduction of the setting condition variability and thus to be able to attribute the difference in exercise performance directly to the different hint text presentations.

References

1. Storrer, A. (2002). Coherence in text and hypertext. *Document Design*. 3 (2), 156–168.
2. Schnotz, W. (1994). *Aufbau von Wissensstrukturen*. Weinheim: Beltz.
3. Foltz, P.W. (1992). *Readers comprehension and strategies in linear text and hypertext*. Boulder (Colo.), Univ., Diss.
4. Kintsch, W. (1994). Text comprehension, memory and learning. *American Psychologist*, 49, 294-303.
5. Weber, G., Kuhl, H.-C., & Weibelzahl, S. (2001). Developing adaptive internet based courses with the authoring system NetCoach. In S. Reich, M. Tzagarakis, & P. de Bra (Eds.), *Hypermedia: Openness, Structural Awareness, and Adaptivity* (pp. 226–238) (Lecture Notes in Computer Science LNAI 2266). Berlin: Springer.

Scrutable User Models in Decentralised Adaptive Systems

Andrew Lum

School of Information Technologies, University of Sydney, Australia
alum@it.usyd.edu.au

Abstract. This research focuses on users being able to inspect and manage large client side user models in a decentralised adaptive system. In particular, users should be able to scrutinise and modify which parts of their model can contribute to a partial user model that shall be made public. An ontology will be used to structure the user model, allowing users to see what can be inferred about them from this partial user model and also to serve as a basis for visualisation. This work will be evaluated in an online learning context and utilise current web standards.

1 Introduction

User models should be considered personal data [1] and under the EU directive [2], they should be accessible to the user. One architecture for personalized systems that would satisfy this requirement has a decentralised storage of the user models [3]. These would be stored on the user's own local machines and be fully accessible to the user at any time. Users need to be able to control which parts of their user model are publicly accessible to a personalized system. We call this subset the partial user model [4].

The focus of this thesis is to make user models scrutable so that users can understand the components of the user model and have control over their access. Even though the user model may be very large with hundreds or even thousands of components, users should still be in charge of what data in the user model can go into their partial user model. It would be extremely useful for users to be able to explore possible inferences that can be made about them by an external source from their partial user model. Being able to see time based inferences, such as changes to the partial user model over time, would also be useful.

For example, in an online auction context, it is very important for the purposes of building trust between buyers and sellers for a user to make public their past transaction history. It would be useful to allow users control over the granularity of the history to be made public: whether to allow for every item or the broad categories to be visible, or restrict it to recent transactions.

P. Brusilovsky et al. (Eds.): UM 2003, LNAI 2702, pp. 426–428, 2003.

2   Proposed Solution

We propose to build an ontology for a course on user interfaces[1]. The ontology will be constructed with our own annotations of the learning resources and running the MECUREO ontology generation tools [5], on an online glossary of usability terms [6]. The ontology will be used to make inferences on the student user model.

VlUM [7], a tool for visualisation of large user models, will then be integrated with the course website. This will allow users to scrutinise their user models. We have already refined VlUM to successfully visualise MECUREO output for a subset of the Free Online Dictionary of Computing [8]. The visualisation for the subgraph generated from the definition Declarative Language is available online[2].

The important goal of our work is to extend VlUM so users can annotate parts of their user model to indicate if they wish to make those parts public. Then a mechanism to mark non-shared components that might be inferred from the partial user model can be developed. We propose to base this on the ontology underlying the user model.

A further area we propose to explore is time-based inference. This would allow the user to see trends in the user model. For example, it might automatically project a monthly partial user model based on what the user has previously released. In our teaching context, students will be able to see their learning trajectory.

The Semantic Web project [9] is also relevant, particularly the Web Ontology Working Group whose aim is to create a web ontology language. This ontological layer would sit above the semantics provided by the resource description format (RDF). We propose to integrate this as VlUM already uses RDF as the format for its user models, and the graph structure is derived from an ontology of the domain.

3   Evaluation

The approaches that are currently being examined and implemented will be evaluated through a series of user studies. A hypothetical user will be created that will represent a student who would be half way through the course.

Users should be able to answer a series of questions and use the enhanced VlUM tool quickly and accurately. These would involve tasks like:

- Find a topic that this user is ready to learn.
- Put the component about the user's knowledge of Fitts' Law into their partial user model.
- Find a component whose value might be inferred as a result of having Fitts' Law in their partial user model.

---

[1] http://www.cs.usyd.edu.au/current_ugrad/handbook2002/third/comp3102.html
[2] http://www.cs.usyd.edu.au/~alum/vlum_decl/

– Find a topic the user should have learnt by now but has not fulfilled the prerequisite requirements.

The solution will be successful if users can understand the user model representation and interface by successfully using it to answer the questionnaire. Logging will be utilised to determine the speed at which users can perform the tasks.

4 Conclusions

It is important that users be able to understand and manage their user models. This task is made more difficult when user models are very large. It is essential that a visualisation should make it easier for the user to understand the domain and the information stored about them. The contributions of this work will be:

– A rich user model that includes time information in the components.
– A visualisation of ontology-based inferences that can be made from the partial user model.
– An evaluation of this approach by implementing these in the VlUM tool.

Allowing users to scrutinise these elements will serve as a basis for increasing their trust and confidence in adaptive systems, and respects the spirit of legislation on privacy and personal data.

Acknowledgements. This research project has been sponsored by Hewlett-Packard.

References

1. Shreck, J.: Security and Privacy in User Modelling. PhD thesis, Universität Gesamthochschule (2001)
2. EU Directive 95/46/EC of the European Parliament and of the Council of 24 October 1995 on the Protection of Individuals with Regard to the Processing of Personal Data and on the Free Movement of such Data. Official Journal of the European Communities (23 November 1995 No L. 281, 1995).
3. Kobsa, A.: Personalised hypermedia and international privacy. Communications of the ACM 45:5 (2002) 64–67
4. Kay, J., Kummerfeld, R.: Customization and delivery of multimedia information. In Proceedings of Multicomm 94, Vancouver (1994) 141–150
5. Apted, T., Kay, J: Automatic Construction of Learning Ontologies. In Aroyo, L and Dicheva, D, (eds) Proceedings ICCE Workshop on Concepts and Ontologies in Web-based Educational Systems, ICCE 2002, International Conference on Computers in Education, CS-Report 02-15 Technische Universiteit Eindhoven (2002) 55–62
6. Usability Glossary: Available at http://www.usabilityfirst.com/glossary/main.cgi (2002)
7. Uther, J.: On the Visualisation of Large User Model in Web Based Systems. PhD thesis, University of Sydney (2001)
8. The Free On-line Dictionary of Computing: Available at http://foldoc.org/ (2001)
9. Berners-Lee, T., Hendler, J., Lassila, O.: The semantic web. Scientic American 284:5 (2001) 34–43

A *Pseudo-Supervised* Approach to Improve a Recommender Based on Collaborative Filtering*

José D. Martín-Guerrero

Digital Signal Processing Group, University of Valencia, Spain
jose.d.martin@uv.es

Abstract. This PhD Thesis develops an optimal recommender. First of all, users accessing to a Web site are clustered. If a user belongs to a cluster, the system offers services which are usually accessed by users from the same cluster in a collaborative filtering scheme.
A novel approach based on a users simulator and a dynamic recommendation system is proposed. The simulator is used to create the situations that one can find in a Web site. Introduction of dynamics in the recommender allows to change the clusters and in turn, the decisions which are taken. Since the system is based both on supervised and unsupervised learning whose borders are not too clear in our approach, we talk about a *pseudo-supervised learning.*

1 Description of the Problem

The problem of finding an optimal recommender has two basic approaches: automatic customization approach and collaborative filtering [1]. In this work, we have chosen the second option because of the characteristics of our approach. Our strategy is firstly to cluster the users and afterwards to use the performed clustering for giving recommendations.

Since the Web sites can be formed by lots of links, it is important to reduce the dimensionality of the feature space where we cluster, from the number of services (a *service* is each one of the possible links which exist into a Web portal) to a lower number of labels (a *label* or *descriptor* is a set of services, all of them with similar contents).

The clustering algorithms must work by default in the space defined by labels because it is more feasible and the obtained clusters are more informative. These labels are usually chosen by the designer but sometimes no 'a priori' choice exists. Then, there are two possibilities: to cluster in the space defined by services or

---

* This work has been partially supported by the Spanish Science and Technology Ministry project FIT–070000–2001–663, by the Valencian Culture, Education and Science Council project CTIDIA–2002–166 and by the University of Valencia project UV 01–15. I want to express my thanks to Drs. Emilio Soria-Olivas and Gustavo Camps-Valls for their direction and advices. I also want to express my thanks to Tissat, S.A., iSUM Department, http://www.tissat.es/, for its collaboration and technical support.

P. Brusilovsky et al. (Eds.): UM 2003, LNAI 2702, pp. 429–431, 2003.

to obtain a good set of descriptors from the whole set of services. The latter can be achieved performing a Principal Component Analysis (PCA) [2] of the services which provides the linear combination of services (i.e., labels) with most information.

When desired clusters are not available, unsupervised learning algorithms must be used. In order to allow the evaluation of algorithms performance, we propose to simulate Web usage sites whose clusters are known. The aim is to develop a general Web simulator which could take into account the whole set of possibilities that could appear. Therefore, algorithms would be tested in every situation in order to know which algorithm is the best in each kind of Web site.

Afterwards, a recommender is implemented in order to give the best recommendation to users by using collaborative filtering. This recommender is based on the best clustering algorithm for this Web usage site, but not exclusivelly; in fact, a dynamic system which takes advantage from both supervised and unsupervised learning is developed. We call it, consequently, *pseudo-supervised learning*.

In Section 2, the proposed methodology is presented. In Section 3, it is described the developed work until now, its conclusions and planning for the future.

2   Methodology

The methodology begins with the development of the users simulator. We have taken into account two constraints which one can observe in all the real *log* files which were analyzed: the number of users who open up a new session decreases when the number of previously opened sessions increases; and, in each session, the number of users who access to a service decreases when the number of previously accessed services is higher. The constraints are obvious; when a user becomes an expert in a Web site, her navigation profile is straightforward but when she is a newbie, her profile is very random.

The simulator generates users in a label space. We have implemented several situations in our controlled experiments, covering most of those possibilities which can appear depending on the Web portal's characteristics. The simulator output offers information about the accessed services and labels by a user in a certain session. This information is coded into two tensorial matrices. The simulation of service accesses is achieved from label simulation. Once the label accesses are known, it is possible to find the number of services which are accessed because the relationship between labels and services is defined. Therefore, it is only necessary to take out the corresponding number of services from each descriptor.

The clustering works by default in the label space but it must be able to cluster users from information about the services because, sometimes, label information is not available. Anyway, it may be very difficult to cluster in the service space when its dimensionality is high. Moreover, one can take out more useful information from a label than from a service because the latter is too specific and it is very difficult to find a users' behaviour with only one service. In fact, if predefined labels are not available, our proposal is to carry out a PCA of the services in order to reduce the dimensionality and to extract the best labels, because it will mean to cluster in the most informative space.

We have taken into account several clustering algorithms, such as, C-means, Fuzzy C-means, Expectation-Maximization algorithm, generic sequential and hierarchical clustering algorithms [3] and Self-Organizing Maps (SOM) [2]. Inclusion of ulterior algorithms in the system is trivial.

Once the clustering has finished, the recommender is based on collaborative filtering, i.e., those objects that were highly rated by other users with similar tastes are suggested. A user belongs to that cluster whose representative point (typically, its centroid) is nearest her. The clusters are dynamic since after the initial clustering, we can take advantage from the new users' behaviour by fitting the clusters to include this new information using a fuzzy scheme of Learning Vector Quantization (LVQ) [2]. This fitting implies that cluster representatives are adapted changing their position.

Summarizing, we propose a modular system with four parts. The first one is the simulator which allows to generate generic Web usage sites. The second is the choice of the best clustering algorithms; despite clustering is based on unsupervised learning, desired outputs are known because we generate them with the simulator. The third is the recommendation and the last one the fitting of the recommender including information from new users. We talk about *pseudo-supervised learning* to explain how the system works.

3   Work Already Done and Tentative for the Future

Users simulator and clustering algorithms comparison are finished. We have observed that very simple algorithms, such as C-means, work properly when the site is not complex. When the overlapping and the number of users' groups and labels increases, another approach must be used; we have observed that hierarchical algorithms work in medium complex sites but they fail when complexity is very high. The most complex sites need a more powerful tool: we have used a hierarchical SOM modifying the two-dimensional mapping with image digital processing and other variations.

Nowadays, we are working in the development of the adaptive system recommendation based on collaborative filtering and fuzzy LVQ. Future work will be related to non-linear tools applied to extraction of the best labels from the whole set of services.

References

1. Perkowitz, M., Etzioni, O.: Towards adaptive Web sites: Conceptual framework and case study. Artificial Intelligence, Vol. 118. Elsevier (2000) 245–275.
2. Ripley, B.D.: Pattern Recognition and Neural Networks. Cambridge University Press, Cambridge, UK (1996).
3. Theodoridis, S., Koutroumbas,K.: Pattern Recognition. Academic Press, a division of Harcourt Brace & Company, San Diego, CA, USA (1999).

Visualizing a User Model for Educational Adaptive Information Retrieval

Swantje Willms

University of Pittsburgh, Pittsburgh, PA, USA
swillms@mail.sis.pitt.edu

Abstract. We will visualize a user model to achieve adaptive information retrieval in a learning environment. User profile components such as user interests and user knowledge are visualized in WebVIBE with the purpose of helping the student in identifying relevant documents for study. We will be able to find out whether this visualization will change the students' access patterns to the study material and whether they will be able to find relevant documents faster.

1 Introduction and Contributions

We will visualize the user model in order to help students more effectively locate educational documents based on their interests, knowledge, and a lecture topic as points of interest (POIs). The user model is represented as vectors of user profile components. These components are visualized as POIs. In the past, relevant documents for the student have been shown as a list, but a multi-dimensional display may be easier to understand. It is more flexible because it can show how the potential study documents relate to the POIs.

The hypothesis is that the students may be able to find relevant documents faster when they have a visualization of their interest and knowledge available and use it to identify relevant study materials. The study will determine whether there is an improved success rate in finding relevant documents within the allotted time frame vs. a control condition using presentation in lists. A second hypothesis is that students are more likely to make use of external material when they can judge its relevance with the help of the visualization.

2 Research Design Overview

The user model will consist of components including the student's interest and the knowledge of the student, each treated as a separate POI in the visualization.

The students express their **interest** by highlighting part of a document that is relevant to them or by rating the document for relevance. In a process similar to that used for WebMate [4]: 1. The highlighted parts (or the positively rated document) are preprocessed (stop words and stemming, and extracting titles). 2. The frequency vector for the document is extracted. 3. It is either added to a set of vectors that represent the student's interests or combined with the one most similar to it.

P. Brusilovsky et al. (Eds.): UM 2003, LNAI 2702, pp. 432–434, 2003.

Student **knowledge** is represented by weighting keywords (from unknown to known) based on test scores. Each multiple choice question in a quiz is associated with some terms or keywords (extracted from a paragraph from lecture material) that correspond to the concept(s) addressed by the question. If the student answered the question correctly, it is assumed that she knows the concept. Increased weight for a keyword (because several questions with the same keyword have been answered correctly) represents increased knowledge (up to a maximum). Apart from the user model another important POI, the **lecture topic**, is represented by keywords extracted from the corresponding lecture notes document (slides). A non-homogeneous lecture will be split into two or three topics if necessary.

We will use a spatial visualization system, called WebVIBE (Figure right). In WebVIBE [1], the Java version of VIBE [2], the POIs (represented by magnets as a metaphor for attraction) define a coordinate system on the display to present a virtual document space. Each POI in WebVIBE is based on a vector of keywords. Users can change the display interactively by selecting and placing the POIs. WebVIBE will be applied in the context of KnowledgeSea [3] (Figure left) which displays a map of the educational documents, with a set of keywords in each cell that describe the documents in this cell. Usually, the user would be linked to a list of documents from the cell. Instead the users will be linked to a WebVIBE display so that they can see how these documents relate to each other with respect to the POIs. The POIs for the WebVIBE display will be generated behind the scenes

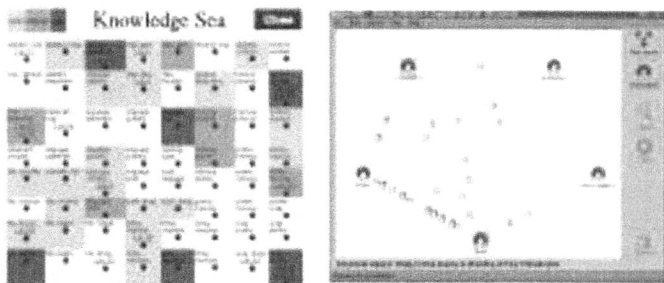

Fig. 1. KnowledgeSea and WebVIBE

based on term vectors generated as described above. The similarity between the POIs and the documents is computed using a similarity measure such as the cosine measure. The position of each document within the WebVIBE display is based on the ratio of the similarity measures for a document with respect to the POIs. A weighted centroid model places the documents according to the strength of their relationship to the POIs.

We will undertake two kinds of experiments involving real users, the students enrolled in a class: 1. Long term observation, and 2. Controlled sessions. In addition, the students' satisfaction with the visualization will be assessed through a questionnaire. Some of the needed material already exists for classes such as "Introduction to Programming". The existing lecture notes in form of slides build the internal document collection. In addition, the students have access to a couple of online tutorials as external resources. These can be referenced by page, the pages for one tutorial making up one collection. Different "sections" of a class can have different conditions, e.g. one with WebVIBE visualization, one without. Over the course of the semester, we will keep track of the documents that the students access. Using these data, we can find out if students are more likely to access external material if they access the documents through the visualization system. In addition, we will schedule a session of specified length in which the student is asked to identify study material relevant to a specific topic, we can assess whether students find relevant documents faster with the visualization. At the beginning of this focused session, the student will state her goal in natural language; a list of keywords associated with this goal could be used as a starting point for the student's interest. In this manner, the student's perceived goal will be adjusted (like the model for the user's objective in METIOREW [5]).

The WebVIBE display the student is presented with will have at least the three POIs: **interest**, **knowledge**, and **lecture topic** as described above. The student will want to learn about concepts that are far away from her knowledge and close to her interest or the topic. The centroid of the lecture can be seen as a target because it is supposed to represent what the student is supposed to know. Therefore, the student may want to explore those documents that relate to both their interest and the lecture topic, and also look at documents that integrate these with her previous knowledge, but not at documents that are related to knowledge only.

3   Future Work

One could extend the user model by (1)(a) the **class interest** as a group model extracted from the interests of individual students or (b) several separate group models based on "categories" of students such as good, average, and poor students; (2) an explicit representation of student **needs** based on test scores weighted inversely to the representation for knowledge and on topics that have been covered in class, but which the student has never accessed. The visualization could provide additional or alternative POIs such as the class/group interest and needs or a POI based on a traditional keyword query. One could add additional document collections such as a glossary.

References

1. Homepage for WebVIBE. URL: http://www2.sis.pitt.edu/~webvibe/WebVibe/
2. Olsen, K.A., Williams, J.G., Sochats, K.M., Hirtle, S.C.: Ideation through visualization: the VIBE system. Multimedia Review **3(3)** (1992) 48–59.
3. Brusilovsky, P., Rizzo, R.: Map-Based Horizontal Navigation in Educational Hypertext. Journal of Digital Information **3(1)** (2002)
4. Chen, L., Sycara, K.: WebMate: A personal agent for browsing and searching. 2nd International Conference on Autonomous Agents (Agents'98) (1998) 132–139
5. Bueno, D., Conejo, D., David, A.A.: METIOREW: An objective oriented content based and collaborative recommending system. Third Workshop on Adaptive Hypertext and Hypermedia (AH2001) (2001) 310–314

Author Index

Lecture Notes in Artificial Intelligence (LNAI)

Lecture Notes in Computer Science

GPSR Compliance

The European Union's (EU) General Product Safety Regulation (GPSR)
is a set of rules that requires consumer products to be safe and our
obligations to ensure this.

If you have any concerns about our products, you can contact us on
ProductSafety@springernature.com

In case Publisher is established outside the EU, the EU authorized
representative is:

Springer Nature Customer Service Center GmbH
Europaplatz 3
69115 Heidelberg, Germany

Batch number: 09490862

Printed by Printforce, the Netherlands